The Rivers Ran Backward

The Rivers Ran Backward

The Civil War and the Remaking of the American Middle Border

CHRISTOPHER PHILLIPS

OXFORD
UNIVERSITY PRESS

Oxford University Press is a department of the University of Oxford.
It furthers the University's objective of excellence in research, scholarship,
and education by publishing worldwide. Oxford is a registered trade mark of
Oxford University Press in the UK and certain other countries.

Published in the United States of America by Oxford University Press
198 Madison Avenue, New York, NY 10016, United States of America.

© Oxford University Press 2016

All rights reserved. No part of this publication may be reproduced,
stored in a retrieval system, or transmitted, in any form or by any means,
without the prior permission in writing of Oxford University Press,
or as expressly permitted by law, by license, or under terms agreed with
the appropriate reproduction rights organization. Inquiries concerning
reproduction outside the scope of the above should be sent to the
Rights Department, Oxford University Press, at the address above.

You must not circulate this work in any other form
and you must impose this same condition on any acquirer.

Library of Congress Cataloging-in-Publication Data
Names: Phillips, Christopher, 1959 November 1- author.
Title: The rivers ran backward : the Civil War and the remaking of the
American middle border / Christopher Phillips.
Description: First edition. | New York, NY : Oxford University Press, 2016. |
Includes bibliographical references and index.
Identifiers: LCCN 2015042282 (print) | LCCN 2016005038 (ebook) |
ISBN 9780195187236 (hardcover : alk. paper) | ISBN 9780199720170 (Updf) |
ISBN 9780190606138 (Epub)
Subjects: LCSH: Border States (U.S. Civil War) | Middle West—History—Civil War, 1861-1865. |
United States—History—Civil War, 1861-1865—Social aspects. | Regionalism—Border States. |
Regionalism—Middle West—History—19th century. | Group identity—Border States. |
Group identity—Middle West—History—19th century.
Classification: LCC F217.B67 P49 2016 (print) | LCC F217.B67 (ebook) |
DDC 973.7/1—dc23
LC record available at http://lccn.loc.gov/2015042282

3 5 7 9 8 6 4

Printed by Sheridan Books, USA

Parts of Chapters 5, 6, 7, and 8 were published previously as "Netherworld of War:
The Dominion System and Federal Occupation in Civil War Kentucky," *The Register of the
Kentucky Historical Society* 10 (Summer/Autumn 2012): 327–61, with permission of Kentucky
Historical Society; "Lincoln's Grasp of War: Hard War and the Politics of Neutrality and Slavery
in the Western Border Slave States, 1861–62," *The Journal of the Civil War Era* 3 (June 2013):
184–210, with permission of University of North Carolina Press; "'A Question of Power Not One of Law':
Federal Occupation and the Politics of Loyalty in the Western Border Slave States during the American
Civil War," in Jonathan Earle and Diane Mutti Burke, ed., *Bleeding Kansas, Bleeding Missouri: The Long
Civil War on the Western Border* (Lawrence: University Press of Kansas, 2013), 131–50, with
permission of University Press of Kansas; and "The Hard-line War: The Ideological Basis of Irregular
Warfare in the Western Border States," in Joseph M. Beilein Jr. and Matthew C. Hulbert, ed., *The Civil
War Guerrilla: Unfolding the Black Flag in History and Myth* (Lexington: University Press of
Kentucky, 2015), 13–41, with permission of University Press of Kentucky. Interstices "House of Cards"
and "The Gates of Zion" were published previously as "The Fall of the House of Underwood" and
"A Storm in Zion" in *Opinionator: Disunion*, March 3 and November 9, 2012,
with permission of the *New York Times*.

For Bill, Jim, Emory, and Mark, for a lifetime of inspiration and support, and for Jill, Grayson, Maddox, and the rest of my family, for a lifetime

You could not step twice into the same river; for other waters are ever flowing on to you.

—Heraclitus, *On the Universe*

CONTENTS

Acknowledgments xi
Note on Terms xvii

"There Is a West" 1
1. Introduction 5

White Salt, Black Servitude 15
1. White Flows the River: Freedom and Unfreedom in the Early National West 21

North of Slavery, West of Abolition 44
2. Babel: Changed Persistence on Slavery's Borderland 49

Vox Populi 78
3. The Ten-Year War: Sectional Politics in a Dividing Region 83

House of Cards 114
4. No North—No South—No East—No West: The Fiction of the Wartime Middle Ground 120

The Gates of Zion 163
5. Netherworld of War: Civilians, Soldiers, and the Dominion of War 169

War of Another Kind 207
6. Bitter Harvest: Emancipation and the Politics of Loyalty 211

The Art of Retaliation   236
7. Shadow Wars: The Crucible of Social Violence   242

A River Between Them   285
8. Southern Cross, North Star: The Politics of Irreconciliation   291

Rally Round the Flags   326
Conclusion   328

Abbreviations   339
Notes   341
Bibliography   427
Index   475

ACKNOWLEDGMENTS

However clichéd, it is inevitable that books make for debts. Books that take nearly two decades to create make for bankruptcies. Unable to pay my crushing obligations, I'll offer gestures of restitution that, however meaningful, will only embarrass by their insufficiency. It is equally a cliché that despite the assistance of so many, errors will have found their way into this book. They are not shared, owned solely by its author.

Authors customarily thank their editors at the end of their acknowledgments. Susan Ferber needs to head my list. Her editing skills are matchless, but more, her counsel, confidence, and steady encouragement that "good books take longer" sustained me through the heavy lifting required to see through what she called a promising proposal to what I call fraught early manuscript drafts to what we both hope is in fact a good book. She allowed me the latitude to construct as I saw fit a book that she has all along called sprawling, believing in my approach and inspiring me to develop and write my story, and stories, better. I can only hope I have.

Although my thinking about this project began in graduate school at the University of Georgia, where a stellar cast of southern historians crafted a dynamic environment for ideas, the real work began in the mid-1990s. Having worked on this project while on the faculty at several universities, I must spread out my many repayments to institutions, colleagues, and friends. For the past fifteen years at the University of Cincinnati, wonderful colleagues like Wayne Durrill, David Stradling, Willard Sunderland, Maura O'Connor, Sigrun Haude, Wendy Kline, Mark Lause, Mark Raider, Zane Miller, Barbara Ramusack, Tom Sakmyster, John Alexander, Roger Daniels, Tracy Teslow, Gene Lewis, and Hope Earls have, in various ways, offered unflagging support and either read drafts, offered letters of support, heard renditions of various portions of the project, or provided vital support for it. The University Research Council of UC provided a generous summer grant that allowed me to conduct vital research in its early stages, and the Charles Phelps Taft Research Center and former faculty chairs Rich Harknett and Jana Braziel provided me with several opportunities for funding and leaves, including a yearlong fellowship that allowed me to draft two important and difficult chapters and a book production grant that allowed me to secure images and generate a map. (Special thanks to Ric Snodgrass for his expert work on the latter.) The McMicken College of Arts and Sciences, in particular deans Karen Gould, Valerie Gray Hardcastle, and Kristi Nelson, supported me with two sabbatical leaves that allowed me to write the project to completion. At John Carroll University, where I taught for a year as visiting professor, Matt Berg and the late David Klooster offered insights, research materials, and warm friendship during my brief residence. At Emporia State University, where I began this project in earnest, the graduate school supported me in the earliest stage of the project with several faculty research grants to conduct primary research at far-flung repositories. Colleagues and friends there, including Greg Schneider, Pat O'Brien, Karen Manners Smith, Phil Kelly, and Charlie Brown, provided open doors for early discussions of this and other creative endeavors during my six years in Kansas on the edge of the Great Plains, where this project began its life.

Outside my university homes, a number of institutions have supported this project from its infancy by a number of generous grants and fellowships. The American Philosophical Society offered a research grant that seeded the project and proved instrumental in realizing early on that it was viable by the voices speaking through rich primary sources I quickly encountered. The American Antiquarian Society provided a Kate B. and Hall J. Peterson Fellowship, during which I was blessed with the company of wonderful historians and scholars, including Jeff Pasley and Peter Baldwin. My thanks to Ellen Dunlap and especially Vince Golden, who pointed me to (and even acquired during my stay) early American newspapers from the middle border region that proved essential to developing my research and story. The State Historical Society of Missouri, Kentucky Historical Society, and Filson Historical Society each awarded me research fellowships that allowed me to mine their collections for extended periods. The helpful staffs of these latter research institutions, as well as numerous others, deserve special mention, especially Jim Holmberg and Jennifer Cole of the Filson Historical Society; Darrell Meadows and Lynne Hollingsworth of the Kentucky Historical Society; Bill Marshall of the University of Kentucky's Special Collections Library; Kevin Grace and Sue Reller of the University of Cincinnati's Archives and Special Collections; James Cornelius, Roberta Fairburn, Boyd Murphree, Glenna Schroeder, and Daniel Stowell of the Abraham Lincoln Presidential Library and Museum; Dennis Northcott of the Missouri Historical Society; Lynn Wolf Gentzler, Laura Jolley, Anne Cox, John Bradbury, and Joan Stack of the State Historical Society of Missouri/Western Historical Manuscripts; Ruby Rogers, Anne Shepherd, and Doug McDonald of the

Cincinnati Museum Center/Historical Society Library; Brandon Slone of the Military Records and Research Branch of the Kentucky Department of Military Affairs; Trace Kirkwood of the Filson Historical Society and the Kentucky State Archives and Library; Steve Mitchell of the Missouri State Archives; Jonathan Jeffrey, Nancy Richey, and Nancy Disher Baird of Western Kentucky University's Department of Special Collections (especially for sharing the transcription of the second volume of the Nazro Diary); Glenn Taul of Georgetown College's special collections library; and Patricia Van Skaik of the Public Library of Cincinnati and Hamilton County. Marshall Hier deserves special thanks for directing me to the Greve-Fisher collection at the University of Missouri, St. Louis's Mercantile Library Special Collections. Ric Snodgrass fashioned a masterful map without the benefit of an adequate historical template. No two persons at any of these repositories deserve more thanks than Gary Kremer, director of the State Historical Society of Missouri, and Lynn Morrow, former director of the Missouri State Archives Local Records Program. Gary accepted innumerable requests and guided me to collections and documents he knew would be essential to my study, and Lynn supervised the digital Union provost marshal records project and shared the database that his staff had compiled for this initiative, and regularly sent me important documents his researchers had unearthed. He and his wife, Kris, have regularly offered me lodging and other comforts on my many sojourns to the Boon's Lick. Many thanks to Rudi Keller for providing me with the "lost" Missouri secession House journal that he found in plain sight by intrepid archives haunting, and to Jeff Patrick at the Wilson's Creek National Battlefield Park, who similarly provided me with the Missouri secession Senate journal.

Individually and collectively, a number of scholars and friends have richly sustained me, professionally and personally, through the long preparation of this book. Dan Crofts, Jim Roark, Jim Cobb, John Inscoe, Steve Aron, Bruce Levine, Mark Neely, Emory Thomas, the late Tom Dyer, Dan Sutherland, Fitz Brundage, Gary Gallagher, David Blight, Ira Berlin, Bill Blair, Lesley Gordon, Amy Murrell Taylor, Frank Towers, John Quist, Diane Mutti Burke, Jenny Weber, Jon Earle, LeeAnn Whites, Mark Wetherington, Glenn Crothers, Russ Duncan, Bill Piston, Bill Parrish, Bill Foley, Jim Ramage, Kyle Sinisi, and the various participants in the Civil War Study Group are but a few who have offered advice, research material, and helpful criticisms of paper presentations and various written iterations of this project, including articles and manuscript chapters, and have written supportively for grants and fellowships. In the process, they have become good friends. Completing this project has introduced me to a number of scholars and specialists who, by their own publications, location at research repositories, or proximity, are vested in studies of the border region in the era of the Civil War: Bill Harris, Jim Klotter, Drew Cayton, Mark Geiger, Dennis Boman, Steve

Towne, Richard Nation, Jim Fuller, and Nicole Etcheson are excellent scholars of, or in, this diverse region, whose work has invigorated fuller understandings of it. Several of them have read early drafts of various portions of this book. Serving the Organization of American Historians as a Distinguished Lecturer has allowed me to present various aspects of this project over the past eight years, and the opportunities for interaction with public audiences have offered the insights that collectively benefited the final revisions of the book.

Friends have helped me in various ways during this long process, and it will likely be impossible to recall, much less to acknowledge, the innumerable acts of kindness that have helped me through the long process of writing this book. Trace and Dana Kirkwood, Jason and Jodi Pendleton, Lynn and Kris Morrow, Gary and Lisa Kremer, Ken Winn, Jim and Sue Denny, John Bradbury, Jason and Jodi Pendleton, and Jim McGhee have been welcoming friends and hosts more than once on my vagabond research trips, as well as offering deep knowledge of these states for many years. Crittenden, Kentucky, and Glendale, Ohio, have been village sanctuaries since we made them home in 1999 and 2002, respectively, and there are far too many friends to thank there, but the Jacksons, Combses, Plvans, Taylors, Curtises, Honerlaws, Karbowskis, Kreidlers, McCormicks, Amongeros, Cengias, Schmahls, O'Briens, Niehauses, and Johnsons, along with the Lawsons, Sparkses, Weingartners, Abbatiellos, and Dashleys head the list. Jim Ringenberg; Pat and Carol Johnston; Dave Mead; Paul and Ann Nordstrom; and Brian, Laura, Bill, and Eileen Polian have been steadfast supporters of my work, whether living in the Midwest or in other American regions, and over many years have offered inspiration and wonderment. Clay and Kim Arnold have been cornerstones of my family's life since our time at Emporia State, and they continue to anchor it, however far-flung our lives are now. Bennie Heard has been like family since my days in Athens, and Kent Nance and Sam St. Clair more recently in other parts of the Deep South. My real families—the various Phillipses in Illinois, DeFreezers in Georgia and Illinois, Conways in Ohio, and Mitchells and Nesbitts in Tennessee—have offered years of support from the farther reaches of the river regions and beyond that have been no less than a life's treasure.

For a decade as coeditor or senior editor of *Ohio Valley History*, I was graced with introduction to a corps of talented younger scholars whose articles and books well reflect our shared belief in the value of studying the border region. I've had the pleasure to publish many of them and have had the benefit of learning from them and supporting their work, as well as others I haven't published, including Matt Salafia, Anne Marshall, Aaron Astor, Jeremy Neely, Brian Craig Miller, Bridget Ford, Joe Beilein, Matt Hulbert, Brian McKnight, Patrick Lewis, Jessica Cannon, Mike Rhyne, Mike Crane, Clint Terry, Chris Dee, Aaron Cowan, Rob Gioielli, Bill Bergmann, Kelly Wright, Zachary Bennett, and Rory Krupp (who generously shared his deep knowledge and research on the western Shakers).

Acknowledgments

My own graduate students have offered me a fruited vineyard, and helping them move to completion their own projects on various border topics, watching them enter the profession on their own terms and contribute to it, and engaging in many full discussions of topics of mutual interest has enriched my own work and my life. In particular, I want to thank Matt Stanley, Zach Garrison, Steve Rockenbach, Jason Bell, Jason Pendleton, Ismael Kimbrough, Marc Charboneau, Matt Hall, Cathy Collopy, Rebecca Wiechel, Jim Streckfuss, Matthew Semler, and Frank Gorrasi. For a scholar, there is no substitute for being involved in a vibrant, research-oriented graduate program.

Finally, I reserve special gratitude for a few individuals who not only have assisted but inspired me, by reading chapters from or the entire draft of this book, as well as other projects. Mark Plummer planted the seed for this project years ago when his interest and expertise in nineteenth-century regional history nurtured my own fascination with its many complexities. That he and Betty have remained good friends over long years is even more important. Emory Thomas and Bill McFeely have been mentors, colleagues, supporters, and friends since our extraordinary time together in Athens, and at various stages offered helpful advice and encouragement. Jim McPherson has supported this project since its inception, generously writing for grants and fellowships, offering close reading of portions, and providing a model for how a celebrated academic and author remains a celebrated academic and author. Bill Freehling was among the readers of my book proposal and has offered unflagging support and sometimes rigorous critiques of the evolving project. His calls for reintegration of narrative and interpretive analysis was something of a North Star even before we met at a Filson event in Old Louisville too many years ago. Mostly, I appreciate his enthusiasm, confidence, and comradeship. T. J. Stiles has been a compatriot since our books about Missouri's complicated Civil War–era narrative appeared in the early 2000s. His exceptional historicism and graceful prose have been an inspiration to me since our early western ventures. Not long before his death, Michael Fellman read the manuscript's bloated first draft in its entirety and offered an invaluable critique. I hope he knew his friendship mattered even more. My parents have heard me talk for far too long about rural midwesterners being southerners once removed. They gave me a life worth living by encouraging me to pursue dreams and to dream big. My own family has lived beside this project through its entirety. My wife, Jill, has patiently endured my absences within and without our home, while our sons, Grayson and Maddox, enlivened the process by regularly asking me whether my book is finally done. I'm happy to tell all of them in print that it is, and to thank them for staying with it, and with me. My biggest dream, of course, has been realized by sharing my life with them.

NOTE ON TERMS

Because their meanings often merged in the words of antebellum contemporaries, I have frequently used the term "middle border" interchangeably with "West" to mean those states bordering the Ohio and Missouri Rivers west of the Appalachian Mountains and south and east of present-day Nebraska, Iowa, Wisconsin, and Michigan. Although many antebellum Americans claimed the West as a descriptor for their own localities within the massive, dynamic region, the contest over regional meanings was most transparent, and most entwined with the Civil War and its aftermath, in this portion of it. Because the term "Middle West" was seldom used prior to the 1890s as a regional delineator for western states, free and slave—including Kentucky, Missouri, Illinois, Indiana, Ohio, and Kansas, as well as the states and territories lying immediately north of them—I reserve use of this term to its proper chronology.

Best seen as the battleground for these terminologies and definitions, in this middle border region's free and slave states a wider spectrum of definitions of proslavery and antislavery existed than modern Americans employ, and their shades of gray were largely more moderate than is presently understood. In this region in antebellum and wartime periods, being proslavery was not necessarily the same as being a fire-eater committed to slavery's perpetuation, any more than being antislavery was the same as embracing abolitionism as a mechanism for slavery's end. Both positions were then considered extreme in the minds of most white westerners. Recognizing that historians have not created precise terms for the wide range of moderate positions on slavery and those who held them, I have also made broadly specific use of them in order to categorize residents' political and ideological stances on this issue that is foundational to the war. I use "proslavery" to refer to those residents who favored slavery for whatever reason, whether or not they themselves owned slaves or hoped to, or who advocated the perpetuation of slavery for any reason in their state, region, or elsewhere. I use "antislavery" to refer to those who, by a wide range of actions and beliefs, saw slavery as problematic and hoped for or worked toward its gradual end in the middle border region or in the nation, yet did not seek abolition by legislative enactments. I use the terms "anti-abolitionist" and "emancipationist" as respective positions within the general proslavery and antislavery constituencies. The term "abolitionist" is reserved for those who actively supported or worked to achieve the statutory end of slavery by means of governmental power.

Given the evolution of the meanings of the terms "North"—and "northerner"—and "South"—and "southerner"—to contemporary white Americans in the middle border region, rather than replicate historians' a postieri use of them, I have tried to use these terms only in the context of residents' understandings, as political descriptors rather than as geographical or cultural references.

The Rivers Ran Backward

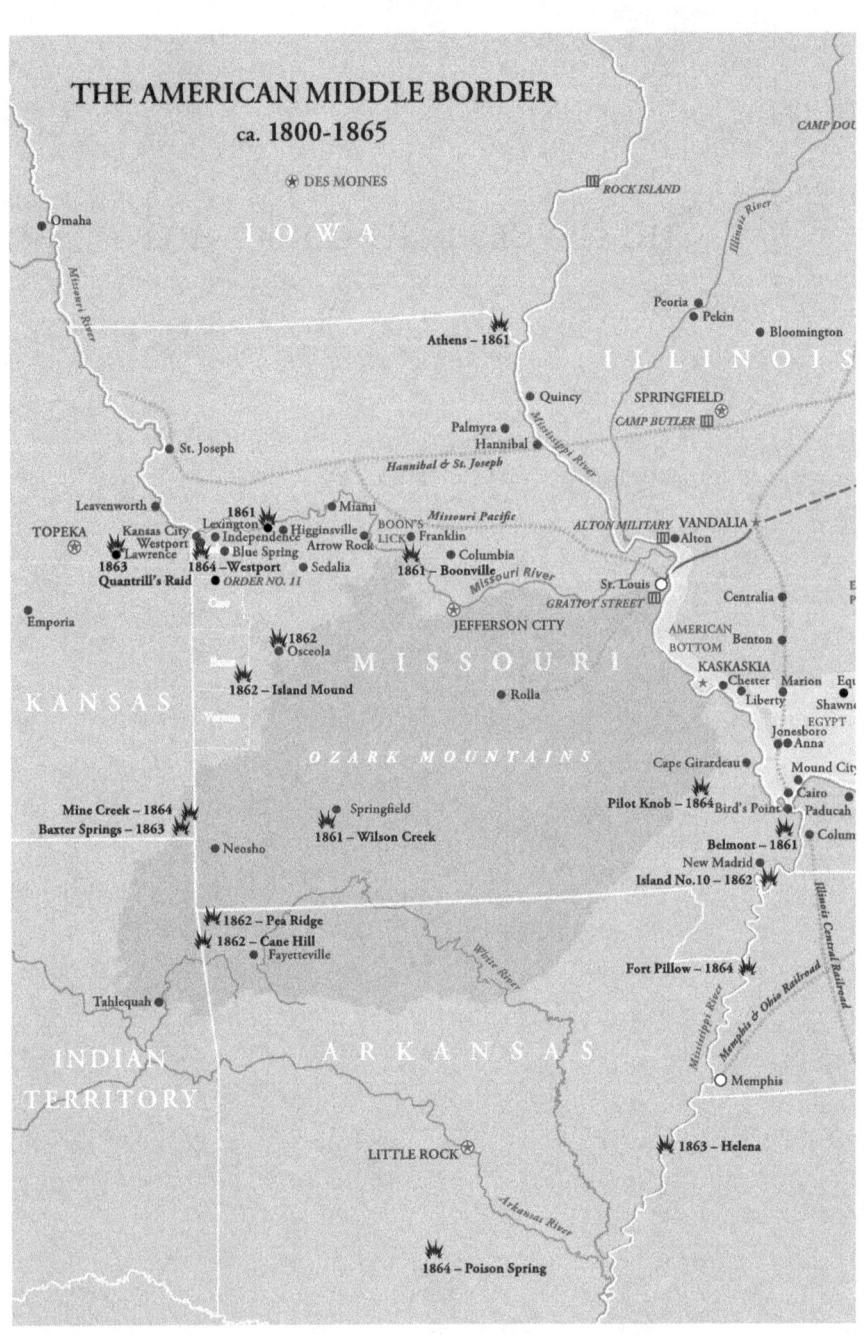

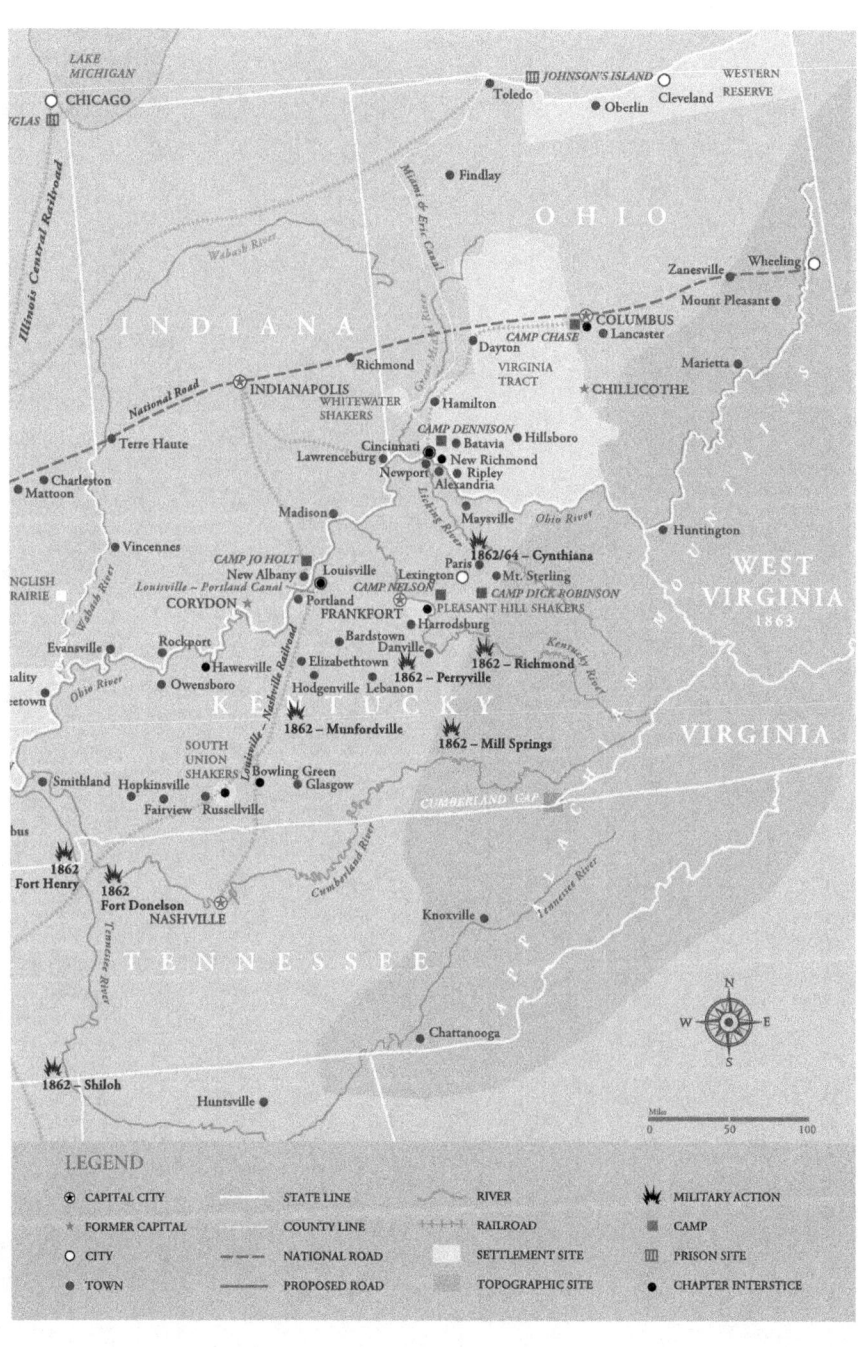

"There Is a West"

They came to renew wedding vows—and to stand witness to the act.

On the cold Thursday afternoon of January 26, 1860, residents of Columbus, Ohio, joined the state's Republican governor, William Dennison, and its congressmen, in joint session in the state capitol. Amid buildings draped with bunting and flags, throngs of people lined the city's streets to cheer the procession of marching bands and militia companies escorting a visiting entourage to the state house, with its steps, windows, and unfinished cupola illuminated by thousands of candles. Packing the chambers of Ohio's House of Representatives, the legislators greeted their invited guests with thunderous applause. Among those guests were the governors of Kentucky and Indiana; the lieutenant governors of Kentucky and Tennessee; and numerous dignitaries, including state judges and members of the various state legislatures and the U.S. Congress.[1]

This grand reception was the last of four such demonstrations that had begun on the previous Tuesday in Louisville, Kentucky, ostensibly to celebrate the opening of the Louisville and Nashville Railroad. Undertaken nearly a decade earlier at a cost of over $7 million, the route would eventually connect the middle border region from north to south by rail just as the rivers had for half a century. The journey would take just ten hours by train, rather than three days or more by steamboat.[2]

None of these gatherings was a simple ribbon-cutting ceremony. Sectional politics were grafted onto regional celebrations. What started in Louisville, where in front of some five hundred attendees, Bluegrass dignitaries warmly welcomed visitors from the other states, soon became self-styled "Union festivals" that continued on to Cincinnati and Dayton prior to the group's arrival in the Ohio state capital. As in each of the other cities, a public banquet was convened, at which guests offered fulsome toasts declaring their solidarity with neighboring Ohio River valley states. In Cincinnati, the Queen City of the West, where the invited "excursionists" had arrived by riverboat after chuffing upriver to cannon salutes and flag-waving, the *Daily Press* triumphantly announced the Kentuckians and Tennesseans as "messengers of peace," and at the "joyous" meeting, "Ohio and Kentucky embraced each other by proxy, and saved the Union without firing a single gun."[3]

Yet somber sectional tones echoed throughout the halls and hotels. In the early weeks of what would likely be a fractious presidential election year—only months after abolitionist John Brown's shocking raid on Harpers Ferry, in the border area of Virginia and weeks after his public execution there—speakers recognized a tense new relationship for old friends, one that the new railroad might help to ease. Invoking the memory of "the noble [Henry] Clay...who knew no North, no South—nothing but his country, his whole country, the Constitution, the Union, and the laws," the dignitaries conjured up all the fraternal imagery they could muster. They pointed to geographic contiguity; shared historical sacrifices; and common cultural and political covenants, causes, and destinies. All such boasts evoked pride in the traditional union of these middle border states as hopeful evidence of the strength of the Union itself. James A. Garfield, a young state senator and president of the Western Reserve Eclectic Institute (later Hiram College), declared in Louisville, "We have long enough heard the story of the North and the South.... God be praised, there is a West." The speakers placed their dependence on the greatest commonality of the sister states: "the beautiful Ohio," as one put it, "which seems to separate us, is, in fact, a bond of union that connects us more firmly together." Ironically, it was this very natural artery that the railroad was intended to eclipse.[4]

Yet the toastmasters' testaments suggested to their audiences that they were clearly worried about a divided region as much as about a nation riven over slavery. None of the speakers was more concerned than Indiana's Democratic governor, Ashbel P. Willard. "All along the border line," he claimed, "the people are friends of the Union." He honed his argument and audience, emphasizing a border made by divisive slavery politics rather than divided white cultures. "There is but one question before this country that imperils the Union," the free state's chief executive claimed.

> That is the relation that exists between the white man and the black man in this country.... Kentucky has no right to say to Indiana, you shall be a slave State; Indiana has no right to turn upon the other side and say Kentucky shall be a free State. [Renewed cheers.] And this quarrel does not grow up between Tennessee and Kentucky, Indiana and Ohio.... But up in the far North, where many men never saw four negroes in their lives, we have a quarrel, and down in the extreme South a great many Southern men are not satisfied with the present state of government. I, for one, and I think I speak the voice of my people, am satisfied where the laws now are. [Applause.][5]

The other speakers quickly took up Willard's cue. They offered toasts expressing outrage at sectional extremists in the North and the South, worlds away from their gathering. To rousing cheers, Memphian Robert G. Payne, who proclaimed himself "a Southern man, with all the impulses of my own glorious South," admitted that the harmony offered by those in attendance roused him not to full trust, but rather to renewed faith that conservatism over slavery in the free West yet prevailed over northern radicalism. "I never yet contemplated a dissolution of this Union," he averred, adding, "if the battle is to be fought, I will fight, but it will be for the Constitution and the temple of the Union." A Kentuckian from the western river town of Owensboro, who eschewed the term "southern man" yet fully understood its politicized meaning, was relieved. "[T]he Union is safe," he wrote. "The friends of the Constitution and the Union had no foe or rivalry except among their own phalanx[e]s.... Demagogues there will be disappointed." The word "there" referred to the states immediately north of his river, where the entourage would soon travel. Indeed, if these unionists had a lingua franca, it was their acknowledgment of a perceived border between freedom and slavery, one that agitators—inside and outside their region, in the Deep North and Deep South—were actively manipulating to undo a traditional white consensus in their western region. Having crossed a soft border into the buffer state of Kentucky, where antislavery demagogues were not tolerated, the prospect of heading north of the Ohio River was more daunting to less proximate "southern men" like Payne. Indeed, a Nashville reporter covering the event, who admitted he had "never crossed the border before," prepared himself for the "Land of the Abolitionists," where he feared an "attack from the ghost of old JOHN BROWN and his friends." Instead, he found nearly universal welcome from Ohioans all along the way to Columbus.[6]

This was not the first time in memory that a nervous diplomatic delegation from Kentucky had crossed the river in wintertime to ease regional disharmony over the "peculiar institution." In January 1839 commissioners from the Kentucky legislature—including former governor James T. Morehead—had traveled to Columbus to negotiate with the Ohio General Assembly for comity in the form of a fugitive slave law that would, like their state's law, punish those who enticed slaves to escape. (A recent unpleasant event, in which a mounted posse from Kentucky had unharmoniously crossed the river and arrested a noted abolitionist and Methodist minister in southern Ohio, led directly to this peace mission.) "[W]ith distinguished courtesy," the Kentucky commissioners were met in the Ohio capital by a largely sympathetic legislative committee, who had themselves recently received more than a dozen petitions from black and white abolitionists in the state begging for repeal of the state's racially discriminatory "Black Laws." Within weeks Ohio's governor, Wilson Shannon, a proslavery Democrat, requested a fugitive slave bill that would both deter inducers of slave escapes and facilitate recovery of those enticed to flee. At least one critic later charged Shannon with being "an extreme Southern man in politics."[7]

Less than a month later, on February 22, the Democrat-held Ohio General Assembly gave Shannon his bill, which he quickly signed into effect as the state's newest and perhaps most infamous Black Law amid both widespread celebration and determined resistance. The law would last less than five years, undone narrowly in December 1843, but not by widespread support for the end of slavery, whether in the form of activists working for its repeal, intrastate and intraparty politics, or an unfriendly U.S. Supreme Court ruling that made it untenable and unpopular. Rather, it lost out to the politics of hard times and expense in the lingering aftermath of a national depression. As one anti-abolitionist and repeal supporter argued, the people of Kentucky "should take care of their own negroes"—a suggestion most white Ohioans applauded and were entirely content to go along with by its fullest understanding.[8]

Introduction

Had they been offered a window onto the future only a year away, the celebrants of 1860 would have beheld a world either incomprehensible or grimly predictable. For a variety of reasons, these "Union festivals" in Kentucky and Ohio challenge accepted beliefs about the coming of the American Civil War. Most historians hold that the Ohio River was a clearly defined and static demographic and political boundary between North and South and, by its distinctive cultures, an extension of the Mason-Dixon Line developed decades after the famed surveyors completed their work in 1764. Once settled, the new states west of the Appalachians formed a fixed boundary between freedom and slavery, extending the border that inevitably produced the war.

None of these beliefs is, or was, accurate, but the centrality of the Civil War and its outcomes in the making of these tropes is undeniable. The Civil War's mythic influence has offered meaning and identity to generations of Americans and has allowed them to experience this conflict in ways unlike any other historical event. The war, as Robert Penn Warren wrote, "may, in fact, be said to *be* American history... our only 'felt' history—history lived in the national imagination."[1]

Schoolchildren learn that the South lost to the North, with no role allowed for the third of the nation's major nineteenth-century regions, the West. In prevailing narratives of the broad expanse beyond the Appalachians, the Civil War rarely serves as a defining event, and other than among military historians, it figures marginally in studies of the war. Ironically, this story's central figure, Abraham Lincoln, was a lifelong resident of the border states of this region, its middle border lying astride not one but two fault lines of that war, running east to west and north to south. This project began as a means to understand how Americans living in this space felt the war as it happened, but in the end it confirmed that those feelings were not bounded by four years of conflict, and that nearly a full century of passions spilled over from that war, changing the area into new and different places.

The complexities of those passions, and places, are best seen in the sectionalized postwar narratives of this western way of war. They stand in stark relief because they offer an alternative history of the war that occurred there. Slavery had not fully divided the white celebrants of the middle border's "Union festivals" in 1860, and long after the war's conclusion, Penn Warren—a western Kentuckian and resident of the once middle-border region, who famously took his stand as an agrarian southerner along with eleven other of the region's most prominent intellectuals in the early twentieth century—had his felt history, his "uninstructed Southernism," proved wrong by its realities in his home region. Close to the semicentennial of the end of the war in 1915, Warren was dumbfounded to learn from his proslavery, maternal grandfather and former Kentucky Confederate that he "had been a Union man," opposed to secession and the war "worked up by fools—Southern fire-eaters and Yankee abolitionists," until he saddled up and rode with Nathan Bedford Forrest and participated in the atrocity at Fort Pillow, Tennessee, in 1864. Like Warren's kin, my own paternal ancestors were western Kentuckians and slaveholders who—as I was equally dumbfounded to learn from archival evidence—were vocally opposed to the Thirteenth Amendment, which ended the peculiar institution. Unlike Warren's kin, mine were confirmed proslavery neutralists, who stayed out of the war as much as possible, serving halfheartedly in their county's home guard. Shortly after 1915, my paternal great-grandfather took his family from the Green River country and crossed the Ohio, heading "up North" to rural central Illinois. There they found anything but a sentimental reconciliation over the war among their rural, almost exclusively white new neighbors. There they were assaulted by taunts of being poor and ignorant, rebels, southerners.[2]

"Forgetting," wrote scholar Ernest Renan, "is a crucial factor in the creation of a nation." If current scholarly interpretations are to be believed, the nation's former bitterness about the war had largely been forgotten by the beginning of the twentieth century. As David W. Blight has argued powerfully in *Race and Reunion: The Civil War in American Memory*, in the aftermath of the war, "American culture romance triumphed over reality, [and] sentimental remembrance won over ideological memory." The divided nation had reunited by the semicentennial of the conflict, as its once-divergent narratives of the war harmonized around a new, reconciled nationalism built on racial subordination, by which white Americans effectively buried the smoldering embers of war divisions. The once deeply felt war seemingly dissipated to mystic chords of memory amid a torrent of white commemorative activity.[3]

As a Kentuckian, Robert Penn Warren cited the historical memory of the Civil War as the parchment for his southernness. Updating the foundational studies of southern political behavior by V. O. Key, in the 1980s sociologist John Shelton Reed interviewed white Americans who characterized themselves as southerners and found that those who resided in the self-described "Border South"—a subregion that did not exist until the twentieth century—especially west of the Appalachians, were most defensive of their identity. According to Reed, these recent southerners clung tightly to this regional identity, in large part from the fear of losing what they considered their cultural distinctiveness to the encroachment of "northern" influences, to which they were geographically closest and thus most susceptible. With his work generally focused on the cultural elements of regional identification, Reed included surprisingly little historical foundation for the various delineators comprising what he has called the modern "One South."[4]

The One South had considerable help in its formation, not the least of which derived from the experience of the Civil War and its reinterpretation by those on both sides of the famed border. As historian Barbara J. Fields argues of the constructed nature of identity, especially regional, "coherence, built on the retrospective aggregation of contingencies, comes after the fact." Nowhere was such latter-day coherence demonstrated more than in the middle border states, including the slave states of Kentucky and Missouri and the free states of Illinois, Indiana, Ohio, and Kansas, where Confederate and Union allegiances were deeply contested and malleable during and after the war and where bitterness at its outcomes intruded beyond traditional wartime allegiances. Between and within these states, white Americans who reputedly reconciled or reunited with former foes after the war created antagonistic counternarratives about the war as deliberate reversals of history, and which have proven remarkably resilient.[5]

Present-day residents often align the war narrative with the traditional sectional binary. Below the rivers, the Civil War was a valiant struggle by Confederate soldiers, who fought in defense of invaded home states and southern cultural institutions, with defiant votes for secession by conventions or rump legislatures in Kentucky and Missouri and the inclusion of stars representing these states on the Confederacy's national flag to being evidence that these bodies did their full duty for the southern cause. Postwar memoirs and biographies of Confederate wartime leaders from these states, as well as works by modern popular writers and even historians, have helped the rebels carry the narrative field in a rout. Yet more white soldiers from Kentucky and Missouri fought for the Union than for the Confederacy, and these numbers increase—nearly doubling for Kentucky—when enlisted African Americans from these states are included.

Equally complicated is any application of a "One North" model to states lying above the western rivers. In this "Lower North," as historians Eric Foner, William W. Freehling, and others have dubbed the middle border's free states, postwar narratives effectively "unionized" their war histories, portraying them entirely as blue-clad, small-town, and farm men, led by Abraham Lincoln and his military triumvirate—Ulysses S. Grant, William T. Sherman, and Philip Sheridan, all from the free border region—who drove the federal armies to victory over gray-clad rebel foes, including Kentuckians and Missourians, who fought largely to preserve their peculiar institution. This narrative wrote out pervasive proslavery sentiment and war dissent in these free states, although more than half of these states' southernmost counties did not support Lincoln. Large numbers of embittered fighting-age white men, called Butternuts or Copperheads by their northern or Republican opponents, evaded or quit the war altogether, supporting the Peace Democrats or waging a subversive war against their Republican neighbors. The arrest of the war's best known dissenter, former Ohio Democratic U.S. congressman Clement L. Vallandigham, and Lincoln's exiling him to the Confederacy without the benefit of trial, became a cause célèbre for wartime dissent and postwar obstructionism. Other than in academic studies, Vallandigham's place in history is remembered mainly as the subject of Edward Everett Hale's allegorical wartime short story, "The Man Without a Country," a biting example of the northernized war narrative's disdain for war dissent.[6]

So too, competing interpretive schools, national and state, have largely replicated the broader wartime alignments, further complicating narratives of the conflict in this western space. Indeed, David M. Potter chided "northern" historians who equate nationalism with northernness and sectionalism with southernness and "southern" historians who overemphasize the distinctiveness of the region's white culture. In both narratives, the North and South are presumed to be fixed and distinctive cultural, ideological, or geographical entities.[7]

Such binary definitions, northern and southern, obscure a third narrative of the war. This former West, the nation's middle border, was less a battleground for the conventional war than for a different conflict. For war-era residents there, the Civil War was the catalytic event in a long struggle between collectivism, imperfectly recognized as northern progressivism, and individualism, equally imperfectly recognized as southern traditionalism. Because the war's meaning was most contingent in this place, these conflicts entwined into bitter, persistent legacies that were only deepened over a century of politics, formal and informal, surrounding the conflict. Between 1800 and 1915, long-harmonized tensions between competing nationalist ideologies were magnified by formal sectional politics over the extension of slavery, then were realized as antagonisms through the war, and were at last transformed by informal cultural politics surrounding the end of slavery, including postwar memories and physical commemorations of the war and its outcomes.[8]

At the center of this extended process was an encompassing "People's contest," as Abraham Lincoln dubbed the war as a whole, one that has largely evaded historical scrutiny. Although Lincoln himself did not anticipate how at once appropriate and inadequate was his choice of words, the conflict in the region he called home was an uncivil, lived war, one that was ultimately overshadowed by broader, traditional narratives of the clash of arms. Unlike the war on the front lines, the middle border's conflict was fought largely in innumerable clashes that occurred at every level: state, county, and municipal governments; within and between communities, families, neighbors, and friends; in parlors, dining rooms, barns, churches, schools, stores, groves, and fields; at public meetings, polling places, and recruiting stations; and along dusty roads, wooded paths, and fences—wherever people met during their daily routines. Through discussions over the right of secession; decisions about neutrality and neutralism; defining loyalty and disloyalty; choosing whether to support or oppose emancipation and the draft; and debating the war's social, constitutional, and racial outcomes, they crafted language and meanings to define themselves and distinguish others like and unlike themselves. This often painful process—negotiated with full knowledge that doing so would likely alter many personal and community-based relationships—forced white border residents to create politicized identities that were central to waging this inner struggle in the midst of what many there considered an outsiders' war.[9]

This book is about how a traditional western political culture that traditionally accommodated slavery was transformed by the era of the Civil War—its coming, its lived experience, and its memory—into the cultural politics of region. It explains how slavery could organize the life of an entire region even as it became the foundation of the conflict while being at once its least attributed and most unreconciled cause among those white residents who endured it. It also explains how in their haste to make a fully formed sectional border divided by slavery historians have largely ignored the centrality of Lincoln's home region—the West—to perhaps the war's most lasting outcome. Beneath the edifice of postwar American nationalism lay newly formed regional identities that were anything but unifying and have proven more enduring than their sectionalized predecessors. Because regionalism is cultural and thus intrinsically political, it has been anything but a "good twin" to the formal politics of sectionalism, as historian Patricia Nelson Limerick has claimed, and its tensions are anything but soft-edged. By sustained and irreconciled postwar cultural politics surrounding the war and its divisive outcome—emancipation—claimants of the former West's promise of liberty changed what was once a lived border of confluence into an imagined and antagonistic border of separation defined as North and South and, more complicatedly, Middle West and Midwest. The formation of regional identities completed the nationalistic struggle that brought the war, and in doing so, the West was effectively written out of the traditional war narratives, accomplishing the moving frontier not by conquering physical space or its inhabitants but by new regional definitions understood as culture.[10]

The politics of exclusivism drove the engines of these identities, just as cultural politics in these states in turn were driven by them. Exclusivism refers to a war-era political process of societal inclusion and exclusion based on a broad spectrum of individual and collective acts of ideological, cultural, and political separation. Through this process, white residents of former western states redefined themselves and those around them into binary constructions: "northern" and "southern." These meanings evolved at specific times, always with politicized usages and accompanying aesthetics, and were contextualized by events occurring during the era of the Civil War. The looming presence of sectional identities might have shaped these negotiations, but the outcome was not dictated entirely by them. Sentimentalizing the concept of region has obscured its potent political purposes, rooted in this western place by a shared racial history and a divisive war that was experienced differently. The resultant regional identities were as, and perhaps more, attributable to the contest over emancipation than slavery.

The experience of that war, as much in victory as in defeat, and then the discrete and often inaccurate memories of its winning and its losing, changed the meaning of the border and with it the nation's regions. The acceptance of this new border, and the mutual understandings of the new regionalism, accomplished the nationalism that in part had spawned the war. Just as slavery had not fully divided the former western house before the war's outbreak, race—with white supremacy and African American exclusion as foundational democratic pillars—could not fully reunite its people after their political culture had been shattered by a war within the states.

The Rivers Ran Backward explains this politicized reversal of historical experience into cultural understandings of American regions, with the Civil War at its heart. The book is largely organized chronologically and topically, moving back and forth as events occurred across the interior rivers, central to the region's history, between the middle border's slave and free states. Chapter 1, "White Flows the River," assesses the coincidence of white freedom and black slavery and servitude as central pillars of a consensus that white culture built in the West during the early national period. Prior to national and regional debates over slavery that would emerge during the 1840s, for most white middle border residents slavery represented more than contradicted democratic ascendance in the West, seen especially in its slave states. Rather than the Ohio River forming an absolute barrier that slavery could not penetrate, and despite the Northwest Ordinance of 1787, which supposedly barred slavery from the "free" part of the middle border, slavery and white supremacy were interwoven into the fabric of the entire western region. Outright slavery existed in Kentucky and later Missouri, but legislative "Black Codes" in Illinois, Indiana, and Ohio and support for the legalization of slavery there sharply proscribed African Americans' freedoms and discouraged their residence.

Chapter 2, "Babel," describes the economic, political, and racial environment in the middle border region that sustained the western white consensus. Even as these states modernized between 1820 and 1850, if at different speeds, resultant demographic and economic expansion and diversity, not slavery politics, irrevocably divided western white populations. To various degrees, political parties in the region (Democrats and National Republicans, or "Whigs") adopted nationalist positions and eschewed the federal government's involvement in the issue of slavery, considering it a states' rights issue. As the debate over abolitionism influenced the West, racialized (or "conservative") antislavery strategies and movements such as colonization and gradual emancipation emerged among white residents to harmonize the region. Abolition, the most strident of the various antislavery activisms, had a conservative western variant. Consistent with the West being slavery's borderland, African Americans there collectively experienced a continuum of racial distinctions, statuses, and circumstances in these slave and free states rather than a sharp division between them as legal statuses.

Chapter 3, "The Ten-Year War," assesses the open national conflict over slavery that drew the West into the vortex of events during the 1850s. In the final antebellum decade, political fault lines compromised the former regional consensus as increasing numbers of white residents aligned for and against slavery. The moderate regional variants of the national parties, including the new Republican Party born in the region, were challenged by sectionalized platforms. Despite the region's slave states having comparatively few bond people, the democratic contours of slaveholding altered their political economy to defend the peculiar institution against "northern" agitators, namely abolitionists. Each successive controversy—the infamous Fugitive Slave Act (1850), the Kansas-Nebraska Act (1854), the *Dred Scott* decision (1857), the ill-fated Lecompton Constitution (1857–1858), the Lincoln-Douglas debates (1858), and John Brown's raid (1859)—sent shock waves through the region and complicated the western consensus. But the controversies did not yet fully sectionalize the region, as evidenced by voters' response to the outcome of the 1860 presidential election, which polarized the North and South politically and ideologically.

Chapter 4, "No North—No South—No East—No West," examines efforts in the middle border's slave states to maintain versions of neutrality as logical extensions of the region's consensus tradition met with failure in wartime. Neutrality and personal neutralism were statements not only of sovereignty, but also of dissent, designed to maintain the traditional balance of unionism and proslavery. These states' middle grounds gave license to partisans to forge terms of loyalty and disloyalty and target those who dissented. "Hard-line" warfare ensued in both Missouri and Kentucky, whereby the politics of slavery were infused into the contours of civilian-military interactions. Occupying federal and Confederate troops regarded neutrality as disloyalty, with slaveholding as an essential measure, and civilians used neutralism to their best advantage to protect themselves and the peculiar institution on their states' untenable middle grounds. As they reconsidered their relationship with the American nation, two proslavery political cultures emerged in these states—southerners of culture and political southerners—struggling to control their states' futures while defining the wartime contours of dissent in contested loyal slave states.

Chapter 5, "Netherworld of War," assesses the profound societal effects of the prolonged presence of military forces, federal and Confederate, in all of the middle border states. In the region's slave states, armies and state militia implemented military occupation to control a divided and often hostile civilian populace, subverting civil liberties at the local and state levels as part of a broader strategy to maintain order, determine loyalty and disloyalty, and obtain resources to prosecute the war. In the mesh of conflicting stances and allegiances, the military presence hastened communities' realignments among loyal and disloyal constituencies. In turn, these residents divided into "communities of allegiance" constituting discrete loyal and dissenting networks.

Chapter 6, "Bitter Harvest," assesses the political and ideological effects of the Emancipation Proclamation, which resulted in a more deeply divided white population in the middle border states in 1862 and 1863, pitting white and black civilians against military personnel. More than any other issue, emancipation disrupted the white consensus of the middle border region, as residents consolidated all other controversial war initiatives: confiscation, conscription, and the suspension of habeas corpus. The term "Conservative" arose in organized politics as a designation among white residents, whether Republicans or Democrats, for a blend of patriotism, opposition to wartime emancipation, protest against racial equality, and even outright support for slavery. The backlash against emancipation and the 1862 midterm elections ignited a civil war within the middle border's free states and troops. Republicans used harsh measures to rein in new Democratic majorities intent on undercutting the federal war effort, and partisanship emerged in the form of the rise of empowered dissenting groups, or "Copperheads."

Chapter 7, "Shadow Wars," examines the intertwined strands of the "war within the war" after emancipation and the 1862 midterm elections, which developed into a civilian home front war that raged between 1863 and 1865. Not all interactions between the middle border's war supporters and dissenters in their struggle for power resulted in violence, but they fueled the hardening of ideological and political positions into a wartime binary that would outlast the conflict. Guerrilla warfare was only the most apparent manifestation of the ideologically based internecine struggle that roiled the middle border region as white residents turned against the government's war. Emancipation and black enlistment ignited a full political war among black and white, slave and free, Conservatives and Radicals, and drew the active and sustained engagement of women amid a "fire in the rear," as Lincoln characterized the antiwar dissent movement. The conflict reached into communities as local, partisan discord and even violence more than as organized electoral politics. Wartime dissent reached a crescendo prior to the 1864 presidential election, only to decline precipitously after Lincoln's reelection and the Republican (or National Union) Party's resounding victory in the West.

Chapter 8, "Southern Cross, North Star," examines the middle border's postwar political struggles and development of exclusivist war memories and meanings that ended the region's former white consensus. Racial aversion in the region's former free states could not contend with racial hatred in the former slave states, and the willingness of white residents to resort to violence in the postwar period provided one measure of difference between former loyal states. However deep and shared their war wounds, they were felt discretely as white residents translated war experiences into distinct postwar understandings. More important to these politics than racial discourse and violence was white residents' conscious distortion, even inversion, of these states' war narratives so as to align them along the emergent North-South binary. The abstruse politics of white sacrifice, formal and especially informal, offered distinct lenses that obstructed reconciliation across what were seen as discrete regional cultures. Despite the similarities of these states' postwar experiences, the cultural politics of war memory and regional white identity divided these middle border states from one another.

§

On August 26, 1863, Abraham Lincoln wrote a letter to supporters attending a war rally in his hometown of Springfield, Illinois, urging them to stay the course through tempestuous times. The recent capture of Vicksburg, Mississippi, by federal forces prompted Lincoln, who understood—and had used—the western waterways as highways to success, to claim the feat as a sign of ultimate victory. "The Father of Waters again goes unvexed to the sea," he wrote confidently. (Faced with questions from his private secretaries about several watery metaphors, Lincoln responded, "I reckon the people will know what it means.") "Thanks to the great Northwest for it. Nor yet wholly to them. Three hundred miles up, they met New England, Empire, Key-stone, and Jersey, hewing their way right and left." For the nation, that victory signaled a new birth of freedom—words he would soon deliver at Gettysburg, the twin victory to Vicksburg—including participation by those only recently enslaved. "The Sunny South too, in more colors than one, also lent a hand. On the spot, their part of the history was jotted down in black and white." His regional references were not made by chance. Only weeks before, ugly draft and race riots had torn through New York and Boston. The president perhaps addressed his detractors more, especially those "dissatisfied with me about the negro."[11]

Lincoln referenced emancipation to speak to his Democratic opposition. Those in his home region would hear a unique articulation of recent troubling events there. In the raw days after Missouri guerrillas had brutally murdered nearly two hundred antislavery civilians in Lawrence, Kansas, the president used alternately sanguine and scolding words to stitch together the various strands of meaning for a changed conflict there—race, slavery, emancipation—to offer a hardened response to the purveyors of retributive warfare in his home region. Ending the not-so-peculiar institution would not only save the nation but also end, once and for all, what one historian has called the resultant "Long War for the West." Control of those rivers that had long actuated freedom for some while denying it for others symbolized another conquest: severing the region's enduring ligaments between freedom and slavery. "[T]his great consummation," Lincoln argued, would occur despite resistance as desperate as in the Confederacy from "some white [men], unable to forget that, with malignant heart, and deceitful speech, they have strove to hinder it.... [A]mong free men, there can be no successful appeal from the ballot to the bullet; and that they who take such appeal are sure to lose their case, and pay the cost."[12]

The president would live just long enough to comprehend the full cost of those appeals. He would not live to see the full payment, including perhaps the war's greatest irony: that the victorious North created a larger, more enduring South than the defeated Confederacy could accomplish for itself, and that his former western neighbors created a border between them after the fact. Claiming the western waterways that during slavery had adhered to his home region, Lincoln's decision for emancipation would make them a symbolic dividing line between the newly defined North and South. Through the Civil War and its aftermath, the rivers reversed their course and, with it, the nation's manifest destiny.

White Salt, Black Servitude

"Let your speech be alway[s] with grace, seasoned with salt," the apostle Paul exhorted his followers, "that ye may know how ye ought to answer every man." His virtuous reference was to the most life-sustaining of natural substances, for centuries nearly synonymous with fidelity, honor, and wealth. Because salt was also a medium of exchange, taxation, and power, it could not have been more appropriate in the nineteenth-century American context that in the same letter Paul offered one of his most oft-quoted and oft-condemned scriptural passages: "Servants, obey in all things your masters."

Readers of the good book on the American middle border, like John Hart Crenshaw, would have entirely connected salt with servitude. The white mineral they so relied on had been produced locally by unfree black hands. Crenshaw's life circumstances were not only a testament to the value of the manufacture of salt, the lucrative business he pursued for a quarter century in southern Illinois—or "Egypt," as locals commonly referred to the wedge of land between the Mississippi and Ohio Rivers, in part because of the annual flooding of their wide, low-lying bottoms. They also revealed the persistence of slavery, unfreedom, and racial subordination in the middle border region in the early part of the nineteenth century.[1]

Born in 1797 on the northern border of South Carolina, Crenshaw was a child of the frontier when his parents moved him far beyond the mountains to New Madrid, Missouri, just within foreign land west of the Mississippi River. Despite Spanish efforts to encourage settlement, New Madrid, a former trading post on the river's west bank, remained a sad river town of about a hundred shanties and cabins. Only a year after their arrival in 1807, one visitor described its population as "a mixture of French creoles from Illinois, United States Americans, and Germans. They have plenty of cattle, but seem in other respects to be very poor." Poverty would not drive the Crenshaws out of the District of Louisiana—known generally as "Upper Louisiana" and soon to be known as Missouri. Indeed, the family held a sizable tract of land. Rather, they fled from a series of four earthquakes that began shaking the area just before Christmas in 1811. The worst quake hit in mid-February 1812, when the ground near New Madrid heaved, trees uprooted, and river banks shifted, then crumbled and fell. In Cincinnati, more than three hundred miles away, it "shook the houses, rocked the furniture, opened several partition doors that were fastened with falling latches and threw down bricks from the tops of chimneys." President James Madison was rumored to have been awakened from his sleep to reports that church bells were ringing in Boston. Indeed, the mighty Mississippi briefly ran backward, permanently lowering the land along the Mississippi and engulfing forests that once lined its low-lying banks. Daily tremors occurred for months. Weekly ones were felt for years.[2]

The Crenshaws were not alone in abandoning what soon became known as the "sunk country." Set against the start of Tecumseh's uprising above the Ohio, disguised as another war with the British, white westerners' mounting fears triggered a religious revival that shook the region as much as the earthquakes. As Methodists, the Crenshaws might well have taken part in the wave of revivalism that began several hundred miles east in central Kentucky. Crenshaw's father, William, soon resettled his wife and seven children some one hundred miles to the northeast, on Eagle Creek, a tributary of the Saline River in newly formed Gallatin County, Illinois. Twelve miles east was Shawneetown, a fast-growing Ohio River port and Illinois's largest town, which the peripatetic Fortescue Cuming noted in 1809 "contains about twenty-four cabins...and more appearance of business than I had seen on this side of Pittsburgh."[3]

In Illinois the elder Crenshaw put faith in the distant federal government, which many like him had come west to avoid. Only the past year surveyors had marked land for future distribution according to Congress's 1785 land ordinance, and the government was set to open a land office at Shawneetown to apportion saleable plots. Crenshaw leased his land directly from the government, and his choice of flinty ridges and a boggy depression of some fourteen acres suggested he was perhaps the West's worst judge of land. But Crenshaw chose the tract on Eagle Creek for a specific purpose. Located just south of the junction of the two main thoroughfares between Missouri and Kentucky, it lay within a sixty-five-square-mile government reserve set aside because of the area's saline "licks," in which for centuries Native Americans had made salt from shallow wells. Because the saline land was in the reserve, Crenshaw and others could not buy it. Once Illinois became a state in 1818, and despite the Illinois territorial legislature's preemption law permitting renters like Crenshaw to buy the land they occupied, the federal government maintained control of it. With government-contract salt-makers having plied their trade at several nearby licks since 1806, "supply[ing] with salt all the settlements within one hundred miles, and I believe the whole of Upper Louisiana," the lease looked safe.[4]

The elder Crenshaw would not live to see the outcome of his gamble. He died in September 1814, leaving the fledgling salt operation in the hands of his three sons. The eldest, John, then seventeen, worked for the family's business only a couple of years. He then leased his own tract a mile to the north, gambling on his own behalf by paying for the higher lease required for acquiring an established salt operation. Collecting the saline water was far easier there than in the boggy bottoms his brothers continued to work.

Salt-making was no easy task. Man- or horse-operated pumps—or, if one was lucky, spurting springs—filled elevated tanks, which in turn fed wooden pipelines, bored from whole tree trunks that had been narrowed at one end and driven together, to bring the briny water to furnace houses. A series of iron evaporating kettles, anchored in brick kilns over fire pits, burning constantly and heated nearly to glowing, received the water. Laborers felled trees and dragged them from the woods nearby. Wood smoke belched into the air as the fires boiled the saline water. When the water had nearly evaporated, workers carried the remaining paste in oak baskets to one or more drying houses, where on plank floors workers sifted the dried paste, turning it into hard crystals. They packed the dried salt into oak barrels and hitched up teams of oxen that hauled the heavy load nine miles to Shawneetown.

Local producers routinely undercut the government and one another, bootlegging salt into Kentucky, sabotaging pipelines, and stealing water. Salt-makers on the reserve soon faced competition. The Kanawha works in western Virginia increasingly shipped their salt westward on river steamers. With salt selling for 37½ cents and more per sixty-pound bushel, and a market that spanned the Ohio, Cumberland, Tennessee, and Mississippi valleys, cutthroat competition was the norm. To keep up, the Gallatin salt-makers pushed their laborers relentlessly. By 1819 these Gallatin County salt springs were producing from two to three hundred thousand bushels of salt a year. In 1824, just one of the nearby salt companies produced an average of nearly five thousand bushels of salt per month, with a potential profit of more than $16,000 a year.[5]

John Crenshaw soon saw salt pay off. He established himself as a local producer, controlling three of the nine works on the reserve. As Kentuckians and other middle migrants streamed into the state, Shawneetown grew rapidly. Land and salt ran the town, with enough wealth to turn it into the state's banking center. The outsized brick and stone Greek revival Bank of Illinois, built in 1838, housed the town and state's wealth and power and symbolized the West's aspirations.[6]

Salt production required hard, dangerous, and ceaseless labor that few free men would perform. Luckily for Crenshaw, Illinois lawmakers had made provisions to guarantee salt-makers in the reserve a ready source of unfree labor. Although Jefferson's 1787 Northwest Ordinance had ostensibly prohibited chattel bondage in the region, the delegates to Illinois's statehood convention recognized the value of the saline reserve to the new state's infant economy.

Members of the convention—the largest contingent of whom both lived in southern Illinois and had themselves migrated from slave states—included a key clause that forbade future importations of slaves into the state but allowed French-owned slaves to remain. The convention also continued the practice of slave labor in the reserve—either by hire or "voluntary servitude," a novel system of contract apprenticeship that secured unfree African Americans in perpetual bondage—or until 1825 by outright ownership of slaves. Black labor would thus continue unmolested for salt-makers in Egypt. Indeed, the persistence of bound black labor in the Gallatin salines prompted another name for Crenshaw's saltworks: the "nigger springs." Ironically, only a couple of miles away lay the new town of Equality.[7]

John Crenshaw drew deeply from his briny wells of opportunity. He set up a steam sawmill at Cypressville to supplement the income from his three salt furnaces; it became so important locally that two separate petitions for roads included stipulations that they pass by his mill. He soon involved himself in large-scale construction projects in the area, including providing labor and ties for a new railroad company's line grade and building a brick railroad depot at Shawneetown. In July 1829 the Illinois state legislature, desperate for money to offset the massive costs of internal improvements that would soon nearly bankrupt it, auctioned some thirty thousand acres of the saline lands. Crenshaw purchased several thousand acres and continued leasing many more. A couple of years later he began construction of a crudely columned, three-story Greek revival house with piazzas on the first two floors, which stood on a sharp eminence overlooking the Saline River. Crenshaw named his at-once garish and rustic palace, completed after nearly a decade of work, "Hickory Hill." Among its earliest overnight guests in the fall of 1840 was a young state representative, Abraham Lincoln.[8]

Rumors had long accompanied Crenshaw's success. For more than a decade his name had been associated with illegal perpetuation of full slavery. He invariably refused to grant certificates of freedom to bonded laborers he hired, although they were required annually by Illinois law for black persons who wished to remain in the state, and obstructed freedom certificates by legal hairsplitting. Indeed, he does not show up in the county's 1830 registry of slaves and servants—although a number of his business competitors did—suggesting that he largely eschewed "annual" labor contracts, which bound workers for as long as seventy-five consecutive years, in favor of chattel laborers at his various salt operations. Since the 1820s gossip had linked Crenshaw, under the pseudonym John Granger, to the region's free black abduction trade, a perverse "reverse underground railroad."[9]

Whispers now circulated about Crenshaw's new house. Oddly, the large second floor had double doors on the back, wide enough for wagons to pull in, as if it were a barn. The third floor, as some heard it, was the home's most curious feature. Accessible only by a narrow, steep, and concealed stairwell, it was no simple garret. A central corridor was flanked by a dozen rooms, some as small as six by three feet. Each had windows and doors to the corridor only, with iron bars, screens, and locks, and inside each cramped room was a pair of crude wooden bunks. Alternately stifling and frigid, the rooms ostensibly confined Crenshaw's "apprentices" in what the family generally called "the quarters." Locals murmured about the iron rings that were anchored to the floor joists, some sized for children, and the whipping posts that stood on either end of the corridor. A registry of servants and slaves during the period suggests that Crenshaw brought "voluntary" laborers from slave states much farther away than Kentucky. Only three individuals had come from neighboring states, while the remainder had come from ten different slave states as far south as Louisiana and as far east as Georgia. More likely, the labor of the largest portion of Crenshaw's black workers was coerced, a far cry from the unfreedom that Illinois in fact allowed.[10]

Only three days after completion of his "slave house," as locals soon called it, rumors exploded into fact. On March 28, 1842, the salt-maker stood accused of kidnapping a free black family who farmed in the area and selling them to a slave trader, who took them down the Mississippi to Arkansas or beyond. That same day, Crenshaw's steam sawmill at Cypressville burned under mysterious circumstances. The two events were certainly not unrelated. Because his mill offered both semiskilled and unskilled work, Crenshaw could not have avoided noticing that Cypressville had become largely a free black settlement, as numerous freedpeople and their families from Kentucky and Tennessee came there to find work.[11]

Crenshaw's indictment was among a string of confrontations that soon engulfed Gallatin County in racial warfare. As the editor of the *Illinois Republican* related, a brother and a friend of the family whom Crenshaw had sold into slavery attacked the salt-maker, who had been released on bond, while on the road. Managing to escape with his life, he quickly had the local sheriff arrest the two. Days later, Crenshaw's own trial began. As it progressed, and periodically after the verdict, armed and mounted white men rode the county's roads, firing guns in the air and spreading word that they intended to "forc[e] all the Negroes, without respect to age, sex, condition or character to leave the county." Calling themselves "Regulators," a term long familiar to former upcountry South Carolinians like Crenshaw, these vigilantes burned nearly the entire village of Cypressville that night in what a local editor termed an outbreak of "Negrophobia." These nightriders, young white men from respectable families in the Shawneetown area, had for a decade recurrently formed paramilitary bands that administered rough justice to perceived black and white miscreants—especially emancipationists—but also engaged in illegal activities, including horse-stealing, counterfeiting, and arson, and threatened law enforcement officials if they interfered. In this latest spate of violence, residents appealed to the state's governor for troops to restore the rule of law. Among the Regulators' illicit activities, suggesting their willingness to defend John Crenshaw, was kidnapping free blacks in the area and selling them into slavery south of the Ohio.[12]

In the midst of the Regulator crisis in southern Illinois, by a narrow 4–3 ruling, the supreme court of Illinois outlawed the state's constitutional provisions allowing slavery and contract servitude. Its legislature then strengthened the state's "Black Code" by requiring current and prospective black residents to post a $1,000 bond to live in the state and permitted white residents to turn them in for even the slightest infractions. Three years later, in 1848, the state's new constitution officially prohibited the ownership of slaves in Illinois. In 1850 Illinois lawmakers banned black immigration altogether. Violators would be sold into slavery outside the state.[13]

Vigilantism, likely more than governmental reform, altered John Crenshaw's white-and-black world of salt. But it did not entirely change it. In the 1850 census, his household listed three black and mulatto members, complete with his surname. Listed also, as Crenshaw's "neighboring households," were a total of sixteen African Americans of various ages and sexes, with at least eight different surnames, born variously in South Carolina, Virginia, Tennessee, Kentucky, and Illinois, mostly males whose occupations were listed simply as "laborer." What the census taker did not record was whether those black households lived freely, or as people less than fully free, on this murky middle ground.[14]

1

White Flows the River

Freedom and Unfreedom in the Early National West

John Crenshaw's long perpetuation of unfreedom in Illinois challenges the image of the Ohio River as a powerful symbol of a divided America. Slavery and freedom are only the most obvious of presumed static barriers that mirrored the timeless cultural divide between North and South. Embedded in the imaginations of generations has been the powerful human drama of fugitive slaves escaping across their "River Jordan" to the free states that lay north, a boundary that to a lesser degree extended westward across the Mississippi, along the Missouri River. For Crenshaw and many white residents of the early western country, the great western rivers offered no more impenetrable a barrier between freedom and slavery than did their often shallow banks against annual floodwaters. Rather than form an absolute barrier that slavery could not penetrate, the rivers served as a collective confluence for both slavery and freedom.

Slavery was not a disunifying institution in the middle border region, precisely because it boasted a cultural mélange drawn largely from states where the institution of slavery was still practiced. The Ohio River was an artery by which people from the middle Atlantic coastal states, the southern states, New England, and Europe poured into the western country, and they transferred various cultural ways to diverse, if clustered, locales. The result was a pluralistic society in which cultural persistence existed alongside societal adaptations. As noted in 1834 by one traveler, Charles F. Hoffman, these new westerners readily acceded both persistence and change in their adopted home. "There is a common phrase in the new settlements of the West—'We all come from some place or another.'" In fact, slavery was among the aspects of the border region that made it difficult to characterize, because white settlers constructed a western political culture and identity that obscured the convergence of cultural elements on this borderland. During the later antebellum decades, Hoffman's adopted region was far more influenced by the slaveholding cultures of the middle and southern states than by those farther north, nearly all of which had disowned slavery.[1]

As early as 1784, after a trip to the western country, French essayist J. Hector St. Jean de Crèvecoeur proclaimed the Ohio River the "grand artery" by which the American West was thrown open to settlement from all parts of the globe. Seventeen years later Adam Rankin, a Presbyterian minister and native Pennsylvanian who had come west from Virginia in 1800, marveled at the diversity of peoples he saw in Lexington, Kentucky. "I suppose we are as complete a mixture of all nations as ever met," he averred. The Ohio and its tributaries, including the Kentucky River, which ran west and south of Lexington, was neither the sole nor the first artery by which the West was settled. Since the 1760s Anglo-Americans had crossed the Appalachians into Kentucky by way of the Wilderness Road through the famed Cumberland Gap. By the time of Crèvecoeur's pronouncement, Kentucky was a tenuous Virginia county boasting a population of as many as thirty thousand, and hundreds more trekked overland there every day, equaling or even surpassing the number floating down the Ohio. In effect, two distinct paths brought migrants from different parts of the extended Chesapeake region into separate reaches of the middle border.[2]

To the chagrin of New England Yankees, who sought in the West to create "the 'greater New England,'" during the first decades of the nineteenth century people primarily from the middle Atlantic states—Virginia and Maryland, as well as Pennsylvania, New Jersey, and Delaware—spearheaded the western migration. The journals kept by Presbyterian minister John Dabney Shane, drawn from interviews conducted with hundreds of surviving members of the charter generation of Ohio valley settlers, indicate that nearly half of Shane's informants, like himself, had been born in Virginia. (Pennsylvania was a distant second.) As late as 1788, George Washington himself believed his Old Dominion, or at least his portion of it, was part of what he called "the middle states" and certainly not part of the "Southern states," a term he reserved for Georgia and South Carolina. Among the earliest to go to the "Dixie frontier," as one historian termed it, were Virginia veterans who, in lieu of withheld pay, settled Ohio's Military Tract, reserved by Congress in 1791 in southern and central Ohio. As late as 1840, Virginia law student John Parson noted the middle and southern cultural influences he encountered in southern Indiana. He warmly accepted invitations to barbecues and relished burgoo, "a rich and well-seasoned soup of many ingredients," crediting the National Road for the migration. "For some years there has been a continual stream of movers from the East, from Ohio, from different parts of Indiana and from the South, into the Wabash country... little Southern carts drawn by bony little Southern horses... and we passed continually these families, sometimes five or ten in a company, wagons, men, women, children, and stock." New Albany was "in many respects... a Southern city." Affluent travelers in Quincy City, Illinois, a growing Mississippi river town north of St. Louis, lodged at its best hotel, the Virginia House.[3]

The Ohio River's south side similarly confounded attempts to sectionalize the West's mixed population. A resident of Mason County, Kentucky, living near the Ohio, wrote in 1794 that his neighbors had mostly "emigrated from New England, New York, Jersey, and Pennsylvania," and forty years later Charles Hoffman complimented the neat fields and hillside farms he encountered in Kentucky's Bluegrass region, likening them to those in eastern New York. As late as in 1856, Frederick Law Olmsted was similarly surprised by the middle border's similitude. "Travelers usually make the observation in descending the Ohio, that the free side shows all the thrift and taste," he judged. "It is a customary joke to call their attention to this, and encourage them to dilate upon it when the boat's head has been turned around without their notice.... The advantage, if any, is slight on the side of the free states."[4]

Yankee migrants often groused about their neighbors' distinctive cultural preferences and practices that they judged as southern. Beyond architectural styles, speech patterns, and the prevailing taste for corn whiskey, perceived differences included cookstove types; tastes for Irish or sweet potatoes, corn or wheat bread, pork or beef; fence-building methods; the shapes and sizes of their cleared fields and other farming methods; and the proper method of enclosing fields or livestock lots. Some broadened their gripes into general condemnations of western society. John M. Dickey, a Congregational minister from Connecticut, concluded bluntly in his correspondence with the tract *Home Missionary* in 1844 that upland "inhabitants of southern Indiana have no *enterprise*, no good *society*, no *intelligence*," blaming this on the "'poor class' of eastern people who had moved into the region twenty or twenty-five years before." New Englanders like Dickey heard everywhere a prevailing dialect they believed worthy of ridicule, full of terms and twangs associated with uneducated southerners. It was in fact a western amalgam. The editor of the *Missouri Intelligencer* thought it necessary in 1823 to publish his "PROVINCIAL DICTIONARY...*For the convenience of Emigrants.*" He offered these readers a number of verbal cues. Unlike Yankees, who called daily excursions in their home villages "outings," most westerners "had came" to the courthouse, and on their way "thar" would have "seen a heap" (quantity) of folks "patering" (ambling along) in town. They might have "reckoned" (supposed) that this year's "crap" (crop) of tobacco would be "tolerable" (decent) and traded "powers" (quantities) of goods in town, and working men—or bondmen—were "up and a doing" their business by "toting" (carrying) sacks of flour and meal to "whar" the customers' wagons were parked. A half century later, when fellow Missourian Samuel L. Clemens entertained audiences as Mark Twain with such vernacular dialect, he did so as a celebrated westerner, and not as a southerner or even a southwestern humorist like his predecessors.[5]

Non–New Englanders in this individualistic western culture, especially outside the region's infant cities, were largely hostile to Yankee newcomers, whose social impulses more often led them to create physical communities and ordered spaces rather than settle in the rural townships. Daniel Boone, who had left Kentucky in 1799, was reported to have decided to vacate his new home on Missouri's "Boon's Lick" frontier not simply because it, too, was "too crowded" with new settlers, but also because town dwellers representing New England culture, especially lawyers, politicians, and merchants, who had dispossessed him of his land, were reputed to have settled west of the Mississippi. "It had not been two years," he complained, "before a d____d Yankee came, and settled down *within a hundred miles of me!!*... It was then that my misery began." George W. Ogden, a Quaker merchant from New Bedford, Massachusetts, claimed during a business trip in 1821 that he had noticed only as far as Pittsburgh that westerners were "extremely jealous of the Yankees, and [they] condemn the whole," while John Stillman Wright claimed of southern Illinois that most settlers "look with a malicious, scowling eye, on the New England men who settle among them." Not all New Englanders were as insular as charged. Charles H. Titus, a native of Maine's Kennebec country, related wryly after two years of living near Madison, Indiana, that he had at last acculturated to the prevailing folkways of "the 'Great West'... and many of my former prejudices set aside. I could now enjoy worship in the sanctuary of God, if every thing was not conducted precisely *à la New England*. I could live on 'hog and homony,' 'flour bread and chicken fixins,' or even 'corn bread and common doings.'" Titus hoped his conspicuous adaptations would "allay the prejudices against Yankees" among his neighbors.[6]

For many individualists on both sides of the Ohio River, Yankee—the term reserved nearly exclusively for collectivist New Englanders and eastern New Yorkers—was synonymous with distrust. Social violence was not uncommon. William Faux recalled an incident in which a New Yorker named Williams was suspected of robbing a store in southern Illinois. When the local judge acquitted him after hearing scanty evidence, the man quickly faced vigilante justice. A committee of four soon came to his house and, in front of his wife and child, warned him that he should leave town immediately or face lynching. As the family headed out of town the following day, a posse with dogs overtook the party, forced the man to confess to the crime, and cowhided him in front of his family. "He was then untied," Faux recalled, "and told to depart from the state immediately, or he should receive another whipping on the morrow, as a warning and terror to all future coming Yankees.... Here was liberty, with a vengeance!" In Illinois, "because he was a walking, working Yankee man, on a journey... [he was] considered as nothing better than, or below, a *nigger*." In 1817 Thomas

Moore Parke, a Connecticut-born and Edinburgh-trained physician living in Mount Vernon, Indiana, ran afoul of his neighbors after "untombing" the body of a neighbor to perform an anatomical dissection on it. Despite his claims that using cadavers in such a way was a common practice among medical students in New England, the act of desecration enraged one neighbor enough that nearly a year later he bludgeoned the doctor with a club, declaring, "I have killed one damn Yankee and now for another."[7]

Westerners and Yankees lived uncomfortably together yet apart on the middle border, as evidenced by the patterns of land tracts that existed in the Old Northwest. Settlers in territories and states south of the Ohio River transferred the topographical "Virginia" metes and bounds system. The system also encouraged disputes, the litigation of which favored large landholders. Congress imposed rectangular land surveys and direct government sales in the Northwest Territory, north of the Ohio, reputedly sparing residents from such disorder. Yet neither became universal. Both systems coexisted, with radial road patterns melding with rectangular towns, metes and bounds adjoining regular land grids. Although in the Western Reserve the grid system prevailed, in the Virginia Military Tract and much of Ohio south of the Treaty of Greenville line roads followed land forms and traditional Indian highways, with rural tracts following their contours, while streets and roads in hub towns were laid out on artificial grids. A quick look at a plat map of Ross County, Ohio, partially inside and partially outside the Virginia Tract, divided by the Scioto River, suggests this blending. Virginians, who in 1850 comprised some 85 percent of the residents of the county, settled the districts west of the river, where irregularly shaped tracts prevailed. Chillicothe, the capital of the Virginia Tract and lying on the west side of the river, and the townships east of the river where nearly all of the county's few New England residents lived, shared formalized, right-angled street grids and land parceling. New Englanders, who arrived late and comprised less than 8 percent of the county's population, nonetheless influenced governance boundaries by settling according to the township system.[8]

A sampling of counties that lay immediately north of the Ohio River suggests the prevalence of southern influences on the middle border. In 1850 a full 41 percent of Indiana's entire population hailed from slave states (especially Kentucky and Tennessee), alongside about 30 percent of Illinois's population. Of the fifty-two Illinois counties that lay on or below the 40° parallel (roughly the southern half of the state), southern-born migrants constituted immigrant majorities in 77 percent of them and comprised the majority of immigrant populations in nearly half of the state's ninety-nine counties. Ohio's southern-born migrants constituted just 5 percent of the state's overall population in 1850, but of all residents not born in the state, southerners made up 21 percent, and emigrants from Pennsylvania and New Jersey made up half of those who moved to the Buckeye State. New Englanders and New Yorkers comprised less than 7 percent of the state's population and just more than a quarter of its immigrants.[9]

This migrational aperture went on for decades, with prominent families exerting significant influence in communities, counties, and states for years. In four prairie counties in south central Illinois, of the forty-nine "old settlers" enumerated there in 1872, 83 percent hailed from states south of the Ohio River, most from Tennessee, North Carolina, and Kentucky. Of those residents of Williamson County, Illinois, in 1850 aged forty and older, a remarkable 94.5 percent were from southern states. Similarly, in Alexander and Gallatin Counties, Illinois, and Brown County, Indiana, they comprised between 70 and 80 percent of the population. A decade later, of the 177,538 residents of Illinois who had been born in slave states, more than half hailed from southern states. Much of Jasper County, Illinois, and portions of surrounding counties were long known locally as the "Blue Grass" for their core of Kentucky immigrants, while neighboring residents called their localities Kentucky, Tennessee Prairie, Southside, Jersey, and New Philadelphia. Although these southern uplanders formed an overwhelming proportion of the earliest settlers north of the Ohio River, significant numbers migrated from the cotton states, a journey that took them far from familiar topography, climates, and crops. Surprisingly, more than 20 percent of residents of Scott County, Indiana, claimed Georgia and South Carolina as their former homes.[10]

Such influence in the lower counties in the Old Northwest is seen in slave state immigrants' domination of their territories' and states' highest offices and land appropriations in their earliest years. Six of Illinois's first seven governors hailed from states that made no effort to exclude slavery following the American Revolution. Moreover, one historian has determined that individual land allocations within Ohio's Virginia Tract were on average ten times larger than outside it, suggesting the influence of the plantation model in this large section of the middle border. By one reckoning, the legacy of weighted land apportionment was present in Ohio some two centuries later.[11]

Recorded dutifully by census takers, families' arduous and extensive westward migrations to the middle border are striking. Many young men moved from Pennsylvania, Maryland, Virginia, or North Carolina, down the Shenandoah valley and across the mountains or down the Ohio River, first to Kentucky or Tennessee, often taking brides there and having several children, only to move again to Ohio, Indiana, Illinois, Missouri, or Arkansas, where they had more children on their small homesteads. A notice that appeared in a Danville, Kentucky, newspaper in the 1820s suggests the composition and destinations of the migration that was passing west from the Cumberland Gap. "Emigrants," it boasted, "the number of movers passing daily through this place westward, is astonishing.... Nine-tenths of these movers are from North

Carolina, South Carolina, Georgia, Virginia, and other southern and eastern slaveholding states; the remainder are our citizens, all pressing to the free states on our western frontier." A Missourian at school in Princeton, Kentucky, marveled in 1830 at the apparently ceaseless rush of upcountry migrants through the western portions of that state toward crossings on the Ohio and Mississippi. Writing to his family, he claimed to be "glad to hear of Missourie filling up more, and aspecilly of our near neighbours as they are quite respectable, and also will keep out other of a quite low standing for I assure you there is a vast number of that kind pass here going to missouri and Illinois but the most of them to the latter place, and the most from Tennessee—Ford that keeps the ferry on the Ohio river is getting very wealthy." In 1860, sixty thousand Illinoisans, sixty-eight thousand Indianans, and fifteen thousand Ohioans claimed Kentucky as their birth state. Many more had preceded them, whether from there or from other slaveholding states. It is small wonder that in 1862 U.S. senator Garret Davis boasted in Congress that "Kentucky has almost peopled the northwestern states, especially Indiana and Illinois.... They are bone of our bone and flesh of our flesh."[12]

§

Other than among the region's few New Englanders, slaveholding was apparently a mark of neither distinction nor indolence among early settlers on the middle border. As physician Daniel Drake recalled of the mixed settlement of his youth near Mayslick, Kentucky, although his New Jersey father never purchased a slave—more out of economic concerns than ideological opposition—he often hired slave laborers from his Jersey immigrant neighbors, all of whom became slave owners.[13]

From its earliest records, unfreedom was woven into the fabric of the western country. Black and red men in chains were a common sight in the western border country, regardless of which side of the Ohio or Mississippi Rivers one lived on. For centuries before and after Spanish and French settlers staked ephemeral claims to the western region, Native Americans practiced forms of involuntary servitude and slavery. Black servants paddled and portaged LaSalle, Marquette, and Jolliet down the waterways of the American interior southward from Quebec to the Gulf. French villages and settlements in Upper Louisiana contained black servants, often in equal numbers to the white *habitants*. The 1712 charter creating Louisiana included the opening of the African slave trade in order to supply the colony, and five years later a second charter included the company's promise of the transport of one black slave for every two white French settlers during the first decade of colonization.[14]

Beginning in the 1720s Upper Louisiana saw the arrival of black chattels. After half a century of French settlement in "les Pays des Illinois" (as they referred to the string of settlements on the east bank of the Mississippi) and despite falling under British rule at the end of the Seven Years' War in 1763, by the early 1770s slavery was firmly entrenched, with a thousand or more slaves laboring there. At Kaskaskia between four and five hundred black slaves served among the five hundred white French settlers; at Prairie du Rocher, eighty black laborers worked for the one hundred white inhabitants; and at Cahokia, eight black residents served its three hundred white settlers. Black slaves worked and lived at the French settlements farther east. At Vincennes on the Wabash, ten black and seventeen Indian slaves labored largely in the households of the 250 white residents and 168 "strangers" who resided permanently or traded transiently. Some of these French traders later moved upriver to Louisville, at the falls of the Ohio, and farther up the Wabash to Terre Haute, taking their chattel property with them. Little changed during the Spanish possession of the territory that lay west of the Mississippi. In 1772, collectively at Ste. Genevieve and St. Louis, 300 black slaves and an undetermined number of Indian slaves, held despite Spain's ban, labored among 975 white residents. When Virginia ceded the region to the United States in 1783, the new state recognized its French subjects' ancient "laws and customs" as it had Anglo settlers' "ancient cultivation" land rights in Kentucky a half decade earlier. By the time of the American acquisition of Louisiana from France in 1804, more than a quarter of St. Louis's one thousand residents were slaves.[15]

The Revolutionary War era only increased the presence of bound laborers in the western country. Grafted onto the ongoing conflict, the violent war of independence fought between Indians and settlers bred a virulent, racialized worldview that defined white residents for generations. Despite the Crown's ban on trans-Appalachian migration for English-speaking colonists in 1763, hundreds or even thousands were already in residence or had claimed large sections of the woodlands west of the mountains long before the war. Among these "long hunters," surveyors, and other backcountry itinerants were black slaves who hacked trails through the heavy brush, skinned hides, kept camp, and fought the Shawnee resisting their presence. Slaves accompanied James Harrod's 1774 colonization venture into Kentucky, and they were among those first settlers who in subsequent years trudged the Wilderness Road to clear and plant the bluegrass meadows and build stations and cabins in the new Transylvania Colony. By 1790, some 12,430 black slaves comprised nearly 17 percent of Kentucky's resident population. During the subsequent two decades, the new state's slave population would grow by 54,000, faster than any other.[16]

Idealists like Thomas Jefferson hoped for a virtuous, free trans-Appalachian West whose example, led by its trade with the East, ultimately would eradicate the stain of slavery from the infant nation. Instead, western elites did all in their power to further their self-interest, including the maintenance of slavery. The creation of the Northwest Territory in 1787 was accompanied by the ordinance's sixth article, which forbade slavery forever north of the Ohio River. In truth, slaves brought by French traders and settlers and their offspring remained there despite Article VI. Many early white migrants who settled in the hills and prairies north of the Ohio believed that Virginia's legal endorsement of Frenchpeople's ancient right to slavery was theirs by extension, regardless of the article. Indeed, French-speaking residents hired Bartolomei Tardiveau to negotiate with Congress for a rescission of the antislavery article. Although Tardiveau made little headway, he helped to convince Arthur St. Clair, the first territorial governor, that Article VI contained a grandfather clause with regard to slavery. The territorial governments, too, made little effort to manumit slaves, often requiring only that residents register taxable property upon settling in their respective counties. Indiana's and Illinois's legislatures made specific provision in their statehood constitutions for the continuance of such bound labor despite the ordinance's prohibition article, guaranteeing de facto slavery in their states. Only Ohio upheld the prohibition upon achieving statehood.[17]

French Vincennesians, or those who did not relocate across the Mississippi to Spanish territory for fear that the Anglo-Americans would actually enforce the Northwest Ordinance's slavery exclusion clause, petitioned the Confederation Congress for assurance that they would not lose their rights to chattel property. Indeed, St. Clair's successor, William Henry Harrison, assumed the Virginia cession's ancient preemption was inherent in Article VI and was designed only to prevent new introduction of slaves into the territory after 1787. Harrison, a slaveholder from a prominent tidewater Virginia family, identified closely with the territory's proslavery leadership that emerged in the Wabash region after 1800. In 1803 he presided over a convention that petitioned Congress for a decade-long suspension of Article VI. In fact, the region's residents delivered five such petitions between 1800 and 1807. One read, "Slavery is tolerated in the Territories of Orleans, Mississippi and Louisiana; why should this territory be excepted?" Later that year, Harrison and the territorial court's proslavery judges adopted an act from the Virginia Code that limited black immigration to those "under contract to serve another in any trade or occupation to perform such contract specifically during the term thereof." Two years later the territorial council enacted an indenture law that allowed outright slavery for a term of years in the territory, followed by an involuntary contract that indentured black laborers for periods between thirty and ninety-nine years. This clear circumvention of Article VI was followed by a series of racially proscriptive territorial laws in 1806—known as its Black Code—that restricted the movements of "Slaves and Servants" and allowed whipping as punishment for trespass, unlawful assembly, riots, and "seditious speeches," along with a stiff penalty for white residents who aided runaways. In 1814 the legislature passed a law declaring that any slave contracted elsewhere and taken to the Illinois Territory "shall for the time being be considered and treated as an indentured servant."[18]

As new settlers streamed into territorial Indiana, they registered a growing number of such indentures in the local courts. Most black residents thus lived as outright or de facto slaves. Between 1805 and 1810 white settlers in Clark and Knox Counties registered seventy-eight individual indentures involving eighty-six African Americans; sixty were from Kentucky, while the remainder were from seaboard states between Maryland and Georgia. The Black Code limited servants' ability to travel, forbade their right of congregation and even speech, and prohibited sale of liquor to them. The legislature sanctioned public and private whippings of black miscreants. In 1810 some 630 black persons resided in the territory, spread among four counties lying in its southernmost portion. Although 393 were listed in the census as being free, the indentures and sales suggest that most were in fact indentured servants or outright slaves preemptioned by either French descent or presence in the territory prior to 1787. Their terms of service were legally transferable by sale or will, provided servants gave "consent" before a notary.[19]

In fact, there was little distinction between slaves and servants. Black servants could not travel without passes, including visiting neighboring "plantations," and could not congregate or attend public gatherings without white supervision. Transfer laws were rarely enforced, subjecting black servants to the real possibility of being sold into slavery outside the territory, facilitated by easy access to Kentucky and by the Ohio and Mississippi Rivers to the other states and territories beyond. Court records suggest that many white residents were eager to break the indenture laws in order to extend servants' terms or claim them as slaves for life. Term servants did have access to the territorial courts, which recognized the legality of slavery and servitude, but those who filed freedom suits took their chances. Despite his public professions of opposition to slavery and his emancipation of some of his own slaves, Thomas Posey, a native Virginian who succeeded William Henry Harrison as territorial governor in 1813, stipulated in his will, written after Indiana gained its statehood, that two slaves should go to each of his three children and that his two indentured servants should be auctioned at Vincennes.[20]

The issue of servitude would remain divisive. When Indiana's delegates met in convention in 1816 to adopt a constitution required for statehood, eight in ten were from states where slavery still existed, more than 60 percent from Kentucky alone. Although six years earlier the territorial legislature had repealed the law authorizing slave importations and indentures, the latter continued seemingly unabated. An east-west schism soon surfaced; delegates from the western prairie counties generally favored the current system of servitude, and those from the ridge and hill country nearer Ohio opposed it. Hastening through issues concerning the structure of governance and frequently borrowing language from the Ohio and Kentucky constitutions, the delegates took up the fractious matter of indentured servitude and slavery. Ultimately, the antislavery delegation prevailed, inserting into the draft, "There shall be neither slavery nor involuntary servitude in this state," but the Vincennes faction managed to qualify the seemingly declaratory clause: "Nor shall any indenture of any negro or mulatto *hereafter made*, and executed out of the bounds of this state be of any validity within the state." Hereafter made, of course, allowed for yet another grandfather clause, allowing existing indentures of black laborers to remain in the Wabash counties. One observer noted there in 1819, "Gentlemen, one or two, here and there, have a negro or two in the house." Probate records attest to the persistence of involuntary servitude in the state, which the state's supreme court failed to address in its several rulings abolishing outright slavery in the 1820s. Indeed, in 1820 some 190 slaves continued to serve legally, nearly all in the westernmost prairie counties, and a dwindling number of slaves continued legally in bondage in Indiana well into the 1830s.[21]

Illinois adopted Indiana's legal construction by inserting its own grandfather clause into its 1818 state constitution for both French-speaking and territorial period servant and slaveholders—and to salt-makers like John Crenshaw in the reserve. Although the convention barred the future introduction of slaves to the state, delegates also included in the constitution a provision designed specifically to circumvent Article VI of the Northwest Ordinance for many years. Black male servants under the age of fifteen would serve until the age of thirty-five, women to thirty-two. All servants brought henceforth into the territory with valid indentures would be held to their contracts, and children born of indentured servants would be free at ages thirty and twenty-eight, respectively, for males and females, although renewals were ostensibly prohibited. So prevalent was the practice of indenture among the state's emergent elite that three of Illinois's first four governors, French as well as Anglo, held such "apprentices." Its first, Shadrach Bond, in 1832 willed "to my wife Achsah... all the rest of my negroes to be disposed of as she thinks best having entire confidence that she will make a proper use of [them]."[22]

The Illinois statehood council's stance against outright slavery was largely political, safeguarding its application against Congress's watchful northern antislavery contingent. Some residents contracted with their black indentured servants as they would with any white apprentice, including offering incentives for faithful service such as the learning of a trade and stipulations against bad behavior. "Cards Dice or unlawfull Games," read one, "he shall not play, not frequent any house forbidden him, fornication he shall not commit, matrimony he can contract, from the service of his said master, he shall not at any time depart or absent himself without his said masters leave or his representative." In reality, such arrangements were rare. Local officials allowed the continuance of perpetual "annual" indentures as delimited by the territory's 1809 indenture law, and the legislature created its own law in 1814 that allowed residents to import hired slaves for twelve-month terms, renewable indefinitely. County clerks recorded them exactly as owners wrote them. On February 13, 1818, William Wilson of Pope County entered an indenture between himself and Linda, "last out of Missouri Territory," for a period of ninety-nine years for a consideration of $400 "in hand paid, receipt of which is hereby acknowledged." The following August, Gallatin County's Oliver C. VanLandingham indentured Daniel, "a free man of color," for "$600 plus food, clothing, 40 years." Just as owners largely disregarded the consent of their "apprentices" that the law required, these slaves likely never saw the money promised in the indentures. The assessed value of slaves in the counties was often considerable, given that only slaves over the age of twenty-one were taxable. In 1826 in Randolph County, in the wide Mississippi floodplain known as the "American Bottom," thirty-six owners were assessed $26,185 for the 121 slaves there; William Morrison held at least fifteen valued at $3,750, and six owners (including former governors Pierre Menard and Shadrach Bond and former territorial delegate and current federal judge Nathaniel Pope) had slave property worth a thousand dollars or more. Nearly half were not French. In 1841 some twenty-six owners there were assessed $20,539 for their slave property; more than half were Anglo-Americans. A year later, eighteen owners were assessed $16,250 for their slaves. Small wonder that upon news of Illinois having achieved statehood, English antislavery colonizer George Flower remarked dimly from his Edwards County cabin that his new home was "as much a slave state as any south of the Ohio River."[23]

Even in Ohio, which upheld the antislavery provision of the Northwest Ordinance, the laws prohibiting slavery were far from airtight. As would later be the case in Indiana and Illinois, settlers who moved from the slave states across the Ohio River during Ohio's territorial period brought their servants, often under the guise of being indentured, and held them as slaves. Although Ohio's 1803 state constitution outright and unconditionally prohibited slavery, that outcome was never politically beyond doubt. Since 1799 Ohio's proslavery leadership had attempted to suspend Article IV of the Northwest Ordinance. Centered in the Virginia Tract, members of the "Scioto gentry" such as John Edgar, Thomas Posey, and Nathaniel Massie argued that an abolition ordinance would deter affluent slaveholding emigrants and speculators from purchasing lands in Ohio's fastest-growing portion. Arthur St. Clair spoke for large landholders—and slaveholders—in the Military District by playing to republican sentiments, arguing that a disproportionately small number of these residents paid the lion's share of the territorial taxes and that statehood should be delayed until Ohio boasted more free residents. When the constitutional convention at last voted for statehood in 1802, it did so by a single vote largely because of the controversy over its antislavery provision. When the call for a constitutional convention was issued again in 1819, voters narrowly blocked it, out of fear that it was a plot to introduce slavery into the state.[24]

Ohio's proslavery element did not come away empty-handed. In order to gain passage of the constitution, the antislavery leadership made significant concessions. With the assent of Thomas Worthington, soon to be the new state's first governor and a man who opposed both slavery and black citizenship, Ohio's Virginia-born leaders legalized the indentures of black residents, although by less strict provisions than in Indiana and Illinois. The constitution allowed the binding of female children until age eighteen and males until age twenty-one, regardless of color. The antislavery statute included in the first constitution suggests the influence of the proslavery legislative contingent. Any pretense of clarity in the statute ended abruptly after its clear procedures for the recovery of fugitive slaves from slaveholding states. Section 2 prohibited the indenture of any "negro or mulatto" adult, save those made with free persons within Ohio for terms not exceeding one year. But a subsequent clause specified that only free blacks could be employed in the state, allowing slaves held legally by citizens of *other* states to reside with their masters in Ohio so long as they did no "useful" labor for unspecified periods of time. These accommodations to slavery and indentured servitude not only afforded opportunities to bring human property into Ohio, but kept all black people subservient, free as well as bound.[25]

Both before and after statehood, sharp-eyed slave owners looking to emigrate to Ohio inspected its laws for loopholes regarding chattel property. In 1801 Nathaniel Massie, aided by his brother-in-law, Charles Willing Byrd, the territorial secretary, threatened to sell one of his servants, Abraham, newly arrived from Virginia and seeking freedom in Cincinnati, "if he did not sign [an] indenture, and by other menaces he was compelled to subscribe to it." Two years later, just after Ohio achieved statehood, Robert Patterson, a native Pennsylvanian, former Kentucky legislator, and one of the original proprietors of the cities of Cincinnati and Lexington, acquired land near Dayton and emigrated there. A proponent of gradual emancipation, Patterson appears to have intended to free his slaves after bringing them to the state, but he also expected that most of his black servants would voluntarily stay with him under its indenture law. He quickly recognized that many settlers from Kentucky and Virginia living in the Virginia Tract believed that Ohio law derived from territorial law, which had accommodated slavery, and that they could maintain former slaves under term indentures. Others believed that the antislavery law would not stand before the full force of migration from slave states. Patterson knew he could not legally hold slaves permanently in Ohio, but relied on pervasive beliefs in racial subordination that he believed held western society together. Patterson managed to evade the state's registration laws until 1806.[26]

Robert Patterson and others found plenty of sympathy for slavery in Ohio, but even more residents opposed full civil and legal rights for free blacks. Ohio's courts, like those in Indiana and Illinois, took a flexible stand on the continuation of slavery and other forms of servitude. Despite the constitutional ban, the vagueness of the state's constitution allowed judges, juries, and attorneys, many of whom in the Virginia Tract were formerly from slave states, to tolerate the persistence of long-term black servitude where popular opinion allowed. Various slave cases tested Ohio's stand on issues involving slavery and comity. Local cases suggest that through the late 1830s Ohio's courts upheld standards that were more accommodating to the interests of slave owners than to those opposed to slavery in the state. Only then did the state's courts begin denying slaveholding citizens of other states the right to bring their chattel freely into the state, even temporarily, and upheld local magistrates' refusals to cooperate in the return of fugitives who crossed the Ohio River. Slaveholding continued illicitly nonetheless. As late as 1838, Marylander John Burns brought "a few slaves" to central Ohio and for five years refused to liberate them, even selling one who tried to escape. His neighbors did not object.[27]

In 1823–24 the most concerted effort to undo the Northwest Ordinance's prohibition of slavery coalesced in Illinois as an effort to secure a plebiscite allowing voters to cast ballots for delegates to a convention to amend the 1818 constitution in order to legalize slavery in the state. The event came about in part because the Illinois political landscape was deeply divided over the exclusion. Voters had recently elected a proslavery lieutenant governor and legislative majority, pitting them against the new state's controversial governor, Edward Coles. Coles was a former Virginia slaveholder who had freed his twenty slaves in 1819 while floating down the Ohio to their new home. An avowed emancipationist, he included in his inaugural address a call for the abolition of slavery's French exemption. Coles's speech ignited a political firestorm and immediately renewed the latent debate over overturning the Northwest Ordinance's sixth article. Within just two years of achieving statehood, Illinois's emboldened proslavery leaders sought a showdown.[28]

Pro-conventionists, likely in collusion with proslavery leaders in Missouri smarting from many Illinoisans' opposition to their neighbor's statehood, capitalized on the sour mood of voters in the midst of hard times lingering after the Panic of 1819. More important, they hoped they could galvanize residents, especially those who had migrated from slave states. Avowing "Convention or death," in December 1823 Illinois's "Conventionists" managed to win passage of the bill—by the exact two-thirds votes required—in both legislative houses of the new state capitol in Vandalia. Supporters celebrated their victory with toasts and speeches. "The State of Illinois—*give us plenty of negroes*, a little industry, and she will distribute her treasures," toasted one, while another offered "*A new constitution, purely republican,* which may guarantee to the people of Illinois the peaceable enjoyment of *all species of property.*" Recognizing that many white emigrants were crossing through Illinois on their way west to the nation's newest slave state, one pro-conventionist taunted, "They are going over to fill up Missouri, and make it rich, while our State will stand still or dwindle, because you wont let them keep their slaves here." Pro-conventionists argued that what nearly happened with Missouri was an unconstitutional attempt by northerners to interfere in the West, that a state had the right to decide its own future, including amending its constitution. They employed tropes that would within a few decades become familiar: immigration of affluent slaveholders would raise property values for all landowners, and slavery would "free" white men by removing them from the most degrading menial labor that "no white man...is willing to risk or able to endure." In the West, only white men should be legally free.[29]

Anti-conventionists, too, used the recent Missouri slave controversy to their advantage. Both of Illinois's senators and its lone U.S. representative had voted for Missouri's statehood. All were slaveholders. Antislavery leaders offered well-worn moral, class- and race-based arguments, claiming that slavery was a violation of the Declaration of Independence and that expansion of slavery would increase crime, depress wages, degrade society in general, and introduce a master class that would lord itself over common men—hardly the egalitarian landscape that drew many to the open lands north of the Ohio. Inherent was the promise of a slaveless West, which would demonstrate the superiority of free societies. For months, newspaper editors in both Illinois and St. Louis—the latter of whom controlled four of the five newspapers in Illinois—harangued readers and smeared one another. Voters left little doubt of most Illinoisans' views. On August 2, 1824, they voted against the convention 6,640 to 4,972, or 57 percent to 43 percent. Predictably, the southern counties voted in the majority for the convention, with several of the state's central counties joining them. The northern counties were uniformly opposed, and many of the central counties joined them. The vexing question of slavery's future in the Northwest, it seemed, was at last settled.[30]

§

If the outcome of Illinois's convention crisis were taken at face value, the story of slavery in the West would confirm the prevailing genesis story of the border region as innately divided. After a brief seduction, idealistic republican settlers on the virgin soil north of the Ohio River threw off the challenge of immigrant southerners and rejected slavery, fulfilling the covenant of the Northwest Ordinance and consecrating the Tocquevillean western democratic promise for America. This tale has been told widely and embraced by residents of the modern Midwest, especially those who see the uniqueness of their region as having turned largely on its residents' rejection of slavery there. Even those who know of slavery's presence above the Ohio often hinge the region's uniqueness on the absence of the peculiar institution in the early nineteenth century. Most often, they give slavery minimal attention or, anticipating the war to come, cast it as doomed from the start. Undergirding much of this is the regional emergence of Illinoisan Abraham Lincoln, identified with effecting the abolition of slavery in the nation.[31]

As the Illinois debates reveal, the free middle border states witnessed a wide diversity of opinion and practice with regard to slavery. Certainly extreme positions were evident already in these new states. Efforts to legalize slavery might have failed in each of these territories' statehood constitutional conventions, but only by close margins. Illinois's political struggle over the constitutional convention was no simple fight between pro-conventionists, who uniformly supported the constitutional right of slaveholding, and anti-conventionists, who just as universally sought its abolition in Illinois and elsewhere. Rather, the mass of residents occupied a middle ground between the ideological extremes that would emerge nationally within a decade. Far more prevalent in the early years of these young western states were those who saw slavery as a negotiable issue in American politics and society, especially in the West.[32]

Chattel bondage's slow death in the Old Northwest was nothing new to immigrants from the reputedly free Atlantic seaboard states. In Pennsylvania, Connecticut, Rhode Island, New York, and New Jersey, gradual emancipation legislation long delayed the freedom of slaves there, offering what historians have called a "two-generation grace period" for chattel bondage. Generally, these states freed only future-born children of slaves, at ages ranging from twenty-one to twenty-eight; those currently enslaved most often remained so for life. Legislatures or court rulings set universal emancipation dates (if they set them at all) well into the nineteenth century, thus guaranteeing that slave owners would sustain little if any capital losses. The Massachusetts Supreme Court dealt slavery's death blow in 1783, only to see the legislature erect a legal scaffolding of racial apartheid in its aftermath. Pennsylvania's universal emancipation did not come until 1847, when the state's last legally held slave died. These laws were passed grudgingly in nearly all of the states, over vigorous proslavery resistance. After New Jersey's supreme court in 1826 had declared as "a settled rule...that the black color is proof of slavery," the state legislature refused to take up the issue of emancipation for twenty years. It then created a legal mechanism by which masters could hold their servants by indentures, much like in the Old Northwest, rather than emancipate them outright. Census takers continued to list them as slaves. In 1830, of the 3,568 slaves held legally in free states, more than two-thirds were in New Jersey under indentures; they labored unfreely in the state until the 1860s. Small wonder that in 1806 William Henry Harrison confidently instructed his agent that several of his slaves be sold there, rather than in Kentucky or his native Virginia, reminding him that unlike those bound for Indiana, "it would make no difference whether they are slaves for life or only serve a term of years."[33]

Neither Maryland, Delaware, nor Virginia abolished slavery during the first, or Revolutionary, emancipation, yet none greatly restricted the practice of private manumission in the years immediately following the Revolution. With compelling economic changes affecting the region, planters abandoned tobacco for grain. These states' legislatures liberalized earlier enactments regarding the freeing of slaves, including passing laws offering manumissions by deed and by will and others designed to ameliorate slaves' conditions. Consequently, all of these slave states witnessed continuously high rates of manumissions prior to 1830. In Maryland the slave population remained the same, and in Virginia it increased by 60 percent. Only Delaware's slave population declined.[34]

With white settlers from these Chesapeake states, along with those from the mid-Atlantic, largely peopling the middle border, avowed opponents of slavery were the most uncommon of westerners. The largest contingent of them appear to have been either New Englanders or foreign born. Morris Birkbeck, a fifty-five-year-old English Quaker, arrived in the Ohio valley in 1817 with utopian ambitions for the West. Birkbeck and George Flower attracted some four hundred English people and seven hundred native-born Americans to their colonies on the "English prairie" in Edwards County, Illinois, near the Ohio River. As Birkbeck wrote, his and Flower's abolitionism drew inspiration from their recognition that "that broadest, foulest blot" of slavery was alive and well in Illinois despite the Northwest Ordinance. Birkbeck was hopeful, his partner less so. Flower saw slavery as the West's great infection, and its white inhabitants were not easily inoculated. Indeed, during Illinois's 1824 constitutional contest many of the English eschewed antislavery sentiments. Nearly half who voted at Flower's colony, Albion, favored calling the convention. "To roll a barrel of salt once a year or to put salt into a salt-cellar was sufficient excuse for any man to hire a slave and raise a field of corn," Flower sneered of his neighbors. His was a pithy variant of Englishman Edmund Burke's earlier reminder of the profound importance and adaptability of chattel property to the liberties of independence-minded American colonists. "Slavery they can have anywhere," intoned the conservative statesman and theorist. "It is a weed that grows in every soil.... Deny them this participation of freedom, and you break that sole bond which originally made, and must still preserve, the unity of the empire."[35]

In America's emerging western empire, more numerous than these early abolitionists were emigrants who left slave states to escape the peculiar institution. Although many nonslaveholders like Virginia-born Thomas Lincoln left former homes—in his case Kentucky—because of an abiding hatred of institutionalized privileges for slave-owning elites, others were less ideological, having sold out to affluent slaveholders in order to afford cheaper land on the less-settled Northwest frontier. Few arrived with single-mindedness on the subject. North Carolina–born Braxton Carriage, for example, recalled that as an illiterate and newly married man in 1821 he had left Tennessee with "no property in the world but a change of clothing and a horse, saddle, and bridle," with his new wife and her children, for their new home in southern Illinois. "I had seen the constitution of the state," he wrote, "and being disgusted with slavery, I wanted a home in a free state, and consented to move there." Disillusionment with the planter hierarchy did not prevent Carriage from considering leaving Illinois for Missouri's slave-rich central Missouri River counties shortly thereafter.[36]

While certainly not in the majority, proslavery Illinoisans spoke for many in the western region. Their language gravitated to the democratic promise of the West, which was incomplete without slavery, a stance designed to appeal to middle- and southern-born settlers of common means. Some argued that wherever black slavery existed, economic prosperity followed, offering equality for all white residents. Others claimed that the dearth of laborers in the region was the greatest impediment to freedom for hard-working residents. "[W]ill any white man... take the slavish employments?" asked an editorialist who signed himself "A Plain Man." "Would a white man for less than fifty cents a day make himself the veriest slave of the community?" Such sentiments echoed elsewhere above the Ohio. An unnamed Virginian, who had settled some ten years earlier in southern Indiana and owned land there and in Kentucky, vented his frustration at the West's undemocratic impulses to Englishman William Faux, who visited him in 1819. "[H]e damns the state government for denying him the privilege of slavery," Faux noted, "and of using his Kentucky negroes, who, in consequence, (he says) are hired and exposed to cruelty." In his former home, "every man did as he pleased. This Indiana [is] a free state, and yet not at liberty to use its own property!"[37]

Decades after this dissatisfied Indianan, other white residents reconsidered their belief that freedom offered in the free states was better than what they had left behind in the slave states (see figure 1.1). Labor needs headed a long list of grievances. In 1841 Englishman William Oliver overheard one riverboat passenger venting about the chimera of white freedom without black, bound laborers above the Ohio River. "I was a post-master in Alabama," he fumed. "I determined on leaving the state, and on going to one where there were no slaves. I went to Indiana, but it will not do, there is no getting any one to work, no getting along. I have sold all off, and am now on my way back to Alabama."[38]

One can question whether many of these migrants had left their homes in slave states specifically to escape the peculiar institution. Oliver's observations of former slave-staters living in Illinois had moved him to question whether the "antislavery" southerners he observed in Illinois had "immigrated to this part of

Figure 1.1 Woodcut published in [Ebenezer Deming], *Western Emigration* (New York, 1839). Both proslavery and antislavery emigrants often found the Old Northwest unsatisfying for settlement owing to the porous nature of the Northwest Ordinance's Article VI, prohibiting slaveholding. Courtesy Abraham Lincoln Presidential Library and Museum.

the country, owing to the dislike they had to slavery" or whether they had left frustrated by "their want of means to become slaveholders, a man's respectability being, in a great measure, proportioned to the number of slaves in his possession." Three decades later, Reuben McDaniel might not have been one of them. A thirty-seven-year-old merchant in Prince George's County, Virginia, with ambitions to migrate west, McDaniel twice headed down the Ohio to Illinois, in 1836 and 1837, to reconnoiter for good opportunities. He found the people of the region's lower free states "polite, genteel, and agreeable as they are in Virginia and much more so than they are in some parts of it," but concluded "Illinois will not do." In 1841 McDaniel settled in Missouri's Boon's Lick, where he became a substantial slaveholding farmer. As late as 1853, a newspaper editor remarked that it was common knowledge that "in the south part of Illinois, a portion of the population" still favored the introduction of slavery in the state.[39]

Kin networks that stretched across the middle border's rivers offered natural fords for such proslavery sentiment. Cross-state land ownership was common as it became more expensive in settled areas of slave states like Kentucky with thriving economies, and residents sought cheap property in the more sparsely settled free states farther west. William Faux noted that an English couple who ran an inn on the "English prairie" claimed, "Much of the land has been thus purchased by capitalists here... because the Kentucky speculators, it is said, would otherwise have bought all up and charged more for it." With both states allowing bondpeople to work and reside on their owners' property for as much as six months of the year, cross-river proprietorships continued well into the antebellum years. In 1840 many of the 331 slaves who labored on Illinois farms, in the shops of its mechanics, and at the Gallatin saltworks were owned by resident Kentuckians and Missourians. As late as 1845, when the Illinois Supreme Court ruled that all slaves born after 1787 or brought to Illinois were free, Henry T. Duncan, a farmer living near Lexington, Kentucky, and owner of sixty-three slaves, took his laborers annually across the river to work the several hundred acres he owned in southern Illinois. Although the 1848 Illinois Constitution stated "there shall be neither slavery nor involuntary servitude in the state, except as punishment for crime, whereof the party shall have been duly convicted," masters like Duncan were freeing legally held slaves as late as 1850.[40]

Proslavery sentiment in these states took many forms. Among Illinois's "exclusionists," as one historian has termed opponents of the 1824 constitutional convention, were many who "professed to be opposed to Slavery and who rail much against it, but yet who are friendly to it," as Edward Coles claimed. Resisting slavery's introduction into their state did not preclude support for its continued existence in other states. Leaders like Coles appealed to those who had migrated from hierarchical social systems because they opposed the privilege and power of slaveholding elites. An 1807 counterpetition to Congress from antislavery Kentuckians in Illinois assured representatives that many from their birth state were "preparing [to immigrate, or had] actually immigrated to the territory, to get free from a government which does tolerate slavery." Exclusionist Abraham Carns spoke especially to these migrants when he addressed a crowd of listeners in September 1823: "Many of us have been long accustomed to living in slave states, and we know the poor people in those states suffer." By employing language that consistently portrayed the struggle as one between an enlightened democracy and an oppressive aristocracy, convention opponents thus spun liberty and democracy as conditions unattainable in slaveholding societies.[41]

The strategy of using language designed to appeal to the democratic sensibilities of hard-working, common farmers had its limitations. Western frontier society, slaveholding and not, hardly resembled the hierarchical system associated with the southern states. "John Rifle" answered Morris Birkbeck's charge that slave owners were elitists by employing a nuanced depiction of slave societies for his readers. "Do the people of Kentucky," he mocked, "ride about, mighty grand, with umbrellas over their heads? We have a great many Kentuckians, Tennesseans, and North Carolinians in this state, and we don't find that they are more grand and proud than other folks. As for working bareheaded in the sun...there is nothing to prevent their covering their heads here." Offering scripture, "The Rev. W. K." reminded hard-working white emigrants, "Both thy bondmen and they bondmaids which thou shalt have, shall be of the heathen that are round about you, and of them shall ye buy bondmen and bondmaids.... [A]nd they shall be your possession; they shall be your bondmen forever."[42]

Indeed, many more exclusionists believed the most important reason to exclude slavery in the Old Northwest was to prohibit black emigrants entirely, free as well as slave. These states enacted "Black Laws," often before achieving their respective statehoods, that were progressively more restrictive the farther west one traveled. Designed to assure the white promise of the West, the laws created a black class that a Maryland jurist recognized as "a sort of middle class, neither slave nor free; exempted from many of the motives for obedience which influence slaves [for life]." They also created a free black population that white residents considered "more idle and vicious than slaves." To many, manumission laws in slave states guaranteed that black faces, whether free, slave, or indentured, would pollute a land that exclusionists and even abolitionists together agreed was to be reserved as a "white man's country."[43]

To correct this looming problem, Ohio, Indiana, and Illinois passed laws designed to prohibit black immigration from states like Maryland and Virginia that had a surfeit of slaves. In 1804, less than a year after achieving statehood, Ohio required free blacks and mulattoes to provide proof of freedom upon entering the state; three years later it blocked residence unless they could post a $500 bond as a guarantee of being able to support themselves. In the same year, the city council of Cincinnati, on the Ohio River's north bank, enacted "An Ordinance for the better security and peace of the town," which required a "special license" for any Kentucky slave to come across the river and enter the town. Further, the ordinance forbade Kentucky slaves from entering the town or moving within its limits on Sundays unless accompanied by their owners or employers, with jail and an hour at the town's pillory, respectively, as penalties for offenses. (Family networks stretching across the Ohio River, travelers from slave states passing through by the river, and complicated rental ordinances combined to ensure that slaves would long be found there, regardless.) In 1815 Indiana imposed a $300 poll tax on all free black residents; three years later it prohibited black residents' voting altogether, as well as testifying in cases involving whites, making interracial marriages, and participating in volunteer militias. Illinois followed suit, as did the middle border states across the rivers. In 1818 Kentucky prohibited the immigration of free blacks from other states (those already living there had to be gainfully employed to avoid imprisonment), while Missouri's controversial state constitution draft, submitted to Congress in its application for statehood, raised fewer hackles by its protection of slavery than by its anti-free-black proviso, which cautioned that it would need to pass laws "to prevent free negroes and mulattoes from coming to and settling in this state, under any pretext whatsoever."[44]

However free the West might have been for white people, it was by design never so for black Americans who might consider moving there. By statute, practice, and prejudice, for white westerners their region was destined to be a "white man's country," where in fact slavery existed and where in name it did not.

§

In 1839 Henry R. Reynolds looked west. Living in Baltimore, Maryland, now crowded after a century of settlement, the twenty-eight-year-old entrepreneur embarked on a business journey down the wide Ohio River to sell iron goods to hungry western markets. But he had other motives. As a developer, builder, and industrialist, he believed that the growth of the West's cities and towns, not its plentiful farms, would lead the nation to its manifest destiny, which as a businessman he considered one and the same. His fervent belief that the West would complete the American colossus derived from an equally deep conviction that it should have no middle ground. Reynolds was a Quaker and staunchly antislavery. As he was keenly aware, chattel slavery had been present in Maryland and his home city since their founding. Yet both were well into an economic transition to free labor, and their slave populations, especially Baltimore's, fell sharply after 1810. Two decades later, Baltimore's slaves comprised just 3 percent of the city's population and 15 percent of it black residents. Reynolds hoped that in the West, on a different border between free labor and slavery, he would find his thinking confirmed.

Yet as his boat chuffed downriver, Reynolds's quarry proved elusive, as he found things other than expected. On both sides of the river, he was impressed by progressive river cities, towns, and even countryside, with orderly farms, well-kept homes, neat fields, and full orchards. Rural residents, like the homespun clothing they wore, appeared to him "truly domestic and democratic...they are genuine hoosiers," the prevailing term for lower-class, rural westerners. Nowhere had he yet found indications that slavery had debauched Kentucky's society, especially in comparison to the free states he saw north of the river. Only at the great river's lower reaches, with plantation-style slavery and its effects evident on both sides of the river, did he find what he sought. At Henderson and Smithland, Kentucky, and at and below Cairo, Illinois, he found "[e]very evidence of amalgamation is seen here" in the form of "copperheads...a mixture of the white and black or partly black races.... yellow girls and copperheads, plenty of every shade and the morals are rather loose." Only in this alluvial part of the river region, rather than in the murky realities Reynolds had seen along the upper Ohio, did the West's wide vistas of freedom give up any of its mysteries of unfreedom.[45]

Henry Reynolds was not alone in being bested. For many others during the first half of the nineteenth century, the western river region blurred distinctions between slavery and freedom that elsewhere were becoming clearer. In the middle border states of Kentucky and later Missouri, slavery became a fixed institution protected by law. In Indiana, Illinois, and Ohio, proslavery legislators enacted state laws that offered exemptions or circumventions to antislavery ordinances or provided home rule—and after achieving statehood, Illinois residents even attempted to overturn the Northwest Ordinance. Despite federal, territorial, and ultimately state laws against slavery, local white citizens took advantage of ambiguities and inconsistent interpretations of those statutes, and the varying enforcement of and wide variations in them in local practice, to deny freedom to black people living there.

Through these early years in the nation, the middle border defied characterization, largely because the white western consensus transcended the rivers that had helped to people it. Yet a sectionalization of sorts was indeed occurring, one focused on the nation's growing cleavage over the issue of slavery and the West. The lines of battle, however, were not so easily drawn. Indeed, the great western rivers ran south.

North of Slavery, West of Abolition

As he looked about his sprawling home city of Cincinnati in 1848, Elwood Fisher was surprisingly dismayed. The self-proclaimed Queen City of the West was by anyone's estimation the region's boom town. When the decade began, the city was sixth largest in the nation and behind only New Orleans in the states west of the Appalachians. By the end of the decade the city's residents had nearly tripled in number. Its population—more than 115,000—crowded into the city's bricked streets, plentiful new row houses filled to bursting and spreading to the bluffs hemming it in on the north bank of the Ohio River.[1]

For the Virginia-born Fisher, a thirty-nine-year-old newspaperman, printer, and attorney, his concern was not about the recent flood of foreign immigrants into Cincinnati. In 1840 some 40 percent of the city's population was foreign-born, doubled from just fifteen years earlier. In 1825 some 80 percent of the city's immigrants had come from the British Isles; now, nearly two-thirds hailed from Europe's German principalities. Indeed, nearly a contiguous square mile of the cityscape was a virtual German Stadt, with street signs and business placards posted in German script rather than in English letters. The city's Tenth Ward, known simply as "Über der Rhein," originated from the area's separation from the rest of the city by the Miami Canal. Many of these immigrants were Catholic, causing consternation to native-born Protestants. "[T]hey are almost all imbued with extreme democratic notions," Englishman Charles Lyell sniffed after his second visit to Cincinnati. "In the city, the New Englanders appeared to have lost political weight since we were last here."[2]

Fisher was no committed nativist, the term applied to those "Know-Nothings" who vocalized their anti-immigrant, anti-Catholic anger, and he did not rail against these foreigners' unmistakable cultural and political influence on the transforming city. Nor was it more than mildly concerning to Fisher that New Englanders far outnumbered those hailing from the slave states. Those from the middle Atlantic states far outnumbered both, and these Germans, predominantly Catholic or Jewish, were engaged in the national political debates largely as Jacksonian Democrats, contributing to Cincinnati's, and indeed the entire middle border region's, conservative political climate. Fisher's angst arose from a subversive zealotry associated solely with the North, one that threatened the economic and social advancement that he had come to expect in his western world. That evil was abolitionism.[3]

Fisher was no stranger to slaveholders or antislavery activists, nor to darkly veiled secrets. He knew the pain laid on by crusaders against slavery. He was born in 1809 in the South River Quaker community in Virginia's Southside, where slavery was prevalent and where his father, Samuel, had moved with his own parents early in life from Bucks County, Pennsylvania. Consistent with the precepts of his and his Virginia-born wife's faith, no bondpeople were owned by Friends in South River Meeting. A few years earlier, Samuel Fisher's brothers and parents had "traveled northwardly on a religious journey" to relocate to Columbiana County in eastern Ohio. Samuel remained with his growing family in South River, running afoul of the local sheriff for nonpayment of muster fines a few months before Elwood's birth. Samuel's troubles in Bedford County soon deepened. In April 1816, when Elwood was seven, the Meeting condemned Samuel, and within months he requested a certificate of transfer to the Ohio Friends' Meeting to join his parents. Although the elders granted a transfer for his family, they denied Samuel's request for unspecified "obstructions." Angry and defiant, in December 1817 he left Virginia with his wife and six children for Cincinnati. Less than three years later, while in Ohio, the South River Meeting disowned him for "dealing... a negro boy who was in his care and later sold into slavery." His appeal was denied, and he was never readmitted to any Meeting. His son bore his father's stain and blamed antislavery meddlers. In 1833 Elwood, then twenty-four, was himself disowned by the Cincinnati Meeting for "disunity."[4]

The precise nature of Elwood Fisher's sin is unrecorded, but it likely resulted from his having disavowed the Friends' quiet morality. He entered the public realm of men, where he sought presence and power. After having taught school briefly in Vicksburg, Mississippi, where he saw plantation slavery and grew to appreciate its commercial benefits, he returned to his home city and engaged in job printing while editing a newspaper, *The Journal*. He was one of the initial managers of the city's Lyceum, which opened in 1831, serving alongside a recently arrived New Hampshire–born lawyer, Salmon P. Chase. Like Chase, Fisher became involved in Democratic politics, but as the decade progressed the two diverged sharply over the issue of slavery. While Chase ultimately chose the party's antislavery wing, Fisher strongly and publicly defended its conservative, proslavery faction. Cincinnati's business interests supported the existence of slavery just as strongly as they did private rail enterprises and limited government assistance with internal improvements to connect the city with the slave states. Though the segment of its population born in those states was small, Cincinnati's reliance on the "southern trade" was indisputable. Each year during the 1830s, at least 100 steam engines, 240 cotton gins, and more than 20 sugar mills were built in the city and shipped south by river. The bulk of the city's massive export trade, especially pork and flour, also went southward, nearly thirty-seven times as much downriver as up, and more than 90 percent of it to New Orleans. Fisher's marriage to the daughter of a shipper would only confirm his belief in free trade. As he would soon argue, what was good for cotton's kingdom was good for the nation.[5]

An emergent abolitionist presence in Cincinnati in the mid-1830s pushed Fisher to work actively to squelch it. Beginning in 1838, with Moses Dawson he edited the city's traditionally rabid anti-abolitionist newspaper, the *Cincinnati Advertiser and Journal*, a paper that immediately preceded the *Enquirer*. Both devoted themselves to "hard" Democratic politics through the antebellum years. Fisher was present at an 1836 meeting in which resolutions were offered against the publication of *The Philanthropist*, a new abolitionist newspaper edited by James G. Birney. The meeting's leadership, comprised largely of the city's commercial interests, condemned abolitionism for jeopardizing "internal commerce." Its purveyors were "pregnant with injury, to the political, commercial and friendly relations between the States." Fisher is not known to have participated in sackings of Birney's paper and the race riots that ensued, or in the 1841 riot that ravaged Cincinnati's black community over four days. But he would soon edit the Democratic paper *The Advertiser*, which offered anti-abolitionism favorable publicity, and he was among those editors who opposed the state's new Anti-Slavery Society, claiming that "the Southern feeling is too strong in this city; the interests of her merchants, her capitalists, and her tradesmen, are too deeply interwoven with the Southern country... to admit of the successful operations of a Society, tending to separate ties that connected the city with those States."[6]

During the 1840s Fisher sold his newspaper to Democrats with deeper pockets, practiced law, and jobbed prints on the side, without remunerative success. Yet he remained a stolid free trade Democrat, and in 1842 at Lockland, Ohio—"a stinking little manufacturing town [where] they think they must be '*protected* by *Government*'"—he railed against Whigs and Henry Clay's American System. At nearly the same time he contributed occasionally to the short-lived *The Cincinnati Post and Anti-Abolitionist*, which began publication soon after the 1841 riots. Three years later he chaired a committee at the Hamilton County Democratic Convention that authored and circulated a scathing critique of the tariff. Anti-abolitionism took hold of Rev. Joshua L. Wilson, who presided over the city's First Presbyterian Church and defended slavery as "a relation recognized as lawful, in both the Old and New Testaments." But antislavery sentiment, both extreme and moderate, was growing in the city and migrating from its upper classes to its working classes. In 1839 the city's New Light Synod endorsed the American Anti-Slavery Society, and the local Presbytery advised ministers to preach "on the sin of slave holding, as often as they preach on the subject of temperance, Sabbath desecration, and other great moral questions." The synod even recommended that slaveholders be excluded from fellowship in the church. In 1844 and 1845 the city was the scene of a series of public ecclesiastical debates over the issue of slavery, soon published and distributed nationally, that divided Presbyterians in the city and region.[7]

On the snowy Tuesday evening of January 16, 1849, Elwood Fisher articulated his frustrations, born of living astride the nation's hardening sections over the issue of slavery. A friendly Democratic audience crowded into College Hall, the third-story auditorium of Cincinnati's rebuilt Young Men's Mercantile Library, recently damaged by fire, to hear his lecture. It was entitled simply, "The North and the South." From his podium overlooking the great river, he gave an often tedious, commercial-based interpretation of the nation's ascendance. Comparing Ohio and Massachusetts with Kentucky and Virginia, and contrary to northern claims, he argued that the slave South had surpassed the North in economic production during the past several decades. These states, and not those of the New England model, offered more general prosperity and a more civilized culture for white Americans.

Fisher went beyond any simple call for a reduction of the infamous tariff, which unfairly disadvantaged southern agriculturalists—an argument he had made to the county's Democrats four years earlier. Having corresponded with John C. Calhoun, he offered a nationalist argument for slavery as a positive good for his home region. The West, he claimed, meaning the middle border states and the Northwest, was predominantly rural, agricultural, and socially superior to the North. The "individual enterprise and independence of farmers," he argued, as well as its "local, sectional and class interest" mandated the "restraining [of] that part of our system [the federal government] within its proper constitutional limits." Contrary to the arguments of free-labor advocates, who claimed that slavery stagnated the nation's economic and social growth, Fisher criticized the northern capitalist "wage slavery" of hired workers and condemned urban extravagance and waste compared with rural pastoralness and thrift. He concluded that slavery was in fact a cornerstone of both the South's and West's integrated economies and shared cultures.[8]

Reasoned and dispassionate, Fisher argued from a traditional western perspective: slave-based southern agriculture and industrial northern modernity were entirely compatible, except for abolitionism. He was more emotional in his plea that the West's conservatism blunt the northern-born sectional divisions over slavery by maintaining its traditional communion with the South. "These two great systems have grown up together," Fisher concluded:

> [The] North could not have so much expanded without a market in Southern agriculture—nor could this have grown so great but for the

demand and supplies of the North.... If either should fall by the hand of the other, the crime would not only be fratricide, it would be suicide; and over the mouldering ruins of both would deserve to be written the epitaph: Here were a people who disputed about the capacity of the African for liberty and civilization, and did not themselves possess the capacity to preserve their own.[9]

Proslavery-ites, especially those in the slave states, quickly lionized Fisher, and printers in three slave state cities—Richmond, Charleston, and Washington—published his pamphlet in the next year. Far more heard a voice emanating at last from a free state sympathetic to southern arguments. "This mirage," wrote Robert Goodloe of northernized criticisms of slavery, "this chimera, which has been generated by a combination of Yankee deceit and presumption, with Southern modesty, and self-abasement, is now forever exploded and cast to the winds, by the good right arm of one man, who has remained free from the infatuation." New Orleans Whig editor J. D. B. DeBow twice reprinted the pamphlet in serial form in his *DeBow's Review* and frequently used Fisher's statistics in his editorials. Proslavery polemicists immediately referenced him. Reviewed favorably by proslavery firebrands Edmund Ruffin and James Henry Hammond, Fisher's pamphlet appeared among prominent southern publications a decade later. Many assumed him to be a southerner, as have many historians since.[10]

By contrast, northern abolitionists heard only the words of a traitor. Within a month, in a speech on the floor of the House of Representatives, Horace Mann, a Whig congressman from Massachusetts, thundered against the pamphlet's "falsehoods," likely more from outrage at a perceived fellow northerner's apostasy than from his argument. "Mr. FISHER, the disunion propagandist," spat the editor of the *New York Times*, "had better go hang himself."[11]

Within a few months, Fisher would leave Cincinnati. Lured by partisan benefactors, including two U.S. senators—South Carolinian Andrew P. Butler and Georgian Robert Toombs—he headed to the nation's capital to employ what his patrons considered a uniquely un-northernized western voice that spoke for the South. Welcomed warmly at public receptions by proslavery Virginians, he had been wooed to head up an upstart publication entitled *The Southern Press*, specifically to counter the city's notorious abolitionist and Liberty Party organ, *National Era*, edited by another former Cincinnatian, Gamaliel Bailey, who had followed Birney as editor of *The Philanthropist*. From faraway California, one antislavery editor smeared Fisher's venture as little more than "[a] sectional paper for the support of the South." The publication lasted two years. Finding his former middle ground no longer habitable, Fisher never returned to Cincinnati, or to the West that he claimed was different from the rest, or at least its northern reaches.[12]

2

Babel

Changed Persistence on Slavery's Borderland

Elwood Fisher could not have provided a better representation of the uniquely nonsectionalized middle border. As the free and slave states of the West modernized between 1820 and 1850, they did so along recognizably parallel lines. Compatible economic systems, commercial production, racial ideology, and even politics tethered the western river region to what it had largely been during its frontier period: a consensus culture of diverse interests and peoples. Only in the late 1840s did Fisher target the harbinger for real change, indeed turmoil, on his changed western landscape. Sectionalization of the slavery issue introduced dissonance to the regional harmony he had long believed would secure the nation's future, but it did not engulf the chorus.

As the debate over abolitionism and slavery influenced the West's politics, "conservative" antislavery strategies and movements such as colonization and gradual emancipation emerged among its white residents seeking to harmonize the national sectional debate and preserve racial subordination. On what one historian has called "slavery's borderland," these same residents demanded gradations of racial distinctions and statuses that sharply proscribed African Americans' collective experience, slave and free, on the middle border.[1]

"[T]he people of the west generally... [and] their eager pursuit of money and restless enterprise and unceasing activity," wrote one early Missouri emigrant, "is obvious to every one and the Kentuckian yields not a whit to the yankee in resorting to every means, however contemptible they might be thought in old Virginia, to amass wealth." The ties that bound these western states across the rivers owed much of their vitality to Kentuckian Henry Clay's "Bluegrass System." This merging of public and private enterprise, city and country, public and private, commerce and agriculture, in pursuit of an aristocracy of production by tying governmental financing to individual initiative was a regional economic system that carved deep inroads into nearly all of the middle border states. Appealing to "the pushing, ambitious, go-ahead bankers and businessmen, canal promoters, land-owning interests, lawyers with an eye to the main chance, and farmers anxious for internal improvements," by 1840 Clay's system was celebrated generally by upwardly mobile white westerners regardless of residence. In fact, the grass on the other side of the great interior rivers soon became noticeably bluer than in Clay's Kentucky.[2]

A practicing attorney when not a politician, the Virginia-born Clay had invested heavily in commercial and manufacturing enterprises in his adopted Lexington. His six-hundred-acre estate, Ashland, a hemp, cattle, and horse farm, was perched on the immediate outskirts of the self-styled Athens of the West owing to its fine university, schools, libraries, galleries, theaters, churches, and shops. (Clay and Lexington's merchant elite touted their home city as the Philadelphia of the West.) He believed in the compromise of competing interests as strongly as he believed that what was good for the Bluegrass was good for the nation. For twenty-seven years he served in Congress with the West in mind, devoting himself to an expanded "American System," which advocated federal support for internal improvements, a strong national banking system, and tariff protection for emerging industries. By 1840 Clay was the ostensible national head of the National Republican or, after 1834, "Whig" Party.[3]

With the rivers as highways, Clay took his regional system onto the national stage as the middle border's population spilled out northward and westward, as if by design. In 1829 the young Edward Everett proclaimed to listeners in Lexington that "beyond the Wabash, beyond the Mississippi—there are now large communities, who look to these their native fields with the same feeling with which your fathers looked back to their native homes in Virginia." In 1820 perhaps two-thirds of those living in Missouri's central river counties had been born in Kentucky, Tennessee, or Virginia, and three decades later more than a third still claimed those states as their places of birth. By 1860 one hundred thousand Kentuckians called Missouri home, more than three times those from any other state. Joined by those from the piedmont areas of Virginia and the Carolinas and from the Nashville basin, they established a second generation, upcountry patrimony that prompted Baptist minister John Mason Peck in 1816 to claim that it looked "as though Kentucky and Tennessee were breaking up and moving to the 'Far West.'" As late as 1860, compendia of federal censuses categorized Missouri and Kentucky as "Western States," alongside those farther north, as compared with the "Middle States" lying on the Atlantic seaboard largely along the same latitude.[4]

Commercial farming beckoned more than self-sufficiency, and in Kentucky and Missouri especially the subsequent arrival of "gentlemen planters" and enterprising merchants and tradesmen—aggressive, acquisitive capitalists with means to economic and social ascendance—soon transformed these former frontiers into new western states. Traditionally, planters and farmers diversified their production, with grain fields and pastures dotting the rolling landscape.

Kentucky's economic base was the broadest of any slave state save perhaps Virginia, and by 1839 it was the second-leading corn-growing state in the nation, behind only Tennessee. By the late antebellum years the middle border states produced nearly 80 percent of all grain crops grown in the slave states, largely exported down the Mississippi to the cotton-producing states farther south. In addition to growing corn, oats, flax, wheat, rye, and barley, they also raised livestock: cattle, hogs, sheep, and especially horses and mules.[5]

The presence of cash crops was no delineator among middle border states, free or slave. Brought westward from the Chesapeake region, tobacco was grown widely on small to middling farms as a cash crop, its broad leaves possessing cultural meaning far beyond economic value. As a source of identity and harmony that buttressed the societal status quo and resisted the tyranny of the market economy, even in gloomy downturns farmers continued to plant and harvest the weed. Although Kentucky led the way, producing more than 108 million pounds by 1860, followed by Missouri, southern Ohioans, Indianans, and Illinoisans grew the crop as well, if in smaller overall amounts, with Ohioans producing nearly the same poundage per square mile as did Kentuckians (if only a third of their overall production). Farmers often grew tobacco to reduce the soil's fertility, necessary for a good wheat crop. What most set Kentuckians and Missourians apart from their cross-river neighbors was hemp, a former Chesapeake crop long stunted by planters' overdependence on tobacco. In the West the hemp industry found its footing. These states' 74,493 tons of dew- and water-rotted hemp represented three-fourths of the nation's production and dwarfed the less than two thousand tons their free state neighbors grew. Ironically, by 1840 southern Illinoisans grew more cotton—two thousand tons, or some five hundred bales—than either Kentuckians or Missourians. Although three decades earlier Missourians cultivated three thousand tons, in 1850 census takers recorded that cotton was not cultivated in the state. Despite cotton prices having nearly doubled during much of the ensuing decade, the 1860 agricultural census lists not one bale produced in Kentucky.[6]

Production of staple or cash crops facilitated the growth of slavery in Missouri and Kentucky, but the peculiar institution was more an equalizing than a corrosive influence there. The prevalence of slave hiring and small-scale slave ownership in these states was evidence of both a diversified, flexible economy and the widespread white belief in slavery as a means of material advancement. Few masters in Kentucky and Missouri had designs on achieving planter status for the sake of social prestige, and many former opponents of slavery soon found their stance softened. A few years after Daniel Drake's antislavery New Jersey family settled near Mayslick, Kentucky, his father and uncles began hiring slave laborers to help work their farms. Vermont-born Abiel and Nathaniel Leonard and Connecticut native John S. Phelps became some of the largest slaveholders in their Missouri locales. Yet they drew firm distinctions between theirs and the slave societies farther south. In 1835 Nathaniel Leonard wrote of Alabama, "All they want here is a large cotton field and plenty of Negroes and they have no other use for money but to buy more Negroes." Border whites often sneered at the slave-rich plantation states as "Africa."[7]

The mixed agriculture of the western states was only one sector of a far-flung yet integrated economy. On both sides of the river, commercial and manufacturing interests of all sorts sprang up, processing raw and agricultural materials such as tobacco, hemp, cotton, salt, maple sap, hardwoods, and grains into salable goods like tobacco plugs, rope, bagging, sugar, paper, lumber, gunpowder, and whiskey. Indeed, Kentucky flour, meal, and pork far outstripped tobacco exports for the first three decades of the nineteenth century. The Bluegrass System's success soon evoked jaunty declarations of utopian westernness. Louisville's *Western Monthly Magazine* trumpeted the "Democratic Principle" of "what is now called the West—the Great Valley," and Irish-born Cincinnati editor and shameless western promoter William Davis Gallagher included Kentucky in his "great interior valley," the most important region of the country.[8]

To link the bustling and newly diverse cities and towns, Henry Clay's greening of the Bluegrass served as a model for the other western states. Its most visible symbol was the National Road, approved by Congress in 1820 as a government-financed, toll-free, macadamized highway extending westward from the nation's capital along the Cumberland Road. After crossing the Appalachians to Wheeling, Virginia, it bisected the settled portions of the Old Northwest all the way to the Mississippi to St. Louis. When Congress ceased funding it in 1840, its westernmost portion was barely cleared, was unpaved, and ended at Illinois's former capital, Vandalia, one hundred miles short of its target. Kentucky poured resources into various turnpike companies to link Lexington, without direct river access, and various interior cities with the Ohio River. In 1838 Kentucky's $2.5 million debt for toll-road construction exceeded all western states and more than doubled all but Ohio's. Its construction of paved roads outpaced any of the neighboring states, leading one historian to denigrate Ohio's comparative "backwardness."[9]

More than roads, harnessing the West's system of navigable rivers was key to sustained regional growth, especially after completion of the Erie Canal. To link the rivers to the lakes, state governments undertook extensive, entrepreneurial banking initiatives in flush times to accomplish expensive canal digging. Regular steamboat service connected the exploding port cities on the Ohio and Mississippi and even smaller towns and landings. Daily packets filled with enterprising businessmen and tourists chuffed upstream and downriver to southern and western Kentucky by the Tennessee and Cumberland Rivers. The efficiency and extensiveness of the western region's river transportation system likely hindered more than helped the canal "boom." With the notable exception of Ohio, where over two decades workers scooped 744 miles of earth from the state's landscape to connect the Ohio River at two points with Lake Erie, most middle border states completed few canals. Indiana had completed just 150 miles, and Illinois and Missouri had yet to finish even one canal mile by 1840. Kentucky, with the most extensive navigable system of any state, managed the feeblest effort to carve canals through its limestone ridges and knobs. Its lone, two-mile Louisville and Portland Canal, bypassing the falls of the Ohio, proved both profitable and long-lived, but only as a means of perfecting river traffic. With it, New Orleans was less than a five-day steamboat trip from Cincinnati in good water.[10]

The immediate outcome of these internal improvements was an appreciation of land values throughout the middle border states. Indeed, settlers who sought the choicest crop land paid far more than the $1.25 per acre minimum price for available public lands. Already by 1827, the best land in Howard County, Missouri, in the heart of the state's Boon's Lick, often cost five times that or more. The availability of such land was soon enough reduced, and prices rose sharply during the subsequent decades as western speculation became the most desirable investment for striving Americans. Foreign investors bought up large tracts of land, and canal and railroad companies received direct appropriations and tax exemptions from fawning state legislatures and even outright grants of public land from the federal government, all of which were eager for development. The annual income from sales of public land increased tenfold between 1830 and 1836, before the bubble burst during the following year's panic. In 1836 alone, nearly twelve million dollars' worth of land was purchased in the middle border states outside Kentucky, relatively evenly distributed.[11]

With his famous talisman, "No North—No South—No East—No West," Clay touted his system as offering regional and national harmony by economic integration. But the 1850s would bring sweeping changes to the middle border, coinciding with sectionalized responses to the national political crisis over slavery. A railroad-building frenzy swept through these states, especially the northern portions, racing past the stodgy river system on which the West's economic system had long relied. Ohio boasted some 3,000 miles of track, seventy-six times that laid in 1840. Illinois was second in the region and the nation with 2,799, and Indiana followed (fifth in the country) with 2,163. Only New York and Pennsylvania had built more. Missouri and Kentucky had themselves engaged heavily in railroad construction, but their 817 and 534 miles of track, respectively, left them lagging far behind even most of the cotton states, much less their immediate neighbors. Two-thirds or more of the track mileage in states north of the Ohio lay above the National Road, where railroad lines influenced town formation and development. Even in Missouri, virtually all of the main railroad lines ran along or north of the Missouri River.[12]

Following the iron horse into the middle border's upper regions were exploding populations. In 1860 Ohio's 2,339,481 people represented a more than 50 percent increase since 1840, making it the third largest state in the country. Indiana's population had nearly doubled, to 1,350,138, and Illinois's and Missouri's growth was nothing short of astonishing. Their populations, 1,711,717 and 1,063,489 respectively, had each more than tripled in the same period. Illinois was now the nation's fourth largest state. The migration filled the prairies of these western states, in Missouri's northern tier and western river counties and especially in Illinois's Rock River country. Assisting with this was a militia army, mostly from middle border states and including a newly arrived Illinoisan, Abraham Lincoln, that in 1832 drove out Black Hawk's "British Band," the last Native American populations in the Old Northwest.[13]

The 1850s saw the floodtide. As late as the 1840s, many of the unorganized areas or fledgling counties of the northwestern region had been sparsely settled. During the 1850s the number of Missouri residents from the northeastern states increased by more than 200 percent, largely to the northern tier and St. Louis. All of the counties of northwestern Ohio, where railroad service began only in the 1840s, saw their populations increase by half or more in the decade; only two other counties in the entire state saw such population increases, and one was the site of the fast-growing city of Cleveland, propelled by the Lake Erie trade. Formerly boggy forests that were drained by industrious canal laborers and settlers, these counties accounted for much of the state's growth in the final antebellum decade. Indiana, Missouri, and especially Illinois had similar patterns, their northern counties grown nearly to bursting and shifting their population base from their traditional loci in the southern or middle portions of their states. Indeed, the proportion of southern Illinoisans in the state's overall population declined from 40 percent in 1840 to just 25 percent two decades later. The towns and villages of the southern portions of these states declined proportionally as well; by 1860, just 13.3, 26.3, and 23.5 percent of the cities, towns, and villages of Illinois, Indiana, and Ohio, respectively, lay in the Ohio valley. This northward shift contributed greatly to the western region's population exceeding those of all others, including the fast-growing cotton frontier of the Old Southwest.[14]

As during the first wave, these new emigrants were acquisitive, middle-class farmers, many having sold farms in their former homes and now staking a solid claim to land in the upper portions of those states. "These emigrants," commented the editor of Columbus's *Ohio State Journal*, "are not needy adventurers, fleeing the pinchings of penny. They are substantial farmers." Many came westward to break the rich prairie sod, formerly seen as infertile, and grow wheat using recent agricultural innovations such as the steel plow and mechanical reaper. The stake they made sought to harness profits to the agricultural revolution that accompanied the transportation revolution, directing farm produce by rail and wagon to the growing Great Lakes port cities, then by the Erie Canal to

New York. Chicago grew almost overnight from a shabby town of just 4,470 residents in 1840 to a major metropolis to 112,172 twenty years later, becoming the fourth largest city in the West and ninth in the nation. No less than eleven railroad lines converged there. Cleveland and Detroit each boasted more than 43,000 residents; neither had even a fifth as many two decades earlier. Farm values appreciated accordingly: between 1839 and 1860, land in Ohio's northwestern counties increased nineteenfold.[15]

Hezekiah Niles observed from Baltimore in 1834 that this new immigration made the upper portions of the western states virtual "northern hive[s]." Swarms of industrious New Englanders breaking the deep-rooted Illinois prairie was certainly a metaphor for their bringing order to a disordered land. The "Yankee" ingenuities of John Deere and Cyrus McCormick, both of whom realized their agricultural triumphs there, were storied. Deere was a Vermonter who invented his famous plow in Grand Detour, Illinois, but McCormick was a Virginian who located his reaper manufactory in Chicago. In fact, Yankees made up a small proportion of these rural populations. A sampling of county census records suggests that the largest portion of these second-wave immigrants came from western New York, Pennsylvania, and Ohio. In 1860 in two northern Indiana counties, Jasper and Benton, New Englanders constituted just 1.4 percent and .5 percent of their respective populations; middle Atlantic and slave state emigrants each outnumbered Yankees by as much as three times. In northern Illinois's Ogle, Grundy, and Jo Daviess Counties, New Englanders represented 7.6, 6.6, and 1.4 percent, respectively, of their overall populations, compared with as many as a third from the middle Atlantic states. By 1860 there were more Ohio-born residents of other states than in their own birth state, while sixteen of Ohio's southern counties actually lost population during the previous decade.[16]

Much like the free states lying across the rivers, Missouri and to a lesser degree Kentucky exemplified this western ideal of progress as village and urban frontiers. According to the 1860 census, Missourians had organized themselves into 728 towns, cities, townships, and districts, a figure seven times that of Virginia. With nearly 90 percent of its entire population living in small towns and cities, Missouri closely reflected Illinois, Indiana, and Ohio, with 934, 1,017, and 1,493 towns and cities, respectively. Kentucky's 66 towns lagged behind neighboring states, but ran well ahead of states farther south. (Georgia, Tennessee, South Carolina, and Alabama had between 15 and 36 towns and villages each.) Although not all white westerners associated with these various districts actually lived within the physical boundaries of these towns, they were still affiliated with the towns nearest their farms. Opportunities abounded in participatory self-governance beyond voting, from holding minor offices to attending community meetings. These westerners practiced what one historian has called a "loose-limbed Union[ism]," celebrating the success of the experiment of republican government and the Constitution while remaining wary of federal power.[17]

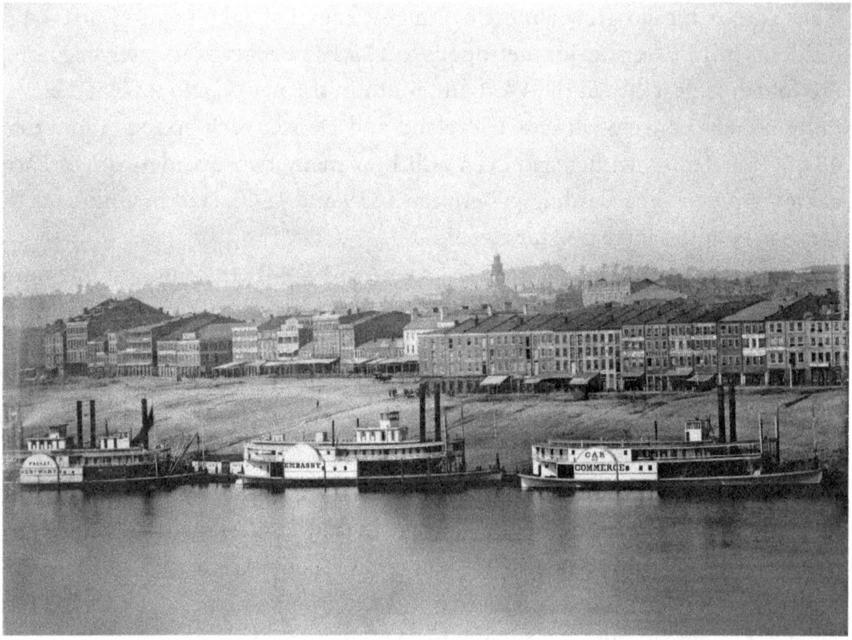
EMBASSY
CAR
COMMERCE

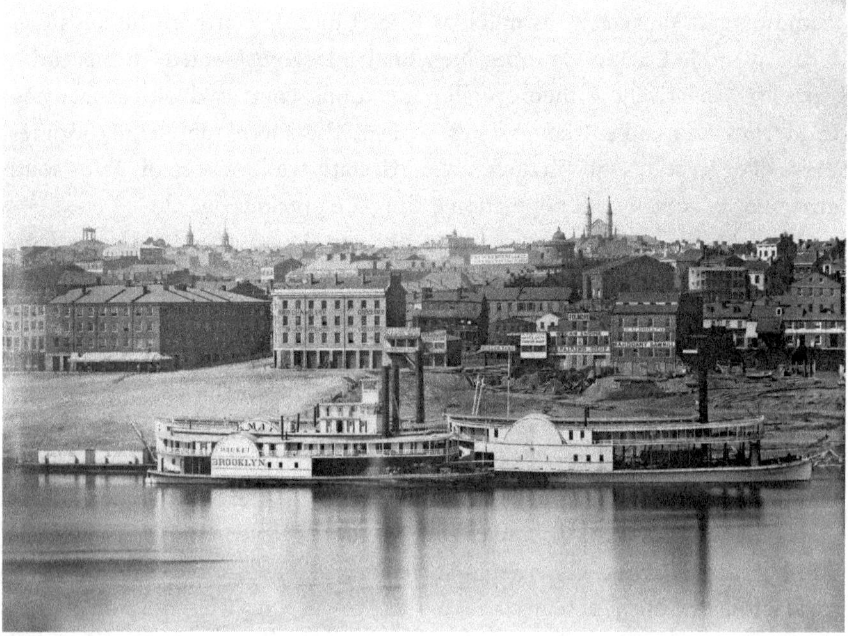
BROOKLYN

Figures 2.1a, b, opposite and c Panoramic photographs of Cincinnati riverfront, September 1848, panels 3, 4, and 5. Taken by Charles Fontayne and William S. Porter from across the Ohio River, the eight separate daguerreotype images came to be known as the Cincinnati Panorama of 1848 and are the oldest comprehensive photographs of an American city. Courtesy Public Library of Cincinnati and Hamilton County.

Even more even than towns, the middle border's cities became the most visible destination of the region's new populations. Indeed, the urban frontier was no longer a frontier. Whereas in 1840 just less than 4 percent of the region's overall population was urban, and only three cities boasted as many as eight thousand residents, by 1860 some 14 percent were living in cities, and fourteen cities had at least ten thousand residents. Evansville eclipsed Madison as Indiana's most populous city by 1840 and by 1860 had grown from 4,000 to 11,484 residents. This former "rude village dispersed among the trees [that] scarcely attract[ed] the notice of the traveller as he swept by her...is now a city," wrote one visitor. Louisville, lying at the falls of the Ohio, had 22,000 residents and more than doubled each decade. Cincinnati doubled Louisville's population by 1840, and a score of years later reached a staggering 161,044 souls, becoming the seventh largest city in the nation. No border city grew faster than St. Louis, ironically the oldest city in the West. With just over 16,000 residents in 1840, by 1860 its 160,773 residents rivaled Cincinnati and constituted more than 13 percent of Missouri's entire population. St. Louis's breakneck industrial growth soon replaced its once commercial dominance. Led by flour and mill processing, sugar refining, and meat packing, by 1860 $27 million of manufactured products ranked it seventh among American cities, and it was sixth in the number of manufacturing firms, bypassing Cincinnati as the largest supplier of beer and flour to the southern markets. Nearly half of the city's new residents came from New England, Pennsylvania, and New York, and by 1850 nearly nine in ten adult New England emigrants were engaged in trade or professional endeavors. They had also launched three-fourths of the city's new businesses.[18]

As cities changed the middle border region on both sides of the rivers, a sea of immigrants filled its cities, towns, and villages. A first wave of German immigration came from eastern cities and from their native homes, disappointed by failed liberalizing movements in 1832 and 1833. "The chief emigration," noted Charles Lyell of Cincinnati in 1842, "has been from Bavaria, Baden, Swabia, Wirtenberg, and the Black Forest." Lured by the promise of the West, they settled in cities as skilled and semiskilled urban tradesmen who opened breweries, tanneries, shops, and markets. By 1850 one in three of those residents of St. Louis was of German origin, compared with just 7 percent of the state's population as a whole outside the city. These first-wave immigrants were often politically conservative. When German-born whiskey merchant Joseph J. Mersman relocated from Cincinnati to St. Louis in 1849, he found nearly mirror cities; the existence or debate over slavery was too inconsequential for him even to mention. Some two-thirds of the German immigrants to Cincinnati, Covington, Louisville, and Evansville were Roman Catholics. Irish people, too, flocked to these western cities, especially after the infamous famine of 1846, drawn by employment opportunities with road-, canal-, and railroad-building companies. St. Louis's nearly ten thousand Irish-born residents in 1850 represented a full 13 percent of the city's population. Though they were often less affluent, educated, and skilled than the Germans, Irish benevolent organizations, Hibernian societies, and other such communal associations safeguarded cultural solidarity and promoted their communities' progress.[19]

This immigrant deluge washed over the middle border. In 1850 census takers found that 47.2 percent of Cincinnati's 115,000 residents were foreign-born, behind only St. Louis among American cities. Foreigners, of course, were nothing new to the Queen City, or to the West, but as recently as 1825, 80 percent of them had been Anglo-Americans. Now, more than thirty thousand, or three-fifths, of these immigrants were Germans and formed the overwhelming majority of the city's influential Jewish population. Of Louisville's 12,532 foreign-born in that year—who constituted just less than a third of its population—60 percent were Germans. Upriver on the Kentucky side, Covington's and Newport's foreign-born constituted more than 20 percent of each city's population, just more than Evansville's. Beyond the cities, they founded towns on the prairies and in the interior river valleys with names from their homelands: Hermann, New Baden, New Alsace, Rhineland, Wittenberg, Dutzow, and Westphalia.[20]

Consistent with Henry Clay's economic and social borderland, political parties in the West reflected degrees of separation more than firmly divisive positions. They articulated interdependent nationalist positions, upheld conservative racial ideology, and eschewed government involvement in local issues. At least initially, the western system's most lopsided benefit was to the party that Henry Clay largely built, the Whigs, who championed progressive economic initiatives. Western voters rewarded them with rapid, if uneven, electoral viability. Kentucky offered Whig candidates their most consistent successes, often three-fourths or more of the votes cast. Between 1836 and 1848 the party was competitive in all of the middle border states, winning elections at all levels. Its appeal was strongest in the region's numerous towns and villages, and thus the Whigs' regional success in part reflected the region's settlement patterns. Ohio and Indiana saw Whigs carry congressional and state majorities in most elections during the period, taking several gubernatorial elections, and voters preferred a Whig candidate in three of the four presidential elections. In Illinois, Missouri, and western Kentucky, Whigs had their least influence, suggesting that the farther west one traveled within the middle border states, the less progressive voters were likely to be. Illinois was the most challenging ground for Whigs. Their candidates occupied only from a quarter to a third of the state legislature during the period, and just one of seventeen U.S. congressmen and no senators won office. Yet despite Abraham Lincoln's dour admission that "the tendency in Illinois was for every man of ambition to turn Democrat," Whigs did well enough among small-town strivers in central Illinois to compete with the party of rural individualists.[21]

However much Clay's Bluegrass or American System overspread the middle border states beyond his Kentucky home, Whig proponents never managed to consistently control their political landscapes. They walked a fine line in a western region where charges of elitism could stain darkly. Western legislators and voters tried to align inherently contradictory notions about liberty and government with alternately traditional individualist and progressive collectivist lines. The Whigs' positive portrayal of an active and even interventionist government to promote economic development garnered suspicion from rural property holders, who regarded an invasive governmental presence at best with suspicion and at worst with outright hostility. While common westerners could and did expect their government to protect their commercial interests, they drew firm lines around its perceived intrusions on their liberties. The more remote the residents' access to transportation networks, the more likely it was that Democratic candidates would best their Whig contenders. Localist economies and communities thrust themselves into the region's political struggles, such as in southern Indiana's hills, in displays of ambivalence to progressivism. Subsistence farming and a widespread distrust of the wider commercial economy symbolized by subsidized canals led voters to shun the Whig Party and vote for local, state, and national Democrats, who espoused distrust of consolidated business interests and governmental intrusions.[22]

Western Democrats, too, were forced to walk a fine line in the middle border's slave and free states. None could oppose the advocacy of regional growth and potential prosperity by the increased availability of domestic and foreign markets. But westerners were divided over individualist support for the states' rights theory of government and the potential for distribution of benefits that the collectivist American System offered. In the region's slave states, this thicket was especially thorny. In Kentucky and Missouri the federal tariff meant opposing protections for hemp, risking losing the support of the rural slaveholding gentry. Supporting the tariff exposed them to the elitist stigma they heaped on their Whig rivals while appearing to obstruct progressive initiatives in order to hold down common farmers. Consequently, Democratic state politicians selectively portrayed consolidated industrial and business interests as tyrannical northern threats to western democratic principles. Both parties claimed the mantle of economic progressives and tarred their opponents as conservatives, "in their eyes, a crime," as a Missourian wrote, when uncoupled from racial understandings.[23]

Fractious political contests whipsawed their states' respective leadership and policies between the Democratic and Whig Parties. One historian has estimated that during the 1840s in one southern Illinois county lying near the Mississippi River, two-thirds of the county's poorest voters and nearly as many of its farmers supported the Democratic Party, while merchants, lawyers, clergymen, and physicians chose Whig candidates 62 percent of the time. This split also emerged along urban-rural lines. Clay's system appealed especially to men who benefited from town-based economic exchange: merchants, bankers, factory owners, and small-town entrepreneurs. But commercial planters and large farmers who needed access to credit, theoretically stood to profit by access to broad national and world markets and should have embraced the Whigs. Most, however, did not. These rural conservatives convinced themselves and their constituents that despite their relative wealth and power, as independent westerners they should reject Whig "federalism" and support the Democratic party.[24]

Western Whigs soon learned painful lessons about economic progressivism. A generation of frenzied modernizers attempted to recast western independence as achievable by, and not despite, government involvement. Led by its local Whig politicians, including Abraham Lincoln, the longest of the mostly Kentucky-born "Long Nine" of Sangamon County, site of Illinois's newest capital, the Illinois legislature made huge appropriations for canal building. Several states like Lincoln's barely avoided defaulting on their debts during the Panic of 1837, and Indiana and Pennsylvania could not stave off such an embarrassment. Indeed, more than two-thirds of Indiana's $13 million debt was attributable to internal improvements. Because Missouri's legislature refused to be drawn into the canal frenzy, the state weathered the Panic of 1819 relatively unscathed. But its economy was less resilient in subsequent economic downturns.[25]

Nationalized roads and banks were the foundations of the Whig's western system, making them individualist Democrats' prime targets. As western Whigs tarred Andrew Jackson and his party for their failure to finish the National Road, "banking aristocracies" became a Democratic rallying cry. No bank was more reviled than the Bank of the United States, for which Henry Clay served as chief counsel. Westerners impulsively blamed "the Monster" for all financial woes. In 1820 in Cincinnati, the center of the western system's entrepreneurism, now mired in the nation's first financial panic, the bank confiscated valuable property for debts and drove angry, democratic-minded voters to turn out local officeholders who supported it. Indiana, Missouri, Illinois, and Kentucky passed laws limiting the collective authority of banks, and a vengeful Ohio legislature belatedly ratified the famed Kentucky and Virginia Resolutions. All of the middle border states but Kentucky voted against Henry Clay in 1824 in his initial bid for the presidency, and in Kentucky the same Clay voters elected as their governor the pro-relief candidate, Joseph Desha, in 1824. Partisan riots bloodied Lexington's snowy streets during the holiday season.[26]

Beyond local and state politics, the entwined debates over banking and internal improvements that contributed to the brief ascendance of the Whigs betokened something more important: an infant fissuring of the western Democratic Party amid pressures of evolving national platforms. All the middle border states bore witness, none more than Missouri. Senator Thomas Hart Benton and other western Jacksonians found themselves cornered by the Whig platform, unable to oppose the idea that increased access to markets would benefit western constituencies, especially farmers. On the one hand, the self-described "party of the common man" espoused states' rights and opposed the exercise of the national government's authority. On the other hand, conservative Democrats recognized their states' need for transportation improvements for access to markets to secure western individualists' freedom. Benton decried Whig competitors as economic nationalists, and those in his own party who supported their platform, largely from St. Louis, were "false" or "business Democrats." What resulted was largely a specious distinction, with Bentonites supporting the National Road and improvements to the river system, but only insofar as they could benefit plain farming folk.[27]

Henry Clay had gotten his wish. His "Bluegrass System" was the western region's, and the modernizing forces that had once benefited his Lexington now benefited the entire middle border. Without clear lines of separation, the West's politics were an amalgam of regional and national positions that nuanced more than divided the parties and platforms. One issue that did not yet divide them was slavery.

§

Consensus in the diverse region suffered an unexpected inevitability. Far more than economic and demographic changes, the political controversy over abolitionism shifted the course of the western river region. As early as 1818 the Scotsman James Flint noticed the emergence of a regional divide over the status of runaway slaves, a "moral boundary" of sorts that pitted slaveholders in Kentucky and Missouri against their free state neighbors. Border region's residents, white and black, had been long aware of an "Underground Railroad," as the network for aiding fugitive slaves later came to be called, running northward by innumerable, shadowy rights of way. Throughout the 1830s and 1840s thousands of freedom-seeking bondpeople escaped slavery, assisted by white and black "conductors." In 1849 the *Louisville Journal* reported that slaves absconding to the free states deprived owners of some $30,000 in property each year.[28]

In truth, moral absolutism on the matter of slavery was in short supply in the middle border states. Most white westerners were unpersuaded that slavery was a moral issue, and abolitionism posed a greater threat to the nation's stability than the extension of slavery. Descriptions of chained slaves being returned to the South aboard riverboats were commonplace among travel narratives. Indeed, during the 1819 debate over Missouri's statehood, half of Ohio's congressmen and one senator voted that slaves already in that territory should remain in bondage after statehood, and that slavery should be allowed into the Arkansas Territory as well. "The question of slavery in the United States," clucked an Ohio editor in 1837, "is a political question. Its character is mistaken by most abolitionists."[29]

As the cant of abolitionism emerged in the North, most white westerners convinced themselves that their consensus was best preserved by traditional stances on slavery. Among the most committed of the West's antislavery moderates was Cincinnati's William Davis Gallagher, a Whig editor who urged peaceable discussion rather than ugly confrontation between abolitionists and slaveholders and refrained from publishing political arguments over slavery. Echoing longtime claims of slave state moderates such New Orleans Whig J. D. B. DeBow, the editor of St. Louis's *Western Journal and Civilian* opined that openness on the issue of slavery in middle border slave state cities would overcome the "want of homogeneity between the people of North and South" of which "[e]very intelligent mind is conscious." After the Unitarian Church, reputedly the most liberal of the nation's religious denominations, issued a public protest against slavery in 1845, it was "divided on the abolition question, as most sects are," as one of its faithful reported, by an East and West schism rather than North and South. The church's Western Unitarian Conference sent out missionaries in the region with explicit instructions that they were without doctrine on slavery, allowing ministers like St. Louis's William Greenleaf Eliot Jr. to build their congregations as best suited their communities and consciences. Eliot's endless equivocation on slavery opened him to national charges of being "a slave-state time server."[30]

For antislavery westerners, moderation on slavery found a voice in support for colonization, the movement to convince slaveholders to free bondpeople, who once emancipated would be relocated elsewhere. Indeed, Henry Clay was a founding member and longtime president of the American Colonization Society, and among its later membership was the upstart Illinois lawyer Abraham Lincoln. Each of the region's states formed branches of the ACS, composed of opponents of slavery but also of those who sought primarily to rid their states of free blacks, and discrete state and local societies soon organized as well. By 1832 Ohio alone boasted thirty-three colonization societies, second only to Virginia and only slightly above Kentucky's thirty-one.[31]

The most conservative of antislavery schemes, colonization initially enjoyed wide appeal in the western border states as a preventative to both abolitionism and free black migration. From Ohio, Englishman Edward Abdy noted in 1834, "All the whites...admitted that [blacks] had been defrauded—but then their color! What right had they to remain where they were? They must go to Liberia." When easterners held out the West as a possible destination for freed slaves, such schemes tempered colonization's appeal there. Missourians were horrified to learn that a number of well-meaning eastern colonizationists advocated the Louisiana Purchase region as a likely destination for the removal of African Americans, much as Native Americans would be forcibly removed by way of the infamous "Trail of Tears." The idea of using the West as a dumping ground for freed slaves, and with it amalgamation, horrified even the most ardent antislavery leaders. Salmon P. Chase admitted to Frederick Douglass that he "looked forward to the separation of the races" and encouraged freedpeople to emigrate to the Caribbean or South America.[32]

Racial aversion, more than empathy, characterized western colonizationism. As Ohio minister John Rankin wrote disgustedly from his river bluff home overlooking Ripley and the far Kentucky shore, it was "evident that the [Ohio] Colonization Society owes it existence to prejudice." Even free state Quakers, the most quietly committed of slavery's opponents, were divided over blacks in the West. In 1841 the Indiana Yearly Meeting of Friends closed its meetings to antislavery lectures, and five years later Indianapolis colonizationists met, according to one observer, "to exhume the Society for manufacturing *prejudice against color.*" The state's governor, Joseph A. Wright, complimented the legislature's resolutions favoring colonization as a barrier to abolitionism, intending to prevail in "the great struggle for the separation of the black man from the white." Western colonizationists empathized with Illinoisan D. J. Pinckney, who declared during the state's constitutional convention in 1847, "I am in favor of removing [free blacks] not only from this State, but from all the States."[33]

Nowhere was the delicate balance between competing antislavery impulses stronger or earlier felt than in the middle border's slave states, where the West's antislavery thrust was born. And nowhere was the line between them so easily crossed. As early as in 1792, Kentucky Presbyterian minister David Rice constructed antislavery foundations in his pamphlet, *Slavery Inconsistent with Justice and Good Policy*. Early evangelicals in the state who held similar views formed the state's first "abolition" society in 1808, calling for gradual, compensated emancipation rather than legislative action against the "moral evil" of slavery. By 1827 eight such societies existed in Kentucky, before colonization societies largely replaced them. Indeed, in 1833 the Kentucky legislature enacted a Non-Importation Act designed to halt the domestic slave trade into the state in order to curb future emancipations. Robert Wickliffe Sr., one of the largest slaveholders in the state, sneered that the purpose of colonization was to rid Kentucky of free blacks, not slaves. For speaking out too strongly against slavery in 1835, the president of newly established Marion College, near Palmyra in northern Missouri, lost his position and was run out of the state. Two years later the Missouri state legislature unanimously passed a law prohibiting the spread of abolitionist doctrines, with life imprisonment as the penalty for a third offense. Passions had hardly cooled by 1841, when the state's newly elected governor, Thomas Reynolds, in his inaugural address, thundered against abolitionists' "head long fury...[to] trample upon the rights of the slaveholding states and expose us to all the horrors of a servile war." He and his western countrymen would be "wanting in self-respect...were we to suffer the least interference with this delicate question, from any quarter."[34]

In antebellum Kentucky, emancipationists—self-styled "antislavery conservatives" who were often committed or disillusioned colonizationists and whose economic, rather than moral, arguments to convince slaveholders to free their bondpeople and legislators to enact gradual emancipation laws often fused with colonization—were uncomfortably tolerated. Abolitionists were stoned. Cassius M. Clay, a distant cousin of the famed statesman, who converted to antislavery in part because of his Yale education, gained national attention while serving in the state legislature by espousing an economic critique of slavery in which the inefficiency of slave labor blunted the growth of slave states' industry and commerce. A former colonizationist, in speeches, editorials, and pamphlets Clay implored: "Give us *free labor* and we shall, indeed, become *'the garden of the world.'*" When northern abolitionists held him up as their southern ideal, he earned infamy in Kentucky. Clay was assailed in public, and his newspaper, *The True American*, was mobbed and briefly suppressed in Lexington in 1845. Fearless, he began brandishing bowie knives and pistols and recklessly fought all comers, even rigging his Lexington residence's front hall with a loaded four-pound cannon and lanyards reaching to his desk in an adjoining room so that he could fire on anyone who might storm the front entrance. After moving his editorial office to Louisville and publishing his paper in Cincinnati, he began speaking nearly exclusively in free states. Minister John G. Fee avoided attacks for a few years by confining his missionary efforts mostly to those areas of the state with few slaves. But when he helped Clay get up a "Radical Abolition party" in Kentucky in 1855, Fee found himself driven from his home state by angry mobs. Although the combative Clay would not admit being forced into a sort of exile from his home state, Fee frequently commented on his "martyrdom" in Cincinnati.[35]

North of the Ohio, residents generally were little less committed opponents of abolition than those south of it. Antislavery westerners often were more concerned with the deleterious effects of African Americans in their midst rather than with the debate over slavery in the abstract. Other than in recognized areas of New England settlement, such as Ohio's Western Reserve, whites reversed their tradition of tolerant pluralism and closed ranks to impede the spread of abolitionism. Even in the Yankee enclave of Marietta, Ohio, across the river from Virginia, advertisements for fugitive slaves ran regularly in most newspapers until the mid-1840s. Efforts at transplanting freed slaves, or using free territory to effect wholesale manumissions, met with hostility. When in 1819 Samuel Gist famously brought some three hundred Virginia slaves to Brown County, Ohio, and freed them, residents protested about the "depraved and ignorant...set of people" and persecuted the freedpeople who stayed. Edward Coles, who offered his slaves both freedom and land in Madison County, Illinois, did so with conditions, requiring continued service and improvements to their 160-acre unimproved parcels before they could receive clear title. Most worked for years for Coles as wage laborers, even as he served as Illinois's governor during the state's decision not to overturn the slavery prohibition. (He later became a committed colonizationist and gradual emancipationist.) Disillusioned, only a few remained with him long enough to get the land he had acquired for them. Most moved on, working as tenant farmers, sharecroppers, and general laborers, rarely becoming landowners.[36]

So long as they did not espouse abolitionism, even the most ardent of antislavery moderates found their efforts unimpeded. Benjamin Lundy, a New Jersey Quaker and lifelong emancipationist and colonizationist, came west to Missouri, and after campaigning unsuccessfully for an antislavery state constitution, returned eastward and settled safely in the Quaker community of Mount Pleasant, Ohio. There he founded the Union Humane Society, dedicated to aiding free blacks, and in 1821 began publishing *Genius of Universal Emancipation*, one of only two such papers in the nation. (The other, *Abolition Intelligencer and Missionary Magazine*, was published by the Kentucky Abolition Society.) The tepid response to Lundy's paper in Ohio convinced him to publish in Baltimore. In Cincinnati, William Davis Gallagher found antipathy more than ambivalence for abolitionist publications. His short-lived *Daily Message* was "altogether too Anti-Slavery (not *Abolition*) a tinge to make it acceptable to business men in Cincinnati who had commercial transactions with businessmen South," and soon after publishing the "Address of the first National Constitution of the Anti-Slavery party of the United States," his paper was "kicked out of the stores on the river tier of Squares," forcing him to quit it. In 1841 William H. Brisbane, a former South Carolinian planter (who, much like Edward Coles, freed his thirty-one slaves after taking them north of the Ohio) and pastor of Cincinnati's First Baptist Church, was dismissed from his congregation for his perceived abolitionism after founding the Baptist Anti-Slavery Society and the local Liberty Party. Within a dozen years, known by then for briefly publishing an abolitionist paper, for assisting needy black residents, and as an active "co-laborer in the cause the slave" with Quaker conductor Levi Coffin, he found himself unable to earn a steady income in the area and moved his family to Wisconsin.[37]

Abolitionists like Cincinnatian Gamaliel Bailey expressed frustrations with the West's racial conservatism, which preserved the region's pervasive moderation on the issue of slavery. "[W]hat a hard place this is! And what a curious sort of abolitionists we have got!" he wrote in 1837, exasperated at his faltering efforts to solicit contributions to the state's antislavery society. "One man told me with a grave face, that it would not do for him to take an *active, open* part in the cause, for it would injure his business!... [I]t is hardly worth while to get men to join us, who are not '*powerfully converted*,' as the Methodists phrase it." Ironically, the itinerant Methodist preacher Peter Cartwright, an antislavery Kentuckian who went to Illinois to escape his native state's "slavocracy" more than slavery, characterized abolitionists as "high-handed.... I have never seen a rabid abolition or free-soil society that I could join, because they resort to unjustifiable agitation." When what he called a "secession" splintered his denomination into sectionalized conferences at its 1844 annual conference in Cincinnati, he blamed abolitionists in the church. (Six years earlier, the Presbyterian Church had similarly divided, with disputes over slavery figuring deeply in the sectionalized schism.) The Kentucky conference, meeting in Louisville the following year, voted 98–5 to withdraw, and five-sixths of Missouri's delegates did the same. In 1845 St. Louis minister William G. Eliot refused to sign the Unitarian Church's "Protest against American Slavery," and in 1857 he and much of his city's delegation withdrew from its Western Conference after the annual meeting declared "the system of slavery as evil and wrong."[38]

By the 1840s abolitionists in small towns and rural areas were met with vocal opposition and even violence. The Quakers' reputation for peaceful antislavery activism, which traditionally included quiet refusal to do business with slaveholders or to sell their goods (see figure 2.2), did not shield them. A speaker at a Milton, Indiana, antislavery lecture was attacked, and law officers refused to prosecute anyone. In 1837 a lecturer employed by the American Anti-Slavery Society, Marius R. Robinson, was tarred and feathered in Trumbull County, Ohio, whose seat claimed to be the "capital" of the Western Reserve, for preaching what they saw as radical Garrisonian tenets of immediate abolition. The next day, he was arrested for having incited the mob. Zanesville and Dayton, Ohio, witnessed anti-abolitionist mobbings in 1839 and 1841. Virginian John Parsons, a proslavery moderate, visited Levi Coffin at his new home outside Newport, Indiana (he had by then left Cincinnati) and discussed the "odium" of abolitionism. "It is not a popular cause," Coffin told his young visitor. "It tries a man's soul to take such a stand in these days, when brickbats, stones and rotten eggs are some of the arguments we have to meet." John P. Parker, a free black conductor suspected of aiding fugitive slaves in getting across the Ohio and northward to safety, lived in constant danger from neighbors on both sides of the river. Even in his hometown of Ripley, Ohio, later the self-proclaimed "terminus of the Underground Railroad," Parker recalled that "the real warfare was waged around these few [abolitionists'] homes."[39]

Figure 2.2 Free Labor store, Mt. Pleasant, Ohio. The Society of Friends, or Quakers, were the most reliably antislavery of the West's varied population, and among their acts of opposition was refusal to market goods produced by unfree labor. Courtesy Ohio Historical Society.

In middle border cities, where discriminatory racial ordinances were commonplace, abolitionists were seen as incendiaries. Winning converts required covert efforts, as antislavery Ohio lawyer Samuel Galloway instructed, including circumventing "unreasonable opposition, manifested to the cause.... [S]ay nothing upon the subject in public, yet they are free to express their opinions, privately." Knowing fully the West's racial antipathy, Lyman Beecher moved to Cincinnati from Boston in 1832 to establish an institution that would instruct budding western clergymen how to preach abolitionism effectively to racially conservative flocks. His commitment to evangelize the West to abolition had financial backing from New York's controversial Tappan family, and Beecher brought his own family there, including his as yet unpublished twenty-one-year-old daughter, Harriet. In addition to his pastorship of Cincinnati's Second Presbyterian Church, Beecher founded the Lane Theological Seminary on the hills overlooking the city and became its first president and an endowed professor of theology.[40]

Characterizing those who supported the cause there as "conservative Abolitionists," Beecher's version of the crusade against slavery was nearly the same as previous antislavery positions in the West. "I am not apprised on the ground of controversy between the Colonizationists and the Abolitionists," he claimed. "I myself am both, without perceiving in myself any inconsistency." Lane's mission was to accomplish emancipation by the "spontaneous action of the slaveholding states," rather than through the national government. Garrisonians, he averred, were "men who would burn down their houses to get rid of rats." In 1835 Beecher published *A Plea for the West*, a call to arms that argued for conservative ministrations to the western flock, quiet teaching rather than vocal sanctimony. "[T]he ministry for the West must be educated at the West," he reasoned, and those who came to proselytize must do so "with the feelings, not of New-Englanders, or Pennsylvanians, but of Americans." To any northern abolitionist considering emigrating in order to enlighten a backward western constituency, Beecher warned "let him stay at home." His conservative abolitionism would soon strain relations with his benefactors, but Beecher stood firm, believing the West held the movement's—and the nation's—best hope.[41]

Inadvertently, Beecher's efforts contributed to the westward migration of Garrisonian immediatism in a very public way. In 1833 Theodore Dwight Weld arrived at Lane Seminary an enthusiastic, older student with a personal endorsement from evangelical revivalist Charles Grandison Finney. He brought students from upstate New York's famously evangelized "Burned Over District" as well as financial support from the famous New York abolitionist philanthropist, Arthur Tappan. Weld was a committed colonizationist when he arrived in Cincinnati, but its harsh racial environment convinced him that conservative abolitionism was little more than a "conspiracy against human rights." He quickly radicalized the mixed-race student body, including Marius R. Robinson and John G. Fee, as well as James Bradley, a former Kentucky slave who was among the nation's first African Americans to attend an American institution of higher education. In February 1834, while Beecher was on a fund-raising tour in the North, Weld conducted more than two weeks of revival-like "debates" that shook the foundations of the new seminary. The following summer students started Sunday schools and evening adult education classes and organized benevolent societies for Cincinnati's twenty-two hundred free blacks, and established an employment service and even a "freedom bureau" to assist them in buying relatives out of slavery.[42]

"Cincinnati was never so convulsed before," one of the seminary's trustees marveled at the angry response to the "Lane rebels." Four years after a race riot had driven out half of its black population, white Cincinnatians now lashed out at the "perverting [of] seminaries... into political debating clubs" and condemned the Lane students for "dreaming to organize a wide-spread political revolution." When Weld published an impolitic response claiming the students' radicalism had only begun, outraged civic leaders and even some Lane faculty pressured the school's trustees—the majority of whom were businessmen with trade ties with the southern states or native-born in the slave states—to "impose restraints" on the students and their leader. "No Seminary of learning, especially no theological one," read the Board's resolutions, "should stand before the public as a partisan on any question." All but eight of the seminary's one hundred students withdrew, and with them went Tappan's future financial support. Forty students, including Weld, transferred to the newly established Oberlin College, located in Ohio's Western Reserve. There, Weld pressured the board into admitting not just African American students but also women. "Oberlinism," spat Ohioan Samuel Galloway, had become the "focus of folly and fanaticism." Beecher returned to find his conservative seminary "obliged to bear up under a load of prejudice as a proslavery institution." As abolitionism radicalized nationally following the Lane rebellion, Beecher needed to appeal to northern applicants and placate suddenly wary investors there. He moved the institution's mission to the center by diversifying its student body. "Our students... come to us... through two ranks of opposition," he wrote in 1840, "Old School and ultra Abolitionists, though the conservatives among the latter confide in and patronize us, and most of our students are conservative Abolitionists."[43]

Animosity from moderate antislavery westerners was in part a response to the activism of western women in the region's abolitionist movement. Forming associations at the county and state levels, these women worked cooperatively and pragmatically on several reform fronts beyond ending slavery: to change the West's racial conservatism, to repeal the region's Black Laws, and to effect women's rights legislation, especially suffrage. They circulated antislavery publications;

raised money; and fed, clothed, and even sheltered fugitive slaves from bounty hunters. Not surprisingly, the largest number of activists were in Ohio's Western Reserve, where in 1836 the Ashtabula County Female Anti-Slavery Society boasted over 450 members. By contrast, Philadelphia's sister society, which would later become one of the largest women's abolitionist organizations in the nation, at that time had less than a quarter that number.[44]

With the crusade against slavery representing progressive social reform generally, anti-abolitionism on the middle border was uncivil and frequently violent. In 1836 former Kentucky slaveholder James Gillespie Birney, a Princeton-educated lawyer and ACS agent whom Theodore Weld converted to abolitionism, freed his slaves, sold his family home, and moved to Cincinnati to form the Ohio Antislavery Society. When he announced plans to publish an abolitionist newspaper, attendees at a series of public meetings in the city denounced him and shouted him down when he attempted to speak. Continued threats of violence forced Birney to relocate temporarily to New Richmond, where he began publication of *The Philanthropist*, but distance and sporadic river mail deliveries soon forced him back to Cincinnati. On July 12, 1836, his press was mobbed. A handbill posted and circulated afterward warned: "ABOLITIONISTS BEWARE." Birney reopened and soon suffered a second mobbing, led by merchants who benefited from lucrative trade with "southern neighbors," whom Birney's "unholy cause [was] annoying." After pitching his press into the Ohio, the mob ransacked homes in the city's free black community, prompting Harriet Beecher Stowe, wife of a Lane Seminary instructor and daughter of its president, to confide in her journal, "The mob madness is certainly upon this city." Birney left again, only to return to Cincinnati, where he remained until September 1837, when he left for New York to become secretary of the American Anti-Slavery Society. Birney's paper continued to be published for six more years, and both he and his son, William, were egged, separately, at speaking events in small Ohio towns.[45]

Perhaps no anti-abolitionist event in the nation was more notorious than the 1837 mobbing of editor Elijah P. Lovejoy, the proprietor of the *Observer* and abolitionism's first martyr. A Maine native, Lovejoy came to St. Louis in 1827, where he opened a school and edited the *St. Louis Times*, a newspaper devoted to reformist causes other than slavery. After studying briefly at the Princeton Theological Seminary, he returned to St. Louis in 1833 and began espousing emancipationism. In May 1836, when he criticized the lynching of a mulatto sailor accused of murder, the Presbyterian minister suffered the lash of conservative Missourians. When a local judge ruled that Lovejoy's inflammatory editorials had provoked such vigilantism, a mob dumped his press into the Mississippi and threatened violence against his family. A few months before Missouri's legislature passed its law prohibiting abolitionist activism, he relocated upriver to

Alton, Illinois. Before he could even unload his press, a mob met him there and again threw it in the river. Twice more, antagonists sought to destroy replacement presses. On November 7, while defending his office from another mixed mob of Illinoisans and Missourians, Lovejoy was shot dead. No one was prosecuted. "Sprinkled with my brother's blood," wrote his brother, Owen, who would honor his brother's murder by dedicating himself to his cause. As Elijah's biographer, the Congregational minister and Underground Railroad conductor would become the most strident abolitionist in Illinois and one of its political and social leaders.[46]

Unlike in New England, where Lovejoy's martyrdom spurred membership in antislavery societies and calls to "free" the West, on the middle border antiabolitionism only gained strength. In Illinois, boasting the nation's strongest comity laws save New Jersey's, proslavery residents routinely broke up abolitionist meetings over the next several years. Rather than condemn Lovejoy's murderers, St. Louis's Anti-Abolitionist Society demanded strict enforcement of the city's Black Code laws. In the spring of 1838 the Kentucky legislature sent commissioners armed with petitions and resolutions from their constituents to the Ohio legislature seeking cooperation in suppressing abolitionists. The following February, under pressure from the Democratic governor, Wilson Shannon, it easily enacted a fugitive slave law that facilitated warrants for fugitives and imposed fines from $100 to $500 for those aiding escapes or hindering arrests. A Cincinnati newspaper hailed the law for "strengthen[ing] those feelings of friendship between Ohio and Kentucky." When the state's supreme court overturned it in 1841, ruling that slaves brought to Ohio were free, Cincinnati's Anti-Abolition Society funded a newspaper, the *Cincinnati Post and Anti-Abolitionist*, to "counteract the pernicious influence of a rank modern mania with which [the city] is beset." Claiming support from eight out of ten of the city's residents, the society asked members to collect and forward to local constables "the names of all negroes residing in [their] ward, who have not given bond according to law, as well as the names of all persons harboring negroes contrary to law." With special delight, the paper published the names of known abolitionists in the city and surrounding area, mistakenly or not, often to the consternation of those identified. Antislavery soon found little literary traction at any level. In 1843, returning to Cincinnati after college stints in Athens and Oxford, Ohio, William H. McGuffey set about revising his popular school primer to sell more *Eclectic Readers*. His publisher there convinced him that he should not offend middle border white residents' moderate sensibilities on the slavery question, whether antislavery or proslavery and on either side of the Ohio. Eliminating or editing key passages, lessons, and lines from its selections that cast slavery in an unfavorable light, the former minister, professor of philology, and college president, who had become ensnared in slavery politics that afflicted his campuses, broke with the prominent western intellectual and educational circle known as the "College of Teachers," which included social reformers and abolitionists like the Beecher family. Sales increased markedly.[47]

Formal politics on the middle border saw abolitionism fare similarly poorly. For all of the national attention it received from northern abolitionists, the Liberty Party, born in 1839 in western New York's Burned Over District and resolving to "demand the absolute and unqualified divorce of the general [i.e., federal] government from slavery, and also the restoration of equality of rights among men," gained little traction in these western states. Its candidate for president in the 1840 election, James G. Birney, polled only forty-seven votes of a total of eleven thousand cast in his former home city, Cincinnati. Four years later, despite having the backing of local lawyer Salmon P. Chase, less than 6 percent of the city's voters supported the party's candidates. As the Liberty Party's appeal stalled in the middle border region, a deep sense lingered among most white voters that western expansion unfettered from slavery politics overrode moral opposition to the peculiar institution.[48]

§

The presence of abolitionists in the 1830s, and the backlash against them, solidified white middle border residents' resolve to limit slavery's perceived pernicious influence. Ironically, they did so not by restricting slavery but rather by targeting the presence of free blacks. For decades, the middle border states and cities, free and slave, had been adopting nearly mirror-image statutes as self-styled Black Laws that restricted the freedom of free persons of color. These included strengthening existing immigration laws, codifying legal definitions of race, disfranchisement, exclusion from membership in militias, and forbidding testimony in court cases involving whites. The public school system that Ohio established in 1829, the same year whites in Cincinnati first rioted against its black community because its city council failed to enforce the state's Black Laws, did not provide for education of black children. Indiana replicated Ohio's certificate requirements and required a $500 bond. An 1829 Illinois law required twice that, as well as proof of freedom, from blacks upon entering the state.[49]

Free black populations were minuscule in all of these western states. Kentucky's never constituted more than 1 percent of its overall population or more than 5 percent of its black population, most in Louisville. Missouri's was smaller yet, and the free states' smaller still. Regardless, between 1842 and 1851 each of these states, slave and free, rewrote its constitution, adding provisions that protected slavery or added or strengthened racially discriminatory provisions. In none could African Americans serve on juries, vote, or join the militia, and all but Ohio's included bans on racial amalgamation. Not one of the delegates elected to Kentucky's 1849 convention was an avowed emancipationist, and its constitution banned free blacks from entering the state and tied future emancipation to mandatory out-state emigration. In Ohio, after years of black and white activists' challenges to discriminatory laws, the legislature repealed some of its Black Laws in 1849, including registration and bond requirements for black immigrants. Prohibitions against black voting and jury service remained, and although the legislature at last provided for black public education, its schools were segregated. As one Ohio legislator remarked, "[P]rejudice against the negro is worse than it ever has been, and it is idle to suppose that this sentiment will ever decrease as long as the two races remain together."[50]

The constriction of freedom for free blacks was of little surprise to those in the West. Many had long understood the region as "the Borderland," to use John Parker's phrase, for its continuum of freedom and slavery without firm borders. For blacks, neither legal status nor social distinction was experienced as a sharp opposite. On the margin of slavery, as one historian has written perceptively, many black residents were acutely aware that "freedom did not offer all the privileges that slavery denied, nor did slavery deny all the privileges of freedom."[51]

More than whites, black border residents were aware of the western region's conflation of the aversive race relations practiced in its free states and dominative race relations that pervaded its slave states. Slaves worked routinely in Cincinnati, St. Louis, Louisville, and other border cities to purchase their freedom from their owners in the region's slave states. One observer estimated that a third of Cincinnati's black residents in "Bucktown" and "Little Africa" were working to earn money to liberate family and friends still in bondage. Neither trudging slave coffles nor galloping patrollers crowded the county roads above the rivers, but posses and marshals pursuing fugitives and kidnappers stealing free blacks away to slavery certainly did. Newcomers, black as well as white, often could not easily distinguish them. Indeed, free black emigrant John Malvin, newly arrived in Cincinnati, saw little difference between slave and free status. He recalled disappointedly, "I thought upon coming to a free state like Ohio that I would find every door thrown open to receive me, but from the treatment I received by the people generally, I found it little better than...Virginia." Englishwoman Amelia Murray recalled a southern couple whose mulatto slave woman was introduced to racial proscriptions in Cincinnati, "hurried back to her mistress...and entreated she might be taken or sent back to the South, 'where black people are free.'" Cincinnati's *Daily Enquirer* reported that one fugitive who had been induced by abolitionists to run to Ohio's Western Reserve returned voluntarily to slavery in Kentucky when reputedly sympathetic whites "treated him as if he was a nigger."[52]

With these border states' diverse economies, and with prevalent slave hiring tangling the workplace web among free black, slave, and free white workers on both sides of the rivers, historians have long puzzled over the fact that the vast majority of the hundreds of thousands of slaves in the middle border's slave states did not take flight. Though laboring in immediate or relative proximity to the free states, only an estimated five thousand fugitive slaves a year reached the free states, out of the nearly fifty thousand who took flight each year in all the slave states. Unquestionably, the largest portion of these escaped from border states. The river industry had long offered employment and agency to both free blacks and slaves in western cities and towns, in slave and free states. Freedpeople used steamboat travel as a source of meager income, whether working as sawyers, coal diggers, stevedores, or carters, or simply by hawking food and other provisions to passengers. Hired slaves formed a sizable portion of Cincinnati's river workforce, and slave owners certainly did lease bondmen to steamboat operators—some two or three thousand in western cities in 1850, by one estimate. Occasionally slaves even captained western boats, and they certainly did escape, often jailed in river towns during overnight tie-ups. The rivers facilitated escapes enough to trouble white residents all along their reaches, especially in upper waters, where racial subordination was reputedly less ironclad. Boat companies had policies denying service to blacks traveling upriver past Cincinnati and St. Louis.[53]

John P. Parker's antislavery activism notwithstanding, as a free black man living on the north bank of the Ohio, he had good reason to constantly be on guard. Between 1820 and 1860 an estimated 375,000 captured runaways were sold south, some 10,000 a year from Kentucky alone. During the 1850s, 22 percent of Kentucky's male slaves aged ten to nineteen were sold, contributing to the heavy flow of working-age bondmen from the border region to the southwestern cotton frontier. Ohio's 1804 law required certificates of freedom for black residents, allowing slaveholders to come into the state to retrieve fugitive property and forcing black residents to prove their own freedom. Unscrupulous white slave hunters entered small free black settlements lying along the rivers, deprived free blacks of their certificates, put them in irons, and whisked them away, often in the dead of night and with the assistance of white posses from both sides. Paducah, Kentucky, near the mouths of the Tennessee and Cumberland rivers, was widely known as a port for kidnapped Illinois free blacks secreted south. The problem was pronounced enough in 1819 for Ohio to enact a law prohibiting the practice and then to strengthen it a dozen years later. In the fall of 1838 slave catchers roamed freely, enough for a Delaware County, Ohio, man to complain that his state was "run over, by the slaveholders and their hirelings." Residents of other Ohio communities, even Oberlin, complained of their homes being broken into by slave catchers, and a correspondent to *The Philanthropist* characterized the state as "a kind of hand-maid to the South." (Ironically, some fugitives ran from forced labor in Illinois and Indiana, and the possibility of being kidnapped and sold south, to slave state cities such as Louisville and St. Louis.) Although localized armed resistance occurred, black and white antislavery residents' efforts were generally more surreptitious than overt. In 1846 Charles Lyell overheard details of one Ohio kidnapping, "in consequence of some flaw in [Jerry Phinney's] letters of freedom, and brought back to Kentucky." After a failed rescue, an antislavery society raised contributions of $500 to purchase Phinney's freedom. Few victims were so fortunate.[54]

Despite the overwhelming drive for freedom, many slaves in the middle border region believed that their future liberty was preserved most tangibly by remaining slaves. The racial realities of the western consensus having entwined bondage with the experience of freedom, owners used the future prospect of freedom as a deterrent to escape in order to secure short-term loyalty and labor from their slaves. They allowed their most trusted and privileged bondpeople considerable mobility and hiring options. Some former slaves stated quite plainly that the prospect of self-hiring, enabling some measure of control over their lives, and self-purchase kept them from running. In 1825 Josiah Henson led a large group of fellow slaves from Maryland to his owner's brother in northern Kentucky by way of the Ohio River. Despite pressure from free blacks during a stop in Cincinnati, he convinced his fellow slaves not to escape, intending to purchase his and his family's freedom in order to secure it permanently. "The idea of running away," Henson later explained, "was not one that I had ever indulged. I had a sentiment of honor on the subject, or what I thought such, which I would not have violated even for freedom."[55]

Henson's admission echoed that of others who saw little gain in seeking freedom on the middle border. Elisha W. Green, a slave preacher whose master allowed him to travel throughout the Bluegrass, recalled riding trains and steamboats with and without passes to reach various Kentucky destinations. On one occasion a train conductor did not throw him off after discovering his slave status. But at Maysville, when he was invited to preach at a funeral in Ripley, Ohio, the ferry owner refused to take him across the Ohio for fear he would escape. "I have had a dozen chances to run off. I do not want freedom in that way," Green argued. He found freedoms within slavery that counterbalanced his wish for manumission. He was allowed to organize an African Baptist church in Paris and drew a monthly salary. After Green purchased his freedom, his liberties were quickly curtailed. "Before this I could go many places without interruption, but when I became a freeman," he admitted soberly, "I was more of a slave after I bought myself than before." Similarly, Lewis Clarke, a slave in Madison County, Kentucky, suppressed his desire for freedom in favor of the relative economic benefits he then enjoyed. He "lived out," meaning that he hired his own time as a grass seed peddler, provided for his own room and board, and paid his master a monthly fee from his profits, an arrangement he believed was economically more advantageous than full freedom. "Now if some Yankee had come along and said 'Do you want to be free,'" he later explained, "What do you suppose I'd have told him?... Why, I'd tell him to be sure that I didn't want to be free; that I was very well off as I was. If I didn't, it's precious few contracts I should be allowed to make."[56]

For the largest portion of border slaves, family ties likely kept them from escaping. Bondpeople understood that group flight was substantially more complicated, and less likely to succeed, than individual escapes. Despite employment opportunities on the rivers and easy access to the free states, many middle border bondmen were not quick to escape. The guilt of abandoning their loved ones played heavily into these decisions. William Wells Brown worked as a slave on steamboats that plied the Missouri and Ohio Rivers and was regularly presented with opportunities to escape. "The remembrance that my dear mother was a slave in St. Louis, and I could not bear leaving her in that condition," prevented him from absconding. In 1834, he at last made his escape in Cincinnati. But he knew he could not remain in Ohio and quickly moved on to Buffalo, New York.[57]

Despite residences proximate to the free states, the majority of middle border slaves did not seek freedom owing to the compromised liberties they believed they would encounter there. The stigma of slavery followed them and often resulted in violence across the rivers. Rather than celebrating the Fourth of July, some black communities secretly celebrated August 1 to commemorate the anniversary of the 1833 abolition of slavery in the British West Indies. In 1848 Lancaster, Ohio's black residents prepared to mark the occasion and publicly announced it as a Sunday School celebration. When white residents discovered the ruse, a mob of "the rough element" attacked the home of the organizer. "The house was badly wrecked and the furniture destroyed. The one hundred or more visiting negroes from Chillicothe and Circleville hastily left the town." When a white resident denounced the mobbing as an "outrage," he drew rebuke from one of its most prominent residents, Ohio's attorney general, Henry Stanbery, for "his incendiary language" and needed a nighttime guard to protect his home.[58]

For the vast majority of slaves, fear prevented them from attempting to seek freedom in the middle border's free states. Lewis Clarke was not alone in understanding the persistent racial boundaries fugitives would find by making risky escapes to the West's free territory. Crossing the frozen Ohio with a group of fugitives from Tennessee into southern Indiana in 1834, Jermain Loguen recalled that a party of white southern Indianans swooped in to arrest them. "D—n the niggers!" exclaimed one, "We don't want them on this side!" After some in Loguen's party brandished and fired pistols, the party of white men moved on, prompting a free black observer to warn them, "My dear fellows, you are little safer here than in Kentucky, if it is known you are slaves.... It is called a free state... [but] your danger is in falling upon enemies. It will not be safe to stop here a moment." As they moved northward through the snow toward Canada,

Loguen and the other fugitives were refused food by white residents and considered returning to Kentucky. In Ohio, he "found the *spirit* of slaveholding was not all South of the Ohio River," and as far north as Cleveland feared he would be caught while searching for passage to Canada.[59]

Their experience in freedom already tempered, free African Americans living on the middle border certainly recognized outright dangers in the pervasively hostile white response to abolitionism. "There is a storm brewing," cautioned a black Methodist minister in 1846 to his Louisville congregation, "owing to some late doings in Ohio, and I hope that none of the membership will get themselves into a scrape." That his congregants were deeply antislavery if not outright agents of abolitionism was readily apparent to local whites. White hostility toward such efforts, and not antipathy for slavery, prompted three race riots in the city in less than a quarter century. The violent combustion of race and class evidenced in Cincinnati saw its counterpart in rural, free state counties, nowhere more than in southern Illinois. In Massac and Pope Counties, isolated in the hills lying along the Ohio River upriver from Paducah, a series of ugly vigilante conflicts raged periodically from the fall of 1846 to 1849, fought ostensibly between propertied Regulators and propertyless Flatheads, the latter a euphemism for poor whites living on the Ohio's bottom land. The precipitating event was an attack on a local farmer and former slaveholder, Henry Sides, who was acting as executor for a neighbor who had brought his freed slaves with him when he moved from Tennessee in the 1830s and left his estate to them upon his death in 1846. Taking these black residents' money was more than simple robbery. By January 1847, one newspaper had counted thirty lynchings in Massac County, and residents reported that Flatheads had supplanted Regulators as racial vigilantes, terrorizing and kidnapping free blacks for sale downriver as slaves. The Illinois Supreme Court's ruling two years earlier, and the current constitutional convention that would soon end slavery forever in this reputedly free state, calculated heavily into the racial violence in the state's former stronghold of slavery.[60]

§

As the West modernized, the changes occurring in the region did not disrupt the region's white consensus. Eschewing government involvement, its variations of the national parties celebrated the western culture of progress and blunted the national sectionalization over the issue of slavery by upholding conservative, proslavery racial ideology. Abolitionism found little support, but its influences would bear fruit. As Cincinnatian Elwood Fisher predicted, the West's debate over abolitionism and slavery would change the middle border by drawing its residents into the sectional debate during the last antebellum decade. Amid a western Babel, middle border residents would soon find themselves forced to translate their world in finite, decidedly nonwestern language.

Vox Populi

In the summer of 1855, as the bluestem grasses parched in the baking heat, William Barclay Napton watched thunderheads gather high on the western horizon. From Elkhill, his 1,760-acre western Missouri farm, Napton, a circuit lawyer and former state supreme court justice who had lost his seat four years earlier when voters rejected his hardened proslavery opinions, looked toward the Kansas Territory, some eighty miles away across the Missouri River. The murmurous winds he felt were in fact political. Just over a year earlier, the Kansas-Nebraska Act had opened the area to settlement by "the great principle of popular sovereignty." By its transformation of American democracy, occupants of the territories, and not Congress, would decide slavery's extension.[1]

Far from fearing the tempest, Napton welcomed it. As the owner or trustee of some fifty-four slaves, he saw Kansas as a gift from Congress. He and his proslavery neighbors claimed that "the natural order of events" would assure the spread of southern culture, institutions, and staple crops. The eastern portion of the territory, especially the Missouri River watershed, was conducive to growing tobacco and especially hemp. (Of the sixteen thousand tons of hemp produced in Missouri in 1850, nearly all came from western Missouri's river counties.) This and latitudinal migration patterns would ensure that, just as Kentucky had been settled by Virginians and Tennessee by North Carolinians, proximity would see Kansas settled by Missourians.[2]

But political events had not proceeded naturally. Napton and many others soon acknowledged that the controversial act had set into motion what had fast become a regional civil war. In Missouri, the free-labor ideology—that "a man can raise himself to the ceiling by taking hold of the seat of his breeches"—had seduced emigrants from the upper portions of the Northwest to come west by way of the new Hannibal and St. Joseph Railroad to Missouri's northern tier. Many were antislavery. "Their population is chiefly from Indiana, Ohio and Illinois—and they cannot be trusted," Napton complained. St. Louis was worse. "Yankee abolitionists and German radicals [who] have gotten possession...have made that place as thoroughly hostile to slavery as Chicago." In the southwestern Ozark counties, white residents' traditionally strong commitment to free-soil ideas and their ownership of few slaves had diluted the southern sympathies of the largely Upland-born residents. Only in the black belt Missouri River counties, where Napton lived and where slaveholding was dense, were residents reliably proslavery.[3]

More troubling to western slaveholders like Napton was the arrival of abolitionist emigrants from New England, who they believed would soon entice their bondpeople to escape. Many saw these migrating Yankees as an immoral, unwanted people. To the secretary of war, Mississippian Jefferson Davis, western Missouri U.S. senator David Rice Atchison offered a chilling historical allusion to collective efforts against the migration. "[W]e are organizing, to meet their organization," he averred. "[W]e will be compelled, to shoot, burn and hang, we intend to 'Mormonise' the Abolitionists." He was referring to an 1837 militia campaign in Missouri's northwestern counties that had violently expelled all Mormon settlers from the state. Atchison now exhorted listeners "to give a horse theif, robber, or homicide a fair trial, but to hang a negro theif or Abolitionist, without judge or jury."[4]

Slave stealing by abolitionist interlopers was bad enough, but more detestable for proslavery Missourians like Napton and Atchison was these New Englanders' organized and publicized swarming of Kansas. With a capitalization of $5 million approved by the Massachusetts legislature, the emigrant aid societies or Kansas Leagues, as they were called, intended nothing like popular sovereignty. What Eli Thayer and Amos A. Lawrence orchestrated was an invasion to populate the region and subvert the spread of slavery. By colonizing antislavery settlers, they intended to do more than replicate the culture of the North in the Far West. These were antidemocratic subversives, a stark contrast to the land-seeking immigrants from the slaveholding South and even the antislavery Northwest, "a Hessian band of mercenaries was thus prepared and forwarded, to commence and carry on a war of extermination against slavery." As Napton railed, "To call these people emigrants, is a sheer perversion of language.... They are hirelings—an army of hirelings—recruited and shipped.... Emigration has followed the parallels of latitude and will continue to do so, unless diverted by such organizations."[5]

In mid-July 1855 Napton was one in an angry group of 240 delegates representing twenty-six Missouri counties, the lion's share from the state's central and western portion, who assembled in the Cumberland Presbyterian Church in the Missouri River town of Lexington. Local meetings held during the previous months throughout the area had elected their delegates to the meeting, which was named the "Pro-Slavery Convention of Missouri." They now articulated their neighbors' frustrations at the alarming regional and national events that threatened the future of the peculiar institution—in other words, Kansas. Proslavery firebrands, such as David Rice Atchison, Sterling Price,

Claiborne Fox Jackson, and the Mexican War hero Alexander Doniphan, were conspicuous among those in attendance. Thirty-eight past, current, or future state representatives; ten state senators; three governors; two lieutenant governors; one attorney general; one state secretary of state; and six U.S. representatives participated in the convention. Several were some of the largest slaveholders in the state. Held in summer heat thickened by river humidity, the three-day meeting was, as one newspaper correspondent described it, "stormy and confused."[6]

On the meeting's final day, as chair of the convention's Committee on Resolutions, Napton spoke to the sweaty crowd. The former judge dutifully submitted to the assembly his committee's work: eleven resolutions drafted to vent collective frustration over events in their region and state. Although not normally given to making public addresses, he offered the assemblage a wide-ranging oration, honed by years of reading on national and world history, laying out historical, economic, political, and legal foundations for the present crisis over slavery. Reminiscent of Elwood Fisher's proslavery talk delivered to a Cincinnati audience more than six years before, Napton's included the timeworn strands of Calhounian proslavery polemicism. He blamed the extralegal actions in Kansas on the federal government and New England emigrants, who sought to wage war against a constitutional right and moral responsibility. His keen logic and unveiled outrage charged the heated crowd, which unanimously adopted the resolutions, "every man in the house rising to his feet and greeting the result with a loud cheer."[7]

The convention's emotional centerpiece was reserved for its final speaker: James Shannon, an Irish-born, converted evangelical minister and proslavery militant who was president of the state university at Columbia. Indeed, five years earlier Napton had helped to install him to replace the free-soil Whig moderate who had rankled the slave-rich river counties' proslavery Democrats. Shannon's address, "Domestic Slavery," amplified many of the points Napton had made but added their scriptural counterpart. The convention delegates thundered in response to the address. Kansas offered redemption for the Democratic Party as defender of the rights of common men, but also for the state's largely proslavery constituency, who saw themselves as crusaders against outside agitators and conspirators.[8]

That such a convention occurred in a state in which slave owners comprised just 10 percent of its overall population, led by a delegation that represented mainly its western counties (two token delegates from St. Louis showed up late), suggests the depth to which proslavery ideology had burrowed into Missouri's politics. Slave ownership was the obvious unifying symbol. Predictably, nine in ten delegates had been born in slaveholding states, especially Kentucky, Virginia, and Tennessee. Of the twenty-three men who served on the Committee on

Resolutions, all but four owned more than ten slaves or served in state or national government.[9]

The composition of the broader delegation is more intriguing; their chattel holdings and occupations offer a more complicated story of the power of the slaveholding mystique in this northwestern-most slave state. Although the convention's leadership clearly drew from the slaveholding elite, the convention was more representative of the middling ranks of Missouri society in terms of slaveholdings. The average delegate owned just over eight slaves, somewhat above the statewide average of six per slave-owning household, and nearly eight in ten owned at least one slave, or soon would. Rather than large planter politicians, a full 63 percent were identified as farmers, few of whom had held political office and, by all indications, they had little political experience. The rest were drawn from a wide array of occupations, including bank cashiers; hotel, tavern, and livery keepers; steamboat captains; preachers; teachers, professors, and other educators; rope manufacturers; millers (both saw and grist); turners; ferry operators; tobacconists; wheelwrights; mechanics; freighters; shoemakers; carpenters; cabinetmakers; turners; coopers; blacksmiths; students; three "gentlemen"; and one "traveller."[10]

Beyond the obvious debate over slavery's western expansion, the make-up of the convention delegation spoke to the region's material concerns. The 1850s were flush times generally for western slaveholders, in Missouri and elsewhere. Indeed, the price of cotton doubled during the decade, facilitated in part by Congress's tariff reduction, and production followed suit, especially in the expanding southwestern states. In five of Mississippi's Delta counties, cotton production increased from threefold to eighteenfold during the decade. Land values in those counties increased even more. With more bagging needed for cotton, hemp prices rose sharply, peaking in the fall of 1856 nearly 75 percent higher than at the start of the decade. With easy river access to the South's cotton frontier, and easier access to the West's farming frontiers, where demand for rope, twine, and sack cloth was incessant, hemp planters in Kentucky and especially Missouri took full advantage of the windfall to buy more land and laborers. "Missouri is now the great hemp State, and will probably long remain so," concluded a Kentucky legislative committee in 1860.[11]

The opening of Kansas triggered a frenzied bubble in land and slave prices in western Missouri, running counter to other border states such as Kentucky—other than its westernmost counties—and Maryland, and even most of Missouri. By 1850 slaves in these western counties were worth an estimated $25 million, and real property values nearly doubled during the ensuing decade. Owners who might have fed the insatiable slave market in New Orleans held their bondpeople in response to the rapid rise in land prices in the state's western counties. As a western Missourian wrote in 1859, "[E]very thing is rising in value—

especially negro property—hirelings went at most exorbitant prices on New Year's day—men generally at about $230 for the year.... Slave labor has never been any thing like so high." Convinced that their potential wealth was as limitless as the Kansas prairie, Missouri's slaveholders looked hungrily to the open lands to their west, now threatened by northern abolitionist mercenaries who, in their minds, had no legitimate rights to their region.[12]

The strong convictions articulated during the Pro-slavery Convention perhaps welled up from its members' changing material circumstances during the first half of the 1850s, which the unfolding Kansas crisis clearly threatened. A sampling of thirty-one delegates from six western counties reveals that during the 1850s the value of their real property holdings nearly tripled, increasing by an average of $10,678. Samuel H. Woodson, a lawyer and former U.S. representative from Jackson County, saw his real property holdings grow from $20,000 to $60,000; Samuel L. Sawyer, a lawyer and farmer from Lafayette County, saw his holdings increase ninefold, from $4,000 to $36,000; and John S. Jones, a farmer and freighter from Pettis County, saw his property holdings increase more than tenfold, from $7,300 to $75,000. Slave property grew as well. Although in 1850 delegates had owned on average six slaves, a decade later they would own nearly ten. Their value grew apace with land.[13]

On the surface, convention delegates railing against abolitionist usurpers hell-bent on racial leveling could easily have been transplanted to Charleston's St. Andrew's Hall, Savannah's Johnson Square, or New Orleans's Customs House. Entirely clear was that the convention served as a coming-out of the reconstituted leadership of Missouri's proslavery elite, who had only recently been cast out for their strident eschewal of the moderate slavery politics of the state's voters. By articulating slaveholding as the province of all white men regardless of circumstance and by criticizing a federal government they believed was intent on denying their inherent liberties, these Marxes of the middling class asserted the majority's claim to the democratic promise of the West, now threatened by a determined antislavery foe. These men, who conspicuously braved three days of suffocating July heat in the pews of a small Missouri brick church in the heart of the richest concentration of slaves in the state, were not the first—or last—striving white conservatives in flush times to shout egalitarian claims to privileged ascendance secured by denying those rights to others. But their unruly protest was perhaps the most transparent.[14]

3

The Ten-Year War

Sectional Politics in a Dividing Region

The famed "Missouri Artist" and former state representative George Caleb Bingham commented grimly in 1854 that "the slavery agitation is too convenient an instrument in the hands of demagogues to be dispensed with." Bingham's barb was aimed at increasing proslavery radicalism in Missouri, but it could have been directed at the entire western region during the 1850s. Over that decade, the moderate impulses that had buffered the modernizing influences could not prevent sectional politics over slavery's extension from carving deeply into the middle border's consensus landscape. Although a New Englander in the West boasted of "a thirty years war" that antislavery proponents had waged for political control of the region, most white westerners would have disputed the vigor of such a claim. Indeed, as late as 1860 the western region was not yet fully sectionalized, and what sectionalization there was occurred within the region's states, free and slave, as much as between them.[1]

Yet as extremism emerged around the polarizing politics of slavery, the threads of the region's consensus social fabric began to unravel. In Kentucky and Missouri a new proslavery militancy emerged as challenges to western expansion drove residents to intolerance of traditionally diverse stances on the peculiar institution. Conversely, above the rivers western abolitionists initiated a political offensive against proslavery neighbors who defended the institution they long believed was synonymous with democratic liberty. In this struggle over contested definitions of liberty, both sides used cultural perceptions to attack those who differed in their views of the future of the West. The result was at best an imperfect sectionalization. The election of 1860 did not divide the middle border states into antagonistic free and slave blocs, but rather subdivided its free states into pro- and anti-Republican constituencies, while in its slave states the vast majority of residents galvanized around moderate proslavery positions to oppose sectional extremism.

Even with the issue focusing on the far western territories, selling any antislavery platform in the free West proved no mean feat. Repulsed by free-soilers' support for restrictions on slavery's extension as well as by their promotion of free land for poor settlers, Democrats made steady gains at the state and local levels in the free western states between 1840 and 1848, especially among their newest residents. In 1844 Democratic candidates won 69 percent of their votes; captured eleven of sixteen new counties in Ohio, Indiana, and Illinois; and seized control of a majority of counties in all three states, each previously held by Whigs. Indianans returned a proslavery Democrat, Jesse D. Bright, to the Senate even as the 1848 election put a Kentucky Whig slaveholder, Zachary Taylor, in the White House.[2]

When the debates over Texas annexation and the war with Mexico forced the slavery debate into the national spotlight in the late 1840s, the middle border's free states heard moderate calls for stemming the sectional tide. Richard W. Thompson, a southern Indiana Whig congressman, castigated extreme northerners and southerners for slavery politics having gone "too far." The Virginia-born legislator took heart that "the *ultra* feelings of neither of these parties have yet—to any great extent—reached the West. Here we occupy a *conservative* position." Conservatism, racial and political, informed Indiana's state Democratic Party platform in 1848, which avowed that residents of the region "know no North, nor South, but like her noble rivers comprehend both extremes." Indeed, when the Illinois legislature sent a memorial to Congress in 1846 urging it to move ahead with the annexation of Texas, it stood squarely alongside most slave states.[3]

But the Mexican War in 1846–1848 signaled the first sectional shots heard in the region, and among its first casualties were antislavery Whigs in its free states. Condemnation of the war with Mexico largely fell on deaf ears among land-hungry westerners, who saw it as a conflict for expansion. Self-described as "ambitious," Whig U.S. congressman Abraham Lincoln gained a national reputation, not entirely in his favor, for disputing Democratic president James K. Polk's claim that American blood had been spilled on American soil and demanding that he come to the floor to point out the precise spot where it happened. As the sole Illinois Whig to win election to Congress in 1846, Lincoln's "spotted fever" cost him, and other dissenters, dearly. Discouraged by the future of antislavery politics in his home state and region and his party's prospects, Lincoln headed into voluntary political retirement. After voting for the Wilmot Proviso barring slavery from territories acquired by the war, in an inflammatory three-hour speech Whig U.S. senator and former Ohio governor Thomas Corwin condemned the Mexican War and admonished Congress to terminate the war by refusing to fund it. When called upon to explain himself to voters near Cincinnati, the Kentucky-born Corwin harangued abolitionists as fomenting discord and denounced the Proviso as a "dangerous issue." For publishing antiwar poetry, Indiana's John Greenleaf Whittier, a Quaker, was damned as a northern pacifist and an abolitionist.[4]

Antislavery free-soilism made for a poor bedfellow with western individualism's hallmark: states' rights. Ohio's "Free Territory" convention, like that of neighboring Indiana, put on record its faith in limited intrusions on slavery's domain. "We do not ask that Slavery be abolished by Congressional enactment in any State," its platform blared. "We do demand Slavery shall cease to control the action of the National Government." The platform of Indiana's state Democratic Party declared "improper" all efforts by "the National legislature (under present circumstances)... calculated to create local and sectional divisions."[5]

Despite its appealing slogan of "free soil, free speech, free labor, and free men," the Free Soil Party, a fusion of antislavery Democrats, Whigs, and Libertyites, offered moderate antislavery westerners a largely unsatisfactory option in the 1848 presidential election. It carried only Ohio's Western Reserve, the West's most reliable antislavery area, and extreme northern Illinois, settled primarily by northern immigrants. Its candidate, Martin Van Buren, polled less than 20 percent of the votes in all but twenty-seven counties in the entire region. Only one of them, in Ohio, lay below the National Road, and none were in Kentucky or Missouri. In Indiana, Free Soil candidates outpolled Whigs in only three counties. The fluctuations of the entwined issues of slavery and western expansion forced many antislavery moderates in the free middle border states to chase fireflies in pursuit of a suitable party. Among them was Cincinnati's Salmon P. Chase. The lawyer, political aspirant, and longtime Whig was a committed colonizationist until attacks on the city's abolitionists, especially James G. Birney, triggered a conversion that could easily have been mistaken for confusion. In 1841 Chase supported Birney as the presidential candidate of the fledgling Liberty Party, then subsequently declared himself a Free-Soil or "Free" Democrat, then a Free Soiler in 1848, and then an "Independent" Democrat. Chase was among the antislavery majority in Ohio's legislature that scored a partial victory against racially discriminatory laws, repealing its registration and bond requirements for black immigrants in 1849.[6]

Growing antislavery politics in these free western states provided tinder for the sudden proslavery militance in neighboring Kentucky and Missouri. The peculiar institution's apparent inconsequence in both states masked rapidly consequential proslavery sentiment there. Missouri's 115,000 slaves constituted just 9.6 percent of its population in 1860, and its 24,000 slaveholders represented just 2.3 percent of its total free population. They and their families represented just 12.5 percent of the state's white families—the lowest number of any of the slave states save Delaware, and a far cry from South Carolina, where more than half of free white families owned bondpeople, and slaves made up between 40 and 50 percent of residents. Kentucky's overall slave population of 225,483 constituted less than 20 percent of the overall population, and it ranked ninth among states still holding slaves in that year. Their numbers grew only 6.9 percent during the 1850s. Nowhere were slaves less visible than in these states' largest cities. St. Louis's 1,542 slaves comprised just 1 percent of the city's population as a whole, the smallest of any major slave state city, while Louisville's 4,903 slaves formed 7 percent of its population, a far cry from Charleston, Savannah, or even Richmond, where bondpeople made up a third or so of residents.[7]

Despite these data suggesting slavery's imminent death, in both states overall slave populations actually grew, in some portions remarkably, during the 1850s. In Missouri, between 1840 and 1860 the number of Missouri slaves nearly doubled, ultimately to some 115,000, a greater increase than in most of the plantation states. In Kentucky the peculiar institution was more entrenched than in any other border state, its slave population nearly double that of its closest rival, Missouri, and more than two and one-half times Maryland's. In these states, slave ownership was not so peculiar an institution. In 1860 Kentucky had numerically more slaveholders than any other state except Virginia and Georgia, and proportionately more than any except Virginia. Kentucky's 38,645 slave owners constituted 22.8 percent of its white population and 28 percent of its families, ranking the state above all other border slave states, but a far cry from the Old Southwest where half or more of residents owned slaves or lived in slaveholding families.[8]

Unlike in the plantation belts, the middle border's slave states mostly saw small farms worked by few slaves. Slaveholders in Kentucky owned on average just 5.4 bondpeople, while in Missouri's Boon's Lick, the wedge of counties astride the western Missouri River where slaveholding was densest, they held an average of 6.1 slaves, considerably lower than the 12.7 typical of the plantation states. In 1860, at the region's slaveholding height, just 4 percent of Missouri's slaveholders owned twenty slaves or more, the common threshold for planter status, a third of those in the Deep South. (In Kentucky, the figure was 12 percent, closer to the cotton states.) In the two states, some 90 percent of slaveholders owned fewer than ten bondpeople. No Kentuckian owned more than three hundred slaves, only seven owned more than one hundred, and just seventy held fifty or more. Only one-fifth of all of Kentucky's slaves lived on farms considered large, compared to a full one-half in the plantation states. More than a quarter of Kentucky's slaveholders and a third of Missouri's owned just one slave.[9]

Dense slaveholding areas existed in pockets in these states and had expanded westward within them. In Kentucky's Bluegrass counties, slaves often comprised nearly a quarter of the population, and in its western and Ohio River counties, they averaged 15 percent. (The mountain counties averaged just 5 percent.) Slavery expanded most in the latest settled counties of these states: Kentucky's Purchase Region, framed by the Ohio, Mississippi, Tennessee, and Cumberland Rivers, and Missouri's Boon's Lick. Between 1850 and 1860 these Kentucky counties saw their slave populations grow collectively by 76 percent and Missouri's by 82 percent. A sampling of thirty-five counties across these western subregions reveals that on average, slave populations increased by a full half in Missouri and by more than a third in Kentucky. In only two of these sample counties, both traditionally large slaveholding counties in Kentucky, did slave numbers decline. In some areas within these counties, slaves constituted nearly half of the population, and there were recognizable trappings of plantation-style slavery, including slave patrols, gangs of field laborers, overseers and drivers, and a white social hierarchy based on the ownership of human chattel.[10]

What set the middle border's slave states of Kentucky and Missouri apart most noticeably from such states east of the Appalachians was white residents' comparative unwillingness to free their slaves. In 1860 free blacks represented just 3 percent of Missouri's and 4.5 percent of Kentucky's black populations, in contrast to nearly half in Maryland, 90 percent in Delaware and the District of Columbia, and even Virginia, where free blacks grew to more than 10 percent of its black residents. By 1860 Kentucky's 10,684 and Missouri's 3,572 free blacks constituted 1 percent or less of these states' overall populations, nearly identical to states north of the Ohio. The dearth of free blacks in the western slave states was not coincidental. Racial proscriptions, including black emigration restrictions, were patterned after those enacted in western free states. In 1851 Kentucky made future emancipations contingent on freedpeople's outmigration within a month.[11]

In both states the year 1849 saw the middle border's first political demonstrations of proslavery militancy. Missouri's Thomas Hart Benton, a Democratic U.S. senator since Missouri gained statehood, found that his decade-long, free-soil advocacy and opposition to annexation left him open to charges of collusion with abolitionists. Bellowing in a three-day speech in 1844 that he would "not engage in schemes for [slavery's] *extension* into regions where it was never known...where a slave's face was never seen," he opened a breach in the state party that would never heal. Led by Democratic "Ultras," the legislature's leadership demanded absolute support for slavery's extension. In 1849, led by state senator Claiborne Fox Jackson, it spearheaded resolutions by the Missouri legislature instructing Benton to vote for bills supporting slavery's western expansion. His refusal would soon cost him dearly.[12]

That same summer, in Frankfort, Kentucky, a constitutional convention accomplished a similar proslavery transformation. Chaired by Henry Clay, half of the delegation owned collectively more than three thousand bondpeople. Yet Emancipationists led by Robert J. Breckinridge, Cassius M. Clay, and James Speed, all hailing from large slaveholding families, offered a spectrum of gradual schemes by which slaves could be freed, including tying emancipation dates to their slaves' ages, much as in First Emancipation states. Denouncing abolitionists' activities, they pointed to the relative wealth of neighboring free states. "After elevating labor to its proper dignity," read one pamphlet published just prior to the convention, "there will be abundant facility in substituting free for slave labor, at the same cost to [Kentucky's] employers." Circumstances severely undercut these reformists' efforts. A cholera epidemic ravaged the entire Ohio valley that summer, fueling hysteria following a thwarted mass slave escape in several Bluegrass counties that ended in a gun battle in a hemp field. Proslavery candidates denounced antislavery advocates for inciting slave violence, linking them to abolitionist radicalism. The legislature quickly repealed the state's Non-Importation Act to overwhelm antislavery sentiment, and hard-line proslavery delegates and proposals dominated the constitutional convention. "Take away slaves," railed delegate William C. Bullitt, a Louisville lawyer and hemp-grower, "and you destroy the production of that valuable article, which is bound to make the rich lands of Kentucky and Missouri still more valuable." The draft—subsequently approved by the state's voters—declared slavery an "inviolable...right of property...before and higher than any constitutional sanction," and prohibited *post nati* emancipation without compensation to the owners. That the new constitution did not further restrict emancipation offered moderates their only victory.[13]

"The idea is up that it is popular to be a decided pro-slavery man," Kentucky Whig state senator Warren L. Underwood scratched cynically in his diary following the convention. In a fluid western democracy experiencing rapid change, the institution of slavery in Kentucky and Missouri was politically vital, even sacred, to the majority of white residents. In Missouri the furor over slavery's extension was too strong even for the Gibraltar of the West. In 1850 proslavery legislators ousted free-soil Democrat Thomas Hart Benton from his U.S. Senate seat. The following year in Kentucky, Emancipation gubernatorial candidate Cassius M. Clay received only 3,621 votes statewide. Portrayed as antislavery, Whigs managed to hold the state legislature in 1851 from insurgent proslavery Democrats by only two seats in the Senate and one in the House, and in the 1852 presidential election (in which Kentucky was one of only four states to show for Whig Winfield Scott over Democrat Zachary Taylor, a Kentuckian), Free Soil candidate John P. Hale received a minuscule 256 votes. In the Commonwealth of the "Great Compromiser," there would be no compromise over slavery's protection.[14]

§

Histories of the sectional crisis commonly portray the federal Fugitive Slave Act of 1850, requiring all citizens to assist officials in apprehending black fugitives in their midst, as having awakened a somnolent North to the dangers of a "slave power" conspiring to spread the peculiar institution to the western territories. Enacted in September 1850 to supplant a weak 1793 law, it required all citizens to assist officials in apprehending black fugitives in their midst under penalty of fine or imprisonment. Outraged free-soilers like Salmon P. Chase, who told a southern Ohio antislavery group that "disobedience to the enactment is obedience to God," united with abolitionists in sympathy or action. Their principled opposition to the odious new law was converted into forceful obstructions to its enforcement, rescuing fugitives from jails and spiriting them off to Canada and hastily passing personal liberty laws. As one historian has concluded, the issue became "the psychological focus of the sectional controversy."[15]

Chase's example notwithstanding, other than among the West's most predictably antislavery constituencies—Quakers, urban abolitionists, and New Englanders, especially in Ohio's Western Reserve—the region's prevailing white response to the law was relief. The Whig editor of Springfield's *Illinois State Journal* called for "national jubilation" over the Fugitive Slave Act, and the *Louisville Journal* trumpeted it as a deterrent to both fugitive slaves and sectional discord. Indiana Democrat Jeptha Garrigus, a native New Jerseyite and self-proclaimed "northe[r]n man with southern Principles," argued that he did "not believe the north have any right to meddle With the subject of Slavery, the South have just as much right to go north and steal horses, as the north have to go south and steal Negroes."[16]

The common presence of plantation slaves aboard riverboats that stopped in middle border river towns caused many white westerners to welcome the Act. Mary Logan, the wife of a southern Illinois congressman, recalled the "weird sight [of] black stevedores, clad only in turbans and trousers, rolling these bales and barrels on to the levee at Cairo by the light of pine torches planted on the shore" before boarding boats and steaming off. Having spent his boyhood and adolescence in Hannibal, Missouri, a Mississippi River town, the fictionalized site of two novels, Sam Clemens knew well the hostility to fugitive slaves in neighboring Illinois and white residents' wide advocacy of the new law. In *Adventures of Huckleberry Finn*, Clemens had Huck and Jim float downriver to Cairo, rather than risk flight less than a mile away to western Illinois. There, they thought they "would sell their raft and get on a steamboat and go way up the Ohio amongst the free States, and then be out of trouble."[17]

Opposition to the Fugitive Slave Act was largely relegated to antislavery locales such as Ohio's Ripley and Salem, the latter a long-standing Quaker enclave and home of the Western Anti-Slavery Society. When the U.S. House reassembled in December 1850, what few local antislavery petitions the western region's congressmen presented came largely from the Western Reserve. None came from slave states, and none of the legislatures in the region's free states passed new personal liberty laws. With such a law on the books, Ohio's legislature did nothing more than vote narrowly for resolutions supporting modification or repeal of the national law. As much as her abiding abolitionism, widespread ambivalence to the act in her former home city, Cincinnati, convinced Harriet Beecher Stowe to write her famous protest novel, *Uncle Tom's Cabin*. Indeed, in 1852, just a few months after Stowe's book was published, Ohio's legislature debated a bill that would prohibit further black immigration to the state and deny those already there the right to purchase or hold property.[18]

Not until 1854 did passions ignite conservative westerners to slavery politics. The Kansas-Nebraska Act, organizing the remainder of the former Louisiana Territory and effectively repealing the Missouri Compromise, allowed popular sovereignty in the region that was long assumed to be forever free of slavery. Stephen A. Douglas, Illinois U.S. senator and chairman of the powerful Committee on the Territories, identified the Missouri Compromise as the greatest political obstacle to the nation's manifest destiny. He introduced a bill that carved the expansive northern portion of the territory into two, Kansas and Nebraska. Latitudinal migration suggested the likelihood of having one or two future states adopt slavery, but the probability of four or more new free states was a small price to pay for national harmony. For a second time in a generation, the middle border, more specifically Missouri, lay at the center of a national crisis over slavery.[19]

When Douglas forecast "a hell of a storm" attending his bill, he spoke mainly of the legislative fight. The contentious debates paled in comparison with those in the westernmost portion of the middle border. Nationalizing what in many minds was a local or regional institution and issue by placing white liberty above sectional considerations, the Little Giant skillfully consolidated the Democratic Party's power by positioning it between the battling sections. Ambitious western "New Democrats" held that neither Congress nor extremists in the North or South would control the western territories, and white westerners would lead the nation to its manifest destiny by territorial settlement. The act drew on broad appeal in the individualist lower portions of the middle border, especially Kentucky and Missouri, and least from the "*infected* portions," as Indiana Whig Godlove S. Orth referred to the collectivist, antislavery northern portions. Douglas's consistent focus on the rights of white men and his dismissal of the notion that slavery was a moral issue drew many nonsectionalists toward his attempt at compromise and away from those "extreme Anti-Slavery men," in Abraham Lincoln's words, who opposed it. A southern Ohioan warned a friend who had organized a private excursion on the Great Lakes "that nobody that is infected with the Nebraska question, or with Kansas outrages shall be admitted, for I might get excited on the nigger question."[20]

However much Douglas tried to convince white westerners that democracy would prove itself on the Kansas plains, his home region broke apart politically over it. For decades, many like Chase and Lincoln had considered the Missouri Compromise's slavery prohibition a "sacred pledge." "Douglas," Chase spat privately, "has out southernized the South." Free-soilers recognized Douglas and the New Democrats as heretics, and he was run from the podium in his home city, Chicago, for "dishonor of a national compact." Even in Cincinnati, free-soilers—especially German-born—organized meetings against the "disgrace to America and this age." For them, Douglas had "forfeited the esteem of every citizen who had the interests of liberty in his heart." As Cassius M. Clay denounced the Nebraska act as a "gigantic evil which threatened even their own liberty" in Springfield, Illinois, one attendee was Lincoln, an antislavery Whig and a committed colonizationist whose idol was Henry Clay and who had long claimed not to "know what to do, as to the existing institution" even "[if] all earthly power were given" him. He knew now he would reenter politics to combat slavery's western spread.[21]

But Lincoln was searching for a party that could transcend the national parties and, as Salmon P. Chase claimed, "hasten the inevitable reorganization of [national] parties... [that] serve the interests of slavery." After Henry Clay's death in 1852, the Whig Party was weakening nearly everywhere in the western states, free and slave. In the former's antislavery belts, Douglas Democrats were made vulnerable by new anti-Nebraska coalitions. After Illinois's Democrats initially followed Douglas's instructions and passed resolutions endorsing the act, "anti-Nebraska" candidates in its northern counties swept the fall 1854 elections despite Douglas's feverish autumn speaking tour explaining his actions. In Ohio all eleven Democratic incumbents lost their seats in Congress, and every elected congressman, as well as nearly all in Indiana and Illinois, publicly opposed his act. Against the new proslavery ascendance, Whigs fared little better in the region's slave states. "[O]urs is a routed party," moaned Missouri's James S. Rollins in 1856. Even in Clay's Kentucky the party struggled. When antislavery Whigs defected largely to the nativist American, or "Know-Nothing," Party, the party lost half of its ten congressional seats and the governorship to proslavery Democrats.[22]

Emboldened antislavery politicians in the free West seized the opportunity to create a new party unencumbered by perceived proslavery moderates. Illinois's Owen Lovejoy, the brother of the famed abolitionist martyr, played a hand in launching this as yet unnamed movement that would trigger the nation's greatest political revolution. Born of regional concerns, the Republican Party was launched at an 1854 convention in Bloomington in central Illinois "to keep the party... under the control of moderate men, and conservative influences," claimed Orville H. Browning. (In Indiana, it was initially called the Fusion or People's Party.) The new antislavery party positioned itself as a western rather than a sectional party, above ideological extremism. In its infancy, western Republicans were less didactic about slavery than those who would later join. Indeed, the Cincinnati *Daily Enquirer*'s advertisement for an organizing meeting called for "public opinion... not tinctured with fanaticism or polluted with sentiments disloyal to the Union." The evening's first speaker prefaced his remarks by reminding listeners that "I am not now and never have been an Abolitionist in the common acceptation [sic] of that word," which was being used "as a scarecrow, to frighten the timid and sensitive," as one Ohio Republican claimed.[23]

The Republicans' rapid rise to national power could not have occurred without moderate westerners' support for their party's regional perspective. Neither Owen Lovejoy nor any other antislavery radicals in Illinois were included on the

1856 state ticket as the national party put up its first presidential candidate, St. Louis's John C. Frémont, the celebrated "Pathfinder of the West." When western moderates in the party leadership met at Pittsburgh and adopted a nominating platform that hedged on slavery, outraged abolitionist delegates like Ohio's Joshua Giddings hardened the national platform adopted at Philadelphia. Conversely, Democrats met in Cincinnati (moving from Baltimore, the party's traditional convention site), using its and the West's large German constituency to diffuse the Know-Nothing controversy, and moderates largely obfuscated party divisions over free soil caused by Douglas's bill, including ousting Missouri's Benton faction as illegitimate amid fisticuffs. The unruly delegation settled on moderate Pennsylvanian James Buchanan to deflect criticism over Douglas and highlight Republicans' perceived radicalism over slavery. The western strategy worked. Frémont carried all the northern states, but lost all the middle Atlantic and middle border states, apart from Ohio (he also lost Cincinnati). Northerners like Charles Francis Adams lamented voters' "cold and apathetic" showing in much of the western region's free states. The first Republican presidential candidate did not even appear on most Kentucky ballots, only three hundred Kentuckians cast votes for him, and Louisville's Emancipationists refused to support the "radical" new party. In its slave states, the Pathfinder's votes came mainly from New Englanders and Germans in Louisville, Covington, and St. Louis to counter the nativist Know-Nothings, who had launched virulent election day riots.[24]

Even to the most untrained of observers, the Republican upsurge widened fault lines in the middle border region. But the degrees of separation over the slavery issue of two antislavery Republicans, Indiana's Caleb B. Smith and George W. Julian, suggest the fine line that antislavery politicians walked on the issue. Raised as antislavery Quakers, both were former Whig congressmen who headed their state's Republican Party. The southern Indiana-born Julian, recently the vice-presidential candidate for the Free Soil Party, stridently opposed the Kansas-Nebraska Act of 1854 and believed that this Democratic portion of his state, along with Illinois's, were "outlying provinces of the empire of slavery." The Massachusetts-born Smith criticized his friend more for his tone than his beliefs. "Our paths have diverged," Smith wrote him. "You are regarded as ultra in your anti-slavery notions, yet I do not know that you have advanced an opinion in regard to slavery... that I cannot endorse."[25]

Beset by a national crisis they resisted, many moderate westerners employed geographical language to explain emergent political and ideological divisions. Indeed, the *Cincinnati Gazette* predicted in 1857 that the slavery agitation "may not divide the country by sectional ties; [it] may similarly divide each section." Moderates sought to convince the nation that a third section of the country existed, whose residents formed a natural alignment of culture, heritage, climate, and geography distinct from the North and South. In 1850 Indiana's lieutenant governor, Democrat Abraham A. Hammond, reaffirmed that Indiana lay between the two sections and belonged to neither, and he hoped would "witness that political death of Northern and Southern Fanaticism upon the subject of slavery." Taking care to separate his region from the antagonistic ones, he averred, "The North has no special rights in contradistinction to the *South*."[26]

In the mid-1850s Lincoln's law partner, William Herndon, saw three distinct states in his adopted Illinois. Politics, more than geography or demography, helped him draw a map of its cultural partitions. The first section was the northernmost tier of counties, including Chicago, whose residents, largely recent northern immigrants, were "all for Freedom" and thus, in 1858 when Herndon wrote, solid Republicans. The second was Egypt, the extreme southern counties, where predominantly "proslavery," southern-born settlers held up the Democratic Party (whose percentage of the state's population was declining rapidly, comprising just 10 percent by 1860). Finally, and to antislavery former Kentuckians like Herndon and Richard Yates the most challenging section, was the belt of central counties whose residents were of mixed backgrounds and who had the most doubtful political allegiance. This was the state's great political "battle ground," where party alignments were jumbled, "discordant elements" as one Illinoisan called them: Republicans, Know-Nothings, conservative Whigs, fusionists, anti-Lecompton (Douglas) Democrats, and National Democrats, doughface supporters of James Buchanan. As former Whigs became Republicans, what Herndon and Yates mistook for unreliability was the maddeningly complex, formerly conservative Whig part of the state, where residents continued to subordinate the slavery issue.[27]

Earlier settled, the traditionalist southern reaches of these free states now offered negative comparisons for the progressive new people of their northern tiers. Amid sectional controversies, overlooking the fact that the largest cities in this region were located there, editors and politicians disdainfully stereotyped these residents as backward and thriftless "Butternuts." William Herndon dismissed them as "pro-slavery and *ignorant* 'up to the hub.'" In fact, most regarded these areas as being part of the South, injecting yet another sense of otherness into the political discourse. Using geopolitical language, a strongly antislavery Chicago editor wrote to Illinoisan Elihu Washburne, a northern Illinois antislavery moderate, that Lincoln was "southern by birth, southern in his associations, and southern... in his sympathies." Knowing that the majority of central Illinois's congressmen were themselves Kentuckians, Washburne disagreed, claiming of Lincoln's antislavery politics, "*I know he is with us in sentiment*." Not surprisingly, at the Illinois convention at which the state's as-yet-unnamed Republican party was born in 1856, virtually none of the 270 delegates came from Egypt, the state's southernmost counties. To follow their party's line, the few Republicans who lived there often subscribed to St. Louis's *Missouri Democrat*, which despite its name was a moderate Republican organ.[28]

§

Across the rivers in the middle border slave states, the furor surrounding the Kansas-Nebraska Act manifested itself among many proslavery moderates as the centrist concept of a middle confederacy, healer to the ailing nation. Virtuous slaveholders could maintain steadfast loyalty to the Republic while supporting the democratic process as the foundation of liberty. Yet the Kansas conflict soon altered their view of the Union, and with it differences emerged in these slave states' commitment to the western consensus. As Kentuckians sought to harmonize their region and nation, Missourians' proximity to the Kansas controversy suddenly turned them into residents of the nation's most militantly proslavery state.[29]

Ironically, however much proslavery Missourians' rhetoric on slavery and social progress invoked the language of southern apologists, most white residents clearly considered the South a discrete, even foreign place. In 1850 Missouri sent no representatives to a "Southern convention" held at Nashville, Tennessee, though the center of debate was the protection of slavery. Boone County proslavery Whig James S. Rollins cautioned his son, a cadet at West Point, to "say to the Northern and Southern cadets—that you belong to *neither section*—that you are a true son of the great West." Attempting to carve a middle ground in the deepening sectional crisis, Rollins advised that Missourians "take a just and conservative position... and arrest the fire brands hurled by the violent and fanatical portion of the North and the South." David Rice Atchison quickly reminded a free middle border state colleague in the U.S. Senate who had differentiated his region from those that practiced slavery that Missouri was indeed "one of the northwestern States, although it is generally, from its *institutions*, classed as one of the southwestern States."[30]

Beyond abstract arguments over slavery and governmental authority, westerners considered the debate over the Kansas Territory in a practical sense. With a strong commitment to the Union intact, southern arguments for the winning of Kansas as "a point of honor" were less potent in the West. The residents of Weston, Missouri, declared as much at a "law and order" meeting in 1854, adopting the motto "The Union first, Union second, and Union forever." Northern, not southern, fervor drew the ire of proslavery residents. Yale student James H. Buckner, alarmed at the "zeal in Kansas affairs [shown by] the close fisted abolitionist of this section of the Union," averred to his brother in Kentucky that "the time is not far distant when that question [of slavery] *must be* settled.... I suppose you will register your vote this fall for the first time." Reflected by the term "the Goose question," proslavery Missourians claimed their "natural right" to expand into the territory immediately west of them. "Let neither Congress, nor state conventions," exhorted one, "enact any arbitrary laws to regulate property... then will *soil and climate* point out where the slave-holders ought to locate."³¹

The grim realization that their "vilest enemies" would use the democratic process to subvert this natural order and manipulate popular sovereignty drove many to extreme positions. As one Missourian predicted, "the Abolitionists will compass sea and land[,] heaven and hell to prevent the establishment of slavery in this Territory." The mobilization of emigrant aid societies to fund colonization ventures for antislavery settlers to Kansas drove many into a frenzy, fearing that abolitionist settlers would soon entice their bondpeople to escape. Hundreds, even thousands, of these "Hessian band[s] of mercenaries," predicted William Walker, were being "sent here as hired servants, to do the will of others, to pol[l]ute our fair land, to dictate to us a government, to preach Abolitionism and dig underground Rail Roads." As dupes of northern money, these hirelings had no legitimate claim to the independent West. *Squatter Sovereign*, a proslavery Kansas newspaper founded by Missourian John H. Stringfellow, predicted a grim future of "great wealth gathering in the hands of the few, the toiling millions struggling for bread; the one class is corrupted by luxury, the other debased by destitution."³²

The fear that should Kansas not become a slave state, Missouri would become the first state bordering a free state to its west, effectively sealing off slavery from further progress and changing the complexion of westward expansion, drove men to link their cause with southerners. "If we cannot carry slavery into Kansas," William Barclay Napton reasoned, "it is quite obvious that we cannot succeed anywhere else. The result will be that no more slave states will be created." Proslavery Missourians concluded, by mandate, that Kansas was theirs to shape. David Rice Atchison declared to a northerner who opposed slavery in Kansas "that I and my friends wish to make Kansas in all respects like Missouri. Our interests require it. Our peace through all time demands it, and we intend to leave nothing undone.... We have all to lose in the contest; you and your friends have nothing at stake."³³

"Kansas meetings" were soon countering emigrant "Kansas lodges" throughout the state, as well as "self-defensive societies," "blue lodges," and other secret societies formed to prevent abolitionists from reaching their destinations. Perhaps ten thousand Missourians pledged allegiance to such organizations, a thousand alone in Atchison's Platte County, just across the Missouri River. William Walker wrote to David Rice Atchison from Wyandotte, Kansas, soliciting aid from the other slave states: "Our Southern friends must be up and stirring. Virginia, Tennessee and Kentucky ought to send her hardy sons out to claim their rights and maintain them too. Missouri, as far as she can, is doing nobly for a new State." Walker's plea did not go unheeded. Missourians and other slave-state men soon formed emigrant aid societies of their own, often armed. "We are in favor of making Kansas a 'Slave State' if it should require half of the citizens of Missouri, musket in hand, to emigrate there," declared Liberty's *Democratic Platform*, claiming that "nothing but prompt and determined action on our part can avert a catastrophe." Thousands—including Atchison and Jackson—crossed the border to claim exemptions or vote illegally in territorial elections.[34]

Widespread condemnation issued from the northern states, while Missourians defended the voting fraud as a virtuous defense of liberty against undemocratic "northern and Eastern States, [whose] avowed purpose [was to] coloniz[e] the Territory with persons of antislavery Sentiments, to the end of making Kansas a free State." Proslavery Missourians had invented a democracy by which the territories were open to settlement only to those willing to extend slavery into the West. "Companies coming from slave States," wrote John H. Stringfellow, "will be heartily welcomed by our citizens, as well as those from free States who are all 'right on the goose'.... There will be many a good citizen settle among us from Illinois, Indian[a], and Ohio, whose notions of slavery are parallel with our own.... No one can fail to distinguish between an honest, bona fide emigration, prompted by choice or necessity, and an organized colonization with offensive purpose upon the institutions of the country proposed to be settled."[35]

Proslavery Missourians were squarely in two lines of fire: abolitionists drawing down on slaveholders generally, and free labor and free-soil advocates condemning slave societies as socially stagnant, lacking incentive, and degrading to laborers, and touting the free West as the key to America's future greatness. Convinced these immigrants intended to level the West's traditional racial and social hierarchies, many found special solace in the imagery of victimization embedded in the concept of "southern rights." As St. Louis free-soiler Franklin A. Dick charged, "the man of property in Missouri; those who have always been old Whigs, are nearly all in favor of the South. This class of People are really in heart with the Southern Cause and hail with satisfaction the exclusion of the common masses from equality of rights with the wealthy."[36]

For these westerners, denying slaveholders their constitutional right to property was in effect the denial of minority rights, yet more proof that northerners and free-soilers—not slaveholders—intended to destroy democracy. Considering their rural world, with its pervasive white egalitarianism, the freest in the nation, free-soil arguments were slanderous attacks on a virtuous people. "'Southern rights,' as they are termed," scoffed one antislavery editor, entwined western individualism with slavery's protection and triggered widespread sympathy with the plight of the beleaguered South. Indeed, in September 1850 the twenty-four-year-old North Carolina emigrant Jefferson W. Limbaugh began publishing a proslavery newspaper, *Southern Democrat*, in Cape Girardeau, to "vindicate the rights of the South, and the principles of non-intervention in the unfortunate slavery controversy."[37]

In direct response to the northern attacks on the South and slavery led by Missourians, proslavery westerners haltingly adopted the mantra of southerners. Prior to the 1840s, little evidence exists of cultural meaning attached to the term "southern." It generally meant slaveholder, regardless of the individual's stance on slavery's extension. By the time of the Texas debates, with the cant of abolitionism having politicized the term, proslavery westerners more widely took up the cognomen of "southerner" as a defense against attacks on the peculiar institution. In 1844, as he first stood against slavery's spread, Thomas Hart Benton affirmed, "I am Southern by birth; Southern in my affections, interest, and connections.... I am a slaveholder, and shall take the fate of other slaveholders in every aggression upon that species of property." Once the debate over slavery's extension had flowered, slaveholders reserved the term's use for antislavery free state residents, those who posed a threat to the peculiar institution. Conversely, little need existed to employ the term with proslavery neighbors. Indeed, in 1853 St. Louis free-soiler Frank Blair defended his ownership of slaves as a product of being "a southern man by birth, and identified with southern institutions by my interest and education."[38]

During the Kansas controversy, the meaning of southernness was fully politicized, transcending slaveholding status or even its support, to describe deepened proslavery politics. When in 1855 one western Missouri newspaper adopted as its moniker the *Southern Advocate*, its Democratic editor claimed pro-Nebraska politics: "[T]hose of every party...who are opposed to *interfering* with the question any longer, are *good friends* to Southern rights...for *therein* consists the *test* of loyalty to the South." Supporters of slavery drew the sharpest distinctions between neighbors based not on sectional or even regional location, but on their adherence or opposition to slavery. "Put confidence in *no man* for any station of public trust who is not known to be true to the institutions of the State and the rights of our citizens," Atchison railed. William Barclay Napton summed up this new political calculus:

> Because a man is born and raised in a slave state does not prevent him from being a free-soiler or an abolitionist. Kentucky is a slave state, yet I will venture that one half of the Kentuckians who emigrate here are free-soilers—one fourth out-and-out abolitionists. They are not slave holders though born and raised in a slave state, and wherever they are they still entertain anti-slavery sentiments.... The political adjuncts of the northern free-soilers stay scattered here and there throughout the South and 'born and raised' in slave states are the most dangerous of the whole tribe. Such declarations are therefore entitled to little or no importance, except that they should cause the men who make them to be closely watched.[39]

The politics of slavery defined border slave state residents more than whether they came from free or slave states. Democratic congressman James J. Lindley addressed the U.S. House in 1856, claiming that Missouri's proslaveryites "assume to have taken into special custody the slave interest of Missouri, and freely denounce as Republicans and Abolitionists men of southern education, slaveholders, and all others who do not conform to and maintain every arbitrary tenet which they set up.... I who have been raised and educated to believe in the propriety of southern institutions, and who have never uttered one word against slavery." The evolution of two Missourian politicians, Kentucky-born Whig state representative Benjamin Gratz Brown and New York–born Democrat Robert M. Stewart, suggest the manipulation of the slave question to accomplish political ends, with often unexpected outcomes. To throw doubt on Stewart, Brown avowed, "I am a Southern man, in feeling and in principle... the place of my birth forbids the ridiculous nonsense of abolitionism!" Yet before the end of the decade Stewart would become one of the state's most committed supporters of slavery, while Brown would lead Missouri's Emancipationists. The fluidity of these new political mandates caused an antislavery South Carolinian to write from his new home in eastern Kansas, "When I am much amongst the Free State men, I begin to get out of patience.... [S]ome of them are so miserable, truckling political demagogues, that I get disgusted, and commence moralising on the dignity &c. of the Southerner; but when I get amongst the pro-slaveryites, and see the rascally efforts to carry matters with a 'high hand and an outstretched arm,' I grow a Free State man, again, all over."[40]

As this internal struggle for Kansas soon revealed painfully to these westerners, the promise of democracy would not be realized in the West. Constant exertions, including armed forays into Kansas; continued interference with territorial elections; and recurrent violence in the hopes of intimidating abolitionist residents would not wrest the territory from what soon became a floodtide of antislavery immigration. This influx came from the northern portions of the middle border states, less moderate than those who editor John H. Stringfellow had mistakenly believed would support slavery in Kansas. Well outnumbering proslavery settlers in Kansas, these free-staters waged their own war with the proslavery element in the territory by delegitimating the legislature and ultimately forcing a congressional showdown when Kansas applied for statehood in 1857. By the time the territorial legislature proffered the ill-fated Lecompton Constitution to Congress for approval, with its infamous option to vote "*for* the Constitution with slavery, or *for* the Constitution without slavery," even proslavery Missourians grudgingly conceded that the document no longer reflected the Kansas constituency and condemned it as undemocratic. "All this is... the work of a few political demagogues," declared the editor of the Democratic *Jefferson Inquirer*, "who are seeking to bring about a dissolution of the Union, and are reckless of the means to which they resort to accomplish their purpose." For the sake of the Union, proslavery westerners bitterly accepted Kansas's destiny as a free state.[41]

§

On July 4, 1857, a large crowd of Kentuckians gathered at the city cemetery just north of Lexington. For five years it had boasted the unadorned remains of the state's most celebrated resident, Henry Clay, whose whistle-stop funeral train had drawn men from their plows and girls in white dresses to stand along its route to honor the western region's most distinguished statesman. Now, construction was begun on a fitting grave monument: a towering, 120-foot Corinthian column topped by a 12 1/2-foot limestone statue of Clay. Adorning the monument to the Great Compromiser, the first person to lie in state in the nation's Capitol, was a simple headstone inscribed with perhaps his most famous utterance: "I know no North—no South—no East—no West." Fittingly, eulogist Robert J. Breckinridge, a noted antislavery activist, lauded Clay as a slaveholder who had no hardened sectional inclinations over slavery.[42]

Had any listeners been in attendance in October 1842 at Richmond, Indiana, they would have recalled a harder, even sectionalized posturing from the great Kentucky pacificator. There, Clay had admonished local Quakers who had presented him with a petition asking him to free his own slaves. Kentucky's laws, he reminded them, clearly and unambiguously recognized "the right of property in slaves," and universal emancipation and amalgamation would trigger a racial "civil war" in his home state. The great statesman condemned meddling abolitionists for their "unfortunate agitation of the subject," and with unstatesmanlike annoyance dismissed "monomaniacs" in the audience "who think with [them]." "Go home and mind your own business," he barked, "and leave other people to take of theirs." Fifteen years later, any of these Quakers who might have been in Lexington would certainly have noticed of the south-facing statue of the deceased Kentucky senator that his non sectional image had been weathered by just a half decade of sectional strife.[43]

Indeed, by 1857 the violence in Kansas had spread tension throughout the middle border as free and slave states offered different responses to the sectional crisis plaguing the nation. Proslavery Kentuckians and Missourians used violence to suppress antislavery subversives in their midst, whether white abolitionists or black slaves. Beginning in 1856, alarming reports of slave revolts, escapes, and near warfare with free state neighbors plagued the commonwealth. When rumors of slave rebellions swept up white residents in Frankfort, Cadiz, Paris, and Hopkinsville, white residents responded by forming county vigilance committees and other paramilitary organizations. Arrests, whippings, and vigilante executions of slaves, free blacks, and white intriguers soon followed. Madison County's vigilantes expelled minister John G. Fee and a hundred residents, black and white, of two antislavery communities he had founded there.[44]

Fugitive slave incidents escalated to mass armed responses as these tensions spilled over the Ohio River's banks. Only weeks before Henry Clay's monument dedication, in what newspapers called the "Rebellion in Ohio," local residents exchanged fire with deputy U.S. marshals and an armed posse of slave catchers from northern Kentucky, preventing an alleged fugitive's arrest. A week later two hundred pursuers fired on a subsequent posse and retrieved the captured men. That fall a Kentucky posse arrested one black and two white Indianans who had assisted a fugitive slave and took all four men across the river to jail in Brandenburg. As a hastily formed rescue expedition waited for boats, the county militia formed and threatened a pitched battle. The prisoners remained in custody, awaiting trial for aiding and abetting a fugitive, until the following July, when just before the trial the two white men's kinsmen crossed the river and sprung them from jail, amid gunfire, leaving behind both black men. When a posse of Louisville constables recaptured one of the men in New Albany, two forces of armed Indianans, dragging a small cannon, crossed the river and encamped near Brandenburg, threatening a "civil war." Two years later, Missouri appeared to sanction such a war when outgoing governor Robert M. Stewart sent an armed expedition to the Kansas border to fight "Jayhawker" marauders like James Montgomery, an Ohio-born evangelical who boasted, "We are neither Democrats nor Republicans, but ABOLITIONISTS."[45]

Far more than political violence, in the middle border free states the widening national breach manifested itself in aversive racial politics over the West's place in the sectional conflict. The well-publicized debates in 1858 between Illinois's Stephen Douglas and Abraham Lincoln, as they vied for Douglas's U.S. Senate seat, drew national attention (see figure 3.1). The debates themselves, part of a larger canvass during which the candidates traveled nearly nine thousand miles and made collectively 122 public speeches, centered not on slavery in the abstract but rather on Douglas's defense of popular sovereignty amid the Kansas controversy. Both men parried before mixed constituencies, especially in central and western Illinois, where four of the seven debates took place. Many attendees hailed from the neighboring slave states, especially at the debates held at Jonesboro, Quincy, and Alton.[46]

Throughout the campaign both Lincoln and Douglas assumed the mantle of Henry Clay, one as a longtime Whig and devotee and the other claiming to be the newest Great Compromiser. One of Lincoln's closest friends confided that he had limited appeal to former Whigs who considered his party (and him) "too closely allied to the abolitionists." Like Douglas, Lincoln initially supported the *Dred Scott* decision and remained silent about the ruling for some months before admitting that he and his party "offer no *resistance* to it," prompting one critic to charge that he was actually "too much on the old conservative order" for his liking. In truth, Lincoln was less uncertain about his position than unsituated in the

"SIT DOWN, LINCOLN, YOUR TIME IS UP"

Figure 3.1 Great Debate at Charleston, Illinois, September 18, 1858. Eleven railroad cars of spectators from Indiana were among those who listened as Abraham Lincoln contested Stephen Douglas's charge that the Republican senatorial candidate favored full racial equality. Courtesy Lincoln Collection, Abraham Lincoln Presidential Library and Museum.

West's new political alchemy. He initially agonized about joining the fledgling Republican Party after being approached by Owen Lovejoy, who led its formation there. His personal belief that African Americans were innately inferior to whites complicated his core conviction that he had "always hated slavery I think as much as any Abolitionist," but his western Whig belief in tempered individualist principles blunted his sympathy for northern "Freedom National, Slavery Sectional" collectivism, which portrayed slavery as a national "great moral wrong." However much he "abhor[red] the oppression of negroes" and the assumptions of middle border whites that "all men are created equal, *except negroes*," as a westerner Lincoln could in 1855 claim to "no more than oppose the *extension* of slavery."[47]

By 1858, still a Whig in a Democratic world, Lincoln the national office aspirant compartmentalized his racial conservatism and political progressivism into a pragmatic antislavery middle ground within the Republican Party. His commitment to free labor—and with it full democratic rights for free citizens—exceeded his commitment to racial egalitarianism, and with prejudice in his region too entrenched for "political and social equality between the white and the black races," he harnessed an even more fundamental western trope—liberty, meaning the access to unfettered economic ascendance rather than any guarantee of political or social equality—to overcome it politically. The nation's founding principle, the natural right of man to life, liberty, and the pursuit of happiness, guaranteed by the Declaration of Independence, gave "every man... the chance—and I believe a black man is entitled to it—in which he can better his condition." African Americans were "as much entitled to these as the white man.... [I]n the right to eat the bread, without the leave of anybody else, which his own hand earns, he is my equal and the equal of Judge Douglas, and the equal of every living man." In contrast, the Constitution, by various measures including its Tenth Amendment, protected slavery where it existed originally but allowed states and, if Douglas was right, territories, to exclude African Americans from citizenship rights in the expanding nation.[48]

With Illinois having banned black immigration just eight years earlier, both Lincoln and Douglas used racial language to appeal to white western voters, though they differed in the degree to which they affirmed racial inferiority and supported black rights. Lincoln's reasoned racialism contrasted with Douglas's overtly racist rhetoric, but their arguments were often parallel. Douglas regularly pandered to central and southern Illinois whites' overt racism, asking whether they wished their state to be "a free negro colony, in order that when Missouri abolishes slavery she can send one hundred thousand emancipated slaves into Illinois, to become citizens and voters, on an equality with yourselves." Listeners responded with cries of "never" and "no," just as northern Illinoisans returned his regular employment of the term "Black Republican" with shouted corrections of "white, white." Lincoln also pandered, albeit in a more principled way, varying his positions depending on his perception of his listeners' level of negrophobia. At Freeport, the northernmost of the debates, an angry Douglas charged that "the color of [Lincoln's] principles are a little darker than in Egypt" and at Charleston he derided his opponent for being "jet black in the North, a decent mulatto in the center, and almost white in the South." Indeed, at the southernmost venue, Jonesboro, to a strongly proslavery audience Lincoln affirmed differences "between the white and black races which I believe forbid the two races living together on terms of social and political equality" and said that "the signers of the Declaration had no reference to the negro whatever, when they declared all men to be created equal." He ineffectually tried to turn the tables on his Vermont-born opponent by trying to obscure politics with birthplace. "Why, I know this people better than he [Douglas] does," Lincoln offered. "I am part of this people. But the Judge was raised further north." Douglas responded by mocking Lincoln's "attempts to cover up and get over his Abolitionism.... [W]here a man was born...has [not] much to do with his political principles."[49]

Positioning himself as a national Republican candidate for the presidency, Lincoln was forced astride another razor's edge: slavery politics in his home region. Neither to the debate audiences nor to subsequent listeners would Lincoln again issue any direct call for slavery's end, as he had in his "House Divided" speech in Springfield in June, just prior to the debates. In September 1859 Lincoln visited central and southern Ohio, where for two years the state legislature had whipsawed over African Americans' legal rights since Republicans had taken control. As Democrats lost and regained the majority in subsequent elections, by straight-party votes it passed, rescinded, then passed again a series of proscriptive Black Laws, among them a quasi-anti-amalgamation law requiring judges to reject the vote of any person whose skin color betrayed a "visible admixture of African blood." ("[T]he word *white*, in the Constitution of the State," argued Ohio Democrats, "*means white*, and nothing else.") Reminding voters "that every Black Republican member of the Legislature voted against the law," Democrats publicly asked: "Shall a few thousand Negroes and Mulattoes rule us?" In his first speeches since the Illinois debates, Lincoln was forced to answer repeatedly about his views of racial equality. On a cool evening in Cincinnati, he fulfilled his promise to "shoot over the line," a reference to reaching out to Kentuckians, by reiterating western Republicans' pledge that he "neither had, nor have, or ever had, any purpose in any way of interfering with the institution of Slavery, where it exists."[50]

A month to the day after Lincoln's Queen City speech, simmering tensions over slavery boiled over on the middle border, a harbinger of what might happen should the Republican candidate be elected president. In western Virginia on October 16, 1859, abolitionist John Brown led an armed raid on the federal armory at Harpers Ferry to launch a general slave insurrection. One of Brown's captured black conspirators claimed that Kentucky would be the next site. New rumors of imminent abolitionist raids from Ohio triggered hysteria, meetings, and arming as Democrats condemned the raid as a product of Republicans' radicalism. A correspondent to the *Kentucky Statesman* predicted that Brown's execution would make him an abolitionist martyr. Fearing for their young party's future, western Republicans including Lincoln scrambled to disassociate from Brown. At a speech in Kansas, Lincoln called him "insane" and admitted he had no objection to his execution for "treason against a state."[51]

In Kentucky's new militance, perhaps no white resident suffered more from preemptive actions against perceived extremists than William S. Bailey. For a decade, the Ohio-born cotton machinist and steam engine builder had published a struggling abolitionist newspaper in Cincinnati. In 1858 he moved across the river to Newport, where he renamed his paper *The Free South*, the first antislavery paper published in the state since Cassius Clay's *True American*. Bailey employed his wife and eleven children in his operation, which promoted Clay's economic arguments for abolition more than Garrisonian moralism. He subsequently espoused the Republican Party and claimed fatefully, given Brown's similar shibboleth, that the war on slavery must be moved to the South. On October 28, 1859, within days of Brown's raid, a mob attacked Bailey's office in full daylight, destroyed his two presses, scattered them in the street, and threatened his family. Bailey filed suit, but the grand jury failed to return an indictment. When Bailey solicited money from northern supporters to re-establish his press and resumed publication ten months later, he was arrested. With the support of northern abolitionists, Bailey relocated again to Cincinnati. Within months Kentucky's legislature enacted its first law prohibiting "any free person [to] write or print [or knowingly circulate], any book or other thing...with intent to advise or incite negroes in this State to rebel or make insurrections."[52]

In the free states, rather than succumb to sectional politics, white westerners responded to anti-abolitionist militancy by supporting more delicate slavery politics. Regionalism under the guise of divergent, obstructive sectionalism became a viable political position that crossed the aisle. In Ohio, reputedly the most antislavery of the middle border states, the state's moderate Republican U.S. congressman Thomas Corwin reminded his House colleagues following Brown's raid that the West yet defied sectionalization. "I know we have but two points of compass now in our political geography—North and South," he chided. "I beg the gentlemen of the South to remember that there is in our country about nine millions of people who reside in the West; that they have an identity of language, manners, and social systems...[and] do not mean to be held responsible to the North or to the South." A week later Corwin's colleague, Ohio Democrat and self-styled "western sectionalist" Clement L. Vallandigham, warned sectional extremists to pay heed to western interests lest the region secede from them. "I am as good a Western fire-eater as the hottest salamander," he preened to laughter and applause, then pointed to the North's economic exploitation of both the South and West. "I am not a northern man," he averred. "I am not a southern man either, although, in this unholy and most unconstitutional crusade against the South...my most cordial sympathies are wholly with her." In

February 1860 Vallandigham would offer a series of resolutions, modeled on John C. Calhoun's idea of concurrent majorities, reorganizing Congress into northern, southern, western, and Pacific voting blocs and requiring bills to pass all of them before enactment.[53]

Anti-abolitionist violence and local civil wars drew strength from a Republican political surge ahead of the 1860 presidential election. Narrow wins in the 1858 midterm elections had gained pluralities in the U.S. Congress and in Indiana's and Illinois's state legislatures, and the party held a narrow majority in Ohio's legislature. In Missouri the Kansas war ginned up support for proslavery Ultras, as they were called, largely as protection against the Republican threat. In the 1858 midterm elections, even in St. Louis, "Free Democrats" Frank Blair and B. Gratz Brown both lost reelection bids. Kentucky's and Missouri's subsequent gubernatorial elections suggest hard anti-Republican politics. In Kentucky, in 1859 Democrat Beriah Magoffin claimed that slavery and the Union were not "antagonizing ideas" but "[t]he Constitution and the Union are threatened" by abolitionist Republicans.[54]

§

On the night of November 6, 1860, in Sandersville, a hamlet a few miles north of Lexington, Kentucky, Joel K. Lyle wrote in his diary. "Ice on the ponds," he scratched, "Earth and water froze some for the first time this fall—so far as I know." Lyle, a thirty-six-year-old Presbyterian minister and strong unionist whose father had founded and edited Paris's *Western Citizen*, had earlier that day cast his ballot for the Constitutional Union ticket of John Bell and Edward Everett. He likely learned within days that Abraham Lincoln had won the presidency. Only 1,364 Kentuckians had voted for him, less than 1 percent of those who cast votes. In fact, he garnered just over 6 percent of all the votes cast in the border slave states, Kentucky's tally being the smallest of them. Bell and native son John C. Breckinridge carried nearly all of Kentucky's counties and some three-quarters of Missouri's. Although he ran dead last in both states, of Lincoln's 27,000-odd popular votes from all of the slave states, some two-thirds came from Missouri and Kentucky.[55]

Yet for Lyle the ponds might have frozen over, but hell had not. Although many in the Deep South saw Lincoln's election as nothing short of a national apocalypse, as a slaveholder Lyle was unruffled by it. Nor was he alone. Despite the "raw, cold, disagreeable [election] day," Louisville's Mildred Bullitt confessed that "strange it is, how calmn I feel, when I know *this* election is fraught with such danger to the Union, which is our pride, and we *have* thought, our security." In Paducah another person claimed, "when this day of election came there was no excitement, no pulling, and hauling to the polls, no fights, no drunkenness. Those who voted went quietly away after voting." Few in these slave states were surprised by the new president's election. Two weeks after receiving the "by no means astonishing news" of Lincoln's election, Lizzie Hardin noted that in Harrodsburg, Kentucky, "[a]t first, men turned and looked at each other, not knowing what to do.... The great majority seemed to think no important movement would follow the mere election of a Black Republican President." Union meetings in Covington "deplored the election of the Kentucky-Illinois rail-splitter, but thought that no sufficient cause for dissolution," and Lexington hemp manufacturer John Hunt Morgan wrote his brother Thomas, at college in Ohio, that he had "no doubt but Lincoln will make a good President at least we ought to give him a fair trial."[56]

Amid sectionalized responses to the election outcome, such seeming calm in the middle border slave states might have resulted from the region's apparent return to consensus slave politics. Days before the election, Alabama's fire-eating former U.S. congressman, William L. Yancey, campaigning for Breckinridge in Cincinnati, received applause and foot stamping at Pike's Opera House for "denounc[ing] the North as 'nigger thieves' [and declaring] ... there was only one kind of union he would maintain, and that was a union that let slavery run wherever it choose to go." Amid newspaper headlines such as "Revolution and Civil War the Aim of Republicanism," the lower portions of the region's free states similarly rejected Lincoln. He lost half of the counties in Illinois and virtually all of those in its southern and west and south central areas—including his home county of Sangamon. In the sixteen southernmost Illinois counties, all of which Douglas won, Democratic candidates outpolled Lincoln more than ten to one. Similarly, he lost most of those counties in Indiana and half in Ohio as well as most of the latter's northwestern counties. Many voted for Douglas or Breckinridge as a clear rejection of the Republican Party's perceived abolitionist platform. The popular votes in these states for Lincoln came largely from their northern counties and their cities—Evansville, Cincinnati, and Indianapolis—in part because of German voters, the most reliably Republican constituency in the middle border region. In northern towns like Winslow, Illinois, Republicans taunted disbelieving Democrats at the election of Republicans not only to the presidency but to the governorships of their state and neighboring Indiana (see figure 3.2).[57]

If Lincoln's election did not evoke panic below the rivers, the Republican victory was seen as a catalyst to emboldened slaves, causing consternation among slaveholders. East of Louisville, rumors flew about the Oxmoor neighborhood that slaves would soon exploit the recent election to place the bottom rail on top. "[M]any of them believed Lincoln was to free them, and they generally think he is a black man," Mildred wrote nervously to her son in Philadelphia. "[S]ervants tell [their owners] they won't work for them much longer, that when Lincoln takes his seat they'll all be free." As Mildred heard it, even the youngest slaves openly demanded retribution against whites. "Mrs. W[inchester] said," she wrote, panic stricken, "[that] a little black child was in her room the other day,

Figure 3.2 "Election bet," Winslow, Illinois, summer 1860. Located in the state's far northern counties, the village's support for abolitionist Richard Yates as the Republican candidate for governor in 1860 surprised moderate residents, forcing one Yates opponent to carry a sign admitting he had "more sand than sense." Courtesy Abraham Lincoln Presidential Library and Museum.

playing with Willy... and commenced to talk about what would be done with the clock, and different articles of furniture, when the black people came in, said if the white folks didn't run fast, the black people would kill them all." "[T]he abolitionists have it all to answer for," William Bullitt railed.[58]

With all branches of the federal government in the hands of Republicans, and with plantation states calling conventions to consider their future courses, Lincoln's victory quickly hardened calls for moderation into demands for restraint. Bipartisan Union meetings argued for compromise measures such as extending the Fugitive Slave Act into Canada, prompting a southern Indiana editor to proclaim that if secession should occur "the line of division must run north of us." On December 20, 1860, Cincinnatian and outgoing Ohio Democratic U.S. senator George E. Pugh argued that border residents demanded "some reasonable plan of adjustment and conciliation... [to] avert a calamity which must fall chiefly upon us." Restraint also meant firm support for the racial status quo. Cincinnati's *Daily Enquirer* claimed the city's black residents celebrated Lincoln's election as "*their triumph*, and... the harbinger of Abolition in the South and negro equality in the North!"; resultant white residents' anger forced a hastily organized black convention to respond that any "joy at the defeat of the Democratic party... [derived from] its rallying cry of '*damn the niggers*'" rather than support for abolition.[59]

To preempt Abraham Lincoln's inauguration as president, forty-five days after the election a South Carolina state convention voted unanimously to exercise a state's ultimate right to withdraw from the Union. Within another forty-three days, six more southern states—Mississippi, Florida, Alabama, Georgia, Louisiana, and Texas—held elections for delegates to conventions that would vote to do the same. As middle border residents watched the secession crisis unfold, a sudden paralysis of business occurred in the river region as banks suspended specie payments. A sense of alarm caused many who had voted for Lincoln to question their choice. In the president-elect's hometown, Asa Washburne believed that many of his neighbors "begin to see that they have been most almightily hoodwinked, and could the election come off again, old Lincoln would never carry Ill[inois]." The following spring, Democrats swept municipal elections in Ohio's five largest cities, including Cleveland in the Western Reserve.[60]

If anything, the secession crisis strengthened the western consensus by weakening Republican support in the middle border's free states. Residents of Illinois and Indiana recognized the tenuous control of their newly elected governors and state legislatures, as well as the new president, who would soon leave Springfield, Illinois, on a whistle-stop train trip to his inauguration in Washington, stopping at cities and towns across the middle border region. Moderates, whether pro-slavery or antislavery, held "Union meetings" that supported compromise and often evinced outright sympathy for the southern states. Cincinnati rabbi Isaac M. Wise claimed that "with every passing day, we get more and more convinced that the secessionists are right, they would not bow down to a set of fanatics who are blind in their zeal to do wrong, who care much less for the white man than for the Negro, and prove themselves faithful to one thing only, i.e. to fanaticism." Indeed, both houses of the Ohio legislature resolved in favor of repealing state laws impeding prosecution of the Fugitive Slave Act as a response to a raft of recent fugitive slave cases that had distanced their state from Kentucky's most recent governors.[61]

Many moderates in these free states suddenly became more supportive of southern rights and even secession. Many were products of the slave states and had slaveholding kin. Indiana congressman James H. Cravens, a native Virginian, suggested the idea of division of his and Illinois's southernmost regions, creating a new state to be named Jackson. "I cannot obviate the fact that our interest is with the South." Perhaps none was more outspoken than Ohioan John Allen Trimble, a fifty-nine-year-old merchant and former postmaster in Hillsboro, in the heart of the Virginia Tract. A longtime Whig, the Kentucky-born Trimble embraced the Democratic Party during the 1850s out of firm support for slave owners' rights. Although he hoped war could be averted, he advocated secession not only as a right but as a responsibility to stay "the Madness and folly of the republican party." Uncertain of Ohio's future course, he was certain "under the lead of Republicans, [it] will be forced into a *wrong* position in Sustaining Lincoln.... [A]ny attempt on the part of the remaining States to use coercion will be the last fatal Stab." Although the Ohio legislature denounced secession, it passed resolutions supporting Kentuckian John J. Crittenden's compromise, submitted in December in the U.S. Senate, calling for restoration and extension of the Missouri Compromise, with slavery guaranteed everywhere below its former boundary, to be stretched westward to California. A Democrat claimed of Ohio, "1/3 of [its] inhabitants are with the south in their feelings and sympathies," and he voted in the 1860 election for Breckinridge "to show the people of the south how many votes in Ohio go for peace and the Union." Salmon P. Chase, soon to be named Lincoln's secretary of the treasury, claimed that as an unconditional unionist, "I find myself in a minority in the Ohio delegation." Indeed, prominent northern Ohio Democrat David Tod, who had once promoted a bill to facilitate the return of fugitive slaves to Kentucky and endorsed the retention of Ohio's Black Laws, vowed that if Republicans should coerce the South, they would do so through two hundred thousand in his party standing shoulder to shoulder.[62]

The sudden surge in consensus politics put many middle border Republicans on the defensive, causing them to amplify their stance on slavery as a local institution by calling vaguely for the "enforcement of the laws." In Indiana, a party convention pledged to preserve the Union, but in the event of war it would act with other "conservative" states to block any coercive measures enacted by radicalized northern Republicans. One county's party leaders resolved that they were "ready to stand and abide" the principle of popular sovereignty that was "as old as our government." The editor of Ohio's *Ripley Bee* complained that coercion "is a much abused word... as if the Republicans proposed to levy war against the Southern States, to lay waste with fire and sword, and carry all manner of 'horrors' among the Southern people, in which there is not a particle of truth." Illinois's Democrats pulled enough moderate votes from the slim Republican legislative majority to pass conciliatory measures and block the introduction of a bill that would help the new Republican governor, Richard Yates, mobilize its state militia should war come. "Secession is deeper and stronger here than you have any idea," Yates pleaded. "Its advocates are numerous and powerful, and respectable."[63]

What the Kentucky-born, deeply antislavery Yates—whom Lincoln had on numerous occasions counseled against both personal intemperance and intemperate slavery politics on Illinois's shifting middle ground—bemoaned as secessionism was the middle border's deepened moderation during the turbulent winter months. Led by Kentuckians, proslavery and Emancipationist, moderates stepped to the forefront of regional solutions to the nation's sectionalization by rekindling the notion of a middle confederacy. Robert J. Breckinridge noted in a speech in Lexington that "it may well become the border slave States to unite themselves into a separate confederacy," while another speaker hoped for the formal establishment of traditional alignments, with "the planting States into a Southern, and the border States (including, perhaps, the Northwest), into a central republic." Congressman Garret Davis envisioned "a great central confederation, embraising Southern New York, New Jersey, Southern Pennsylvania, Delaware Maryland and the whole area of country lyeing within the basin of the Mississippi—excluding the extreme North and the extreme South—I think that country would live together in peace."[64]

Without clear state mandates, the western consensus would fray should the defense of the Union demand a united stance on "Freedom National, Slavery Sectional." Kentucky's and Missouri's governors nuanced their bellicose proslavery rhetoric. Just after Lincoln's election, Beriah Magoffin chastised Republican dismissals of slave states' rights "and equality in the Union" and reminded southern secessionists they had less cause for grievance against slave property violations than slaveholders in his state. "Let passion be allayed," he implored, "let moderation, forebearance, and wisdom guide our counsels, and the country may yet be saved." Magoffin honed a hard proslavery edge to his unionism. "No more concessions... no more compromises," he demanded, urging slave states to "resolve not [to] discuss the question of slavery any more." In the summer of 1860 Magoffin had impelled the organization of the state militia (see figure 3.3), authorized by the legislature, and sent its commander, Simon B. Buckner, to neighboring states with purchasing authority for arms and powder. Within days Missouri's governor-elect, Claiborne F. Jackson, who had only recently supported Stephen A. Douglas for president, was less moderate. "Let there be no threats, no bravado, no gasconading," he wrote in a public letter. "Let us preserve the government if possibly in our power, but if after having tried all the remedies within our grasp, if these should fail—as I fear they will—then I say let us dissolve the connection and maintain the rights which belong to us AT ALL HAZARDS AND TO THE LAST EXTREMITY."[65]

Unlike Kentuckians' devotion to a regional defense against sectional extremes, western Missouri's proslavery extremists believed that the western consensus was compromised by the Kansas defeat. After immigrant free-staters voted overwhelmingly against slavery by rejecting the dubious Lecompton Constitution, talk of a regional confederacy was nothing more than abolitionists' subterfuge. "Efforts will be made here to hold us on—by talking about—[a] *Western* Confederacy and an Independent state," William Barclay Napton sneered. "All this is only a *pretext*—the object is to abolish slavery here." To summon secession sentiment among proslavery unionists, they articulated southernness as a defense against Republican extremism. In 1860, a decade after Missouri voters had unceremoniously dumped Claiborne Fox Jackson, the state senator who introduced the resolutions instructing Thomas Hart Benton to vote for slavery and

Figure 3.3 Kentucky State Guard, Louisville, ca. 1860–1861. The Kentucky legislature's vote and the Missouri convention's posture for neutrality in the spring of 1861 were complicated by a variety of military organizations. Recruiters from both governments enlisted volunteers in these states, and state troops massed along their borders. In both states, organized militias acted as rival forces, with Confederate sympathizers organized as state guards and unionists as state militias and home guards. At the local and county levels, allegiances ran the gamut. Courtesy Filson Historical Society.

then ousted him as a proslavery radical, they elected Jackson as their governor, no longer content to be "controlled by 'Northern Men, with Southern principles.'" On January 3, 1861, in the Missouri House chambers in Jefferson City, a joint session heard outgoing governor Robert M. Stewart plead for renewed moderation, while Jackson tied a passionate opposition to federal authority with the defense of slaveholding, urging southern identity as a common political cause. "So long as a State continues to maintain slavery within her limits, it is impossible to separate her fate from that of her sister States who have the same social organization," he argued. "The identity, rather than the similarity, of their domestic institutions...all contribute to bind them together." Blending traditional ties of culture, heritage, and economic pursuits with the overarching ligature of slavery, he transcended *"stand by the South"* with the cant of southernness—Missouri *was* the South. Jackson's speech triggered thunderous applause, and within ten days lawmakers set February 18 as the date for electing delegates to a convention that would "consider the then existing relations between the government of the United States."[66]

The western consensus's last chance to forestall war took the unlikely form of a Republican-led effort to protect slavery. On February 27, 1861, during the closing days of the 36th U.S. Congress's session, Ohio U.S. congressman Thomas Corwin, Republican chairman of a select "Committee of 33," introduced in the House a proposed constitutional amendment. "No amendment shall be made to the Constitution," the joint resolution read, "which will authorize or give to Congress the power to abolish or interfere, within any State, with the domestic institutions thereof, including that of persons held to labor or service by the laws of said State." Despite outcries against the proposed amendment, procedural efforts to table it, and an initial failed vote, the following day the House approved the resolution by a vote of 133–65, one more than the two-thirds required. Three days later, in the late night hours before adjourning, the Senate did likewise by a vote of 24–12, exactly the number required. Middle border state delegates, free and slave, voted nearly in lockstep in favor of the Corwin amendment—49 to 13 overall, with each of the House delegations voting nearly three to one in favor, Kentucky's unanimously. Just hours before his successor's inauguration, the president, Pennsylvania Democrat James Buchanan, endorsed the amendment, forcing the Republican president-elect to make a hasty addition to his speech, offering awkward and mild support. In May 1861 Ohio's legislature ratified it, and a year later Illinois followed, controversially, by constitutional convention and not by legislative vote, as stipulated. The only other state to ratify was yet another border state, Maryland. No other even put it to a vote. By the time they could have done so, northern legislators had little interest in a reputed antislavery westerner's eleventh-hour compromise of what would have been a proslavery Thirteenth Amendment.[67]

§

In 1860, less than five years after proslavery western Missourians had publicly taken their stand for the tradition of a slaveholders' democracy on the middle border, their intellectual leader, William Barclay Napton, offered a gloomy prediction. "There is now going on another political revolution here and...it will end in a civil war, first a border war, but soon a general state of hostility between the two sections of the Union, slaveholding and non-slaveholding." Napton's conclusion was certainly not surprising. In fact, it was barely prescient. More than a decade of attacks on slavery's extension had already roused the middle border's militant proslavery constituency to violence. From his perspective, only a looming war aligning the West with the other sections remained to settle the great national debate over slavery.[68]

Napton's sectionalized regionalism was at once thoughtful and not. His binary did away entirely with cultural geography, reducing its strife to its barest essence, slavery politics. Some in the western states had sectionalized, fully or partially, linking themselves loosely with northern states by arguing that democracy and liberty were incompatible with slavery. Many others saw slavery as the buttress of white freedom and supported the southern section of the nation. Wrongly, he overlooked that the mass of white westerners, in free and slave states, sought to remain between the warring sections, believing that extremism in defense of liberty surely was a vice. The long open national conflict over slavery had shaken Napton's and other border residents' middle ground of regional identity. In only a few months, the bedrock that most sought in their western consensus would be shattered forever by the emergent realities of a war for region fought within the contours of a national war between sections.

House of Cards

For Josie Underwood, her family's hilltop farm, Mount Air, lying just a mile east of Bowling Green, Kentucky, was "the dearest old home in the world." Among the largest farms in the entire region, Mount Air seemed an island of stability. Fields of corn and wheat waved heavily in the rich bottomland of the Barren River as it looped north and east around the farm's thousand acres. Whitewashed and handsome, the two-story, federal-style house differed little from the modest farm homes that dotted the middle border region. The grounds were Mount Air's crown, from the stately oak-canopied avenue leading to the main house to its stone-fenced gardens, pastures, woods, and orchards. Nestled into the sloping landscape, it was, as one Pennsylvania visitor claimed, "the realization of all he had read and imagined of a hospitable Southern home." For this observer at least, among its distinguishing features was the knot of slave cabins that lay off the main house's east gable. To the north, the house overlooked the newly completed main line of the Louisville and Nashville Railroad. Modernity and tradition in harmony, Mount Air was the West personified.[1]

For Josie and her six siblings, their home farm was an anchor for the entire region as much as the limestone beneath its auburn soil. So too the Underwood family. Josie's father, Warner, had been until recently a U.S. congressman, and his older brother, Joseph, was a former state supreme court justice and U.S. senator. They were Virginia-born, college-educated lawyers and Whig slaveholders, whose ownership of some thirty-five slaves between them had once made them targets of congressional abolitionists. As unconditional unionists as well as proslavery moderates, they differed over slavery's future. Joseph was a practicing colonizationist, while Warner was unsupportive. Yet having lived several unhappy years in Texas's cotton kingdom, Warner eschewed fire-eating proslavery extremism. He and his brother worked assiduously to oppose Kentucky's secession, believing "she may some way avert a war and bring about reconciliation between the sections."[2]

Privately, the growing national extremism over slavery caused Warner to be gloomy about the future. Although both native Kentuckians, neither the federal nor the Confederate president, he feared, would compromise, even at the expense of war. Warner knew and even liked Lincoln, believing him "honest in his convictions and his desire to do what is right." But his antislavery politics would likely prevent peace, "his ideas differ[ing] with the great Union party of Kentucky and other conservative states." Even less encouraging, Underwood also knew Jefferson Davis, having shared committee assignments with him in Washington. "[R]ecalling many conversations," Underwood was convinced "he has long been anxious to see the Union dis[s]olved." Should war come, the border slave states, he knew, would inevitably bear its brunt.[3]

Raised in a slaveholding family, sixteen-year-old Josie—whip-smart and politically informed—believed the people of their region were more sensible than those in either of the belligerent sections. Like her mother, Lucy, "the most intense Southerner I ever knew," Josie considered herself a southerner by culture, believing her family's right of slaveholding was guaranteed within the Union and that their peculiar institution raised the social order by stability and paternal race relations. As secession debates raged in her home state, she was troubled that her family's southern footing was no longer sure on fissuring western ground. Extremists were politicizing, and thus changing, understood meanings of white southernness. Antislavery unionists charged slaveholders as latent secessionists, and the latter responded, as Warner learned painfully during an exhaustive series of speeches, by tarring proslavery unionists as not being "consistent Southerner[s]" and as being under the influence of "Lovejoy and the abolitionists."[4]

In truth, southernness on western soil had already confounded Josie's cultural understandings. Over Christmas 1860 she had spent a stormy six weeks with family in Memphis, Tennessee, where her outspoken unionism had made her an outsider among those she believed were cultural kin. "We have every phase of sentiment represented in our own home," she confessed, "though all are southern born." Secessionists were boisterous among Bowling Green's two thousand-odd residents, most of whom were ostensible unionists. But crowds of "rowdies" shouted "hurrah for Jeff Davis" at trains passing through town on the L and N, convincing her that most in her town were disloyal. "[T]hough the Union sentiment is much the greatest in Kentucky," Josie wrote, "the Rebels have so many rowdies they make the most noise."[5]

These secessionists offered more than political noise. They controlled political language, and by it forged exclusivist meanings. "[W]hen they slur at southern men who side with the North against the South," Josie fumed, "I can't take it quietly—the secessionists intentionally put it all the time that it is just North against the South, when that isn't it at all." Hardened lines suddenly separated Bowling Green's white residents. Social encounters soon devolved into political arguments, as farmers "come to town to get 'the news' and getting it the discussions and excitement keep them there all day and fights are constantly occurring." Neighbors re-evaluated and assailed one another, manipulating an array of political stances into simple and sharp categories. "Mrs. Baker is 'Union' and Miss Polly 'secesh' and the bitterness of this difference is added to their former dislike of each other," Josie observed. Josie's Literary Society meetings became so intense that its leader declared political discussions "Taboo." Unionist schoolboys fought with young "secesh," including her younger brother, outside the gate of Mount Air after taunts of "'Ab, Ab'—meaning Abolitionist and that is what no southern boy will stand being called." The Underwoods privately foreswore all political conversations outside their home.[6]

Neutrality quickly became unsustainable, privately and publicly, after news of the firing on Fort Sumter and Lincoln's call for seventy-five thousand volunteers to put down the southern insurrection. "[T]hat position can't be held much longer and is really only in name—for every man, woman and child is on one side or the other," Josie noted. "Sumter had turned a number of waivering people to secessionists, for they argue now there is no chance of saving the Union and right or wrong they want to go with the South." Encouragingly, "the staunchest and most prominent men in the town—are all determined still to stand by the Union, and save the country from being broken up."[7]

Autumn had commenced what would become a long nightmare for the Underwood family. While fighting raged in Missouri and western Virginia, on September 3 Confederate general Leonidas Polk had crossed the state line and seized the Mississippi River bluffs above Columbus. Two weeks later, "Philistines," as Josie termed the mixed force of Confederates and Kentucky and Tennessee state militia, rushed up the L and N and occupied Hopkinsville and Bowling Green. The town teemed with rebels, who pulled down the national flag flying over the depot and replaced it with the "stars and bars," as most already called the Confederacy's first national flag.[8]

Within days Mount Air was a Confederate camp. The 1st Missouri Infantry spread out into the orchard and barn lot and used the front pasture as a parade ground. The rebel commanders had carefully chosen the farm, seeking out "the strongest Union man in the county, to destroy anything they can belonging to him," as a resident wrote. Soldiers burned fence rails; dug potatoes out of the garden; and raided the milch barn, kitchen, and smokehouse, while ax-men felled oaks and walnuts to build artillery emplacements on the high ground at the back of the farm. Warner was "humiliatingly helpless" to stop it, something his twenty-eight slaves noticed. "The darkies can't yet understand that it is possible for their 'Marster' to be so 'run over,'" Josie wrote despondently.[9]

Josie and her family learned that these rebels would harshly turn the tables on the Underwoods' perceptions of cultural southernness. When soldiers approached the house asking for food, "The men laughed as they turned away and I heard them say 'Yanks' as they strolled on down through the orchard." Shocked that their politics now defined them, Warner remonstrated to the commander,

Lt. Col. Lucius L. Rich, about damages to his property, only to be told "southern Union men needn't expect much respect shown them or their property." Josie inverted the insult, asking the Missourian about his heritage. "He said he had the misfortune to have been born at his mother's home in Ohio, but he had always lived in Missouri, and was doing all he could to wipe out that misfortune." She pounced. "I don't believe you can do it. We southerners you know notice characteristics that would be imperceptible to you 'Yankees.' Oh! but he was mad, and the other officer laughed." The officer would soon take his own vengeance. Warner came under suspicion for relaying information on the troops to federals in Louisville, especially after Warner Jr. slipped away to enlist in the federal ranks. Shockingly, officers entered the house and warmed themselves by the fireplace in their mother's bedroom, even as she lay sick in bed.[10]

After a gloomy holiday season, during which soldiers pilfered the Underwoods' lone remaining turkey, Confederate general Albert Sidney Johnston summoned Warner to his office in town. On New Year's Eve, he made a last ditch effort to convince his fellow Kentuckian of "the advisability and advantage of his (Pa's) giving up his unionism and going over to the secessionists—or with his section as the Gen. put it." Warner refused. The next day, rebel officers delivered an order instructing the family "to vacate the premises immediately by order of the General commanding." The family's slaves loaded what they could onto wagons while soldiers and officers exulted. "This is only a *small confiscation* we call it," sneered the Missouri colonel. In a drizzling rain and sleet, the Underwoods' "sad procession" rolled eastward to a leaky, two-room cabin more than a dozen miles away. Josie noted of the poorer unionists who came by with food, they "want[ed] to talk with Pa and have him 'Prophesy' as they say—what the outcome is to be and indeed it is prophesy for no one knows."[11]

Despite their best efforts, the family's location was soon discovered. Tipped off by a friendly city councilman that a squad of rebel soldiers would arrive the next morning to arrest him, Warner Underwood hurriedly packed his bags, saddled his horse, and with the help of a guide slipped through the lines northward to Louisville. There he learned that the Confederates had taken all the family's working livestock.[12]

Believing the worst was over, the family soon learned otherwise. On February 12 a note arrived from the Missouri colonel at Mount Air informing Lucy that the Confederate troops were withdrawing and that she should return to their home "at once lest evil persons destroy the buildings." At first light they struck out westward for town, in a driving winter storm. A few miles from their home, they noticed that low-hanging clouds glowed red. After crossing the river bridge on the Louisville Pike, Lucy ordered their slave driver to tear across their fenceless fields toward the house, their emotions giving way first to heartbreak, then to rage:

> We had not gone very far through the fields before we saw that the trees around the house were all charred and burned and that only the gable end of the house was standing, a smouldering smoke rising about it and as we drove up through the garden—all trodden down like an old common—the last standing wall fell in with a crash and we arrived only in time to witness this last catastrophe and standing there helplessly watched the smouldering ruins.... Both orchards were cut down—the avenue of big trees leading toward the town were all gone... and only the barn and two cabins in the quarters left of all the buildings. Ruin devastation and desolation everywhere![13]

After spending the cold night in the slave cabins, they were awakened by dull thumps of cannon fire announcing fighting at Fort Donelson, some eighty miles to the southwest. About 11 o'clock a sharper cannon report to the north announced the arrival of federal troops at Bowling Green, approaching by the snow-covered pike opposite the river. Amid shouts of "The enemy is upon us," shells screamed down around the depot and town square. Josie and her family, who had gone into town for food, took refuge in a cellar. "Soldiers were rushing wildly through the streets—cavalry and infantry—horses were being taken anywhere and everywhere found—citizens, men, women, and children, white and black were fleeing over the hills to get out of reach of danger—whilst the steady Boom—swish—shriek and bang—of cannon shot and shell went on—most of the balls and shells falling with wonderful accuracy in the space around the Depot and the snow and slush preventing many of them bursting."[14]

After a day of shelling, burning buildings lit the late afternoon dusk as retreating Confederates hastily set fire to the depot and two bridges. Many secessionists evacuated with the rebel troops for what they hoped was temporary exile. Unionist townspeople saved the depot as federal troops forded the swollen river and entered the town. Cheers quickly quieted as these unionists realized their liberators were "a lot of hungry coarse Dutchmen!" Josie grumbled that the Louisville troops were "not much more regardful for personal property than were the Rebels." They soon ransacked many of the town's homes "from garret to cellar," especially those abandoned by southern sympathizers. On the night following their arrival, drunken federals set fire to half of the remaining buildings on the town square. "[N]othing could have been more unfortunate for the Union cause in this town and section," as Josie saw it. "We gave these men breakfast and others came and the servants and all of us cooked, and fed till 12 o'clock, that day and still they poured into the town, going to various houses demanding food and in one or two instance treating Union women with a great deal of rudeness, calling them 'dam Rebels' and ordering them to get them something to eat 'D—quick'.... [T]hey destroyed in a few days more Union sentiment than the

Rebels had been able to do in six months." Witnessing the grim face of war brought an unexpected comfort: among the arriving federal troops were Warner Underwood and his son.[15]

Alongside civilians and soldiers in Bowling Green, the Underwoods lived amid the misery of lingering sickness and death behind the new war front. Josie and Lucy helped in the temporary hospitals set up in the depot, churches, and nearby public buildings, which were full to overflowing—the "soldiers' graveyard," as Josie referred to them. Private residences were not spared. Indeed, in their rented home Josie was soon forced to give up her parlor sofa bed for a feverish young federal lieutenant. "[T]he town is full of filth," claimed a worried visitor to the city, "the stench from the imperfectly buried dead is such as to sicken you.... The inhabitants are in fear of a pestilence." To complete the eleven fortifications ringing the town, federal troops took down buildings for lumber, including at the local college, and cleared hundreds of acres of timber around town. Many families' slaves—including some of the Underwoods'—soon went missing, reportedly having slipped off behind federal lines. Efforts to find them met with officers' indifference.

If the Underwoods' tragedy serves as a cautionary tale for the war's coming to the American heartland, the pieces do not make for a precise fit. Despite being slaveholders and self-proclaimed southerners, the Underwoods unflaggingly supported the Union. The wanton destruction of their Kentucky home occurred at the hands of invading Confederates, not federals. Worse yet, fellow border slave-staters set the torches.

Within weeks, word of Mount Air's destruction spread throughout the state. Of war's destructive appetite in Bowling Green, an observer concluded, "This thing ought not to have been commenced. It was a huge miscalculation on the part of its projectors and a huge wickedness on the part of all who had any agency in bringing it about.... [T]he death struggle...may well be terrible." Far more than this witness, who had so far lost nothing to the war, the Underwoods' suffering taught a painful truth. Amid armies and partisan civilians waging an uncivil war, the contours of allegiance were trampled by military boots. Wartime residents searching for gray in wartime found their world turned black and white.[16]

4

No North—No South—No East—No West

The Fiction of the Wartime Middle Ground

In wartime, as it is often said, truth is among the first casualties. So too is in-betweenness. The onset of war sparked deep divisions among white middle border residents, many of whom assumed neutral or nonpartisan stances as their state governments attempted to avoid the war by refusing to join either belligerent. Especially in the region's slave states, inner struggles among unionists, neutralists, and secessionists raged alongside public conflicts among uniformed federals, Confederates, and militia. Together they laid bare the fiction of the middle ground in wartime.

Rather than forestall war, neutrality and neutralism empowered extremists, both unionists and secessionists, to manipulate these positions to their own advantage. Claiming these states as theirs, partisans constructed definitions of loyalty and disloyalty and targeted not only adversaries but also those who refused to choose sides between slavery and the Union. Under extreme pressure, the spectrum of political understandings that once defined the middle border quickly began to collapse into exclusivist identities, northern and southern, under new, war-born definitions.

As former Kentuckians were inaugurated as presidents of respective nations, the slave states of these men's home region walked the tightrope between the peculiar institution and the Union. Residents of Kentucky and Missouri boasted a spectrum of stances on the conflict, including unconditional unionism, conditional unionism, conditional secessionism, unconditional secessionism, neutralism, and pacifism—especially strong among the region's many utopian religious groups such as Quakers, Shakers, Mennonites, and Amish.

Candidates identified themselves not along party lines but rather as supporting one of three general principles regarding their states' future relation to the union of states. At one end of the political and ideological spectrum were unconditional unionists, generally antislavery Republicans or Old Line Whigs. "I am for the Union, without an *if* or a *proviso* of any sort," wrote Virginia-born Missouri attorney Thomas J. C. Fagg. At the other extreme were states' rightists, who demanded constitutional protections for slavery or outright secession. Overwhelmingly proslavery, many had voted for Breckinridge. Secessionism often came without overt support for the Confederacy. Admitting that he was "a party by myself" in his neighborhood, Kentucky secessionist Will T. Hart nuanced his position. "If we cant go with the South let us quit the North and not be like a free negro at a Barbecue unable to speak till they have all left."[1]

Most numerous by far were conditional unionists, moderates who advocated staying in the Union so long as the federal government did not interfere with a state's right to determine local affairs. Compromised unionism, however, did not mean qualified opposition to secession. "If God should tell me I had either to go to Hell or the Southern Confederacy I should ask for a week of deliberation," wrote a Kentuckian to kin in southern Indiana. Nor did it mean pessimism about remaining between the sections. "I would a thousand times rather be where we are," he averred hopefully, "and that's where Kentucky is going to stick."[2]

In these slave states, concerns about racial order figured deeply into the mutual caution of most anti- and proslavery white residents. Over the winter months Missouri and Kentucky hosted emissaries from several Confederate states who were attempting to woo these border states to secession by appealing to their slave belts, in the same way that they had convinced nonslaveholding yeomen in white belts of their own states. Among the inevitable outcomes of the Republican victory were "the ultimate elevation of the negro to civil, political, and social equality with the white man" and even race war, accomplishing "amalgamation ... to gratify the lust of half-civilized Africans." But racial rhetoric soon found its limits. One Kentuckian admitted quickly that he was "sick of politics and more than sick of nigger, nigger, nigger." Another, Thomas H. Shelby, a state representative from one of Kentucky's Bluegrass counties and a member of one of the state's largest slaveholding families, overheard fellow congressman St. Clair Roberts, representing a county in the mountainous northeastern portion of the state, loudly advocating for his state "'taking a position' and 'asserting her rights'" by seceding. When he asked why the man supported secession, he received the reply "to maintain his rights and property." Shelby pulled rank. "What kind of property? Slave property. How many slaves do you own? Well I dont own any myself but my 'people' do. How many have 'your people'? *Twenty nine*! Well sir, tell 'your people' to bring their slaves to me and I'll buy every one of them and then your *damned* County will have no excuse for going out of the Union."[3]

Whether or not they owned slaves, most white Kentuckians and Missourians believed the status quo—loyalty to the federal government—was the best protection for their property. However threatening the Republican victory, secession was more so. "Old Howard is for the Union," wrote Vermont-born Abiel Leonard, owner of fifteen slaves, from his slave-rich Missouri county. "Our slaveholders think it is the sure bulwark of our slave property.... If Missouri is forced out of the Union you and I and every other man who has any thing—land or slaves[—]are ruined." Another Missourian wrote to his local newspaper, "To go either way, *exclusively*, is *annihilation*."[4]

Historian Carl Degler cleverly termed this fence-straddling proslavery stance "peculiar unionism." Border slave-staters, as well as many in the near free states, found nothing peculiar in it. In fact, they saw this as a pragmatic continuation of past practices: "the Constitution as it is, the Union as it was." Supporting the Union and slavery was the only way to preserve the nation and prevent catastrophe. Louisville's Robert Morris urged disregard for partisan characterizations of the two sections. "Brethren of the North! you are misinformed upon the subject of slavery," he implored. "It is not the hellish evil you have been taught to believe it.... Brethren of the South! you are misinformed as to the general feeling of the Northern people relative to slavery.... [I]n the broad lands of the North and West, and even in Canada, the popular sentiment is to let the subject alone."[5]

With Republicans controlling all branches, the federal government's coercion of states, more than the question of slavery, most threatened the nation's stability. The editor of Cincinnati's *Daily Enquirer* argued that the choice was "Union by conciliation, or Disunion by coercion and civil war." John Marshall Harlan, a Frankfort attorney and former Whig, wrote: "The chief cause of the excitement now in Kentucky, Maryland, Virginia, North Carolina, Tennessee and Missouri is the constant fear that Lincoln's administration will attempt coercion, or war commence between 'him' and the Seceding States." A public meeting in Kentucky's Meade County approved a series of resolutions that "regard[ed] the coersion of the ceceded States by the Federal Government as unconstitutional and Subversive of the principals of free governments and fraught with all the evils to her anticipated by Civil War."[6]

Admittedly, qualified loyalty, supporting the national government so long as that governments did not intervene in the states' affairs, was a paradox. But supporting secession, claimed one proslavery Missourian, was "to advocate treason, insubordination, reckless disregard for law." For these westerners, war would bring "bloodshed, devastation and ultimate subjugation of our country by foreign powers." Pressure for side-taking among them clearly favored the South. In the spring of 1861 Salmon B. Axtell, a Vermont-born lawyer living in Cleveland, rode extensively through the southern portion of Ohio and Kentucky. He found residents who "cannot yet see it our duty to take up arms against the south: They are particularly of our blood[.]—There is hardly an old family in Kentucky, but had living and cherished branches in the seceding states." Most turned against the nation's "fanatics north or south" while "proclaim[ing] to W[est] and S[outh] the above sentiment."[7]

Sympathy with southern concerns was not the same as declaring for the South. A decade earlier, neither Kentucky nor Missouri had sent delegates to the "southern convention" in Nashville, and in February 1861 both sent delegations to a peace conference that assembled in Washington. Northern delegates, mostly Republicans, dominated the meeting and sought little common ground with moderates. After three weeks of closed-door, often acrimonious discussion and debate, the compromise report to Congress patterned itself on the Crittenden Compromise. The Senate's Committee of Thirteen rejected the measure along free state–slave state lines. "[A]mazed at the Radical Hostility" of the northern commissioners, Kentucky's Joshua F. Bell was forced "to the conclusion though very reluctantly that... it was impossible that we should longer remain together; and the sooner the Union was dissolved the better for the whole country." The angry report of the state's six commissioners prompted the governor, Beriah Magoffin, to call a special session of his legislature to consider secession.[8]

Missouri voters had long since taken this step, and its convention would show unequivocally for the Union. On March 4, two days before the presidential inauguration, voters cast ballots for convention delegates. Antisecession candidates received nearly 80 percent of the 140,000 votes cast. Not one avowed secessionist candidate received election to the ninety-nine-member delegation. Yet neither did Missourians reward those known to be Republicans. Only four were elected, all from St. Louis. "The result was a surprise to every one, and a bitter disappointment to the South," recalled Thomas L. Snead, editor of the proslavery *St. Louis Bulletin*. Within a month delegates would vote 98–1 against secession, making it the only state convention to decide not to secede. "[N]o adequate cause [existed] to impel Missouri to dissolve her connections with the Federal Union," it resolved.[9]

However strong the Missouri convention's opposition to secession, slavery's protection drove it to support an undeclared neutrality. It was also un-neutral. Issued on March 9, the Committee on Federal Relations's report placed slavery at the center of its relationship with the federal government, approving the Crittenden Compromise recently rejected by Congress and calling for constitutional protections of slavery where it existed. It reaffirmed Missouri's devotion to "the institutions of our country." The report also noted the irony that should Missouri secede to protect slavery and enter "into a slaveholding confederacy," its residents would likely lose their slaves to soldiers of the government that currently protected them. Moderates defeated a second amendment pledging Missouri "to take a firm and decided stand in favor of her sister slave States," then approved another that requested the president withdraw federal troops from "the forts within the borders of the seceding States where there is danger of collision between the State and Federal troops." Claiming that coercive measures ran counter to state sovereignty, proslavery moderates castigated unconditional unionists. "*Abolitionist! traitor! and renegade!* were stereotyped words in their vocabulary of abuse," wrote one newspaper editor.[10]

No such convention was called in Kentucky, where the vast majority of unionists believed any call for one was tantamount to secession. Even a legislative vote, declared Garret Davis, "without submitting it to the people should be met by an armed resistance." Marshaling this groundswell of unionist support was the recent secretary of war, Joseph Holt, who had taken the position after John Floyd decamped for the Confederacy in December 1860. While in Washington Holt, a Kentucky attorney and stalwart unionist, had corresponded regularly with other unionists in his home state for information. After Lincoln's inauguration, Holt returned home and stumped against secession. His most important contribution was a thirty-five-page letter to Joshua F. Speed, which unionists subsequently published and distributed in pamphlet form. Secession, he claimed, represented the denouement of a decades-long conspiracy of "fraud and violence" carried out by a deceitful minority bent on destroying the Union because of their "unholy lust for power." Holt dismissed southern leaders' claims that they simply wanted to protect their "institutions." He argued that they triggered a sectional revolution by agitating the slavery question despite the federal government's concessions and compromises. Secessionists, not Lincoln or his administration, were the aggressors. "[T]he only southern right now insisted on, is that of dismembering the republic."[11]

As an unconditional unionist, Holt denounced neutrality, but conceded that within limits he construed it as something less than secessionism: "If, from a natural horror of fratricidal strife, or from her intimate social and business relations with the South, Kentucky shall determine to maintain the neutral attitude assumed for her by her Legislature, her position will still be an honorable one, though falling far short of that full measure of loyalty which her history had so constantly illustrated." Strict neutrality, however, which Missouri's convention supported and Kentucky's legislature was considering, was as unconstitutional as secession. "The troops of the federal government have as clear a constitutional right to pass over the soil of Kentucky, as they have to march along the streets of Washington," he reasoned, "and could this prohibition be effective, it would not only be a violation of the fundamental law, but would in all its tendencies be directly in advancement of the revolution, and might, in an emergency easily imagined, compromise the highest national interests."[12]

Holt's most powerful argument against his state's secession played uniquely to the concerns of slaveholding border residents and their understanding of geography, whether cultural, political, or strategic. Using border imagery, he cleverly turned the tables on secessionist Kentuckians by nationalizing their emergent sectional identity. Playing on long-standing feuds with neighboring free states over runaway slaves, Holt reminded audiences that the federal fugitive slave law served as a crucial protection for slavery. Secession would in effect *create* an antagonistic border, and Kentucky would "virtually have Canada brought to her door" by denying slaveholders legal protections to prevent enslaved people from fleeing northward to freedom. "Powerful free states, whose population relieved of all moral and constitutional obligations to deliver up fugitive slaves, will stand with open arms, inviting and welcoming them, and defending them, if need be, at the point of the bayonet." In effect, slavery's future "as a ball of snow would melt in a summer's sun." Charging that secessionists saw the border slave states as "a breast-work, behind which the Southern people may be sheltered," he played on prevailing fears of an imminent federal invasion. To disarm arguments for secession based on cultural affinity, he skillfully linked southern sympathy with nationalist traditionalism. "The people of the South are our brethren," he averred. "Their country is our country and ours is theirs and...we [cannot] permit it to be destroyed by others."[13]

Despite a governor who, if not outright favoring secession, sought a convention nonetheless, strong arguments against secession effectively countered the efforts of Kentuckians who organized as a "Southern Rights Party." The state legislature only sporadically considered the governor's request for a secession convention, and like Missouri's convention, its Federal Relations Committee presented a report in January recommending that remaining in the Union was the best protection for states' rights. But distrust of the Republicans in control of the national government prompted the legislature to affirm the Union Central Committee's recommendation that Kentucky "*ought to hold herself independent of both sides*, and *compel both sides to respect the inviolability of her soil.*"[14]

Historian James M. McPherson has written that Kentucky's and Missouri's support for neutrality was tantamount to secession. For most border state residents, nothing could have been further from the truth. Viewing with resolute seriousness their place in the nation, residents recognized that they, lying between the polar extremes of northern abolitionists and southern secessionists, would serve as mediators and deterrents of the gathering storm. Their declarations of neutrality were also intended to force Lincoln's hand to make good on his public pledges to protect slavery where it existed. As Confederate states claimed state sovereignty as the constitutional cornerstone of secession, border slave state residents believed their duty lay in defending state sovereignty against extremism *within* the Union. Until the federal government attempted to make war upon a sovereign state, or to coerce one of the loyal states to make war on the seceded states, neutrality and neutralism were anything but secession.[15]

More subtly, neutrality and neutralism actually strengthened unionism in these moderate yet divided states in the anxious secession months. By coalescing the spectrum of positions held by unionists who evinced a strong sympathy for the South, it affirmed individual rights, especially to property, threatened by the Republican ascendance. Winning only narrowly in the West, the new party was possibly a flash in the political pan. "How long is [Lincoln's] rule to last?" Archibald Dixon questioned a Louisville audience. "In the history of nations, what is four years?" Neutrality offered the opportunity to wait them out. As one Kentucky unionist averred, "Give the North time to Repent and undo their misdeeds.... Our people are for all their rights but believe they can get them in the Union—They want Revolution to be the last resort."[16]

§

On April 12, 1861, the fiction of neutrality revealed itself on the middle border. Before dawn, Confederate batteries opened on Fort Sumter, fire streaking across the inky moistness over the harbor of Charleston, South Carolina. Three days later, after Kentuckian Robert Anderson had surrendered the fort, Abraham Lincoln called for seventy-five thousand volunteer troops to put down what he called a rebellion in the southern states. As the crisis unfolded, telegraph operators in New York reported that "the West is all one great Eagle-scream." Certainly, in Cleveland and Chicago ringing bells, festive parades, flag raisings, and picnics, along with thronged streets, churches, opera houses, and filled meeting halls, showed support for the federal Union by condemning the Confederacy's treason. There, Lincoln's call for volunteers occasioned home guards, vigilance committees, and militia units to rush quickly to the colors for a "ninety day war." By the end of 1861 Ohio's enlistments had exceeded the state's quota by 27 percent, Indiana's by 58 percent, and Illinois's by a whopping 71.5 percent.[17]

But in the region's lower cities and towns during the heady weeks after Fort Sumter, war demonstrations were more somber affairs. Patriotism tinged with caution hardly amounted to eagle-screams, serious meetings about union replacing public celebrations. On the rainy day that news of the fort's surrender arrived in Cincinnati, the wife of a store clerk noted that she was "home all morning feeling very gloomy." In Indianapolis, "men closed their shops—and thousands of old men walked solemnly with faces pale—and tear wet cheeks." That evening Ohio's Jacob D. Cox recalled of Columbus: "[N]o torches, no music. A dark mass of men filled full the dimly lit street." Stephen A. Douglas's reception in the state capital offered a stark contrast to the cheering throngs who had welcomed the president-elect only weeks earlier. Of Douglas's encouragement to support Lincoln's administration, Cox wrote "I do not think we greatly cheered him, it was, rather, a deep Amen that went up from the crowd." Cincinnati mayor George Hatch issued a proclamation "requesting [residents] to refrain from the discussion of all exciting topics in public and enjoining upon them to discourage and avoid all congregation of crowds in the streets." Many heeded his advice. Cincinnati lawyer Rutherford B. Hayes, who had ridden on the inaugural train with the president-elect and who as recently as late January had advocated that the government "let them [the seceded states] go," decided at the city's union meeting to "put down my foot that I would not think of going into this first movement."[18]

In the war's first days many communities, especially those nearest the rivers, effectively shut down. Rockport, Indiana, "right on the border" on the Ohio River, was one. Sally Dorsey, a native Kentuckian whose husband and brothers would enlist in the federal army in the summer of 1861, quickly "recognized the unwisdom of exposing flammable material to possible sparks.... Women did not go out of evenings except on urgent affairs." No less outraged at the South's aggression, unionists in the lower counties were shocked at the militancy of Republican war supporters, especially in the upper counties. Ohio's Democratic leader, Cincinnatian Thomas M. Key, grumbled that "the people have gone stark mad!" while an Indianan complained, "D__n such love for the Union.... War against the South for the sake of war is a bad idea." The editor of the Madison *Courier* urged the Indiana state legislature to meet with Kentucky's lawmakers to settle their recent differences over fugitive slaves in order to avoid making the Ohio River a hostile boundary.[19]

Abraham's western house was especially divided over war with its slave state neighbors. Even in Ohio's Western Reserve, as the *Ashtabula Sentinel* admitted, "the people of the border [are] in favor of peaceful separation.... [T]he idea of coercing or fighting them to make them stay in, is looked upon as ridiculous." As "messengers of peace," a delegation from Louisville hastily traveled to Cincinnati to assure residents that "Kentucky has no desire to go to war. She wants the amicable relations between Ohio and herself... pledging their word that we of Ohio could rely upon the fidelity of Kentucky in preserving an 'armed neutrality.'" Ohio governor William Dennison recommended the "unconditional and early repeal" of its personal liberty laws, which the legislature resolved but never enacted as legislation. Ohio's Democrats approved an appropriations bill to support its volunteer troops, but not a muscular war policy. When Dennison seized control of the state's railroads and telegraph lines for military use, allowed Cincinnati boat yards to begin outfitting riverboats as gunboats (see figure 4.1), and called for his state troops' entrance into Kentucky and Virginia, moderates in the state's Republican Central Committee balked. Rather than be punished at the polls in an election year, they joined with war-supporting Democrats and Constitutional Unionists to form a moderate "Union Party." For the fall gubernatorial election, the fusion party's leaders soon dropped Dennison as their candidate in favor of David Tod, a War Democrat, who won easily.[20]

For unconditional unionists, neutrality was disloyalty by another name. "We want no enemies in disguise," one wrote to a Cincinnati newspaper. Editor Henry Reed, unfazed by the recent parade of conciliatory Kentucky delegates

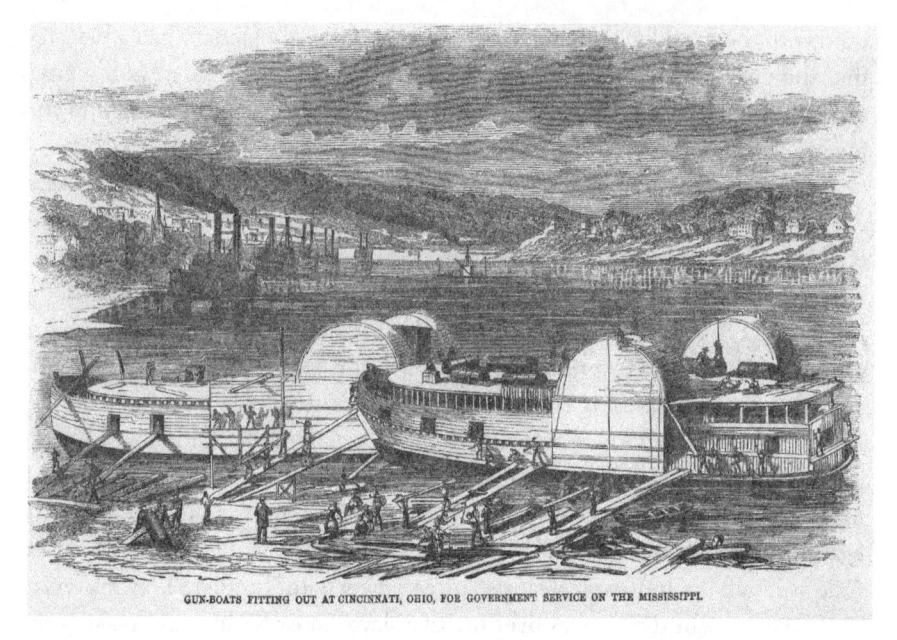

Figure 4.1 Federal gunboats outfitted at Cincinnati, July 1861. Control of the interior rivers was seen as critical to both federal military strategy and state sovereignty, quickly pitting loyal western free and slave states, and hard-liners and moderates, against one another. Courtesy Filson Historical Society.

to his city, condemned the state legislature's May 24 decision for neutrality. "This is no time for deception. Minced words will not do," he fumed. "In this contest there can be no neutral position.... He who will sustain the Government is its friend, and he who will not, is its enemy.... [O]ur enemies, [are] those who are not for the Union." No longer were these voters good, if misguided, slaveholding unionists. They were latent traitors, buying time before seceding. "Kentucky is to-day out of the Union to all intents and purposes, and should be treated as such," wrote an "Old Citizen" to the newspaper.[21]

Such feelings drew from divided realities in portions of their own free states. Amid broad support for the Union in the rural lower, or "Butternut," counties, opposition to war and even pockets of outright secessionism soon surfaced. In one community in Ohio's Virginia Tract, Confederate sympathizers wore secession cockades, flew the palmetto flag, and intimidated local unionists. When instructing a grand jury, a circuit court judge in Chester, Illinois, noted that "the disturbed state of the country might soon leave them without any government, in which case, they could adopt such organization as they thought best calculated to secure their protection and rights." The editor of the *Cairo Gazette* declared that "the sympathies of our people are mainly with the South," while a resident there reported to the Illinois governor, "Some of them say... they are going to hang cut throts and shoot every Republican in egypt." Public meetings in Illinois's Pope, Williamson, and Jackson Counties resolved to "refuse, frown down and forever oppose" a coercive war against the South that would "drive all the Border States from the Federal Union." One resident of Williamson County, native Tennessean Henry C. Hopper, invited residents to what unionists called a "pro-secession rally" that quickly adopted resolutions supporting southern rights. Following the arrest of a Democratic state legislator, Hopper led a company-sized contingent to western Tennessee, where they enlisted in a Confederate regiment. Lincoln offered a colonel's commission to Illinois congressman John McClernand and sent him to recruit in southern Illinois with specific instructions to "keep Egypt right side up."[22]

Although Butternut disloyalty was more quarantined than epidemic, clustered among families and in neighborhoods and hamlets, it triggered long-standing cultural prejudices against these states' southern sections and hardened unionists' responses. An Illinois lieutenant marching southward through his home state judged the "illmannered and slovenly clad people of Carlinville... [as] 'Secesh' in sentiment... from the almost entire absence of any exhibition of joy at our arrival." "Peace meetings," such as the one in Marion, Illinois, quickly found themselves squelched by local Union vigilance committees and hastily formed home guard units. Near Centreville, Indiana, on the National Road, one committee questioned farmer John Ketler about raising a company of "southern rights" men to enlist in the rebel army. After the men had forced him to say that his effort was "all in jest," the local newspaper editor warned readers: "He who is not for us, is against us." When Indiana's John Poague left his Marion County home to fight for the Confederacy, his property—some two hundred acres—was confiscated and sold at auction under the terms of Congress's First Confiscation Act. Despite these Butternuts' dissent, most counties exceeded their enlistment quotas by as much as half. More than 80 percent of voting age men in Massac County, Illinois, went into federal regiments. The number of men from the president's adopted state who joined the Union war effort was greater than all states but New York, Pennsylvania, and Ohio, and Indiana's enlistments as a percentage of its eligible men ranked it second.[23]

As the young men of the middle border's free states volunteered en masse for military service, they found recruiting camps—often hastily established at county fairgrounds—inadequate to organize, enlist, and train them. The Illinois legislature rushed into special session and approved a bond issue to provide war funds, as well as a new militia organization. The new plan established official camps at Alton, Caseyville, and Cairo in southern Illinois, among others, placing training centers nearer to the anticipated theater of conflict. Indiana's and Ohio's legislatures did likewise, establishing Camp Morton in Indianapolis and Camps Dennison and Clay near Cincinnati and creating the state-service "Indiana

Legion" to accommodate overflow recruits. Another impetus for these camps of instruction to be established on their southern borders was distrust of secesh, both across the rivers and homegrown. "In the event of an attack upon Cinc[innati]," averred war dissenter John Trimble, "every Citizen of Ohio will be liable to be called upon for repelling it." Exclusivist patriotism became only more pronounced when soldiers prepared to cross the rivers into slave states. "There is a great difference between the people of free states (Yankees) and those of slave states (Kentuckians) and their striking characteristics are quite discernable in this part of the West," wrote one antislavery Illinoisan.[24]

Across the rivers in neighboring slave states, the news of war sparked unlimited caution. With the nation's largest rivers flowing through or along them, avenues to the Confederacy, Kentucky's and Missouri's geographical positions made these states gateways through which federal troops would reach the South. Kentucky boasted nearly 500 miles of Ohio River frontage, along with some 65 more on the Mississippi River and more than 400 miles on the Tennessee and Cumberland Rivers, while Missouri's 500 miles of Mississippi River and 550 miles of Missouri River frontage similarly accessed the rebellious states. The federal government would surely demand security in these loyal states.

Official or not, neutrality offered cold comfort when set against the hostile responses in nearby free states. Among the government's supporters, a fatalistic unionism prevailed. By remaining ostensibly between the antagonists, putting them at the mercy of both, anguished residents felt tormented in the spring and summer of 1861. "I am glad I have no boys to fight you may think I am not very patriotic I must confess I do not feel so...this war is so perfectly unnatural," a Louisvillian wrote to his brother in New York. A Missourian wrote similarly to a Kentucky friend: "[A]ll is uncertainty these days.... I am wearried with hearing of secession, and wars, and rumors of wars; truly these are troublous times.... Is there peace and tranquility in your region[?]" In Kentucky, the image of the Great Compromiser found itself resurrected in Kentucky alongside overt war dissent. While Lexington unionists met at Henry Clay's unfinished grave monument in preparation for Fourth of July festivities in 1861 to "obtain a renewal of our love of Country," in nearby Richmond residents held a "peace and anti-war tax" picnic to oppose the Lincoln administration's warmongering.[25]

Secessionist sympathy in these slave states was more widespread, but no less shackled by strong unionism and infuriating neutralism. "This State is not like Va and Tenn, divided into sections, East and West," wrote western Kentuckian Mildred Sayre to her father, famed Virginia firebrand Edmund Ruffin. "But there is division every-where throughout the State." Bevie W. Cain knew by their private war talk that a large number of her central Kentucky neighbors were supporters of the government. "[P]eople talk of nothing else. We are still for the Union that is not all of us (for there are some *very* strong secessionists here), but the majority is for the Union." One Kentucky secessionist "was much chagrined and mortified to hear many of our citizens express no preference for either side which to my mind amounts to a very decided preference for the North."[26]

Rather than march away proudly in columns, federal recruits in these states more slunk off to war. "No noise or music, nothing heard but the occasional word of command in a low steady tone," wrote a Hopkinsville, Kentucky, woman as a company passed her gate. Enlistment quotas were mostly unmet in Kentucky and Missouri. "This fact is known to anyone who has observed with what difficulty volunteers are gotten here," wrote a unionist from Lexington, Kentucky. "In this strong Union (so called) district... they have been unable to obtain one regiment, while several companies have gone South... the majority of the fighting population is on the other side." Volunteer companies from across the rivers frequently crossed into neighboring slave states to enlist. The 9th Missouri was comprised entirely of Illinoisans, while the majority of companies of the 13th Missouri hailed from Ohio and Illinois. Although these states' governments offered varied terms of service to attract more local recruits, the shallow well soon ran dry. After an initial burst of enlistment in May and June 1861 in Covington, Kentucky, during the remainder of the war only 5 more men joined the 93 men already in uniform in Company D, 2nd Kentucky Volunteer Infantry, and for ninety days only.[27]

Under such labels as "Union and Southern men," a new political geography divided white residents. In its city council elections in early November, Hannibal, Missouri's candidates ran as "Union" and "Secession," and secessionists won in two of its four wards. Schools soon suffered politicized strife. In Danville, Kentucky, finishing schools facing one another on the same street were known as union and secession. The latter soon closed because "the principal it was said intended joining the Southern army." In the weeks following Lincoln's election, Georgetown College's students quarreled, took unexcused absences, and violated rules. But after Lincoln's call for troops secessionist students hoisted the stars and bars from Giddings Hall and refused to lower it, requiring a trustee to climb to the roof to haul it down. On April 23, 1861, the unionist trustees suspended classes until fall "[o]n account of the increasing excitement among the students caused by the agitated condition of the country." The school remained closed until January 1863, briefly reopened, then shut its doors for low enrollment. Called out by southern rights faculty and cadets at the nearby Kentucky Military Institute, Ohio cadet John B. Neil declared himself an unconditional unionist and Lincoln man. "They determined that he should leave the institute" to protect him "from insult or violence." To exact retribution on latent secessionists, he would enlist in the 2nd Ohio Volunteers and return to Kentucky.[28]

As much as opposition to coercion by blue-clad troops, fear of racial disorder drove locals to quick action. Vigilance committees reconstituted as citizen or home guards avowed their purpose, as in Charleston, Missouri, "for the protection of the wives, their children, and their houses." Kentuckian Thomas W. Parsons claimed his home guard formed "in the present state of excitement [over the possibility that] the Negroes might break out and much mischief could be done before we could organize." In Kentucky's Purchase area, vigilance committees drove out and even executed unionists and slaves. "The negroes are showing signs of discontent, and some have already been shot," one Kentuckian wrote in 1861, while residents of Polk County, Missouri, formed a protective organization to ensure "that no negroes (Free or Slaves) shall be allowed to transcend the rules of decorum." They also scrutinized any "suspected [white] person [who] holds opinions at Variance with our laws and interests, and persists in tampering, and intermedling with our institutions."[29]

Protection of slavery undergirded white unionists' professions of loyalty, as it did for many claiming support for the Confederacy. A Kentucky Confederate soldier ridiculed any "southern man" who would "not fight for his principles.... Tell him 'you come home with me and I will have my father to give you a negro and then you will have something to fight for.'" Missouri U.S. congressman John S. Phelps claimed of his Ozark district that "men who were born north of Mason's and Dixon's line, and who had been there only a short time, were in nine cases out of ten the most violent and rabid secessionists in the community, and especially if they did not own negroes." "We are fighting for our liberty," wrote another soon-to-be Confederate to his prominent Louisville father, "against tyrants of the North...who are determined to destroy slavery." Careful with public statements, Missouri's William Barclay Napton let down his guard upon learning the news of Virginia's secession after Fort Sumter. "Thank God," he exclaimed, "K[entuck]y. and *Missouri*, I hope, will follow soon.... I would rather give up every negro I own and lose them all and my land too, than...submit to menaces of this Abolition despotism now ruling the North."[30]

Among the range of responses to war of proslavery citizens in the middle border's slave states was a political and cultural awakening. The largest portion of these residents rejected secession and with it the Confederacy. As they considered their relationship with the warring sections of the American nation, two slaveholding political cultures emerged—southerners of culture and political southerners—waging a bitter inner war not only over their states' political futures but also to stake the boundaries of white southernness.

Unionist slaveholders soon saw their sectional understandings redrawn by exclusivist loyalty politics in the West. Hoping to convince Illinois leaders of continued relations as a private agent for the governor of his slave state, Kentuckian Isaac Shelby Jr. was in Chicago "an object of suspicion to the entire community...on [account] of the prejudices." He cautioned his wife: "Keep Politics out of your letters, as it is dangerous ground that all Southerners in the

North now stand upon." But Josie Underwood learned the same in Memphis, Tennessee, where she saw its dramatic outpouring of public sentiment prior to that state's second-wave secession. "If Lincoln's name happens to be mentioned, it's like a match thrown into powder," she wrote in her diary. "This is one of the hard things for the Unionists to contend with...hav[ing] to fight his extreme views as well as the secessionists." Watching or participating in competing torchlight processions on alternate nights, she snarled, "I think I will send [secessionists] a dictionary with the word *Loyal* marked—for they have forgotten its meaning."[31]

In an unraveling nation, both Kentuckians clung to formerly safe relationships as slaveholding unionists while pursuing alternative southern courtships. Shelby conjured southernness to defend against predictable, northern-style, antislavery prejudices against him as a member of a prominent family from a slave state. By contrast, Underwood believed her family's twenty-eight slaves were proof of southernness despite her family's unyielding support for the national government. But Tennesseans turned the tables, requiring that "loyal" southerners, regardless of slave ownership, favor secession. "[W]hy not fight for Southern rights *in* the Union—why wish to divide this great country that your forefathers and mine sacrificed so much to establish[?]" she questioned one secessionist beau as they danced at a ball. "The only way...is for the South to remain in the Union if she would maintain *any* of the 'Southern rights' she is clamoring for."[32]

Having long accepted the ownership of slaves as a defining feature of distinctive southernness, and more recently, political support for its protection, many unionist slaveholders, especially large owners, considered themselves southerners of culture. Believing deeply in the superior ideals of a plantation society, they occupied a broader swath of Kentucky's population than Missouri's. They disavowed the linchpin of the embattled rebel nation—rejection of the Union—while supporting the South's grievances against abolitionist attacks. As Missouri Whig editor William F. Switzler, a proslavery moderate, wrote in his Columbia newspaper on the day Lincoln called for federal volunteers, "*Of* the South, we are *for* the South." Switzler's claim was no statement of Confederate allegiance. Rather, it was a reiteration of cultural distinctiveness as the national struggle strengthened feelings of solidarity with other slave states. "I know you will call it prejudice," wrote a Kentucky minister after he had been exiled to Canada, "but, the character and virtues of the Southern people, including of course all the Slave States; her civilization, her religion, her glory, are full of charms for me, and greatly superior to those of any other nation."[33]

With a resounding no, loyal southerners of culture answered secessionists' employment of the "language of ancestry," laying claim as the legitimate heirs of their forebears' revolutionary tradition to a "Second American Revolution." By maintaining the political will to suppress extremism in the nation, they, and not Confederates, were heirs and defenders of the founding patriots' gift to subsequent generations: the republican form of government. "[M]y mind secured to the scenes of the Revolution when our noble ancestors freely shed their blood and laid down their lives to achieve and establish not for themselves but for us and future generations the best government the world ever saw with its attendant blessings," wrote Kentucky federal officer Benjamin Helm Bristow to his family in Hopkinsville, from his camp near surrendered Fort Henry. Knowing that many of his cousins had chosen not to enlist, he claimed he "thought of that government and what it had done for my friends and myself." The war was a revolution indeed, and many southern unionists employed the term freely, especially to describe as illegitimate revolutionaries the proslavery radicals who ignored generations of compromise as they sought to break up the union of states. When unsuccessfully cautioning his son, a West Pointer and officer in the federal army, against joining the Confederacy, John J. Crittenden argued that decades of national ascendance had proven the national union inviolate, and such traitors had "*No Nation*, no National Flag."[34]

Commitment to the institution of slavery complicated ideas of nationalism for loyal southerners of culture. Conditional unionism implicitly attached strings to such conceptions, the protection of slavery being the strongest of them. "I am as out-and-out a Southern man as anybody," claimed the unionist slaveholding minister Joel K. Lyle early in 1861, denying Confederates' claims that slavery and union were antagonistic and that war was being waged over their peculiar institution. Many came to believe otherwise. Those who remained loyal to the national government often found their cultural identity as southerners challenged by extremists, secessionists, and unconditional unionists. Though an affluent slaveholder, Kentucky's Henry Duncan Jr. was unwilling to accept that slavery was the cause of the war. During much of 1861 he disentangled the primary thread of communion between loyal and disloyal slave states, one that the Confederate commissioners had tried assiduously to tangle, and moved beyond slavery to embrace a compromise position. The war was "being waged for an abstraction...which as it then stood and now stands, is—government or no government?" He promptly rejected the premise, as well as the constitutional theory that underlay the Confederacy's existence. Recognizing cultural distinctiveness while disavowing the right to be a separate nation became the fundamental dilemma faced by unionist southerners of culture in wartime.[35]

But a small portion of these southerners of culture immediately declared themselves secessionists or outright Confederates, supporting the legitimacy of the rebel government. More required introspection to make the decision to support the South. Kentucky's Lizzie Hardin recalled being tortured by the nationalist symbols with which she had been raised. "The words 'Star-spangled Banner', 'American Eagle', 'Glorious Union' were the 'Open Sesame' of my heart," she reflected. Thinking deeply about her conception of the Union, she came to a realization. "[S]trange as it may seem, my love for the Union arose only from an idea that it was beneficial to the South.... At the end of two or three weeks I donned the blue cockade."[36]

For southerners of culture like Duncan and Hardin, affecting southernness was founded on abstractions beyond slavery as the foundation of cultural distinctiveness. Cora Owens was a Louisville schoolgirl whose family and slaves were driven from their home in southwestern Kentucky in 1861 by Confederates, not the federals, a circumstance embarrassing enough to her not to mention it to classmates. She admitted to her journal that but for slavery, she was an outsider to the Confederacy, and even to the South. But her "*Southern right*" was to claim by association the white culture she considered her own: "I cling fondly to the idea that the South is my native country and I feel like I ought to be there.... I would love to visit there soon, at least and if only to freshen the memory with purely Southern associations. I know of no place that I desire so much to visit, as my native Country, which is natural."[37]

More natural were the racial orthodoxies based on the slaveholding imperative within such southern associative bonds. Among southerners of culture who ultimately turned against the federal government was William Preston, the former U.S. congressman and ambassador who, with U.S. senator John C. Breckinridge, left the state after the arrival of federal troops and served as a Confederate brigadier general. Like many Kentucky Confederates and sympathizers, the Virginia-born, Yale- and Harvard-educated Preston agonized for nearly a year about his loyalty, believing racial leveling by the Republican ascendance more than proslavery extremism threatened the nation. Deciding it "better to remain with two republics, than one tyranny," in April 1862 he explained his decision to his children at home in Louisville, anticipating that "if we should be conquered you will hear me called a rebel and traitor." He argued that he did not wish for war, but understood the southern cause. "By many you will be told that this war is for slavery," he wrote. "Doubtless it is the most prominent cause... but it is not to perpetuate slavery that I have taken sides with the South." Rather, "the zeal and bigotry of the abolitionists," he reasoned, "would overwhelm the white race with ruin, and therefore [I] resisted them."[38]

The complicated politics of slavery, loyalty, and true and false southernness were not native-born white residents' alone to unravel. Recent emigrants from free states were quickly forced to untangle redefined political and cultural identities in the middle border's slave states. Fresh by rail from his rural Pennsylvania home, Missouri schoolteacher Allen P. Johnson—no Lincoln supporter—found his own cultural conceptions complicated in mostly nonslaveholding Rolla. "[T]he native Missourians," he admitted, "are not a people after my own heart." But as a proslavery Democrat he felt at home, enough to set straight his fiancée and her solidly Republican family about catching secessionitis. He had not "become a regular southerner in the west.... I detest the 'fire eaters' of the south; but no more than the ultra Republicans, or abolitionists of the north. I am a union man throughout, knowing no north or south." Other "western men with southern principles" became ardent states' rights hotspurs. Frank F. Steel, a southern Ohioan, was influenced to enlist in Confederate regiments. "The truth is that the North has been deceived by the elections in this State," he wrote to a friend. "They have supposed that the people here were for the Union, when they were only for Neutrality and Peace.—these gone their interests and sympathies lead them with the South."[39]

Among those who manipulated the new politics of loyalty and southernness were the governors of Kentucky and Missouri. As earnest or hopeful secessionists, Claiborne F. Jackson and Beriah Magoffin did not need to foist secession upon their constituents. Their states' majority support for noninterference and widespread opposition to the Republican Party and the new president allowed them to employ passive-aggressive strategies. Inevitably the federal government would march troops across their borders, violating their states' neutral positions. Conjuring notions of their states' vulnerability to counterunionist legislatures, both men proclaimed their paramount devotion to their states. Jackson remained cautious in wielding his public authority, knowing that the best chance for Missouri's secession lay in maintaining the role of protector rather than provocateur. Leading unionist newspapers soon declared him "against secession" and applauded him for his "peace policy." However politic his public actions, Jackson privately maneuvered for the state's secession. On April 19, 1861, the day armed Massachusetts troops and unarmed Pennsylvania militia met mob resistance en route to the nation's capital in what quickly became known as the "Baltimore Riot," Jackson urged the president of the Arkansas secession convention: "Mo will be ready for secession in less than thirty days; *and will secede*, if Arkansas will only get out of the way and give her a free passage." Focusing on the federal arsenal at St. Louis, fortified by Regulars recently arrived from Kansas, Jackson sent an emissary to the Confederacy to obtain mortars and siege artillery to "batter down [the] walls, and drive out our enemies." When he received word that captured arsenal guns from Baton Rouge would come upriver, Jackson "look[ed] anxiously and hopefully for the day when the star of Missouri shall be added to the constellation of the Confederate States of America."[40]

Jackson's strategic use of armed neutrality to effect secession found private support among many Missourians. "Secession is tremendously popular," wrote a buoyant state officer, "the great difficulty now is to Keep secession back awhile.... [Sterling] Price will call the convention shortly. He says he Know[s] they would pass an ordinance of secession in a day." When the Blairs convinced the president to remove the commander of the Department of the West, William S. Harney, a proslavery moderate, Jackson provoked the legislature in special session to accelerate events. On May 6 militia units from all over the state converged on their various district encampments, a measure prescribed by the 1858 Militia Act. The St. Louis district's was located at Lindell's Grove, on the western edge of St. Louis. The commander, Daniel M. Frost, a known secessionist, named it Camp Jackson.[41]

Kentucky's Magoffin proved even more cautious than Jackson. His neutrality proclamation had claimed Kentucky would throw its support from whichever belligerent should first invade it. His venomous rejection of the president's quota of four regiments was coupled with a similar refusal to the Confederacy. But responding to a letter from an Alabama secessionist commissioner, he was confident that "when the time of action comes (and it is now fearfully near at hand) our people will be found rallied as a unit under the flag of resistance." Magoffin did nothing to prevent secessionists from organizing, recruiting, and offering their services to the Confederate government or to squelch southern rights associations' organizing in local communities. After his election he had stockpiled guns, uniforms, equipage, and munitions for the state militia and appointed West Pointer Simon B. Buckner as its operative head. Buckner solicited materiel from former federal armories in seceded states and from Tennessee's provisional army. (Tennessee had entered into a military league with the Confederacy as its legislature considered secession.) Magoffin did nothing to prevent Buckner from operating a camp of instruction there, at which he recruited not for the state guard but rather for the Confederate army.[42]

§

Judging neutralism as creeping secessionism, unconditional unionists immediately launched a counterrevolution. "The cry of 'making war upon a sovereign state' so freely used in the convention and out of it was a subterfuge," charged U.S. attorney James O. Broadhead, a St. Louis member of Missouri's secession convention. Louisville's Lovell H. Rousseau ridiculed his peers in the state legislature for "attempting to preserve a neutral attitude in the present crisis." In both cities, hard-line unionists like Rousseau and Frank Blair armed ostensibly for self-defense, enlisting thousands into home guard units while actively soliciting government arms and ammunition. Both reached out to their cities' most reliable Republicans, German Americans. Louisville's unionist papers soon reprinted Leonard Streiff's address to the "Germans of Kentucky," calling for them to "beware of all the tricks and treachery of Disunionists.... Tell the rebel... [w]e all left our fatherland because we desire to rid our necks of the heel of the tyrant." Louisville's William Preston Johnston, whose father would soon command the Confederacy's western department, was alarmed by the preemptive radicalism of his state's unconditional unionists. "Should secession be attempted," he informed his uncle, William Preston, "there is a strong enough Union party here to create a civil war in *our State* without interference from other States.... Can you see any hope of salvation for us?" In St. Louis, Blair soon convinced the War Department that secessionists, or "Minute Men," intended to capture the federal arsenal. When he and Nathaniel Lyon, a rock-ribbed antislavery zealot (and antiabolitionist) in command of the federal troops at the arsenal, enlisted and armed "Black Dutch," a western pejorative for antislavery Germans, Blair threw the city into a frenzy. In the March city elections, Republicans lost control of the government they had held for the past four years as voters evinced a clear distrust of the new president many had recently helped to elect.[43]

Within days Missouri saw armed conflict. Two weeks after the Baltimore Riot, on May 10, 1861, St. Louis exploded in violence when Lyon and Blair ordered a preemptive strike. After Confederate cannon arrived by steamer from Baton Rouge and were secreted to the militia camp, they marched some 6,500 members of the home guard from the arsenal to Camp Jackson, forcing the surrender of 669 openly secessionist militia, two-thirds of the entire force. Then, in a grandiose display of might, Lyon and Blair marched the prisoners under guard nearly the entire six miles from the camp to the arsenal, through hostile throngs. A fracas near the center of the column caused the barely trained home guard units to open fire, resulting in twenty-eight deaths and as many as seventy-five injuries. For days, rioting tore through the city streets, and thousands fled the "murdering dutch": government troops who many believed were "shooting women and children in cold blood." Within hours rumors of Lyon's troops heading for the capital caused a special session of the legislature to pass Jackson's long-debated military bill, granting the governor sweeping military powers "to repel such invasion or put down such rebellion." Within a week the legislature authorized Jackson to take possession of the state's railroads and telegraph lines and mobilize the state militia. The *"coup de tat* at St. Louis," as one writer called the Camp Jackson affair, galvanized Missouri's countryside, turning thousands of conditional unionists into southern rights advocates or outright secessionists. Even St. Louisans like Uriel Wright, once a unionist stalwart who had voted decisively against secession at the March convention, were outraged. "If Unionism means such atrocious deeds as I have witnessed in St. Louis," he proclaimed, "I am no longer a Union man." As the state's attorney general, J. Proctor Knott, wrote, because of the Camp Jackson affair "the boys from the hills are pouring into town today by hundreds with their *squirrel killers* and our usually quiet little city is now a military camp.... [M]ark me a bloody day of retribution will come."[44]

In Kentucky, St. Louis's violence weighed heavy on the Border State Convention that convened in Frankfort on May 26. Its seventeen delegates, mostly Kentuckians, reminded the nation that "all the slave States except four are arrayed in hostility to the General Government" and called for a constitutional amendment to protect slavery. "We ask no concession of new or additional rights," they claimed, "we do not fear any immediate encroachment upon our rights as slave States." If anything, the convention revealed the incompatibility of slaveholding unionists in a nation fast dividing into sectionalized polarities.[45]

Secessionists were also taking preemptive measures. Days before the Border State Convention opened, secessionists in western Kentucky confiscated nine hundred arms and six cannon from the state guard armory at Paducah, loaded them onto rail cars, and secreted them across the Tennessee line to the state guard encampment. "I fear we shall have war between the parties themselves," gloomily wrote Kentucky minister William Moody Pratt. Unconditional unionists, including neighboring Republican governors, pressured the new administration to arm loyalists in these states, and the War Department quickly created the Military Department of Kentucky and assigned Robert Anderson to enlist troops and "restrict exports thence by land and water." Joshua F. Speed soon obtained Lincoln's promise to arm Kentucky's home guard units. The commander of the new Department of the Ohio in Cincinnati, George B. McClellan, promised to see the muskets reach the right hands. "About the latter part of this month or first of July the ball will very probably open," Garret Davis wrote McClellan on June 8, the day Tennessee seceded.[46]

On August 24 the ball began. On the heels of a final secessionist recruiting parade in Louisville, some twenty-five hundred soldiers in federal service crossed the river to Louisville, including Indianans, Ohioans, and Lovell H. Rousseau's Kentucky "Legion," who had trained for six weeks at Indiana's Camp Jo Holt. Together they evoked "a good deal of excitement amongst a certain class of old fogies about the government troops [from] across the river." Rousseau was not the first unconditional unionist to violate Kentucky's neutrality. Days earlier, with War Department authorization, William "Bull" Nelson, a U.S. Navy lieutenant and native Kentuckian on special assignment, had established Camp Dick Robinson in rural Garrard County to recruit federal troops alongside those "principally from Ohio and Indiana," as Lincoln's secretary John Nicolay admitted. Lincoln rebuffed Kentuckians' complaints, categorizing these troops as an indigenous force. Conditional unionists were outraged. The editor of the *Kentucky Yeoman* howled, "If Kentucky suffers one of the belligerents to occupy our soil," he fumed, "she cannot expect the other to keep off."[47]

As Kentuckians sweated out neutrality violations, Missouri bore witness to war. Jackson prepared the state for defense against invasion. Appointing Sterling Price, the former governor who chaired the nonsecession convention, as commander of the state guard, he dispatched squads from the reorganized state militia to guard vital railroad bridges, dispersed the state's powder stores around the countryside, and removed the treasury funds. The governor's efforts found widespread support from all portions of the state, and thousands flocked to state guard recruiting stations. "My blood boils in my veins when I think of the position of Missouri, held in the Union at the point of Dutchmen's bayonets—I feel outraged." One enlistee at Jefferson City proclaimed of the state militia that "they are ordered here to defend the Capitol, and they firmly believe that the Government is the worst of enemies, intending to invade unlawfully the Soil of Missouri."[48]

Missouri's secessionists did more than just enlist in the state guard. They quickly sought to drive unionists, especially northern-born, from their midst to pressure their slaveholding state's qualifiedly loyal stance. "I love the Union, and beg and plead for peace," pleaded one. "I have no slaves. I do not want to fight— and for all these things I am charged with being a Submissionist, a Black-Republickan—a friend of the North and an enemy to the South…and if I do not fight for the South I will be hanged." Despite being a slaveholder with a long public proslavery record, Connecticut-born U.S. congressman John S. Phelps found himself vulnerable to charges of submissionism in Springfield. In nearby Rolla, Allen B. Johnson watched as a mob drove out of town prominent unionists— including the new postmaster—shouting "no man should hold office under 'Abe Lincoln.'" When secessionists "openly proclaim[ed] that no law can be had for northern men, and are taking the opportunity…of seizing on the property of northern, or union men on the smallest pretense," he left for St. Louis "in disgust, hoping to meet them only with the opportunity of administering summary punishment." He got it—by enlisting in an Illinois federal regiment that soon returned under arms to Missouri.[49]

The last gasp for Missouri's affected neutrality took the form of a brief attempt to balance federal and state military authority. When the War Department restored William S. Harney to command, the native Tennessean forged an agreement with Sterling Price that so long as the state government suppressed secessionism, federal troops would not intervene militarily. Missouri's moderates were pleased, but hard-liners censured the agreement. "Our friends here and the friends of the Government were very much dissatisfied with the terms of the arrangement," wrote James O. Broadhead, "in as much as it seemed to leave that protection in the hands of the very power by which it was imperiled." Just a week later, an aide of Frank Blair served Harney with orders relieving him of command for a second time, with Lyon again assuming command. Events escalated rapidly. On June 11 Lyon and Blair met with Jackson and Price in the governor's suite at St. Louis's sumptuous Planters' House hotel. The state leaders proposed strict neutrality, while Lyon refused to concede any point on federal authority. After four heated hours, Lyon declared bluntly, "Better, sir, far better that the blood of every man, woman, and child within the limits of the State should flow, than that she should defy the federal government." Hastening back to Jefferson City, the following day Jackson issued a proclamation calling for fifty thousand volunteers to repel the federal government's troops bent upon the coercion of peaceable Missourians. "Rise, then," it declared, "and drive out ignominiously the invaders who have dared to desecrate the soil... consecrated by your homes."[50]

Within hours of Jackson's proclamation, Lyon embarked with two thousand men on a military expedition to Jefferson City, traveling by commandeered steamers up the Missouri River. Jackson and his staff frantically gathered state papers; appropriated much of the currency, treasury records, and the official seal; and ordered the destruction of three railroad bridges west of Jefferson City to impede pursuit. As they and other state officials left the capital by steamer that evening, the legally elected government was fugitive. Two days later, Lyon's troops occupied Missouri's capital and on June 17 routed a small force of state guards at nearby Boonville. Missouri's "governor in the saddle" and his state troops fled headlong toward the southwestern portion of the state, pushing aside a second federal host that moved to intercept them at Carthage. In late July Confederate and Arkansas state troops entered Missouri to give battle to Lyon's federal troops, encamped near Springfield. Jackson left the state, trying to convince Confederate commanders in western Tennessee to occupy southeast Missouri, then heading to Richmond, Virginia, the new Confederate capital, to secure financial assistance from the Confederate government.[51]

On July 22, when the Missouri convention met again in emergency session in Jefferson City, unconditional unionists vacated the governor's seat, along with those of members of the General Assembly who had accompanied him, and moved to fill those offices. The convention then seated Hamilton R. Gamble, a lifelong Whig, slaveholder, and firm unionist and centrist on the slavery issue, as provisional governor. Under Gamble's leadership, the provisional government would maintain steadfast support for the federal government for the duration of the war.[52]

Within days of the provisional government's creation, on August 10, 1861, the West's first major battle occurred at Wilson's Creek. Lyon lay dead on the field, and federal troops were in retreat to St. Louis. Telegraph and newspaper reports prompted thousands to strike out by wagon or carriage, on horseback or on foot, to help in the relief effort. Corpses rotted in the fields, carrion for buzzards, wild hogs, wolves, bear, and coyotes, or were dumped in sinkholes. "[T]he stench from the dead and dying is so offensive as to be almost intolerable in some quarters," wrote one wounded Kansan. "Springfield is the most offensive place you was ever in." When Sterling Price led the state guard northward to reestablish the authority of Missouri's elected government and gain recruits, he succeeded mainly in bringing more bluecoats into the state, who remained for the duration of the war.[53]

Conciliation between federal and state troops similarly failed in Kentucky. On June 8 state guard commander Simon B. Buckner entered into an agreement with the federal commander in Cincinnati, George B. McClellan, balancing federal sovereignty and the state's official neutrality. Like the Harney-Price agreement, such concord was quickly broken when unconditional unionists convinced federal officials of secessionist threats. "I doubt not that two-thirds of our people are unconditionally for the Union," wrote Garret Davis to McClellan, but "timid and quiet... they shrink from convulsion and civil war, whilst all the bold, the reckless, and the bankrupt are for secession."[54]

The Bluegrass State's anxious neutrality ended abruptly on September 3, when Confederate troops occupied southern Kentucky, including Columbus, Bowling Green, and Hopkinsville. Three days later Ulysses S. Grant occupied Paducah and Smithland, securing the mouths of the Tennessee and Cumberland Rivers. Perhaps no federal military commander more fully understood the border region's strategic importance. Born only a few yards from the Ohio River in Point Pleasant, Grant graduated from West Point and married into an affluent Missouri slaveholding family. Less antislavery than his father, Grant nonetheless freed the only slave he owned, but did not free his wife's domestic servants; he hired slave laborers and stayed with the Democratic Party. Only months before the war, failures at farming and a poor head for business had forced him to seek refuge in Galena, in northern Illinois, to clerk in his father's store. The town's only West Pointer and a decorated Mexican War veteran, Grant reluctantly accepted the colonelcy of its volunteer regiment and marched off to war-plagued Missouri. Political connections finally got him a promotion to brigadier general, and his competence and energy earned him the command of troops at Cairo, the chief naval depot and port for the brown-water fleet, or Western Flotilla, that would steam deep into the Confederacy. Grant saw this mudhole as the most strategic point on the continent that would win or lose the war, and with an unerring sense of both water and events, he took the wheel of victory on the western rivers. "What I want," he wrote his wife, Julia, in late October, "is to advance." His superior officer, John C. Frémont, ordered him to clear marauding rebels from swampy southeastern Missouri and occupy the Iron Banks at Columbus, Kentucky, the northern terminus of a vital railroad spur. Confederate general Leonidas Polk beat him to it, sending troops by river and road to the bluffs, where they sealed off the Mississippi River by stretching a massive chain across its span, creating a self-styled "Gibraltar of the West." Kentucky's solidly unionist legislature instructed the governor to order the Confederates, not the federals, to withdraw from the state and overrode his veto of its call for forty thousand troops "for the purpose of repelling said invasion." The Confederacy alone, it argued, had violated the state's neutrality. "The axe has at length fallen," seethed J. Proctor Knott, Missouri's deposed attorney general, from back home in his native Kentucky, having been imprisoned and disbarred for refusing to take Missouri's loyalty oath.[55]

Grant quickly showed his brand of forceful impetuosity. Columbus was vital to securing both Missouri and Kentucky, and McClellan had already drafted a plan of occupation. All summer, locals told Polk about "secret service" missions by border patrols and home guard scouts and, more recently, armed river forays by squads of federal troops from Cairo aboard timberclad gunboats, and their capture of civilians. All were clear violations of Kentucky's neutrality. Grant declared confidently to stony local citizens, "The strong arm of the Government is here to protect its friends and to punish only its enemies." Columbus's pro-Confederates scolded the legislature for supporting the federal occupation as a violation of the state's neutrality. Despite Frémont's orders to make "demonstrations [without] attacking the enemy," in early November, aboard timberclads and transports, Grant steamed three thousand men downriver to take Columbus. Across the river at Belmont, Missouri, Polk repulsed the surprise attack and nearly cut off Grant's bloodied command before it narrowly escaped to Cairo.[56]

In the fall of 1861 both federal and Confederate troops poured into Missouri and Kentucky, in separate occupations. These states' authority structures offered mirror images. In Missouri an exiled government headed by elected, pro-Confederate administrators but repudiated by unconditional unionists claimed sovereignty over a provisional government it decried as fraudulent—a point Lincoln was forced to concede—while in Kentucky the elected, loyal government did the same to a self-constituted, pro-Confederate provisional government that claimed legitimacy behind rebel lines. Sheltered by the brief advance and retreat of the state guard after Wilson's Creek, Claiborne F. Jackson used Price's pyrrhic victory at Lexington to mold public opinion toward immediate secession, which Jefferson Davis demanded for Confederate military and financial support. When Price was forced to retreat and establish protective military lines in the southwestern portion of the state, Jackson issued a proclamation calling the General Assembly to meet at Neosho on October 21 to effect "an immediate and unconditional connection with the Southern Government."[57]

Reports of a quorum—nineteen senators and sixty-eight representatives—and even vote totals appeared quickly in some newspapers. Their reliability is questionable. One contemporary source reported that only two people were initially present and that the governor spent the entire first week securing enough members, likely appointing proxies. By the end of the first day, October 28, both houses of the rump legislature voted in favor of a secession ordinance, elected senators and representatives to the Confederate Congress, then hastily adjourned after receiving reports of an advancing federal force. Jackson signed the secession ordinance and excitedly sent copies on to the Confederate administration without holding a ratification referendum. On November 28 the Confederate Congress admitted Missouri as the twelfth Confederate state. William F. Switzler, editor of Columbia's *Missouri Statesman*, ridiculed the act: "The people of

Missouri for three weeks past have been in Dixie's happy land, without knowing it.... But what a mockery is this."[58]

In Kentucky a convention of delegates largely appointed or elected by Confederate soldiers met on October 29 in Russellville, shielded by the Confederate occupation. Headed by John C. Breckinridge and U.S. congressman Henry C. Burnett, it met again in mid-November and declared Kentucky a free and independent state and elected a provisional government. The governor, George W. Johnson, who headed Kentucky's State Rights Party, believed secession would check Republicans. The Confederate Congress recognized this provisional government and adopted Kentucky as its thirteenth state on December 10, 1861.[59]

§

A widely cited chestnut ascribed to Abraham Lincoln has the burdened president nearly in prayer, wishing God on his side but insisting that Kentucky be there. However fervent his wish, it might have been less a supplication than a demand. Just weeks after federal troops crossed the Ohio into Kentucky, Lincoln wrote to Orville H. Browning, a former Whig, native Kentuckian, and Republican U.S. senator holding Stephen A. Douglas's seat after his sudden death earlier that summer. "[T]o lose Kentucky," Lincoln cautioned his friend, "is nearly the same as to lose the whole game. Kentucky gone, we cannot hold Missouri, nor, as I think, Maryland."[60]

Having lost only one popular election in his entire political life, Lincoln was not accustomed to losing at all, much less the whole game. His renown for legal success in Illinois, especially in the seventy-one cases in which he had represented various railroad companies, had earned him the simple yet enviable sobriquet "the railroad lawyer." Lincoln knew already in 1861 that he must have the border slave states, and he intended to keep them. A third of the white population of the slave states resided there and produced just less than half of the value of the region's manufacturing products. For the first year of the conflict, the Lincoln administration's military and political strategies and goals entwined as the ground war forced a broadening of once limited definitions of military necessity. In these same states a hard-line war against civilians and their property originated in the war's first year, as the president allowed federal commanders and militia nearly free rein. Rather than work at cross-purposes, this tandem strategy effectively held these troublesome yet vital states by controlling their divided populations.[61]

As a newly elected president and head of a party accused of being led by hardliners and abolitionists, Lincoln did surprisingly little in the frenzied months after his election to soften his image. On February 11, 1861, at Indianapolis, he forcefully averred the federal government's power over states, prompting newspapers in Louisville and St. Louis to condemn his speech as "a war proposition... without a declaration of war." Reasoning that "the words 'coercion' and 'invasion' are much used in these days; and often with some temper and hot blood," Lincoln scoffed at "professed lovers of the Union...who spitefully resolve that they will resist." The following day—the president-elect's fifty-second birthday—at a brief stop in Lawrenceburg, Indiana, on the Ohio River, his impromptu remarks to a strongly unionist crowd sounded little like an olive branch. "I suppose you are all Union men here," he queried, to cheers and cries of "Right," "and I suppose that you are in favor of doing full justice to all, whether on that side of the river (pointing to the Kentucky shore) or on your own." (Immediately shouts rang out: "We are.") By the time he delivered his inaugural address three weeks later, such provocative language had been modified considerably, on the recommendation of several advisers and cabinet members, especially his secretary of state, William H. Seward.[62]

"My policy," the pragmatic president often told his advisers and critics, "is to have no policy." Judged an "idiotic notion" by his secretary of the treasury, Salmon P. Chase, hard-liners thought this meant Lincoln had no principles. Far from it. The neutral stances of Delaware, Maryland, Kentucky, and Missouri having darkened Lincoln's sunny opinion of southern unionism, he had become increasingly convinced that strong measures were necessary to secure the border slave states. The South was in revolution, and revolutionary measures were required. "It is revolutionary times," wrote then general in chief Winfield Scott when ordering William S. Harney's removal on April 30, "and therefore I do not object to the irregularity of this"—an order that Lincoln himself endorsed that day in thick black ink. Indeed, only three days before Lincoln had suspended the writ of habeas corpus in Maryland, declared martial law in areas there, and allowed federal troops to take control of transportation lines to Washington. He quietly authorized "the bombardment of cities, if necessary," and federal troops began suppressing secessionists during the summer. Although dominated by states rights Democrats, Maryland's legislature, like Kentucky's, refused to consider an ordinance of secession and supported its moderate unionist governor's recommendation for neutrality. In August, just prior to the legislature's convening, Lincoln permitted the arrest of a number of the state's legislators, a "strange move," one historian notes, "five months after the secessionist impulse appeared spent." These coordinated arrests of public figures were clearly linked to an early hard-line strategy in Maryland. As a Bostonian wrote in November 1861 after the release of one public figure, "I believe he is one of the men who ought to be on our side and if so would be of great value to us when the time comes for conciliation in Maryland."[63]

The border slave states' neutrality stances caused angry northern hard-liners to condemn Lincoln for any conciliation toward them. As writer and Harvard professor James Russell Lowell scoffed in 1861, a "little Bopeep policy of Let them alone, and they'll all come home Wagging their tails behind them" only courted disloyalty. Their decision to maintain ties with the Confederacy rendered their professed unionism little more than a veneer. "We believe, then, that conciliation was from the first impossible," Lowell railed. "The only way to retain the Border States was by showing that we had the will and the power to do without them.... The way to insure the loyalty of the Border States was to convince them that disloyalty was dangerous."[64]

On July 4, 1861, the president's message to Congress offered a hard edge to military authority emerging in the middle border states. He unambiguously condemned neutrality as de facto if not outright secession and those "*professed* Union men" who favored it as disloyal. Under the "guise of neutrality... the border States, so called—in fact, the middle states [claimed] being almost *for* the Union," Lincoln sneered, dismissing "'armed neutrality' [as] disunion completed" designed to "tie the hands of the Union men." This falsity, he argued, "recognizes no fidelity to the Constitution, no obligation to maintain the Union; and while very many who have favored it are, doubtless, loyal citizens, it is... treason in effect." Lincoln clearly approved of the reordering of those states by the elevation of unconditional unionists over elected officials. "[T]his government," he reasoned, "has no choice left but to deal with [insurrectionism], *where* it finds it." Less than two months later, on August 24, Lincoln coldly answered the letter of Kentucky's Beriah Magoffin complaining of federal officers recruiting unionists to the state guard in his neutral state "without the advice or consent of the Authorities of the State." He refused to remove these officers, whose presence the majority of Kentucky unionists opposed. "It is with regret," he snarled, "I search, and can not find, in your not very short letter, any declaration, or intimation, that you entertain any desire for the preservation of the Federal Union." Viewing conditional unionism as in fact disunionism, he wrote to a Maryland congressman a year later, "I distrust the *wisdom* if not the *sincerity* of friends, who would hold my hands while my enemies stab at me. This appeal of professed friends has paralyzed me more in this struggle than any other one thing."[65]

As part of what historian James M. McPherson has termed his "strong-arm strategy," Lincoln soon gave a long leash to federal commanders in the middle border states who demonstrated the inclination and capacity for aggressive military measures. In the war's first year, he often appointed politicians to rank and promoted officers, regardless of political affiliation, who assumed the most bellicose postures. Lyon, Frémont, Franz Sigel, David Hunter, James Henry Lane, and John Pope were the earliest, all in Missouri. Lincoln allowed them latitude to formulate what one historian has called "positively draconian" policies toward the civilian populations. Those who urged caution or conciliation—favoring a moderate policy toward middle border slave state civilians that would allow time for majority unionist populations to rise up, disavow the Confederacy, and bring their states back into the fold—soon found themselves "with [their] backs in a ditch," as a Lincoln associate described the president's former courtroom mastery of opposing counsel. Harney, Scott, George B. McClellan, Robert Anderson, and Don Carlos Buell, all proslavery and from middle border states, were among the first. Lincoln might have tolerated such moderation in the war's infancy, if only as a way to keep the Union war coalition in place, but he appears not to have lingered long on this stance in the middle border states.[66]

Whether or not specific directives on loyalty and disloyalty came directly from the president, pressure for nonconciliation in the border states came down from the war administration. Within two weeks of the rioting in St. Louis, the adjutant general, Lorenzo Thomas, wrote on the president's behalf to William S. Harney, ostensibly reminding the general to protect "loyal citizens" from alleged partisan outrages. "The professions of loyalty to the Union by the State authorities of Missouri are not to be relied upon," Thomas directed. "They... are too far committed to secession to be entitled to your confidence.... The authority of the United States is paramount, and whenever it is apparent that a movement *whether by color of State authority or not* is hostile you will not hesitate to put it down." Regardless of its governor's private secessionist intentions and actions, Missouri's elected state government had yet to demonstrate hostility to the federal government, and the state guard commander, Sterling Price, had chaired the state convention that rejected secession and advocated armed neutrality. Neither Lincoln nor any other administration official publicly questioned Lyon's preemptive military incursion, which exiled the elected state government and drove the state guard nearly from the state in 1861.[67]

Such handling of conciliating superior officers received support from hardline subordinate officers, who saw no room for a middle ground in the border slave states. Indeed, in Maryland former U.S. senator Nathaniel Banks agreed that those whose disloyalty was "prospective" needed to be suppressed. "The government," he averred to Secretary of State William H. Seward, "must make these men feel its power just as a matter of argument." In states whose governments had declared themselves qualifiedly loyal and among populations with hopelessly disarrayed political stances, conciliatory inclinations that might have begun to take root were quickly undone. "The citizen who has chosen the position of neutrality," decreed John McNeil, a Canadian-born, St. Louis Yankee forced to suppress partisans in southwestern Missouri, "and who claims or has claimed to have 'done nothing on nary side,' is not loyal." Federal commanders were authorized to treat all citizens as disloyal until they were proven otherwise, and officers who tried to act even-handedly soon found the heavy burden of consistent treatment among divided civilians. Over the 1862 New Year's season, Charles Whittlesey, a Connecticut native, West Pointer, and antislavery attorney and editor in Ohio's Western Reserve then in command in northern Kentucky, received a communication from a local officer asking how to treat known southern sympathizers who were "quiet and perfectly peaceable." Having served in Missouri, where he saw much overt disloyalty, Whittlesey responded immediately. Stay the hard hand, he instructed, only selectively. "Moderate Measures will probably restrain the Moderate Secessionists—The active and rabid ones need expect no mercy."[68]

Other federal commanders were less restrained in their treatment of civilians. Many acted capriciously and harshly, even shockingly so. The Kansas-Missouri border, long the site of violence, witnessed the earliest and most transparent military violations of civil rights. Kansas abolitionists James Montgomery and Charles R. Jennison were among the most zealous prosecutors of hard-line war, making clear their intentions to exact justice for decades of sins by proslavery residents. In early 1862 a unionist in Jackson County complained that Jennison's men had stolen horses, insulted and assaulted women, robbed families and even the local post office, and committed more extreme acts of terror, including burning homes and "put[ting] ropes around innocent mens necks threatening to hang them."[69]

James Henry Lane's once free state radicalism carried immediately to Missouri. The Republican U.S. senator from Kansas was no stranger to Lincoln, obtaining a brigadier general's commission directly from his friend the president at the urging of key northern abolitionists. Despite many complaints about Lane's extremism, Lincoln saw fit to remind his secretary of war that "we need the services of such a man out there at once" and doing so immediately "will get him into actual work quickest." Lane's work would go well beyond recruiting Kansas jayhawkers and, later, Redlegs. Boasting that he would "play hell with Missouri," he made proslavery civilians "feel the power of the government.... If they don't want slavery to perish, let them lay down their arms... When you march through a State, you must go march that traitors will feel the horrors of war." "If we are jayhawkers," he sneered, "we are jayhawking for the Government." Far from restraining his men, Lane instructed them to plunder and burn the homes of perceived disloyalists: "Take the Union man by the hand, but lay waste the property of traitors." Lane spared little time or effort discerning who was who. After a skirmish, on September 23, 1861, he bombarded Osceola, Missouri, a hilltop town overlooking the Osage River, and "the place was [then] burned to ashes." Among the residences destroyed was that of his colleague, Waldo P. Johnson, who would soon be expelled from the U.S. Senate for disloyalty. After a hastily convened hearing, Lane executed nine male residents, constituting half or more of the body count there.[70]

Kansas jayhawkers were not the only westerners to carry hard-line war into neighboring Missouri. Many eager Iowa and Illinois recruits, having witnessed a decade of misery along the Kansas-Missouri border, intended to stamp out disloyalty in the neighboring states. Threats of violence against Iowa unionists emanating from armed bands across the border with northern Missouri, as well as rumors of impending predations to "burn out 'every d____d abolitionist" living there, prompted one Missourian to claim that residents there shared "frightful stories as to what the soldiers would do if they came into the State [that] preceded them on their approach to a place." On the early morning of June 15, 1861, a detachment of the 2nd Iowa Volunteers, moving westward on a rail expedition ordered by Samuel R. Curtis to secure the Hannibal and St. Joseph line in northern Missouri, disembarked at Stewartsville, a sleepy rail town lying east of St. Joseph. At several prior points, Curtis had reported encountering those he called rebels, arresting some and firing upon "several who fled." Within minutes of arriving "at the front," as one participant referred to this area of northwestern Missouri, a member of the regiment shot to death an alleged disloyalist, nineteen-year-old Donald McDonald. Although later reports charged that the young man flew a secession flag, in his official report Curtis declared that the death was a "homicide." But for the fact that the killing occurred in a loyal state, the event was nearly the inverse of a northern Virginia secessionist's much-publicized shooting of Illinoisan Elmer Ellsworth, a federal officer and a former law student of the president's, only two months earlier. Lingering charges of murder associated with the young Missourian's death appeared to have little troubled the detachment's commander, Lt. Col. James M. Tuttle. "[P]erhaps I am responsible," he defiantly responded when confronted publicly with the incident years later. "If so, I have nothing to take back. Our business down there was to put down the rebel colors and of course we commenced as soon as we saw where the work commenced.... His flag came down and so did he."[71]

Some of the harsh treatment of civilians by military personnel occurred spontaneously. At precisely the moment when calls for strong action were loudest, untrained military personnel lacked the capacity for restraint. But they drew legitimacy from deeper ideological and political wellsprings. Emerging federal policy in the border slave states thus centered on the identification of loyal and disloyal constituencies within broader populations. The presence of sizable populations of neutralists, secessionists, and conditional unionists made it difficult, perhaps impossible, to discern one from the other. Cultural prejudices aside, military personnel took their cue from the president's conflation of overt secessionists and neutralists as disloyalists. For practical purposes, they consolidated the spectrum of ideological stances into a binary amid the chaos of war. "The military look upon the contest as one between the whole people of the South and the people of the North," Montgomery Blair cautioned the president. William T. Sherman, an Ohio brigadier general who by 1862 was Grant's most trusted subordinate, quickly adopted such a dialectical view of loyalty. "When one nation is at war with another, all the people of the one are enemies of the other," he wrote to the secretary of the treasury, Ohioan Salmon P. Chase. "Most unfortunately, the war in which we are now engaged has been complicated with the belief on the one hand that all on the other are *not* enemies."⁷²

Federal authorities' consolidation of disloyalty distinctions quickly led to suppressive measures against perceived disloyalists—"overwhelming physical force," as George B. McClellan advised Lincoln after leaving his middle border command (see figure 4.2). In July 1861 northern Illinoisan Stephen Hurlbut, a staunch Republican though born and raised in South Carolina, prosecuted in northern Missouri the type of warfare that Lane and others had initiated in the western part of the state. When Hurlbut's men learned that John McAfee, the speaker of the state's house of representatives, was at his home in Shelby County, he "was arrested and required by General Hurlbut to dig trenches in the hot sun...all day," a unionist remarked. "Hurlbut himself told me he set him at it...still it was admitted that it was very doubtful if any charge could be maintained against him.... I fear he will be able to do us much more hurt than heretofore.... Such outrages will make more enemies than thousands of men can quell." He claimed Hurlbut ordered McAfee strapped to the top of a locomotive, but his men refused to comply. Within two months of his release McAfee joined the rump legislature in Neosho, presiding over the secession ordinance. After Hurlbut empowered local home guards in northern Missouri to determine loyalty and disloyalty by "dispers[ing] and break[ing] up by force any and all gatherings and assembly which may be held by persons hostile to the United States," John Edwards, lieutenant colonel of an Iowa home guard regiment, immediately disarmed all Missouri home guards and replaced them with his own. "[L]oyal men of both States, separated merely by an imaginary line, have the same sympathies in a common cause," he assumed, in contrast to "the neutrals and a great many terror-stricken secessionists." Occupying troops gave support to entreaties of local unionists about their neighbors' disloyalty. Fellow northern Illinoisan John Pope refused to accept locals' professions of ignorance of the identities of saboteurs of a key railroad bridge in northern Missouri. "If people who claim to be good citizens choose to indulge their neighbors and acquaintances in committing these wanton acts, and to shield them from punishment," he snapped, "they will hereafter be compelled to pay for it." Pope judged them disloyal until they proved themselves otherwise. Residents who could not offer "conclusive proof" that they had actively resisted saboteurs or informed federal authorities of their identities would be levied for damages, and local officers would label residents based on their loyalty, assisting in the creation of "committee[s] of public safety" as civilian arms of the military.⁷³

Not surprisingly, antislavery hard-liners like these were quickest to judge loyalty and disloyalty along a slaveholding axis. In the western states, politicians (especially Republicans), federal officers, and soldiers who first entered

Figure 4.2 Militia on parade, ca. 1861–1862. These home guard troops, believed to be part of Col. William Bishop's "Blackhawk" battalion, were raised in northern Missouri during the first summer of the war as one of the many, varied organizations that sought to control local civilian populations. Courtesy State Historical Society of Missouri.

neighboring slave states did not easily divest themselves of long-held ideological predilections gained from years of struggle and even violent confrontations with slave state citizens over slavery. Few saw need to conciliate proslavery residents, much less slave owners. As James Russell Lowell argued in 1861, "There can be no such thing as a moderate slaveholder,... moderation and slavery can[not] coexist." The provost marshal at Palmyra, Missouri, Ephram J. Wilson, was just as blunt. "[A]ny man [who] would hold a slave with very few exceptions is neither a Christian, a patriot or a loyal citizen," he wrote, a charge echoed by a Missouri militiaman who fumed that "[t]he Americans who are slaveholders are the enemies of the government." Prejudice among many free state federals derived from culturally absolutist views of inferior populations of slaveholding states that easily led to conclusions of widespread disloyalty. "[T]here being so many of that class of people in Missouri," stated Edward Daniels, colonel of the 1st Wisconsin Cavalry garrisoning Cape Girardeau, as he lectured a crowd of residents that "the demagogues and secession leaders befooled them.... [I]ndeed the great reason of the whole rebellion is, *IGNORANCE*.... The Col. told them this in plain words, and extorted [*sic*] them to *educate their children*." Federal soldiers from the northern portions of the West labeled these border slave state residents as more than "secesh." In Missouri, they were "pukes."[74]

Many free state soldiers evinced distrust, even disdain, for the mass of residents, owing to their antipathy for a slaveholding society. Williamson D. Ward wrote to his family about a farmer outside Louisville, who he and his comrades "believe[d was]...a Secessionist [although] he said he was union. He owned several Slaves and a farm of 600 acres I asked him if that was not too much for one man to have he said no I told him if a man in Indiana had a farm of 160 acres he had all he wanted to take care of." Norman G. Markham, who served in the 18th Michigan, was surprised to find when his regiment entered Lexington, Kentucky, that residents "had flags strung across the street and they cheered us and hurrahed for the Yankees.... [S]o you see there is some good union folks in Kentucky." But he found it difficult to separate his conceptions about the slaveholding society he saw from those about the South he had expected to find. "This is the only place we have been in since we came into Kentucky where the folks act as if they were glad to see us," he grumbled. "The farmers are very wealthy. They own large plantations and lots of niggers. They have the finest buildings that I ever saw, have nice horses and carriages and nigger drivers.... I think when this war ends these big plantations will be cut up some."[75]

Lincoln's open unilateralism influenced such perceptions that the presence of or support for slavery was the singular barometer of the disloyal South. In a hard-line war, many free state soldiers drew a hard line on political geography: the border slave states were part of the Confederacy, and their white residents by extension were southerners and thus disloyal. More than one in the first months of the war boasted to the folks at home that after arriving with their regiments in Louisville, "We have at last got into 'Dixie's Land.'" Just a few miles into Kentucky an Indiana soldier wrote to his hometown newspaper late in 1861 that "[t]he people and the country are about twenty years behind the times: they appear to think and talk of nothing but negroes and tobacco. This is their comfort by day and their song in the night; their hope, their salvation, their all.... They claim to be good Union men, but press them a little and they very soon let you know that they are Southern-rights men; in plain terms, they are rebels, the last one of them." Charles C. Williams put on record the intentions of his Illinois regiment when they crossed into southeastern Missouri. "[We] come to teach braggarts and bullies who have mistaken barbarism for courage, and the quiet order of civilization for cowardice," the second lieutenant published in a regimental newspaper in Fredrickstown, "that as much as they love peace they love *their* country more."[76]

Further challenging federal commanders who sought conciliatory administrative policies was the rapid proliferation of armed irregulars, guerrillas, bushwhackers, and partisans during the summer of 1861 in Missouri and southeastern Kentucky. The ability to identify and suppress them quickly hardened or evaporated would-be conciliation. Henry W. Halleck, a published expert on international and military law, showed in Missouri little of his reputation for overanalysis and restraint. Initially opposed to Lane's and Jennison's "outrageous abuse[s] of power and violation[s] of the laws of war," his concern for such behavior lasted only a week. In early December, vowing that "[t]he mild and indulgent course heretofore pursued...[had] utterly failed to restrain...unlawful conduct," he prescribed capital punishment for those who assisted or joined insurgents "[who] threaten and drive out loyal citizens and rob them of their property." Rather than shrink from his predecessors' respectively less hard lines, Halleck asked permission to be tougher on the state's civilian population, which the president himself went on record as supporting, albeit with the notable exception of emancipating slaves. "We cannot at the same time extend to rebels the rights of peace and enforce against them the penalties of war," Halleck declared. "They have forfeited their civil rights as citizens by making war against the Government, and upon their own heads must fall the consequences.... Peace and war cannot exist together." Having been stationed only a month in Missouri, Halleck announced, "The time for conciliation, I am sorry to say, has passed. Nothing but the military power can now put down the rebellion and save Union men in this State. It is useless now to try any other remedy." A few months later a southern Kentucky unionist wrote to the district commander that "the Rosewater policy will not do here.... Loyal men have almost despaired and are ready to sacrifice their property and leave." Indeed, the assistant secretary of war, Peter H. Watson, temporarily heading this vital department, advised another commander there, "If guerrillas were shot without challenge as enemies of mankind their bands would soon disperse, and the...barbarities practiced in irregular warfare would soon [end]."[77]

Pressure for hard-line war similarly emanated from below. Burdened by their inability to discern with certainty the allegiances of the mass of civilians, and battling enemies visible and invisible, military personnel were influenced by unconditional unionists, who encouraged local federal commanders to reject conciliatory treatment of all but the avowedly loyal. "Among our citizens there are all shades of opinion," observed William Greenleaf Eliot, the noted St. Louis Unitarian minister and New England–born unconditional unionist, "from what is called neutrality, which is little better than treason, through all the grades of lukewarmness, half-way measures, and hesitating zeal up to the unqualified loyalty." A moderate Kentuckian feared that with so many "shades of opinion... how readily we might run into anarchy." "Draw a line, and divide the Sheep from the Goats," a St. Louis marble merchant wrote to Halleck in February 1862. "No measures can be too harsh and no punishment too severe on the thousands in our midst that would welcome the armies of the rebels to our City.... [C]an no measures be adapted to protect, *and patronise* all true Union loving men, and prevent the fostering of our enemies in our midst?" To these hard-liners, the president was too charitable. "[Lincoln] is emphatically, not a war man, he is for peace and easy blows," wrote Franklin A. Dick in October 1861, "always watching the lines of the Constitution, and looking for rays of peace and good intentions amongst a set of determined Rebels, and he does not act as if he knew the only safety was in subduing them."[78]

Subordinate officers within the western armies often had no truck with conciliation. A St. Louis officer in command of a federal regiment in western Missouri recommended executing the sole two civilians in his district who refused to take the oath. "I think if I have them shot and make an example," he wrote Halleck in December 1861, "I can have peace and the parties who take the oath will regard it in future." Although Halleck appears to have demurred, other commanders sympathized. "I always acted on the supposition that we were an invading army; that our purpose was to move forward in force," recalled William T. Sherman, who, fresh from the chaos he had witnessed in Missouri, offered an impassioned call for hard-lining the war to the secretary of war, Simon Cameron, in the autumn of 1861. "The rebellion could never be put down, the authority of the paramount Government asserted," he railed, "and the union of the States declared perpetual, by force of arms, by maintaining the defensive... [I]t was absolutely necessary the Government should adopt, and maintain until the rebellion was crushed, the offensive." To drive the rebels from Kentucky alone would require two hundred thousand men, an estimate the secretary found preposterous. In the spring of 1862 in western Tennessee, Sherman asserted his views of conciliation to a Memphis newspaper editor who complained about the federal armies' depredations on civilian property there. "This [waste]... is an expense not chargeable to us, but to those who made the war; and generally war is destruction and nothing else."[79]

Beyond simple foraging, which all residents complained about regardless of the troops' political inclinations, targeting of southern sympathizers' homes and farms occurred throughout these states and even in the free states. "I think it perfectly right to take the hog and leave them none," wrote one Illinois soldier stationed in southwestern Missouri in October 1861, "and then if they ain't Satisfied I am fore banish[ing] ever Rebel and rebel simpathiser from the U.S." A Kentuckian complained bitterly of the hard treatment residents suffered when federals occupied their county. "I find those of our neighbour[s] who did not treat them *decently* fared very badly—ruining their places in many respects.... *fiddlestick we* could not help ourselves we only gave them what they *asked* and they would have taken it any how—as they did *others*." Similarly, in the spring of 1861 soldiers from the 11th Illinois Volunteers, stationed at Cairo, Illinois, "engaged in lawlessly killing animals belonging to citizens," meaning Illinoisans suspected of being southern sympathizers. (This lack of restraint would result in the largest portion of the regiment being mustered out in July before ever leaving their home state.) A Jackson County, Missouri, resident calculated his losses from six raids on his farm between January 1861 and August 1863 at just over $4,100, 84 percent of which occurred on one raid, when federal troops destroyed his house, barn, carriage, wagon, kitchen, and smokehouse. Frustrated, Henry W. Halleck complained that many Kansas troops and their officers stationed in Missouri "are no better than a band of robbers; they cross the line, rob, steal, plunder, and burn whatever they can lay their hands upon. They disgrace the name and uniform of American soldiers."[80]

Once the largest portion of the armies had left for the South, garrisoning troops readily showed their disdain for secesh—"mostly the lower Class of people," as one Ohioan newly arrived in Louisville wrote. This often ran beyond benign antagonism to outright violence, despite the laws of war. Confederate soldiers found at home often were given summary punishment. In the fall of 1862 Paulina Stratton, the unionist wife of a small slaveholder in Missouri's Boon's Lick, was shocked to learn that local militia had executed two brothers, both Confederate soldiers home on leave. "John Rice was taken out and Shot the night of 7 of Oct," she wrote reprovingly a few days afterward. "His brother Jim was taken from his bed and Shot in August. Oh that such things could be stoped." The previous fall, an embarrassed southern Illinois soldier had confirmed such behavior in a letter to his wife. "Our army is doing some very disrespectful and disgraceful things. A perfect reign of terror, starvation and hatred we leave behind us as we go.... Annihilation and destruction seems to be their motto.... We never can be successful in this mode of warfare."[81]

The willingness to employ hard-line tactics emanated not from belief in conciliation for proslavery unionists but rather belief in the punishment of those who opposed the union under the guise of neutrality. When Don Carlos Buell issued what amounted to a conciliation order for his command in late February 1862, at least one officer howled in protest. "The poison of rebellion has penetrated deeply into the systems of our Southern people," railed longtime Cincinnatian Ormsby M. Mitchel, a well-known abolitionist and radical Republican. Conciliatory behavior in a slaveholding state was a "blunder... [that] needs some powerful antidote." Rather than "leave the grass to grow under our feet," Mitchel carried hard-line war to Kentucky residents, regardless of their political stance. "I adopted a very simple policy at the outset," he stated firmly. "I determined to make every individual feel that there was a terrible pressure of war upon him, which would finally destroy him and grind him to powder, if he did not give up his rebellion.... [N]egroes are our only friends." When Buell faced a military commission over charges of ineffective leadership of his department, he was accused of disloyalty for not having implemented adequately hard-line policies toward civilians in Kentucky and Tennessee. Submitting its report to the war department the following April, the "Buell Commission" concluded that Buell had "violate[d] no orders because there were none... [for] what is familiarly known as the conciliatory policy... at that time understood to be the policy of the Government." In August 1862 Grenville M. Dodge suggested burning out Kentucky's entire Purchase area because local residents "paid no attention to the oath" and "feed and guide the rebels."[82]

Even moderates found themselves conflicted over how to view and handle the divided populations in the border slave states. An Ohio major captured the ease with which soldiers countenanced hard-line war already in 1861. "As I go through this traitor country," wrote Cincinnatian and Massachusetts native Edward F. Noyes from western Missouri, "two impulses are struggling in my heart, one to lay waste as we go—like destroying angels, to kill and burn and make the way of the transgressors hard—the other is to wage a civilized warfare.... [O]ur boys only wait for the word, to make the land desolate." By December 1862 a militia officer in western Missouri sought assistance from the federal commander, Samuel R. Curtis, on the contours of loyalty so as to stay the hard hand if possible. "I write to you for information in regard to what it takes to constitute a loyal citizen.... We want to deal with all our citizens, in strict accordance with your orders, and not knowing how you define a loyal citizen, touching those of our citizens who at one time did sympathise with the rebelion; but who now claim to be loyal, and are quiet and peaceable and law abiding men." Other soldiers were far less willing to show restraint. "The people here are bad *Secesh* people," wrote one southern Illinois lieutenant from southeastern Missouri in the spring of 1862, "and have be whipped like bad children to make them good." An Ohio private, having marched from Kansas City to Springfield, Missouri, soon after the battle at Wilson's Creek, then back to Sedalia for garrison duty, boasted: "Missouri may well repent the day she ever went out of the Union. she is ruined. there isn't enough corn hay, apples, oats, or anything else left to winter a grass hopper and rails are all burnt, perfect desolation reigns all over southern Missouri." A federal sergeant from St. Louis, exasperated already at what he had seen while stationed in the southern portion of his home state, put the matter grimly to his fiancée: "Nothing that I can see now short of extermination will save Mo."[83]

Strange conciliation, this, in nonseceded states whose residents were still overwhelmingly loyal. What rings most clearly in these federals' respective words is the limited value of conciliation as a policy descriptor, beginning with the commander in chief's rejection of neutrality and neutralism. Ironically, only as the western department's troops prepared to march or steam from Missouri into the seceded states of Arkansas and Tennessee did Halleck stress the importance of conciliation. Civilians in those states who had not aided the rebellion, women and children especially, as well as "merchants, farmers, mechanics, and all persons not in arms... are regarded as non-combatants, and are not to be molested either in their persons or property," he ordered. "They have been told that we come to oppress and to plunder.... We will prove to them that we come to restore, not to violate, the Constitution and laws." Yet the flagrant and widespread "violation of private rights" of border state residents caused Missouri's exasperated provisional governor, Hamilton R. Gamble, to complain to the president. "[I]t is seldom in modern times that such abuses have the express sanction of officers high in command."[84]

Federal commanders recognized that their early advocacy of hard-line war in the border states was reaping the whirlwind. Harsh actions by occupying bluecoats, Henry W. Halleck warned, "are driving good Union men into the ranks of the secession army. Their conduct within the last six months has caused a change of 20,000 votes in this State.... The bitter animosity created against these troops is naturally transferred to the Government which supports them and in whose name they pretend to act." He feared that such conduct would soon make the border states "as Confederate at Eastern Virginia." Only weeks later, John M. Schofield fumed of indiscriminate outrages by federal volunteers near Warrenton that "their conduct has been absolutely barbarous—[a] burning disgrace to the army and to the Union cause.... In spite of all my efforts to the contrary they have plundered and destroyed the property of citizens (many of them the best Union men in the State) to the amount of many thousands of dollars.... If something is not done soon there will be very few Union men in this part of the State." Halleck soon cautioned the general in chief that should this conduct continue, the government "may resign all hopes of a pacification of Missouri." By December 1861 Franklin A. Dick wrote from St. Louis that "late reports represent the whole interior of the State as under the dominion of the Rebels; and I know that there are many Union men amongst them.... [T]he real question will soon be one of boundaries.... if [the war] goes on and on the spirit on our side must become as it is on the Other, Wolfish."[85]

On the other side in this cauldron of divided loyalties, with federal troops leveraging local communities in favor of unionists, the boundaries of southern sympathy soon boiled over as a new class of dissenters—political southerners— emerged, especially from the ranks of small and nonslaveholders (see figure 4.3). Among them was Missourian Peter Collins, a thirty-seven-year-old, Ohio-born farmer living in Buchanan County. Questioned by garrison troops in late February 1862, Collins claimed that he was "openly opposed to the United States and that he was a proud Southern man. He offered his horse to anyone that would take up arms against the United States but could not go himself because of convenience. He would, however, if forced, go into the field with his gun and die as a Southern man rather than live as a Northern man."[86]

Unlike among southerners of culture, slave ownership was less resonant with political southerners than opposition to federal war-making against proslavery

Figure 4.3 "Political southerners," ca. 1863. The Jacob Moulder family of Warren County, Kentucky, were among those who converted the war's realities into new considerations of the meaning of being southern. The image notes "that the family is war weary and the ladies are dressed in home spun and the discharged men are wearing the pants of their Civil War uniforms. They were in the police [home] guard." Courtesy Department of Special Collections, Western Kentucky University.

residents. Despite disagreements "over the old grinds, 'nigers' 'Southern rights,' etc.," the fact that "the North is something they didn't understand" allowed slavery to figure into their response. Armed federals used support for the peculiar institution against neutralists and even unionists, only deepening a growing alienation from these soldiers' government. The driving engine of this new political identity was grievance, personal or collective, against the federal troops, conjured easily by accessing the sense of victimization built during the decade-long struggle over slavery. In combination, many residents began to see themselves, their neighbors, and the blue-coated soldiers around them—especially from other states—as antagonistic peoples, northern and southern.[87]

Under such circumstances, political southernization could be rapid. A Kentucky unionist remarked of the transition in his community, "This secession is a disease—a disease, Sir. It can be caught in a night. I have seen people go to bed as good Unionists as there are in the country and wake up in the morning Secessionists." What he termed secessionism was in fact an emergent, clandestine culture of dissent among white border residents. With soldiers and unionists openly targeting known Confederate sympathizers, opposition to the federal war effort was forced underground, replaced by a generic and ultimately safer southern identification not so easily judged as being disloyal. Political southernness allowed dissent without treason, identifying oneself as a citizen, beset by an aggressive antislavery host, who peacefully defended the nation's republican tradition of slaveholders' rights *within* the nation. Important to conditional unionists, affecting the badge of southerner often meant opposition to excessive force by federal troops, a position that spread quickly enough that a railroad superintendent claimed in August 1861, "There are far less Union men than two months since." Like Peter Collins, many *"for the South"* had no direct cultural connection with the Confederate states and even, as a Kentucky unionist minister whose kin were all in the seceded states wrote, "know very little of the South or her institutions." *"Politics,"* he complained of the southernized congregants who sought to remove him in the early summer of 1862, "they falsely call Patriotism and Treason and their conflict."[88]

As a retributive counterweight to the federal presence, political southerners conflated unionists and blue-coated soldiers as Yankees by association, meaning New England abolitionists, a label they knew many free state westerners loathed. Although an Illinois federal referred to his army's "Northern regiments" specifically as antislavery troops "from Wisconsin, Kansas, Minnesota, and Iowa," such hairsplitting did not dissuade one such Kentuckian. "I knew those North Western people would rather you should call them devils than Yankees," clucked Lizzie Hardin. Alongside southerners of culture, "the old Kentucky families who came out of Virginia," as one woman claimed, political southerners "reproached the Unionists with being Yankees and those allied to the Yankees." The politicized nature of exclusivist identities on both sides was obvious to Cora Owens, who observed of her Louisville school, "Two girls are down from St. Louis and any stranger might judge them to be Southern, but both are Northern in politics, and one is a yankee."[89]

Ethnic and class prejudices ignited the politicized cant of southernness. The sudden presence of uniformed immigrants within their communities—"aliens Dutch, under the garb of soldiers... [yet] whose patriotism has been aroused by the promise of 15 dollars per month"—deepened residents' resentment of the national government's prosecution of the war. A full third of Henry W. Halleck's trans-Mississippi army was foreign-born, and six of Ohio's earliest regiments were nearly entirely German and and Irish, along with two of Indiana's, four of Illinois's, and the first five of Missouri's. To prove their patriotism and often to settle scores, many ethnic soldiers targeted proslavery civilians despite commanders' orders. In search of arms, a squad of the 24th Illinois, nearly entirely Chicago Germans and commanded by a hard-liner and abolitionist Forty-eighter, threatened the family of a prominent slaveholding farmer and merchant in southeast Missouri. As this resident concluded angrily, the German soldiers were little more than "unprincipaled cowards, who find a 'Secesh' wherever they find property unprotected." Such treatment easily transcended ethnocentric and racial prejudices to exclusivist antipathy. "Germans had no business to bear arms and become soldiers," one Kentuckian grumbled, "because they value the country so little just like the Negro." Another concluded, "I used to think any white man was better than a negro, but I had rather sleep or eat with a negro than a dutchman."[90]

With hard-line war driving the new politics of loyalty, the risks attendant on political southernness often accelerated conversion to full Confederate. When Kentuckian Thomas Parsons's unionist home guard captured an armed secessionist party near Mount Sterling, they interrogated local residents. Parsons asked one, "What is your politics Mr. Ross?" to which the man replied, "Well now these are mighty squally time, but I am never afraid or ashamed to tell my politics.... I am a Southern man." When the man asked theirs, they replied they were southern as well. This "rebel ruse" encouraged the man to speak freely of his knowledge of the secessionist militia they sought. "'That is what all of us southern men think,' said someone," after which Parsons revealed that his squad was unionist and arrested the man. Rather than a traitorous act, joining the Confederacy was often an act of defiance against such behavior or against its perceived political foundations. "[A] rebel I admit he is," Martha M. Jones explained to her unionist father of her husband's painful decision to enlist in the rebel ranks in the spring of 1862, "from the whole abolition faction and dominion." Nearly simultaneously, after months of conflicted "Southern" feelings and federal troops being in firm control of his Kentucky home, Thomas W. Bullitt and his brothers made their decision to fight for the Confederacy. The Bullitt family's house, much like the president's, was deeply divided. Reading law in Philadelphia, another border city with a middle temperament whose most prominent families were of Virginia origins and to varying degrees in sympathy with the South, they watched helplessly after Fort Sumter as angry unionists sacked their Chestnut Street businesses; burned horse-drawn carts loaded with bales of cotton; and then turned on suspected disloyalists, attacking and savagely beating at least two men and threatening several prominent Democratic military leaders at their homes, demanding pledges of allegiance. The following spring, traveling to Kentucky in disguise and at night to his home, Oxmoor, before striking out for Tennessee, Tom avowed his "Southern birth, and southern acquaintance... The South is my home." A few months later, after the federal military had exiled him to Canada, where "the People for the most part are a set of unmitigated Abolitionists; Negro equality is the idea," dissenting Kentucky Presbyterian minister Thomas A. Hoyt declared, "There is little left within [me] but the South."[91]

§

In the fall of 1861, as turning leaves bathed the Ohio River bluffs in golden splendor, John A. Roebling paused. He was not a man given to inaction. This German immigrant had come to the American West in 1831 after imbibing the democratic beliefs of his former philosophy professor, Georg W. Hegel, while a

Figure 4.4 John A. Roebling's "Ohio River Bridge," 1862. The war interrupted construction of the nation's longest suspension bridge, from Cincinnati, Ohio, to Covington, Kentucky, leaving only the pier foundations completed until 1865. A military pontoon bridge crossed the Ohio near the unfinished piers. From *Harper's Weekly*, September 27, 1862. Courtesy Cincinnati Museum Center.

student and after reading Gottfried Duden's sunny promotions of Missouri. Restless and intellectual, Roebling, a naturalized citizen, inventor, utopian community organizer, and published author, was a noted suspension bridge builder whose magnificent expanses—over the Ohio River at Wheeling and the Niagara River near its mighty falls—positioned him for greatness.

But his great project stood incomplete—the longest single-span suspension bridge in the world, a full 1,057 feet above the Ohio River between Cincinnati and Covington—stalled nearly since its inception by forces larger even than his boundless drive and ambition. First, jealous Ohio business interests had failed him. Steamboat operators had lobbied strongly enough for the respective city councils to agree that the toll bridge would not line up with existing streets despite the two cities' mirror grids. Then, the Ohio legislature had long withheld funds, fearing that the bridge would encourage slave escapes from Kentucky and thus depress white property values in Cincinnati. (The irony was inescapable. The idea for the bridge came from Lexington businessmen in 1839 to compete with Louisville.) The frigid winter of 1856–1857 interrupted construction, and then the ensuing financial panic froze funds and nearly bankrupted the bridge company. In the spring of 1861, construction ceased.

Roebling's "Ohio River Bridge," as he would always call it, stood unfinished because of a war between a North and South that he sought with steel cables over western rivers to unify (see figure 4.4). The massive piers for two sandstone and limestone towers offered a visible symbol not only of the divided nation but also of neutrality's failed attempt to bridge its most recently built political border. Until 1866 the only bridges thrown over the Ohio below Roebling's Wheeling bridge lay on army pontoons, over which federal soldiers would tramp relentlessly southward.[92]

The Gates of Zion

Perhaps no group better reflected the West's uncomfortable diversity than the Shakers, a sect of charismatic Christians who counted thousands of members from New England to the Ohio River valley during the mid-nineteenth century. And perhaps no people suffered the middle border's uncivil war more than the Shakers of Kentucky.

The utopian faith, originated in England in the eighteenth century, was formally known as the United Believers in the Second Appearing of Christ. Brothers and sisters referred to themselves as Believers, but neighbors called the curious group "Shaking Quakers" after their ecstatic worship services, which included nighttime public group dancing and singing. Their tenets included communal property, strict celibacy and taking in orphans, and racial and gender equality. Shaker families soon established communities in New York and other northern states, and by the early 1800s they had established staid western enclaves that stretched southwestward from Ohio's Western Reserve into southern Ohio and Indiana and into central and southern Kentucky. There were two main Shaker communities in Kentucky: South Union, with 223 inhabitants, located on the Logan County prairie where the state's southwestern tier gave way to the Mississippi's floodplain, and Pleasant Hill, a village of 347 people in the Bluegrass's Mercer County on a meadowed plateau above the looping Kentucky River's steep palisades.[1]

Initially their new western neighbors found the Shakers threatening and occasionally resorted to arson to scare them off. The Shakers largely overcame reproach and hostility by their industry, quietly going about their business, putting their hands to work while pledging their hearts to God. Their gardens, orchards, and fields, surrounded by neat limestone fences, were pictures of order in the western landscape. By the 1850s a modus vivendi had developed between the western Shakers and their "worldly" neighbors.[2]

This tolerance partially resulted from their strict eschewing of politics, including voting. Keenly aware of the political issues of the day—many avidly read non-Believers' newspapers—Shakers recognized their vulnerability and, unlike the region's Quakers, hid their antislavery predilections. They respected their neighbors' right to own slaves, in part because slavery supported their profitable seed business in those states, and hired bondmen for seasonal work in their ample fields while quietly purchasing the freedom of slaves of new members. By mid-century their worldly neighbors recognized that among the Shakers' simple gifts was moderation in all things.[3]

The Shakers understood from the beginning what the war was really about. "The whole country is at present greatly agitated from one end to the other, on the question of negro slavery," wrote a Pleasant Hill deaconess in her journal. "Under the plea of their cherished institution of slavery being endangered, [the South] thereby, revolted." She and her brothers and sisters wisely refrained from sharing their beliefs, especially with fellow Kentuckians, but as unionists practiced an un-neutral neutrality.[4]

All was thrown into crisis by the arrival of war in their midst. Moderation was as difficult to balance as worldliness, especially in Kentucky. The unionist Shakers strictly observed days of prayer, Thanksgiving, and fasting, whether proclaimed by the president or the governor. Like Amish, Quakers, and Mennonites, they were "conscientious objectors" to war, and quietly forbade their men to enlist on either side. "My kingdom is not of this world," wrote a Pleasant Hill eldress, "therefore my servants do not fight." (This approach was not entirely successful; an estimated 60 percent of Indiana's Quakers would ultimately serve.) When several Shaker brothers slipped off to join mostly the federal army, elders hastened to nearby camps to retrieve them.[5]

Because both Pleasant Hill and South Union were prominent and well-known locations on well-traveled Kentucky thoroughfares, the war quickly forced itself into their business endeavors and their community streets. "Shakertown," as neighbors called both communities, was used for mustering both Union and secessionist home guards. While Pleasant Hill's Shakers were merely the targets of recruitment efforts, South Union fully suffered "the ravages of War," as an eldress wrote in her family's journal. Secessionists especially harassed the Believers for their pacifism, and when the Confederates occupied Bowling Green, Kentucky, in 1861, the nearby Shakers quickly became targets for rebel strong-arming.[6]

Cavalry under Nathan Bedford Forrest, who "very civilly" paid for corn and oats after the Shakers fed their men well, did not fully prepare them for the full cost of the occupation, which they would endure for nearly half a year. Horses and wagons soon disappeared, pointed out by local secessionists who knew the lay of their six-thousand-acre property. Thousands of troops camped on the Shakers' grounds, demanding grain, flour, beef, and milk. Outlaws dressed as Confederates frequently rode through the area, demanding horses, goods, and money and threatening "to burn every building on the place." The Believers employed survival tactics by day and prayer by night. Though blessed with a good harvest, they soon found their stores depleted.

The Shakers did what they could to protect transportable property. Under the cover of night, they dismantled their remaining wagons and hid the parts deep in woods and sinkholes, far from outbuildings and the main road. When search parties came for horses, they rode only old and lame ones, hiding their best until they could move them to safety. As quickly as they could that fall, they secreted a few hundred of them in southern Indiana and northern Illinois for the duration of the war, at a cost of some $24 a month.

In December 1861 Confederate recruiters blanketed the region, fueling rumors of an imminent draft by the rebel government to force young Kentucky men "to take up arms against the Government of the United States." Like many unionists in the area, several South Union brothers fled northward, assisted by other Shaker communities, who sent money, horses, and even guides through Confederate lines to safety.[7]

In late February 1862, during the final days before the rebels withdrew southward, South Union's Shakers saw and smelled the smoke from the burning of Bowling Green and felt the earth shake from the cannons at Fort Donelson, some eighty miles away in Tennessee. Before the rebels left, they occupied several of the Shakers' buildings as hospitals for sick soldiers, many feverish with measles, and Kentucky's provisional Confederate government forced the Shakers to pay a levy to support its soldiers, either $20 or one gun per person. Confederates encamped in the west lot, burned one of their buildings and hundreds of their fences, and traded rations for baked bread. Confederate general William J. Hardee's order that forbade confiscating "more forage nor any thing of the kind... from our people for the use of the army" licensed soldiers to refuse to pay for coats and other goods they demanded of their Shaker hosts. His use of "from our people" denoted only those loyal to the Confederacy and excluded unionists, who they believed were not true southerners. As the Confederates retreated, setting fire to surrounding depots and mills, the Shakers kept an all-night vigil after rebel "marauders" threatened their village. "They say they are determined, the Federals shall have no mills to make flour, and Shaker town shall go too," one eldress wrote fearfully. The war hardened secessionists' once genial feelings toward their utopian neighbors. No longer were they "religious, orderly people," as one described them, but "Lincolnites" and "abolitionists." One cursed the pacifist Shakers as cowards, taunting that federal soldiers had "to fight their battles."[8]

When the Confederates left South Union in February 1862 and a squad of federal cavalry arrived a few days later, the Shakers welcomed them as liberators. But they found themselves again hosting a military force on their property, with vital buildings commandeered for convalescent troops and their railroad depot for government transportation. The federal soldiers burned their bridges and culverts to prevent a Confederate counter-advance. Over the spring and summer, troops passed daily through their property on both the state road and the nearby railroad, calling at all hours for bread, well water, vegetables, and wood. Meanwhile, the South Union Shakers were forced to apply for passes when they traveled to conduct business.[9]

Pleasant Hill's Shakers, too, would soon learn the steep price of Union allegiance. Other than the "hard times" that slowed business, and omens their millenarian neighbors used to commence the region's newest series of revivals, the war seemed far away, unlike at South Union. A hot summer soon turned into the worst drought in memory, plaguing the entire middle border. For more than two months no measurable rain fell. Daily temperatures rose into the mid-nineties, as the ground cracked and springs, ponds, and creeks slowed or dried up. Songbirds departed, and mature trees dropped their leaves or died altogether before turning color, while crops withered under the blazing sun. The heat continued well into October.

Visits and letters received from South Union brethren informed those in Pleasant Hill of their hardships under the Confederate occupation, warning of the destructive nature of this "uncivil war." "I never would wish to see or here of such a large collection of land pirates nowhere on earth any more," wrote elder James Ballance. "[W]here ever they set their unhallowed feet, famine and distruction followed, they stol'd burt and poisen'd evry thing they could get their unhallowed hands on." A fracas between two near neighbors at Pleasant Hill's post office, where worldly neighbors received their mail, which resulted in drawn pistols and someone being wounded, confirmed that the seemingly distant war could at any moment come uncomfortably near.[10]

Pleasant Hill's Believers soon saw the real war up-close, with a full-scale Confederate invasion of Kentucky. In September 1862 the mails stopped, and the Shakers heard of fighting at Richmond, Cynthiana, and Munfordville. Confederate armies under Braxton Bragg and Edmund Kirby Smith had entered eastern and central Kentucky, trailed by a larger federal army under Ohioan Don Carlos Buell, converging on the central Bluegrass. Tense glimpses of John Hunt Morgan's Confederate cavalry, which drove out federal garrisons in nearby towns and passed through on the way to and from Lexington, now full of rebels, suggested South Union's former agony would soon become Pleasant Hill's. These Shakers soon secreted their horses, livestock, and "valuables, such as cloth, flour, preserves" in the wooded valleys and shallow caves on their six-thousand-acre farm. On the last day of the month, the Believers "learn[ed] that 15,000 Confederate troops are now at Harrodsburg. War with all its horrors seems to be approaching quite too near to our sacred borders!" At gunpoint, Confederates impressed what horses, cattle, and wagons they could find, "travers[ing] the fields and pastures in search of them" and paying in "worthless hash," meaning Confederate scrip. Nearly daily, Confederate horsemen, some of them former neighbors, passed through the main street demanding food, water, and horses. "This is Southern rights, liberty and freedom from oppression and bondage is it?" sneered an elder. "Well that is enough of such deliverance!"

On October 6, 1862, a Confederate infantry brigade and supply train camped on a lot in Pleasant Hill, along the river. Seemingly endless lines of starving, thirsty troops—"ragged, greasy and dirty, and some barefoot, looking...more like the bipeds of pandemonium [than]...the angels of deliverance from Lincoln bondage"—descended on the town. As one elder related: "Large crowds marched into our yards and surrounded our wells like the locusts of Egypt, and struggled with each other for the water as if perishing with thirst; and they thronged our kitchen doors and windows, begging for bread like hungry wolves. We nearly emptied our kitchens of their contents, and they tore the loaves and pies into fragments, and devoured them as eagerly as if they were starving. Some even threatened to shoot others if they did not divide with them."[11]

Things would soon get worse. At dawn on October 8, exacerbated by "weary nights of watching, fatigue and anxiety," the roar of more than two hundred cannon awoke the brothers and sisters. Troops hurrying along their dusty street informed them that a full battle between armies numbering more than seventy-two thousand was raging along the shallow Chaplin River near Perryville, just seventeen miles to the south.

Streams of refugees sought safety in Lexington as the guns "belch[ed] forth death and destruction" for a full day. Then the Shakers watched helplessly as Confederate wagon trains creaked through the village and camped in their north pasture, where horses and mules foraged in their cornfield. "As far as the eye could see on both ends of the road," retreating Confederates arrived from every direction, accompanied by even closer artillery fire. The first rainfall in months offered the day's only comfort.[12]

On a cool Sabbath morning, the war nearly exacted its fullest measure from the Pleasant Hill Shakers. On October 12, exhausted from days of feeding soldiers and stragglers, the brothers and sisters prepared for worship. A regiment of Morgan's cavalry formed into line at the north end of the village and put out pickets in the streets themselves. Cannon fire opened immediately west and southwest of the community as thirty thousand federals approached. Pleasant Hill appeared on the verge of becoming a battleground. "How awful to think of a wicked and bloody battle Occuring in the midst of Zion on earth!" exclaimed a shaken elder. After several tense hours, Morgan himself gave the order to withdraw across the river toward Lexington and ordered his troops "not [to] disturb the tranquility of our people any longer." By the evening, the entire southern sky was aglow with campfires as the retreating rebel army occupied the southeastern hills, while the exhausted federal army remained fifteen miles southwest near Perryville. Only the dull thud of artillery fire from the southeast and stragglers who showed up for days and surrendered to federal troops reminded the villagers that the rebels had been there—that and the Shakers' empty storerooms, hundreds of wounded rebels left at Harrodsburg and other surrounding towns, and the fresh grave in the village cemetery of a feverish Georgia soldier who had died in the Shakers' care.[13]

The Believers had only a month to breathe easy. On November 15 a regiment of Illinois troops marched through their village, well dressed, flags flying, and band playing—a decided contrast to the Confederates. A day later they received word that a brother in the North Union community in New Lebanon, New York, had been enrolled for military service. That same month, with conscription imminent, one of the North Union brethren, Ezra Leggett, represented the western Shakers in a visit to Washington and met with the president, Abraham Lincoln, and secretary of war, Edwin M. Stanton, seeking a general reprieve from the draft. Lincoln, a descendant of Quakers and sympathetic to the Shakers' pleas, encouraged Shakers to submit sworn petitions for permanent exemption from service in the federal armies. Such an exemption would not come until 1864, but the president's demeanor was hopeful. "This affords great relief relative to the important military subject," wrote a Pleasant Hill elder.[14]

As the scene of fighting moved south, the presence of large armies gave way to frequent raids by mounted Confederates and pursuit by federal cavalry. For the Shakers at Pleasant Hill and South Union, the name John Hunt Morgan sent shivers through their communities and forced brethren home from business. But the occupying federals soon became nearly as onerous as the rebel nightriders, who were "about as insolent as the secesh," as an eldress grumbled. In November five regiments under William S. Rosecrans occupied South Union overnight and consumed 12 tons of hay, 245 bushels of corn, and 10,000 bundles of fodder and oats, and burned some 2,500 fence rails. They offered vouchers for less than $400. The following month the Pleasant Hill elder bemoaned federals having "sank all the boats on the Kentucky River in this vicinity, to try to prevent John Morgan from crossing if he should come this way, as he is now in the Green River country on his third raid into Kentucky." The word "guerrilla" at last appeared in the Shakers' vernacular, added to other imprecise terms for roaming, armed horsemen, such as outlaws, marauders, robbers, thieves, and banditti. One word, however, was unmistakable: measles. This disease, a Pleasant Hill elder wrote, "in a malignant form, [is] prevailing throughout the Society, brought into this region by the soldiers who are engaged in this wicked and cruel war."[15]

As this war raged in the middle border region, as much for the boundaries of civilians' allegiance as between contending armies, this middle ground once known as Zion on earth had fallen a casualty to hell's full fury.

5

Netherworld of War

Civilians, Soldiers, and the Dominion of War

By the spring of 1862 federal forces were in firm possession of the middle border. Federal advances in the late winter drove out rebel armies and saddle-sore rump governments from southern Missouri and Kentucky, exiled to the Confederacy, with only brief returns for the rest of the war. Dueling state governments might have claimed sovereignty, but legitimacy was no longer in doubt. Their capitals and largest cities, and virtually all river, rail, and communications networks, were occupied by large federal armies, often named for the West's great rivers. Seventeen regiments each from Indiana and Ohio and another ten from Illinois were stationed in Kentucky, along with several from Pennsylvania and Michigan, constituting thirty-five thousand soldiers standing alongside fifteen thousand Kentucky county militia. (Citizens' estimates, always unreliable, doubled this number.) Half as many occupied Missouri, along with troops from Kansas and Iowa. Its state militia's ranks swelled with men independent from those in federal service, all of whom intended to suppress disloyalty.[1]

When the armies advanced, the ostensible war front moved into the seceded states. Left behind was a war within the war—for allegiance, authority, and meaning—that was only just beginning. When the Yankees came, they brought with them clear distinctions between loyalty and disloyalty and rejected the assumption that professed unionists were above suspicion. An inner war front formed in these middle border states, influencing the civilian experience in free states above the rivers and hastening the realignment of communities into loyal and dissenting memberships. Military commanders often tolerated the subversion of civil liberties at the local level as part of a broader strategy to keep order among divided populations, determine allegiances, and prosecute the war. What ensued was a military occupation by the federal government of states that had not seceded from it. When Confederate armies returned to Kentucky in 1862, they too upended loyalty and forced residents, white and black, to confront the new realities and vulnerabilities in a region not safely behind the lines.

In many parts of the nation, communities went to war. In the middle border states, the war came to communities. In the mesh of conflicting stances and allegiances across the middle border, the war hastened their realignments into loyal and disloyal constituencies. In response, newly fashioned communities of allegiance, comprised of discrete loyal and dissenting networks, competed for local legitimacy as the lines of military and governmental authority developed around them.

On both sides of the rivers, as federal troops established garrisons to protect railroads, telegraph lines, and bridges, unionists initially breathed easier. Dances, picnics, parties, concerts, tableaus, and other frivolities offered a semblance of normal life, with a military flavor. Businesses' newspaper advertisements either offered remedies specific to soldiers' needs or adapted military terminology for profit—"MORE VICTORIES! GOOD NEWS! The Enemy 'Skedaddle!... HEAD QUARTERS—1862: A NEW AND SPLENDID STOCK OF GOODS FOR THE SPRING AND SUMMER CAMPAIGN"—briefly rendering the war little more than a commercial opportunity. Living with in-laws in Dayton, Ohio, Missourian Sarah Jane Full Hill found "peaceful and well ordered lives of people going about their usual avocations, apparently without thought or concern regarding the war. Seldom was a soldier in uniform seen...a startling change from the rush and feverish excitement of the past year."[2]

But war proved not to be merely a passing season. Its rhythms were foreign, its demands intrusive and irregular. The armies' incessant hunger caused inflation, deprivation, and worse. Handbills of the most recent military orders, published in newspapers and posted on street corners and at rural crossroads, contained a bewildering array of restrictions on behaviors once considered rights and liberties. They caused inconvenience and resentment among residents who once welcomed the presence of federal troops in their communities. The brutal western battles in 1862 shattered hopes of a larkish war. Spring planting was interrupted by horrific reports of battles at Mill Springs, Fort Donelson, Elkhorn Tavern (or Pea Ridge), and especially Pittsburg Landing (or Shiloh), all federal victories and each progressively bloodier than any yet fought on the continent. Within a single season, special editions of newspapers were filled with the names of those dead or wounded on not-so-distant fields. Bits of news circulated illicitly of brave deaths on battlefields or senseless ones in the camps behind the lines, of wounded soldiers freezing to death and their mercy killings, of unmarked mass graves, and of prisoners' being scalped by rebel Indians and merciless guerrillas. More frightening, armed nightriders stole indiscriminately, broke into homes, pistol-whipped or harassed known white unionists, captured or shot free blacks and slaves, and burned houses and barns. This, residents soon learned, was wolfish war—less to be won or lost than endured or survived.[3]

As church bells tolled and families grieved, funerals—often without caskets—offered small comfort. An Indiana woman recalled that after hearing rumors of local men in these battles, "those at home would wait and wait for news, wait and hope and fear for days. There might be various reports that could not be confirmed, a grape-vine message or a word from someone travelling through. Sometimes more than a week would elapse before even a meager account came." Most faced the grim fact that they would neither see their loved ones again nor put flowers on their fresh graves. Wounded soldiers returned home to convalesce, often disfigured or crippled, becoming new branches of the war grapevines, federal and especially rebel, as they were beset by "a host of friends [who] hurried to see us and hear of their brothers and husbands and sons who were out in the Southern army." What news these witnesses passed on to families left out details of agonizing deaths, more haunting than comforting.[4]

Panic drove thousands, especially mothers of young men in service, to travel to battle sites to care for wounded husbands or sons or retrieve and bury them properly. "[T]here are several leaving this place to bring their dead children hom[e]," wrote one woman after Shiloh. "I expect to hear every day that Jimmy is killed, but am thankful that I nevred encouraged him to go." They saw firsthand the carnage left by real war. When fetching home her wounded brother, Josie Underwood mistook

> what I at first took to be a big dog.... [she] then discovered to be a poor bent old woman... [who] had managed to get down here from New Albany, Indiana, hoping to find her son.... [S]omebody told her her boy was dead.... [She] never had nobody *belonging to her but jess Jim.'* ... "she couldn't get back"—her money was all gone—she had taken possession of an old abandoned shanty on the edge of the Camp ground—eking out her miserable life with the help of the little food some charitable negroes near by gave her.... The poor old soul was in faded calico rags...gathering up all sorts of trash, rags of cast-off soldier clothing, canteens—a few beans in an old can.[5]

Never had war seemed at once so far away and so close. Unionists in river communities who had hallooed at the frequent riverboats heading downriver filled with "troops or Government stores" stared at boats loaded with rebel prisoners, often malnourished, sick, and wounded, heading upriver to newly established prison camps. Initially troubled about detaining them in river cities with deeply divided populaces like Cincinnati, Louisville, and St. Louis, Henry W. Halleck was forced to overcome his fears as the war expanded. By December 1861 St. Louis's Gratiot Street Prison, designed for five hundred men, contained two and a half times that number. Within months, with the army needing to

Figure 5.1 Galvanized Yankees at Rock Island Prison, ca. 1863. Kentuckians held at Louisville were among the first Confederate soldiers to be transferred to Rock Island Prison, in the northern Illinois stretch of the Mississippi River. Some of these soldiers had been drafted into the Confederate army, then enlisted in the federal army after being captured at Vicksburg. Courtesy Abraham Lincoln Presidential Library and Museum.

detain some eleven thousand Confederate prisoners after their surrender at Fort Donelson, enlisted men were hauled to Camp Butler, Camp Douglas, and Rock Island in Illinois (see figure 5.1); Indianapolis's Camp Morton; and Ohio's Camp Chase. Paroled officers initially feted by St. Louis's "home grown rebels" were soon sent to military prisons at Alton, Illinois, and Ohio's Johnson's Island.[6]

As prisoners headed north, the withdrawal of the rebel armies sent a wave of refugees, who accompanied them to the Confederacy rather than face the advancing federals. Left behind were "marks of the desolating effects [of the Confederate occupation]... visible on every hand," wrote a federal soldier from southeastern Missouri in March 1862. "Houses are vacated, and some of them burnt.... A few who held slaves fled at the approach of our troops, going south, because 'Lincoln wanted their *niggers*.'" In Bowling Green, Kentucky, William and Mary Van Meter loaded their wagons and slaves and headed to northern Mississippi, where they tried to grow cotton despite having no experience. The war found them in November when federal troops arrived, ransacking homes and farms, and several of the Van Meters' slaves ran off. Rather than face the Yankees again in a strange land, Mary spent three months traveling home to her father's household. "I now sit by the window all day, and scarcely recognize a familiar face," she wrote dejectedly. "Alas, I know too well they [her former friends] are exiles far from home."[7]

When the regular war marched or steamed away, bruised secessionists who elected to remain took off their blue cockades or white rosettes and hauled down their secession flags for fear of hostile federal troops. Many were merely biding time, as one slave informant related to arriving Illinois soldiers in Missouri. "A negro came into camp and seemed quite talkative, when one of the 'boys' asked him if the people here, were for the Union he replied, with a very knowing look: 'Dey all say dey are, before you face, but behind, dey all just as dey used to was, Secesh.'" Investigating a tip near Manchester, Missouri, troops discovered a "massive" flag sewn inside a girl's quilt. She told them "she had slept under it, and that she loved it, and that fifteen stars was not so terribly disunion, in her estimation, after all." The bluecoats disagreed.[8]

Many secessionist families found refuge in St. Louis, Louisville, and Lexington, believing their safety was best preserved by silence and the massed federal presence. Others fled to the Confederacy or to neighboring free states as families broke up (see figure 5.2). These "rebel refugees" tussled with unionist neighbors, often bringing down home guard retaliation or local vigilance committees, who warned them to leave unwelcoming communities. Owing to a Missourian's "ill fame, and bad character," southern Illinoisans soon notified him "that the peace and morals of this community will be promoted by your removal." Others used the cover of night to terrorize local unionists, who often took their families from war-torn counties rather than face threats or worse. "Many timid Union men, who have seen secessionists grow more numerous, bold, and threatening," wrote one despondent resident, "have left the State or are intending to leave it, while perhaps a larger number think it is of no use to struggle against it, and bow to the storm."[9]

White unionist refugees from the Confederacy often fled by river to settle in cities and towns in neighboring states, slave and free. Many appeared to be from their society's lower rungs. "The refugees are comeing here by scores," marveled one Illinois woman. "We receive a fresh supply nearly every day there is several families here from Black River Ark near Jacksonport I do really pity the women, they look as if they had never had an hours health, or a day's happiness in their lives." Other newcomers were anything but poor. "Thousands of Tennesseans are now in Kentucky—men, too of property, position, and reputation—men of character and courage," wrote a soldier, "not the riff-raff of any population so often composing an army." A southern Illinois woman wrote, "This old town is rather more populous than when you left most of the inhabitants are women and children there is a family in every house and two in some.... we get along very peaceably their Children and ours play together sometimes." Fewer welcomed these newcomers. In September 1862 residents of Batavia, Ohio, were "in a

Figure 5.2 Secesh Leaving Home, ca. 1862. Thousands of war-weary residents of the middle border's slave states left their homes as refugees, seeking safety in free state communities, where they often met with local resistance. Lincoln Financial Foundation Collection, courtesy of Allen County Public Library and Indiana State Museum.

continued state of excitement and dread" owing to their county being "filled with refugees from Kentucky and we are in a state of perfect confusion," enough to ask the governor to call out the militia. By one estimate, half of the population of four counties in southwestern Missouri, mostly unionists, left their homes as entire neighborhoods emptied and headed north in search of protection.[10]

Refugees soon taxed these communities with epidemic outbreaks of measles and smallpox, dwindling supplies of wood and food, and doubling prices. The more affluent rented vacant homes and rooms, driving housing costs skyward. When winter arrived, the poor desperately searched for warmth and shelter, pleading with federal commanders for assistance. Many could do no better than build brush huts and makeshift hovels. Relief agencies such as the Western Sanitary Commission and the Ladies Union Aid Society struggled to shelter and feed them. Some towns and cities established poor, or "industry," houses for them, while in others local governments or almshouses refused to provide for them. In late 1864 one steamboat in Cincinnati deposited four hundred "destitute refugees," all women and children, requiring the quick formation of a refugee relief commission, whose leaders solicited clothing, shoes, food, and money. One commissioner realized charity alone could not provide for them. "They are not adapted to city life," he wrote, "and it is absolutely necessary that they should be sent to the country…where they can with their hands provide food for themselves and their Families."[11]

Displaced newcomers contributed to the disruptions that middle border communities faced during the war's early months. However deep their political differences, some residents initially found ways to accommodate one another. In late 1861 Lizzie Ridgway described the amity that yet prevailed among her divided Kentucky family. "Father is a good Union man and so is mother," she wrote, "although her southern sympathies are so strong, after all, that we call her, laughingly a secessionist[.] Clara and I agree in being disgusted with both sides." Pro-Confederate women especially still felt safe demonstrating their political views. "The secesh are still impudent," wrote Kentuckian Ellen Sudduth. "Mrs John Young has twins she calls the Boy Sterling Price and the girl Albert Sydney Johnston." Social events often accommodated both union and secession tastes. In January 1862 Mary Louisa Reed of Shelbyville, Kentucky, went to a party at which the war seemed to encourage more than dampen conviviality. "[T]here was Lincoln cake and confederate cream, Union Sherbet confederate jelly—so all tastes were suited.... Everybody is talking about the late [Mill Springs] victory—some lamenting—some exulting. Mrs Logan says she is not going to purchase another dress until the S. C[onfederacy] is acknowledged."[12]

In many more places, divided allegiances paralyzed social relations. Driven by war tensions, the breakdown of community institutions ensued. Societal organizations locked their doors for months and even years "in consequence of secesh Ribilion," as the moderator of Kentucky's ill-named Harmony Baptist Church noted of his congregation's six-month interruption owing to its members' private conflicts. In the late winter of 1861 another Baptist congregation saw the "peace of the church" shattered when one brethren's statements in support of the Confederacy evoked a female congregant's vow "to go before the legislature praying them to preserve the union." A committee of elders "consider[ed] whether the church did not do wrong in suffering sister anderson to talk in church speaking hard things," but when she refused "[to] answer for her misconduct," the elders dismissed her. So too did many county courts, especially in the region's slave states, such as in Kentucky's McCracken County, whose court was closed from late 1861 until the spring of 1863. The real war in Missouri only reminded residents across the rivers of their vulnerability. "The booming of Cannon must have made you feel that war was at your door," wrote John Preston Mann to his wife in Liberty, Illinois, in late October 1861. "What a state of things we would have, if the Mississippi River was not the line of Mo. you would all have to leave."[13]

Political sentiments were rarely so amicably expressed as those Mary Louisa Reed witnessed. Often neighbors found themselves unable to socialize at all. "Festivities of any kind," recalled one Cincinnati woman, "were very rare, so deeply was the nation impressed by the horrors, taking place at the front." While traveling on a stagecoach through southern Illinois, a Kentucky woman commented that she "felt as though I was in a funeral procession.... [T]he passengers seemed sunk into a state of apathy bordering stupefaction." Sally Dorsey recalled of Rockport, Indiana: "Naturally in so small a village the politics of every one was known, the army men soon discovered which houses sheltered the loyal families, which the disloyal. Life ceased to be a matter of pleasant neighborliness and instead was often marked by sharp antagonisms. Union and Confederate families had slight dealings with one another." Later that year Kentuckian Lizzie Hardin claimed of her Harrodsburg community that she had "never seen such bitter feelings as there was between the two parties," and Josie Underwood wrote, "The lines between secessionists and Union people are more and more marked and the Union or Rebel feeling is drawing people together who never before had any association. None of my friends have fallen away as... but I *feel* a difference. We are always trying to avoid the subjects we are each most interested in, which spoils a friendship." A year later Josie admitted, "Lizzie Wright sits on her porch just across the street and I on ours and merely the coldest bows and never a visit now." The presence of federal troops only magnified such incivility. In the spring of 1862 residents of Hopkinsville, Kentucky, burned their town's fairgrounds "to prevent the Union Army from benefiting by them."[14]

Community members became distant, even hostile, their interactions ranging from polite disdain to outright conflict. Saloons and hotels became known as either unionist or secesh, and thus closed to opposing patrons. Schools were rent by partisan divisions and often broke up as a result. In New Albany, Indiana, they closed in June 1861 and did not reopen for more than three years. In the early summer of 1862 southern Illinois schoolteacher Alfred M. Mann wrote of the isolation he felt. "I hav no *associates*," he lamented, "only the School children Simply because they are *Secessionists* and I will not hav anything to do with any Such." When his sister-in-law, Nancy Mann, applied for a teaching position after the former schoolmaster had been dismissed for his political convictions, she was told that "the employers would very much prefer a man there is very bad boys here very bad indeed." Mann concluded that gendered excuses were only a cover. "[I]t [is] all a *Secesh* matter that is causing all the troubles and the union men are bound [to] have their way." In Lexington in early 1862, Frances Dallam Peter's unionist family had ceased all contact with their secessionist neighbors. She noted that when one of them "dressed to represent the 'Bonny Blue Flag'" to taunt the town's federal convalescents, "a number of people who had witnessed her behavior, collected together, followed her, and began throwing stones and would have mobbed her... if they had not been prevented."[15]

Nowhere were the battle lines more joined than in the pulpits and pews of the middle border's Christian congregations, realigning old communities of faith as new communities of allegiance. "Christian Warfare," according to a Kentucky Baptist circular, splintered churches throughout the region. The debate over slavery having widened theological and denominational crises over biblical authority, the war's political disruptions assaulted churches' sacred spaces. Charges that opponents were unchristian gave new immediacy to partisans' claims of legitimacy within often divided congregations.[16]

Churches soon acted to facilitate politicized definitions of loyalty. Each of the major evangelical denominations, even Catholics and Episcopalians, who largely declared themselves neutral on the subjects of slavery and the war, had dissenting church factions that challenged supporters of the president, the war, and especially abolitionists. In Republican-majority congregations, Democrats fought back against galling charges that "a Copperhead can not be a Christian" with doctrinal imperatives but also with injunctions against "pulpit politics," meaning partisan sermonizing. Published pamphlets by northern clergymen—John Henry Hopkins's *Bible View of Slavery*, Henry J. VanDyke's *The Character and Influence of Abolitionism!*, and Nathan Lord's *A True Picture of Abolition*—largely confirmed for Republican readers that conservative Democrats were obstructionists. David Christy's 1862 response, the book *Pulpit Politics*, excoriated Protestant ministers for preaching abolition. A Cincinnati geologist and former American Colonization Society agent, Christy blamed northern Republicans' abolitionist wing for the debilitating church wars. "[T]he country must be convinced that the agitation in favor of emancipation has been uncalled for," he railed, "and that Christian ministers, therefore, have been inexcusable in agitating the subject of slavery, so as to distract and divide the Churches." Democratic newspapers throughout the border region promoted the book as a "Great Work of the Age." Republicans condemned it. "Satan has joined the Church," one propagandized, and an Ohio provost marshal seized copies of the book as incendiary "contraband."[17]

The popularity of Christy's book among middle border Democrats derived from the evolving realities of congregational politics. Even as the conflict began, congregants or soldiers chased off rural circuit ministers for their politics, leaving pulpits unfilled. Ministers in mixed or majority dissenting congregations found themselves beset for politicized sermonizing. Republican ministers such as Indiana's J. W. T. McMullen, who in the fall of 1861 "called upon God Almighty to damn the rebels," found their political views challenged by dissenting congregants. One southern Illinois minister reputedly placed a revolver beside the pulpit Bible and prayed for God's curse of extermination for all rebels in arms, resulting in a fracas that ended the morning service and permanently splintered his Methodist church. "I don't blame you for not wanting to go to hear a Secesh preacher," wrote Indiana soldier Thomas Prickett to his wife. "I believe that I could not patronize such a minister even though he did preach my doctrine. I fear that there a good many 'wolves in sheeps clothing.'" Democratic flocks complained bitterly about politicized sermons and prayers that "utterly discarded thousands [of sympathizers and dissenters] from the benefits of the atoning blood of Christ, and invoked war, pestilence, famine, fire... and the destroying angel to be unloosed." In turn, they accused Lincolnite congregants of "holy bloodthirstiness" and castigated them as "war dogs... who thank[ed God] for the war and for prolonging it." Published by Democratic newspapers, the invocation at Illinois's Republican convention—"Old Abe is a special gift from God Almighty and if we reject him... we reject God Almighty"—offered dissenters proof that their daises were really bully pulpits. In March 1863 one Baptist congregation in Lincoln, Illinois (named for the future president), comprised largely of Republicans, reputedly denied the family of a dead soldier use of their church for his funeral because he and his family were Democrats.[18]

Similarly, dissenting flocks on both sides quickly drove out ministers who espoused support for the war. Presbyterian minister Joel K. Lyle found himself distrusted by many in his Lexington, Kentucky, congregation soon after casting his vote for Lincoln in 1860. After publicly praying for the leaders of both governments, several church elders voted to replace him with a secessionist minister. His congregation's attendance soon lagged, as many dissenters quit the church, while others questioned Lyle's manhood as a noncombatant and an abolitionist. In the spring of 1862, after Lyle wrote a soldiers' tract for the American Tract Society, congregants demanded that "Parson Lovejoy" stop "preaching to the Negroes" in the neighborhood, then threatened to shoot him in his own front yard. He soon left for West Liberty, Ohio.[19]

Beginning in 1862 unionist congregations applied politicized definitions to denominational doctrines in order to proscribe dissenting ministers. Military intrusions upon ministers' civil liberties, such as the arrest of Louisville's Stuart Robinson, were sometimes well publicized. Despite offering frequent prayers for the president, Samuel B. McPheeters, a popular pastor of St. Louis's Pine Street Presbyterian Church, baptized a baby named Sterling Price, and his brother joined the Confederate army. Unconditional unionists convinced military authorities to shut down his church and banish him and his wife from the city. He protested directly to Lincoln, who admonished St. Louis authorities for taking such strident measures merely "upon the suspicion of [McPheeters's] secret sympathies," but refused to interfere.[20]

War-dissenting ministers found politics and pulpit mixed when they were brought before conferences or synods to answer for their political views. Disciplinary proceedings often implemented political tests as measurements of religious faith, and witnesses were often known partisans. Congregations with Republican majorities adopted constitutions that explicitly professed support for the national government and its troops and used votes for or against as a litmus test of loyalty. In the spring of 1862 a central Missouri woman was appalled to learn that her local Presbyterian church, used as a hospital following the battle at Lexington, was in turmoil. Its congregation's "Black Republican" unionists forced a vote on the minister after writing the synod "stating the church in his care was vacant.... He and the majority of his congregation [in] favor of the South.... Has, or is it coming to this that church and state affairs are to be combined[?]" Oliver H. McEuen of Pike County, a Methodist deacon, was tried and dismissed for sowing dissent, among other charges, for allegedly claiming, "The time has come when the Church must be divided, and a conservative Church must be organized, and every Democrat must leave the Church." After criticizing the administration, in 1862 central Illinois Methodist minister William C. Blundell, a Democrat, retired rather than face charges of "*Disloyalty* to the Government of the United States" for "failing to pray in public for the President or Armies of the United States." In southern Indiana, Thomas Marshall, later the nation's vice president, recalled his grandfather telling about his family's 1862 withdrawal from their Princeton church after being "notified by the Methodist preacher... that they would have to strike their names off the roll if they continued to vote the Democratic ticket. My grandfather announced he was willing to take his chances on Hell, but never on the Republican party." The family soon moved.[21]

Democratic congregants in majority unionist congregations also found ways to disrupt formerly filled churches. Quoting biblical precepts such as "Render unto Caesar that which is Caesar's, and unto God that which is God's," many refused to take part in the president's annual Thanksgiving proclamations and national fasting days, withheld tithes and other contributions, and refused church work. In the fall of 1863, Hancock County, Illinois, newspapers announced the formation of a new "Independent Methodist Church" that was "purely Democratic" and whose minister would preach the gospel "rather than politics, war, bloodshed and devastation." Democratic congregations often pooled their resources to pay commutation fees or replacement bounties for drafted ministers or congregants. "I am told that the[y] have got 5 or 6 of our Church Members," wrote one Kentucky clergyman. "The people here [are] very much excited about it, Sir the[y] have cause for excitement." Such behavior drew the ire of local unionists, especially Republicans, who were eager to prove these residents unpatriotic or disloyal. Democratic newspapers happily responded with similar stories about draft-evading Republicans, ordained and not.[22]

In slave state congregations with dissenting majorities, unionist ministers found themselves similarly besieged. Sermons based in scriptural passages supportive of civil authority or loyalty, even beyond those questioning slavery, were condemned as "purely political subjects." A Kentucky elder claimed that secessionists and Confederates dominated the leadership of a local Baptist association, with "very few union men present... or noticed more than if they were dogs." Dissenting congregants "denounce as abolitionists not only those who preach what they regard as political sermons, but also those who merely pray for the President... and his constitutional advisers." William Moody Pratt, a Baptist minister in Lexington, Kentucky, complained in June 1862 that despite being a slaveholder who had long served the city's oldest such congregation, "The political disturbances of the country have alienated a great many of the Congregation from me, for being so positive an Union Man... they dont come to meeting... some here got miffed and joined other denominations, and many have neglected to fill their places in the house of God." At an August quarterly meeting, the outspoken Pratt—a native New Yorker—prayed aloud for Lincoln and the Union. "I found that quite a number of Secessionists had either left the house or were leaving, vowing they would never hear me pray or preach again.... I found some person had run against my buggy and broke one wheel." With Sunday attendances routinely in single digits, he was soon dismissed.[23]

The Fourth of July became an annual flashpoint for competing loyal and secesh networks within these communities of allegiance. In Kentucky one observer wrote, "Barbacues have become quite common there was one in Pendleton Co about two miles from here last week, and last Saturday there was two in this county only 3 miles apart one Secession and the other Union both was largely attended." Another noted that the Fourth of July celebrations were unattended by secessionists and even neutralists, with "patriotic speeches, and flag presentations, and National Songs sung by little girls in white, with banners waving in every direction, it was really an interesting day to the *Union* folks, at least." The garrison commander at Jackson, Missouri, ordered the cancellation of the town's 1862 "Festive Day" activities, which were replaced by a patriotic speech that he delivered to attendees. Federal and militia commanders used nonattendance as a marker of disloyalty and often retaliated. The family of Missourian Elvira A. W. Scott, an Indiana-born wife of a Whig merchant and slaveholder, opted to go visiting rather than attend the local Fourth festivities held at the fairground in Miami, Missouri, despite an order from the garrison commander requiring all residents' presence. "We did not feel like celebrating, under the circumstances," she confided in her diary. "It would be more appropriate to fast and mourn in sack cloth and ashes over the desolation of our once beloved land," she argued, claiming that none of the village's Confederate sympathizers attended. Five days later she received an order requiring her to report weekly to the garrison commander and the provost marshal. The following day, John Scott was arrested publicly at his store, and the commander, Lt. Adam Bax, German-born and an abolitionist Republican, brandished a pistol and chastised his frantic wife. "Madam, you shall not insult the flag of my country, or I will teach you [not] to," he snarled. Taken to jail in Marshall and set to face a military commission upriver in Lexington, John was released three days later after taking the oath. He quickly closed his business and left on a steamer for St. Louis.[24]

In the unfolding war, tensions wrapped in loyalty politics wracked families, communities, and consciences. They quickly influenced even intimate relations and marital decisions. In early November 1861, as the Russellville convention met about fifty miles away to deliberate secession, one western Kentucky couple sought out a local minister for a hasty wedding. On their marriage license return, he was moved to write "the spirit of secession drove them from home to marry." Women of marriageable age, especially in garrison towns, commonly described their attraction to young men in loyal uniforms while expressing revulsion for those in enemy coats. Unionist Annie Leslie McCarroll admitted a brief flirtation with a rebel officer who was occupying her Kentucky hometown, but rejected him owing to his allegiance and ultimately married a local federal officer. Kentuckian Benjamin F. Buckner often complained of his fiancée's outspokenness as "talking secesh" after he enlisted in the federal army. "You are just as much entitled to your opinions as I am to mine," he chided her on his way to Cincinnati to buy a uniform. "I only regret that we both can't think alike.... I won[']t quarrel with you if you are a rebel. I had so much trouble to get you to fall in love with me." Susan Terrell Scrogin, a Kentuckian whose two brothers would enlist in Confederate service in Missouri, postponed her wedding owing to political differences with her fiancé, a federal officer.[25]

§

William Tecumseh Sherman had long foreseen the difficulties in keeping peace in the middle border region. The freshly minted brigadier general, who had lived in the South and whose brother, John, was a moderate antislavery Ohio Republican U.S. senator, witnessed St. Louis's Camp Jackson riot, throwing himself into a shallow ditch to shield himself and his young son when the shooting began. Not even this brush with death prepared Sherman for what he would face in Louisville later that year. The outright secessionism he saw everywhere shocked him. "A young lady [tore] the American flag from its staff and whipe [sic] her feet on it," wrote one resident, while others "snatch[ed] one from the hands of a child and [tore] it in rags. Yet such things occur here, in loyal Kentucky." Sherman understood that his army could not simply keep the peace, but would have to win it. "The people of Kentucky...themselves are neutral or hostile," he wrote despondently in mid-October, and "will not rally in my Judgment but turn on us who came to save them from the Despot of the South." Sherman's overweening pessimism drew a visit from the secretary of war, Simon Cameron, who questioned the general's state of mind but was nonetheless convinced that "[m]atters are in a much worse condition than I expected to find them." Two weeks later, Sherman was removed from command and sent briefly to central Missouri before returning home. Newspapers claimed he had gone "stark mad."[26]

Strategic concerns did not drive Sherman mad, even temporarily. Uncertain loyalties among mixed populations caused widespread, often hidden internecine conflict. In the late summer of 1861 Barton Bates, a prominent Missouri moderate, wrote to his father, Lincoln's new attorney general, that this conflict was emerging from the ground up. "The state of Missouri is in a strange condition. With (as I firmly believe) a large majority now decidedly for the Union, it is difficult to keep the peace among ourselves." Nearly simultaneously, Missouri's attorney general, J. Proctor Knott, saw the conflict as top-down. Arrested and paroled by federal officials and soon to be replaced, he wondered whether "Kentucky and Missouri [would] become parts of the great centralized despotism to which our government is so rapidly drifting, or whether they be destined to remain the cherished homes of Constitutional liberty after the present ravaging storm shall have passed by." Although their wartime lenses were clearly different, as lawyers they both recognized that the contest between state and federal authority was eroding civil liberties in these loyal states.[27]

As Knott learned painfully, Missouri's and Kentucky's state governments implemented official allegiance mechanisms to suppress or purge disloyalists. Between the fall of 1861 and spring of 1862 their legislatures enacted restrictive loyalty definitions centering on a mandatory "test" oath for civil officials—"from the highest to the lowest, whether municipal or otherwise," as Missouri's law stated—swearing allegiance to the federal and state governments and promising not to aid or abet the rebellion. Those who refused faced expulsion. (Many local communities soon required similarly fashioned municipal oaths for their civil servants.) In Missouri the "convention oath" would "be used as long as we have a Provisional Government and traitors among us who are either in, or aspire to, office." Missouri's governor Hamilton R. Gamble made wholesale replacement appointments for state officials who refused to take the new oath, including all three state supreme court justices. Both state legislatures expelled their U.S. senators—Kentucky's John C. Breckinridge and Lazarus W. Powell, and Missouri's Trusten Polk and Waldo P. Johnson—for sympathy with the Confederacy and elected unionists to fill their seats. (Breckinridge, Polk, and Johnson would take seats in the Confederate Congress.) Powell successfully fought his expulsion, arguing that the charges against him rested on his support for the state's neutrality and his opposition to furnishing troops and funding the war. Kentucky's legislature disfranchised Confederate "expatriates," whether civilians proved to have joined the Confederacy, persuaded others to do so, or returned to the state under arms, and required a test oath for all male citizens, who had to swear that they had neither served nor supported the Confederacy. In 1862 unconditional unionists forced the resignation of the state's governor, Beriah Magoffin.[28]

With Kentucky's and Missouri's military forces commanded by hard-liners, allegiance quickly shaped distinctions between citizens. In Kentucky, Jeremiah T. Boyle reimplemented the blanket arrest strategy that Sherman had tried to suppress. Boyle, a state's attorney, railroad entrepreneur, and local scion, was an unconditional unionist who had actively recruited men into federal service. That he was a known emancipationist in a slave state likely confirmed his loyalty. Immediately upon taking command on June 1, he issued a series of orders that required Confederate sympathizers to give up firearms, take the federal oath, post bond for future good conduct, and avoid "anything [spoken]...with the intent to excite to rebellion." Violators faced imprisonment or execution. Boyle's self-styled "sifting" policy, which received approval from the army's judge advocate general, Kentuckian Joseph Holt, would continue "until the last Jeff. Davis sympathizer is cleared out." Baptist minister William Conrad recalled the local sheriff being instructed by federal officers that "every man of able body and good mind was to take up arms against any body who was for the Sesesh and that any body who did not obey was to stay in his house and would be shot down if he left it." Local jails and prisons, such as those at Newport Barracks and Camp Chase, were soon full to the brim again with alleged "enemies in our camps," including women. Widespread outrage caused federal officials in Louisville to order that the names of those arrested no longer be published in the city's newspapers. In September 1862, with Confederate troops in the state, the new secretary of war, Edwin M. Stanton, ordered Boyle to halt all arrests unless ordered by Kentucky's governor. Six weeks later he received new orders from Buell: "All persons who have actively aided or abetted...rebel troops within the last three months will be immediately arrested and sent to Vicksburg, Miss., and forbidden to return to Kentucky."[29]

Confederate sympathy as a punishable measure of disloyalty was only the most visible exercise of wartime military authority in the middle border states. Beneath it lay less perceptible strata of loyalty measures exerted by Confederate, federal, and militia troops, especially in the region's slave states. In the troubled western portion of Missouri, a similar sifting policy was at work in February 1862. Unionist George Caleb Bingham saw civilians there

> subjected to a kind of winnowing process by which the "tares" were to be separated from the wheat—the loyal from the disloyal portion of the inhabitants. In effecting this desirable end, it was not, for a moment, deemed necessary, that any investigation, in form, should take place. The statement of a single individual, who had been for some years a resident in such community, was to be taken as conclusive in reference to each case.... [Commanders] drew a line, sufficiently legible, between Unionists and Secessionists, without exhibiting the latter in colors so dark as to render their redemption hopeless. The separation completed, the doors of the good old Union church were charitably thrown open.[30]

Bingham was not alone in sensing redrawn loyalty lines. But many residents were convinced that federal troops used slaveholding as a measure, barring shut the doors to loyalty that Bingham believed open. The same month, David Bailey, a War of 1812 veteran, who like most of his neighbors was a "Slave holder and opposed to Emancipation and do[es] not wholley approve of all of the acts of the present Administration," complained that he was among "the class of Citizens that those in Power think proper to designate as Secessionist, disloyal Rebels and Sympathizers and treat them as Such." Based purely on their ownership of slaves, local federal troops had "taken all their armes from them they have arrested them and taken them to headquarters, and made them take the oath and give bonds in Large amount—they impressed their Horses and their waggons and teams and Slaves just where and when they please in the most insulting manner."[31]

Nearly at the same time that these Missourians recorded their separate observations, Henry W. Halleck in St. Louis concluded: "Our army here is almost as much in a hostile country as it was when in Mexico." With secessionism, neutralism, and unionism coexisting—and with no mechanism for precise measurement of any of them—he and other federal commanders recognized their greatest security challenge was to judge civilians' allegiances. As Halleck wrote, winning the peace in these states would require "a strong hand": a hostile occupation.[32]

Although it would prove the most expansive and lasting, this "strong hand" was not the first suffered by residents of the middle border's slave states. Over the fall and winter of 1861–1862, as their troops filled St. Louis and Louisville, rebel armies had initiated full occupation of the southern portions of their states, including creating military districts and garrisoning towns. Squads rousted local unionists, confiscating horses and other supplies from farms and requiring oaths of allegiance. "[P]eaceably-disposed citizens" who refused were often "driven from their homes because of their political opinions, or... left from fear of force and violence." In early August 1861 the Confederacy allowed recruiting in the border slave states, and new squads circulated throughout the region behind Confederate lines, enlisting or impressing fighting-age men and levying local unionists for arms, equipment, food, and forage. It also enacted a Sequestration Act that allowed the confiscation of property of "alien enemies" of the Confederate government. Rebel commanders could seize and sell such property for the benefit of Confederate citizens who had lost property to the federal government. Confederate officers often applied narrow definitions of loyalty and disloyalty as a military necessity to confiscate property, and residents found themselves in a perpetual "no man's land" squeezed between the competing legal, constitutional, and military claims of the belligerent nations.[33]

Once rebel armies were pushed out in early 1862, citizens saw developing around them a more lasting federal occupation, a dominion system of sorts, accomplished by an integrated yet imperfectly administered knot of counterinsurgency measures by both federal troops and state militia and conducted mostly by low-level, volunteer post commanders. Administering this system required interaction between these troops as well as home guards and citizens, which placed real impositions on local populations. To establish control of a "chaos of incendiary elements," as one commander referred to local, often armed populations whose loyalties were often uncertain, such leaders often tolerated the subversion of civil liberties as part of a broader strategy with which to prosecute the war. Although this dominion system's primary burden fell on the middle border's slave states, its restrictions spanned the western rivers into the lower counties of the free states.[34]

Although ad hoc measures began as early as a month after the war commenced, each of the six pillars of the dominion system was in place by the summer of 1862. First, military districting at once focused and diffused military command, trying to regularize the myriad of orders and regulations that soon blanketed district commanders' offices while affording them latitude to implement policies. Each district contained garrisoned towns, occupied by squads of federal troops—generally cavalry—and supported by local home guards or state militia. Second, unconditional unionists provided commanders with names and evidence of known or suspected secessionists; compiled evidence against them; and led them to their often rural homes for investigation, questioning, or arrest. Lists of loyal, neutral, and disloyal became tools for identification and control. Third, provost marshals, generally civilians with military rank but independent of garrison commanders, had a wide range of powers and responsibilities to maintain local order, including policing towns and environs, issuing travel passes and permits, fielding complaints and arbitrating disputes, and acting as liaison between troops and municipal governments. Fourth, oaths of allegiance and surety bonds, administered and cataloged by provost marshals, required civilians to declare loyalty before witnesses both aloud and in writing. Those who refused could be levied for unionists' property damages and deaths or banished, and their property could be confiscated. Fifth, the ad hoc martial law declarations mandated restrictions of civil liberties and individual rights, including the suspension of habeas corpus and the creation of military tribunals (or commissions) for civilians under military arrest, superseding civil authority. Finally, federal military authorities established local trade regulations and empowered local trade boards composed of unconditional unionists, who together, as treasury secretary Salmon P. Chase termed it, "*let commerce follow the flag.*"[35]

Garrisoning towns required the commandeering of physical structures for the army's use, often including private homes. As a soldier in Kentucky wrote, "Calhoun...might be called an hospital, or army store house, a large part of the houses being occupied by the sick, the Quartermaster's stores, and factors Stores. Then there is two or three taverns which are now Soldier's Eating houses, and nothing else." Damage or destruction often followed, as did confiscation of private property. A resident of Jackson, Missouri, complained in August 1861 about soldiers occupying dwellings and carrying off "most of household goods... her cooking utensils, her table ware, chairs, bedclothes, towels napkins were taken and carried into camp... [to] then ship them to their own families." Already by February 1862 the federal occupation had all but wrecked Westport, Missouri, a once thriving, southern rights river town. "[S]oldiers are quartered in the dwellings and horses occupy the storerooms," wrote a Union officer. "The hotel was burned down three days ago. The houses are torn to pieces... the mantles used to build fires, and doors unhinged. I presume the place will be burned as soon as the troops leave." Many residents fled these occupied towns, leaving "crops ungathered, houses deserted, barns and stables falling to pieces, fences torn down, and stock running loose and uncared for.... But one family I think is living in the town. The remaining buildings are now standing empty with their door and windows open or broken in except those which are occupied by soldiers or their horses."[36]

Cavalry patrols, large and small, regularly roamed the countryside on "scouts" looking for disloyalists, saboteurs, and guerrilla bands, who operated strictly on their own until April 1862, when the Confederacy passed its Partisan Ranger Act, commissioning officers to organize bands of partisans. The nearly two-week, two-hundred-mile mission of a battalion of Lewis Merrill's 2nd Missouri "Horse" Infantry through Saline and Lafayette Counties, the heart of Missouri's slaveholding district, in December 1861 was characteristic of heavy patrols. Three hundred mounted militia and three companies of regular cavalry under George C. Marshall left Sedalia and rode "northeast through Richard Gentry's farm and encamped at Union Church, on Dr. Cartwright's farm," where they took several prisoners. The following day they went northeast fifteen miles to the reputed rendezvous of a large group of guerrillas, the advance guard taking fire from an estimated sixty horsemen who "then retreated into the brush," and the patrol confiscated "kegs of powder and a quantity of parts of cavalry equipments." The force camped overnight on a nearby farm, then rode fifteen miles farther north, taking prisoners, horses, and mules before encamping "on the farm of the notorious Claiborn[e] F. Jackson, and raised the Stars and Stripes over the traitor's house." The following morning, at Arrow Rock, "we found several kegs of powder concealed in warehouses; destroyed the ferry-boat, and while doing it our men were fired upon by a few men from across the river; the fire having been returned, the enemy ran." Continuing northward along the Missouri River, at Saline City they captured arms and powder and Confederate recruiting officers, and near a Glasgow mill a detachment surprised a force "caught playing cards and others getting breakfast... and getting their arms, ammunition, teams, cooking utensils," and took twenty-eight prisoners. After camping overnight on yet another farm, the column moved west about thirty-five miles, claiming stolen "government wagons, 5 of which we brought with us and destroyed 3, being unable to get mules or harness to bring them with us." Encamped on a known secessionist's farm, rebel horsemen under cavalryman Joseph O. Shelby, who was recruiting locally for the Confederacy "annoy[ed] us by firing at our pickets and to try to scare us by bombarding us with a 10-inch mortar loaded with mud." The next morning, December 10, the column rode into Waverly and at Shelby's ropewalk confiscated nine kegs of powder, a cannon carriage, "and the mortar concealed under a platform," all likely stolen in April from the Liberty Arsenal. After dispersing Shelby's horsemen, the federals rode southward some sixty miles, reaching Sedalia three days later.[37]

More reflective of the daily implementation of the dominion system were small, squad-based actions of federal troops, such as by Charles Whittlesey in northern Kentucky over the winter of 1861. Whittlesey, a New England–born, West Point–trained Ohio lawyer and editor, was ordered to take command in Gallatin, Grant, and Owen Counties in December. "Still continue to search, the premises of those quiet and inoffensive sympathizers with the south," he reported. "The *Union Men* discourage this." Between December 28, 1861, and January 14, 1862, Whittlesey received nine written tips from local unionists about disloyal actions by local residents, ranging from holding weapons, to harboring or aiding known guerrillas or guerrilla bands, to firing a gun in anger across the Ohio River. Threats against unionists were the most common complaint, including one who vowed to "kill his brother Dick for joining the Union army to cut his heart out, boil and eat it." Whittlesey ordered two raids of two companies each, the first riding to a mill of a known secessionist, looking unsuccessfully for a guerrilla, and then on to New Liberty, where they occupied public buildings on either end of the hamlet's main street and declared martial law while they searched for arms and ammunition. The second went to a hilltop hamlet of Mount Zion, where the squad arrested twelve suspected guerrillas, parole violators, or aggressive Confederate sympathizers. Of the fifteen men arrested during the action, Whittlesey paroled several with stipulations, while holding the others indefinitely for alleged disloyalty.[38]

Beyond the bias against these slave state citizens held by many free state troops, personal disputes and feuds lurked beneath this hidden warfare, offering what one Kentuckian called an "evening-up time ... [when] many a man became a violent Unionist because the ancient enemies of his house were Southern sympathizers." The war opened old wounds that, having festered for years, became scores to be settled—by accusations and arrests. Another Kentuckian lamented that a unionist neighbor "has made it his business to arrest all his rebel friends that he has a spite against," while an Indiana soldier wrote in his journal that his regiment's provost guard arrested a Baptist minister near Louisville on an elder's claim that "while in church he took out a Rope and threatened to hang the union men with it." The many layers of this personalized conflict prompted John M. Schofield to complain that the war in Missouri, indeed in the border region generally, was largely "the result of old feuds, and involves very little, if at all, the question of Union or disunion." Southern sympathizer John P. Scott's disagreement with a like-minded customer over the Missouri merchant's apparent friendliness with the federal garrison landed him in custody, fending off disloyalty charges. A Kentuckian claimed "the secret clue to this seeming capriciousness was the private business affairs of the two parties." She continued, "If a Southerner held the note of a Union man and the day for payment approached nothing would save the best government the world ever saw but the transfer of the Southerner to Camp Chase." Class resentments drove many such complaints against prominent landowners. As one Missourian of moderate means later sneered, "the cry of 'disloyal' could be very easily raised against any man who happened to have a superabundance of property."[39]

Home guard and state militia who supported or replaced garrisoning troops both contributed to this private war and were caught in its crossfire. A resident of Elk Fork, Missouri, complained that his local home guard "came from all parts of the County and Some of them have little grudges at their fellow Citizens and they make use of their opportunity to avenge themselves." Lincoln himself heard similar complaints "that arrests, banishments, and assessments are made more for private malice, revenge, and pecuniary interest than for the public good." Distrustful slaveholders believed that the war was a ruse for class warfare. "Dutch and Irish laborers...who by becoming 'Home Guards' can prey upon their neighbors, or jayhawk... openly boast that they will have possession of their fine farms, and they think that the time has arrived for them to take the time to better their fortunes." Abuses of civilians by home guards were pronounced enough for John C. Frémont and Sterling Price, commanding Missouri's largest opposing military forces, to issue an unusual joint proclamation in November 1861, declaring "future arrests or forcible interference by armed or unarmed parties of citizens...for the mere entertainment or expression of political opinions shall hereafter cease;...the war now progressing shall be exclusively confined to armies in the field." Six weeks later, with little having changed, Henry W. Halleck pledged to disband home guard units in Missouri "as rapidly as I can supply their places" with state militia.[40]

Widespread military arrests often made "on the slightest and most trivial grounds" occurred throughout the border slave states. Prisoners jammed courthouse jails and other sites of confinement, "arrested without any cause, except that they were reported secessionists." Henry Clay's son James and Kentucky's former governor, Charles S. Morehead, a Whig delegate to both the Peace and Border State Conventions, were imprisoned for criticizing the Lincoln administration. In Louisville the large number of arrests made of suspected secessionists, especially prominent ones, on flimsy or circumstantial evidence troubled William T. Sherman: "So many improper arrests were made by self-constituted authorities that there was a physical impossibility of keeping them." Sherman instituted a policy by which commissioners, generally prominent unionist county judges or justices of the peace selected by a trusted U.S. Supreme Court judge, would be stationed in garrisoned towns to judge evidence before ordering civilians' incarceration. Historian Mark E. Neely closely examined the federal government's arrest records during the war and concluded that some thirteen thousand civilians were arrested throughout the nation, the largest portion in the border states. His figure does not include Missouri, where fragmentary evidence suggests a "formidable if not staggering" number of civilians likely were detained. From April 1862 to October 1863, in excess of two thousand were incarcerated at St. Louis's Gratiot Street Prison alone.[41]

On the heels of arrests, formalized oaths of allegiance became the most ubiquitous tools of federal authority in these states. Printed on blanks and sworn at provost marshals' offices or in local courthouses, signed copies of sworn oaths had to be carried by those judged disloyal or neutral, much as free blacks had to do. The need for travel, with oaths necessary for obtaining passes, subjected white residents to the same requirements as slaves, a fact not lost on the Harrodsburg Board of Trustees. In October 1861, at the monthly meeting, they appointed a committee to "wait on the military authorities at the Camp and request them not to allow the travel along the public roads to be interfered with by the Soldiers under this command." Two months later, having gained no satisfaction from the garrison commander, the members doubled the town's police force to "keep the slaves off the streets and in subjection" and forbade night meetings "at any African Church" over the Christmas holiday. Verification of disloyalty often required the testimonial of unionist neighbors, some of whom were only too happy to provide it.[42]

For a variety of reasons, many unionists objected to forced oaths. A soldier at Columbia, Kentucky, scoffed at their objections. "It dont hurt a union man to take the Oath," he admitted, "but we find once in a while one that hates to take the Oath but durst not say anything Once in a grate while they are catched by some of us that over hear their conversation and then put them under an arrest." Many residents objected to the oath as "simply a test of adherence or submission to party, a most false test of loyalty in any true sense," thereby rejecting the legitimacy of their state governments, whether elected or provisional, or a Republican-headed federal government. As residents of loyal states, many considered these oaths superfluous or unconstitutional, assuming guilt before innocence and thus abrogating First Amendment rights. Missouri's "convention oath" was reviled because many saw the convention as extralegal, and public officials and public servants, such as teachers and ministers, who took a state oath when assuming their positions, believed subsequent oaths suggested disloyalty. Bettie Terrell, a student at Kentucky's Midway College, was fearful that her professors would be arrested for disloyalty, forcing her school to close. "I saw in the paper a few days since that no one would be permitted to teach unless they took the oath, and Dr Cosby says he will go to Camp Chase first." Within a year, Terrell and other women would have greater worries. Commencing in 1863, women who demonstrated hostility toward occupying troops found themselves before a federal swearing officer, threatened with exile for refusal. Many responded by treating federal troops "civilly—[while] Hating them most cordially."[43]

Oaths largely failed as devices for measuring loyalty. One woman spat that "every one has been required to take the oath—they are then called Loyal—What a mockery." Local residents frequently manipulated the oath, taking it disingenuously to retain a semblance of normalcy in their daily lives. "[I]t is at best but a desperate effort to make it appear that a majority of the people of state are Loyalists, but it is certain to prove the contrary if it proves any thing." However "loyal" their taking of the oath made them officially, their true loyalties lay hidden. Oaths drove some Confederate sympathizers underground, feigning loyalty. A Kentuckian wrote that some of the residents around him "say that they did not mind taking the oath as they did not consider it binding on them, in fact they would rather take the oath than not as it gives them protection and they can get passes to go where they please." Department commanders and provost marshals routinely required accompanying verification of witnesses' own loyalty. Mistakes occurred frequently, followed by complaints or requests for corrections, forcing commanders to discern the reliability of information they received. "Sir, you have the name of Hansbrough of Downingsville on your list as a rebel," wrote C. H. McElroy to his local commander in Kentucky. "[T]he parties who furnished you with his name say that it is an error; that he has always been an active union man—The error probably occurred from having used his name as a reference in regard to some traitors."[44]

But as "partisan weapons" originating from the belief that many residents pretended to be loyal or neutral, oaths were an effective means of creating new communities based on allegiances. Pious residents' refusal to take either federal or state oaths smoked them out, especially the final words: "SO HELP ME GOD." Western Kentuckians who signed an oath before the provost marshal at Smithland certainly noticed its last line: "The penalty for a violation of this oath is Death." Condemned as "the Republican mode of carrying on war," oaths carried an implicit ideological dimension. "They believe this war is waged against slavery," wrote Joseph C. Maple, an Ohio-born Baptist minister. "[T]he one side is abolition and the other side proslavery.... Hence they do not wish to take an oath which will cut them off from giving aid to the South." The oath sharpened the lines to the advantage to the federal government, as Barton Bates saw it. "I believe we are really better off having... [t]he doubtful men... avowed against us than as pretended neutrals," he boasted to his father. "[B]ut the promises of vigorous action lately are bringing them out more decidedly some on our side, and some more openly in a position in which we can whip them."[45]

However unpopular, oaths had practical value. With identification of secessionists perhaps the greatest challenge for federal authorities, lists of oath-takers—and refusers—were essential tools. Frances Peter noted "a black book that he (Col Gracie) kept in which were marked down the names of everybody, whether they were union or secesh, and what they had been doing for the last 9 months back against the Confederacy and even the division in families." Many, especially neutralists, did not want to face the consequences of being labeled disloyal. As Fanny Gunn wrote to her sons in the federal army about their Lexington, Kentucky, neighborhood, "a large number of them have taken the oath voted the Union Ticket and declare if any one says they ever were cecessionist they will sue them for slander." Bonds posted to gain release from arrest, from a few hundred to thousands of dollars, guaranteed future good behavior or more. In the Liberty, Missouri, district, in 1862, provost marshals required 612 persons to post bonds totaling some $840,000. The provost marshal in Palmyra, near the Mississippi River, reported taking in as much as $1 million that year. The terms of the $6,000 bond for western Kentuckian R. B. Steele, whose son was charged as a guerrilla, stipulated that he remain in his home county throughout the war and "provide information of hostile movements, conspiracies, &c."[46]

As the most visible symbol of governmental coercion of personal liberties, oaths precipitated a crisis of honor and conscience for many civilians. They resented that local military personnel forced oaths on residents who did nothing more than speak in favor of southern rights, however defined. "[A]lthough they have not committed any overt act," wrote one officer in southern Kentucky, "in conversation they have defended the cause of the South in a very noisy and offensive manner. Some of these, I have placed under bonds and obliged them to take the Oath of Allegiance." Worse, oath-takers were marked. As an oathed Missourian wrote in October 1862 after sending away a known disloyalist from her home, "I was fearful that some of the Negroes about the house might see him. The danger was greater to us than to him." Lincoln left to department commanders the discretion to judge loyalty, writing to one officer in Missouri that such vital determinations "must be left to you who are on the spot."[47]

Oaths visibly divided local communities. Suddenly, "some people [are] very uncomfortable about both themselves and their friends," one Kentuckian groused. Reprisals often followed, resulting in societal divisions that in some cases worked to the government's advantage. Just as unionists, government troops, and home guards used the oaths against neutralists, southern sympathizers, and secessionists who refused to take them, residents often chastised those neighbors who did take them as cowards or disloyalists to the southern cause. Samuel Haycraft, a former unionist state senator in Elizabethtown, Kentucky, wrote in 1862 about an ominous visit paid by one of his neighbors under the cover of night. "[S]ome unknown person cal[l]ed at my gate and in a strange voice asked me to come there," he wrote in his journal. "I asked his name twice. [H]e refused to give it but still insisted on my coming[.] I refused to do it as it was dark[.] [H]e then cursed me for a black hearted rascal and said he would shoot me." Ettie Scott complained of unionists' trickery to expose latent disloyalty. One plied a young man with whiskey "but did not drink himself—heard all he had to say—came back the next evening with a posse of soldiers, took [him] prisoner: his brother got him to take the oath which he does not consider binding—but so it is Young B_____ is branded by his former associates as a spy—and they shun him at every corner." Shunning was only the most benign form of retribution against oath-takers. Many others were insulted, threatened, and attacked for their capitulation, or were turned in to garrison commanders as closeted disloyalists.[48]

However unpopular oaths were as visible symbols of federal authority, even more reviled were assessments, or levies, to compensate "undoubted Union men" for property damage by guerrillas and saboteurs. A revision of forced wartime contributions initiated during the eighteenth century, the controversial policy was begun by John Pope in 1861 in northern Missouri and transferred with him the following year to the Shenandoah valley. Subsequent commanders authorized local boards of assessment, comprised of both military and locally prominent unionist civilians, who used loyalty lists to levy fines against registered disloyalists. As one commander in Kentucky noted, levies drove home the point "that it costs something to be disloyal." Many judged them to be little more than government-sponsored robbery.[49]

Levies gave teeth to the oaths. "[T]he charity of men known to be hostile to the Union," reasoned Halleck with open sarcasm, would reimburse the city for its human burden. Drawing on his understanding of the "laws of war," Halleck implemented the policy briefly in St. Louis County in December 1861. He delineated three gradations of disloyalists: "1st, Those in arms with the enemy who have property in this city; 2d, Those who have furnished pecuniary or other aid to the enemy or to persons in the enemy's service; 3d, Those who have verbally, in writing, or by publication given encouragement to insurgents and rebels." Notified by provost marshals, sixty-four assessed persons were given five days to furnish evidence of loyalty or be levied. Most levies ranged from $200 to $400, but one person was assessed $1,000. For those unable or unwilling to pay, federal authorities confiscated and auctioned off their property, with a 25 percent surcharge. The new secretary of war, Edwin M. Stanton, praised Halleck's

St. Louis experiment, but Kentucky U.S. senator Lazarus W. Powell asked the president to stop it. Lincoln refused, and local commanders soon extended it across Missouri, often by means or loyalty tests. An Illinois soldier related, "This country is frightened out of 'propriety' and are now paying the penalty of their treason. All kinds of property is being taken and brought in—even one man took a *Jack* [mule] and rode it into camp."[50]

As assessment policies expanded, they often created as many problems as they solved. Oath-taking did not preclude assessments, with the burden of proof lying with the accused to "satisfy the committee that they are and have been thoroughly loyal, or, if ever disloyal." Assessments included reparations to the families of those killed by marauders: $5,000 for every soldier or unionist killed and $1,000 to $5,000 for those wounded. In the summer of 1862 John M. Schofield in Missouri and Jeremiah T. Boyle in Kentucky initiated assessments to arm and equip state troops, namely the new, unionist Enrolled Missouri Militia (EMM) and Kentucky's county-based home guards. Boyle soon allowed provost marshals to assess "the weak-back Union men" and forced "secessionists and domestick rebels...to furnish timber and their wagons to aid in the work" of rebuilding sabotaged railroad trestles. The levies could be well within residents' means to pay, but they were often unreasonable. In January 1863 John McNeil ordered $300,000 collected in the District of North Missouri, exempting only widows and children with property of less than $5,000, "unless they have given aid and comfort to the guerrillas." With the stigma of being assessed often as much the goal as raising revenue, levies did little to check bushwhacking. Federal troops—and especially militia and home guards—often regarded assessments as authorization for plundering homes and farms of those on lists. Lincoln heard that two-thirds or more of one Kentucky county's assessment take was siphoned off before auction. Many liquidated assets, especially livestock, to avoid their being confiscated. Complaints against assessments by prominent unionists in both states were plentiful, and when latent secessionists infiltrated assessment boards to retaliate by levying unionists, they begged that assessments be suspended. Boyle soon encountered resistance from Kentucky's governor and his superior officer in Cincinnati, who ordered a temporary suspension of the policy. More important, assessments seemed to be fueling the insurgency. One St. Louis clergyman feared that "[t]he bitterness of feeling likely to be engendered by the progressing assessment will renew the personal hostilities which were beginning to disappear, and, thus fanned, the secession element will refuse to die."[51]

Widespread charges of these assessments' "great abuses," as Missouri's governor claimed, caused Lincoln to quietly suspend assessments there and in Kentucky in 1863. He did not, however, countermand these assessment orders, recognizing their strategic value. He continued to endorse assessments in spirit and practice and allowed discretion to commanders to implement them "sparingly," arguing later that "experience has already taught us in this war that holding these smoky localities responsible for the conflagrations within them has a very salutary effect." Many unionists saw things differently. The foreman of a western Missouri board reported in November 1862 that because property damage throughout the county was so extensive and so many residents had fled, assessments were futile. Judged as a "Union defeat," assessments continued sporadically in both states for the duration of the war as hard-line commanders used them largely as a political weapon against dissenters.[52]

Martial law, or the suspension of civil authority in favor of military rule, and trade restrictions were the most widely felt impositions of the dominion system, and both extended over the rivers into the region's free states. Most often declared ad hoc, for local areas rather than for entire states, coincident to a perceived threat from guerrillas or Confederates, martial law gave fangs to the dominion system. Civilians could be arrested, or worse, by soldiers suppressing seditious discourse—spoken, sermonized, written, or printed. Gatherings of perceived disloyalists were forbidden, and in some places "persons are not allowed to stand in groups to talk." Insults hurled at federal troops evoked harsh responses. In central Kentucky, Jeremiah T. Boyle issued a circular in June 1862 requiring arrest for seditious language "that excites rebellion," and rumors circulated that those who "hurrah[ed] for Jeff Davis on the street [would] be shot down." An anxious Missouri woman, repeating a chestnut common in the region, wrote that "if one Secessionist wanted to speak to another he had to go into a cornfield and put out pickets." Young men with loose tongues—or as one Missouri official charged, "Union when sober, rebel when drunk"—often brought retribution upon themselves or their families. "Edd Hensley of our town—but the truth was the young man drinks too much whiskey—and talked too much himself," wrote one Kentucky woman, "and so his family are blamed."[53]

Secessionist or southern-sympathizing citizens quickly became targets. "Our city is now under *martial law*," wrote Bethiah McKown in St. Louis. "[T]he [numbers] of all the houses and the names of all the occupants has been taken down, in order to tell who are Federals and who Secessionists." Banishment, curfews, and even occupation of homes were common. In the summer of 1862 rumors about John Hunt Morgan's approaching rebel cavalry reached Lexington, Kentucky. The federal commander, William T. Ward, declared martial law and sent most of his troops, including both home and provost guards, to the earthworks outside the city. Those on the disloyal list were ordered to remain inside their homes, while the most prominent of them, including the Confederate leader's mother, Henrietta, "were sent out of town as the people threatened to level their houses with the ground, and Major [F. G.] Bracht said he could protect them no longer." The city council then issued an order that all other secessionists would shoulder muskets to defend the city; those who refused were jailed.

As one resident saw it, the order was retaliatory, a response to pro-Confederate residents' verbal abuse of the home guard, "only done to scare them a little... and the soldiers took their revenge by that order."[54]

Newspaper editors in garrisoned towns and cities learned the lesson painfully, as vigilance committees and federal troops suppressed their papers. One historian has claimed that suppressions of newspapers during the war, either by military authority or civilian mobs, exceeded all others in American history. Among them were, in Missouri, St. Louis's *Missouri State Journal* and *Herald*, Boonville's *Patriot*, Weston's *Platte County Conservator*, and St. Joseph's *Tribune*, and in Kentucky, Frankfort's *Kentucky State Flag*, Louisville's *Courier* and *Presbyterian Herald*, and Paducah's *Daily Herald*. Editors who did not flee arrest often found themselves shackled in front of military commissions. In Columbia, Missouri, Edmund J. Ellis's *Boone County Standard* was seized in February 1862, ostensibly for publishing information that could be of use to the enemy and for printing pamphlets encouraging resistance to the federal government. After Ellis was found guilty and banished to Illinois, the army confiscated his press, equipment, and furniture. Some arrested editors fought off suppression of their papers, but they were often targeted recurrently. Others voluntarily stopped publishing or, by de facto suppression, were forced to cede editorial responsibilities to unconditional unionists, which (as Ellis soon learned) occurred frequently in Butternut counties of neighboring free states. In the summer of 1863 in southern Illinois, George H. Dickinson temporarily gave up the editorship of the *Marion Record*. "The office having been taken possession of by the military authorities," the former editor wrote, he ceded control "[to] the gentleman appointed by the Provost Marshal." Confiscated printing property frequently found its way to local federal regiments, whose personnel published progovernment newspapers with titles such as *The Kentucky Loyalist, Cape Girardeau Eagle*, and *The Advance Guard*. Unionist editors, too, faced pressure. One historian has found that 60 percent of Indiana's Republican papers received threats of suppression or actual violence.[55]

Until 1863 women were exempt from taking the oath, but they were not exempted from punishment for aiding and abetting the enemy. Those "giving information to or communicating with the enemy, will be arrested, tried, condemned, and shot as spies. It should be remembered that in this respect the laws of war make no distinction of sex; all are liable to the same penalty." Many faced military commissions that often judged harshly. Lincoln himself commuted sentences of death to imprisonment, and department commanders mitigated prison sentences to bond and parole. In February 1863 a St. Louis commission found two women, Laidee and Augusta Bagwell, guilty of writing and trying to send antigovernment letters to Confederate soldiers in the field. For one, the commission recommended parole and bond, but for the other bond and banishment to the South. The department commander, John M. Schofield, mitigated the sentences to banishment to Canada, but increased their bonds substantially.[56]

Of the dominion system's various mandates, trade restrictions most overtly politicized loyalty designations. Because access to or control of navigable interior rivers underlay both federal and Confederate military strategy, both sides tried to secure them by different methods. In hopes of enticing the western states to secede, the Confederate Congress quickly moved to protect the traditional trade relations between the South and the West by enacting generous river navigation and trade laws, including tariff exemptions for western farm produce and many manufactured goods. Federal officials undertook construction of the ironclad Western Flotilla to accomplish the "Anaconda" plan and strangle the Confederacy by encircling it.[57]

If in-betweenness worked in any way to the advantage of the middle border's slave states, however temporarily, it was in the matter of trade. Neutrality meant unregulated trade with both belligerents, and cities like St. Louis and Louisville, connected by river as well as rail, initially took full advantage. By way of the Mississippi and the newly completed L and N railroad line, ever heavier amounts of freight, even arms, found their way to Nashville, Memphis, Chattanooga, and even New Orleans. State and federal troops garrisoning river cities quickly interdicted such traffic. On May 2 the War Department instructed the commander of troops at Cairo not to block southbound river shipments so "irritating to Kentucky and other States bordering on the Ohio.... That this may not be used as a means for extending the spirit of secession." This conciliation would not last. In fact, it would not survive the day.[58]

Trade policy soon empowered special agents, treasury officials, and army officers with making judgments about the loyalty of those who shipped or received goods. Fearful that these cities' merchants were putting business ahead of war, on May 2 the secretary of the treasury, Salmon P. Chase, issued a circular to nonmilitary customs port officers in western river cities requiring examinations of manifests and searches of "all steamers, flatboats and other water crafts... railroad cars and other vehicles... destined for any port or place under insurrectionary control." Agents on the ground agreed that Kentucky, especially Louisville, was the weak link. As one Cincinnati editor fumed, "'[N]eutrality' seems to consist in perfect freedom to furnish our enemies the wherewithal to make war upon us." (Not surprisingly, within two weeks Kentucky would declare neutrality.) When Lincoln relaxed interior trade policy to conform with select coastal cities, including New Orleans, leaving room for smuggling from the border states by boat and rail, Congress authorized commercial interdiction with "insurrectionary" states. In September the administration stopped trade altogether with western Kentucky, and Ulysses S. Grant stopped southbound boats at Cairo and confiscated contraband goods despite "serious doubts whether there is any law authorizing this seizure." In October 1862 Samuel R. Curtis refined the policy in Missouri by forbidding "public trade or commercial business... except by persons strictly loyal," prohibiting permits and licenses for all others and requiring bonds from those who received them. By the summer of 1862, all southbound trade on the Ohio below Wheeling and on the Mississippi below the northern border of Missouri required permits. The Confederate Congress reciprocated, including Kentucky and Missouri, and troops interdicted upriver shipments at Columbus.[59]

Recognizing that compiling identifications taxed an overburdened army, especially in large cities, the War Department's order authorized special treasury agents, with guidance from commanders, to appoint local boards of trade "by whose approval and permission only... goods, wares, or merchandise... shall be unloaded or disposed of." In effect, these boards determined who could, and more important who could not, conduct trade, perhaps the most potent weapon wielded by the federal authorities against civilians short of arrest and punishment for treasonable activities, and affixed their names to disloyalty lists if they were determined to have engaged in contraband trade. By March 1862 boards of trade operated in most of the cities lying on navigable rivers and in many interior towns.[60]

With these boards, business interests soon influenced the emerging calculus of loyalty and order on the home front. Although unconditional unionism was the baseline criterion for membership, nearly all were prominent businessmen, editors, manufacturers, or public officials. The boards often selected provost marshals, and many were members of boards. Their ostensible willingness to forego personal gain or to put aside business or private relationships in order to stop illicit trade with the Confederacy, as well as connections with the administration, got them their positions. In Centralia, Illinois, editor Edward S. Condit was named his district's provost marshal in 1864 owing to his "thorough-going business qualifications.... The locating of the Head-quarters at Centralia will naturally draw a considerable amount of business to the city."[61]

Because patriotism and profit were not mutually exclusive impulses, trade restrictions did not stop widespread smuggling. Mismarking barrels and boxes and bribing federal marshals, deputies, and inspectors were standard practices, and army officials blamed local boards of trade for suspect ethics and even loyalty, especially in the border slave states. "These Boards cannot possibly fulfill the purposes for which they were created," wrote an exasperated commander in Bowling Green, Kentucky. "Supposing it possible to find three unconditional Union men so to act (a fact I am not disposed to admit as for as some towns are concerned),—their very isolation places them at the mercy, and under the control, of the disloyal population around them." Nightriders targeted board members, forcing some to flee upon hearing rumors of approaching horsemen. "Add to this family and social ties, and the chances of protection for the Government against the abuses they were appointed to correct, amount to nothing." Commanders thus devised other means to reduce the illegal trade, including allowing limited traffic in some contraband goods to encourage broader compliance with restrictions. Even loyalists were often detained for hours or even overnight as they waited for passes, resulting in "most unfriendly comment and acrimonious feeling." An exasperated Grant issued a short-lived order expelling Jewish traders from Paducah and his department owing to widespread prejudice over latent disloyalty and illicit pursuit of profit over patriotism. In August 1864 the army halted all trade in and out of Kentucky by known disloyalists.[62]

The same political motives that influenced agents and boards of trade to overlook illicit trade also drove implementation of trade policies. In divided border states, free and slave, where changing circumstances made loyalty and disloyalty uncertain and fluid, letting commerce follow the flag demanded strict measures of unconditional unionism. In the fall of 1862 Jeremiah Boyle ordered in central Kentucky that persons could not "engage in the buying, selling, or shipping of merchandise or groceries without having first obtained a certificate signed by six Unconditional Union men of good standing, that said person himself is an Unconditional Union man." Politicized manipulations of such distinctions by boards of trade and army officers led to widespread abuses of the permit system, compelling Kentucky's final wartime governor, Thomas E. Bramlette, to complain to Lincoln that "many *loyal men* are driven out of business...for no other reason than their political preferences." When the army refused to honor the Treasury Department's rescission of trade restrictions in Kentucky in early 1864, the governor condemned the permit system as "a most shameful and corrupt system of political partisan corruption and oppression."[63]

In the middle border's free states, which in 1862 were less affected by overt disloyalty than states across the rivers, trade permits became the vehicle for partisan politics. Boards of trade expanded their responsibility to stop trade with the enemy by pressuring businesspeople who opposed the Lincoln administration, while rank-and-file Republicans more easily received approval for monthly applications for the southern trade than Democrats. When the president of Cincinnati's Chamber of Commerce, Joseph C. Butler, telegraphed the new secretary of war, Edwin M. Stanton, with the appointments of three members of the local board of trade, he noted that all were prominent Republicans who had received government contracts for war materiel or transportation services. The potent stew of trade, politics, and loyalty distinctions soon boiled over in the western river states, enough to cause many businesspeople to complain. When John Skiff, a Cincinnati merchandiser, admitted to attempting to smuggle south a load of butter marked as ale through Kentucky in May 1861, he claimed he "had done no worse than others" and grumbled that his greatest crime was to have voted for John Bell, and not Lincoln, in 1860.[64]

This web of trade restraints cascaded through the population on both sides of the rivers. In May 1862 a visitor to Louisville, by then a teeming federal supply center, remarked that the city had "suffered terribly" from a year of conflict, its nonmilitary economy stagnant, its storefronts boarded, its factories silent, giving it a "sleepy, drowsy look." Businessmen who could not conduct business could then not pay workers, who in turn could not pay their bills. Many were left destitute, forced out of their lodgings and into those of friends, neighbors, and relatives, or they relocated to where they could find work. Some moved into abandoned homes and buildings or left altogether. Louisville's Alexander Jeffrey, who owned and managed several gasworks in the region and in Mississippi, fell afoul of federal authorities in the city for his outspokenness against partisanship in awarding trade permits. After he was placed on the disloyal list, his businesses were ordered closed and he fled the city, leaving his family behind to prevent their home from being vandalized. Without income in Lexington, he tried to obtain clemency from the district commander and to hire or sell several of his male slaves. Jeffrey found employers unable to pay his wages or prohibited by the local board of trade from conducting business. A frustrated Jeffrey wrote to his wife, "I really think it is better to live any where than here.... Ky is a subject province under the most arbitrary military despotism.... I do find myself getting very savage."[65]

In early 1862 Bernard G. Farrar, Missouri's provost marshal general, huffed from his headquarters in St. Louis, "It is now purely a question of power not one of law." At nearly the same time, that state's lieutenant governor, Willard P. Hall, spoke more laconically, if not quite accurately, about conditions in Missouri. "Amidst armies," he asserted, "the law is silent." Farrar's and Hall's candid views of the authority of an occupying army among a hostile citizenry were placed, curiously, in the context of instructions to desist in arresting civilians around the state merely on suspicion of disloyalty. But they spoke rightly to the circumstances in these middle border slave states, where martial and civil law coexisted, at least in theory. Where lines of loyalty were drawn in the sand, law and power were often nearly indistinguishable.[66]

§

After a string of shocking Confederate defeats west of the Mississippi—Mill Springs, Fort Henry, Fort Donelson, Pea Ridge, New Madrid and Island No. 10, Shiloh, and New Orleans—for southerners in the West the spring of 1862 was a season of despair. At the onset of summer, federal armies and navies (100,000+ men) controlled most of Tennessee, Arkansas, and Louisiana, and occupied the region's largest cities. Felix Zollicoffer, Ben McCulloch, Albert Sidney Johnston, and even George W. Johnson, Kentucky's Confederate governor, had been killed in battle, and others, like Gideon Pillow and Simon B. Buckner, had been ignominiously captured and paroled. The war had moved deep into the lower Mississippi valley, far from the middle border states, safely enough for the secretary of war, Ohioan Edwin M. Stanton, to close all recruiting offices and release "political prisoners," as the Lincoln administration referred to civilian detainees in military custody, upon their taking the oath. Residents could only listen to rumors or refuse to believe the largely unionist newspapers and hope for a reversal of fortunes.[67]

For two nightmarish months the real war found Kentucky, revealing what the people of the South were daily enduring. Starting in mid-August, some forty thousand gray-clad soldiers waving battle flags emblazoned with slogans such as "Kentucky Shall Be Free" headed into the state in three, uncoordinated wings. The first, six thousand men under Edmund Kirby Smith, moved northward toward Lexington from east Tennessee; a second, forty-six hundred under Humphrey Marshall, came eastward over the mountains from western Virginia; and a third, trailing the others, thirty thousand men under Braxton Bragg, headed toward Louisville from the central southern tier. John Hunt Morgan's twelve hundred cavalry operated independently, in advance of the infantry columns. The only sizable federal force, the forty-thousand-man Army of the Ohio under Don Carlos Buell, was en route from Nashville, without use of the L and N Railroad after Morgan and Nathan Bedford Forrest destroyed a number of vital bridges and tunnels. Facing an unimpeded invasion, both Cincinnati's and Louisville's citizenry panicked. Federal commanders rushed to defend these cities, forcing civilians—largely African Americans—to labor with soldiers on earthen fortifications across the Ohio River. A Louisvillian claimed that days of "general panic" were made worse by "a warning for the women and children to leave accompanied it was said with the avowal on Genl [William] Nelsons part that he would lay the whole city in ashes before the Confederates should possess it."[68]

By September the southern and central Bluegrass was filled with rebel soldiers. A summer-long drought seared the entire region, with daily temperatures in central Missouri as high as 107 degrees in late July. The drought continued well into the fall. "The dust lay on the roads a foot thick and filled their eyes and mouth, blinding and almost suffocating them," wrote one Kentuckian of the armies' choking march through the Bluegrass, "no water to be met with for miles, but stagnant pools and slimy ponds redolent of the odor of the cattle of the neighborhood."

On August 13 Kirby Smith's force moved into Kentucky. Working independently of Bragg, he occupied Barboursville and captured a federal wagon train loaded with supplies. Learning that a federal force of some sixty-five hundred, mostly Indianans and Kentuckians under William "Bull" Nelson, was positioned south of Richmond, he hastened into the southern Bluegrass. On August 30

Kirby Smith overran the green force in a short fight, capturing more than four thousand along with ten thousand stand of arms, nine cannons, and a complete wagon train, and moved on to occupy Lexington and Frankfort. As citizens swarmed over the battlefield searching for discarded items, the rebel armies stripped farms of vital foodstuffs and livestock and stores of clothing and provisions, paying if at all with worthless rebel shinplasters. "Skedadlers" skulked in the woods, foraged from barns and springhouses, and threatened to harm residents if they informed on them.[69]

Low on supplies and facing what he called a hostile population—"their bluegrass and fat grass are against us"—Kirby Smith never joined Bragg, who entered Kentucky on September 14. Buell occupied Bowling Green the same day. Bragg meandered northward with his Army of the Mississippi, wasted precious days nearly besieging a four-thousand-man federal garrison protecting the railroad bridge at Munfordville, then rested his men another full day after he forced its surrender. Goaded into action by his recent near-removal by the president, Buell drove northward along the Louisville Pike, securing Kentucky's largest city and vital federal supply center, and augmented his force with the twenty thousand troops there. He inched southward toward Bragg's scattered columns.[70]

The desperate need for water in part drove portions of both armies toward the small village of Perryville, along the nearly dry Chaplin River in the rolling hills east of Bardstown, which lead units of both sides fought to secure for themselves. On October 8 Bragg, with rampant straggling reducing his ranks to 16,800 men, impetuously attacked Buell's army, by then numbering 55,000. He was saved from a devastating defeat largely by the Ohioan's failure to bring to bear more than half of his force against the Confederate assaults. Some 7,700 soldiers lay dead, wounded, or missing on the field, and the remainder crouched thirsty and exhausted largely where they had begun the brutal day. The Confederate army withdrew throughout the night, and soon from the entire state, along with those in and around Lexington. In the following days locals gathered the dead for hasty burial near the field, while many more sheltered and nursed the federal and rebel wounded in their homes. Nearly all of Danville's public buildings, including Centre College, were filled with sick and wounded soldiers. As if in approbation, the rain at last began to fall.[71]

The Kentucky campaign commenced on the pretext that residents were eager to enlist. "[T]he region inhabited by my friends," blustered Humphrey Marshall to the Confederacy's vice president, Alexander Stephens, "and they have been looking for me as their deliverer from accursed bondage.... [T]he people will flock around my banner as the Italians did to that of Garibaldi." A "Kentucky bloc" pressured high-ranking Confederate officials into believing that they should prioritize the war in the West. Even Jefferson Davis was convinced that his birth state was a conquered federal province, its residents needing only to have the federal occupation thrown off to demonstrate themselves as true southerners. Anticipating a crush of Kentucky recruits, all of the wing commanders issued calls for recruits by employing flowery language linking Kentuckians to the southern states, certain they "have only been thus far kept from joining us by the infamous misrepresentations of the Yankee leaders and newspapers."[72]

Yet the recruits never came. The unwillingness of Kentuckians to answer the Confederate call when they entered the state exasperated rebel commanders like Kirby Smith, who complained: "Thus far the people are universally hostile to our cause." As Bragg famously also complained, "We have so far received no accession to this army.... We have 15,000 stand of arms and no one to use them." Edward O. Guerrant offered perhaps the most jaundiced remarks about Kentuckians' cold reception of the rebel armies. "We came into the state to meet and deliver *friends*," he lamented. "We met clenched teeth, and closed doors.... We treated all men as *friends* and *freemen*. Most of them treated us as *enemies* and *robbers*."[73]

The perception that Kentuckians put their purses ahead of the Confederacy's cause likely spoke to inconvenient truths. Doubt bled through these Confederates' first public words. "Kentuckians!" cooed Kirby Smith. "We come to test the truth of what we believe to be a foul aspersion—that Kentuckians willingly join in the attempt to subjugate us, and deprive us of our property, our liberty, and our dearest rights.... ARE we deceived?—Can you treat us as enemies?—Our hearts answer, No." Desperation likely prompted Bragg to absent himself from his army to hold a farcical ceremony in Frankfort to install the state's provisional governor, Richard Hawes. On the statehouse lawn, his inaugural speech denounced the federal dominion system's "insult, persecution and cruelty.... Seizures and imprisonment of persons without warrant or trial; confiscations of estates; forced loans and military exactions; the utter suppression of speech and the press." Within hours, cannon reports sounded from the palisades across the Kentucky River, announcing the arrival of federal troops. The Confederate delegation fled, burning bridges behind them and offering precious little encouragement of victory.[74]

Likely more debilitating was the Confederates' rough treatment of civilians during their ten-week stay. Prominent unionists, especially those who worked for the federal government, fled their homes lest they be persecuted. John W. Calvert, a southern Kentucky farmer and newly named federal revenue collector, was forced to "skedaddle" and to live "constantly on the 'wing'" for several months, having "burn[ed] all my political papers in order not to compromise the safety of my uncle, with whom we are staying" and to enlist the aid of a "'Body-Guard' (i e, all the Niggers in the neighborhood)." Residents of all political stripes contended with these armies' impositions. "[T]he Friday before the

Battle at Richmond I was notified that a [federal] Regiment would be camped in my *yard*," wrote a southern sympathizer. "I have now an Encampment of Confederates in my *Pasture* without any consultations of my wishes." Rebel cavalrymen's confiscations of horses drew the loudest complaints, but empty smokehouses, missing livestock, destroyed fencerows, and fields stripped of sparse corn brought deeper, more lasting deprivations. Long wagon trains full of plunder followed by droves of cattle and horses trailing the rebel armies confirmed that the Confederates were little better than thieves.[75]

Heavy cavalry raids offered many residents their first glimpse of regular Confederates since their armies had been forced south. Home guards fled, useless against such numbers, and raiders tore up railroad lines, destroyed bridges and depots, and entered communities. For many southerners these horsemen were bold cavaliers and, as one political southerner described them, "the forerunner of the glorious day when the Southern army should hold Kentucky." Rumors swirled all summer of the imminent arrival of rebel horsemen. "One day the report goes that FORREST is coming, and the next, that JOHN MORGAN is coming from Tennessee," reported one Kentucky paper. Lizzie Hardin described the response of Harrodsburg's Confederate community to Morgan's long-awaited arrival in July 1862: "At last they came! Oh! the grand and glorious sight it seemed to us! Eleven hundred Southern horsemen, rushing on at full speed amid the waving of caps and glancing of steel. It sounded as though the shouts of an innumerable multitude rent the air, while from the foremost regiment rose the chorus of the 'Bonny Blue Flag.'" The bearded Morgan, wearing a plaid short jacket, knee boots, and plumed hat, was "exactly my ideal of a dashing cavalryman."[76] (See figure 5.3.)

These bold dragoons represented more than culturally idealized warriors. Rebel cavalrymen offered a chance to demonstrate political sentiments that the occupation had driven underground. But boasts of chivalry for these horsemen obfuscated a war they were already experiencing in the West that was anything but noble. Political southerners especially sought revenge for unionists' complicity in the dominion system. The rebels would surely "spread fear and consternation throughout Yankeedom," as one Kentuckian wrote. When Lizzie Hardin waved her handkerchief at Morgan's cavalrymen, her mother begged her to stop. "You are watched," she whispered. For a fearful unionist who fled the harsh treatment he expected to receive from Confederate "devils," Hardin had little sympathy, having "many a time... seen our men dragged off to prison but I have never seen the Union men on their knees to prevent it." Hardin cruelly tormented a young girl in her community who lived in a divided household. When the child asked "what the rebels would do" when they arrived, "I told her that they were in the habit of eating little children," then boasted of inducing the child's "natural tears shed."[77]

Figure 5.3 "The Rebel Morgan With His Guerrillas Bivouacking in Court House Square, Paris, Bourbon County, After Levying Contributions on the Inhabitants," 1862, wood engraving from sketch by artist Henry Lovie. Morgan, a Confederate commander, was among a number of cavalrymen who entered the middle border states between 1862 and 1864 on heavy raids, including one across the Ohio River into Indiana and Ohio. From *Frank Leslie's Pictorial History of the American Civil War* (New York, 1862). Courtesy Department of Special Collections, Western Kentucky University.

Thousands of uniformed horsemen contrasted with the bands of nightriders that plagued the countryside, but their treatment of unionist civilians soon merged with the region's harder kind of war. With their southern neighbors, even children, acting as rebel informants, raids on garrisoned towns put unionists' property in harm's way. Samuel Haycraft noted that when Morgan's horsemen sacked Elizabethtown in October and December 1862, they robbed the post office, "searched the Clerks office and some private houses...committed various robberies of horses, Store goods, money, etc....Took all the horses nearly in Town and for miles around and many thousand Dollars worth of dry good, boots, shoes, &c." Another wrote, "The Union people met together in solemn groups at the corners of the street, and I noticed whenever I passed them they had just arrived at the part of the story where occurred the words, 'horse thieves, gang-robbers, guerrillas, &c.'" But unionists could expect more than mere ransacking. A resident of Harrodsburg claimed that only local secessionists' entreaties prevented Morgan "from hanging all the Union men," while St. Louisan Sarah Jane Full Hill watched in horror as some twelve hundred rebel horsemen under Forrest turned on unionists in a northern Tennessee town after attacking its federal garrison. "It was here their brutal savagery was shown," she wrote. "They charged up and down the streets, firing wildly into houses among unoffending women and children. They went into the homes of citizens who were suspected or known to favor the Union cause.... Many houses were burned to the ground and their occupants turned out homeless in the winter weather. Stores were looted. There seemed to be no discipline or restraint. They were turned loose in that little town and in a few hours had destroyed more property belonging to their own people than had been done by the Federal thousands that had occupied the place for months."[78]

This unionist's use of language—"their own people"—suggests the hardened lines of allegiance dividing the southern cultures in slave states. Having lost their middle ground, self-professed "Southern rights unionists" were especially outraged at rebels' persecution. Hauled under guard before Morgan solely for his political sentiments, Albert Wallace of Hopkinsville, Kentucky, no longer shared "that sense of security [among] southerners." But for many new political southerners, the hard treatment at the hands of rebel horsemen crushed the illusion of the superiority of the South and its culture. Lizzie Hardin recalled neighbors' trepidations when hearing rumors of Morgan's cavalry descending on their community and "tried to quiet the people by telling them our army did not molest private individuals or private property, but they had seen too much of their own men to believe that soldiers could ever behave well." Rather than shore up support for the rebel cause, such behavior reconverted many political southerners into unionists. "Allen Higgins has come home with his Family," wrote a Bluegrass woman of a neighbor who had fled southern Kentucky after the rebel invasion. "Allen says he is completely cured of cecession he is a Union man from this [time] out the rebbels burnt his cotton and his neighbours."[79]

Gauging this population's shifting allegiances is an imprecise task, but enlistments—and nonenlistments—offer a historical benchmark of sorts. Some 25,000 of the state's native white men ultimately fought as volunteers in the Confederate ranks, while nearly twice that number fought for the union. Not a single Kentucky infantry regiment accompanied Bragg northward, and only five served in the Confederacy's entire western theater, compared to twenty-eight then in federal service. Left untallied are the 187,000 white Kentuckians who avoided military service altogether, ranking the state, as one historian has found, "last among southern states in percentage of whites who fought for the Confederacy and first in percentage of whites who fought for no one." Missouri's totals were less anemic, but more imbalanced, with more than 100,000 serving in federal ranks and just 30,000 in the Confederate armies— some 90,000 Missourians stayed out of the fight altogether. In a war that appeared to offer no winners, most found no side to serve them, so they served none but their own.[80]

§

On a rainy February evening in 1863, Mary E. Van Meter sat down to write in her journal at her father's home in Bowling Green. "Houses burned to the ground, fences taken from around most yards and gardens. The streets which used to be our pride are almost impassible for pedestrians." Stoked by a deep sense of betrayal, Mary wrote acrid words: "How have we been deceived in regard to civil liberty in Kentucky. I came back to the state of my adoption believing civil law reigned supreme, but alas it is not so. Military despotism rules with its rod of iron, and woe to those who dare question the justice of this tyrannical enemy.... The land I gaze upon is ours by the laws of all countries, yet it is in the hands of hirelings brought from other states by an Abolition president, to wrest from Kentuckians their lawful rights in property, freedom of speech, and all else a brave and free people hold dear."[81]

This political southerner wrote primarily of the federal military occupation that the recent Confederate incursion had failed to relieve. But beneath her words lay another, more bitter belief: that she and her people had been deceived. Indeed, by then a new wartime reality, the emancipation of slaves, had plunged her middle border region deeper into the netherworld of war.

War of Another Kind

Robert Winn knew something about borders. Born and raised near Durham in northern England, he spent his early life within sight of the famed Hadrian's Wall, which for two thousand years had stood sentry against invading Scottish barbarians. More recently they had descended not as raiders or reivers but as quasi-countrymen. Winn thus knew the wall less as a barrier than a symbol, a demarcation between peoples at once alike and different.[1]

Winn found in America a new wall of sorts. In 1852, when he was sixteen, his father, a coal manager, moved to Hawesville, Kentucky, a thriving cannel coal town like the family's former Tyneside home. Located where the hills of the river's upper reaches gave way to the lower river's broad floodplain, Hawesville was in fact two towns, one nestled below the sharp river bluff and the other perched atop. The upper town was protected from the river while the lower was annually drowned. So too the county; its 148 slaveholders and 800 slaves lived and labored downriver in the lower, flat, grain- and tobacco-producing half, while upriver in the hills its many foreign-born residents, like the Winns, dug for bright-burning coal. Devout Presbyterians, the Winns found the region's spiritual soil as familiar as the shaly ridges from which they scooped their futures.[2]

More than coal dust, the war clouded Robert Winn's dream of inclusive American freedom. In October 1861 he was in federal uniform, enlisting in the 3rd Kentucky Cavalry. His decision to don the blue coat was entirely nonpolitical in the traditional sense. Astonishingly ambivalent about political matters, he had no strong opinion either of the Confederacy or the Union, or even a passion for victory. In the army he served alongside native-born men he considered commoners, unsuited for political participation, but who saw him as below them. "[T]hey look upon us as mere mercenary's," he wrote to his sister, Martha, who read his letters aloud to his illiterate wife, Amelia. Yet he resented even more those who did not serve at all. Unable to decipher leveling American democracy, he gave up trying. "[I]t is perfect nonsense for Englishmen to try Americanism."[3]

Winn's peculiar patriotism was paired with unpeculiar antislavery beliefs. Like most native white westerners, he had no love for people of color, slave or free; his father competed against local coal companies that employed or owned slave laborers. "Whip the Damned Nigger and send him home," he wrote approvingly of the beatings soldiers in his regiment administered to fugitives in their camps before returning them to their masters. Widespread support in his adopted region for slavery, he believed, had encouraged the South to inaugurate the "dirty buisness." All Americans shared blame for a destructive war "carried on in the interest of slavery each party trying to outdo the other in their devotion to the Institution," he wrote in the summer of 1862. Sadly, "the punishment is sure to fall upon both sections."[4]

Luckily for Winn, while serving in Don Carlos Buell's Army of the Ohio, he managed to miss fighting in its early battles. After Shiloh he assisted with burial details amid the stench of April death, and in early fall endured the long, dry march to Kentucky in pursuit of Bragg's invading army. He did not see the elephant at Perryville because his regiment had been held in reserve.[5]

In the fall of 1862 he did see war, but of another kind. A political revolution swept the western soldiery in response to changed war objectives. "Confiscation and Abolition and Desertion are the staples of Conversation," he wrote. In July the adjourned Congress provided the president with expanded authority. It passed a militia law to replenish the armies' ranks, depleted by the ongoing war, authorizing Lincoln to enroll three hundred thousand more three-year men. Then, after the summer defeats in Virginia, the War Department required state governments to mobilize another three hundred thousand nine-month militia. Many opposed this "militia draft" for its excess, for violating the states' rights by nationalizing troops, and for flooding the western army with inferior soldiers.[6]

Denying that slaveholding was a constitutional right, Winn mildly supported emancipation as a means of ending the war. But he saw Lincoln as a despot who used the war as a pretense for centralization of federal power and the government's infringement of civil liberties. He disapproved of the Second Confiscation Act, especially the "ironclad" or "test" oath requiring slaveholding citizens to declare that they had never voluntarily borne arms nor given aid to the Confederacy to regain confiscated slave property.[7]

The summer's congressional acts also signaled that slavery and African Americans would assume a new centrality in the federal war aims and the armies' efforts. A clause in the Militia Act—passed over the objection of border state politicians—authorized the War Department to enroll "persons of African descent" for "any war service," including soldiering. A new Confiscation Act, passed on July 17 and more expansive than the previous version, punished all disloyal citizens by seizing their property, including slaves as "captives of war [who] shall be forever free."[8]

Winn marveled at the "almost universal" opposition of white western soldiers to this unconstitutional intrusion on civilian property rights, not excluding human chattel. "The western army is thoroughly devoted to the Divinity of Slavery," he concluded. "I hear among both Kentucky, Ohio, Indiana and Illinois troops that Congress has no right to free the Slaves of even Rebels in arms, and such an attempt would justify a revolt of the troops in favor of the South." Mass desertions would follow. "[I]f radicalism must sever the Border States and Nor[th]western States," he predicted, "it will prolong the war indefinitely and probably cause defeat, and thus make another war necessary." Winn counted himself among the disaffected. "As to re-enlisting," he avowed, "I dont imagine I suit the service any better than it suits me."[9]

When the president issued a preliminary emancipation proclamation on September 22, one that did not yet exclude any border states, Robert Winn saw violence engulf the countryside of his adopted slave state. Ending the war by any means now became his paramount aim, including prosecuting a hard-line war. "Let a vigorous Confiscation policy and proper execution of all the laws punishing treason be begun—with a proper force to carry it out," he intoned, "and impress in the rebel states every thing necessary to the army, from friend or foe paying friends only." He shrugged off charges that federal troops were preventing loyal citizens from voting. "Does anybody suppose that Kentucky...[is] more loyal than Mississippi or Louisiana? I don't." Full loyalty meant accepting the end of slavery. The war, whether in the field or at home, would not end "till everybody is a different kind of chap than he is now."[10]

One who was not Winn's "different kind of chap" was fellow Kentuckian Benjamin F. Buckner. A unionist who steadfastly opposed emancipation, at the outbreak of the war Buckner had been a twenty-six-year-old practicing lawyer in Winchester. In late September 1861 Buckner enlisted in a federal regiment, the 20th Kentucky Infantry, and held the rank of major. His was one of the state's "first families," and Buckner lived in not one, but two, divided houses. Publicly, cousins Richard Hawes and Simon B. Buckner served the Confederacy, while privately his fiancée, Helen Martin, the daughter of a large slave owner, was disloyal under the terms of the new measure. "I know dearest that I need not write to you about politics," he added soberly, "that we can't agree and we had better agree to disagree than to endeavor to convince one another by fruitless argumentation."[11]

Following emancipation, Buckner's politics underwent a sea change. Accompanying the president's proclamation was a suspension of habeas corpus and authorization of military trials for "Rebels, and Insurgents, and aiders and abettors [who] discourag[ed] volunteer enlistments, resist[ed] militia drafts, or [were] guilty of any disloyal practice." As the fall elections approached, civilians and soldiers dissented against the president's emancipation initiative. Buckner was among them. "Union Kentuckians are most shamefully treated," he ranted. As soldiers, "we find ourselves in arms to maintain doctrines which if announced 12 months ago, would have driven us all... into the ranks of the Southern Army[.]"[12]

Like Winn, the war made Buckner an outsider. "We joined the people of the North (a people whom we did not love)," he railed, "to fight the South (a people with whom we were connected by ties of relationship interest [and] the identity of our habits and institutions) merely upon principle." Of proslavery unionists, Buckner asked, "Where can we go[?]"[13]

He answered his own question by a dual declaration—of independence from the federal army and of allegiance to slavery. "No Kentuckian can have any heart for this contest," he wrote Helen. "You are anxious for me to leave the Army. I assure you that I am myself *most* anxious to do so....I cant fight against my principles and those of my friends in order to satisfy the absurd desire of a faction at the north." By the end of November he had tendered his resignation. He was certainly not alone. In his regiment alone, "sixteen already resigned because they are required to remain in the South, when their property and that of their friends is being stolen by our supposed friends." Only their colonel, Charles S. Hanson, remained; he said "that he intends to leave the Service—that he will not fight to free his own negroes." Buckner believed emancipation alone had changed the game. "We are all opposed to secession," he wrote dejectedly. "We who are in the army feel that we have been grossly deceived by the President and the party in power.... I am thus utterly indisposed to fight for Lincoln abolitionism." In April 1863 he returned home to his welcoming fiancée, and they married later that year.[14]

Buckner's dissent spared him a greater indignity, or worse. After a listless defense of the L and N Railroad depot while garrisoning Lebanon, on July 5, 1863, a portion of his demoralized former regiment surrendered to John Hunt Morgan's cavalry raiders. Colonel Hanson, who had not left the service, was nearly murdered outright by his rebel captors, enraged at the death of Morgan's popular younger brother, Tom. After burning many of Lebanon's public buildings, Morgan paroled his fellow Kentuckians, including Hanson, a close friend of Morgan's before the war, whose own brother—like Morgan, a once-secession opponent turned Confederate brigadier general—had been mortally wounded at Stone's River on January 2, the day after Lincoln's final emancipation proclamation took effect.[15]

With the war now seen widely as one to free slaves, neither Buckner, Hanson, nor their men saw the surrender as particularly shameful. Instead, they took the opportunity to leave a now shameful war.

6

Bitter Harvest

Emancipation and the Politics of Loyalty

For more than a century military historians claimed that the twin federal victories at Gettysburg and Vicksburg, secured simultaneously on July 4, 1863, constituted the war's turning point, the famed "high water mark of the Confederacy." More recently wartime emancipation has become the defining event of a changed conflict, driving scholarly arguments about the nature of the war: for the Union, or against slavery. As "a beacon that reached deep into the Confederacy," in Ira Berlin's words, emancipation initiated a revolution for freedom rather than simply a restoration of the Union.[1]

That beacon shone brighter on the middle border than in either the Confederacy or New England. In a region struggling for union *and* slavery, dissenting white residents consolidated antiwar responses to Lincoln's and congressional Republicans' war initiatives in the summer and fall of 1862, including confiscation, conscription, and the suspension of habeas corpus. All buttressed the president's announcement of emancipation and black enlistment, with racial antipathy adhering the various strands of dissent.

As much as it unified dissenters, emancipation broke open a region rent by political and ideological fault lines by splintering the moderate western consensus and driving a wedge between the middle border's free and slave states. Definable political factions emerged. In the free states, as Peace Democrats opposed the continuance of a war against slavery and Lincoln as its chief prosecutor, pro-emancipation Republicans consolidated around support for the issue and used it not just as a fulcrum for forceful nationalism against "Copperhead" war opponents, but as the middle ground of dissent against the new war measures. Under pressure, War Democrats and moderate Republicans in those states faced an unacceptable or unsustainable option: become either pro-emancipation war supporters or anti-emancipation war opponents. In the slave states, where hard-line war included an expansive dominion system and new loyalty mandates and demanded civilians' support for the end of slavery, broad opposition to emancipation forced a deadlier choice between anti-administration dissenters and pro-Confederate disloyalists. Consequently, emancipation strengthened a struggling southern nationalism, previously stunted by reflexive unionism and Confederate invasions. Caught between were white federal soldiers divided over whether to use emancipation as retribution against hostile proslavery populations or refuse to support it as a war aim, and African Americans, free and slave, who saw the war as the springboard to freedom for themselves or their families.

In these states especially, freeing slaves by dint of war was perhaps the conflict's worst-kept secret. Long the staple of the region's Democratic newspapers, vicious attacks against "ranting Negro-suffrage, Freedom-screeching Black Republican[s]" only heightened their rhetoric. Only days after Fort Sumter, Ohioan Salmon B. Axtell returned from the southern portion of his state and neighboring Kentucky, having heard widely, "This war *is to become* and is now *to becoming* a war for the *liberation* of the whole slave *population*."[2]

Speculation by middle border whites about imminent wartime intrusions on slavery had begun almost with the war itself. As early as May 1861 St. Louis unionist Thomas T. Gantt, a West Pointer and member of the state convention, related to department commander William S. Harney the concerns of a rural Missourian, "whether I supposed it was the intention of the United States Government to interfere with the institution of negro slavery in Missouri or any Slave State." Harney responded, "I am not a little astonished that such a question could be seriously put. I should as soon expect to hear that the orders of the Government were directed towards the overthrow of any other kind of property as of this in negro slaves." White Kentuckians were mostly unwilling to trust government officials to answer this vital question. By year's end Anton H. Bullenhaar, a German-born Cincinnatian and farm laborer in Kentucky, wrote that the "unaccustomed, murderous hue and cry of war" centered on the widespread belief that "the object of the war is the abolition of slavery." Indeed, Joshua F. Speed believed, "It may be regarded as a fixed public sentiment, and the man who encounters it had as well attempt to ascend the faces of Niagara in a canoe as to meet it, brave it, or change it."[3]

Led by middle border representatives, debates in Congress in the summer of 1861 only fueled anxious conversations at home. When in July the House passed Illinois Republican Owen Lovejoy's nonbinding resolution declaring that it was "no part of the duty of the soldiers of the United States to capture and return fugitive slaves," Kentucky senator Lazarus W. Powell introduced an amendment to an army organization bill forbidding the use of military personnel "in subjecting or holding as a conquered province any sovereign State now or lately one of the United States, or in abolishing or interfering with African slavery in any of the States." Powell's amendment touched off a furious Senate debate about slavery and the war that revealed a fraying western consensus. Although moderates like Ohio Republican John Sherman advocated strict limits on Congress and "the non-slaveholding states" interfering with slavery, only 10 of 37 senators voted for Powell's amendment, all but one from middle border states. On August 6, despite vigorous opposition by middle border senators, Congress passed a confiscation bill that provided for the seizure of all property used by disloyal citizens for "insurrectionary purposes." Recognizing the bill's definition of slaves as persons rather than property, proslavery Democrats howled. Kentucky congressman Henry C. Burnett condemned the bill as "wholesale emancipation," and his Illinois colleague William Kellogg demanded that only the labor of "contrabands" be confiscable, and "not the slaves discharged therefrom." When the Senate agreed to the bill, four of the six nays were from the middle border slave states. (Burnett left for Kentucky the same day, and soon took a seat in the Confederate Congress.)[4]

Within the month the teetering western consensus was in crisis. On August 30, as part of a declaration of martial law, John C. Frémont, commanding the Western Department, ordered what amounted to a limited emancipation proclamation in Missouri. "The property, real and personal, of all persons in the State of Missouri who shall take up arms against the United States," it declared, "or who shall be directly proven to have taken an active part with their enemies in the field, is declared to be confiscated to the public use, and their slaves, if any they have, are hereby declared freemen." Frémont extended the army's reach even beyond that authorized by Congress's recent Confiscation Act.[5]

While northern Republicans applauded the measure, it divided middle border unionists in slave and free states alike. "I am of the opinion that if the policy adopted by Genl Fremont is sanctioned by Mr. Lincoln," wrote a Massachusetts-born St. Louisan to Edward Bates, "this state will be irretrievably lost to the Union." In Kentucky, Garret Davis claimed to Salmon P. Chase that the proclamation came upon residents like a "bombshell.... It has greatly disconcerted and I fear scattered us." Several Bull Run–type defeats, one unionist warned, could be more easily endured. Robert Anderson telegraphed that a company of federal volunteers in Louisville disbanded after the "disastrous" proclamation. Not all slaveholders withdrew support for the Lincoln administration after Frémont's ill-timed proclamation. One self-professed "large slaveholder" from near Hannibal blamed secessionists such as those in his northern Missouri neighborhood for any "confiscation act [that] shall be freedom to some of the slaves, the Government nor the President cannot thereby be blamed, for they have not forced the war." But many more slaveholders heard the warning of Louisville's *Courier*, claiming the proclamation was the first shot in the coming war on slavery. "Remember Missouri, Kentuckians," its editor intoned, "and be ready."[6]

Free state westerners were also critical of Frémont's proclamation. Many praised its declaration of martial law and capital punishment as a means of quelling guerrillas, giving a jolt to the administration's "apparently don't know what to do" policy toward them, but Democrats and even antislavery Republicans condemned the emancipation clause as a bald effort to convert the war into one to end slavery. "[S]everal Gentlemen of prominence and Republicans from Indiana," wrote Joshua F. Speed from Louisville, "say that it meets almost universal condemnation there." On the day news of the proclamation reached the newspapers, one northern Indiana paper proposed that all of the state's volunteer regiments emblazon on their flags, "Non-Interference by Congress with Domestic Institutions of the Slave States."[7]

Knowing that emancipation was the most revolutionary issue of the war, Lincoln had a middle border dilemma. With most of his cabinet and closest advisers hailing from the region, he understood that victory hinged on protecting these states' fragile unionist coalitions. "Southern Ohio Indiana and Ills. are our immediate neighbors," Speed wrote him immediately about the Confiscation Act. "If the North is divided the South will triumph." Radical Republicans like Indiana's George W. Julian seized on the issue to realign free states in their region with the North. Lincoln's "Border State policy," he argued, "tried to pet and please the power that held the nation by the throat." Supporting "loyal" slaveholders was tantamount to losing the war, argued the editor of Cincinnati's abolitionist *Free Nation*, as they were "reckless enemies of our country" who supported the institution that had brought about the war over the nation. Facing a divided Congress, Lincoln believed waging an overt war on slavery was impracticable. Cautious, the president forced Frémont to rescind that portion of the proclamation, then ultimately removed the aspiring Great Emancipator from command in Missouri.[8]

But the president would soon face a changed Congress. Ardent southern rights' Democrats from middle border slave states—namely Kentuckians John C. Breckinridge and Henry C. Burnett and Missourians Trusten Polk, Waldo P. Johnson, and John W. Reid—had been expelled. Proslavery "Conservatives" in free states soon found themselves similarly targeted and replaced with strong unionists. In February the Senate cast out Indianan Jesse W. Bright—who as a slave owner had largely taken up residence on his Kentucky farm amid calls at home for his resignation—for writing a letter of introduction to Jefferson Davis acknowledging him as president of the Confederacy. After off-year fall elections in some states, in March 1862 Republicans would outnumber Democrats and Unionists 106–70.[9]

But as Joshua Speed later claimed, Lincoln saw a need for wartime emancipation "long before he issued it, but was still anxious to avoid it." In December 1861, in his first annual address to Congress, Lincoln had advocated confiscation and colonization, suggesting his willingness to consider other strategies to end slavery. Gradual or compensated emancipation offered the best chance to forestall border states' secession. As early as November, Lincoln had consulted with Delaware's lone U.S. congressman, Union-Republican George P. Fisher, as well as the state's largest slaveholder, who were drafting bills for the state legislature. "This is the cheapest and most humane way of ending this war and saving lives," he told Fisher of compensated state-level emancipation, assisting him with his bill in hopes the initiative would extend to other border slave states. Widespread opposition among state legislators prevented "the president's bill" from being introduced. But the cat was out of the bag.[10]

Over the winter, doubts about Lincoln's sincerity about sustaining slavery eroded many citizens' loyalty to the general government. On January 1, 1862, Charles Whittlesey, colonel of the 20th Ohio Volunteers, received a missive from James M. Vanice, a nonslaveholding house painter in Warsaw, Kentucky, a county seat on the Ohio River downriver from Cincinnati. In it Vanice, then twenty-seven and supporting a family, "*pledge[d] my word* that I will neither aid nor take up Arms for the South, so long as the thing remains as it is, that is so long as the Government is not for the Freedom of Slaves." Vanice's family owned no slaves. Bondpeople were luxuries he could not afford, but he now risked arrest by publicly staking his own future on the president's pledge that his government would not destroy an institution he now supported as deeply as the largest slaveholders in his county.[11]

On March 6, 1862, Lincoln urged Congress to pass a joint resolution offering the government's "pecuniary aid" to compensate slave owners in states that would adopt plans of emancipation. The middle border's response was hardly receptive. The *Cincinnati Daily Enquirer* intoned, "But for such agitation there would have been politically no North and South in this nation," while Garret Davis denounced the president's plan as an invitation to a western race war. With Illinois and Indiana having long forbidden black emigration, Missouri U.S. congressman John S. Phelps asked the president what was "to become of these two or three millions of negroes... [e]xpelled from the southern States, where are they to go?" The answer: to middle border slave states like Missouri, or to Ohio, soon to be "the Botany Bay for the negroes from Kentucky and Tennessee."[12]

On March 13, two days after a meeting between Lincoln and border state congressmen failed to convince them to embrace his offer of compensated emancipation, Congress passed an article of war that forbade army officers, regardless of the masters' loyalties, from returning fugitive slaves in their camps to "any persons to whom such service or labor is claimed to be due." The middle border's slave state leaders went on the offensive, condemning the article as indisputable evidence of congressional Republicans' abolition intent. Lazarus W. Powell called Lincoln's plan "a pill of arsenic, sugar-coated" intended "to inaugurate abolition parties in the border slave states," while Missouri's Elijah H. Norton claimed the now "firm and religious belief that by remaining in the Government they will lose their property" would spur disloyalty in these states, overt and covert.[13]

Free state Democrats were only slightly less restive than slave-staters at Republicans' apparent strong-arming to accomplish emancipation. With unanimous approval from Republicans and despite nearly unanimous opposition from middle border representatives—slave and free—Congress adopted Lincoln's compensated emancipation plan for the District of Columbia. Before Lincoln signed the bill into law on April 16, 1862, with additional funding for voluntary colonization, former Ohio U.S. senator William Allen denounced it as a means of accomplishing a divided nation by pressuring border slave states into "a northern confederacy of free states... in which they may rule supreme." Only weeks earlier, at Cincinnati's Pike's Opera House, Tennessee's fiery unionist editor and minister, William G. "Parson" Brownlow, just released from a Confederate prison, had railed against northern abolitionists driving the war engine. At the same venue, noted abolitionist Wendell Phillips was shouted down, stoned, and egged. When he refused to yield, audience members rushed him, crying "Lynch the traitor" and "Hang the nigger." Phillips was shoved from the stage, leaving the president, his party, and their policies and politics in its hot center lights.[14]

§

Among the many ironies of the war, the middle border slave states that offered Lincoln his thorniest political problem were the first to feel its coming high-water mark. Even before Congress's wrangling over the army's authority over black fugitives, in these politically sensitive states federal troops and black slaves on the ground were commencing the process of wartime emancipation.

By the summer of 1861, in western Missouri, before Ben Butler's controversial contraband policy in the Confederate states, Kansas Jayhawkers were known widely as "negro thieves" because of the regularity with which they confiscated slave property from Missouri's citizens (see figure 6.1). Within days after the attack on Fort Sumter, James H. Lane and James Montgomery were in contact with prominent northern abolitionists, proclaiming their intention to liberate slaves if granted army commissions. When speaking against the Powell amendment, then U.S. senator Lane boasted, "[T]he institution of slavery will not survive, in any State of this Union, the march of the Union armies." As a new brigadier general, Lane used his troops to liberate slaves held by "the wives and children" of Missouri men in rebel service and boasted that his Kansas Brigade would be joined by "an army of slaves marching out." Exasperated, Henry W. Halleck referred to Lane's fall raids as "great jayhawking expedition[s]... [to] prostitute [his men] into negro catchers." They liberated hundreds of Missouri slaves from disloyal and loyal owners "more than a year before the 'Immortal Lincoln' issued his proclamation," as one of Lane's subordinates recalled. Lane then employed freedpeople as teamsters, cooks, and guides and resettled others as laborers on Kansas farms or in refugee camps.[15]

Missouri offered fertile ground for military personnel to exceed the authority of the Confiscation Act. By autumn 1861 Iowa and Illinois troops in northern and

Figure 6.1 Fugitive slaves escaping in wartime. Although the interior rivers proved obstacles to escape, and despite the exclusion of slaves in border states from wartime emancipation until 1863 and 1864 and the ensuing conflicts over it in the western armies and middle border states, thousands of African Americans gained freedom starting in the war's first months by running away to federal camps, large cities, and free state towns. Courtesy Cincinnati Museum Center.

southeastern Missouri were enticing slaves to abscond, and commanders engaged them as servants for "fair wages" throughout. On September 30 a squad of John A. Logan's 31st Illinois Volunteers, on a reconnaissance mission in Missouri, seized all forty-five slaves of a "strong Secessionist" and took them back to Cairo. A Cape Girardeau County resident wrote nearly at the same time of another regiment: "All the negroes of Stephen Bird, (some 25 in number) were persuaded to run off from their master who was sick in bed and come to the camp. They were told that they should be free if they would do so." With slaves offering information about guerrillas and disunionists, emancipation moved along with the military forces. As he pursued retreating Confederates southward in the fall, John C. Frémont would not allow contraband slaves to be returned to masters claiming them in southern Missouri. When fugitive slaves crossed the rivers to Cairo, John A. McClernand issued a confiscation order there despite local whites' remonstrances that the western federal armies appeared to be "waging war for the purpose of abolishing slavery."[16]

In Missouri especially, mere rumors of troops approaching encouraged slaves to take to their heels. In October 1861, near Hannibal, a group of runaways informed their captors that "their masters told them that all the Union men are Abolitionists, and, there being some U.S. soldiers in the neighborhood, their masters told them to step out until the soldiers had left, and they just kept stepping out." By the following spring Benjamin Gratz Brown concluded that "there [were] scarcely any slaves... remaining in the counties along the northern, southern and western borders of the state." The federal military set up contraband camps along the Mississippi River at Helena, Arkansas, Cairo, Illinois, and Columbus, Kentucky, and on Island No. 10, ostensibly for slaves confiscated from the Confederacy. But slaves from Missouri and Kentucky were among them.[17]

Recognizing that both commanders and slaves used the presence of federal troops to effect freedom, in November 1861 Henry W. Halleck implemented an "exclusion policy" for his Western Department. It barred unauthorized persons—slaves and owners—from federal camps. "The military are neither slave-stealers nor slave-catchers," he wrote an Illinois garrison commander. Although antislavery critics attacked Halleck for his exclusion policy, Democratic officers soon extended it well beyond Missouri. "The military problem would be a simple one could it be entirely separated from political influences," George B. McClellan reminded Don Carlos Buell. Curbing the "political," meaning antislavery, conduct of federal troops was more important to success or failure in the middle border slave states, he believed, than regular military operations. To assist, the War Department tried to garrison Kentucky largely with Kentucky troops and officers.[18]

Implementation of the exclusion policy soon became onerous, with discretion falling on subordinate army officers who often cared little for slave owners or slaves. The First Confiscation Act required that only fugitive slaves employed by Confederates be allowed to stay within federal camps. Arbitrating between owners' professions of loyalty and slaves' testaments to the contrary became a constant "annoyance," as one officer called it. "Congress troops should be permitted neither to steal slaves nor to catch and return them to their owners or pretended owners," Halleck wrote to an exasperated subordinate. "To avoid all difficulties about this matter keep fugitives out of camp and let the question of ownership be decided by the civil tribunals."[19]

In Kentucky especially, federal officers drew a hard line against confiscating slaves. In late 1861 William T. Sherman reminded a northern Illinois subordinate accused of sheltering fugitives in his camp that "all negroes shall be delivered up on claim of the owner or agent. Better keep the negroes out of your camp altogether unless you brought them along with the regiment." By the following spring Gordon Granger scoffed at Kentucky's fugitive slaves "forcing themselves into our camps... [believing] that their day of redemption has come... to be free from the constraint of all authority." Granger blamed slaves' misperceptions on white unionists' widespread characterization of federal soldiers as eager abolitionists. Long after Congress's article of war was issued, military personnel in Kentucky, many of them slaveholders, upheld the exclusion policy. As Boyle instructed a subordinate, "I want men of my command to have nothing whatever to do with negroes. This must be understood." Buell went further, ordering officers to assist with recapturing fugitive slaves.[20]

With the war going badly in the summer of 1862, the impetus for harder and broader federal war policies gained momentum. Slavery became a primary focus. Indiana Republican George Julian warned his colleagues in the U.S. House that "the rebellion [was] the child of slavery.... This is a war of ideas, not less than of armies... [and] no servant of the Republic should march with muffled drums." The president was among the converts. "[W]e had about played our last card," Lincoln remarked later, "and must change our tactics, or lose the game!" Having signed into law a congressional bill that abolished slavery in federal territories and expecting imminent passage of a more expansive confiscation bill, on July 12 Lincoln summoned slave state congressmen and senators, including from eastern Tennessee and western Virginia, to the White House. The president offered them a classic carrot and stick. Tying his offer of compensation for gradual emancipation to colonization, he warned that they must make "a decision at once" because "pressure is still upon me, and it is increasing," a reference to Radicals' calls for immediate emancipation. Only a day later, having remarked to Owen Lovejoy that the border states' obstruction threatened "all of us... [with] hav[ing] lived in vain!" Lincoln stated grimly "that we must free the slaves or be ourselves subdued.... [S]omething must be done." Two days later he received a written rejection of his offer bearing the signatures of twenty of the twenty-eight in attendance. That afternoon Lincoln submitted to Congress his own draft of a compensated emancipation bill, which it declined considering, then adjourned.[21]

In less than a week, enacting measures that Lincoln had considered "radical and extreme" only a few months before, Congress changed the course of the war. On July 17, 1862, it passed two bills, both of which the president signed—although he issued a statement listing his objections to one. The first was the long-debated second Confiscation Act, which authorized the confiscation of slave property from disloyal owners. The second was the Militia Act, authorizing enrollment of three hundred thousand men between the ages of eighteen and forty-five for nine months' service in the federal armies. The new Confiscation Act allowed the president to declare "forever free" slaves of those who would "assist and give aid and comfort to such rebellion," while the Militia Act empowered Lincoln to enroll "persons of African descent... [for] any war service for which they may be found competent," including as soldiers, and to liberate their families.[22]

Lincoln's willingness to sign these bills hinted that the "pressure" he had mentioned to the border state representatives was in part self-applied. As commander in chief he had come to recognize "the indispensable necessity for military emancipation" to win the war and then rebuild the Union. Lincoln saw clearly that the loyal slave states tied his hands. Indeed, as he later wrote to a Kentuckian after the border state representatives "declined the [compensated emancipation] proposition.... I was, in my best judgment, driven to the alternative of either surrendering the Union, and with it the Constitution, or laying strong hand upon the colored element. I chose the latter." As federal armies and self-emancipating bondpeople destroyed slavery in the Confederacy, its erosion in these loyal states would undercut conditional unionists' political strength and allow unconditional unionists the chance to gain control and end the war.[23]

Calling his full cabinet to his office on July 22, Lincoln presented a draft of an emancipation proclamation he had been working on most of the summer. Having shown the draft to trusted Kentuckians then in the nation's capital—Joshua and James Speed, along with Cassius Clay—he expected sharp divisions in the middle border. (Only Clay supported the president's plan.) The cabinet's response was similarly divided, though not along free and slave state lines. Edward Bates and Salmon P. Chase supported it, while Montgomery Blair feared the proclamation had given western Democrats "a club... to beat the Administration." Indiana's Caleb Smith, secretary of the interior, was furious over the enlistment of black troops. "[B]efore God," he had argued, white soldiers would "protest being thus put on an equality with Negro soldiers in their ranks." Smith's increasingly distant relationship with the president over new war measures would soon lead him to resign his cabinet position.[24]

Knowing middle border states, slave and free, would strenuously object, Lincoln was not yet ready to leverage a full revolution by enlisting black troops everywhere. "[R]ecruiting slaves of loyal owners *without* consent *unless the necessity is urgent*" would "do more injury than good... [and] would produce dangerous and fatal dissatisfactions in our army," especially in the West. "[H]alf the Army," he averred to a delegation of the region's Radicals, "would lay down their arms and three other States would join the rebellion." In his famously measured public response to editor Horace Greeley, who scolded him for not emancipating slaves despite the Second Confiscation Act, Lincoln credited widespread opposition to "the counsels... of certain fossil politicians hailing from the Border Slave States." The president's border state dilemma was foremost when he reasoned, "My paramount object in this struggle *is* to save the Union," which in fact left his options wide open.[25]

Before Lincoln completed the final draft of his emancipation proclamation, black troops were in military service on the middle border. Kansas Jayhawker Charles R. Jennison was reputed to have led an entire company of liberated western Missouri bondmen, under command of a black officer, on a raid in November 1861. In January 1862 James H. Lane formed the 1st Kansas Colored Infantry, the first black regiment of the war. To enlist them that August, he loosely interpreted recruiting instructions from the War Department as well as Congress's authorization that the president employ "as many persons of African descent as he may deem necessary and proper for the suppression of this rebellion." Despite

Stanton's admonitions that they should not be received, Lane's black enlistees, comprised of slaves from Missouri, Arkansas, and the Indian Nations, filled nearly two regiments. In October black detachments of them saw action, repulsing repeated attacks by white Missouri horsemen at Island Mound, the first armed black participation in the war.[26]

By the time these troops took to the field, Lincoln's border state dilemma had become a crisis. With rebel armies still in force in Kentucky, on September 22, 1862, Lincoln issued the preliminary draft of his emancipation proclamation. His concern not to disrupt the middle border's fragile coalition of Republicans, War Democrats, and Conservatives in advance of the election of 1862 lost out to deeper military and political convictions. Effective January 1, 1863, in states then "in rebellion against the United States.... [A]ll persons held as slaves... [would] be then, thenceforward, and forever free." Although the preliminary draft did not name any states specifically, the loyal slave states were excluded by an entire paragraph devoted specifically to delineating rebellious and nonrebellious slave states. Pledges of compensation for gradual emancipation and for colonization were retained. Two days later Lincoln suspended the writ of habeas corpus throughout the country, ostensibly to enforce the militia draft against "insurgents... their sympathizers... [and] a most efficient corps or spies, informers, suppliers, and aiders and abbettors of their cause."[27]

§

On December 18, 1862, John Preston Mann Jr., a second lieutenant in the 5th Illinois Cavalry, predicted a thin winter not only for a drought-starved western region but for the entire nation. Although New Orleans and Memphis were in federal hands and armies were poised to secure the Mississippi, the unconditional unionist wrote gloomily to his wife that "a dark picture overshadows our land.... [T]he 'rebel sympathizers' (under the lead of men calling themselves Democrats to hide their Treason) are opposing the 'administration', and doing everything they can to annoy the Government and prevent the Successful prosecution of the war." Aboard a riverboat above Memphis, an angry Mann had "a few talks... with *Secesh* passengers who were trying to pass for Union men. I told them [to] join the Rebel army and cease trying to pass as loyal as the[y] could not do successfully."[28]

Mann bemoaned the recent midterm elections that had occurred just weeks after Lincoln announced his preliminary emancipation proclamation. Nationally, Republicans retained an overall majority of twenty-five in the U.S. House and even gained six seats in the Senate. But in Mann's home region Democrats increased their congressional seats by eighteen and outnumbered Republicans, and they won legislative majorities in Ohio, Indiana, and Illinois. In two of its free states and in Missouri and Kentucky, the damaged Republican Party largely ceased to exist, replaced by a more generic "Union Party." Supporting the new war measures was, by one measure, "standing upon a Volcano." The rapid "revolution in public sentiment," as a Cincinnati editor described it, was unmistakable but nonetheless shocking to Lincoln's party. "Up to the day of the election, they were denouncing the majority of the people of the State as Secessionists, traitors and copperheads," he clucked. "Conservative men saw the coming change—felt it in the political breeze which set in strong, especially after the President succumbed to the Abolitionists and issued his Emancipation Proclamation."[29]

Placing emancipation at the center of a larger political storm could not have been more right. In 1862 the president and congressional Republicans had broadened the definition of both military necessity and the Union, from one perpetual and complete, "as it was," as Lincoln's Democratic critics demanded, to an evolving, more perfect union, "as it should be." Benefited by an absence of southern Democratic legislators, the 37th Congress had enacted a series of laws expanding the power of the federal government—including a homestead act, a land-grant college act, an internal revenue act, a transcontinental railroad act, a national tariff, a legal tender act, and a national banking act—which western individualists grumbled was a bald consolidation of power sure to enslave them to the northern "money power." Opposition to conscription might have fueled the fires of dissent in the free states of the middle border, but in the summer months enrollment proceeded peacefully, and their quotas were mostly met, according to the region's newspapers.[30]

Dissent against new war measures found its catalyst in the western backlash against emancipation, quickly eroding Republicans' influence. Many editors admitted that voters had cast their ballots largely against emancipation. Indiana Democratic congressman Daniel Voorhees, who blamed the war on abolitionists' "bloody, dripping sword of irresponsible power," won overwhelmingly in his Terre Haute district. In Ohio, after the Union coalition had swept the state elections only the previous fall and despite subsequent legislative gerrymandering, Democrats now won fourteen of the state's nineteen seats. Edson B. Olds, arrested and detained for disloyal speech in 1861, was elected to the state legislature while still in a New York military prison. After losing his bid for Congress in his Virginia Tract district, Ohioan Hezekiah S. Bundy "thought until this year the cry of 'nigger' and 'abolitionist' were played out, but they never had as much power and effect in this part of the state as at the recent election." Even the most prominent of the state's Republicans were suddenly vulnerable. The state legislature barely returned Benjamin Wade, one of the most hard-nosed Radicals and chairman of the Joint Committee on the Conduct of the War, to the U.S. Senate, mainly to prevent antiwar Peace Democrats from gaining the seat. One seat Ohio Peace Democrats did not hold was Clement L. Vallandigham's, whose district was gerrymandered after a biting war critique charged Republicans with fighting a ruinous war for the benefit only of slaves.[31]

Loyalty politics drove fractious political conflicts as Republican governors in Indiana and Illinois, Oliver P. Morton and Richard Yates, fought anti-emancipation waves. Although Morton organized Indiana's Union Party to curb Radicals and quell Democratic dissenters, in 1862 Democrats won seven of eleven congressional seats and one of its U.S. Senate seats. In Lincoln's Illinois, where partisan divisions ran deep, Yates's appointment of Republican Orville H. Browning to Stephen A. Douglas's U.S. Senate seat quickly exposed him to charges of partisanship. In early 1862 a constitutional convention saw more than twice as many Democratic delegates as Republican ones, who castigated the assembly's majority as disloyal—even subversive—and condemned its resultant "Copperhead" constitution. Democrats swept the midterm elections after winning the central counties and controlled the state legislature and Illinois's congressional delegation by winning nine of fourteen seats. The new state senate soon elected a Peace Democrat, William A. Richardson, to the U.S. Senate to replace Browning. "Secession," wrote Yates, "is deeper and stronger here than you have any idea."[32]

What Yates took for secession was dissent fueled by a summer of racial unrest prior to Lincoln's proclamation. With the amended rallying cry, "The Constitution as it is, and the Union as it was, *and the Niggers where they are*," western Peace Democrats who favored an immediate end to the war took aim at Republican candidates. "The great issue to be decided to-day at the polls," blared Cincinnati's *Daily Enquirer*, "is the FREEDOM OF THE WHITE MAN." Contrabands would soon arrive by the "hundreds of thousands, if not millions...and will either be competitors with our white mechanics and laborers, degrading them by the competition, or they will have to be supported as paupers and criminals at the public expense." Consequently, race riots—not draft riots—erupted in middle border cities that witnessed an influx of contrabands and fugitive slaves and whose employers replaced white workers, especially immigrants, with blacks. In Chicago, Toledo, Indianapolis, and Evansville, working-class whites ravaged black residential sections. In New Albany, Indiana, five days after Lincoln signed the confiscation and militia bills into law, amid Democratic newspapers' editorials claiming "the city is overrun with worthless runaway slaves," armed white supremacists roamed the city's black community to rid it of "strangers." Cincinnati's violence outstripped all others, especially after blacks retaliated by burning homes in "Dublin," its Irish section. William Wells Brown, a former Kentucky slave and prominent abolitionist, claimed that "hatred of the negro" was worse in Cincinnati "than in any other city in the West."[33]

In Illinois, by more than a five to one margin, voters upheld the state's bans on black immigration, suffrage, and officeholding. Two-thirds of Republicans joined Democrats in affirming the exclusion clause, which included new provisions such as a $1,000 fine and five years in prison for those who might bring them into the state, while fugitive slaves would be returned to their masters and black emigrants sold South into slavery. Only days before Lincoln issued his preliminary emancipation proclamation, southern Illinoisans' collective anger at the change in the war's direction boiled over. On September 18, to alleviate overcrowding at refugee camps, the secretary of war, Edwin M. Stanton, ordered contrabands to federal camps near Cairo and authorized their use as laborers to assist labor-strapped farmers with their harvests. Its post commandant was instructed to turn women and children over to local committees of "humane and benevolent persons," who would provide them with employment.[34]

White rural Illinoisans erupted in fury at the Republicans' bald intention to "Africanize" their state in violation of its exclusion law. "[T]he state of illinois will have mor negroes than tenese in one year more iff the war lasts," wrote one resident. Many communities and counties held mass anticontraband meetings and passed ordinances prohibiting black employment on farms. "[I] tell you John if tha sende Eney Nigers hur ther will be a fight hur shure," one Pike Countian wrote to his brother in the army, "fore the people is thur ly roused hur." Freedpeople who managed to find work were often subjected to violence. A mob of angry men drove off forty contrabands from a farm in Union County who were assisting in planting cotton, while a local woman informed her husband, then in the army, "Some person set fire to those houses of Father's in the bottom where the blk folks were the fire was put out before it did much damage the man that brought them there took them to Cairo and then I think to Island No 10." Many of the black refugees quickly fled back to Cairo, where the post commander drew a stern rebuke from Stanton after accusations that he had "refused to render them any [protection], upon the ground that you have no sympathy with Abolitionists." Stanton ordered the cessation of contraband shipments, but the political fallout was widespread. Robert Smith, an Alton War Democrat, and many others lost their seats from "votes made against me, on the Negro question." The editor of the *Belleville Advocate* warned that racial undertow from anti-emancipation politics assured that "the Radical of yesterday... will be a Conservative to-day."[35]

The furor over emancipation drove white free state men and women to open war dissent. The impending draft conspired with anti-emancipationism among rural white women, who now realized that their husbands and sons might be forced into the army, leaving them at home to work their farms. Elizabeth Millikan spoke for many southern Illinoisans when she stated publicly that "she wanted the south to whip and Jeff Davis to Rule over the north, [that] the war was not to save the union but it was to free the Negroes and that old Abe Lincoln was as black as hell in Principle.... [S]he did not believe that there was a drop of honest blood in the veins of any Abolitionists." An Ohio soldier claimed that his sister "is under the doctors care all the time. She is ver[y] much troubled about the Negroes." For many with slaveholding kin, the bile of long-suppressed proslavery beliefs rose alongside anger at Republicans, especially during the postemancipation harvest season. "Cellie has been cutting wheat ten days, and I have had all the cooking to do for 6 men, besides the family and he will not get through in less than ten more," one central Illinoisan wrote to her family in Kentucky. "Whether I shall keep up or not I think doubtful, if you had that to do, dont you think you'd like to have a darkie. I would, God knows I would."[36]

In the region's slave states, especially Kentucky, where Confederate troops were still in full force, the proclamation shook the faith of loyal unionists, slaveholding and not. "Stop him! Hold him!" wrote Hugh Campbell of St. Louis to the judge advocate general, Joseph Holt. "Beg him to write no more letters to newspapers, and never to publish a proclamation.... Can you not prevail on him to be entirely silent on 'negro-ology'?" After touring fourteen counties of Kentucky, an Ohioan wrote to the *New York Tribune* that "halfway conditional [Union] men have become advocates of the South, and secessionists have broken their silence with traitorous speeches." After sitting on their hands while federal troops confiscated the slave property of disloyal residents, restive slaveholders in Lexington, Missouri, led by one of the state's ousted supreme court judges, now questioned the motives of military authority. "The President's Proclamation of 1st Jany '63 does not embrace Missouri," they complained. "Why should the radicals enforce it here, at the point of the bayonet?... We ask a repeal of this abolition order; this military license to steal our negroes."[37]

Racial fears that accompanied the announcement of emancipation prompted a sea change in unionist slaveholders' loyalties. To a friend "*almost* as far *north* in your sentiments *as I am South*," Kentuckian Bevie W. Cain admitted that "I *was* for the Union myself until [the proclamation]; but I am far enough from it now." As former unconditional unionists who endured what she called "secession bondage," even having two of their slaves confiscated by the rebel troops during the Kentucky Confederate occupation, Ellen Wallace and her husband, Albert, of Hopkinsville quickly transitioned to full proslavery dissent. Ellen was an active member of her community's "loyal ladies" and frequently sent generous contributions of food and other aid for their support, while Albert, over sixty, served in the home guard and fought against "gurillars" who threatened their town and home. "Lincoln's proclimation liberating all the slaves in January is the finishing stroke to all these horrors," Ellen wrote angrily on the day she learned of it. "[T]he blood of the helpless women and children will flow... St. Domingo over again." Within days she admitted "spitting blood in small quantities." "[S]hudder[ing] with horror," as she watched "contraband negroes in a body and with a banner... two had guns" as they passed on their way to Fort Donelson, and she vented her anger: "The hot blood of our best Union men is up. They feel keenly the insults heaped upon them by the negro administration.... We look upon [Lincoln] as a wretch only fit to rule over the most degraded part of the negro population."[38]

Despite the national drum taps that steadily announced emancipation, in Kentucky and Missouri Lincoln's proclamation and the ensuing election spurred party realignments. Caught between pressures of loyalty and disloyalty, national and state authority, and military and civil imperatives, moderate proslavery coalitions were pressured to defend their middle positions against emancipation. In Kentucky the dichotomy between unionists and secessionists weakened amid galvanized proslavery responses, while in Missouri the opposite occurred, with disloyalty being more firmly linked with opponents of emancipation. Kentucky's Union Democrats closed ranks in opposition to the president's proclamation, and the state senate voted overwhelmingly that slavery was a state and local institution. Little goodwill remained for Emancipationists led by James Speed, and the faction died in all but name. The most ardent anti-emancipationists reconstituted as a rejuvenated states' rights party calling itself the Peace Democracy. By contrast, Missouri's Emancipationists gained sudden strength. Just after Lincoln issued his proclamation, he appointed Samuel R. Curtis, a firmly antislavery Iowa Republican, to command. He instructed provost marshals to arrest "pretended loyal men" and to grant certificates to slaves entitled to freedom by the second Confiscation Act. Self-styled "Radicals" (or "Charcoals" as opponents dubbed them) defected from Hamilton R. Gamble's provisional government and held their own convention, a coalition of St. Louis Republicans and hard-line War Democrats, many of them Germans. Gamble grudgingly urged slaveholders to support Lincoln's gradual emancipation plan, but the fall election saw Radicals or Emancipationists take six of the state's nine congressional districts and gain sixteen seats in the state legislature. In December 1862 Missouri's outgoing U.S. congressmen introduced measures for compensated emancipation.[39]

§

In 1863 Lincoln's attorney general, Edward Bates, once supported widely by the West's proslavery moderates as a presidential aspirant, was not unfamiliar with divided houses. As counsel for the Lincoln administration, he encountered constitutional crises arising from an array of controversial war measures. As a Missourian, he had sons fighting in belligerent armies. But he railed against the *"moral forgery"* by which Radicals were misusing emancipation politics. New definitions and ideological labels replaced party names and distorted longtime understandings, and he clearly understood their political uses and misuses. *"Loyalty"* was defined as little more than "adhesion to *my* clique.... Heretofore and until lately, the Democratic party gloried in calling itself *the party of Progress*, and in denouncing its adversaries as *Conservatives*.... But now their presses and public orators claim for them the merit of *conservatism*." By contrast, "[p]olitically, a *Radical* is a man who is always dealing with the *root*, the origin and foundation, of society... *as he understands them*... [and] can, at pleasure, abrogate all former laws and constitutions.... He always claims to act in the name of the *Sovereign*

People, and is armed with all their powers." Believing Radicalism had pervaded the president's administration, within a year he and other proslavery moderates would leave it.[40]

Nowhere were the ambiguities of conservatism as meaningful as on the middle border, where the war offered a vehicle to settle warring nationalist definitions—northern, southern, and western. In the region's slave states, the Old Republican version of nationalism, in which slavery and union were compatible, entwined race and conservatism as a discrete political faction. Ironically, "Conservatives" appropriated western free state Republicans' use of the term to denote antiblack attitudes within the fledgling party. (In 1860 Indiana's *Evansville Journal*, a German organ, had argued that Lincoln was the conservative, or white man's, candidate.) By 1863 Conservative Unionists were unwelcome in the Republican Party, and they no longer supported Union coalitions that were pro-emancipation. With its constituency searching for a viable alternative, that summer Cincinnati hosted a convention of "OLD LINE WHIGS—WAR DEMOCRATS—CONSERVATIVE MEN, without regard to former party predilections." In Kentucky and Missouri, Conservatives found strength as a counter to supporters of emancipation, whom they derided as "Radicals."[41]

Bates saw rightly that the politics of ending slavery licensed exclusivist politics at all levels of society. Inherent in the new array of party designations—War and Peace Democrats, Radicals, Unionists, and Conservatives—was an intent to obscure the ideological extremes entwining wartime loyalty politics with venomous partisanship. As Republicans hard-lined Democratic majorities intent on undercutting the federal war effort, their political counterinsurgency fueled a new, politicized intolerance among home-front communities. "The excited people," wrote a Kentucky unionist, "seem willing to endure nothing which is not all on their side. Not a syllable must be conceded to the other side."[42]

As owners of emancipation, middle border Republicans employed a coercive nationalist strategy to redefine their opponents. Beginning in the summer of 1861, Republicans pejoratively labeled dissenting Democrats "Copperheads," likening them to poisonous snakes that strike without warning. As a western epithet for mulattoes, it only hardened negativity toward Republicans and the post-emancipation war effort. Republicans' strategy to regain and hold political power against newly empowered dissenters led not to compromise, but to consolidation. To Peace Democrats' familiar charge that "the Administration is not the Government," Republicans responded: "In time of peace we may oppose the policy of the Administration... but in war if we do so in a manner to weaken the Government we strike hands with the enemy." That enemy was on both the battlefront and the home front.[43]

To win this discursive war, Union League Clubs, or "Loyal Leagues," became the operative means by which Republicans exacted home-front loyalty. Begun in late 1862 by anxious central Illinois Republicans, they quickly spread to other northern cities and small towns as "patriotic fraternities" to counteract defeatism and war-weariness. By the summer of 1863 the leagues had spread to eighteen free states; by 1864, some 140,000 members were enrolled in Illinois alone. Enlisting the aid of sympathetic editors, the leagues sought "by moral and social influences" to raise troops and supplies and blunt rising disaffection. Distributing pamphlets and holding debates to promote the war effort were accompanied by economic pressure exerted by the business community, who offered rigid tests of national patriotism centering on support for emancipation. Leveraging employment and the dominion system's trade permits, these elite soon pressured wage workers and small business owners to support the now unpopular war. "Disloyalty must be made unprofitable," argued one.[44]

Hard-selling nationalist war aims among localist, rural constituencies in the western free states required hard propagandizing. In May 1863 John W. Fletcher became the new editor and proprietor of the *Centralia Sentinel*, a weekly newspaper in southern Illinois. An abolitionist from western New York, Fletcher was recruited by Centralia's anxious Republicans for his unwaveringly loyal voice to regain political control of their state and region. "Every man that has got the sand will throw off on the Lincoln Government now after the proclamation setting the nigger free," wrote one Illinoisan to a soldier in blue. "Ill[inoi]s is bound to go with the Southland." The first issue of the *Sentinel* announced the paper as "The Voice of the Loyal League," to "disseminate true and loyal sentiments, counteract the pernicious effects of a corrupt and disloyal Press, stir up her business men to more enterprise and public spirit, advertise their interests, foster education, cultivate intelligence, and encourage morality and religion." Even moderate Republicans saw rightly that opposing emancipation would expose them to political attack. "[He who] hates the cause which the League advocates, is not a loyal man," Fletcher declared.[45]

Emancipation soon became these predominantly Republican organizations' purity test for loyalty. The Pekin organization proclaimed itself a "home guard ... [to] put down treason and traitors ... maintain the laws ... [and] keep inviolate the principles of the constitution and the Declaration of Independence." The choice of language was telling; western individualists differed with northern collectivists over racial interpretations of America's fundamental documents. Radicals interpreted the Declaration of Independence as a condemnation of slavery and racial exclusions and elevated it as the nation's guiding principle over the traditionalist Constitution. Moderates and conservatives alike believed in black inferiority, but the former upheld the declaration's appeal for equality before the law, while the latter argued for constitutional guarantees for white supremacy. Faced with anti-emancipation dissent, loyalty was the wedge that Republicans used to divide moderates and conservatives and realign the union coalition among western traditionalists. Edward Bates was shocked at how quickly emancipation became the litmus of loyalty. "[A]bolition seems to be the strongest rallying point, and men who dont care a fig about it, have become all of a sudden, very zealous in that cause.... The radicals are making great efforts to create the belief that they are *the* Union men, and all others are against the Union," he grumbled. "And they succeed in driving on some *cowardly patriots.*" When black Cincinnatians founded the newspaper *The Colored Citizen* in 1863 to advocate for universal wartime emancipation (see figure 6.2), a Cincinnati dissenter complained, "They brand every man as traitor who does not Kneel at the footstool of 'Abraham' and say Amen to every edict and Proclamation that emenated from his pen," while another wrote, "Though you give your flesh and blood to put down the rebellion, if you do not favor abolition you are denounced as a rebel sympathizer."[46]

Many white westerners opposed emancipation on more than racial grounds. Just as southern nationalism grew by closing ranks in response to sustained threats to liberty centered on slavery, emancipation laid bare northerners' intent by dint of war. Moral nationalism was only the latest weapon of northern expansionist goals to accomplish the "greater New England," and many white residents bitterly opposed this denouement of "Freedom National, Slavery Sectional." The day after the Emancipation Proclamation had taken effect, a unionist in Paducah, Kentucky, argued that Yankees believed "what constitutes a loyal citizen was an ardent zeal manifested by great outward show to raise oneself to the social, political and moral status of the Negro." Another scolded his friend at college in Franklin, Indiana, that he hoped any "absorption from the *partially Puritanical Yankee* element in which you now live...has not entirely obliterated the *sympathy* which *once* existed in your mind for the *South.*"[47]

These westerners saw this regional war within a war not simply to restore the Union as it was, but as it would become by shaping the contours of the West. As historian David M. Potter wrote, nationalism did not function independently of local loyalties; rather, they were nested in a "mutually supportive relation to one

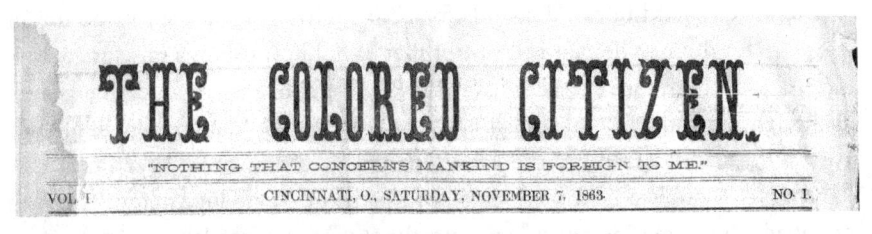

Figure 6.2 Masthead from the first issue of *The Colored Citizen*. Published sporadically from 1863 to 1869, this newspaper was edited by African American citizens in St. Louis, Chicago, Louisville, Indianapolis, Columbus, and Cincinnati. Courtesy University of Cincinnati Archives and Rare Books Library.

another." In truth, most white westerners found themselves caught between competing nationalist fires. Western dissenters like Ohio's Clement L. Vallandigham sensed that the changed war signaled the eclipse of his idea of western nationalism. The depth of western Democrats' opposition to the Republicans' hijacking the war's direction transcended ideological abstractions about republican versus federal forms of government or debates over strict and loose constructions of constitutional theory. Northerners had orchestrated an unpopular takeover of the war's direction and now targeted opponents of emancipation, the most reviled of its wartime initiatives. Many westerners fought back. As exiled Presbyterian minister Thomas A. Hoyt observed in February 1863, "The most remarkable thing is the growing feeling against New England ideas and men. The Western and Middle States begin to see that they have been made a catspaw of in the war, and that they are past becoming subjected to the wild and insane fanaticism of the 'Yankees.' There is danger of a counter revolution here in the North, by means of a collision between the States and the Federal Government."[48]

As a nationalist weapon, loyalty discourse soon turned descriptive terms to exclusivist epithets. When dissident Democrats who had long labeled their opponents as abolitionists and "black Republicans" turned to states' rights arguments, Republicans responded by calling them Copperheads, secesh, and traitors. In the days following emancipation, Missouri abolitionist Adolph Frick wrote, "Mr. Eimer says the North will lose," concluding that "he has enjoyed too much southern sun and *blackness*... he's probably become a *Democrat* too." Questioned why Radicals equated opposition to emancipation with disloyalty, one election official reasoned that "differing [with the administration]... is calculated to embarrass the government, and will always more or less give encouragement to rebels.... I support every act of the administration for [that] purpose, without questioning it when such measures are the means of enforcing the laws and suppressing rebellion and treason." A southern Ohio newspaper declared, "*There are now but two parties in this country—the friends and enemies of the Government. Every man who does not stand up for* ALL MEASURES *that may be adopted for the maintenance of the honor of the country... is* A TRAITOR *at heart!*"[49]

Republican hard-liners' demands for all-or-nothing patriotism made for an easy step for them to demand all-or-nothing Republicanism as a measure of loyalty. As a southern Indiana editor complained, Republicans "conduct themselves as though 'patriotism' in these days is exclusively designed for the benefit of their party." The state's Republican senator, George W. Julian, would later admit that "loyalty to Republicanism was... accepted as the best evidence of loyalty to the country." The terms "northern" and "northerner" described loyal supporters of emancipation and the new war measures. "[W]e call on Northern thinkers to emancipate themselves, in order to save their own section from destruction," wrote one Cincinnatian in the spring of 1863. The collective North consisted of states with unionist majorities sharing a commitment to the president and preserving the Union by victory. Sectional terms now became political designations as political geographers made the "Loyal North" synonymous with acceptance of emancipation as the central strategy for winning the war. In the inverse, all who opposed were part of the disloyal South. Rebranding more than simply renaming politics found public form in March 1863, when a gutted former Cincinnati steamboat that "once held a place in the front rank of the Western boats" had its machinery "placed in the new steamer, Luminary." The destroyed boat's name: *The Southerner*.[50]

Fueling this home-front political war were western federal soldiers on the front lines who faced the prospect of becoming "practical emancipators." Many from the free middle border states believed it was not their mission to either support or interfere with slavery. Most western soldiers, wrote Richard J. Oglesby, an Illinois brigadier general, "cared nothing about the negro, or party politics[.] They wished to put down the rebellion, restore the Union, and restore the authority of the constitution and laws and let all other questions alone." A Kentucky German American soldier was appalled at the racial antipathy of western soldiers. "[T]he Free States' Americans give the Negro much worse treatment than those who belong to the Slave States," he wrote. "The Kentuckians treat the Negro more humanely, the others treat him like a dog. The former call him Negro, the latter call him Nigger." Serving in slave states often confirmed negative racial views even among antislavery troops. A Michigan sergeant garrisoning in Danville, Kentucky, confessed: "I am not half so much of an abolitionist as I was before I came here.... I would not turn my hand over to see the whole lot of [slaves] free." For many, the wellspring of outrage was the threat to white supremacy posed by black enlistment. "If you make a soldier of the negro you can not dispute but he is as good as me or any other Indiana soldier," wrote one southern Indiana private to his father. "Woud you love to see the Negro placed on equality with me?" Popular among western soldiers was a minstrel show variant of a jaunty marching song: "It's a funny thing to me, That the 'nigger' now should be, The question everybody wants explainin'. When there's not a single man for the niggers cares a damn, But they'd send 'em to the happy land of Canaan."[51]

Rather than "turn black" or "radicalize," hundreds of officers and enlisted men from the region's free states tendered their resignations or took "French leave" in protest against the president's proclamation. Nowhere was this backlash against emancipation stronger than in the ranks of southern Illinois's volunteers. Within months of the final Emancipation Proclamation on January 1, 1863, two Illinois regiments, the 109th and the 128th, both largely from Egypt and stationed at Holly Springs, Mississippi, and Cairo, respectively, virtually disappeared as a result of mutiny and mass desertion, refusing to fight against "their southern brethren" or worse to assist "that class of patriots [who] go in for 'exterminating the Southern people.'" In response, Ulysses S. Grant put the former under mass arrest for "disloyalty," and both regiments were soon disbanded. One soldier estimated in the late spring of 1863 that desertions had reduced several of the newer regiments in his brigade by half, "mostly caused by the disloyal of Illinois writing down here and pursuading them to desert." Many soldiers, from other free states, vowed they would never reenlist. "A large majority can see no reason why *they* should be shot for the benefit of niggers and Abolitionists," reasoned an Ohio editor. Enough made good on their promise to leave the army to prompt the Democrat-controlled Illinois legislature briefly to consider recalling its regiments. The situation became so dire that William S. Rosecrans, commander of the Department of the Ohio, and Secretary of War Edwin Stanton employed strong measures to prevent a general crisis.[52]

The home-front war over emancipation roiled the western armies nearly as much as the proclamation itself. With partisan response in their home communities threatening war sacrifices, the federal soldiery from the middle border's free states soon assisted in the labeling of unpatriotic home-front dissenters. "It is almost a mystery to us why traitors at home are allowed to utter such vile sentiments in a free and enlightened country," wrote a southern Indiana soldier when learning of anti-emancipation resolutions drafted by Democrats in his home county. "Such proceedings are denounced with indignation by Soldiers in the field." Republican community newspapers soon ran soldiers' letters castigating unpatriotic displays at home and employing hard language drawn from the political war raging in the ranks. Indianan Orville T. Chamberlain counseled no tolerance for anything less than full patriotism from "Northern traitors who uphold with their voice what they *dare* not support with arms.... Your letter shows you to be a cowardly traitor. No traitor can be my friend... *you are my enemy*." So noticeable was the conversion of the federal armies' sentiments against the fire in the rear that one Indianan wrote confidently in April 1863, "All the copperhead sentiment has left the army, and it is again really patriotic." Louisvillian Alfred Pirtle found his mind changed on the matter by the summer of 1863. After having threatened to resign his commission should Lincoln renege on his promise not to free slaves, he wrote to his sister, "I am afraid that I am getting to be an abolitionist. All right! Better that than a Secessionist."[53]

Among slave state soldiers, especially Kentuckians, opposition to emancipation was more universal. Soldiers fought for "this Best government on earth," as one Kentucky unionist wrote, because it represented the protection of slavery and the stability of their social order. John T. Harrington, a nineteen-year-old private in the 22nd Kentucky, complained that he had "enlisted to fight for the union and the constitution but Lincoln... has us Union men fighting for his abolition platform and thus making us a hord of suffagates, house burners, negro thieves, and devastators of private property." Open violence often accompanied soldiers' debates. An Ohioan claimed that emancipation caused such poor morale among Kentucky regiments that Confederate troops "don't fear the Ky troops attol," and a St. Louis private claimed, "I dont want the negro freed. I dont think I will do much fighting to free the nasty thing." He was not alone. Angered by being forced not only to accept but to enact emancipation, many more enlisted men from middle border slave states left the army than from free states. More than a hundred soldiers in the 24th Kentucky deserted, and when the remainder were ordered from Frankfort to leave the state for the front, they mutinied, requiring an Ohio regiment to force them onto train cars at the point of bayonets. In January 1863 a Missourian in the ranks in the lower Mississippi valley claimed that one "Regiment in our Brigade stacked their arms the other day but were prevailed on by their Col. To take them again. They say they are going home the first March." One Illinois officer wrote in late 1862 that Kentucky's enlisted men were "more than half opposed to the North, and in sympathy now with the South," and that the officers were "more than half Rebels."[54]

Many slave state officers protested emancipation by obstructing orders. When John McHenry, colonel of the 17th Kentucky, issued orders that barred slaves from his camp and threatened those who remained with allowing their masters, loyal or not, to reclaim them, he was dismissed from the army. Other such refractory officers were similarly cashiered, while hundreds more tendered their resignations. In November 1862 a Wisconsin regiment nearly triggered riots by emancipating Kentucky slaves on the march, and members of an Illinois regiment fought outright with Kentucky federal troops—and locals—who demanded the return of sheltered runaways. Thomas Gunn, serving in the army in middle Tennessee, wrote home that "many of our officers have been complaining and murmuring during the past few days on account of alleged interferences in Ky with private property (niggers) on the part of some northern Regts.... [T]hey are just tired of the Service and are trying to find a pretext for resigning so as to go home and live off of their kin and spend what little they have made off of U.S." A Kentucky private spoke for many in the ranks from his state when he wrote home, "This is nothing but an abolition war."[55]

Emancipation had forced even prominent unionist officers to prioritize their patriotism. Kentucky editor Orlando Brown managed to convince his son, a federal captain, not to defect to the Confederate army by arguing that the proclamation would not stand constitutional muster, and dissenting officers who remained would assist in undermining it: "[I]t is so universally regarded as unconstitutional that it will not be enforced. Public opinion in Military as well as Civil affairs is a power in the state and has its weight with soldiers and civilians." Like many officers, John Marshall Harlan privately tendered his resignation in the early spring of 1863 "to settle his business matters" after his father's death, but he made his unhappiness with Lincoln's proclamation well known upon his return to Frankfort. The former Constitutional Unionist would soon win election as his state's attorney general as a Union Democrat, and Harlan would campaign for Lincoln's opponent for the presidency in 1864, arguing in New Albany, Indiana, that abolitionists had "trample[d] upon constitutions and laws with impunity" and that the war was "not for the purpose of giving freedom to the negro."[56]

The political divisions over slavery that had long festered within the Regular Army officers' ranks broke apart even the close fraternity of former West Pointers. Republican federal officers chafing against what they believed was a Democratic majority soft on slavery among the army's brass used all-or-nothing emancipationism as a partisan weapon, writing congressmen serving on the Joint Committee on the Conduct of the War asking for their removal as latent traitors, Copperheads in wall tents. Lincoln firmly defended Ulysses S. Grant, a closeted Democrat but a not-so-closeted critic of abolitionists, to "loyal men" who claimed Republican officers were opposed to him as a "proslavery man." By contrast, Missouri Radicals touted John M. Schofield's abilities owing to the fact that "he is an abolitionist and emancipationist." After a discussion of slavery and politics with his division commander, a German colonel wrote, "Yesterday I had quite a spat with Jeff. C. Davis, he is a proslavery General and he is down on the Abolitionists.... I have no good feeling for him, and I have made up my mind that I will not go into another Battle under his command." (After a confrontation unrelated to slavery politics, in September 1862 the Indianan Davis shot dead his superior, Kentuckian William "Bull" Nelson, in the lobby of Louisville's Galt House, for which he received no official punishment.) When Don Carlos Buell replaced Kentucky-born Ormsby M. Mitchel as commander of the Department of the Ohio, the prominent Cincinnati abolitionist was exasperated at being subordinated to a slaveholder who was "hamper[ing] the army... by [his] political intrigues." In the fall of 1862, amid the furor over the Emancipation Proclamation, Lincoln sacked the proslavery Buell, whose antislavery subordinates accused him of being "not a loyal man." John M. Palmer, an Illinois abolitionist and brigadier general, wanted only Republicans in command in the West lest the eastern armies oppose emancipation. "Let our present army be made efficient," he implored Lyman Trumbull in December 1862, "consolidate the radical regiments and be careful in doing so to retain only loyal incorruptible officers."[57]

§

Emancipation declared, the war against the Confederacy required a war against slavery—at home and at the front. Despite the Lincoln administration's "conservative" border state policy, allowing proslavery sentiment to coexist with unionism in order to appease loyal yet divided populaces, the president's supporters, in uniform and out, found the policy impracticable. With support for or opposition to slavery now the measure of loyalty and disloyalty, they must wage war in earnest against all those who actively supported the peculiar institution. The new imperatives demanded that the old spectrum of allegiances tolerated, even cultivated, by ameliorative federal policies could no longer coexist peacefully.[58]

With the war front now hundreds of miles to the south, western residents who faced the chaos that followed emancipation demanded a binary along loyalty lines that were in truth framed as antislavery and proslavery politics. In the middle border's slave and free states, community wars were raging within and apart from the broader conflict. Local motives and national imperatives converged in innumerable struggles, often hidden from view except to those who experienced them, as what one scholar has termed "welters of complex struggles." They in turn intensified and expanded the scope of local retributive conflicts as "feuds writ large." Residents newly polarized over slavery would put "private violence to public use," erasing the disappearing frontier between individual and collective behavior. Communities of allegiance, hardened by overt political struggles, emerged in new, deadlier forms as they fought hidden conflicts that would remake the wartime western region.[59]

The Art of Retaliation

If pain is the artist's muse, George Caleb Bingham found a full palette of inspiration in Missouri. Raised in the western Missouri River valley, he stretched the canvas of misfortune that would define his life. As a boy he watched the silt-brown river take his grandfather and brother in successive floods and his father die of another of its unwelcome offerings, malarial fever. Only the greatest of luck saved the family's small farm in Saline County from the hungry creditors who took nearly all the rest, and Bingham's mother, Mary, moved them to the new town of Arrow Rock in 1827. From there the young man with a penchant for woolgathering and a talent for drawing left for art training in the East, only to return and use portraiture to stroke the vanities of affluent white Missouri families in order to earn enough to support his real ambition. As a painter, the western rivers and people served as motifs in his exuberant works of genre art depicting daily lives and democratic politics of the common folk of his region, popular enough to gain him national and even international prominence as "the Missouri Artist." His own vanity was challenged by a case of smallpox, which left his face scarred and his head entirely bald, forcing him to resort to wearing a wig for the remainder of his life.[1]

As a slaveholding Whig and "emotional nationalist," Bingham served one term in the state legislature in the 1840s. The political arena soon proved that artless moderation was no match for brute partisanship over slavery. In 1849, as chairman of the House Committee on Federal Relations, he offered a set of counter-resolutions to try to head off the infamous Jackson resolutions that elevated Missouri's proslavery Ultras nearly to the voice of the state. Though a moderate, Bingham's politics could be emotional. Local legend holds that when Bingham had applied the last brushstroke to the portrait he painted of Saline County neighbor William B. Napton, an unflinching proslavery Democrat and seated state supreme court judge, he said, "One Napton in this world is enough," pulled out a derringer, and shot the likeness between the eyes. Proslavery Missourians' unprincipled pursuit of Kansas convinced Bingham to become an Emancipationist, and in 1856 he boasted that he had "gone clear over to the black republicans." By 1860 abolitionist extremism had forced him again toward proslavery moderation, and he supported John Bell rather than Lincoln for president.[2]

When the war came, Bingham nonetheless declared himself an unconditional unionist who approved the "wisdom and practicability of Coercion" by the presence of the federal military. "The neutrality policy which our friends have been generally urging has never struck me as being manly or patriotic," he blustered naively. "To pronounce Secession treason in one breath, and in the next to declare neutrality between the traitors and the Constituted authorities who are endeavoring to maintain the government, seems to me to be twin brothers to the treason.... The fact is Governments are for purposes of Coercion alone." Impulsively, he joined a Kansas City home guard. Suffering through battle and surrender at Lexington, the artist was soon convinced he did not have the constitution of a soldier. In January 1862 Hamilton R. Gamble appointed Bingham state treasurer to replace the elected official, who refused to take the provisional government's test oath.[3]

All romantic hues of Bingham's war canvas faded entirely when he saw federal troops and militia inflict "predatory warfare" on proslavery civilians in western Missouri. "[T]hey have made war upon Union Men as fiercely as upon Secessionists," he railed. In the summer of 1863 hard-liner Benjamin F. Loan threatened to execute "the first half dozen Secessionists whom he could find nearest to the Spot" of guerrilla depredations and ordered the burning of private dwellings "consisting of women and children chiefly... charged with *no offense whatever.*" Bingham complained to department commander John M. Schofield that these troops were "turn[ing] peaceable and quiet citizens into desperate guerilas."[4]

The artist's moral outrage at federal troops' and militias' predations on civilians would find its match in murderous Missouri guerrillas. On August 21, 1863, William C. Quantrill, a notorious guerrilla chieftain, culminated a recent flurry of violence by boldly attacking Lawrence, the "abolitionist capital" of Kansas. Ostensibly, Quantrill seethed after the August 13 collapse of a Kansas City building used as a prison for southern-sympathizing women, killing five, some of them relatives of his men. In fact, he had been planning the raid for weeks. His choice of Lawrence for his band's "revenge" was nothing short of obvious. Long the locus for Kansas abolitionism, Lawrence was now a place of refuge—and enlistment—for fugitive Missouri slaves. More, it was the symbol of a changed war since Radicals had seized control.[5]

Screaming "Jennison!" and "Osceola!," allusions to destructive Jayhawker raids on Missouri, some 450 raiders descended on Lawrence at dawn. By mid-morning nearly two hundred townsmen lay dead or dying, many executed in front of their families. For nearly four score years, this massacre was the largest wartime loss of civilian life in American history. Eighty widows and 250 orphaned children were among the survivors. Virtually all of the town's businesses on sloping

Massachusetts Street and a hundred of its private homes lay in smoldering ruins, totaling some $2 million in property. Quantrill had lost only one man, whose body was soon dragged by horsemen through Lawrence's streets amid the stench of burned death. Federal cavalry pursued from Fort Leavenworth, but they could not catch Quantrill's raiders as they scattered across the bluestem prairie toward Missouri.[6]

Heading the delayed pursuit was Thomas Ewing Jr., commander of the newly constituted District of the Border. Scion of a prominent moderate Ohio political family whose foster brother was William Tecumseh Sherman, Ewing condemned abolitionists and proslavery extremists alike. In 1861 he had been made chief justice of Kansas's first supreme court. Ewing opposed the president's Emancipation Proclamation, fearing it would expand internecine violence, but he soon underwent a conversion on slavery as a war issue. Those who supported armed resistance to protect the peculiar institution needed to be shown the harder hand of war, and in late June 1863, Ewing had vowed to "set the border right in ninety days." In truth, he was less a hard-liner than James H. Lane and attempted to contain the various bodies of armed, mounted Kansas "Red-Legs," the antislavery bushwhackers, who Ewing believed were "stealing themselves rich in the name of liberty." The quote was quickly reported in northern newspapers.[7]

To deter violence from both sides, Ewing intended to create a veritable no man's land. More properly, it was a no woman's land. As much as the building collapse, Ewing's public targeting of women had likely fueled Quantrill's raiders' fury. As early as August 3, Ewing had proposed driving out families of known and suspected guerrillas to undercut the civilian lifeline to thugs like Quantrill. Arguing that two-thirds of residents were kin to guerrillas, Ewing issued General Orders No. 10, requiring subordinate commanders to arrest and forward to the Kansas City provost marshal all men and women "not heads of families" who had knowingly aided guerrillas. Federal disloyalty lists around Independence soon consisted entirely of women.[8]

The "Lawrence Massacre" demanded an immediate, hard-line response. The U.S. senator James H. Lane called for vengeance—an unauthorized war of "devastation and extermination" in Missouri—and Lincoln himself wrote that "no punishment could be too sudden, or too severe for those murderers." "[T]ormented... beyond endurance for months by both sides" in Missouri, the president ordered Schofield "to take hold of the case." The department commander believed "that nothing short of total devastation of the districts which are made the haunts of guerrillas will be sufficient to put a stop to the evil" and issued a draft order authorizing the deportation of all "disloyal people... with such of their personal property as they may choose to carry away" and the destruction of the "houses, barns, provisions, and other property." Crops and livestock would be confiscated and distributed to unionists.[9]

On August 25, 1863, Ewing issued General Orders No. 11, a "burnt-offering to satisfy the just passion of the people." At the start of the harvest season, it required all residents of Missouri's Cass and Bates Counties, virtually all of Jackson, and the northern half of Vernon County who lived more than a mile from the four military posts in the area to be certified as loyal by military authorities within two weeks. Those who received loyalty certificates would "be permitted to remove to any military station in this district, or to any part of the State of Kansas, except the counties on the eastern border of the State. All others shall remove out of this district." Of the some forty thousand people who had inhabited the area at the start of the war, whether unionist or not, none could stay in their homes. The military requisitioned loyalists' foodstuffs and paid in vouchers, while disloyalists' property was either confiscated for the troops' use or destroyed. Refugees migrated into neighboring counties; by one estimate, half crossed the Missouri River northward, crowding into the homes of kin, renting available lodging, or squatting in abandoned barns and outbuildings. Others left the state entirely, trudging southward to former homes in the Confederacy or striking out for Kansas or beyond.[10]

More than one historian has concluded that Order No. 11 "was not a retaliation for the massacre." Surely it was. Absence of evidence did not deter the federal government's first-ever forcible removal of white, propertied citizens from their homes. Anyone "not within the protection of a Military Station...and [who] is not molested [by guerrillas] is [judged] a rebel or rebel sympathizer." Although Lincoln questioned the wisdom "of removing the inhabitants of certain counties *en masse*," the president supported the expulsion of "guerrillas, marauders, and murderers, and all who are known to harbor, aid, or abet them." Ewing ordered Kansas cavalry, led by known hard-liners, to enforce these deportations and destructions. In truth, only the prairies were entirely purged of people. Guerrillas continued to find refuge in hilly sections and creek bottoms. A St. Louis editor ridiculed the notion of "the only pure spot on the globe—the only spot in the whole Union where none but loyal people live."[11]

By design, women and children bore the brunt of the order. Few men remained, especially loyal, most having long since left the area rather than fall prey to Jayhawkers' or guerrillas' persecutions. "I think if we get rid of the women," wrote Bazel F. Lazear, a Missouri state militia officer, "[it] will have a good effect. It may prove hard on some few Union people.... I intend to send all the families of Bushwhackers out of this and Johnson county [Missouri] just as fast as I can give them notice to leave." A resident remembered that "the road from Independence to Lexington was crowded with women and children, women walking with their babies in their arms, packs on their backs, and four or five children following after them—some crying for bread, some crying to be taken back to their homes." One former refugee recalled "every body in the country moving at one time the wether dry hot and dusty the dust so thick on the fences a person could gether it up by hands full, white women and children looked like negroes." One officer remarked a day after the order was implemented that the border was largely "[a] desolated country of women and children, some of them allmost naked." Local unionists were largely unmoved. The garrison commander at Liberty issued an order prohibiting refugees from the border counties from stopping in Clay County "to reside," while one unionist commented "god knows where they are all going for I don't nor do I care so we can get rid of them in Missouri[.]" For decades, locals called these counties simply the "Burnt District."[12]

The outcry from unionists elsewhere was immediate and harsh. After hearing from a wide array of critics, Schofield surveyed the damage and forced Ewing to cease destroying homes, crops, and pasturage. Ewing later admitted being shocked at the destruction, noting only one inhabited dwelling between Kansas City and Independence. Radicals and moderates alike condemned the order. Charles D. Drake called Order No. 11 a "barbarous order [that] belongs to the dark ages," and Frank Blair, then a brigadier general in the field in Tennessee, denounced it as an "act of imbecility." By fall, Sterling Price welcomed Quantrill's men into his camp in southwestern Arkansas and solicited a full report on their activities since the Lawrence raid, claiming them a just response strategy to the federals' war to the knife in the western states, intending that his own report would serve "so that the Confederacy and the world may learn the murderous and uncivilized warfare which they themselves have inaugurated, and thus be able to appreciate their cowardly shrieks and howls when with a just retaliation the same 'measure is meted out to them.'"[13]

Like Ewing and Quantrill, blood was on George Caleb Bingham's hands. Or it appeared so. His ownership of the collapsed Kansas City building, made public in newspapers, suggested complicity in the Lawrence catastrophe. Whether because of the guerrillas' vow of retaliation or his clumsy attempts to get reparation for his destroyed property, within days of the publication of the order Bingham headed to Kansas City for a private meeting with Ewing. Allegedly, when the general refused to rescind the order, Bingham offered a prophetic warning: "If you persist in executing that order, I will make you infamous with pen and brush as far as I am able."[14]

Before Bingham had managed to transfer his rage to canvas, the artist's self-styled "War of Desolation" raged on. Within a month of the order, Jo Shelby's cavalrymen were raiding Missouri, killing or capturing thousands of federal troops and inflicting millions of dollars' worth of damage. In October Quantrill's guerrillas attacked a four-hundred-man garrison that included black troops at Baxter Springs, Kansas, killing a fourth of the men, many after they had surrendered, in a scenario that would become too common in the West, most notably at Fort Pillow and Poison Spring. A year later, as his foster brother, William T. Sherman, was marching across Georgia, Ewing transferred his expulsion strategy to war-torn southeastern Missouri to "renovate" it. "In one way or another the worst rebel families... must be got out before corn planting." The western way of war had become the nation's.[15]

7

Shadow Wars

The Crucible of Social Violence

If the essence of politics is expedience, the essence of war is fear. By the summer of 1863 residents of the middle border were indeed fearful. Thefts, arson, and violence occurred with frightening frequency in many communities. An Illinois newspaper cautioned readers "to have their door and window fastenings safe and secure and ... to have a good revolver in readiness," while a southern Indiana woman recalled, "if any unusual noise was heard of[,] if there was a knock on the door, the light was blown out. Any one with a legitimate errand had to make himself known unmistakably.... Those who lived in two-story houses were likely to sit upstairs after nightfall, leaving the lower floor darkened and securely locked."[1]

The introduction of fear into the broadest constituencies was the most expedient means of waging war in its fullest form. The middle border region saw little of the conventional war after 1862, but its residents suffered a diffuse home-front war fought not between opposing military forces or even between military and civilian combatants. Rather, this war raged *within* them, men and women, white and black, as neighbors, relatives, friends, slaves, and strangers entered the spectrum of conflict alongside federals, partisans, guerrillas, and rogues.[2]

The violence that emerged from these "everyday forms of ideological struggle" was the expression of a mature home-front insurgency that sought more than simple security. Often hidden from view, its combatants fought for wartime power and advantage. These shadowy conflicts produced various forms and targets once emancipation fully entwined political and military goals, but increasingly they narrowed into the political and ideological binary that the war demanded. Once military necessity included slavery's destruction, a "desperate side of the Civil War," as Daniel E. Sutherland has aptly termed it, emerged on the middle border, through which violence became a medium of social exchange and political warfare. Although this violence was prevalent in all the region's states, the degree of violence was not experienced evenly between free and slave states and would divide the middle border region accordingly as the war came to its bitter close.[3]

§

That the word *guerrilla* translates as "small war" is only the most obvious of the ironies surrounding the internecine warfare that engulfed the middle border region in 1863. Guerrillas might have been the most feared purveyors of political violence, but they were only one of many interest groups to traffic in it. Guerrilla warfare did not begin with the Confederacy's Partisan Ranger Act, introduced by middle border representatives (led by expelled U.S. senator and Confederate senator Henry C. Burnett) and passed on April 21, 1862. Independent irregular bands had roamed parts of the nation for nearly a year. Indeed, the pervasive fear of "marauding parties" of pro-Confederate bushwhackers, real as well as imagined, had driven unionists in southern Nebraska, Iowa, Illinois, and Indiana to organize border patrols and home guards with the sanction of their anxious legislatures. Some crossed the state line or rivers and acted as bushwhackers as much as the gangs they sought. Retaliatory warfare soon followed. In the war's first months, unionist newspapers reported robberies by "Secession marauders who...allowed no Union men to 'sass' them." Nightriders stole horses, and saboteurs destroyed railroads, trestles, and bridges. But they soon enough attacked other symbols of federal authority, including trains, riverboats, and stagecoaches, and often interrupted mail, fired at moving boats, or stopped and looted or burned others (see figure 7.1), or derailed trains while women and children were aboard, frequently enough for a Missouri editor to claim it "degrading to think white men would do [this]." Confederate armies in the state spurred the accretion of nightriders, real or imagined. In Missouri during the days surrounding the battle at Wilson's Creek, home guards and vigilance committees reported so many guerrillas blanketing the countryside that Ulysses S. Grant—who had seen such warfare in Mexico—instructed subordinates to "be careful about crediting reports you receive from citizens."[4]

The full guerrilla war came slowly, gaining strength as the Confederacy found itself losing the war in the West. One 1861 estimate numbered horsemen who would soon plague widespread parts of Missouri in the hundreds, and few references mention guerrilla warfare of any kind in Kentucky prior to the summer of 1862, prompting a unionist there to conclude hopefully that the provost system would "Keep things in Order...a death blow to any thing like 'Guerrilla parties' being formed." When control of the lower Mississippi valley became the strategic linchpin in the fall of 1862, a string of defensive outposts in garrison towns across the Ozark plateau and Kentucky's southern tier offered a demarcation of the southern extent of federal occupation in the border states. They also blocked the return of Confederate parolees with a range of motives, as Schofield wrote, including "the hope of being permitted to remain at their former homes in peace, while some have come under instructions to carry on a guerrilla warfare, and others, men of the worst character, become marauders on their own account,

Figure 7.1 Guerrillas burning steamers on the Cumberland River, ca. 1863. With increasing frequency after the announcement of emancipation in 1862, armed irregular bands captured and destroyed trains and steamboats in the middle border states, interrupting government transportation, capturing mail, and often executing federal troops and unionist civilians on board. Courtesy Indiana Historical Society.

caring nothing for the Union nor for the rebellion." Many had run to Arkansas or Tennessee already to avoid federal service, only to return to their homes to avoid Confederate service. Sweeps by both armies resulted in arrest, imprisonment, or exile of many deserters trying desperately to get home. Jeremiah T. Boyle ordered provost marshals to stop releasing captured deserters and "repentant Guerrillas" under oath and bond; once taken up, men claiming Union loyalty were given the choice of proving it—by enlisting in the federal army.[5]

National conscriptions drove many alienated federal soldiers out of the ranks and into the brush. With recruitment and enrollment squads operating in their states, many men hid from military authorities in hilly and mountainous areas, such as the Ozarks and eastern Kentucky. There, evaders and deserters "committ[ed] all kinds of mischief, plundering the families of the soldiers who are serving in our [federal] regiment." An exasperated garrison commander in the "brushy portion" of Kentucky's central counties claimed that "it was impossible for the Union men of that locality to live in security, while these men remained in their midst." Ostracized and on the run, many found it difficult to remain peaceful, much less loyal. One released Louisville Confederate found that he "could not go to church, without having his horse and saddle taken from

him... he was treated at home, by them, as though he was not their equal....
[H]e said that he must fight the enemy." Many others also went back under arms.
Paroled and rearrested in the fall of 1862, Missouri's Jacob Snowden boasted that
"he would be God-damned if he did not go to the brush again... that he would
bushwhack as soon as the leaves came out." By November 1862, after Confederate
armies had withdrawn from his state, a western Kentuckian claimed that its counties were "completely overrun by armed bands of hostile troops and marauders."[6]

Debates about federal and state authority in the middle border's slave states
combined with unionists' concerns about an expanding guerrilla war in "which
only loyal men are the sufferers" to delay or limit militia drafts to state ranks.
Although he badly needed soldiers, the president feared that any arms the government might provide to new Kentucky militia would be "turned against the
government." The president of Kentucky's Union League concurred, claiming
that "every draft... puts more men into the rebel than in the Union Army."
Consequently, no middle border slave state district required a federal draft
before 1864.[7]

The enrollments that accompanied militia drafts gave guerrillas opportunities
to gain recruits and to target federal and militia garrisons and local unionists.
The enrollment lists supplemented those kept by provost marshals of the loyal
and disloyal, identifying those who had offered a substitute or paid the $300 commutation fee to avoid enlistment. Garrison commanders informed them that they
were now "consider[ed] and treat[ed] as an enemy." Another concluded that "in
buying a substitute *before* the draft a man is *surely* put into the enemy's ranks." Of
the 438 "disloyal men" between the ages of eighteen and forty-five in Andrew
County, Missouri, who in 1863 took the oath and were enrolled, sixty-six had
once served in the Confederate army, forty-six had given bonds of as much as
$1,000 (in one case an improbable $70,000), and three paid the commutation
fee to avoid service. Seventy-six enrolled voluntarily, while 327 were arrested,
administered the oath, and enrolled, the latter constituting nearly 20 percent of
the county's white male population of enrollment age. Even Andrew County
men over enrollment age judged as disloyal or sympathizing found themselves
listed, some 238 of them, and some as old as seventy-eight. Robert Elliott, aged
seventy, demanded that the enrolling officer, William Heren, "enter my protest
against my name being used as a suchess [secesh] sympathizer." Rather than be
drafted or targeted by guerrillas, many left their states entirely, heading to the Far
West, Nebraska, or Canada. As one Kentuckian claimed, "all *who can*, leave the
country, and their places are filled up with Preachers, Negroes, and 'strong
minded women' from the North."[8]

Draft evasion, whether Confederate or federal, also contributed to the rise
of postemancipation guerrilla warfare. Singly and in groups, many "who could
not enlist for service in the field," as a southern Indianan characterized them,

enlisted in state or county militias or home guards, to avoid the federal enlistment or the draft, to infiltrate and disrupt these militias, or to prevent armed unionists from targeting their families. A federal officer in Kentucky concluded that the guerrillas in his area were largely "composed of men who were drafted for our service." Many men who refused to serve found themselves compelled to take up bushwhacking. In southeastern Missouri, partisan leader Tim Reeves, a former Baptist minister, conscripted local men into service under threat of execution if they refused. "[I]f a man cannot join one or the other party he has no business here," wrote one Missouri woman, "he is between fires."[9]

Conscription alone did not account for the irregular war raging through parts of the middle border's slave states. If postwar recollections of former guerrillas are reliable (they certainly are not unbiased), self-styled southern residents who took up arms against the government in the war's first year were responding to more than threats to their capital investments. Many took to the brush out of ideological conviction, namely that the war was over slavery. After Kansas Jayhawkers burned their family's home in western Missouri and state militia murdered and robbed their father, Cole Younger and his younger brother joined William C. Quantrill's guerrilla band. Despite his family name, Samuel Hildebrand claimed that his long-standing antipathy for his southeastern Missouri township's antislavery German American majority, largely antislavery Republicans, began his guerrilla career. "The union men were making war upon me," Hildebrand claimed later, "but I was making no war upon them, for I still wished to take no part in the national struggle." When the vigilance committee in his community "became a machine of oppression," persecuting those judged disloyal, and an "unscrupulous mob" had driven him from his home, hanged his brother and an uncle for guerrilla activities, and brought down a squad of militia cavalry to ambush and nearly kill him and burn his home, Hildebrand rode into the woods. "The die was cast—for the sake of revenge, I pronounced myself a Rebel." He soon "rejoiced" in his killing of German soldiers, often by hanging them. That both Younger and Hildebrand hailed from slaveholding families was likely not a mere literary device.[10]

Pro-Confederate Missourians like these hailed disproportionately from the upper strata of rural society, and for years they engaged in for-profit commercial agriculture and invested heavily in railroad construction during the 1850s. Consequently, many were deeply indebted to local bankers. When federal and state authorities took over the banks in late 1861, they saw their farms and slaves auctioned off to pay these debts, denying these families' dispossessed sons their inheritance of social standing. Many responded not by enlisting in the Confederate service, but rather by becoming irregulars, who would wage war on those who had robbed them. In the Boon's Lick, four-fifths of identified "bushwhackers" came from indebted families whose property was sold in estate sales. The families of guerrillas in one western Missouri county were three times as likely to have owned slaves (and were twice as likely to have possessed real wealth, including slaves) as an average white Missouri man, and they held on average nearly twice as many bondpeople as the average slaveholding family in their home county. As bushwhackers, these slaveholding scions made common cause with desperate men from the bottom of their society. A slaveholding Missourian legitimated retributive violence as a response to the federal hard-line war against slavery. "[J]ayhawkers were plundering their neighbors, burning their houses, and laying waste the country, stealing Negroes and everything they could lay their hands on," wrote Elvira A. W. Scott. "People have and will retaliate; it is human nature."[11]

Federal desertions over emancipation also fed the guerrilla ranks. According to one Missouri newspaper, a year after the Emancipation Proclamation some 1,987 Missouri soldiers had deserted the state's twenty-five federal infantry and cavalry regiments and artillery batteries. Countless more had abandoned the state militia. Many there and in Kentucky headed for the brush as bushwhackers. When he was captured as a guerrilla near Lewisport, Kentucky, federal authorities identified Martin V. Asher as John Wallace, a deserter from an Indiana regiment. Manlove Cranor, whose once-unionist county home guard was disbanded by Iowa hard-liners in northern Missouri, was by the spring of 1863 "denounc[ing radicals] as unconditional negroes, and does all he dare do to encourage rebels and dishearten Union men." He headed a new militia band largely to suppress emancipationists, "until we (the radicals) quit hallooing for Jim Lane," opening him to charges of bushwhacking and leadership of a subversive secret society.[12]

Imprecision assisted with the politicization of the shadow warriors who bedeviled federal and state troops in the middle border states, blurring the lines between regular and irregular warfare, guerrillas and cavalry. Unionists indiscriminately referred to armed men roaming the roads—whether draft dodgers, partisans, outlaws, or even Confederate cavalry—as guerrillas. Southern sympathizers claimed them as a modern incarnation of "partizans" who had helped to win an earlier war of independence. Even as some threatened to burn her home, Elvira Scott characterized bushwhackers as "good-looking, polite, and intelligent... the best and bravest of the land, who have been wronged and outraged beyond endurance and have resolved to avenge their wrongs." Unionists like George D. Prentice, the irascible editor of Louisville's *Journal* and by 1863 a harsh critic of Lincoln, ridiculed such hairsplitting, condemning John Hunt Morgan as a guerrilla for attacking under flags of truce while disguised in federal uniform, a common ruse in neighboring Missouri.[13]

In late summer 1862 the spreading guerrilla war in Missouri caused the new federal commander in the state, John M. Schofield, to devise a new approach to suppressing them. On July 22 Schofield authorized the enrollment of all able men between the ages of eighteen and forty-five into the Enrolled Missouri Militia

(EMM) specifically to combat irregulars plaguing parts of the state. By November some seventy regiments had been raised, supported nearly entirely by levies and confiscation of property, including horses, mules, furniture, and valuables. (In 1864, horses and mules were valued between $125 and $160 each.) Schofield's militia call required even the disloyal and Confederate sympathizers, past and present, to report to local posts to take the oath, enroll, and give up weapons. Although they were allowed to return to their homes and live out the war so long as they "in no way [gave] aid or comfort to the enemy," those who refused were marked as disloyal, and those who paid a $10 commutation tax were regarded with distrust. Citizens were expected to assist the militia in finding and capturing bushwhackers, or they should expect punishment. Schofield then announced his intention to combat guerrillas with renewed ferocity. "The time is passed when insurrection and rebellion in Missouri can cloak itself under the guise of honorable warfare," he declared. Schofield's policy ordered summary justice for irregulars, a revival of Frémont's earlier policy and Henry W. Halleck's order that "predatory partisans, and guerrilla bands...are liable to the same punishment which was imposed upon guerrilla bands by Napoleon in Spain and by Scott in Mexico." Those "caught in arms" would be shot down where they were.[14]

Although implementation of these policies in Missouri was soon ensnared in political wrangling, the impact was immediate. Executions of suspected guerrillas were carried out in earnest throughout the state, enough for Schofield to boast in 1862 in his diary that guerrillas "were, under my orders executed on the spot when captured, and hundreds of sympathizers banished or imprisoned." Specific terms of banishment often forced such sympathizers to remove to free states east of Illinois, burdening Indiana and Ohio with what one provost marshal claimed were "bad men from Missouri."[15]

Confederates and southern sympathizers blamed the explosion of this desperate war on the hard-line war brought by occupying federals and state militias, but emancipation figured deeply in such retaliatory warfare. Within two weeks of Lincoln's proclamation, on October 11, 1862, Theophilus H. Holmes, new commander of the Confederacy's Trans-Mississippi Department, complained to Samuel R. Curtis of the "barbarous" executions of civilians. "The war of extermination thus declared against the men of the South is infinitely more such a war when extended to the women and children of the South," he warned. But the real "infamy" was in truth far broader. "The proclamation of your President apparently contemplates, and the act of your officers in putting arms in the hands of slaves seems to provide for, even that extremity. It cannot in such a situation be expected that we will remain passive, quietly acquiescing in a war of extermination against us, without waging a similar war in return." Just a week later Holmes received an answer to his pledge of retaliation in the form of the mass execution of ten Missouri prisoners, uniformed as well as civilian, for the abduction of a local unionist. Immediately labeled the "Palmyra Massacre," it followed a lesser known execution of eleven prisoners charged with bushwhacking. Having watched the war in their state turn retributive, among those who first saddled up to ride as guerrillas the following spring were Frank and Jesse James.[16]

The rapid expansion of guerrilla warfare in 1863 that resulted in Ewing's unprecedented order had a national dimension. The previous summer, the army's general in chief, Henry W. Halleck, was frustrated at the many and varied irregular fighters plaguing the war effort from behind the lines. He solicited Francis W. Lieber, a published expert on international laws of war then lecturing at Columbia University, to offer a legal framework for combating them. A former slaveholder turned abolitionist, Lieber traveled to Virginia and met with Benjamin Butler, who famously refused to return slave "contrabands," before setting to work. The essay he produced emphasized the centrality of slavery to the war effort and condemned most irregulars as outlaws who should be denied rights as legitimate soldiers. At Halleck's invitation, Lieber headed a War Department committee that fashioned carefully ranked categories of irregular combatants by which to assign appropriate punishments. As the most recent scholar to study him has concluded generally, Lieber established limits to wartime behavior of armies and governments, especially to retaliatory targeting of black soldiers and their white officers, while advocating "the more elastic limit of military necessity" to respond to guerrilla warfare. Lieber included the term "guerrilla" among such terms as "robbers, pirates, armed prowlers, and war-rebels," in effect classifying all irregulars as outside the "laws of warfare" and denying them the rights of legitimate soldiers. Calling for the military's restraint in administering punishment, he subjected civilians to it who aided guerrillas, including women. In April 1863 Lincoln approved what was issued as General Orders No. 100, known since as "the Lieber Code," defining as military necessity all measures "indispensable for securing the ends of the war." The order provided constitutional sanction to many of the Lincoln government's recent initiatives—martial law, suspension of habeas corpus, confiscation of the property of the disloyal, and emancipation—as well as allowing for capital and summary punishment of guerrillas. Lieber's expanded vision of military necessity had a political complement. Delivering a jeremiad to New York's Loyal League entitled "No Party Now But All for Our Country," he offered Republicans an exclusivist blueprint for all-or-nothing patriotism against home-front dissenters. For Lieber, the "genesis" of his code, and for guerrilla or other partisan warfare, was slavery.[17]

Evidence drawn from the Official Reports (OR), submitted to the federal and Confederate war departments by commanders in the field, suggests Lieber was probably right. A chronology of the escalating guerrilla war in Missouri and Kentucky coincides with the announcement of emancipation. The irregular war escalated rapidly in the summer of 1862, exploded in the fall of 1862, resumed in the spring of 1863 but eased over the summer, then spiked again after Order No. 11 was issued, reaching its peak during the spring, summer, and fall of 1864. Searching the terms "guerrilla," "guerrillas," "bushwhacker," and "bushwhackers" reveals that a disproportionate number of reports involving them are dated after January 1, 1863, when the final Emancipation Proclamation took effect. After combining these totals, just 14 percent of these reports were made before this date, while 86 percent were made after it.[18]

Quantified evidence from Missouri files in the Union Provost Marshal Papers bolsters this chronology, while suggesting overlap with the hard-line war then raging in the state. Of the 822 (of 933) dated files that include these same terms, only two are dated before 1862. The 1862 and 1863 files, when quantified by month and date, exhibit a startling pattern. Of the 238 files for 1862, 61 percent describe events that occurred after September 22, Lincoln's announcement of the preliminary emancipation proclamation, meaning that a majority of the year's total guerrilla-related incidents happened in that year's final three months. Of the 151 files reporting guerrilla-related activities for 1863, just under 75 percent describe events that occurred in the early spring and summer, a likely extension of emancipation-related violence. After a late summer lull, the announcement of Order No. 11 caused the guerrilla war to explode anew, including a heavy raid by Jo Shelby's cavalry that commenced, likely not coincidentally, exactly on September 22, 1863, the proclamation's first anniversary.[19]

Resisting authority at all levels, guerrillas used targeted violence against garrisons and government officials, federal and county, from postmasters to judges, enough to suspend services, often for years. They eagerly hunted down those who assisted the government's war-making, such as draft board members. Nelson McDowell, a Missouri probate judge, was captured by a band of what he estimated to be about five hundred guerrillas in August 1862 and forced to resign his office "by signing an obligation not to hold office &c. under the present rulers of our once happy, but now distracted government." Unionist legislators, regardless of their stance on slavery, were among the first to be targeted. The U.S. congressman Aaron Harding left his Greensburg, Kentucky, home for Washington that fall "lest the guerrillas might fall behind our army and seek an interview with me." To undermine local governments, raiders and guerrillas destroyed court, tax, and other documents in these courthouses, and unionists were terrified that mail exposing their political views might fall into the raiders' hands. In late January 1863 Benjamin F. Loan, a militia commander in central Missouri, wrote to Curtis that "in several counties in the district no courts of record of any kind have held a session for several terms past.... The records have been stolen, perhaps destroyed, and the civil officers driven from the country." Thirty-five Missouri courthouses were destroyed, damaged, or disrupted by Confederates or guerrillas during the war, more than half of them in the southern part of the state, where the federal presence decreased in the winter of 1862. All but two occurred after the announcement of emancipation. Twenty-two Kentucky courthouses were burned during the war, nearly all after emancipation.[20]

Guerrillas and partisans employed their most eradicative violence against those civilians who represented or supported the end of slavery. In November 1862, around the same time that John Hunt Morgan's field newspaper claimed "any man who pretends to believe that this is not a war for the emancipation of the blacks... is either a fool or a liar," South Union's Shakers claimed of his raiders that "[free] negroes are often hunted by these soldiers, like wild beasts." They were often hanged. A few months later, one western Missouri bushwhacker vowed to Curtis that he waged war "for no other cause than being opposed to the negro-thieving policy of the Administration." For this, he would show no quarter. Another vengeful Missouri guerrilla threatened to "kill a Radical for every house that is burnt." In December Hiram Carver, a prominent Kentucky unionist and recent candidate for office who had helped to capture three notorious guerrillas, only to see them released, claimed they and other residents now "hunted [him] with dogs, like wild beasts." Similarly, a western Kentucky congressman claimed that guerrillas had "driven to bay" the local circuit judge, who was "forted in the court house where he had practiced law and administered justice for twenty years."[21]

State and county militias and home guards roiled by emancipation politics blurred the lines between guerrilla predations and military protection. Slaveholding officers like Kentucky-born Odon Guitar believed proslavery militia might best protect locals, but he soon found out otherwise. State guard troops occupying Calhoon, Kentucky, arrested three citizens in the middle of the night and extorted $490 for their release. Outraged at the president's proclamation, southern sympathizers and outright disloyalists infiltrated the militias to act as "Negro Regulators." In February 1863 residents in Chariton County complained that the county's EMM commander, William Moberly, had ordered his men to arrest unionists, enrolled former Confederates as officers, abused slaves who expressed support for the government, and confiscated them from unionist owners to harvest tobacco. Widespread criticism led to efforts to purify militias that proved ineffective. Missouri's provisional government authorized the Provisional Enrolled Missouri Militia (PEMM), constituted of loyal men who claimed to support emancipation, to replace the EMM. Within weeks of Order No. 11 being issued, two of the new regiments in several northwest Missouri counties, where proslavery and antigovernment sentiment were intense, were disbanded for mutiny and their leading officers tried for treason. Hard-liners vilified these "Paw Paws," as they were called, for their apparent sympathy with the guerrillas, charging that some were former Confederate soldiers (see figure 7.2). "[T]hey would declare for the Confederate flag," wrote one provost marshal in December 1863, then

Figure 7.2 "Paw Paw" militia, ca. 1863. In northwestern Missouri, to end raids by Kansas Jayhawkers, these county home guard units were composed of men who had been enrolled as disloyalists but were armed and paid by the state. When they were used as counterinsurgent forces after emancipation, in 1863–1864 accusations of sympathy with guerrillas (and even being former Confederate soldiers) clouded their efficacy. Courtesy State Historical Society of Missouri.

attack known "radical[s], as we say... from the bushes, or as guerrillas, or as the army of the supposed Confederacy." By war's end, the epithet "Paw Paw" was synonymous with disloyalty among Missouri's unionists.[22]

While serving in the militia or home guards, unionist "guerrilla hunters" wreaked havoc among known southern sympathizers, leading one Missourian to conclude that "one half the Bushwhackers seen is the enrolled militia." Vigilante executions became commonplace. "Men are shot or hung every few days on the most trivial of pretexts," wrote a Missouri woman in November 1862. "It has become so common that it excites no remark." Civilians fought back as vigilante gangs, shooting nightriders who approached their homes. Southern sympathizers often fled to the camps of known guerrilla bands for protection. "The [hardline] policy pursued has caused hundreds of good men to leave their homes and fly to the bushes," an officer reported, "believing that they would be less liable to danger there than at their homes.[23]

Nighttime became the sanctuary of guerrillas on both sides. "Another week of sleepless anxiety," wrote Missourian Elvira A. W. Scott in July 1863, after watching helplessly as shadowy men chased her hogs. "I cannot sleep, but listen, listen all night long, at every sound, in terror.... There is such a general insecurity that many are getting ready to leave the country." Indeed, the spiraling violence and uncertainty drove thousands more white Missourians and Kentuckians, loyalists and disloyalists, from their homes, either to the region's cities or to small towns in neighboring states, "all gone some where or other, in what ever direction suited them," wrote a western Kentuckian in 1864. With nowhere seemingly safe and no middle ground left, Scott concluded soberly "a man has nothing left but to choose sides." For many in these states, those sides had been chosen by the war's presence. M. Todd White ventured to the middle border but wrote from the comparative safety of northern Alabama in 1864, only to confirm his choice:

> I found many changes in Ky.,... old friends estranged and a bitter feeling against Southern people.... property being confiscated and all unlawful means employed to render a Rebel perfectly at a loss now to act or to keep his property, prisons full of political arrests, &c the country being full of loathsome diseases drunken soldiers, dead horses and disagreeable generally, letters intercepted, spies to follow everyone, and families divided to such an extent as you could not visit with freedom or pleasure.... Mo has suffered all that Ky must—this blindness seems so strange I can hardly comprehend.... We were asked to take the Oath—declined.[24]

§

White middle border residents were fearful of more than marauding guerrillas, federal troops, militia, or quarrelsome neighbors. Driving many civilians to violence was the looming presence of black troops in their midst. Although the Emancipation Proclamation initially excluded the border slave states, many believed the federal army's presence there doomed slavery. The delayed enlistment of African Americans saw an unprecedented rise in political violence.

Among occupying free state soldiers, interaction with recalcitrant anti-emancipation civilians deepened anger against slaveholders. "[T]he cry was, and still is, blood! blood! give us the blood of slave holders," warned one Missouri newspaperman. German American soldiers were often the most ideological of those stationed in these states, holding that "the Americans who are slaveholders are the enemies of the government." In January 1863, in a conversation on a crowded train, Elvira Scott became aware that a uniformed officer was eavesdropping. "[I]f he had the power," she wrote that the German American said to her, "there would be no peace in Missouri until the cursed institution of slavery and all that upheld it was swept out of the State.... All he wanted was the power to arrest me." Communities in dense slaveholding areas saw the chances of reprisals by federal troops greatly increased. Nearly half of the families in Jackson County, Missouri, experienced some form of sanctioned reprisal from federal troops or militia, either having their property searched, seized, or destroyed, or having family members arrested, detained, bonded, exiled, or executed.[25]

Many of these troops used practical emancipation as a bludgeon against slaveholders' disloyalty. Illinoisan Jasper Barry stated that he was "not in favor of freeing the negroes and leaving them to run free and mingle among us," yet nonetheless believed it wise to "take a way the main root of Evil and confiscate all [slaveholders'] property [so] they will have nothing to fight fore heareafter." Bolstering the claim of a Michigan soldier that nine-tenths of nonnative federal soldiers stationed in Kentucky intended "to use up slavery," one historian has found that of the 108 federal units from ten states stationed in Kentucky between August 1861 and March 1863, 87 percent violated the state's slave laws, including all of those from Illinois, Indiana, and Wisconsin. Antislavery officers employed fugitives or "secesh negroes" of disloyal masters as teamsters and laborers to work on fortifications and stockades and even allowed them to muster and drill as if they were soldiers. In August 1863 Missourian Elvira A. W. Scott witnessed the establishment of a contraband camp near Miami, signaled by a procession passing her home led by a squad of German federal soldiers "carrying a flag...headed by eleven six-mule teams drawing wagons filled with Negro women and children. Behind them was a large procession of two hundred and forty Negro men." So many free state officers sent freedmen on boats and trains to relatives or friends at home that Horatio G. Wright, commanding the Department of the Ohio, published orders not to transport slaves out of Kentucky. Lot Abraham, an Iowan stationed in Louisville, disregarded the order and sent home a freedman named Henry bearing a letter. "Before you now appears *a man of the South*," it read, "take a good look at him and tell me what you think—*he[']s black but that[']s no matter*."[26]

What did matter in accomplishing emancipation in the middle border's slave states was the conversion of white residents, especially rural, who accepted the end of slavery for their personal security and societal harmony. A wavering Kentucky woman wrote to her brother, "I sometimes think that God is now punishing our whole count[r]y for its sins, more especially for the sin of human slavery." An editor claimed that "all who own negroes are willing and anxious to give them up. The masters have been so harrassed about their chattles, that they have tired of the thing." The spiraling violence caused a Missourian to opine: "We must have emancipation, in some shape, before we can have peace.... [T]he two elements, Border Ruffianism and Secessionism.... cannot be put down while slavery has a permanent footing." In a published letter, Kentuckian Leonidas Metcalfe, son of a former governor and a federal officer, made his conversion clear. "I was born a slave owner, and am now a slave owner, and have been a pro-Slavery man," he wrote "until I see plainly that my country is in danger from that institution."[27]

Many more proslavery middle border residents acted to protect their peculiar institution out of widespread fear that black enlistment would follow emancipation. Missouri masters sent slaves to Kentucky for safekeeping with rural family or friends or to Louisville's slave markets. In November 1863 federal army officials estimated that a thousand Missouri slaves had passed through the city's slave markets in a two-month period. Officials at all levels enforced the state's slave laws, prohibiting the employment of slaves without their masters' permission, preventing the transportation of slaves without their masters' permission within or outside state boundaries, and threatening lawsuits against operators of railroads and riverboats. Kentucky's constables and sheriffs jailed contrabands and advertised or sold them, and militia and home guards often acted as slave patrols, even kidnapping free blacks. One EMM officer pulled a revolver on an antislavery German who obstructed one such incident, calling him a "God damned Dutch Son of a Bitch," and threatened to kill him, while another replied defiantly in the local newspaper to accusations of using soldiers to return freedmen to bondage. "If this be a disloyal act, I can state that the Callaway militia are 'disloyal,'" wrote Isaac M. Snedecor, sarcastically challenging the new loyalty orthodoxies with regard to slavery. Disloyalty, he argued, was "an abolitionist and negro thief and those who are in the name of loyalty endeavoring to overthrow... that Constitution and divert this war from its legitimate object and purpose."[28]

The politics of emancipation had different outcomes in the middle border's slave states. In Missouri the shifting political winds that demanded emancipation as a measure of loyalty swept in the new Radical Union Party, many of whom believed ending slavery was critical to defeating guerrillas and Confederates. Charles D. Drake's meteoric rise to the head of the party both exemplifies and belies his ideological evolution to wartime abolition. A longtime gradual emancipationist and anti-abolition Whig, Drake was a St. Louis lawyer whose views quickly hardened in wartime. Protection of slavery was the "watchword [for] disunionists... [and] the struggle now going on here, though ostensibly connected with the subject of Emancipation, is, in reality, *between Loyalty and Disloyalty.*" Elected to fill a vacancy at the 1863 convention, Drake openly favored immediate emancipation in Missouri. Encouraged by the Radicals' surge, Lincoln was nonetheless wary of Drake's "almost *fiendish*" political opportunism, especially his advocacy of black military enlistment. After a tense meeting at the White House, according to his private secretary, John Hay, the president condemned the Radicals as "utterly lawless—the unhandiest devils in the world to deal with—but after all their faces are set Zionward." Effectively leveraging the brutal internecine warfare now raging in Missouri, they gained enough support in the provisional government to allow Missouri soldiers to vote in the field and enacted a stringent "test oath" that disfranchised an estimated 75,000 Democratic voters, neutralists as well as disloyalists. In Andrew County on the Iowa border, some 353 voting-age men were excluded from voting for "sympathiz[ing] with the Rebellion." Radicals charged proslavery moderates, including governor Hamilton R. Gamble, with being in league with secessionists. Gamble was forced to backpedal on his anti-emancipation stance, and in June 1863 he took a gradual plan to a special session of the convention. Approved on July 1, 1863, the legislation stated that Missouri's slaves would receive terms of freedom beginning in 1870, although none would actually be freed until 1876.[29]

In Kentucky wartime emancipation found more systemic opposition. The state's elected leaders refused to consider it, and a state legislative committee issued a report vilifying congressional Republicans for being "bent on the destruction of the Constitution and the Union" and intending to "elevate [blacks] to an equality with the white man." Following the instructions of the governor, James F. Robinson, the legislature resolved that the proclamation was "unwise, unconstitutional, and void." Kentucky's States' Rights Party saw a rapid infusion of unionist slaveholders, and in a state election that Lincoln followed closely, Conservatives won outright. Former federal colonel Thomas E. Bramlette, an anti-emancipation Union Democrat, garnered nearly 80 percent of the vote, then warned against any "uncalled for and needless experiment" of black enlistment.[30]

As these political conflicts raged, seeking to solve his border state problem, Lincoln converted to the Radicals' advocacy of black enlistment to accomplish universal emancipation as military necessity. Suspending the recruitment of slaves of disloyal masters in Missouri and Maryland, he quietly ordered the army to conduct a census of free black male Kentuckians between the ages of eighteen and forty-five—precisely the age of military enrollment. In November 1863, after he quietly ordered black enlistment begun in Maryland and Tennessee, "whether [recruits] be free or not," with an additional stipulation that loyal owners be compensated $300 for each male slave enlisted in the army, Lincoln briefly upheld the ban on recruiting in Missouri and Kentucky. In November he authorized Schofield to issue General Orders No. 135 authorizing the recruitment of black volunteers—slaves, contrabands, and free blacks—in Missouri for federal military service. Compensation was available, provided loyal owners filed deeds of manumission. Most refused to apply. When Paulina Stratton's husband died suddenly later that month, she "expect[ed] to keep Ike and hire out the rest But Griffin says he will be a soldier." In January all of her slave men began leaving; only two bondwomen remained. Although the army stipulated that the families of enlisted slave men remain at home to be "made useful in securing the grain," they too soon left their owners' farms.[31]

Missouri's white population quickly threw up impediments to slave enlistment, suppressing the initial surge of black men. Although increasingly desperate for laborers, farmers warned slave men not to interfere in "a white man's war" and offered wages or promised freedom at a future date if their bondmen would not enlist. They also threatened violence against women and children who remained behind. Many evicted the families of enlisted soldiers after crops were harvested. Local governments enacted strong measures restricting the hiring of fugitives, and Missouri's governor proposed sending agents abroad to entice immigrant white laborers. Bondmen who ran to army posts often found violence among white soldiers that matched or exceeded that from which they were fleeing, and the likelihood of harsh treatment of their families prevented many black men from enlisting. By the summer of 1864, black federal enlistments in Missouri had nearly ground to a halt.[32]

Federal military leaders countered the rapid decline in slave enlistment with a forcible strategy: impressment. No longer limited to the margins of the state or to slaves of disloyal slaveholders, recruiting squads, often consisting of black soldiers, moved into the state's interior. Believing the "best place for idle dis[s]olute Negroes is in the Army," as one recruiting officer wrote, they took all enlistable black men. When Missouri masters took unruly male slaves to enlistment sites and demanded they be taken, recruiters often impressed them. Free blacks with means purchased substitutes, but more crossed the rivers to neighboring free states rather than enlist or be drafted, often finding refuge in Freedmen's Homes, sponsored by aid societies such as the Western Freedmen's Aid Commission, headed by Quaker abolitionist Levi Coffin.[33]

More even than emancipation, the enlistment of black troops in Missouri signaled the disintegration of slavery in the middle border states, a fact not lost on loyal slaveholders, who one federal officer now estimated as "about as one to one thousand." A "loyal man faithful to the Union and the constitution of the U. States" condemned enlistment as "[e]vil by civil process," and pled his case directly to the president. "I wish my rights to be protected," he wrote, "that the people may see that there is property in being a loyal man." Having heard Radicals call for retaliatory violence, many slave owners feared for their lives. Before leaving for St. Louis in August 1863, Elvira A. W. Scott witnessed the establishment of a recruiting and contraband camp near the river town of Miami. "[T]he sound of fife and drum was heard, beating up Negro recruits," she wrote. "White men who hated us and persecuted us were around me.... All day the marching of the blacks went on.... It was my last day in Miami... forced to leave our home under fear of violence and assassination."[34]

Slaveholders' fear of violence at the hands of former bondpeople was not entirely unwarranted. Black men under arms had been part of Jayhawker squads that raided citizens' farms in western Missouri since 1861, and contraband camps and enlistment and recruiting sites became sources of anxiety for local whites. A freedman at the camp near Miami boasted "they were sent here to tear up the secesh root and branch and that they were going to do it." Though these were more often boasts than threats, some encounters were deadly. In July 1863, near New Madrid, white bodies washed up on the banks of Missouri's Kentucky Bend. Three armed black men, at the insistence of antislavery officers at the contraband camp on Island No. 10, murdered six members of the slaveholding Beckham family, including children bathing in the river. (The men were subsequently court-martialed and hanged.)[35]

Despite white Kentuckians' best efforts to forestall emancipation, military demands soon drove the issue. Slaveholders' and federal troops' resistance to the use of contraband laborers—"Rock (i.e. Pelt) every Nigger out of Town you find in the Streets," recalled one Kentuckian of the instructions given to a garrison patrol—caused Jeremiah T. Boyle in 1863 to order impressment of slave men in central and southern Kentucky as laborers on roads, railroads, and fortifications. He did not intend to free slaves; indeed, most slaves returned to their owners after their terms of service. With contrabands flowing into Kentucky, Boyle believed most laborers would be gathered from Louisville's crowded military prisons and slave pens. He set up Camp Nelson, south of Lexington, for what would become fourteen thousand slaves.[36]

De facto enlistment of Kentucky's slaves had long since begun. Enlistment brokers offered bounties for slaves to serve as substitutes for white soldiers from other states to fill local quotas. Recruiting stations operating just outside Kentucky's borders offered ample opportunity for escaping slaves, estimated at hundreds per day in two southern Kentucky counties, to cross the border and enlist. By one officer's estimate, by January 1864 seven thousand slaves had fled Kentucky to recruiting camps and other military installations in neighboring states. Four hundred black recruits at Cairo in early 1864, according to one report, were "escaped negroes from this State.... Governor Yates would have no objections to their being enlisted." Recruiters for what would be known as U.S. Colored Troops (USCT) regiments from outside the state were enlisting freedmen in Louisville and Lexington and began to enlist impressed and escaped slaves ostensibly from Tennessee and Arkansas.[37]

Slaves were rushing to federal camps from all parts of the state. Kentuckian Ellen Wallace claimed that bondpeople had begun vacating her Hopkinsville farm as early as February 17, 1864; three days later, trying to prevent a general exodus, her husband threatened "the women that when all the men left they would have to go, that he could not support them and their children in idleness." By the end of April virtually all of their slaves had left their farm, taking most of the mules. Many owners took slave men against their will to recruiting stations and filed claims for compensation, while others enlisted them to offset the chance for a draft in their district or offered them as substitutes for drafted sons. County leaders often asked that absconded enlisted slaves count toward their draft quotas. According to the records of one federal commander, Edward Hobson, sixty-nine owners in Green County, Kentucky, applied for compensation for the loss of 157 enlisted slaves. Slave traders found a brisk business as masters tried to sell their slaves before they absconded or enlisted. One resident claimed in July that Bardstown had "more traders than in any other town and County in the state." In Kentucky's westernmost counties, recruiting stations operating at Paducah and Columbus spiked guerrilla violence and Confederate raids. Nathan Bedford Forrest's cavalry quickly raided the area, attempting to massacre black garrisons at Paducah and Columbus and succeeding just over two weeks later at Fort Pillow in Tennessee.[38]

Impressment in Kentucky provided the springboard to full slave enlistment there. With Missouri enlisting black men and Kentucky's enlistment quotas unmet, in February 1864 Lincoln signed a bill amending the Second Confiscation Act by authorizing black enrollment in all states, despite opposition from five of Kentucky's eight congressmen. With a provision for compensation to loyal owners of slave recruits, enlistment in Kentucky was slated to begin on March 7. Confusion reigned about whether owners' permission was required, as per Kentucky's state laws against enticing slaves to escape. Provost marshals, often assigned squads of black soldiers to enroll slaves, resigned in protest or claimed they could find no officers in their districts willing to carry out the order. Stephen G. Burbridge, the new department commander in the central counties, devised a nightmarish system of paperwork requiring prospective slave recruits to fill out and sign witnessed declarations that included their owners' names and county of origin in order to get a pass to travel to the nearest provost marshal's office. The stalemate paralyzed enrollment for several months. In May 1864 the War Department removed all restrictions on slave enlistments. By the end of the war 8,344 African Americans, or just under 39 percent of Missouri's black male population eligible for service, had enlisted in the state's five USCT regiments. Kentucky's contribution was nothing short of remarkable. More than 24,000 of the state's African Americans, overwhelmingly slaves and constituting 57 percent of the state's black men of military age, enlisted in the federal armies, exceeding all other states save Louisiana.[39]

Furious white Kentuckians and Missourians resisted this social revolution with unprecedented violence against federal garrisons, home guards, slaves and free blacks, and white unionists. As a War Department official who toured Kentucky averred, "the moment that Government attempted to draft men and enlist negroes, the true feeling of these people was evinced." A near-riot occurred in Danville, Kentucky, in which many of the 250 black recruits were injured, and Centre College students joined residents in hurling rocks as they left for Camp

Nelson. The sheriff of Linn County, Missouri, organized a posse to "drive the negroes and negro recruiting officers out of the County," and in Green and Larue Counties, Kentuckians flogged provost marshals, a recruiting agent, and slaves who tried to enlist. On a single day in Lebanon, Kentucky, garrisoning federal troops twice shot at the local provost marshal while he walked the town streets. Indeed, seven provost marshals in Kentucky were slain either directly or indirectly as a result of the agitation over black enlistment. In January 1865 a force of western Kentuckians "under pretence of military authority" forcibly retrieved some 150 black recruits from Mound City, Illinois.[40]

Waves of racialized guerrilla violence now tore through the Kentucky and Missouri countryside. One bushwhacker claimed that he had been "instigated by the late slave owners to hang and shoot every negro he can find absent from the old plantation," while others threatened farmers for holding or employing slaves. "[I]f you dont make dam negroes leve there ride away," one scrawled to a farmer in Missouri's Ralls County, "i will hadn [hang] the last negro on the plase and you will fair wors for we cant stand the dutch and negroes both." Slave men who left their masters were pinned among hostile federal troops, civilians, and guerrillas, and "fear[ed] to present themselves for enlistment because of [their] presence." An Illinois woman wrote to her Kentucky sister that she had "read an account of 20 [black recruits] being shot from a steamboat on the Mo river the 'Sam Gaty' perhaps you will see it." Alongside executions of surrendered white troops at Centralia, armed white Missourians and Kentuckians took part in massacres of wounded and surrendered black soldiers at Baxter Springs in Kansas, Poison Spring in Arkansas, and Simpsonville in Kentucky. Lydia Montague, who arrived in Jefferson City, Missouri, in June 1864 to open a freedpeople's school for the American Missionary Association, survived a guerrilla raid that targeted her school and students. "The Guerrillas are it seems trying to rid the State of every radical voter," she exclaimed. "In many instances they have scalped them, after murdering them in the most savage manner.... [T]his class of men, have not dared to sleep in their houses this summer." One Missourian claimed that of the thirty guerrilla-related murders committed in his county during the past year, "we do not know of but one case... of any one having been killed by bushwhackers that was not a *Radical*."[41]

To combat this surging violence, the Lincoln administration quickly promoted military hard-liners to command in these states, albeit with moderate slavery politics. In Missouri William S. Rosecrans, an Ohio War Democrat, replaced long-suffering department commander John M. Schofield. While in Tennessee Rosecrans had vigilantly executed guerrillas and federal deserters alike. In Kentucky Stephen E. Burbridge convinced his army superiors that he would wage hard-line war in earnest against the sudden insurgency. Once in command, he punished antiemancipation dissension in the army and state government. Lincoln approved the transfer to western Kentucky of outspoken abolitionist Eleazer A. Paine ("a good true man... but I do not know much of his military ability," the president admitted), who had enraged superiors and local unionists alike in Tennessee with his hardest form of war.[42]

Beginning in the fall of 1863 a brutal federal counterinsurgency raged in both states, including use of black troops and increased executions of guerrillas. Squads of militia, home guard, and federal cavalry, white and black, blanketed the countryside, burning the homes of known guerrillas and hunting down and summarily executing all those found in arms. In July 1864 Rosecrans ordered that loyal Missouri citizens form anti-guerrilla county home guards or vigilance committees to combat the "reign of murder, robbery and arson." That same month Burbridge ordered: "Whenever an unarmed Union citizen is murdered, four guerrillas will be selected from the prison and publicly shot to death at the most convenient place near the scene of the outrages." With enrollment quotas suspended "on account of... the presence of guerrillas" in western Kentucky, Paine implemented seven weeks of what he styled a retributive "plan of salvation," executing forty-three reputed guerrillas, often using squads of black soldiers, who fought not only against guerrillas but all whites who obstructed African Americans' claims to freedom. In late 1864 black soldiers approached a slaveholder's home near Louisville and "fired a number of shots into the Building, and they stole a number of children, and carried them off also committing other acts of violence." (One of the soldiers was the children's father.) Joseph Holt estimated that more than 150 executions of "outcast robbers and murderers" occurred statewide in June and July 1864. So many had been granted amnesty that Rosecrans and Burbridge asked discretion for summary punishment, to which a frustrated Lincoln readily assented, and again allowed levies in western Kentucky as a "retaliatory tax" that if unpaid would result in banishment. Instructing Burbridge to "run a red-hot ploughshare through them and all their works," as a source close to the president put it, in July Lincoln ordered martial law in both Kentucky and Missouri. It remained in force for the rest of the war.[43]

The sudden fusion of racial and guerrilla violence in Kentucky resulted in internecine misery that Missouri had already suffered for years. Residents witnessed public roadside executions, "awful agonizing crushing scenes of woe," as one woman related after seeing one near Hopkinsville, "horrors of these times no language can paint." Near Bardstown and Midway in November 1864 eight guerrillas were shot "in retaliation for the murder[s] of two negroes" and a local white unionist, and eight more were shot in Louisville for the murder of a local white doctor and two black residents in Henry County. One woman claimed that putting white men to death for killing blacks spurred "*hate, hate, hate,* if it required anything to make me hate [federals] continually, for I *could* not hate them with a hatred *too bitter.*" One resident warned of "a general uprising to the rebelious portion of the population of Ky.," including a "masacree [of] all the negro troops [in Louisville]." In December guerrillas murdered fifteen of twenty black recruits whom they had hauled from a freight train near Frankfort, and a month later they ambushed a detachment of black cavalrymen who were herding cattle from Camp Nelson to Louisville, killing thirty. At Mount Sterling John Hunt Morgan's raiders set fire to the town's business district, defended by unionist home guards, in order to gun them down as they escaped. After Morgan's 1864 attack on Cynthiana, Kentucky, residents buried dead Confederates in the city cemetery "in a beautiful spot (selected by Morgan)... while the Union soldiers were buried *in the negro burying ground.*" Wrote another Kentuckian, "If any Union person had told me of these things.... I could not have credited it, but we saw them."[44]

Subjected for the first time to a merciless war brought by marauding night-riders, guerrillas, and militia, many residents, slaveholding and not, abandoned what middle ground remained within their communities. Moderate unionists often became devout hard-liners, prevailing upon federal commanders to "[p]unish the wicked, protect the innocent, and redeem our loved state from savage rule and cruelty," as a Kentuckian wrote in the spring of 1864. Many avowed disunionists lost their Confederate idealism in the face of the chaos they saw. "I have from the day South Carolina seceded been a secessionist and at that time all I thought about was the South," wrote one resident of Hannibal, Missouri, to a Kentucky acquaintance. "Now I am willing for every one to think as they please and I do the same." Many more longtime unionists suddenly became overt disloyalists. When Confederate cavalry occupied Hopkinsville in early December 1864, driving out recently enlisted black troops, former unionist Ellen Wallace "leaped for joy at the sight, after being subjected to Negro bayonets and black republican outrages." Among the converted were Kentucky's Underwood family. In late 1864, the once prominent unconditional unionists were infuriated at the commencement of black enlistment in their state. Finding their home town garrisoned by black troops, rather than serve either "the low tyrant Lincoln" or a war marked by "tyranny, oppression and injustice as a matter of course" in which none now fit, the Underwoods left for San Francisco, California, to live out the war. As a Confederate sympathizer watched a train full of soldiers leave Louisville for the southern front, she noted "There were 12 cars. Inside were white yankees, outside were black ones."[45]

§

The postemancipation violence that swept the middle border's slave states and the political transformations, high and low, that followed could not have occurred without the active and sustained engagement of white women on both sides of the new loyalty line. As both participants and victims in this shadow warfare, these women did more than simply facilitate dissent; they provided much of its divisive energy. With nearly half of all men, and well more than half of age-eligible men, serving in the war, whether in federal or Confederate regular units or state militias, "cities of women" mobilized to support or oppose the war. Especially after black enlistment, they became leaders in the communities of allegiance that fed the spiraling postemancipation violence. Nowhere was this more evident than among dissenting women. Beyond the crisis of gender and domesticity that accompanied the war-driven absence of men, white women found themselves invested in the crisis of nationalism—and of politicized identity—that the war forced upon them.[46]

The war's hardest line was drawn only when it affected dissenting women in the middle border's slave states. Francis Lieber's 1863 code and Thomas Ewing's Order No. 11 extended the field of battle to the home front by defining women who provided comfort and provisions as quasi-combatants, operating what one historian has called a "domestic supply line" to the irregular war. Women were active partners in and leaders of contraband smuggling rings. Letter-running, a cottage industry among sympathizing border state women, exploited gender conventions and proscriptions by concealing mail packets and other communiques on women's persons, even in their undergarments. The guerrilla conflict and the emergent dissent movement crystallized federal efforts against such subversion. Widened searches of homes for evidence of treason, whether weapons or membership in secret societies, became common, and offenses committed by absconded menfolk brought retribution down on women in these households, including commandeering their homes for federal officers. "[A]fter Pa shot that soldier we could not do as we pleased," wrote Laidee J. Bagwell from St. Louis in February 1863. "He lived four days after he was shot, and the night he died four great black hearted villains came bolting into Ma's room and damned us to everything they could, and not a soul in the house but her and I.... We moved everything over to Mrs Johnson's, and slept on the floor in our clothes and shoes for six weeks, and every night was warned to leave the house, that it was going to be burned. We could not live so, and all we could do was to take some of the highest officers in our house to board."[47]

Women whose husbands were in Confederate service or who were found to have aided the rebel war effort were subject to house arrest, surety bonds, banishment, or imprisonment. More than 360 women accused of disloyalty passed through the St. Louis provost marshal's office. In May 1863 Cincinnati's *Daily Enquirer* noted that "quite a number of ladies, residing in and near Demossville, Pendleton County, on the line of the Covington and Lexington Railroad... have been arrested within the past few days, and will be sent South." Federal authorities established women's prisons in Louisville and Newport, Kentucky, to house such offenders. At the latter, women were forced to "sew for the Yankee soldiers." In 1864 families of Confederate officers, such as Louisville's Margaret Preston, were informed that they "must leave Kentucky the succeeding day or... be sent South." Storing most of her possessions with friends, Preston fled with her children and their most portable belongings to Canada. Across from Niagara Falls,

Preston found a community of refugees with whom she had little in common but shared politics. "It is Southern territory," she concluded, "I hear more secessionism than they dare talk in Kentucky."[48]

With uniformed men waging hard-line war, dissenting women found themselves pressured by a gendered kind of political warfare. With most of those men in blue, the weight fell most on dissenting women. "We think about nothing scarcely but soldiers," complained one Louisville woman, "we have them in and around us all the time." Walking unescorted among garrisoning soldiers or riding aboard trains and riverboats occasioned unwelcome importuning and convinced many not to travel or to stay off the streets, often resulting in virtual house arrest. Refusing to care for convalescent soldiers in their homes or delivering aid packages to rebel prisoners, failure to observe fasting days designated by the president, and allowing into their homes suspected deserted soldiers threatened to reveal or suggest private disloyalty. Singing or playing southern patriotic airs brought immediate scrutiny, even arrest.[49]

Federal officers targeted occupied women in these states with a gendered form of warfare. "[S]he-rebels," accused one pro-Lincoln Kentucky editor in 1864, "were unworthy of the name of *women*... [having] unsexed themselves by their open and avowed disloyalty, and indecent and *unwomanly* acts in aid and comfort of John Morgan's gang of thieves, and other rebel guerrillas." Lizzie Hardin, who faced taking the loyalty oath, imprisonment, or banishment for waving at Morgan in 1862, pleaded her case before Jeremiah T. Boyle, who snapped, "The women think they will rule Kentucky but I will show them they can't do it." Along with her mother and sister, Hardin chose exile to the Confederacy over submitting to such pressure, including use of language as a measure of disloyalty. When Missourian Elvira Scott was summoned to her local garrison commander's office to explain her use of the term "abolitionists" to describe federal troops, he used gender against her. "A Ladies place is to fulfill her household duties, and not to spread treason and excite men to rebellion." After threatening to send her husband to prison "until the commanding officer is fully convinced that you behave yourself as a Lady Ought," the lieutenant lectured Scott that "the women were at the bottom of this devilish rebellion—their influence."[50]

Knowing that troops, unionist neighbors, slaves and free blacks, and even family members were eavesdropping on conversations to expose concealed disloyalty, dissenting women tried to keep private their political notions. As one Kentuckian remarked in 1864, dissenting women were "more careful in speaking, and guarded in giving expressions to their opinions." Another remarked simply, "The secesh don't talk very much now." By preference and for protection, gatherings of women were intensely political. In March 1863 one western Missouri woman's home quickly became a neighborhood meeting place after a militia raid. "The women kept gathering in," she marveled, "until we had a room full of the most ranting, torn-down secesh you ever saw.... Hurrah for Price but Devil take the abolitionists." One Kentucky unionist woman confided to a cousin, "I am very quiet at home on account of the children particularly Ella who will talk." Relating the details of a visit from a female acquaintance, St. Louis's Euphrasia Pettus engaged only in exclusivist conversations. "You may be assured that she talks Southern, or I wouldn't have talked with her," she informed her sister. "We were entirely alone and we almost talked ourselves to death." By contrast, in mixed company most dissenting women, admitted Laidee Bagwell, "do nothing but lie."[51]

Decorum and hospitality, hallmarks of western and southern societies, were challenged by loyalty politics among opposing women. Public travel now occasioned hard stares and harder words. One Indiana woman was on a boat steaming up the Ohio in 1864 when it took on wood and a detachment of black troops. "From the deck above the Southern women mocked them, and when they began to board the boat spit on them." When they exclaimed, "Isn't it terrible to have niggers on the boat!" the Indianan retorted, "I'd rather have niggers than rebels." Having taken the oath, southern sympathizer Mary E. Van Meter was shocked at the cold reception she got from a unionist family when returning to her home in Bowling Green in the late winter of 1863. Offered shelter in a small cabin, she began discussing politics, only to be ordered from the house, "accompanied by the most abusive epithets I ever heard from the lips of the one wearing the garb of women.... We soon learned they were blind, bigoted, worshipers of old Abe."[52]

With their public behavior being scrutinized, dissenting women found their social spheres politicized and limited. Private gatherings became exclusivized. "I would not *dare* to give a large party now for fear the ladies would all get into a free fight," wrote one Kentuckian late in the war. With weddings attended by federal or illicit Confederate military personnel often bearing arms and laden with martial pageantry, marrying across the loyalty line disrupted families and friendships. Shortly before her exile to Canada, southern sympathizer Cora Owens, the daughter of a Louisville iron merchant, lamented the news that a friend had wed "a yankee lieut., who had been paying her a great deal of attention.... [O]ften have I spoken to her of how heartless it is in girls, who are Southern—to be marrying Federals.... I cannot account for it, unless she thinks that there is no one else to marry." Accepting invitations to social events required risk assessment, as Owens realized when she was invited to a picnic in a largely unionist rural district. "Pewee Valley is a very gay place in the summer season, ever since the war. So many...seem to know or feel nothing about the war.... I have seen but one girl or young lady since I've been here that did seem to be a real Southern girl.... I do not wish to go."[53]

Children were scarcely shielded from their families' war-borne divisions. "Even the children were partisans," recalled St. Louis's Sarah Jane Full Hill. "With these counter influences, the children of '61–'65 were veritable little warriors, with their tongues, if not with more deadly weapons." A young Louisville mother lamented that "hear[ing] nothing... but, *war, war, war*! The children catch the spirit. Ed talks about the war, guns, pistols, Jeff Davis, Abe Lincoln, etc." Many unionist parents taught their young ones to honor the national flag, while a St. Louis woman recalled that "those who discarded the flag instructed their children to walk around and not under it, should they meet it on the way to school." More people probably used their children to mask their southern sympathies. "The baby, now a year old, had been taught to wave at any man wearing the blue uniform." Many children acted out their parents' divisive political positions, and war-induced vocabularies could make for newly disruptive daily routines. Mary Louisa Reed overheard a discussion between her older children while they were undressing for bed. "Pa is a union man, Tavé are you for union? I'm tetsh [secesh], I'm Jef Da[vis] boy!" Another mother recalled a playmate insisting that another "should be a 'rebel' in their plays... Phebe revolted and turned on Alice with the declaration that she was not going to play with [her] any more, for she would not be a 'turncoat.'" In the new climate of fear, young children repeating private conversations in public could trigger swift retaliation, and dissenting parents feared that their children would expose their political views in mixed company. Cora Owens recalled an 1863 gathering in her parents' Louisville home at which several of the girls played music for the attendees. "Bertie [Beckett]... is very fond of the Federal officers.... She sang 'Glory Halliluah.' The first part she sang by the Union words and the last by southern words .... All the time she played and sang, Mr. B. was looking daggers at her."[54]

As protectors of home and hearth during their menfolks' wartime absences, dissenting women were put in a precarious position. Those with incarcerated male family members often sent children to deliver food to prisoners in jail, hoping the soldiers would take pity on them. For many, providing for their children was a growing daily anxiety as the war progressed. "Their great cry is for bread," wrote a federal officer in Louisville in 1864, knowing disloyalists would receive no army assistance. In fact, Paducah's post commander requested that surplus funds from trade permits be earmarked for the benefit of the "suffering loyal poor," especially widows and orphans. Destitute Confederate widows often resorted to prostitution in garrison cities and towns, forced into what amounted to compulsory service to the government and war that had taken their husbands.[55]

Already burdened with the impositions of the federal military presence, dissenting white women often faced the impossibility of protecting their children from the manifold dangers of wartime. The experience of Kentuckian Susan Grigsby offers a compelling glimpse of prominent women's often precarious existence. Granddaughter of Kentucky's first governor, she and her eight children and lawyer husband, John Warren Grigsby, resided at Traveller's Rest, the ancestral Shelby family home south of Danville. In August 1862, after not following the state guard to Tennessee the previous fall, John, a native Virginian, was driven south by an arrest warrant for disloyalty and was commissioned as a colonel in a Confederate cavalry regiment, leaving Susan in charge of their large family and thirty-two slaves. In October 1862 four of Grigsby's children, all between eleven months and eleven years old, contracted diphtheria and died within days of each other. After a squad of federal soldiers burst into her home, killed the man hired to guard the family, and demanded money, the grieving Grigsby received another blow. She learned her husband was gravely ill in eastern Tennessee.

Panic stricken, she determined to leave immediately with her remaining children to head south to nurse her ailing husband. She managed to rent out her home with a yearlong lease to a local judge, hired out their slaves, and obtained a pass that allowed her to travel through the federal lines toward Knoxville. There, she learned that the commander of the Army of the Cumberland, William S. Rosecrans, would not allow her to finish her journey. Traveling back to Louisville, she obtained a river pass through Cairo and to Memphis, intending to travel overland from there nearly four hundred dangerous miles to Knoxville. She then was informed incorrectly that her ailing husband was to be transferred across the lines to Camp Dick Robinson, near her home. Returning to Kentucky, she lived at her exiled uncle's empty home near Versailles, helpless as encamped federal troops took the corn and oats from the fields and burned virtually all the trees and fences at Traveller's Rest. Smuggled letters indicated that her husband had regained his health, but in April 1863 Grigsby received news that he had been wounded in fighting in middle Tennessee. She began the process again, at last receiving permission from Ambrose E. Burnside and other federal commanders to travel to her husband.[56]

As vulnerable as dissenting white women and their families were, slave women were more so, especially if their husbands and fathers had enlisted in federal service. Caught in the backlash, wives and mothers were often unable to protect themselves, much less their children, from masters and other white residents who sought to impede their struggle for freedom. Beyond the extra work required of the women when slave men were impressed, black enlistment enraged masters enough to beat enlistees' wives and children and throw them off their farms rather than support them. "Let old Abe Giv them Close," sneered one Kentucky master, while another asked federal troops at Bowling Green to bar his expelled slaves from ever returning "and warned them never to come on his Premises again if they did he would shoot them." Slave dealers combed the Missouri countryside soliciting farmers for the wives and children of black enlistees to sell in Kentucky. Army officers confronted evidence of how easily innocents became casualties of this hidden, personal warfare. In August 1864, after learning about the jailing of the wife of one of his soldiers whom civil authorities in Bowling Green had arrested as a fugitive, the commander of a USCT regiment in central Kentucky feared for her abandoned child. "The woman has a young child and if something is not done soon the child will die," he pleaded. The military offered even less protection for black women and children than the masters did. Distrustful of military authorities, hundreds crowded into Louisville's large refugee camp, hastily established in the late summer of 1864 with support from the Western Freedmen's Aid Commission and the city's free blacks' mutual aid societies. When Kentucky federal troops similarly expelled the families of enlisted men from Camp Nelson into the harsh early winter on November 23, 1864, and then burned their lodgings, more than three-fourths of those four hundred African Americans driven into the snow were children, and an even higher percentage of the hundred who subsequently died of exposure were children. This and other callous acts toward black women and children quickly reached the president's ear, their brutality symbolizing the shadow wars that now raged on the nation's middle border.[57]

§

As political violence plowed up the middle border's slave states into no man's—and no woman's—lands, black and white, across the rivers such violence proved more disruptive than destructive. In the western free states' version of small wars, emancipation and black enlistment were viewed similarly as by their slave state neighbors—as threats to racial subordination. But the defense of the "white man's country" offered insufficient cause to fight a full insurgency as in Missouri and Kentucky. With few African Americans in their midst and preventative anti-immigration laws in their states, Copperheads' dissent was more abstract than real, its fighters more agnostics than atheists. Although widely used labels suggest powerful politics of rage in these states—for Democrats, Ultras, rebels, secesh, traitors, and Copperheads; and for Republicans, Radicals, woolly heads, and nigger worshipers—their engine of dissent was fueled by racial ideology. Unlike the ideological warriors who rampaged across the rivers in defense of an economic and social system based on a dominative racial order, free state dissent lacked the tangible economic and social threat posed by the eradication of slavery.[58]

Copperheadism, or the antiwar movement that Lincoln earthily referred to as the "fire in the rear," has been interpreted by its leading historians as either a will-o'-the-wisp figment of Republican propaganda or a potent, organized threat, subversive and political, to the Union war effort. Among the early outgrowths of the various waves of dissent were organized secret societies that harassed war supporters and troops, discouraged enlistments, supported desertion and deserters, fought conscription with armed force, and voted, if they were allowed to, against the president and his party. Reports of secret societies circulated widely among home-front unionists left vulnerable after so many early volunteers had enlisted. In Indiana, by one estimate in 1862 some ten thousand such subversives were operating in the state; an Illinois newspaper estimated that number in southern Illinois alone. Knights of the Golden Circle (founded by former Cincinnatian George L. Bickley), Sons of Liberty, and the Order of American Knights were but three of the mélange of dissenting groups that adopted the mystique and framework of fraternal organizations, popular during the century. They now conjured righteous historical imagery in order to portray themselves as sacred fighters against despotic authority. Secret signs, countersigns, passwords, handshakes, badges on clothing, stars over doors, and occasional mobbings announced a shadow insurgency against local military presence. More ominously, with Confederate agents they plotted the overthrow of the middle border states' governments and the establishment of a Northwestern Confederacy, which would break with the Union, unite with the Confederacy, and dictate the terms of peace.[59]

The western Peace Democracy drew from several wells. Wage laborers, Irish immigrants and upland southerners, Catholics, and former Whig merchants made up the ranks of urban dissenters, constituting as much as half of these cities' populations. In small towns and rural areas, "Butternuts" with birth or family ties to the slave states formed the majority of Copperheads. However vituperative their words, most limited their dissent to personal spheres of influence—family, friends, and neighbors—and refrained from participating in the violent demonstrations erupting in nearby cities and states. However vocal, mass public dissent, organized and not, was often relatively peaceful, even with firearms present. At Mattoon, Illinois, in August 1863, a procession of an estimated three thousand Democrats, mostly farmers, ended at a mass meeting at the fairgrounds. One in five bore arms. "Contrary to the expectations and predictions of Most of the citizens the event passed quietly without a single outbreak," wrote an army officer sent to monitor the gathering. But, he added, "the Republican Masses were Much excited and with difficulty suppressed their wrath at this Warlike demonstration."[60]

Dissenters rejected variously the pillars of the Lincoln administration's new wartime policies. With enrollment, conscription, emancipation, and the suspension of habeas corpus were coupled other centralizing congressional acts—greenbacks, war bonds, postal regulations, homesteads, land grants, revenue taxes, high tariffs, and a transcontinental railroad—all passed without southerners' opposition owing to their absence and cross-border state opposition. Together these policies gave the impression that Republicans, and especially the president, had dictatorial powers and were intent on usurping local governance. As one historian has argued, western Copperheadism was an "intermingling of different constituencies...with different agendas," including urban workers, who saw freedpeople as an insurmountable threat to their tenuous place in the American social hierarchy, and rural farmers, whose main interest was protection of localist, republican ideals that the federal war authority now threatened.

Moderate Democratic leaders opposed anarchy yet supported popular sovereignty as a check against Republican-led wartime interference, especially in the electoral process. Decidedly less prevalent were anti-emancipation revolutionist cells intent on gaining independence from the rest of the Union.[61]

Whether they supported the Confederacy or simply wished to end the fighting, independent white westerners used the democratic system to subvert the war effort in order to forestall northern-style Republican social engineering. An investigator in southern Illinois found the earliest dissenting organizations were often led by lawyers, judges, physicians, merchants, ministers, and elected county officials. But striving young men who supported the Democratic party's individualist politics were the dissent movements' shock troops. One of two competing protective organizations in Danville, Illinois, was "composed of almost entirely ardent, impulsive young men," according to one recruiting officer, while "the other is composed of middle aged men property-holders, made up out of both parties but all good union men." Antiwar Democrats gleefully appropriated Republicans' political epithet, Copperhead, as a badge of homespun localism while ridiculing their opponents as fanatics, authoritarians, racial egalitarians, and Yankees.[62]

Anxious Republicans' concerns about pervasive dissent derived from their full understanding of the diffuse wartime conditions in towns, cities, villages, and rural hamlets. They freely collapsed distinctions about war dissent as disloyalty in order to attack it politically. "It is generally understood that when we speak of Democrats and Butternutts that they both mean the same thing," wrote an Illinoisan, referring to the terms' conflation of dissent with disloyalty; dissenting residents with southern roots supported Confederate traitors. Or they were Butternuts, southerners, tarred by the same loyalty brush as Confederates. Believing the Democratic Party was fully in league with secret societies, Republicans found an antidote to the racial venom that western Peace Democrats spewed after emancipation. "Copperhead Democracy to-day means traitorism," blared one southern Illinois newspaper in the summer of 1863. "Those that are not for the Government *must* be against it." They claimed that dissenters were drawn largely from the lowest classes and sought to usurp respectable citizens' place in society. In cities these were worthless inebriates, uneducated dockworkers, or immigrant layabouts, especially Irish Catholics. In rural areas they were poor, uneducated bottom-dwellers, river rats, hill people, and mudsills. "We have for our enemies," inveighed John W. Fletcher in the summer of 1863, "every Southern sympathizer, every rebel in arms... the peace men, the ignorant and depraved... men who put in their time bawling about the Constitution, who never read it; men whose constant cry is, 'abolition,' 'abolition,' and yet are too ignorant to even define the meaning of the word." An elderly rural Illinois woman was "very much troubled about what color she should have her Jean, not wishing to have it butternut as that is called Copperhead," while a Kentuckian exiled in Ohio was derided in 1863 by local Republicans, who taunted, "Where is the boasted Chivalry the love of liberty the patriotism of Ky[?]—Gone South."[63]

The midterm elections in 1862 only deepened political and social warfare in these contested free states. The Republican governors of Indiana and Illinois were obstructed by Democrat-controlled state legislatures. They fought back vigorously by neutralizing their states' legislatures and allowing the federal military—now headed by Ambrose E. Burnside, looking to redeem his reputation after his disastrous defeat at Fredericksburg, Virginia—to exert more authority over their states' dissenters. In Indiana, facing a Democratic majority intent upon curtailing the powers of the state's Republicans, Oliver P. Morton led a backdoor assault on his newly empowered opposition by encouraging his party's legislators to "bolt" on days of key votes, preventing quorums and obstructing business. When the partisan session adjourned in March without having approved a funding bill, the governor did not recall the legislature and carried the government largely on his own. Accused of rampant constitutional violations— having "Yankee on the brain"—Morton was condemned for allowing martial law, owing to his belief not only that the Hoosier state was on the verge of rebellion but that the entire middle border region was "trembling in the balance." In Illinois, when Democrats attempted to constitute an appointed commission for spending and appointment of military officers, Richard Yates prorogued the state legislature for the remainder of the war. Outraged, some forty thousand Illinois voters—including some of the most prominent men in the state—attended an antiwar meeting in Springfield in late June. They called for delegates to a peace convention to be held in Louisville that would negotiate the end of the war and resolved against martial law, arbitrary arrests and confinements, and other perceived violations of civil liberties.[64]

Rumors of dissenters' efforts to form a seceded Northwest Confederacy terrified elected Republican officials, but few organizations had sufficient infrastructures to effect grandiose plans. Organized groups, estimated at anywhere between a few to hundreds in various locales, devoted themselves largely to subversive democracy to undermine Republicans' political and economic authority, propagandizing as local "law and order" propertied classes who drove business and controlled newspapers. As one Union County, Illinois, newspaper editor conceded of subversive Copperheadism: "Few really sensible men (aside from demagogues and aristocrats) have come under its influence in this county. It is so shallow in its outside appearance... that none but unsuspecting men have been *drawn* into it."[65]

Yet the Republican counterinsurgency began locally around the time the war began and strengthened after the 1862 elections. Within weeks of the attack on Fort Sumter, a Kentuckian living in central Illinois claimed that Republicans "were forming Vigilance committees to scout the country and find out the principles of every man (and woman too I suppose) those that were not loyal to Lincoln.... Cellie declares he[']ll die before he[']ll ever hollor hurah for Lincoln and they going round and making men do who did not vote for him." One Indianan was outraged when he learned in the fall of 1861 about "the election at the school house for a teacher the plan that was taken to get a *secesh* Teacher elected." In one village in Illinois the following winter, after learning that a local teacher was allowing the school to be the site of secret society meetings, residents "thrashed Old Lakenan about that school... as the old traitor deserved it." Many dissenting organizations formed openly as mutual protection societies to counter threats by opposition hard-liners, whose "partyism rises far above their patriotism," as noted by one dissenter in Terre Haute, Indiana. Some had initially joined the Union Leagues, until they were ostracized for opposing war measures. They formed "Democratic regiments" to deliver blows, political and otherwise, as the muscle arm of the local Peace Democracy, resisting authority that might compel them to support the war. Far more often than actual riots, subversion took the form of terrorizing anxious local unionist constituencies, either by violence or by rumor of their presence, and the sabotaging of bridges and trains. Indiana recruits heading south by rail to Indianapolis in October 1861 were detained half a day by a pair of subversives who derailed the troop train with stacked crossties.[66]

Communities quickly became battlegrounds as residents contested wartime politics with physical force. Normally placid village streets witnessed what amounted to mob warfare. When residents of Liberty, Illinois, celebrated the unexpected news of the surrender of Fort Henry a few months later, "we had a little battle on a small scale in town yesterday.... [S]ome Seceshers came up from the bottom, armed with revolvers and knives, they flourished their arms on the street and hurrahed for Jeff. Davis.... [The] others surrounded the enemy opposite George Walters store, ran them into the store, charged upon them not with bayonets, but with stones.... [I]t appears cruel to beat men so."[67]

As the war's growing burdens weighed on free state dissenting families, women's lives diverged along loyalty lines. Sheltered by federal troops and militia, unionist women found practical and political causes and communities in various venues of war work: voluntary benevolent associations; hospitals; soldiers' aid organizations; convalescent homes; sewing circles; sanitary fairs; tableaus, balls, and other fund-raising efforts, for both soldiers and refugee families; and local women's auxiliaries to the Loyal Leagues. The weight of local protection, with paramilitary warfare raging just over the rivers, fell on unionist women in the absence of garrisoning troops. "We ladies here have been consulting together to adopt some course to persue in case of an attack from guerrillas," wrote one southern Illinois woman in 1862, "there is but few men here, and they are not armed, so I think that they had better leave town to save themselves, and let the women and children take care of themselves as the[y] can best."[68]

Social violence roiled communities of allegiance into adversarial collectives, and free state women eagerly engaged in boisterous war politics. "The Jones Creek ladies have formed Union League they met at our house yesterday afternoon," wrote Illinoisan Nancy Mann in 1863. "I have not joined as I am somewhat opposed to secret Societies some of the ladies call me Copperhead and other pet names." When, on a dare, a southern Indiana woman snatched a butternut pin off the coat of a dissenter, a group soon surrounded her home and forced her to return it to the owner by threatening her property. Loyalty politics pressured women even within their own marriages. In the summer of 1863 William R. Stuckey, a private in an Indiana regiment in middle Tennessee, challenged his wife for attending a social gathering hosted by a dissenting neighbor. "I though[t] you was more of a union woman than to go to a Butternut dinner," he wrote her. A Cincinnati unionist informed federal authorities precisely when and where her husband would attend a disloyalist gathering in northern Kentucky so they could arrest him. Dissenting women were no more exempt than men from federal authority if they voiced their politics in public. In 1863 in McLeansboro, Illinois, Lizzie Morton's newspaper, *Vox Populi*, replaced one that had recently been suppressed. In her first issue she declared herself "a strong Democrat, and therefore a loyalist [and] unconditionally, and unequivocally for the UNION, *as it was, the* CONSTITUTION *as it is*, and the poor negro, right where he has been for the last hundred and fifty years." Loyal Leaguers immediately condemned Morton, and federal troops suppressed her paper and auctioned her equipment to a reliable Republican.[69]

Lizzie Morton's effort loomed small among the Democratic presses stirring the fires of dissent and retaliation in the West. Chicago's *Times*, Columbus's *Crisis*, Dayton's *Empire*, and Cincinnati's *Daily Enquirer*, as well as small-town newspapers in Chester, McLeansboro, Olney, Salem, Paris, and Jonesboro, Illinois; Terre Haute and Rockport, Indiana; and Circleville, Ohio, voiced full-throated opposition to the president and his war policies. But starting in 1863 and especially after mid-May 1864, Lincoln's patience with opposition editors frayed. Soldiers home on furlough or citizen mobs often threatened or arrested these newspapers' editors, sacked their offices, and suppressed their papers, temporarily or permanently, alleging that their editors were in subversive secret societies. Some editors, like John I. Morrison of Salem, Indiana, gave up their dissenting positions in favor of the government's cause. They often had an incentive. John W. Kees, editor of Circleville, Ohio's *Watchman*, was freed from arrest only when a state congressman intervened and convinced military authorities that he was insane.[70]

In rural areas, dissenters mostly limited themselves to terrorizing their neighbors, openly or surreptitiously. Robbery, killing stock, crippling horses, and arson were the most prevalent forms. Anson Babcock of Anna, Illinois, claimed that his "rebel neighbors" had poisoned his horses, destroyed his fruit orchards, "thr[e]w down my fences and annoy[ed] me in various ways because as they say 'my politics dont suit' I am 'a d____d Lincolnite' and [that] they... intend to drive me out of the neighborhood." Dissenters focused much of their energy on postmasters, furloughed soldiers, and potential informants, who occasionally found themselves mobbed or stoned in daylight or intimidated by nighttime saboteurs, who "often Black[ed] themselves." "It is said that Andy Humphreys has issued *his* Proclamation," wrote one discharged Indiana soldier, "setting forth that within 30 days from the date thereof, every Union family in the county shall leave or be hanged until they are *dead dead*!! Wether this is all gass or not we do not know." In several counties in southern Illinois and Indiana, dissenters murdered local unionists for assisting with the enrollment, while many others received or narrowly escaped such punishment for feeding soldiers who were enforcing the draft. In Carbondale, Illinois, one resident related that two men called out a unionist in the night, claiming they were soldiers sent to ferret out deserters and needed a guide. "[H]e of course went," he wrote, "and after getting in the woods they then told him he had thare to take his choice be tied to a tree and whipped or be Shot. That he was a d____m abolitionist and voted for Lincoln the man refused to be tied up but broke and ran for life they fired on him but in the dark he escaped."[71]

Following the 1862 elections, many dissenting groups organized as paramilitary companies, numbering from a few dozen to hundreds. "Prominent men are scouring the country holding meetings of secret societies almost nightly, and often daily," wrote an alarmed officer, noting that these groups drilled at night or in hill valleys and creek bottoms or on prairies in rural areas. Provost marshals and commanders alike frequently received "annonymous [sic] letters from nearly all the little towns, saying they fear an outbreak, and fear to communicate their names." They accosted Union Party speakers, shouting them down or attacking them. Some interfered with local enrollment by blocking roads, or worse, ambushing enrollment officers. And they sought military arms. One dissenter, a physician, claimed in an affidavit that he "advised his copperhead friends present, 'to organize and drill publicly, not in the night as the damned abolitionists were doing, in order to be ready for the conscription, when the abolitionists commenced to enforce it.'" In Hancock County, Illinois, their boldness drew federal troops with instructions to shoot to kill.[72]

Strong undercurrents of dissent contributed to escalating rates of desertion and nonenrollment. By one estimate between 40,000 and 50,000 men had skedaddled from their regiments by 1862, joined by another 161,244 in 1863 and 1864, the latter figure constituting more than 20 percent of all draftees. Southern Illinois's Charles C. Tarpley received a letter from his father encouraging him to desert, including instructions for evading federal patrols. "When you get with the secesh," he advised, "be one and when you get with a union man be one and when you get with black Republicans be one." (Tarpley did not in fact desert.) Volunteer quotas in more than half of the congressional districts in the free states were unmet in 1863, and by 1864 that figure had risen to three-quarters, triggering the draft in most of the nation. As the war progressed, the northernmost counties of these states were the most reliable. The Ohio congressional district that encompassed Cincinnati was among the most evasive draft districts in the country, behind only Louisville's. With the free border states ultimately sending well over half of their age-eligible white men to the war—Indiana's and Illinois's being the highest enrollments in the free states—many decried the enrollment's overt classism. The editor of Illinois's *Quincy Herald* railed, "*The rich are exempt!*" One study of draft resistance in Illinois has found that 30.5 percent of those enrolled failed to report. In Egypt as many as half failed to report, and in the summer of 1864 not one district met its quota. By 1863 the draft and mounting casualties had driven many younger and poorer men into the ranks of dissent. Unable to afford the steep $300 commutation fee or to procure substitutes—in Kentucky they cost anywhere from $1,000 to $3,000, if they could be found at all—these men flocked to dissenting organizations.[73]

The growing numbers of draft evaders and deserters gathered in remote areas of rural counties and fringe areas of cities, where they were often sheltered and supported by family members. One such group in southern Illinois met often at night in blacksmiths' and carpenters' shops, schoolhouses, churches, and mills and openly solicited knots of "deserters from the hills" to attend meetings, at which they "talked war and politics." Politicized charges of cowardice soon mixed with unionists' cries of alarm about armed deserters in their communities. "[T]here were more men that I had the least idea was in the country all together," admitted one Illinois woman in 1864 to her soldier husband. "We hear continually that all the Democrats are in the Army and none but the other side are home and that this country could not possibly spare another man, and all such, but really I could hardly miss a man from the number two years ago."[74]

By the summer of 1863 these "Home rebels," as Republicans referred to them, were often former federal soldiers. Daniel Mooneyham claimed at an antiwar rally in Benton, Illinois, "that he resigned 'because it was an unholy war, and a nigger war'; that 'the South were better fighters', and we could 'not subdue them'; Tilman B. Cantrell at the same place said that Gov Yates, and Pres Lincoln were bigger traitors than Jeff Davis." In some places, uniformed dissenters gained enough local support to exert authority. When discharged Illinois soldiers burned the offices of the Chester *Picket Guard*, they levied local Republicans for damages of $2,500 and called a mass meeting to threaten retaliation if they were not paid. "[T]he copperheads are largely in the majority and have there [sic] Golden

Circle organizations in nearly every precinct in the County," wrote a public official in Quincy, Illinois.[75]

To shield their young men from the draft or deserter squads, local dissenting communities, urban and rural, engaged in subtle forms of collective dissent. In one township of Indiana's Johnson County, "very few would help with the war for the Northern side, [and] would not donate any supplies or food nor help in any way." Others circumvented the various conscriptions by organizing and pooling enrolled residents' resources into "bounty funds" or general "insurance" funds from which to hire substitutes or pay commutation fees for any dissenters who were actually drafted. "In this way," opined one Democrat, "the object of the Government is effectually defeated, at a very small cost to the individuals liable to the draft." Suspected of shielding deserters on his farm, one dissenter heard voices at his gate in the night. When he investigated he was advised by four horsemen "to tell the boys [they] had to leave in ten days or they would see some way for them to get away." By the spring of 1865 these clandestine acts had given way to mass meetings of entire city sections, such as in Cincinnati's Eighth Ward, which had once filled its quota, attempting to raise some $4,000 "to free the Ward" from an imminent draft.[76]

Allegations of open, daylight meetings of secret societies filled with deserters and dissenters put garrisoning federal troops on high alert. Knowledge that guerrilla bands from Kentucky and Missouri crossed into Illinois and Indiana to train mounted dissenters drove residents to militant unionism. Near Shawneetown, Illinois, a thousand state militia fought off two hundred invading Kentucky guerrillas, killing and wounding several. In 1863 Ohio's White Water Shaker community, west of Cincinnati, shed its official neutralism and invited local Republicans and War Democrats to a joint Fourth of July celebration at which, one attendee recalled, "Shakers themselves were pleased and delighted beyond measure that they could so well contribute their share, in their way." With reports of large quantities of powder, saddles, and even weapons being purchased "for 'Mere Sporting purposes'" and shipped to Butternut neighborhoods, federal commanders now acted. Ohioan Jacob Ammen, a native-born Virginian and West Pointer who was once a playmate of Ulysses S. Grant, was uniquely suited to this counterinsurgency. Placed in command of the District of Illinois, Ammen was characterized by a War Department official as "of the old school" and brooked no criticism of harsh measures toward civilian dissenters, believing them an extension of the chaos he had witnessed in neighboring slave states.[77]

Undermanned and dispersed federal garrisons and enrollment squads did more than compel enrollees and round up skulkers. With the assistance of local unionists, they used their authority to weave strong webs of restraint. In provost marshals' offices, lists of newly designated disloyalists lay alongside enrollment lists and those of known deserters. In Wayne County, Indiana, three categories of sympathizers existed—"Union, Traitor, Doubt"—with notations such as "go to the devil" for traitors and "may be saved" and "don't give up" for those in doubt. More often, such as in Fulton County, Illinois, lists contained little more than names of local Peace Democrats, draft evaders, or those who paid commutation fees. Increased arrests for dissenting speech or traveling without a military pass in nearby slave states made it difficult for moderates to avoid running afoul of military authorities. When Ohio's Robert Neil, a former Whig, received a box of clothing from relatives for him to deliver to a Kentucky soldier confined at Camp Chase, he was summoned to the local provost marshal's office for violating the most recent restrictions.[78]

Blaming suspicious calamities, such as the burning of churches, on "dark lantern, slung-shot and bowie-knife 'peace' men in the neighborhood," Loyal Leagues organized as paramilitary home guards and vigilance committees that often overmatched dissenters' secret societies in number and intensity. Beyond propagandist broadsides that ridiculed Democrats' Fourth of July celebrations as open-air subversion (see figure 7.3), as "union regulators" they rooted out dissenters' assemblages, infiltrated their organizations, assisted squads of troops in arresting leaders, and attacked individual dissenters. "[W]e dont want to fight a fare fight" admitted one Illinois unionist, while another claimed his town's Union League could "raid *one hundred men* in this town for service in scouring the county and driving these 'fellows' out on a few hours notice." Galesburg, Illinois's mayor asked Jacob Ammen "how to proceed to exterminate the rebels" in his area, and another resident wanted to "Scatter Some of tham Old loffers out of our part of the country." Reports of "50 armed butternuts" across the state line near Richmond, Indiana, sent three train carloads of armed Illinoisans to assist soldiers in capturing and arresting most of them, then they remained "to gard the jail."[79]

Federal enlisted men harboring deep resentment against dissenters became eager counterinsurgents. "[M]et 4 or 5 young men that ought to have shouldered their muskets and stood up in defense of our beloved government," wrote one soldier who was visiting a neighboring community while on furlough in early 1863. "I must confess that I found hatred rising in my heart toward these fellows." That summer, acting on local intelligence, federal troops aboard a commandeered riverboat raided two locales near Chester, Illinois, arrested vocal dissenters, and marched them at bayonet point to the boat. They then whisked them upriver to St. Louis "amidst the Cheers of some and the curses of other of the citizens." The lines between such groups were commonly blurred, leaving residents unsure of the uniformed bands in their midst. Residents of border counties all along the Ohio complained of squads of Kentucky troops who crossed the river to hunt guerrillas, then in fact acted like them. "[W]hen the laws are infringed upon beyond the civil arm," warned a local unionist, "the military

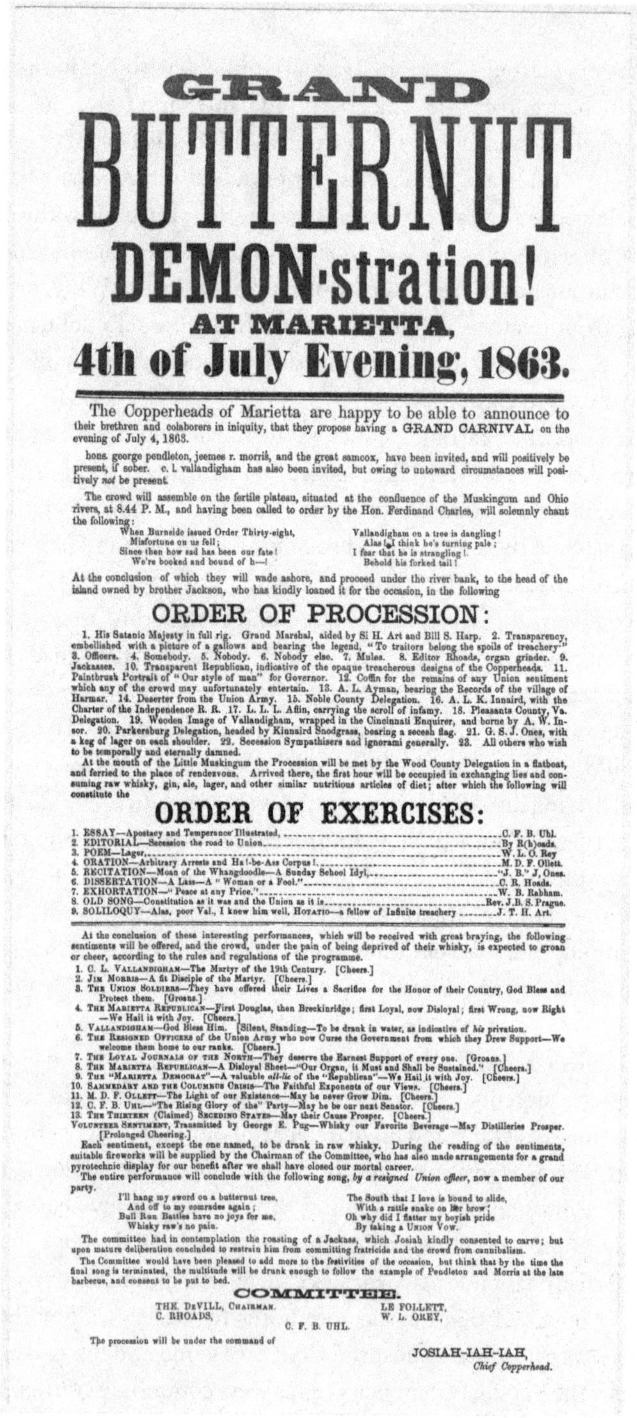

GRAND

BUTTERNUT DEMON-stration!

AT MARIETTA,

4th of July Evening, 1863.

The Copperheads of Marietta are happy to be able to announce to their brethren and colaborers in iniquity, that they propose having a GRAND CARNIVAL on the evening of July 4, 1863.

hons. george pendleton, jeemes r. morris, and the great samcox, have been invited, and will positively be present, if sober. c. l. vallandigham has also been invited, but owing to untoward circumstances will positively *not* be present.

The crowd will assemble on the fertile plateau, situated at the confluence of the Muskingum and Ohio rivers, at 8.44 P. M., and having been called to order by the Hon. Ferdinand Charles, will solemnly chant the following:

When Burnside issued Order Thirty-eight,
Misfortune on us fell;
Since then how sad has been our fate!
We're booked and bound of h—!

Vallandigham on a tree is dangling!
Alas! I think he's turning pale;
I fear that he is strangling!.
Behold his forked tail!

At the conclusion of which they will wade ashore, and proceed under the river bank, to the head of the island owned by brother Jackson, who has kindly loaned it for the occasion, in the following

ORDER OF PROCESSION:

1. His Satanic Majesty in full rig. Grand Marshal, aided by Si H. Art and Bill S. Harp. 2. Transparency, embellished with a picture of a gallows and bearing the legend, "To traitors belong the spoils of treachery:" 3. Officers. 4. Somebody. 5. Nobody. 6. Nobody else. 7. Mules. 8. Editor Rhoads, organ grinder. 9. Jackasses. 10. Transparent Republican, indicative of the opaque treacherous designs of the Copperheads. 11. Paintbrush Portrait of "Our style of man" for Governor. 12. Coffin for the remains of any Union sentiment which any of the crowd may unfortunately entertain. 13. A. L. Ayman, bearing the Records of the village of Harmar. 14. Deserter from the Union Army. 15. Noble County Delegation. 16. A. L. K. Innaird, with the Charter of the Independence R. R. 17. L. L. L. Afiin, carrying the scroll of infamy. 18. Pleasants County, Va. Delegation. 19. Wooden Image of Vallandigham, wrapped in the Cincinnati Enquirer, and borne by A. W. Insor. 20. Parkersburg Delegation, headed by Kinnaird Snodgrass, bearing a secesh flag. 21. G. S. J. Ones, with a keg of lager on each shoulder. 22. Secession Sympathisers and ignorami generally. 23. All others who wish to be temporally and eternally damned.

At the mouth of the Little Muskingum the Procession will be met by the Wood County Delegation in a flatboat, and ferried to the place of rendezvous. Arrived there, the first hour will be occupied in exchanging lies and consuming raw whisky, gin, ale, lager, and other similar nutritious articles of diet; after which the following will constitute the

ORDER OF EXERCISES:

1. ESSAY—Apostacy and Temperance Illustrated, ... C. F. B. Uhl.
2. EDITORIAL—Secession the road to Union .... By R(h)oads.
3. POEM—Lager, ... W. L. O. Rey
4. ORATION—Arbitrary Arrests and Ha!-be-Ass Corpus!. .... M. D. F. Ollett.
5. RECITATION—Moan of the Whangdoodle—A Sunday School Idyl, ... "J. B." J, Ones.
6. DISSERTATION—A Lass—A "Woman or a Fool." .... C. R. Hoads.
7. EXHORTATION—"Peace at any Price." .... W. B. Rabham.
8. OLD SONG—Constitution as it was and the Union as it is .... Rev. J.B. S. Prague.
9. SOLILOQUY—Alas, poor Val., I knew him well, Hotatio—a fellow of Infinite treachery .... J. T. H. Art.

At the conclusion of these interesting performances, which will be received with great braying, the following sentiments will be offered, and the crowd, under the pain of being deprived of their whisky, is expected to groan or cheer, according to the rules and regulations of the programme.

1. C. L. Vallandigham—The Mrtyr of the 19th Century. [Cheers.]
2. Jim Morris—A fit Disciple of the Martyr. [Cheers.]
3. The Union Soldiers—They have offered their Lives a Sacrifice for the Honor of their Country, God Bless and Protect them. [Groans.]
4. The Marietta Republican—First Douglas, then Breckinridge; first Loyal, now Disloyal; first Wrong, now Right—We Hail it with Joy. [Cheers.]
5. Vallandigham—God Bless Him. [Silent, Standing—To be drank in water, as indicative of *his* privation.
6. The Resigned Officers of the Union Army who now Curse the Government from which they Drew Support—We welcome them home to our ranks. [Cheers.]
7. The Loyal Journals of the North—They deserve the Earnest Support of every one. [Groans.]
8. The Marietta Republican—A Disloyal Sheet—"Our Organ, it Must and Shall be Sustained." [Cheers.]
9. The "Marietta Democrat"—A valuable *all-lie* of the "Republican"—We Hail it with Joy. [Cheers.]
10. Sammedary and the Columbus Crisis—The Faithful Exponents of our Views. [Cheers.]
11. M. D. F. Ollett—The Light of our Existence—May he never Grow Dim. [Cheers.]
12. C. F. B. Uhl—"The Rising Glory of the" Party—May he be our next Senator. [Cheers.]
13. The Thirteen (Claimed) Seceding States—May their Cause Prosper. [Cheers.]

Volunteer Sentiment, Transmitted by George E. Pug—Whisky our Favorite Beverage—May Distilleries Prosper. [Prolonged Cheering.]

Each sentiment, except the one named, to be drank in raw whisky. During the reading of the sentiments, suitable fireworks will be supplied by the Chairman of the Committee, who has also made arrangements for a grand pyrotechnic display for our benefit after we shall have closed our mortal career.

The entire performance will conclude with the following song, *by a resigned Union officer*, now a member of our party.

I'll hang my sword on a butternut tree,
And off to my comrades again;
Bull Run Battles have no joys for me,
Whisky raw's no pain.

The South that I love is bound to slide,
With a rattle snake on her brow;
Oh why did I flatter my boyish pride
By taking a Union Vow.

The committee had in contemplation the roasting of a Jackass, which Josiah kindly consented to carve; but upon mature deliberation concluded to restrain him from committing fratricide and the crowd from cannibalism.

The Committee would have been pleased to add more to the festivities of the occasion, but think that by the time the final song is terminated, the multitude will be drunk enough to follow the example of Pendleton and Morris at the late barbecue, and consent to be put to bed.

COMMITTEE.

THE. DeVILL, Chairman.
C. RHOADS,
LE FOLLETT,
W. L. OREY,
C. F. B. UHL.

The procession will be under the command of

JOSIAH-IAH-IAH,
Chief Copperhead.

Figure 7.3 Anti-Copperhead poster, Marietta, Ohio, 1863. Home-front Republicans, often organized as Union Leagues, confronted postemancipation dissent with concerted pressure, including violence against Democrats. Communities quickly became battlegrounds, as residents engaged in social warfare. Courtesy Ohio Historical Society.

[must] be called in to maintain their supremacy.... [A]s soon as armed rebels lay down their arms and return to their old allegiance, the military power will be removed."[80]

Unionist women in many communities organized Women's (or Ladies') Loyal Leagues, to complement the men's leagues and reinforce sagging unionist morale Their members did far more. They warred where men would not, surveilling disloyalists among them and occasionally meting out blows against women and even men. In the summer of 1863 at New Lisbon, Ohio, a group of thirty unionist women, accompanied by five men dressed in women's clothing, "started out, with tar and feathers, after the Democratic women of that town." They punished seven of them, one recently widowed. When an Illinois teacher made a political statement suggesting his opposition to Lincoln and the war, some of his female students responded with unanticipated aggression. "The Wilson girls who thrashed the rebel teacher at Douglas are members of the Ladies League," wrote one neighbor. "[T]he members of the league tendered them a vote of thanks for their praiseworthy conduct."[81]

Brooding melancholy and seething anger soon grew into a combustible mix that often ignited at community events, turning increasingly into violent affairs. Gathering days—court days, celebrations, picnics, and especially elections—were recurrent sites of violence. On the Fourth of July in 1863, separate celebrations in Liberty, Illinois, "wound up with a fray they got into a free fight in which there was three hundred men and boys engaged there was not lives lost but a number of noses flattened and eyes—blackened." Less than a week before election day, at a political rally in Carmi, Illinois, two men got into an argument that resulted in one combatant being stabbed ten or twelve times. "I will be so glad when Tuesday is over," wrote one witness, "then I hope there will be no more publick gatherings and that will decide the conflict any way and it will not be to quarrel over any longer." A unionist lawyer in another Illinois community, before a session of court, was "[p]urposely hissed on and was being agged on by a Crowd of Jeff Davis Democrats" and responded violently; he "took up a Club and Struck the Copperhead a Stunning blow on the head." Public dissent meetings were often met with mob violence. When a group of dissenters "tried to have a peace meeting" in Liberty, Illinois, "the Union men went in and broke the meeting up and made old Lake[nan] Hurray for the Union." Once unionists discovered it, Ohio's Butler County Mutual Protection Company, which rural dissenters (many from Indiana) had formed in July 1863 and which met in one of its remote township houses, barely survived the month. Many union vigilantes were discharged soldiers hardened by their own sacrifices. One vowed he had "suffered to much—endured to much and risked to much on account of this infernal Rebellion—to allow a man to enjoy life and liberty under the Stars and Stripes—while secretly wishing success to our enemies and glorying in the Reverses."[82]

The ferocity of unionists' counterinsurgent responses caused even soldiers to call for restraint. After reading about a fray in his Rush County home following a Democratic meeting in June 1863, Indianan Daniel L. Thomas acknowledged, "No doubt had I been at home on furlough I would rushed madly into this affair (for it is exciting)." Although he "believe[d] they do deserve it," he cautioned against violent reprisals. "If *wisdom* and *moderation* was *ever* needed in that community it is *at the present*.... How wise Gov. Morton was to order the Greensburg Home Guards to stay at home. Had they went they would have inaugurated war immediately." In June 1863 Orlando B. Willcox, commander of the Department of the Ohio's division that included Indiana and Michigan, requested the disbanding of *all* secret societies, including Loyal Leagues, for the sake of public peace. "[T]hey are a constant source of dread and mistrust, and divide and provoke hostility between neighbors, weaken the dignity and power of courts of justice, expose the country to martial law, and [are] discouraging the people from enlisting in defense of the nation."[83]

By the late summer of 1863 the frenzy of military efforts had gone far to quell the disturbances in many areas. In December 1863 a Cincinnatian found several boxes of "Butternut breast-pins... left behind intended for some Butternut procession, which never came off. If meant for this county, there was no demand for them after the election." But in 1864, when full-flowered conscription combined with political fever surrounding the approaching national and state elections, suppressive violence exploded anew in many locales. "[A] feeling of enmity, hatred and general conduct bordering on insanity... [prevailed] throughout this beautiful Western country," reported one resident of Alton, Illinois. More dissenters now calculated the risks before acting. One dissenting group in Indiana weighed whether they should "fight [the draft squads] now or wait until after the election" and opted for the latter.[84]

Amid widespread suppression, Copperhead vigilantism did achieve success. Not surprisingly, given Democratic racial rhetoric, armed dissenters and secret societies targeted African Americans in counties in the border free states, especially in their Butternut regions. Regulators in Illinois attacked and killed prospective black recruits on their way to enlist at Quincy and Shawneetown, and a gang of dissenters stabbed to death Evansville, Indiana's, prominent African Methodist Episcopal minister. Between the fall of 1863 and the winter of 1864, dissenters involved in the Sons of Liberty in hilly Washington County, Indiana, north of Louisville, murdered or drove out virtually all of the county's nearly two hundred black residents, "who would not leave the neighborhood," believing that following emancipation "negroes would receive citizenship." Most left for Evansville and Indianapolis.[85]

These waves of political violence peaked in the summer of 1864 with the presidential election. As grand rallies competed in middle border counties, racial rhetoric took center stage, with Republicans characterizing Democrats as "all nigger" and Democrats tarring Republicans with a recently invented term, "miscegenationists." Democratic county conventions regularly erupted into shouting matches, with "Peace men" shouting down "War men" who "had better go over to the abolition party where they belong," while an anti-emancipation soldier claimed "one thing is certain is that our men is too much of white men to mix with the negroes or abolitionist[s]." At the national party's "Copperhead Convention" in Chicago, the divided delegation compromised around a War candidate, Lincoln's former general in chief, George B. McClellan, while Peace delegates drove through a platform drafted by a committee headed by Ohio's notorious Copperhead, Clement L. Vallandigham, back from exile in Canada and publicly risking rearrest. Vallandigham's presence caused Lincoln to instruct his generals to desist.[86]

With the assistance of the military, Republicans intensified efforts to quash more organized dissent. A concerned resident of Crawfordsville, Indiana, wrote to the commander of the state militia that "companies are being organized composed exclusively of partisans, and each hostile to the other, [see] that you let no arms come to this county, to any company." Intimidating, and if needed, obstructing Democratic voting was a pervasive strategy. Many solicited and received captured arms from soldiers in the field, while others sought muskets and even artillery from their state and the federal government. "Men are hurrying to and fro with guns on their shoulders shooting them off, cleaning and reloading," wrote one woman in Carmi, Illinois. "The gun John sent came just in time," this same woman informed her husband in the army. "This evening is the first time Father has attempted to shoot it.... I am going to learn to use it." On March 28, 1864, in Charleston, Illinois, a violent series of furloughed soldiers' provocations led dissenting citizens to organize a Democratic rally. Many came armed. Federal soldiers and local Republicans clashed with dissenters in the town square. The incident, which occurred in a county known for dissent—perhaps not ironically, only a few miles from the farm near which Lincoln's father was buried and where his stepmother yet lived—lasted only a few moments. Before relief troops could arrive by train from nearby Mattoon and Indiana, nine men were killed and twelve were wounded. In July the provost marshal at Quincy gave clear instructions to deputized subordinates that although his authority limited him to arrests of "deserters, spies and persons who resist or obstruct officers engaged in the enrolment or draft," organized unionists should protect the polls by deadly force if necessary. "[I]f you meet with armed resistance you will give your opponents your best show of fighting without any hesitation, and in such cases use no blank cartridges."[87]

Republicans had for a year been hedging their party's bet. After the bitter fall 1862 election defeats, fifteen states, all with Republican-controlled legislatures, enacted legislation allowing military suffrage, bringing the total to nineteen. An Ohio regiment begged the state senate to allow the soldiers to vote, arguing, "The country has already suffered from disloyal men sneaking into office, in consequence of the absence of so many voters in the army." "[W]ith patriotic self-denial," twenty-two of Indiana's twenty-six infantry regiments signed a resolution opposing their state's military disfranchisement law. Much to Lincoln's dismay, three middle border states—Illinois, Indiana, and Kentucky—would not allow absentee voting. An anxious War Department authorized commanders to furlough as many troops as practicable to go home.[88]

In September 1864 the Confederacy launched its final effort to use war to achieve thwarted political goals. An invasion into the middle border sought to swing the presidential election by invigorating the western dissent movement. Sterling Price's newly named Army of Missouri, totaling twelve thousand cavalry and dragging fourteen guns, streamed northward from Arkansas. Among his subordinates were former partisan commanders and guerrilla chieftains. After taking heavy losses by frontal attacks on Thomas Ewing's smaller, fortified force, which included black troops at Pilot Knob, Price moved northward toward St. Louis, then turned westward along the Missouri River. His troops destroyed railroad bridges and miles of track, impressing recruits, horses, livestock, and supplies and pillaging and burning the homes of unionist "Tories." They executed home guards and especially rural African American and German civilians, leaving their bodies for hogs to devour. At Boonville, Confederates claimed they *intended to kill* and *burn*"—to "Mormonize," as one boasted—the town's many Germans. The slowness and size of Price's five-hundred-wagon supply train, loaded with booty and trailed by five thousand head of cattle, allowed William S. Rosecrans and Samuel R. Curtis to mobilize federal forces more than twice Price's number to trap the invading army.[89]

On October 23 Price attacked the converged federals at Westport, where for two brutal hours opposing lines of horsemen charged and countercharged over the rolling prairies and wooded creek fords in the largest cavalry action of the war. For the Confederates, it was a disaster. Price's forces fled southward as a disorganized mass of horsemen, cattle, refugees, wagons, and unarmed men. Skirmishing continued nearly daily, and on October 25 Price lost more than a thousand men and most of his artillery, captured at rain-swollen Mine Creek in southeastern Kansas. Vengeful federals, especially Kansans, executed many of the rebel prisoners. Price then dispersed his forces and marched into Indian Territory. He lost between four thousand and six thousand men, perhaps half of the force he had brought with him, mostly to desertion.[90]

Two weeks later Lincoln won an electoral landslide, the first president since Andrew Jackson to win reelection. Heading a National Union Party ticket alongside Tennessee Democrat Andrew Johnson, Lincoln's national margin of victory was more than 10 percent; in most middle border states, where margins four years earlier had been thin, the president won comfortably. In Ohio the Union Party's majority was 60,055, and it carried seventeen of nineteen congressional seats. But Lincoln received overall just 380,000 more votes in 1864 than in 1860, and without the soldiers' votes he might have lost Indiana and Maryland. Entire federal regiments had jammed trains and riverboats heading northward. Many who did not held mock elections and published the results in local newspapers before the election, hoping to sway voters. Overall, more than 80 percent of soldiers gave their votes to the president. In Illinois Republicans stationed troops at polling places, intimidating dissenting voters with loyalty challenges and threats of exile and property confiscation. Republicans swept the Illinois state legislature, taking eleven of the state's fourteen congressional districts, as well as the governorship. Indiana's congressional delegation included seven new members, all but one a Republican. Four had served in the war.[91]

In the middle border's slave states, where federal troops manned polling places and test oaths banned disloyal voters, Lincoln won Missouri but lost Kentucky. In the two states, just less than 40 percent fewer voters went to the polls than four years earlier. So complete was disfranchisement and depopulation in Missouri that, although Lincoln had received just 10 percent of the popular vote there in 1860, he received nearly 70 percent in 1864. As one dissuaded voter explained, he "would not risk his life, liberty and property in any vain attempt to vote for McClellan with the vain hope of regaining our lost liberties." Kentuckians were defiant. Lincoln was trounced by nearly 40 percent, giving McClellan his widest margin of victory. Cries of "Curse the president. Damn this Lincoln government" were heard freely at polling places.[92]

§

In late February 1865, as Lincoln was completing a reconciliation-themed address for his second inaugural pledging the nation to embrace the end of slavery "that this mighty scourge of war may speedily pass away," he wrote to Missouri's new governor, former federal officer Thomas C. Fletcher, puzzled by persistent violence and distrust among civilians there: "[W]aiving all else, pledge each to cease harassing others, and to make common cause against whomever persists in making, aiding or encouraging further disturbance.... At such meetings old friendships will cross the memory, and honor and Christian charity will contrive to help." Six weeks later, just days after Robert E. Lee's armies surrendered in Virginia and amid daily unionist celebrations, middle border residents would learn that the president had been murdered. Few missed the fact that a fellow border slave-stater, Maryland's John Wilkes Booth, reputedly a member of the Knights of the Golden Circle, had fired the fatal shot, offering the horrified audience at Ford's Theater a pithy variant of James Ryder Randall's poem, "My Maryland," long since turned rebel battle hymn and associated with his occupied loyal state, to warn against overweening governmental power: "Sic semper tyrannis!" The opening salvos of what would become a "war after the war" had been fired.[93]

Before the present war was officially over, the black-creped funeral train carrying the slain president's body, alongside that of his son, Willie, had passed 1,654 circuitous miles from Washington through thronged cities and bonfire-lit villages in Pennsylvania, New York, and Ohio. Hundreds of thousands of mourners lined the tracks or filed past the displayed casket, a tribute not seen for nearly thirteen years, when Henry Clay's body had traveled to Lexington, Kentucky. Unlike the earlier procession, Cincinnati was not one of those cities allowed to host Lincoln's casket or even see the funeral train. In fact, the train traveled a new stretch of track between Columbus and Indianapolis, accompanied by its heaviest security guard of the entire route, then northward to Chicago, quite consciously avoiding the "disloyal" areas of these western states, free and especially slave.[94]

Had the president lived, he would have learned painfully that amity would be difficult to find on the middle border. The wracking internecine conflicts its states had suffered during the last years of the war would extend well into the postwar period as often violent struggles for political control, outliving the broader conflict by a half-century and defying national reconciliation. Waging it required redefining white cultural identities while constructing new meanings of the war, the border, the region, and in fact the nation.

A River Between Them

On Tuesday, July 4, 1876, residents of New Richmond, Ohio, as did many other communities, celebrated the nation's centennial year. Picnics and speeches filled the steamy summer afternoon, and evening fireworks displays illuminated the village's long-planned anniversary festivities. Four days later these same residents held a more spontaneous festival. Evil had been among their earlier party guests, but the "Late War" would attend this later celebration.

On Saturday morning, sickening rumors interrupted the townspeople's good spirits. Amanda Abbott, the seventeen-year-old daughter of a local teamster, claimed tearfully that she had been raped and nearly murdered in the woods north of town. With finger-shaped bruises on her still-swollen throat, she recounted how a man, offering references of mutual acquaintances and kin ties, lured her away from her parents' home under the pretense of hiring her for several weeks to keep house, something she often did for meager wages. He said his pregnant wife, Mary, was "confined" in the last stage of her pregnancy at their farmhouse with their other children, and she needed household help.

The accused was George Williams, a thirty-nine-year-old tenant tobacco farmer and itinerant laborer who claimed to live near the site of the alleged attack. Williams had led her north away from town on foot by the Cincinnati road. His horses, he said, were plowing corn—an obvious lie, given the month—and so they must walk. After a couple of miles, he stopped at a rural store; telling her he would be detained while trying to sell a load of tobacco—again a lie, tobacco harvest being more than a month away—he urged her to walk on ahead of him. Williams likely was trying to throw off neighbors who might have seen them walking together. Once he had caught up to Abbott, he claimed there was a convenient shortcut up a creek ravine through the river bluff and led her off the road into the countryside. They walked eastward for another mile or so across several crop fields.

At noontime, an hour after the pair had left the girl's home, Williams attacked Amanda in a wooded area near Pond Run. "[H]e threw me down, and in the dirtiest language he could use he told me what he was going to do to me," she recounted. Her entreaties were to no avail, and though she "fought him as long as I could," he raped her repeatedly. He warned that if she screamed, a gang of men would come to kill her at the sound of his whistle. After four terrifying hours, with a summer storm rapidly approaching, Williams pinned her down, beat her into unconsciousness, and hastily strangled her. Leaving her for dead, he hurried back to town.[1]

Miraculously, Amanda survived her ordeal. She stumbled home Friday evening and tearfully told her father and mother—whom the newspapers described as "poor... and [whose] daughters have always worked"—of her ordeal. Within minutes of Amanda's reappearance, news of the attack spread, as well as Williams's boast to her that only a day earlier he had done the same thing to another of the village's young women. A local family, the Hoopers, realized with horror that their daughter, Mary E. Bennett, a twenty-six-year-old mother who was living with her parents while her husband, a carpenter, worked in distant Dayton, had gone with this same man on Thursday under the same pretense by which he lured Amanda. She had not been seen since.

Meanwhile, Amanda's father, Elisha, rushed at once to the town's constable, William Fitzpatrick, who promptly discovered Williams in one of the town's saloons, drinking with the dollar he had obtaining by selling Mary Bennett's basket and shoes to a local black woman. Fitzpatrick arrested the rogue and locked him up overnight in the town jail. Williams had scratches on his face and arms, just as Amanda had said he would when describing her efforts to fight off her attacker. A dozen witnesses, including both sets of anguished parents, identified him as having been seen with one or both of the women.

Williams was hastily arraigned and claimed innocence before the local judge, who remanded him to jail. In one of its two first-floor cells, Fitzpatrick questioned the man about the alleged crimes. Williams admitted assaulting Amanda Abbott and that he had devised his plan at the centennial picnic, where he had first seen her. He claimed to have been "put up to it by two other parties... under the influence of drink." Hastily arranged search parties combed the area around Pond Run for the missing Mary Bennett. The constable obtained little more reliable information, other than that Williams's second wife and three children lived in Bethel, some fifteen miles east of New Richmond, and not near Pond Run.

Late that afternoon Fitzpatrick's interrogation in the stifling cell was violently interrupted. As many as fifteen hundred men and women milled about in the dusty street in front of the jail, many on horseback from rural Clermont County. Among them was the brother of the missing girl, Jim Hooper, who had reached town only minutes before aboard a riverboat, on which he worked. He soon joined the others who were "harangu[ing] the crowd in favor of the immediate execution of Williams." Sensing the events to come, the constable quickly locked Williams in his cell, bolted the inner door to the cell room, and rushed to the front door. Within minutes the townsmen battered down the door and broke into the front hallway, where Fitzpatrick met them. The constable tried to dissuade the enraged crowd from going further, claiming he was about to get information about the whereabouts of Mary Bennett, who Williams claimed was alive. Crying, "We won't give him another God damned minute!" and "Let us hang him on the spot!," the mob rushed forward, flinging the fifty-seven-year-old Fitzpatrick into the street. The constable quickly fled the scene. Having neglected to get the keys from him, the mob used a large wooden joist to batter down the door to the cell room. Unable to beat in the iron-barred cell door, some in the crowd threatened to burn down the building with Williams in it. Instead, they used a large ax and crowbar to pry open the bars of the cell. After twenty minutes the mob dragged out the prisoner, pinioned his arms behind his back, tied a rope around his neck, and dragged him into the dusty street.

Amid shouts of "hang the son of a bitch," the crowd—"composed of the very best and most influential citizens in the town and surrounding country... and many of them prominent church members" and including black as well as white residents—became frenzied. "[M]addened, cursing, struggling," the human torrent rushed Williams across the street to a large sycamore tree. A dozen men scrambled up into its ghostly white limbs, dropped down the rope, and prepared to put the noose over the man's neck. Only the pleas of Emma Kautz not "to see the man hanged on her place" prevented a ghastly spectacle from occurring in her front yard. Williams sensed a chance to save himself. He whispered his own plea to one of the leaders. The other girl was dead, but he had not killed her. "Silence, everybody, for a moment," a man cried out from atop a nearby stump. "He says, if we will let him he will take us to where the body of Mary Hooper lies. Shall we give him a chance?" Although some still howled for Williams's immediate hanging, the lure of discovering the girl's body won out.[2]

Williams, "all the time being led by the rope which was around his neck which was pulled so taut that his tongue at times protruded," fought for air as the sea of townsmen, including some who protested the extralegal justice that seemed inevitable, swept him out of town. Eastward they climbed up the steep Nicholsville Pike, where he had claimed they would find the girl's body. At about nine o'clock, near the foot of Ashburn's Hill, the procession halted under two trees on opposite sides overhanging the road. A Lutheran clergyman who had joined the teeming mass attended briefly to the gasping prisoner and pleaded with him to reveal Mary Bennett's whereabouts so that his life might be spared.

Suddenly, Williams roused himself to face the crowd. Whether from desperation born of a grim realization that the mob would carry out its object with or without his information or the urgent need to torment his tormenters with words that conjured a dark sense of place and past they all understood, he made a bold admission—but not about the missing girl. He was not who they thought he was. "[H]is real name was George Mangrum," one onlooker recalled the prisoner declaring hoarsely yet defiantly, "and he came from Alexandria, Kentucky." Once again, Mangrum was obscuring the whole truth. Although Alexandria lay just across the river, he was in fact from violence-plagued, rural, western Kentucky and had moved to the Alexandria area shortly after the war. Propertyless, he worked as a farm laborer before moving his wife and children over the river just before the attacks.[3]

His latest identity lie mattered little compared with his place of origin. A reporter for Cincinnati's *Daily Enquirer* was among the sweating procession. Having arrived by riverboat that morning to get his scoop, he would witness retributive justice far longer in the making than the past few days. Breathlessly, he watched the New Richmonders' violent reaction to Mangrum's final testament and their fury at his having come from the south side of the Ohio River:

> The crowd was now wild with its thirst for vengeance, and could no longer be restrained, even had there been anybody anxious to restrain them. The loose end of the rope was passed over the limb of a tree by the upper side of the road. Between the tree and the road there was a deep drain. When the rope was pulled tight, forty ready hands, black and white eagerly grasping it, [Mangrum] was jerked off his feet and struck the opposite side of the drain with a dull, heavy thud. The next minute he swung almost clear with his feet just touching the sloping edge of the drain. It was now dark, but by the fitful light of the moon, which was just struggling through the tree-tops, some one discovered that his feet were not clear. "Pull him up a foot higher," was the clear, ringing order from one who seemed to be tacitly acknowledged as a leader, and who was in the tree above him, and in a flash he was dangling in the air.— Three hearty cheers greeted the death, which was almost instantaneous. There were also sexually-explicit derisions, such as "He'll never log upon Pond Run again with a woman," and "How do you like it, old fellow?" Then an inquisitive fellow who was on a level with the hanging man lit a match and held it to his face to see how he looked. The crowd on the road laughed at this uproariously and cried, "Turn him around till we see him." Other matches were then lit and he was turned round to the edification of the whole crowd.... It is a rare thing in Ohio, this thing of lynching...the solemn, slow-going law be mocked by that dangling corpse that swings in the glimpses of the moon.... Hanging was too good for him.

Suddenly, someone in the crowd alerted others to the reporter's presence. Warnings to "see that he gets no names" hastened the reporter back to town. As he quickly descended the pike, not silence but echoes accompanied him. Bouncing off the hillside was singing, a hymn of sorts—"We'll hang George Mangrum from a dead elm tree." The reporter could not have failed to recognize the refrain. It was only the latest of many adaptations of "John Brown's Body," sung by federal soldiers and unionist civilians during and after the war to mock their vanquished Confederate, disloyalist, and Copperhead foes. The echoing tune would not have been unfamiliar in this neighborhood south of town, nor in New Richmond, known for its community of abolitionists. A couple miles upriver, atop the same bluff, sat Massachusetts-born abolitionist minister Daniel Parker's Clermont Academy, where white and black, male and female students had been taught together for nearly three decades. Long considered a waystation for slave escapes, it had been a target of proslavery harassment before the war.[4]

The Late War's return to town by this macabre event was obvious to locals, as was the grim realization that neither was in fact over. The next morning search parties discovered the "bruised and mangled" body of Mary Bennett, lying in a ravine less than a mile from where Amanda claimed she had been assaulted. Her decomposing body was partially clad, her jaw and neck broken, and there were hobnail marks on her forehead. Her dress and bonnet lay some two hundred yards away. Her funeral and interment in the town burying ground would draw nearly "the entire population of the town." As the village prepared for it, Mangrum's corpse swung all night, a hideous reminder of the "scene of retribution" for curious onlookers who ventured out during the dark night. Almost at the same time that Mary's body was found, village authorities cut the body down and hauled it off "on a dray, like he was a dead hog, or something" and quickly buried it south of town in a sandy riverbank, ostensibly to prevent angry townspeople from carrying out threats to burn it or throw it into the river. The coroner's inquest ruled that Mangrum's death had occurred "at the hands of parties unknown." Newspaper accounts soon claimed that he was a serial rapist who had spent time in the Kentucky penitentiary, whose previous victims included the Louisville widow of a federal soldier killed in the late war.

The war's sudden reappearance in New Richmond invited others from the other side of the river to participate as well. Standing *"incognito,"* according to newspaper reports, among the onlookers at Mangrum's derelict burial was the dead man's younger brother, Dick. Working at a local brickyard under the assumed name of Stoneburner, he had actually been solicited by unaware New Richmond townsmen to join the mob that murdered his brother. Embittered at the dishonorable treatment of his brother by these Yankee Ohioans rather than shamed by his kinsman's crime, he left his employer immediately, stating that "he would stay around no d____d town where they hung a man for nothing." As his brother's bare plank box was lowered into the ground, Mangrum loudly threatened revenge upon New Richmonders by means all too familiar. "This is the worst thing that New Richmond had ever done," he growled, vowing that "he would burn the damned town down." Mangrum and an unnamed Kentucky companion then spurred their horses southward along the river road toward Neville, where they crossed the river. "Armed parties are now in search of him," one newspaper claimed, and like his murderous brother, "it is thought he will stretch hemp." A Cincinnati newspaper declared that the dead man's crimes were in fact "venial... in comparison with those of his brother Dick[, who] is regarded as a more vicious man than his dead brother, if that were possible." For weeks armed nighttime patrols roamed the town's streets and county roads.

The veiled language employed by this Kentuckian—and the several Ohio newspapermen who covered the violent story—spoke volumes to local readers. Apparent experts in the brutal business of retributive violence and living now under assumed names, both Mangrums had likely ridden as guerrillas or partisans in the late war. This was not the first time New Richmond, the longtime target of Kentuckians' enmity as an abolitionist hellhole, had received threats from the south side of the river alarming enough to spur a paramilitary response. In September 1862 townsmen had mobilized county militia after receiving credible reports that rebels near Alexandria, armed with artillery, planned to shell their town from the opposite river bluff. They had in fact kidnapped "Union men" from near New Richmond and held them as hostages, to be exchanged for civilian prisoners at Camp Chase. The local home guard had crossed the river to "clean out the Guerrillas" and rescue the men.[5]

Unquestionably, in the minds of these Ohioans, Kentuckians like the Mangrums were brutes, inferiors, southerners. These characterizations were now entwined, as was the now widespread perception of the pervasive and violent nature of southern culture in contrast to the orderly peace of Ohio, which these townspeople's retributive act now belied. On the very pages on which Ohioans and Kentuckians read the grisly details of George Mangrum's hanging, the newspapers carried other news articles. Some five hundred miles to the south, hundreds of armed white southerners were rampaging through Hamburg, South Carolina, killing black militia and Republican public officials, black and white, in what historians have called the last battle of the Civil War. Some two thousand miles to the west, an army of Native American warriors had slaughtered a force of federal cavalry under the flamboyant Ohioan and federal war hero, George A. Custer, the first defeat in the nearly decade-long series of military campaigns against Plains Indians that newspapermen called simply the "Western Wars." Redemptive violence, it seemed, knew no borders or regions.

8

Southern Cross, North Star

The Politics of Irreconciliation

As the horrors in New Richmond attest, eleven years after the war's close its shadows yet darkened the landscape for survivors living on the middle border. At the time of the national centennial, those shadows had only lengthened, with unreconciled war enmities expressed in innumerable forms as cultural antagonism. The incongruence of a white man's lynching in Ohio with our historical understandings of cultural violence in America is fully matched by the undeniable overtones of war strife in this incident.

But the tragedy offers a further complication. The absence of a pronounced racial dimension and the presence of black and white Ohioans at this act of retribution suggest that postwar racial harmony existed where slavery had not existed, and that racial violence reigned where slavery had died. The end of slavery was certainly experienced differently in the middle border's free and slave states, but racial hostility was pervasive in all of these states as white residents sought to blunt or obstruct the fuller social revolution that the war and its aftermath had brought.

The racial politics that overspread these states after the war might have offered a brief opportunity for retreat to the white western consensus. Instead, the opposite occurred. Racial aversion in the former free states could not contend with racial hatred in the former slave states like Kentucky and. Indeed, both saw "rehearsal[s] for Redemption," as historian J. Michael Rhyne has aptly termed violent postwar politics in states barely bound by Reconstruction mandates. Reversing the logic of sovereignty that the federal government had employed in an earlier wartime rehearsal when exercising war powers to occupy its own states, in peacetime it stayed those powers by allowing residents of loyal states, slave and free, autonomy to settle the fractious and often violent politics of emancipation.[1]

The New Richmond incident notwithstanding, the willingness of postwar white residents to resort to violence, racial and otherwise, to preserve or undo the war's outcome provided a marked measure of difference between these neighboring states. However deep and shared their war wounds, they were felt discretely as white residents reordered their societies by translating war experiences into distinct understandings of the war and themselves. More important than racial discourse and violence to these politics were white residents' conscious distortion, even inversion, of these states' war narratives so as to align them along the emergent North-South binary. As the abstruse politics of white sacrifice, formal and especially informal, demanded distinct interpretive lenses, similarly sacrificed was regional reconciliation. By innumerable incidents, these states' postwar cultural politics ended the former white western consensus. Replacing it was a hard border, symbolized by the former western region's wide rivers.

In March 1865 a federal commander in Missouri's Boon's Lick region exulted at the Confederacy's imminent defeat, claiming "redemption draweth nigh." But he was grimmer about his district and state, awash in violence at the statutory end of the peculiar institution there. "Slavery dies hard," he told a St. Louisan. "I hear its expiring agonies and witness its contortions in death in every quarter of my district.... [T]he emancipation ordinance has caused disruption of society equal to anything I saw in Arkansas or Mississippi in the year 1863." Accomplished by different mechanisms, slavery's death triggered years of postwar violence and decades of racial politics in these states. Although they would initially take different political directions, the war and emancipation lay at the heart of widespread rage and competing perceptions of sacrifice and retribution.[2]

With Radicals in control of Missouri's state legislature, Thomas C. Fletcher signed an executive proclamation on January 11, 1865, declaring the immediate emancipation of slaves, overturning by edict the state legislature's eighteen-month-old gradual emancipation ordinance. The convention would soon draft a constitution that would codify the governor's decree. Missouri thus became the first state to outlaw slavery after the late president had won reelection. The others—Maryland, Arkansas, West Virginia, and Louisiana—had done so earlier in 1864, none without considerable political opposition.[3]

Missouri's Radicals accomplished more than a simple end of slavery. They offered political retribution to the state's proslavery majority. Led by Charles D. Drake, a state constitutional convention approved a draft that included an ironclad oath for voting and officeholding as well for jurors, lawyers, preachers, teachers, and corporation officials and trustees; mandated racial equality in property and legal rights; authorized black testimony in court; and empowered the legislature to establish black schools. The convention ousted all of the state's judiciary, from the supreme court to the local level, as well as court clerks, recorders, circuit attorneys, and sheriffs, replacing some eight hundred law enforcers with Radical appointees. When adjourning, Radicals offered a biting chorus of "John Brown's Body." In June, aided by the disfranchisement of many white voters, the constitution passed by just 1,862 of 85,478 votes cast, a margin of just over 2 percent, carried largely by soldiers' votes. Rather than face unionist violence, or treason trials, or a color-blind world, former Confederate officers and legislators like Waldo P. Johnson, Jo Shelby, Trusten Polk, and Sterling Price initially chose exile in Mexico, invited by Emperor Maximilian, who exempted these Confederates' colonies from the republic's constitutional ban on slavery. When Maximilian was deposed and executed in 1867, most grimly returned to their home state.[4]

Slavery died harder in Kentucky. As the Thirteenth Amendment worked its way toward national ratification, its embittered Democratic legislature refused even to take it up, resulting in a legal and social netherworld of slavery and freedom. In the summer of 1865 Lizzie Hardin, returned from a two-year exile in Georgia, saw "slavery in such a condition that neither masters nor Negroes know whether it exists or not, lawlessness of every shade, and in the midst of it all, between Southerners and the Union people a hatred, bitter, unrelenting, and that promises to be eternal." Hoping to forestall violence, the governor, Thomas Bramlette, a former federal officer, suggested what amounted to a plan of term slavery by which current bondpeople would serve their current masters for ten years. The legislature never seriously entertained it. African Americans celebrated emancipation as an accomplished fact. Anticipating full citizenship, including voting, colored men's conventions began meeting in Kentucky in 1865 (patterned after an "equal rights" convention held earlier at St. Louis) and used Fourth of July celebrations as emancipation celebrations, at which former federal officers and emancipationist legislators addressed large black crowds. Ironically, many returning Confederates celebrated at Fourth of July picnics for the first time in four years. John C. Breckinridge and William Preston were not among them, having sought refuge in Cuba and Canada; others, known as "Irreconcilables," would create permanent colonies in Brazil, still a slave nation. Many, most them from western slave states and known there as "Confederados," would return to their former homes when slavery began to die in their adopted homeland in the late 1860s.[5]

White unionists in Kentucky were in no mood to celebrate. "Where are our liberty poles," one asked bitingly, "our fireworks, the ringing bells, and the loud resounding report of cannon?" He spoke not about the celebrations of returning rebels, but about freedom celebrations held in cities throughout these states for those many considered legal slaves. Even before the war ended, thousands of African Americans relocated as families to cities like St. Louis, Lexington, and Louisville; to the latter came as many as two hundred a day, increasing the city's black population by nearly 16,500. By 1870 St. Louis's black population had grown fourfold since the start of the war, and blacks comprised nearly half of Lexington's population. Former congregants in white churches reformed as new or established black congregations. Within a year of the war's end, the remaining thirty-one black congregants of Paris, Kentucky's, First Baptist Church became members of its African Baptist church, numbering 250. In the fall of 1865 black men and women in St. Louis founded the Missouri Equal Rights League—comprised, unlike the Union Leagues, of "representative colored men"—which sought full citizenship rights, including suffrage. A year later black Missouri veterans similarly founded the Lincoln Institute in Jefferson City, and former Kentucky soldiers were instrumental in forming Berea College as a biracial college, much like Ohio's Oberlin.[6]

In Kentucky the avowed goal of slave liberation by the state's federal military authority deepened white retributive anger. John M. Palmer, an avowed abolitionist and an organizer of Illinois's Republican Party, received the department command in his native state from the president specifically to implement military policies to end slavery there. "[D]etermined to 'drive the last nail in the coffin' of the 'institution' even if it cost me the command of the department," Palmer carried out Lincoln's directive "to do as I pleased" by enlisting all able-bodied slave men despite the legislature's strident objections, sustaining martial law to supersede the state's civil courts, legitimating slave marriages to protect the wives and children of enlisted men and establishing refugee camps, releasing slaves from jails and workhouses, and issuing thousands of travel passes enabling freedpeople to move freely in search of employment. (Black Kentuckians called them "free passes," while whites disgustedly called them "Palmer passes.") "My countrymen, *you are free*," Palmer told attendees at a freedom celebration at Louisville, "and while I command in this department the military forces of the United States will defend your right to freedom." To his wife, Palmer wrote exultantly in October 1865: "Slavery is dead in Kentucky and my Mission is accomplished." His private celebration was premature. The state's courts claimed that only slaves of *disloyal* masters were free, and the supreme court struck down Congress's law liberating black soldiers' dependents. Unionists who employed black refugees, especially those armed with Palmer passes, soon faced indictments from angry grand juries. Palmer was indicted by a Louisville grand jury for aiding fugitive slaves and faced a wave of lawsuits from dispossessed Kentucky slaveholders, including U.S. congressman Brutus Clay and U.S. senator Garret Davis. "Negro's are getting verry saucy in Ky," wrote David C. Phillips, "they go to speaking [to] hear their Apostles, advacating the doctrine of their freedom[.]"[7]

With military protection for Emancipationists who claimed the mantle of political leadership, Conservatives fought back against northern-style social reforms. "Negrophobia in its worst form," as one officer characterized white Kentuckians' recalcitrance, swept through these states. During the first five months of 1865 Camp Nelson admitted 2,782 black refugees, mostly women and children, and municipal governments such as that in Harrodsburg, Kentucky, quickly enacted proscriptive ordinances against African Americans now "densely crowded" in their midst. In August 1865 the town's trustees unanimously approved ordinances that prohibited "Free Negroes or Negro[es] claiming to be Free or fugitives" from settling in town, ejected them as vagrants or forced them to work on the town streets, and established fines of two dollars a day for white residents who rented them lodgings. Lexington's civil authorities forbade black gatherings and required masters to retrieve bondpeople "at large" in the city. Hannibal, Missouri's, city council changed its relief law so that "by a new officer called the overseer of the poor who is a conservative[.] Hannibal is no longer the Negroes' paradice that it was under Radical rule." Violence against black garrisons, "d___d smoked Yankees... obnoxious to our people," as one Kentuckian sneered, drew armed responses, and local officers received letters and petitions from white residents charging that these soldiers acted worse than guerrillas. Former provost marshals and troops joined Conservatives to target unionists. In September 1865, at a fair in once-solidly unionist Danville, Kentucky, a white mob exchanged fire with black troops until arriving white troops quelled the disturbance.[8]

A four-way struggle raged among occupying Union forces, freedpeople who tried to exercise the rights of freedom, white unionists, and former Confederates or their supporters, many of them disfranchised, who warred to limit those rights. Many of the obstructionists were current and former soldiers, federal and militia, who "court the favor of the rebel sympathizing portion of the citizens, and do all they can in opposition to the colored troops." In June 1865 a federal officer in southern Kentucky observed dimly that "when color is involved in the contest for right," too many would be "leaning to the side of Injustice." Guerrilla violence was endemic enough for the Kentucky state legislature to keep its militia mobilized and in service until 1866. Unionists in many communities called for troops to protect themselves and support civil governments, and garrisons arrested large numbers of miscreants. Others begged to have troops removed, especially black ones.[9]

This violence, as well as the presence of troops in these states, was as much political as racial. Even before the war had ended, the first national Reconstruction crisis arose in the border states during the ratification of the Thirteenth Amendment. After Missouri's Radical legislature voted on February 6 to ratify it, the first among slave states, Kentucky's legislature was the second to reject it, after Delaware. (New Jersey rejected it as well in these first months.) In Kentucky the amendment hung in the balance all summer against the looming state elections, which could reverse the legislature's rejection if Emancipationists gained control. With sixty-five thousand to seventy thousand slaves still held in legal limbo, many white Kentuckians employed all means of obstruction. "Take these bayonets out of the state and we will shew you whether slavery is dead or not," wrote a Bowling Green resident. In Grayson County just weeks before the election, David C. Phillips witnessed a political assassination. Caleb Stinson, a pro-amendment candidate whose son served in the federal ranks, was murdered after giving a speech. "[I]t won't do to run men, who has occupied his position at this crisis... to command the union vote, not the AB's [abolitionists'] vote.... Old Grayson is right on this question." Garrison commanders refused to prevent disloyalists, former Confederates, and even known guerrillas, from voting, and election judges certified the votes in districts where secession flags hung in sight of polling places. Through the end of 1865 even unionist owners "enforced *their* ideas of Kenty law" by refusing to release their slaves until and even after the amendment became law. Only after the fall election did the War Department demobilize remaining troops, removing them altogether from Kentucky and Missouri in the spring of 1866. They were replaced in certain sections by Freedmen's Bureau agents. Prior to their removal in mid-1868, these agents had limited success assisting freedpeople or protecting them from violence that matched or exceeded that in the former Confederacy. Defiantly rejecting this federal authority, in December Kentucky's legislature repealed its four-year-old Law of Expatriation, re-enfranchising former Confederates.[10]

Once slavery had ended officially, former guerrillas and paroled Confederates "chafing under their defeat" waged overt racial warfare throughout the former slaveholding areas of both states, especially Kentucky. "All of the pent up bitterness of their Rebel natures," wrote one alarmed unionist, "seems to belch forth in redoubled fury, against the poor Negro." In some towns, gangs of paroled Confederates still in uniform murdered freedpeople and warned others to leave or die. Others proclaimed their gangs of nightriders to be "Regulators," "Negro Regulators," or "Ku Klux"; fired into private residences; and taunted unionists that "Nigger Orders are played out." Numbering in the hundreds, they employed terror tactics to maintain the political and racial status quo and to undermine new political mandates. "Some of thos men say they entend to cill the last negro soldier that coms to this County," wrote an alarmed resident of western Kentucky, "all of this Class of men are return Rebl soldier." In western Missouri, Jim Jackson's former guerrilla band threatened entire towns with mass slaughter if all black residents did not leave the state, and a garrison commander in the Ohio River town of Warsaw, Kentucky, noted that "negroes coming from the interior are forced to cross the river into other States." The counties of the southern Bluegrass, where Ku Klux Klan activity was worst, lost on average 17 percent of their black populations. While one white Kentuckian boasted he was "a posed to eny black stripes in the ould american flag," a black emigrant driven out of the state by violence in 1865 remembered, "Dat Ohio shoah shure looked prutty."[11]

With most federal troops removed, returned rebels subjected communities to virtual re-enactments of the late war, both regular and guerrilla-style. Lines of "southern men" exchanged shots with "Union men," often former federal soldiers, while "uncompromising Union men" and peace-seeking former Confederates alike found themselves beset by mobs of "lynch men" and "midnight intrusions.... No house is safe outside the town." Ungarrisoned towns were little safer. At Russellville, Kentucky, unionist residents suffered from returning Confederates who "dress and parade the streets in their Confederate uniforms, fully armed with Revolvers... [and] constantly fire weapons, especially at night." With martial law removed, they "make bold to express their real sentiments which they dared not do before." Federal veterans suffered "contemptible prejudice... that to wear the U.S. uniform and at the same time be a gentleman, are two things which are incompatible." Those who fought back often suffered worse. Frankfort's John Marshall Harlan and Danville's Speed S. Fry, the reputed killer of Confederate general Felix Zollicoffer, were terrorized into leaving their homes. As a recently returned Indianan claimed, "Killing a guerrilla is called murder, in the vocabulary of Kentucky copperheadism," and a white Kentuckian averred "the radical Union men may as well dig their own graves if they have not already done it politically." In March 1866, Kentuckian Robert Winn reflected despondently: "Our State keeps its celebrity as the Champion of Conservatism—and has pardoned all her rebel soldiers, and all thieving gangs whose politics (if they have any) entitled them to the title of Guerrillas.... Nigger hate, and Yankee hate—as bad as ever—with the power of the country in the hands of rebels—or what is the same thing, Slavery-loving, and Liberty-hating Oligarchs."[12]

Indeed, postwar politics embedded with racial and allegiance-based antipathies soon led to ritualized violence against former unionists, black and white. Beginning in the summer of 1865, a wave of lynchings accompanied the return of Confederate veterans and guerrillas in Kentucky and Missouri. Mocking the authority of military law, vigilantes often sent garrison commanders and provost marshals taunting reports of their "Proceedings" and "Docket[s]," recording—often in graphic detail—testimony, sentencing, and punishment, including executions of white and black unionists. After nearly hanging to death a local editor, one emboldened vigilante "judge" warned "all other Newspaper Men... that they *Must* desist from Calling My Court a mob." On Christmas Eve in Danville, Kentucky, hundreds of whites dragged a black man, arrested for exchanging shots with a police officer, from jail and lynched him near the town square. One historian has counted 117 lynchings between 1865 and 1874, two-thirds of whom were African Americans. One Freedmen's Bureau special investigator who toured the state found there had been numerous whippings of black women and shootings of black men, many of them federal veterans, which he characterized as "severe and inhuman." Bureau teachers, women and men, were attacked or arrested and their schools often burned (those who came to douse the flames were often fired upon); white landholders frequently whipped black residents in their employ; and local authorities often did little to assist agents to bring miscreants to justice. Freedpeople often resisted such attacks. Easter Campbell recalled her veteran father fighting back against these vigilantes. "De Ku Klux cum after him one night en he got three of dem wid dis [military] pistol, nobody eber knowed who got dose Kluxes" Many more who resisted with force were soon beset. A group of freedmen in Scott County, Kentucky, wrote, "We are mobed and beat and our houses pulled down on us.... We are all Slaves in this naborhood." Many were driven from their homes. By 1870 Kentucky's black population had declined by nearly fourteen thousand, or just less than 6 percent, but some estimates double this figure. Missouri's black population declined less than Kentucky's, but nearly a quarter of its 118,071 black residents were in St. Louis.[13]

Vowing that they "had been treated like dogs by the people of Ky long enough," many federal soldiers, white and black, struck back by organizing as paramilitary Union Leaguers or "Union Regulators." To "extirpate... enemies of all order," as Harlan vowed, a St. Louis "Loyal and Union" Club posted a circular with the banner "To All Who Were Rebels, Traitors, Sympathizers and Their Friends During the War," claiming: "That if Union men cannot live in peace and quiet where you are in the majority, you cannot enjoy peace and quiet here.... Remember 1862; be warned... we will burst you into atoms... death and desolation will follow the L. and U. A. Avengers." Radicals at Sedalia, Missouri, passed a series of resolutions, declaring that "we will protect ourselves against these thieves, murderers and rebels... peaceably if we can, forcibly if we must." Reconstituted as paramilitary units, these bands intimidated or assassinated Conservative candidates, assessed and confiscated property of Confederate families, and hunted former rebels and guerrillas. In Kentucky one witness wrote, "The men of [Basil] Dukes command... were attacked by bushwhackers—or State Militia who operate much after their own hook and... say they had the hardest fight in their experience—Indian fashion." Midnight wars resulted, as one frightened resident wrote, with opposing forces "try[ing] all the time to kill each other.... They waylay the Roads for each other."[14]

§

The published dispatches of Petroleum V. Nasby did little to harmonize the middle border's battered postwar landscape. Nasby, a semiliterate inebriate, one-time secessionist, and committed Copperhead, once hailed from the northwestern Ohio hamlet of Wingert's Corners. There, mostly white, "trooly Dimecratic," residents

> didn't bleeve in the war—we wuz opposed to it in the beginnin; we wantid the gurment revolooshnizd to keep Noo Ingland, wich is spredin herself all over the West, frum submergin the entire Dimekratik party. Our bark wuz on the sea—slaivry wuz its anker, its jib-boom, its rite forrerd mast, its bow-sperit, its keel, its all.

These Ohioans had seceded immediately from their free state, and claiming "Ameriky for white men," resolved against black emigration and passed an ordinance authorizing slavery. Rather than be drafted, Nasby enlisted in and then deserted the Confederate army, returned to Ohio to found the "Church uv St. Vallandigum," then quit the state in 1864 after Lincoln's and Ohio Republicans' overwhelming election victories. After wandering border states with divided allegiances, he settled in Confedrit-X-Roads, described wryly as a "typical village in the unreconstructed South.... Kentucky didn't secede, and therefore within her borders secesshenists are safe. Thank the Lord for Kentucky."[15]

Nasby was in fact a fictional character born of the fertile imagination of Ohio newspaperman David Ross Locke, a native New Yorker who moved west and began publishing his column in Findley in 1861. "Nasby's Letters" became a wartime sensation, gleefully skewering pro-southern sentiment in Locke's adopted state. Carried in serial form, it became a western Republican staple. When introduced to the letters in 1864, Lincoln reputedly claimed that, had he the author's genius, he would swap places for the good of the country. He personally thanked Locke for "stirr[ing] people to right thinking and decisive action," meaning solidifying Republican wartime loyalism. In October 1865 Locke moved to Toledo to write for *The Blade*.[16]

In the postwar period, Locke's principal foil in his Nasby column was the nightmarish violence unfolding across the river in Kentucky following slavery's end. Exempted largely from Reconstruction measures and thus free to defy them, Kentucky was the perfect representation of the violent politics of southernization. But his satirical target was the politics of white supremacy that rent his adopted state after the war. Indeed, Nasby's Conservative villagers sent "greetin to their brethren uv Ohio, with thanks for their prompt and effectooal squelchin uv the idea uv nigger superiority."[17]

What was in fact unfolding in the middle border's former slave and free states were discrete inversions of Carl von Clausewitz's famous dictum, as white residents employed politics as another means to achieve war goals. Against the background of social Reconstruction measures, especially the controversies over the Fourteenth and Fifteenth Amendments, a war of sorts raged between wartime communities of allegiance writ large. Racial politics drove the engine of dissent against the Radical Republican agenda, whether as Conservative Democrats or Liberal Republicans, with the middle border its epicenter. Despite similarities in racial discourse and ideology that spanned the rivers, white residents above and below them forged discrete war legacies by defining distinct political identities. Through such politics, high and low, formal and informal, the war's realities were appropriated to rewrite war narratives to conform to or oppose the war's national outcomes. Nasby's genius was manipulating cultural politics to influence them to Republicans' advantage, a process also at work in former slave states in inverse, with Democrats the victors. Winning these wars fully divided these former free and slave states from one another.

In Nasby's adopted Kentucky, and soon enough in Missouri, appeals for racial solidarity took the form of appeals to native white men to join the "Rebel Democracy," the pejorative term unionists used for the Conservative movement. Because Missouri's Drake Constitution disfranchised former Confederates and "stay at home rebels," Radicals secured control of the legislature. But Kentucky's militant Confederates swept into office in 1866, replacing the state's former unionist Conservatives. "[T]hose old Democrats that stayed at home are only a little less unpopular than Union men," groused one newspaperman, while "the returned rebels are the pets of the people." Emancipationists like Louisville's Lovell H. Rousseau, elected to the Kentucky legislature only the previous year, quickly converted to the "Rebel Democracy." Not all unionists, especially former soldiers, were so easily persuaded to convert to the new Conservative coalition. In August 1867 "loyal" Kentucky federal veterans representing each of the state's regiments met at Louisville and resolved to march on Frankfort to retrieve their stored battle flags. These relics of their collective sacrifice were now in the hands of rebels, "unfit custodians," many of whom had fought against them in the late war. Rumors swirled that the war would break out anew on the capitol's front lawn as many former rebels vowed to stand a post for their state against federal enemies, symbolically inverting the course of the war while affirming its civilians' perceptions of its outcome.[18]

The turn to a "Rebel Democracy" would take longer in Missouri, but racial politics would build steam ahead of it following the withdrawal of federal troops in April 1866. In the summer of 1866 *The Weekly Caucasian*, a Lexington newspaper, had begun publishing, and in the spring of 1868, after former Mississippian Peter Donan took over editorial responsibilities, it became a leading national voice in the fight against Reconstruction. Donan directly tied the struggle of local white Conservatives to the resistance efforts by Ku Klux groups in Kentucky and former Confederate states, whose advertisements he ran openly. The *Caucasian* pushed disfranchised white readers to resist the state's Radical constitution by registering to vote, duplicitously taking the ironclad oath, suing in courts, and establishing alternate polls for fraudulent voting. Months before assuming the *Caucasian*'s helm, Donan had offered similar white supremacist tropes to angry western Missourians in his *Missouri Vindicator*, published in St. Joseph. "We are Caucasian in blood, in birth, and in prejudice," the editor blared in his first issue. In Osage County, Missouri, wartime unionist Lebbeus Zevely refused to sign the loyalty oath required by the Drake Constitution and founded a newspaper to rail against it, the *Unterrified Democrat*.[19]

When largely urban "Charcoal" (or Radical) leaders called for black "freedom and franchise" in 1868, Missouri's rural white insurgency quickly eroded the teetering unionist coalition. Despite editors' claims that "the people were swarming in the streets, bands of music were playing the soul-stirring strains 'Missouri is

Free.'... Every man felt himself a brother to his fellow-man," Radicals' hold on the state's politics was tenuous even in its urban strongholds. The Drake Constitution had lost in St. Louis, and many Germans in southeastern Missouri voted against it. Conservative "Claybanks" soon found strength among urban workingmen, many of them German, who resented freedmen migrating to cities from the countryside. Although he feared re-enfranchising the "old rebel element," St. Louis's Frank Blair, their former leader and Lincoln stalwart, condemned the Radicals' "malignant passions... [of] exasperation, retaliation, and revenge" and rejoined the Democratic party.[20]

By 1873 Missouri's rejuvenated Democratic Party was dominated not by moderates but by former Confederates. A year later the Rebel Democracy would regain power in the state, and in 1875 a constitutional convention met to "wipe from the statute books that 'sum of all villainies' the Draconian Code, which for studied malignity and concentrated malice has no parallel in the history of the human race," as one St. Louis Democrat characterized the Drake Constitution. All but eight of the sixty-eight delegates were Conservative Democrats; three-fourths had been born in slave states, twenty-four in Kentucky alone; and more than half of those present had either served in the Confederate military or government (the chairman, Waldo P. Johnson, had done both) or were sympathetic to them. The group quickly overturned the proscriptive provisions of the Radical constitution and passed measures making it difficult for any government, whether federal or state, to restrict individual rights, by disallowing the suspension of habeas corpus, tightening definitions of treasonable activity, and prohibiting the state government from confiscating property.[21]

Former Confederates swept into state offices, including rebel governor Thomas Caute Reynolds, who served in the state legislature. In 1875 the legislature elected Francis M. Cockrell, a former Confederate general, to replace the Radical and perceived German carpetbagger Carl Schurz in the U.S. Senate. Four years later George G. Vest, who had represented the state in both houses of the Confederate Congress, joined him there. (Cockrell served three decades in the Senate; Vest stayed nearly a quarter century.) The delineation of state politics based on former wartime allegiances—and more important, the power of the former Confederates in the political landscape—caused Reynolds to write to Jefferson Davis in 1880 that "my experience among some Missouri politicians of their inclination to 'remember to forget' matters which may affect their present aspirations." The political reversions had become so pronounced by 1883 that the editor of the *St. Joseph Herald* remarked, "Ever since the Democrats have been in power in the State there has been a division of offices by common consent between what is known as the Union element and the Confederate element.... Next year [Jo] Shelby proposes that the Confederates shall also have the Governorship." The rebel Shelby got his wish. In 1884, less than two decades after the war's conclusion, John Sappington Marmaduke, the former Confederate general and nephew of its celebrated "Governor in the saddle," assumed the reins of power.[22]

Across the rivers in the region's free states, racial violence and resultant black outmigration from Kentucky and Missouri cast their own shadows. Former slaves surged across the rivers to these free states, especially to cities and towns in border counties. One southern Illinois county saw its black population increase by as many as fifteen hundred during the summer of 1865, and Cincinnati's population grew by more than seventy-four hundred during the decade, prompting the city's only black newspaper, *The Colored Citizen*, to remark "the negro is so much on the increase that the highways and byways, the alleys and open lots are crowded with them." Indiana's Democratic legislature ratified the Thirteenth and Fourteenth amendments, but did not repeal its black immigration law, making it the nation's only former free state to keep racial exclusion laws on its books in the postwar. Freedpeople nevertheless moved there, and most lower Ohio River counties saw their black populations double and even triple by decade's end. "Slavery is abolished, but the 'nigger' cannot be abolished," wrote Cincinnati's archbishop Edward Purcell in the summer of 1865. "They say, we have bought the elephant, and know not what to do with it.... Shall we suffer the illiberal plans of New England to mature?... What is to be done with the nigger?"[23]

Pervasive racial antipathy and outright violence in these states portended a realignment of their southern counties with former slave state neighbors as the national debates entwined the "Negro question" and "southern question" with its western variant. In August 1865 Evansville, Indiana, witnessed the lynching by a mob of exiled Kentuckians of two jailed black prisoners accused of rape and the burning of black homes and tobacco warehouses where many were employed. Residents upriver at Madison asked that a superintendent be assigned to attend the "many persons of colour... coming within our limits... in consequence of the unsettled condition of things in the State of Kentucky." At Cairo, Illinois, with its once-contraband camp now bursting with some three thousand freedpeople, the post commander wrote that same month, "The prevailing sentiment among the white population of the city is disloyalty to the Government and *extreme* hatred of *Free* Negroes.... [A]n effort is being made to intensify this bitter feeling to such an extent as to drive the Negroes from the City entirely." Democratic newspapers sensationalized stories of black misdeeds in town and predicted "a series of bloody riots," causing the War Department to name a Reserve Corps officer as the post's superintendent of freedmen. In Cincinnati the following spring, alongside claims agents' advertisements offering "*Particular attention*" for back pay, bounties, and pensions "due to COLORED SOLDIERS and their families," *The Colored Citizen* reported attacks on black veterans by recently returned white federal soldiers.[24]

Despite such harsh racial realities in these free states, the politics of wartime sacrifice largely blunted the chance for a southern-style Democratic redemption after slavery, as in neighboring middle border states. War triumphalism overrode Democrats' Negrophobic rants as Republicans effectively used emancipation as a purity test for postwar loyalty and tied Democrats to Confederate traitors. In Indiana's fall 1865 elections, one editor clucked that "copperheads had no ticket—they are played. The shadow of the negro was not large enough; the 'undying democracy' have died...wiped out, as clean as a the great rebellion, the bloody termination, and logical conclusion of their nefarious dogmas of Secession, Sedition, State Rights, and sum of all iniquities." "The negro demands at our hands an expiation of the wrongs he has endured for years. He shall have it," claimed one Ohio editor in 1867. In the spring of 1867 white former federal officers and Republicans in Chillicothe, Ohio, in the state's dissent belt, hosted Frederick Douglass, the nation's most prominent black orator, who drew large crowds on successive nights.[25]

These politics of sacrifice manifested themselves at the state level as fierce contests that mirrored their wartime divisions and in turn deepened political animosities carried over from the war. Unlike in the states across the rivers, this political struggle for home rule soon became known, if with different meanings, as the "bloody shirt." At the state level, less to promote black equality than to torment Democrats in Illinois and Ohio, now Republican-controlled legislatures quickly ratified the Thirteenth Amendment and repealed their states' Black Laws, save for suffrage prohibitions. Among the first to link the war overtly to postwar political warfare was Oliver P. Morton, Indiana's embattled Republican wartime governor. On June 7, 1866, at Indianapolis's Masonic Temple, shortly after a Democratic meeting at Louisville at which Indiana representatives had met with Kentuckians, including former Confederates, Morton drew down on these traitors and linked them overtly with southerners. "Every unregenerate rebel lately in arms against his government calls himself a Democrat.... Every man who labored for the rebellion in the field who murdered Union prisoners by cruelty and starvation who conspired to bring about civil war in the loyal states who invented dangerous compounds to burn steamboats and Northern cities... calls himself a Democrat.... In short the Democratic party may be described as a common sewer and loathsome receptacle into which is emptied every element of treason North and South and every element of inhumanity and barbarism which has dishonored the age."[26]

Following Morton's lead (he would be elected to the U.S. Senate in 1867), Republican and Democratic congressmen at the national level routinely used war wounds as weapons to debate greenbacks, the tariff, postwar corruption, and above all Reconstruction. As northern Radicals like Thaddeus Stevens, Charles Sumner, and George Julian sought to deter any reverse of the Union triumph by extending rights to citizenship to freedpeople, conservative western Republicans drew sharp racial limits to the Union Triumphant trope, often refusing to embrace even minimal political rights and social privileges for African

Americans. Complicating western unionists' contest over the war's memory were African Americans' postwar commemorations of emancipation and Union victory. The postwar organization and expansion of African American societies routinely defined the legacy of the war as one to end slavery. Mass public emancipation day parades continued, such as that at Louisville in 1883, with Frederick Douglass as the primary speaker.[27]

Federal veterans led this new political warfare and in turn benefited from it. Commanded by the Union's "Great Triumvirate," Ohioans Grant, Sherman, and Sheridan, and confident that their armies, rather than their eastern counterparts', had led the nation to victory by a western style of war, many returned home with deep enmity for those who either had not supported or had outright opposed their cause. "Men cannot go through a prolonged emotional crisis and not pay the price," admitted one Illinoisan. "It makes people hysterical." Although prevented by their officers from exacting full vengeance on southerners, as "Lincoln's Avengers" they now abused Democratic "home rebels." Affectations of reconciliation, blared one Ohio editor, whether in his own state or former slave states, "illustrate the hollowness of that sickening lip-service, which is intended solely to effect a purpose." Federal officers turned partisan politicians, like Illinois's Robert G. Ingersoll and Ohio's James A. Garfield, told veterans that "every scar you have on your heroic bodies was given you by a Democrat."[28]

Veterans' organizations supported these politics of sacrifice, and they in turn whetted former federals' partisanship. While still in the field, the Society of the Army of the Tennessee (SAT) formed in April 1865. Composed nearly exclusively of western officers and headed by Illinoisan John Rawlins, Grant's aide, and later William T. Sherman, the SAT held its first meetings in 1866, followed soon by similar western veterans' societies for the armies of the Cumberland and the Ohio. They held annual reunions for the next four decades, exclusively in western cities. Also in 1866, following the model of the Union Leagues, the Grand Army of the Republic (GAR) organized in central Illinois as a veterans' "secret society," with John M. Palmer its first state commander (see figure 8.1). Illinois generals would follow as national commanders for the next five years. The first of them, John A. Logan, borrowed from observed "Decoration Day" practices of southern black and white women, and in 1868 ordered May 30 to be a memorial day for remembering the sacrifices of fallen comrades. The GAR, which later spread to northern states, held its first national encampment at Indianapolis that summer. With its sibling organizations and women's auxiliary, the Ladies of the Grand Army of the Republic, it joined other western veterans' organizations to embody the Union Triumphant, and initially all became virtual arms of the Republican Party. Veterans, particularly those bearing wounds, were universal presences at the party's political rallies, helping Republicans maintain control of Illinois's state legislature for the next quarter century.[29]

Figure 8.1 Grand Army of the Republic parade, Trenton, Missouri, ca. 1877. Organized in 1866 in central Illinois as a "secret society" for federal veterans, the GAR was segregated in western states like Missouri. By the 1870s the organization was in steep decline there because of tensions over the emancipationist cant, black suffrage, and, in former slave states, the "Lost Cause." Courtesy State Historical Society of Missouri.

Voting like they shot, federal veterans drew down on Democrats in electoral warfare. Virtually all Republican candidates at the local, state, and national levels were themselves federal veterans, usually officers. Even when veterans headed Democratic tickets, Republicans, as claimed one Ohioan, "cannot and will not vote it when headed by men, who gave all the aid and comfort to rebels they could, and denounced the executive as a usurper of power, and us as dogs, villains, cut throats, Lincoln hirelings, knaves, etc., while the rebels were starving our brave comrades." An announcement for a fireman's benefit in southern Ohio in the spring of 1867 solicited "the gallant defenders of our lives and property and the *life of the Nation* by *all means* be represented.... '[L]et us all make a long pull, and a strong pull, and all pull together.'" The Democratic candidate for mayor of Dayton, Ohio, found himself assailed by innuendo about his wartime disloyalty. "The grey suit which Mr. MORRISON wears would conceal a heap of Confederate bonds," sneered the local Republican paper. "He is to be respected for his sincerity, just as JEFF. DAVIS is." Democrats often were unable to contend, leading an Illinoisan to splutter, "One hundred soldiers of the late war have more influence politically, in any community, than two hundred citizens who never robbed hen roosts or masticated Hard-Tack in range of Rebel guns." From 1868 to 1900 every Republican presidential candidate but one had a military record. Five of them were Ohioans, the first being Grant, the federal war hero, who was elected in 1868 by wide margins in these states.[30]

As wartime loyalty offered currency for postwar sacrifice, daily political warfare in local communities saw unionists, women and men, hurl the epithetic terms "rebel" and "Copperhead" at former dissenters to bar them from church membership and communion. In Hamilton, Ohio, Republicans took aim at Democratic schoolteachers, "northern rebels... whose active sympathies are unblushingly given to treason." Local partisanship, uniformed and not, quickly manifested in insults, lawsuits, business boycotts, and threats of or outright violence. Singing anti-Copperhead songs, as one Ohio music instructor learned by anonymous letter, "will get your damn nose broke.... I will be at your singing and if I hear that song, down goes your meat house." Many partisans were Democratic veterans who claimed they too had fought and bled for a just cause, the Union as it was, and returned home unrepentant. In once southern-sympathizing Williamson County, Illinois, dozens of men died in postwar feuds that followed war loyalties and service or nonservice. Because women actively participated in this partisan personal warfare, they were not spared. A "female teacher, expressive of the wish that Grant, Sherman, Lincoln and others would take the cholera and suddenly die!" was dismissed when she vowed "she should not carry a Union flag to the proposed pic-nic of the scholars but that she intended to carry a rebel flag." Imputing disloyalty, Republican newspapers gleefully published the names of local female writers of wartime dead letters addressed to recipients in the slave states and held by dutiful Republican postmasters. The pervasive postwar violence raging through neighboring former slave states caused many to ridicule claims of wartime federal officers' and soldiers' disrespect for gender norms buttressing their discrete white culture. "[S]outhern women, like southern men, have fallen from grace, and nothing short of 'reconstruction' will save them."[31]

Free state Republicans defined emancipation as key to saving the Union, in order to redefine Democratic opponents as disloyalists and southerners. But race soon eroded the Republican edifice in middle border states. When the president, Andrew Johnson, sought popular support for his vetoes of Reconstruction measures protecting freedpeople's civil rights, including establishment of the Freedmen's Bureau, in 1866, he swung west on a speaking tour. At Cincinnati and Louisville, especially, large crowds welcomed Johnson warmly, after a near brawl in Indianapolis. The next year, although the legislatures in all of the middle border states save Kentucky ratified the Fourteenth Amendment guaranteeing black citizenship, the legislative votes were tied to state election outcomes that were nowhere certain or even convincing. In Illinois and Indiana Republican candidates won in northern counties, virtually deadlocked in central counties, and lost in the southern counties. Decrying the "absurd state suicide theory," many former antislavery hard-liners refused to vote with northern Radicals for racially progressive bills. Votes for Democrats increased in all sectors. In Ohio, after an acrimonious debate over the Fourteenth Amendment in 1866 and its ratification in January 1867, voters restored Democrats to control of its legislature. In January 1868, by resolution it rescinded its ratification, and for nearly a century and a half subsequent legislatures did not override the vote.[32]

Radical Republicans' completion of Reconstruction by the Fifteenth Amendment, which granted black suffrage, permanently tore apart the wavering Republican coalition on the middle border. As late as 1868 only eight former free states allowed blacks to vote, and none were in the middle border region. Fourteen previous black suffrage referendums in these states had failed, including in Ohio, where Democrats had fought the repeal of the Black Laws in 1865 specifically because of fear that it would lead to African American voting rights. "The dominant party is engaged in a regular crusade against that word 'white,' and must strike it out of the Constitution," claimed the Democratic editor of Cincinnati's *Daily Enquirer*. Ohioan Jacob D. Cox, a former general and racial paternalist despite being the son-in-law of abolitionist Charles G. Finney, did not include African Americans in his northernized exclusivist "Yankee race" narrative of western culture above the Ohio River. Believing that regional reconciliation depended on "*a peaceable separation of the races on the soil where they are now*," he had agreed to accept the Union Party's gubernatorial nomination in 1865 on the condition that the platform would not endorse black suffrage.[33]

During the debates over the Fifteenth Amendment, race similarly divided the western veterans' organizations like Cox's GAR. Between 1865 and 1870 a westernized narrative of the war emerged under the construction "Loyal West," by which white soldiers claimed they had fought "solely to suppress the rebellion," meaning for the Union and the national government, and not for emancipation or black citizenship. By their sacrifice the nation was proved inviolable, and slavery, the national impediment, was destroyed as a war measure and was not part of the cause. Nationally, the GAR overtly promoted black suffrage, and its northern posts welcomed black veterans into its ranks, but in the western states its posts were nearly all segregated, with the few all-black posts relegated largely to cities. Many chose to surrender their charters and reorganize as local veterans' organizations rather than accept black members. By 1870 the national GAR was in steep membership decline, especially west of the Appalachians. By contrast, with no black members and having ignored Reconstruction civil rights controversies or refused to promote them, the western veterans' societies for the armies of the Cumberland, Tennessee, and Ohio were thriving.[34]

The proposed Fifteenth Amendment put Republicans in a defensive posture not seen since 1860. Only Illinois, with its Republicans conscious of a martyred president's emancipationist legacy and in control of the legislature, ratified it. Indiana's state house and senate Democrats resigned their seats to prevent a quorum, and by special election all were re-elected, only to resign a second time for the same reason. Only a controversial interpretation of the state constitution's quorum requirements allowed a vote with the Democrats absent, resulting in ratification. In Ohio the amendment met with outright defeat in the Democrat-majority legislature. Even self-styled western Radicals opposed it, leading Cincinnati's *Gazette*, a Republican organ, to conclude, "a Legislature could not be chosen in Ohio which would adopt it." The same state that Lincoln, immediately after his 1864 re-election, reputedly claimed had "saved the Nation" now became the first to reject the amendment intended to complete the murdered president's legacy.[35]

Racial politics fueled retributive violence in rural areas of the middle border's former free states, especially during and after the Fifteenth Amendment debates, suggesting a Conservative alignment with neighboring former slave states. Borrowing from the region's long tradition, Regulators or "White caps" lynched local miscreants throughout the former Copperhead regions, increasingly targeting African Americans as vestiges of the war's emancipationist turn. One historian has found there were eighty white-cappings in just two Indiana counties in the twenty years after 1873, and in the half century after the war's end white vigilantes lynched no fewer than twenty African Americans. Many of these "Ku Kluxers," as they proudly called themselves, had migrated during or after the war from neighboring slave states. "During the late war and toward its close... [many] left Tennessee and Kentucky and... brought with them the relics, the practices indulged in throughout the South," an Illinois editor noted. One former Kentucky slave, Nancy East, living in Middletown, Ohio, remembered, "Nevah heered nothin' 'bout [Ku Klux] atall until we come up here, and dey had em here." Posses and militia on several occasions were called to quell mobbing, and often met armed resistance from Democratic war veterans, their vigilantism now blended with war partisanship. At an 1872 Ku Klux lynching of two white men jailed for rape near Van Wert, Ohio, members of the mob offered "three cheers for Jeff Davis during the hanging." Illinois witnessed at least twenty murders in its southern counties, led by "Bloody Williamson," the state's once-Confederate and Copperhead capital, prompting the state's House to pass a bill appropriating $3,000 to suppress the violence. The county's name, one resident wrote, became to Republicans "a hiss and a by-word."[36]

By wide margins, both of the middle border's former slave states rejected the Fifteenth Amendment, and its national ratification in February 1870 unleashed racial frenzy in each. What one Kentucky resident called "the Black Peril," the first election allowing African Americans to vote potentially to correct the wrongs of the slaveholding past, saw the formation of armed state militias to intimidate black voters from exercising their new political rights. Fueled by rumors of "Negro Kuklux" companies being raised in Lexington, attorney Benjamin F. Buckner, the former federal officer who had resigned his commission to protest the Emancipation Proclamation, raised a battalion of Citizens' Guard that mustered into the Kentucky National Legion. They fought alongside paramilitary Klan groups on election days against armed black voters at Versailles and Lexington in 1870 and at Paris and Lancaster the following year.[37]

However unifying, the politics of race would not easily undo the politics of war sacrifice on the middle border. The Liberal Republican movement, a conservative factional challenge to Radicals' orthodoxy over punitive treatment of southern states and corruption in the Grant administration, emerged in the region specifically during the Fifteenth Amendment debates. Born in St. Louis in 1870 issuing calls for "conciliation" and "self-government" for southern states, the Liberals' coded platform was for amnesty and home rule, namely, for undoing the Radical Republicans' racial revolution. Regarded as free market reformists, and with civil service and the tariff heading their national platform, racial ideology and war animosities underlay the Liberals' western orthodoxy during its brief national insurgency. An Illinois Republican newspaper characterized its state's Liberals as a "sorehead and copperhead" party, while Wendell Phillips sneered that the splinter party was "nothing more than Ku-Kluxism disguised."[38]

The Liberal movement emerged from the ranks of disaffected western Republicans. Former Missouri Radicals like U.S. senators Carl Schurz, who spoke for German Americans who remained supportive of rebel disfranchisement ("Germans do not like the company of Copperheads," one wrote), and Frank Blair, as well as Governor Benjamin Gratz Brown, all one-time Emancipationists, broke with the Republican party over black suffrage. Campaigning as Liberals or Fusionists, they merged uncomfortably with rebel Democratic Conservatives in the middle border's former slave states into the "New Departure" to appeal to white southerners and "Loyal Westerners." In May 1872 the Democratic nominating convention was held in Cincinnati, in the heart of the Copperhead region and near Grant's birthplace. Joined by former Emancipationists and Lincoln confidantes such as Illinois's Lyman Trumbull, David Davis (the president's 1860 campaign manager), and John M. Palmer and former Radicals like Indiana's George W. Julian, who decried the "mercenary element of Republicanism," they tarred the president, a former Democrat, as a turncoat. Northern Radicals decried the "southern nomination" as wanting only to "overthrow what they call negro supremacy and carpet-bag supremacy." Grant won the election in a landslide, and the Liberal movement collapsed, the last gasp of the white western consensus.[39]

§

Just as formal politics shattered the fiction that racial subordination accomplished white reconciliation in the West, the cultural politics of irreconciliation established the middle border as a front for the war after the war. As the fictional Nasby, David Ross Locke did more than satirize former rebel Kentuckians and Ohio Copperheads in the postwar years. He established for his largely western Republican readership the contours of southernness: racial bigotry, Democratic affiliation, stultifying localist ignorance and lack of education, unrestrained violence, and Confederate identity. By creating for his readers a negative reference point, Locke also confirmed for readers on his side of the rivers the contours of northernness: principled restraint from violence, abiding respect for law and order, educated support for progressive modernity and fluid social classes: and above all else, advocacy of the Republican Party.[40]

Locke had plenty of help in forging war-driven definitions. In the free states, newspapermen and politicians busily highlighted the rampant violence wreaking havoc on the countryside in Kentucky and Missouri in contrast with the pervasive nationalist Union Triumphant ethos. Lawlessness in these "loyal" former slave states originated with the same "rebel spirit" that crippled Reconstruction in the former Confederate states. Ulysses S. Grant sent his attorney general to Kentucky and Missouri to investigate Klan activities there, and efforts to court immigrants, free state or foreign, to these states to fill labor shortages were short-lived or doomed—especially in Kentucky—by ruinous partisan violence.[41]

Nearly three decades of "commemorative separatism," as historian Anne E. Marshall has called the discrete white southern and northern myth-making required to explain the wartime sacrifice of some 750,000 people, completed the cultural border that would redefine this former West. Funereal and burial politics, manifested largely by women since the war's outset, led to segregated grieving and interment. Kentucky's and Missouri's Confederate dead were buried largely in unknown or mass graves in distant states, while those interred in family or church graveyards served as the war's first commemorative monuments. They in turn served as instruments of power by segregating postwar memory narratives in these divided states. To honor and politicize the federal dead, by 1895 the federal government had created seventy-eight national cemeteries in twenty-two states and the District of Columbia. Thirteen were in the middle border states and another two in Kansas, most in cities or towns or former federal camps located in or immediately across from the region's former slaves states. Of the 34,797 dead interred in them, just 3,639, or 10.5 percent, were Confederates. Not one was buried in Kentucky's six national cemeteries, as compared with 1,117 black soldiers. Combined, they were visible reminders to white southerners of the high price of wartime disloyalty.[42]

Commemorative civic rituals among middle border slave state unionists preceded those of Confederates and sympathizers. Dedications of public monuments were among the first, especially for federal dead in states like Illinois, Indiana, and Ohio. With far fewer erected in former slave states amid crushing and widespread violence, they offered little assistance in constructing a unionized narrative of the war. In September 1865 in Springfield, Missouri, defiant unionists were among the nation's earliest memorialists to the federal cause, already assailed in Missouri. The Lyon Monument Association took $1 subscriptions to commemorate the federal army's first general to fall in battle at the state's most well known battle site, Wilson's Creek. In 1889 the federal government paid for a Union monument to be erected in Springfield's newly designated national cemetery.[43]

In both former slave and free states, the earliest war memorials were erected where the Union Triumphant was most secure, and the end of slavery was portrayed as the war's principal claim to victory. In Ohio, seven of the eight monuments erected between the end of the war and 1869 were located in the onceabolitionist Western Reserve. When Ohio's Ross County Memorial Association began its fund-raising at a benefit picnic in 1867, dissenters were considered akin to Confederates, meaning "[Andrew] Johnson, R. E. Lee, Vallandigham, [George E.] Pugh, et al." were traitors to the Cause. Vallandigham's accidental shooting death in 1871 was a self-inflicted wound to dissenters' war memory in the state. When residents of Marietta, Ohio, gathered to consecrate their war monument, listeners in this former New England enclave heard Thomas C. H. Smith, a local attorney and former brigadier general on the staff of hard-line war architect John Pope, offer far more than sanctification of the dead. He justified vigilant exclusivism by reminding them that their sacrifice demanded cultural subordination within a "distinctively American nationality." Western "free states" must by "intelligent, voluntary, and ready obedience to law...thereby compact...[with] the Union sentiment of the North." By contrast, in slave states "a difference of spirit...[pervaded that] grew out of a peculiar institution, and... the spirit which that institution bred may survive it, and on other issues work mischief in the land again."[44]

Former dissenters dismissed Republicans' efforts to redefine their states by northernized standards. Amid centennial celebrations confirming the national victory, the editor of Dayton's *Daily Democrat* tried to exhume Vallandigham, and principled dissent, by condemning the northernized rewriting of the war in that region:

> The substance of a Radical stump speech nowadays is about this: There was once a war between the North and the South. The Union army is all Republican, with Republican officers, and Republican soldiers, paid entirely out of the pockets of Republicans! Democratic officers, Democratic soldiers and the money of Democrats were carefully excluded.... Let no one be deceived. Instead of reform they mean to array the North against the South, to keep up in time of peace a feeling of hate and revenge.[45]

As Republicans in the region's former free states crafted a victory narrative that wrote out dissent, across the rivers in the middle border's former slave states, former Confederates had quickly begun writing alternative war histories that coincided with, and even preceded, what Virginia newspaperman Edward A. Pollard termed the Lost Cause. In this literary exclusivism, the South's defeat lay neither with its gallant soldiery nor in its honor-based culture or slaveholding way of life, but rather in overwhelming force from a jealous North bent on their destruction. In these former loyal states, writers bore a greater burden than other Confederate authors. To overcome their collateral place in the Confederate nation as well as the stigma of internecine chaos there, both during the war and after, their pens had to prove mightier than their swords. As a southerner charged grimly, "[I]f all Kentuckyans and Missourians and Marylanders had taken up arms when [the Confederacy] did the cause would not now be styled the lost Caus[e]."[46]

Acceptance of Lost Cause precepts facilitated the evolution of southernness for wartime Confederates in these former quasi-Confederate states. The postwar emergence of what historian Gaines M. Foster has termed the "Confederate tradition" shaped the memory of the war for many white residents in undisputed Confederate states. Those who had not fully supported the live Confederacy did so after the war by becoming "belated Confederates," as historian Aaron Astor has termed them, ironically by recognizing that their cause was lost by their states' having remained in the Union. Several interrelated elements leavened an abiding sense of violation into this new southern exclusivism. Wartime sacrifice to federal troops in the form of humiliation, property loss, injury, or death only deepened their sense of belonging. Resisting invading federal troops who violated their sovereignty and the Constitution "as it was" proved their courage and loyalty. As southerners they saw themselves as upholders of the founders' vision, as well as keepers of the social and cultural ideals on which the nation had formed and prospered. Slavery was the linchpin. It had preserved the moral and racial imperatives of a superior agricultural, homogeneous, and cultured white society over an inferior industrialized, heterogeneous society that might have won the war, but only by brutality and superior numbers. Proximity to northern social and political imperatives, including racial and ethnic pluralism, in contrast with the traditionalism of former slave states, heightened their sense of southernness. As one Kentuckian argued in 1865, "[I]t requires no prophets eye to see that the Negro and the Yankee become the lords of the land and the southren people become Slaves[,] not only southren people of the Cotton States but the rebels and Copperheads of the border Slave states also.... [O]n the down fall of the South the inhabitance of this country will be a meaningless Mongrel crew made up of Yankee, Negro, Irish, Dutch, Rebel and every other kind of blood on the face of the earth." Having opposed the war and the federal occupation, by shared sacrifice they cast their lot with the southern people. Closest to these influences, these newly minted southerners recognized their vulnerability to these influences and, by affecting southernness, resisted them. "We may be provincial," one vowed. "We *are* conservative but we are safe." That safety lay especially in postwar resistance to Republican-led attempts at full social and racial equality.[47] The first salvos of the West's southern literary surge were fired in 1867, ironically, and not from Cincinnati, which saw its own version of the border war among the city's printing houses, clamoring for sales of partisanized war histories. That summer, fresh from insurgent violence in Mexico and now a reporter for St. Louis's *Missouri Republican,* cavalryman John Newman Edwards published his *Shelby and His Men, or the War in the West,* followed that fall by Kentuckian Basil W. Duke's *History of Morgan's Cavalry*. Rushed into print, both books were decorative accounts that claimed their states had served their unique Lost Cause by having remained in the Union. Recognizing that the actual Confederate experience applied only to a small portion of middle border residents, both authors strove to link their states' wartime traumas with those of the invaded Confederacy.[48]

The image of violent guerrillas rampaging over innocent civilians was an obvious impediment to crafting an valorous southernized war narrative. Edwards joined a number of other writers who countered northern journalists' portrayal of Missouri as a lawless "Robber State." By 1870 Edwards was collaborating with the state's most notorious postwar robber, former guerrilla Jesse James, for editorials and correspondence printed in the *Kansas City Times* and elsewhere. In 1877 Edwards published his opus, *Noted Guerrillas,* a largely fictionalized account of irregular warfare in western Missouri, intent on vindicating especially the infamous William C. Quantrill. "Whitewashing guerrilla history," as one historian has labeled this work, Edwards portrayed his subjects as freedom fighters who, against hopeless odds, defended their homes as well as honor and liberty against abolitionist invaders and Radical traitors, a potent blend of Lost Cause symbolism and rugged individualism. Subsequent guerrilla memoirists took the cue. Sam Hildebrand's autobiography's subtitle referred to him as the "'Unconquerable Rob Roy'...[who] lifted the black flag in self-defense...as became a free man and a hero."[49]

Confederate counter-narratives found aid from an unlikely variety of embittered middle border southerners, whether former Confederates, guerrillas, or former federal officers. Waves of civil lawsuits filled local court dockets, arguing for restitution for wartime property destruction and dispossession, evidence that partisan anger over the war was fresh in people's minds. In 1867 Missourian David Bowles, judged to be a wartime "southern man," sued various locals over what he argued were unlawful sales of his property by the local provost marshal in 1864 and 1865. He asked for a change of venue from his home county, believing that the judge's bias raised "questions involving the question of loyalty." As civilians successfully challenged wartime arrests and postwar oaths in higher courts, in 1870 St. Louis minister William M. Leftwich published *Martyrdom in Missouri,* a "true history of the war" that charged the federal military with "recklessness of life and wantonness of destruction... its most shameless, and revolting, and nameless crimes perpetrated upon the unoffending, the innocent and the helpless." Artist George Caleb Bingham made good on his pledge to paint the war as it was. Having protested the state's ironclad oath by his pensive 1866 oil painting, *Major Dean in Jail*, portraying the Baptist minister incarcerated for refusing to take the oath, two years later he made infamous Thomas Ewing's depopulation of the border with an oil painting titled *Martial Law, or Order No. 11*. Issued as a lithograph that Bingham initially intended to be named "The War of Desolation," it became something of a Last Supper for war dissent once it was sold nationally. Even as they sat together in the U.S. House, Bingham attempted to ruin Ewing's reputation for his "crime against humanity," thereby forcing Ewing to defend his controversial order to audiences of federal veterans and former unionists.[50]

Middle border southern women were ready adherents to these victimization narratives and proved early on that they were eager to bear the task of commemorating war sacrifices. Having lost husbands, children, larders, and homes during the war, they now privately decorated graves. Denied the right to bury their dead publicly or even at home, they understood the powerful politics of sacrifice pervading their home states and linked their sacrifices with the Confederate experience. As custodians of the past, for a half century they crafted the architecture of southernized memory and collective identity to, as one historian has claimed, "transform military defeat into political and cultural victory." In fact, by their unique circumstances they led the southern ranks into battle in this cultural war after the war.[51]

This process predated any elsewhere in the nation. Within a year of the war's end, members of the Atlanta Association for the Reinterment of the Kentucky Confederate Dead—exiled Kentuckians who either refused to return to their home state or remained in Georgia voluntarily—began relocating the remains of fallen Kentuckians from the battlefields around Atlanta. In hopes of soliciting funds and spawning local affiliates to move their remains to Kentucky, the organization began corresponding with widows of prominent Confederates. Among its members was Emily Todd Helm, half-sister of Mary Todd Lincoln, whose extended presence at the presidential mansion in Washington during the war had led to charges of disloyalty against the former first lady. Reminding donors that Kentucky's "sons who fell on the opposing side in this contest will receive the fostering care of the Government" in the form of national cemeteries, the organization's avowed purpose was far larger than simply raising money or reburying remains. "With the object in view accomplished, not only you survived them as comrades in the field... but your children, in common with the children of the South." By consecrating occupied soil alongside defenders of the southern cause forced to fight elsewhere, they would claim southern soil in their home states plot by plot against "the threatened forgetfulness of the grave and the obloquy which the world would heap on us."[52]

These Kentucky women were not the first to realize the commemorative power of the middle border's Lost Cause. Even before the war had ended, a group of dissenting women in Missouri claimed cultural authority for southernized war memory, in fact firing its first shot. In September 1864 in Independence's Woodlawn Cemetery, townswomen erected the first-ever monument to Confederate dead, only the second war monument erected in the entire nation. They secured funds to put up a marker over the graves of unknown soldiers killed at a skirmish with the 2nd Colorado federal cavalry and Missouri militia two months earlier. These were not in fact rebels, but bushwhackers under former Quantrill lieutenant George Todd, killed after a raid through the area during which they murdered some eight unionist civilians "before the eyes of their wives and children," along with a slave killed "for fun" before sacking Weston and Platte City. The conflation of regular and irregular southern war memory in this Missouri stone was also the first example of what were later called "martyr monuments," consecrating the resting places of civilians, guerrillas, or captured or surrendered Confederate soldiers killed or executed by federal troops. In Kentucky between 1870 and 1901, several communities erected markers to Confederate soldiers shot as a direct result of Stephen G. Burbridge's eradicative order in 1864, including a marker at Eminence memorializing three Confederates executed to avenge the deaths of black soldiers. In 1907 Missouri put up the last of these monuments on the courthouse lawn in Palmyra. The town's Confederate Monument Association etched the names of the ten civilians and soldiers executed there by state militia in 1862, a direct response to John McNeil's retort in 1889 that this action had been "the performance of a public duty." As a gesture of reconciliation or atonement, the local GAR post contributed part of the obelisk's $2,000 cost.[53]

By erecting the earliest southernized memorials, white middle border women anticipated subsequent Lost Cause commemorative politics that solidified former slave states into the "One South." In both states, their cause was anything but lost. Begun in Missouri in 1890, the Daughters of the Confederacy (DOC), a direct forerunner of the United Daughters of the Confederacy (UDC), soon spawned various local organizations, such as women's Confederate Monuments Associations. (The UDC formed officially in Kentucky and Missouri in 1895 and 1898.) In addition to monuments, the UDC chapters in these states marked soldiers' graves, sponsored various patriotic programs, and raised funds to return and reinter the remains of Confederates who had died in federal prison camps across the rivers. In 1920 more than fifty-three hundred Kentucky women were members of UDC chapters in some seventy towns; in Missouri, ninety-five chapters boasted twenty-two hundred members. Of the twenty-nine war monuments erected in Missouri before 1935, most of them by the UDC, nineteen were devoted to the Confederate cause. Kentucky's monuments were even more imbalanced. By 1925, of the thirty monuments erected in cemeteries and on courthouse squares, all but three were dedicated to the memory of the Confederacy. In both states, one—erected only recently in Kentucky—commemorates African Americans' war service.[54]

Granite soldiers standing silent vigil over a constructed Confederate memory in loyal federal states coincided with recognition that living Confederate veterans were embodiments of middle border southerners' collective sacrifice. Among the earliest commemorative demonstrations in these states were local reunions for returned Confederate veterans, seemingly without protest from former unionists. In Kentucky, prominent Lexingtonians began meeting as early as 1868 to decorate graves in its city cemetery, and their Missouri counterparts gathered in Lexington in 1871 for a "Confederate Reunion," including the state's most distinguished generals, Confederate and even federal. Infrequent and with limited attendance for two decades, by the end of the 1880s these efforts had coalesced as national commemorative organizations such as the Confederate Veterans Association, later reformed as the United Confederate Veterans (UCV). Founded in 1889, the organization had fifty-eight active camps in its Kentucky division and forty-seven in Missouri, and by 1896 its auxiliary, the Sons of Confederate Veterans (SCV), had formed in both. (UCV and SCV camps were also in existence in Illinois, Indiana, and Ohio.) The leaders of the UCV's Kentucky division were Louisville's Basil W. Duke and Bennet H. Young, who in 1900 would strenuously lobby the national organization to host the national reunion, claiming that "Louisville is a southern city... [that] will make you always love Louisville and Kentucky, who did not fight for their homes, but fought for you."[55]

Cooperative philanthropic commemoration in these quasi-Confederate states coalesced in the establishment of Confederate veterans' homes. When Missouri's veterans gathered in 1889 for their annual reunion in Higginsville, they spearheaded the founding of a Confederate Home Association alongside the state's DOC. Led by the St. Louis chapter, it and other women's organizations raised funds to purchase 365 acres of farmland just north of Higginsville and took cash subscriptions and pledges to construct and furnish residence dwellings on the site. In April 1891 the Confederate Soldiers Home of Missouri opened. Chronically short of funds—the state took financial control in 1897, with a board of trustees made up of Confederate veterans—over the next six decades the home housed more than sixteen hundred veterans as well as their families. Recognizing that no Confederate monument had yet been erected on a Missouri battle site, and that the state's only existing Confederate cemetery adjoined the national cemetery at Springfield (its 566 unknown dead were segregated from federals), the DOC established a memorial cemetery on the grounds and funded the interment of some eight hundred veterans. A dozen years later, in November 1902, Kentucky's Home for Confederate Veterans opened in wooded Pewee Valley, east of Louisville. The city's UCV post had raised $21,000 to acquire a hotel and adjoining property there, and the state legislature appropriated a per capita allowance for its maintenance. Although the dwelling had room for 125 veterans, in 1902 only 66 veterans resided there, but by 1922 some 350 veterans with "physical and financial inability to support themselves" had found refuge at the home. Although they were not allowed to live there, "wives, widows, sisters or daughters of Confederate soldiers" could serve as matrons or housekeepers for the veterans' room and board. A mile away, the legislature established a veterans' cemetery.[56]

Irreconciled southern political identity in these former slave states burgeoned alongside the cultural successes of Confederate veterans' and women's organizations. Henry Watterson, who succeeded George D. Prentice as editor of Louisville's *Journal* (soon combined as the *Courier-Journal*) in 1868, was among the most opportunistic of them. Raised in a politically connected family in Washington, D.C., Watterson was a strong unionist before the war and actually stood at Lincoln's elbow during his first inaugural. After turning down an appointment in the War Department and a military commission, he returned to Nashville, Tennessee to try to prevent the state's secession. He soon succumbed to war fever and enlisted briefly in a Confederate unit before turning to journalism. In 1864 he fled to Cincinnati, riding out the war and even editing a Republican newspaper. Unable to boast unionist or Confederate bona fides, Watterson decided to avoid competing war narratives. Recognizing Louisville's unique political geography and seeing an opportunity to capitalize on divided war allegiances by softening the edge of emergent southernization on the middle ground, he moved there.[57]

In Louisville, Watterson was among the first to articulate the "New South Creed," a pragmatic propaganda that one historian claims "bespoke harmonious reconciliation of sectional differences, racial peace, and a new economic and social order...all of which would lead, eventually, to the South's dominance in the reunited nation." Rather than point out any Confederate affiliation, he linked Kentucky with the South by sentimentalizing its shared cultural traditions and war sacrifices, opening himself to lampooning by the northern press as "a resurgent rebel, yelling for war" and caricature by political cartoonist Thomas Nast, who had illustrated Nasby's book on Kentucky nine years earlier, as a Confederate Kentucky colonel. Watterson cleverly conjured the former western consensus in an effort to legitimate southernization, appealing to white conservative unionists who had opposed the radicalization of the war and Reconstruction while romanticizing Kentucky's Confederate identity to deflect criticisms of his state to northerners wary of recent violence in the region. Louisville was a perfect locale, a former unionist enclave and federal army center struggling to regain its commercial base against its upriver rival, Cincinnati (about which Watterson later wrote, "there is nothing Southern," and which held little more than "malignity toward Southern people"). He encouraged free trade, railroad construction, and industrial development, and mindful of white supremacist readership on both sides of the river, supported the New Departure to undermine Radicals and end Reconstruction. Intending to "out-Yankee the Yankee," in 1895 he pronounced the nationalist "ambition of the South" while famously throwing open the New South through his city: "[I]gnorance and prejudice North and South... finally removed, all will be well."[58]

Fully recognizing their waning influence in these states' politics of war memory, former unionists in the 1880s sought to reoccupy their contested home front. They found themselves offering variant narrations of national purpose and destiny, toeing the line of wartime emancipation. The Union Triumphant trope clashed with resentful memories of hard-line warfare in loyal states, and the widespread opposition to the emancipation of slaves threw up obstacles to reconciliation among civilians and veteran officers of the western armies. Joseph W. Keifer and Albion W. Tourgée, Ohio Republican legislators during Reconstruction, published books portraying emancipation as a watershed to "restore decency and selflessness" to a once-flawed nation, while in 1886 Illinoisan John A. Logan, a once proslavery Democrat now turned Radical Republican U.S. senator, offered an irreconciliationist cultural history of what he called "Two Americas." Celebrating Lincoln and the destruction of slavery as the wartime triumph over a "great conspiracy" by southern elites to nationalize slavery, Logan argued that the conflict became destructive only when violent southerners unleashed a war of desolation, forcing the war into one for liberation. The persistence of a historical North-South binary demanded that loyal westerners align with the side of victory, with northern understandings and structures driving the progressive nation forward.[59]

Just two years after the city had hosted a Southern Exposition, as Ulysses S. Grant lay dying of cancer, unionist overtures to reconciliation found an even more uneven middle ground in Louisville. Unionist civic and business leaders, led by attorney and former federal officer Thomas Speed, organized a birthday celebration for the former president and federal general. They proffered reconciliation by prominently placing local former Confederate officers among the parade of speakers "to bury our differences, at least for the moment." Effusive praise for Grant's magnanimity to the surrendered rebels and his unwillingness to prosecute Robert E. Lee included no references to emancipation or Reconstruction. But it barely masked participants' raw war wounds. Regular references to Louisville as a southern city were virtual admissions that the victors of the peace had once worn gray. When Speed published his books, *The Union Regiments of Kentucky* (1897) and *The Union Cause in Kentucky* (1907), both of which denigrated the "manifest aversion to the Union Cause" in his state in favor of Confederate histories that "miserably misrepresent Unionists" and virtually ignored the role of black soldiers from his home state, he and other prominent unionists had little chance to reclaim their state's wartime narrative. Not coincidentally, these self-proclaimed Kentucky unionists refused to claim the mantle of southerners.[60]

With veterans at the heart of enduring tensions over these middle border states' irreconciliation, in 1895 Louisville, the site of Henry Watterson's reconciliationist address, hosted the GAR's national encampment. During a decade of fall encampments held in former unionist cities like Columbus, Detroit, Indianapolis, Milwaukee, and Minneapolis, the organization's choice of this city was the most controversial. Northern veterans and civilians alike complained about holding the meeting in "a Southern City, south of the Mason and Dixon line." The sectionalized controversy over the Louisville encampment was not the first into which slavery and Confederate identity had crept. Respectively in 1882 and 1887, Baltimore and St. Louis had hosted the first such encampments in wartime slave states. Although in Baltimore black units had participated, none were invited to the western cities, despite the existence of 3 black posts in the 344 GAR posts in the Missouri Department. Kentucky's 4 black GAR posts had long since been suppressed by partisan violence, and several of its 8 white posts were inactive. Louisville was the publication site of two Confederate veterans' periodicals, *Illustrated Confederate War Journal* and *Southern Bivouac*, the latter edited until recently by Basil W. Duke. A few years later they were joined there by *Lost Cause*.[61]

While Kentucky's southern women led the charge against this "friendly invasion" of Yankee soldiers, black Louisville veterans actively sought full participation, with the support of northern editors who called for full inclusion not offered previously at St. Louis. Fearful of poor white attendance, local organizers and GAR leaders debated erasing the color line in a former slave state. (Ultimately, some five thousand black veterans would march in the encampment's grand parade, and they were housed in segregated camps.) Cleveland's GAR posts refused to attend, and the affair elicited partisan sniping that generally followed war allegiances. The controversy reached the president, Grover Cleveland, who as a Democrat had raised Republicans' ire recently by vetoing a veterans' pension bill. His invitation to attend "the first [encampment] held in a Southern State" drew hostility and even assassination threats from "ruffians of Iowa and Kansas," led by former general James M. Tuttle. The partisanship was directed as much at the president's reconciliationism as at his veto. "Nothing has been found for him wherein he asserted a belief that the North was right," declared a Cincinnati editor, while another critic blared, "The whole affair has at least served to exhibit the Grand Army as a political organization auxiliary to the Republican party." In St. Louis William T. Sherman quipped, "Instead... of meeting only in the loyal states of 1861, I am in favor of their meeting hereafter at Nashville, Chattanooga, Atlanta, and Richmond, following the example of our armies in the war for the Union."[62]

The choice of Louisville having been sustained, Watterson's *Courier-Journal* greeted arriving veterans to "the Gateway to War in 1861... [and] the Gateway to a Prosperous South." Clouded reconciliationism soon gave way to war-borne storms that overhung the encampment more even than at St. Louis. The blizzard of national flags and Union Triumphant imagery could not obscure the rebel presence in the city. As a jarring welcome to the former soldiers who had occupied the city for more than four years, less than two months earlier Louisville's UDC and SCV had unveiled a monument to their state's Confederate dead. Having worked for years to raise funds, its fruit grew heavy after the announcement of the GAR encampment, when the Kentucky Women's Confederate Monument Association reminded the state's southerners, "All over the North [and South] costly monuments symbolizing the affection of the people have been erected... but Kentucky, so far, has been sadly neglectful... of her never-daunted sons who, on the Confederate side, offered up their lives in defense of their principles and their convictions."[63]

Seeking to harmonize the irreconciled middle border region during the brief flowering of sectional reconciliation that accompanied the Spanish-American War in 1898, in October 1899 a local GAR post in Evansville, Indiana, hosted the first national Blue-Gray reunion. Trumpeting their river city as "the Great Gateway between North and South," organizers tried to harness "real reconciliation" in pursuit of "business relations." Evansville's location astride the lower reaches of the Ohio River allowed reconciliation to be used as a tool for economic self-promotion as much as for sectional harmony. City leaders insisted that its tobacco-related industry, conservative racial relations, rail and river connections, and a population of both former Confederate and federal soldiers made Evansville, as much as Louisville, a gateway to Henry Watterson's New South. The city fairground witnessed florid reconciliationist speeches, fireworks, and sham battles, not between former Yankees and rebels but rather among a unified and nonsectional host of Americans. In awkwardly reconciled form, these displays of national unity had been bested the previous year, when surviving veterans of John Hunt Morgan's cavalry attended the national GAR encampment in Cincinnati as special guests of an Ohio cavalry unit that "Morgan's Men" had captured during the war.[64]

Even the most cursory displays of what one historian has called "symbolic reconciliation" did not extend to the nation's westernmost, and most irreconciled, war border. Where the war before the war had started, the first of a long series of war reunions had gathered under the guise of sectional harmony. In October 1898 near Blue Springs, Missouri, former combatants and their wives and children met for a two-day event billed as informal "country picnics" for "patriotic, home-loving, and peaceable" rural farmers, as the *Kansas City Star* and other local papers pronounced. In fact, its attendees were surviving compatriots of the war's most notorious guerrilla, William C. Quantrill. Claiming to be nonpartisan social gatherings designed to bury the proverbial hatchet, or knife as it were, these reunions sought far more. The first site was carefully and politically chosen, Quantrill having hatched the 1863 raid on Lawrence on a nearby farm. One featured speaker was Francis Cockrell, a former Missouri Confederate general and now a U.S. senator with a UDC post named for him. The other was Frank James, the former bushwhacker whose brother, Jesse, spearheaded and symbolized the entwinement of Confederate and partisan war narratives into a pantheon of southern patriotism, invoking Lost Cause bromides. Held in the heart of one of the counties depopulated by Thomas Ewing's Order No. 11, several of these reunions fell not coincidentally on the anniversary of the Lawrence Massacre, a day of commemorative gatherings its survivors had begun a few years earlier. (See figure 8.2.) By 1913, on the fiftieth anniversary, speakers at Lawrence condemned the Quantrill reunions as "reminders of the barbarism of slavery" and threatened vengeance against participants. Entirely aware of the

Figure 8.2 Quantrill reunion, Independence, Missouri, 1906. Site of the first Confederate monument erected in the nation in 1864 and dedicated by local women to guerrillas killed on a raid, and with Missouri being the birthplace of the forerunner of the United Daughters of the Confederacy, Independence was the scene of several annual reunions of veterans, wives, and widows of the war's most notorious guerrilla band, led by William C. Quantrill. These reunions were often held on or coincident to the anniversary of the raid on Lawrence, Kansas. Courtesy State Historical Society of Missouri.

sanctity that Lawrence had afforded John Brown and wartime Kansas Jayhawkers, and with the active assistance of the Missouri UDC, the "Quantrill Men" responded with deadly partisan weaponry. Of the raid, one participant claimed, "None of us has ever regretted it."[65]

Three decades after the end of the war, white southerners could not have won what amounted to a cultural victory in former middle border slave states without broader appeal than Confederate war narratives. County histories published by amateur historians and professional genealogists routinely offered readers stilted, southernized narratives of their home communities, and especially the war in them. Literary sentimentalism about the Old South found far larger audiences, such as Kentucky novelist Annie Fellows Johnston's *The Little Colonel* series, published between 1895 and 1907. Johnston's twelve children's novels, set in an idyllic and fictional Bluegrass town, used war and Lost Cause regional stereotypes to confirm northern readers' sectionalized conceptions of Kentucky as a Confederate state while appealing to southern readers with gauzy images of the region's benign antebellum slaveholding past.[66]

The politics of sacrifice would undergird the issue of veterans' pensions, offering unionists in these states a pyrrhic victory in the middle border's long war after the war. In 1890 Congress had passed the Dependent Pension Act, supporting honorably discharged veterans of the federal armies, white or black. When Confederate veterans were excluded, southern congressmen argued unsuccessfully for inclusion in the pension system. Long after most former Confederate states offered pensions to indigent veterans, the legislatures of Missouri and Kentucky had not yet acted. With few veterans residing in the state, in 1911 Missouri approved pensions for them, but not for their widows. (By 1927, with 1,472 living pensioners residing in the state, less than three thousand claims had been filed.) With more veterans, Kentucky witnessed a larger and more partisan struggle to provide them benefits, with Lost Cause rhetoric woven into historical justifications for secession and war. In 1910 Kentucky's governor, Augustus Wilson, a native New Yorker, vetoed a pension bill for Confederate veterans, arguing that the state had not seceded from the Union. Two years later, with a new governor, James McCready, a Confederate veteran, the legislature passed another bill to grant pensions to veterans and widows of deceased soldiers. When the governor signed the bill, the state's auditor, a former unionist, denied payment to claimants. The state's court of appeals ruled that because the federal government had failed to recognize the "public service" of all Confederate veterans, the state must honor them. From August 1913 until 1931, the commonwealth spent nearly $5 million on some forty-seven hundred Confederate veterans or their widows. Confederacy's legitimacy and Kentucky's place in it having been settled legally, the politics of wartime sacrifice affirmed southerners' cultural victory.[67]

§

As the war's semicentennial approached, Kentucky offered the apotheosis of exclusivist war commemoration and posed a conundrum to regional memory. Among the state's aging Confederates, plans were underway to acquire twenty acres of Jefferson Davis's former family farm near Fairview, in the state's southwestern portion, one of many hamlets that sprang up after the war "without a sense of belonging in any particular place or having any particular history... anything but an old Southern town," as former resident Robert Penn Warren recalled. When the former Confederate president could not purchase the small tract and the family's four-room cabin, locals bought it and then sold "the park" to the UCV. When Davis's death in 1889 triggered a frenzy of Confederate commemoration in states that claimed southern heritage, veterans and other commemorative organizations envisioned his birthplace as a site for the "crowning glory of Confederate monument work... [as] memorable to the South as Lincoln's to the entire nation." Funding woes delayed further progress.[68]

Another national birthplace shrine in Kentucky also was in the making, situated only a hundred miles north, near Hodgenville. With nationwide contributions from black and white membership as well as an appropriation from the Kentucky legislature, the New York–based Lincoln Farm Association laid the cornerstone of what would become a monument to the martyred president. Construction began in 1909, the centennial of Lincoln's birth, and two years later, during the semicentennial of the start of the war, thousands thronged to dedicate the monument. The neoclassical, granite structure sat atop a hillside three miles south of town, carved out into fifty-six entrance stairs that housed a log cabin billed as the assassinated president's birthplace. Among them was New Yorker Theodore Roosevelt, who ascended the bully pulpit to claim that Lincoln had saved the nation by ending slavery.[69]

Southerners demanded a response. Long awaited, construction began on the Jefferson Davis birthplace memorial, led by former Kentucky Confederates such as its governor, Simon B. Buckner, and Louisville's Bennett H. Young, a "Morgan Man" who, after being captured, had escaped to Canada and led a company of "Retributors" during the 1864 St. Albans Raid. Young also served as an adviser on the UDC's construction of a monument to Andersonville prison commandant Henry Wirz, the only Confederate executed after the war for war crimes. The Jefferson Davis Home Association soon took charge of the sluggish fundraising, and a reunion of the Orphan Brigade in Glasgow in 1907, coincident with the Lincoln birth site efforts and the ensuing Civil War semicentennial commemorations, goaded organizers to broaden their efforts. (Congress had also appropriated the construction of a Lincoln Memorial in Washington, for which Kentucky would contribute native "Bowling Green" marble.) In 1916, at the national UDC meeting in Dallas, Texas, delegates voted to take on the Davis monument as theirs, spurring contributions especially in the former Confederacy.

"OUR MONUMENT"
Second highest monument in the world. Will be 351 feet when completed.

This obelisk is now being erected by the people of the South to the memory of Jefferson Davis at his birthplace at Fairview, Kentucky.

Figure 8.3 Contribution solicitation card for Jefferson Davis birthplace monument, Fairview, Kentucky, ca. 1918. Begun in 1916 with contributions from the national United Daughters of the Confederacy and local groups, the monument was dedicated on June 7, 1924, at a final cost of nearly $200,000. An estimated ten thousand people, including former Confederate soldiers as well as Kentucky unionists and federal veterans, witnessed the dedication. Courtesy Filson Historical Society.

Ultimately the national UDC contributed $20,000, and the state chapter advanced plans to raise funds for a Jefferson Davis highway system, paving a web of roads to link isolated communities throughout the counties surrounding the monument site.[70]

The following year construction began on a concrete obelisk "three hundred and fifty-one feet in height, the second highest monument in the world and the greatest structure of its kind ever built by private contributions" (see figure 8.3). The end of World War I, during which nationalism had again been victorious over wartime dissent, and the sudden onset of a postwar economic depression, again stunted fund-raising and put off its completion. At last, on June 7, 1924, at a final cost of some $200,000, an estimated ten thousand people, including former Confederate soldiers as well as Kentucky unionists and federal veterans, witnessed the dedication of what Robert Penn Warren remembered as "a faint white finger pointing skyward." Only months earlier, as the finger was nearing completion, the local Ku Klux Klan had burned a fiery cross on the spire's yet unpeaked top. Its unmistakable physical and symbolic presence announced that this former contested ground south of the Ohio River had been claimed by way of the anything-but-dead Confederacy for the living, and now completed, South.[71]

Rally Round the Flags

On May 30, 1923, a year before the dedication of the Jefferson Davis birthplace memorial in Fairview, Kentucky, a fracas marred Louisville's annual Memorial Day celebration. The city's American Legion post, principally comprised of World War I veterans but also boasting some from the Spanish-American War, planned a special parade that would include a first-ever joint observance by former Civil War foes. The procession would march eastward on Broadway to the city's national cemetery, where the old soldiers would together lay a wreath to honor fallen comrades. In the afternoon, these men were symbolically to reunite this once bitterly divided middle border city. Yet even before it began, the event was marred by uncivil discord—and with it, visions of reconciliation of that seemingly distant conflict.

Shortly after noon, twenty-four residents of Kentucky's Confederate Veterans' Home in nearby Pewee Valley arrived as the American Legion's invited guests to take their place in line. Several had also fought in Cuba, wearing the government's blue uniform. They now wore their rebel uniforms, with shined buttons and creased pants, carrying "at their head the Stars and Stripes and the Stars and Bars." Within minutes of their arrival, GAR participants, hailing from both sides of the river, objected. Having not been informed of the invitation to the gray-clad veterans, they said "they could not march under the banner for which they fought...the flag of the Lost Cause." The source of the dispute was the verbal invitation—although not the written one, which American Legion organizers freely admitted to sending—which offered that these aged men could "bring their colors," as they did routinely to Decoration Day and Lee-Davis Day commemorations. Believing they were free to choose which "colors" to bring—the Stars and Stripes or the Stars and Bars—the rebel veterans had brought both. "Our men are as loyal to the Government as any G. A. R.," protested the commandant of the Confederate Home. "It was understood that we would have our old flag with us." Unyielding, the GAR's commandant retorted, "One God, one Country and one Flag is the motto I have always been taught."[1]

"[H]aving 'swallowed the insult' to bear it like soldiers should," rather than submit to the bluecoats for yet another ignominious defeat, these rebels withdrew from the parade and returned home later that afternoon. Many of the eight thousand onlookers hissed their exclusion, and the local UDC chapter refused to march in the procession, which went on as planned albeit without rebel participants. One marcher, Louisville physician Forrest Gabbert, a Spanish-American War veteran who had ridden with Teddy Roosevelt at San Juan Hill, complained loudly. "What's the use of waving a bloody shirt after the fight's over?" he railed. "I don't care who ordered the Confederate flag out of the parade, it was narrow-minded. Half of my ancestors were Confederates and the other half on the other side." A litany of denunciations appeared in local newspapers over the next few days.

The controversy prompted the American Legion's post commander to issue a formal statement expressing "deep regret," framing the war along reconciliationist lines that did not mention slavery or emancipation. "The Civil War arose out of a conflict of honest opinion as to the proper construction of certain provisions of the Constitution of the United States," it read. "It is known of all men that the people of the former Confederate States accepted in good faith and abided by the results of the Civil War." Sixty years after the war, for its white veterans harmony was still elusive, a fact the GAR commandant himself recognized. "[W]e feel that in the celebration of future Memorial Days, Jefferson Post ought not, as a body, take part in a joint celebration except when all matters of possible conflict between the veterans who wore the Blue and the veterans who wore the Gray have been amicably settled in advance."

Just over a year later, on July 4, 1924, in Frankfort's Green Hill Cemetery, the Colored Women's Relief Corps, an auxiliary of one of Kentucky's four black GAR posts, unveiled the first monument to the state's African American soldiers. None of these war veterans in attendance had been invited to march the previous year with white soldiers in Louisville, nor had they been invited to the dedication of the Jefferson Davis birthplace monument just a month before. A mile closer to town and near the venerated remains of Daniel Boone, the city's Confederate monument stood sentry over the capital of this former loyal state, as it had already done for more than three decades. Within two years the Kentucky legislature would adopt Stephen Foster's sentimental antebellum "plantation" song, "My Old Kentucky Home, Good Night," as its state anthem. That it was conceived in Cincinnati by the same composer who was reputedly inspired by Harriet Beecher Stowe's novel *Uncle Tom's Cabin* and was banned as a play in Kentucky mattered little. The war had at last been won, and by whom was in no dispute. Left behind was a border, between white and black but also between war legacies lived as newly defined regions.[2]

Conclusion

The antagonisms that remade the former middle border region were not the result alone of semicentennial commemorations of the Civil War. A half-century of politics—formally at the national and state levels and informally as innumerable, personalized war experiences retold by countless civilians and soldiers on both sides of the rivers— emplaced exclusivist cultural narratives of that bitterly lived war that themselves lived on in discrete American imaginations, maintaining divergent yet not fully divested claims to the West as a white man's country.

In the region's former slave states, white residents did more than distort a quasi-Confederate past. Pushing past war boundaries, they articulated a southernized narrative of their states in order to transcend the immediate celebration of a Confederate heritage and achieve cultural identification with the Old South. Commemoratively, they bridged the Confederate tradition to obscure their loyal wartimes by accessing their slaveholding pasts and articulating the shared experience between the antebellum and the postwar South. Deeply contested, the halting construction of white southern identity buttressed their opposition to the destruction of slavery, to freedpeople's acquisition of citizenship rights, and to all those who had accomplished the latter.[1]

One such southerner was Missouri's William Barclay Napton. In 1880, after losing his seat on Missouri's supreme court, this native New Jerseyite resigned himself to living out the rest of his life at Elkhill, his rural Saline County home. He would do so largely alone but for his memories, in which the war was central. In 1861 he had lost his seat by refusing to take the loyalty oath, and late in December 1862 his wife had died in childbirth amid harassment by federal militia over Napton's dubious allegiance. Within days of her death, which left Napton with ten motherless children, unionist state militia twice raided his home and then banished him to St. Louis for the rest of the war. All of his forty-five slaves were soon gone, either by escaping or through military confiscation, and most of his nine sons—including the two eldest, who fought for the Confederacy—fled the war to the Far West and remained there. In the marginalia in his personal issues of *Living Age*, Napton characterized effusive sentimentalities about the late president as "malignities," and in his photo album he tucked a carte de visite of Lincoln's assassin alongside a tintype image of his oldest son, William Jr., standing proudly in his Confederate frock coat. Napton merged it all into a Lost Cause narrative. So would many of his neighbors in the former slaveholding and political locus of the state, the western counties along the Missouri River. They would spearhead the state's Confederate tradition, making Kansas City its commemorative capital, standing sentry against Jayhawker invaders and overlooking Missouri's earlier lost cause: Kansas. As if to affirm the dualism of the war's outcome in this once loyal state, the city's growth as a shipping center for agricultural products contrasted with northernized St. Louis, the entrepôt for federal military authority in the late war and known among rural white Missourians as the state's "Yankee capital."[2]

The war had destroyed all that he considered civilized, and Napton saw himself as a victim. His place as a respected jurist and large landholder was entwined inextricably with his former status as a slaveholder, which, once the North and the federal government had inaugurated its war against the South, overshadowed his former qualified support for the Union. By criticizing the federal government for unlawful intrusions and by maintaining the southern racial and social order against the North's leveling chaos, he suffered at the hands of soldiers and politicians. Through hard wartime experience, this former westerner lay associative claim to southern heritage. By the time he died in 1883, he had become a southerner by right, enough for one of his sons to recall, "I heard him say once toward the latter part of his life that there was not a drop of 'Yankee' blood in his veins—if there was 'I would take a knife and let it out' to use his own words. No native Virginian ever disliked a Yankee more than he." In 1910 his eldest son, a Confederate veteran, would publish his county's defiant, southernized history.[3]

Many other southerners responded similarly to northerners' portrayal of the war as a treasonous slaveholders' rebellion. A year after Napton's death, Kentucky businessman Henry Hillenmeyer warned Lexington listeners that northern radicals used the issue of slavery to malign even the most sacred of the nation's heroes. To Hillenmeyer and his audience, these patriots were maligned because of their heroic defense of individual rights. George Washington "fought for the holy cause of liberty, for the sacred rights of mankind... and yet he has been branded with the name of *Rebel*.... Yes Gentlemen *rebel*! Washington! A *rebel*!... But let it be remembered that the first principle of jurisprudence is: that the laws of every country must be conducive to the welfare of its inhabitants.... [T]o violate an unjust law is to violate no law... therefore in the true signification of the term Washington was *NO Rebel*." When in 1890 Leeland Hathaway, a former "Morgan Man," spoke to Lexington's UDC chapter, many of whom had endured the hellish war at home, he was likely sensitive to charges of guerrilla-style activities. He lauded Jefferson Davis as a patriotic home-front defender who "loved his country and worshiped her flag," he claimed. "But he loved the South better and he loved his state and home best. This is what makes the *Patriot*—The local attachment—the Clinging to our spot dearer than all others—the love of State County town, Home[!]" Born in Missouri's Burnt District the same year as Hillenmeyer's speech, Harry S. Truman heard renditions of this portrayal as a boy in Independence and ascribed to his "debt to history" the irregular war memory, "the Southern side of the thing, the Confederate side." He described family lore about hiding silver and slaves from Kansas Red Legs; vigorous defense of Quantrill's men, including by a maternal relative, as home-front defenders; vilification of Order No. 11; condemnation of Reconstruction as a mistake; and adoption of solid Democratic politics. Despite his national reputation as a plain-speaking midwesterner, such collective family experiences of that war and its aftermath made Truman a proud, lifelong and self-conscious southerner.[4]

The skillful and intentional melding of the slaveholding and Confederate traditions affirmed southern cultural exceptionalism. Former farms now referred to as plantations, and white-coated and white-haired planter "colonels" with their boundless hospitality and bourbon whiskey now considered genteel traditions, are all in stark contrast to hard-working, miserly, and uncultured men and women on small rural homesteads above these states' borders, giving potency to their southernized version of history. For many residents of these former loyal states, bitterness over the end of slavery and the imposition of northern racial imperatives undergirded the widespread adoption of the Confederate tradition. After 1902 the entwinement was seen no more clearly than were the Kentucky UDC's efforts to ban stage productions of *Uncle Tom's Cabin*, the greatest blight on southerners' carefully cultivated Old South imagery. Long a favorite of performing troupes in the western free states, after the war the play's widespread adoption of blackface minstrelsy attracted full houses comprised of working-class white audiences. "Uncle Tom and his cabin seem to have a place in the hearts of the people," wrote one Kansas editor in 1878. Audience receptions varied, from raucous approval of Simon Legree's brutal whippings, to indignant laments over its attack on "southern life," to egging and even mobbing of cast members and the destruction of sets. Productions in the state's major cities were often accompanied by parades and heavy African American attendance.[5]

The opposition to the play acted as a catalyst for full adoption of the Confederate tradition in Kentucky. With the state being the novel's (and play's) primary setting, its negative depictions of slavery there proved an affront to UDC members. Four years of petitions, replete with racialized language and Old South imagery, and support from UDC and SCV chapters in other former slave states pushed the Kentucky legislature to ban stage performances of *Uncle Tom's Cabin* in 1906. Counter-petitions from the state's African Americans and other interest groups resulted in a similar ban on productions of Thomas Dixon's *The Clansman*. Ostensibly passed for the sake of social harmony, the ban made it "unlawful to present plays in this Commonwealth that are based on antagonism alleged formerly to exist between master and slave, or that excites race prejudice." Beyond arbitrating the competing memory narratives of the war and its coming, the law's primary goal was to confirm southern racial norms hard won by postwar political conflicts. Only nine years later, Kentucky filmmaker D. W. Griffith's *The Birth of a Nation*, an adaptation of Dixon's novel and thus exempted from the state's "Uncle Tom Law," shattered box office records, despite being banned in states like Ohio and Kansas and in cities like Chicago and St. Louis.[6]

In thousands of white Kentucky households, the postwar politics of memory edited the history of the war, their state, and themselves. In Louisville, by 1910 Tom Bullitt had long forgotten what he once called uncertain "southern feelings." This Confederate veteran—whose slaveholding family with its divided allegiances had railed against abolitionism, yet who waited until 1862 to enlist and then took a wartime bullet and survived a lengthy imprisonment in Ohio, knowing that his older brother, Joshua, Kentucky's wartime attorney general, had been arrested for refusing to carry out wartime emancipation—helped to secure his city's and state's lost causes. Bullitt's postwar years had been good ones, and he had gained wealth and prestige through his thriving law practice. He and his youngest brother, Henry, both of whom farmed portions of their sprawling family farm, Oxmoor, became deeply involved in the Confederate Association of Kentucky as well as the local UCV chapter. Tom attended Confederate reunions throughout the South, assisted with the Southern Expositions in Louisville in the 1880s, and helped organize the UCV reunion in Louisville in 1900. Both Tom and Henry contributed to Louisville's thriving Confederate periodicals, which sought to create the New South by rooting the city and state in the Old South. Bullitt's magnolias distorted his memory of Kentucky's antebellum past. His slavery apologia, *My Life at Oxmoor*, completed in time for the war's semicentennial, framed a gauzy portrait for his antebellum family and state that bore only an oblique resemblance to either.[7]

In 1926, two years after the dedication of Kentucky's Jefferson Davis birthplace memorial, historian E. Merton Coulter offered readers a wry adage summing up the Civil War and especially its southernized aftermath. "Kentucky," claimed Coulter, "waited until after the war to secede from the Union," an inference to politicized obstruction as a means of defying Congress's Republican authority during and after Reconstruction. As for southern states generally, their experience of "frustration, failure, and defeat," and especially the end of slavery by dint of war, proved the linchpin to what historian C. Vann Woodward has argued was the making of the modern South. Indeed, historian James C. Cobb writes of those living in states of the former Confederacy that "the loyalties of white southerners...had actually converged not primarily on their nation-state but on their common struggle with the North." As they appropriated an embittered, southernized historical consciousness alongside white residents of the former Confederacy, these border residents transcended the Confederate tradition, reimagining southern patriotism as a response to their respective states' own ill-fated stances within, rather than without, the Union. The halfhearted embrace of the postwar reconciliation in these states evidenced the fact that many white residents had affiliated with the new, obstructionist southern order. Only after the war's semicentennial did the widely used antebellum term "border states" give way to its modern iteration, the "Border South."[8]

Above the Ohio River, the Civil War's legacy found different, more complicated forms. More divided at the end of the war than at its beginning, these former western states hallowed their ground by competing scriptures, reinterpreting the war's meaning for divergent communities. During Reconstruction, Republicans saw their military victory eroded on two fronts. The anti-emancipation "Loyal West" cant in these states found particular strength in their lower, rural portions, where intense postwar struggles over nationalism and traditionalism saw the entrenchment of conservative racial traditions and resistant white supremacy in the form of black exclusion ordinances, sundown towns, and "whitecappings." By the late 1870s, in the aftermath of the Liberal Republicans' defeat, the term "Middle West" emerged to distinguish the region, and more specifically to resist the emancipationist cant so closely associated with the North. For progressives there, the latest erosion of the fuller war victory and northern Republicans' postwar revolution was nearly as threatening as the Lost Cause narrative and the southern renascence in neighboring Kentucky and Missouri. Fighting another insurgency required conjuring the war yet again, by rejuvenating the collective image of antimodern traditionalists in the lower portions of their own states for southerners below the rivers: irredeemably backward, violent, uncivilized, and irreconcilable, in stark contrast to northerners' progressive, lawful, and modern society. Northern journalists portrayed the postwar violence in those states as antecedent to the war itself, whether referring to feuding in Kentucky's Appalachian counties, nightriding in its western counties' dark tobacco-producing "black patch," gunfights in town squares in Missouri's Ozarks, James-gang-style railroad and bank robberies in its central and western counties, or vigilante wars waged in cash-strapped counties against local officials trying to collect prewar railroad bond debts. After the opening of John A. Roebling's Ohio River bridge in 1867, Cincinnatians purposefully referred to it as the "Gateway to the South," while a year later an Iowan wrote to Kentuckian Samuel Haycraft (whose invitation to Lincoln in 1860 to speak in his birth state spurred the then-presidential aspirant to ask, "Would not the people Lynch me?"): "We [are] up here in *North* America and you in the other quarter of the world '*Old Kentucky.*' "[9]

As the century neared its end, Ohioan Wilbur H. Siebert offered a consciously northernized narrative for his state and region. Born to German immigrants in

Columbus a year after the war ended, Siebert had graduate training in history at Harvard and returned to his hometown in 1891 to teach at the state's new land grant university. This progressive Republican was deeply angered at conservative Democratic resurgence in his home state and the fact that memoirs and narratives published by northern writers, white and black, about a legacy of the Civil War largely ignored the contribution of his former western region to the emancipationist legacy: the famed Underground Railroad. Eager to lay full claim, Siebert and his students gathered materials; corresponded with aged former western abolitionists, conductors, and their descendants; and sent out surveys. He compiled the responses, along with newspaper and journal accounts and other sources, into a collection of vague and often exaggerated reminiscences of the shadowy escape network in his home region that proved a refraction of the actual activities of those who served on the self-styled "Liberty Line."[10]

In 1898 he published his pathbreaking book, *The Underground Railroad from Slavery to Freedom*, centered primarily on his home region. The work drew criticism for promoting the movement's legend more than chronicling its history, but it quickly became influential. Historian David W. Blight has written that the book "reflected the sentimental retrospection of many Northerners as the century came to a close." Especially receptive were white women and noncombatant men, who sought an "alternative veteranhood...a way of saying that they too had served in the great cause." By helping to destroy the peculiar institution, these civilians were nearly as responsible for winning the war as the veterans themselves.[11]

Siebert's northernizing impulse was driven in part by the contested legacy of the war in his home state. Overwriting wartime dissent and his region's inconvenient slaveholding past might help to temper his state's recent Democratic resurgence and pervasive Jim Crow proscriptions, obstructions to full embrace of the Union tradition. Indeed, in 1887 the state legislature had shipped a second statue of an Ohioan to display in the U.S. Capitol's "Statuary Hall," alongside that of James Garfield. Siebert was among those Republicans embarrassed by the fact that the new statue depicted William Allen, the former proslavery Democratic U.S. senator, governor, and outspoken wartime critic of Abraham Lincoln.[12]

The placement of Allen's statue offers a window into yet another war narrative forgotten amid the regional realignment of the former West. Many rural residents, especially in these states' Butternut counties, rejected the postwar northernization of the Middle West's new cities—Cleveland, Milwaukee, Indianapolis, and especially Chicago—whose residents benefited from economic nationalism as an engine of victory to transform the upper portions of their region. Indeed, by the 1920s the second incarnation of the Ku Klux Klan found its strongest membership and national leadership in the former Butternut region, led by southern Indiana, where a half century earlier the nation's first recorded incident of racial cleansing had occurred as a violent protest against emancipation in the midst of a civil war raging within the region. Seeking to confront the persistent contradictions there, small-town Progressives like editor William Allen White of Emporia, Kansas, coined the term "Midwest" ornamented with tropes of pastoralism, social progress, independence, democratic egalitarianism, and civic virtue. Ironically, their crusade was as much against the modernizing urbanism that was by then controlling parts of their region as against the rural traditionalism that marred their progressive vision for it. Rather than denote "an absence of region," as commonly argued of the modern Midwest, the term in fact illustrates its yet unreconciled intraregional contest over the meanings and broader outcomes of that distant war.[13]

By then the enduring complexities of the middle border had goaded northern academics to employ war narratives as exclusivist, cultural interpretations forged by westward migrations and the former presence—or absence—of slavery. Reuben Gold Thwaites, the Massachusetts-born former journalist and Yale-educated director of the State Historical Society of Wisconsin, chronicled his six-week "revival" trip down the Ohio, making frequent allusions to the distinctive cultures that Yankees and southerners had created on respective banks of the river. "Doubtless before the late civil war,—all the ante-bellum travelers agree in this,—when the blight of slavery was resting on Virginia and Kentucky," the transplanted Yankee concluded, "the south shore of the Ohio was as another country." Like Thwaites, Archer Hulbert, a historian at Ohio's Marietta College in the West's original Yankee colony, wrote in 1906 that the Ohio River border was merely a "projection of Mason's and Dixon's line.... That slavery clause in the masterly Ordinance [of 1787], kept sacred by the conscience of immigrants from all parts of the seaboard, was a flaming sword stretching from the Alleghenies to the Mississippi."[14]

Academic exclusivism was countered by the powerful literary voice of a self-conscious westerner who determinedly complicated the argument that slavery had formed the hard border that led to the war, and emancipation had led to full freedom as its celebrated outcome. Writing as Mark Twain, Missourian Samuel L. Clemens offered national audiences a discordant narrative of the war's meaning and outcome. Clemens recalled that his mother believed slavery was "right, righteous, sacred," and had believed it himself, enough to enlist in a quasi-Missouri State Guard company. Charged with disloyalty after refusing to take the state's provisional oath, Clemens quickly left the state for the Far West, in large part to avoid war service, so his main war contribution was a semiautobiographical short story about the brief misadventures of the pro-Confederate Marion Rangers. *The Adventures of Tom Sawyer*, published in 1876, offered a benign view of antebellum life on the middle border's rivers and his boyhood hometown of Hannibal, feeding northerners' perceptions of cultural persistence in his former slave state, not only as racially conservative but culturally southern. "Mr. Clemens describes things as they really were, in Missouri," boasted a critic, "and as they still are." In fact, he ridiculed romantic notions of honor that "had so large a hand in making Southern character... that is in great measure responsible for the War."[15]

Having achieved literary success, in the mid-1880s Clemens embraced neither the hypocritical triumphalism of the North nor the feigned reconciliation of the South, and he confronted his state's and region's complex history of slavery by satirizing racial subordination as the war's primary national legacy. Much like *Uncle Tom's Cabin*, Twain's *Adventures of Huckleberry Finn* wove a redemptive borderland tale of humanity within the inhumanity of slavery. Employing a male slave as one of the novel's main characters, Twain offered Huck's moral decision to assist his friend Jim to escape—"All right then, I'll go to hell"—as a symbolic condemnation of his home region's pervasive white supremacism, antebellum and postbellum. Fictionalized St. Petersburg sat across the Mississippi from western Illinois, where Jim could not safely escape, and spoke directly to the unreconciled racial outcome of the war. For carving through exclusivist stereotypes in *Huckleberry Finn* that he had helped to make, he now drew wide criticism from northern reviewers. As one groused, Clemens "demolish[ed] something that has no place in the book." Taken together, Clemens's books served as much as they attacked the emergent cant of southernness. By that time he was no longer living in the "Far West" of his boyhood, or in fact in any West, but rather in Hartford, Connecticut, where he fully embraced the modernization that resulted from the war and was nearly bankrupted by bad investments. He managed to financially support the dying Union hero, Ulysses S. Grant, as he wrote his war memoirs. Like Grant's Ohio, Clemens's native state, Missouri, was to most of his readers no longer "out West." Unlike the state above the Ohio, Missouri was now "down South." The Far West lay in Nevada and California, where Clemens had been a journalist after leaving the war, across the newly purposed Continental Divide, no longer a natural landmark since the completion of the transcontinental railroad but rather a political boundary between East and West, and an aspirational symbol of national unity to heal the jagged regionalism dividing the North and South. Americans either conveniently forgot the wartime violence that occurred there, such as the Dakota Sioux hangings and the Sand Creek massacres, or viewed them as part of the ongoing Indian Wars. Collectively, these entwined conflicts redefined Twain's former West by moving its boundaries to the nation's newest imagined frontier. There, as Ohio Radical Republican U.S. senator Benjamin Wade judged, "disunion could [not] possibly take place." Only a few years later, in 1875 Philip Sheridan wrote from the Rio Grande in this new West to his fellow westerner, William T. Sherman (the two had been raised less than ten miles apart in southern Ohio) of the unfamiliar cultural mélange he encountered in this newest West: "It is hard to tell who is who, and what is what, on that border," he admitted. "The state of affairs is about as mixed as the river is indefinite as a boundary line." Only a decade and a half earlier, before the war that remade America's regions, this letter might have been written by any of these men to describe not a fully formed border but the rivered borderland of their youth.[16]

§

The stretching shadows of the Civil War have proven persistent and complicated on this former middle border. Using historical events, marketers employ "Border War" imagery to lure collegiate sports fans to athletic contests between state universities in Kansas and Missouri, and Missouri and Illinois. Kentucky and Missouri schools boast mascots with war-born, cultural names such as Rebels, Cavaliers, and Colonels, while north of the rivers one finds their complements, including Railsplitters, Generals, and Farmers. At Bardstown, Kentucky, the Federal Hill mansion, former residence of Pennsylvania-born judge John Rowan and the centerpiece of the Old Kentucky Home State Historical Site, is referred to as the inspiration for Stephen Foster's famous "plantation song." This and other latter-day "plantations" in Kentucky and Missouri welcome visitors to their states' genteel southern pasts, extolling their former owners' luxuriant hospitality and benign narratives of slavery. (Ironically, Foster's lyrics, most of which are unsung as the state's official song, reflect the lament of a slave sold south to Louisiana.) North of the rivers, aversion to southern cultural perceptions influences public representations of distinctiveness. In the 1990s the board of a fast-growing north suburban Cincinnati school district voted to build simultaneously two identical new high schools. It soon faced a naming problem. Though the land tracts for the schools lay several miles directly north and south of one another, the board chose to name them Lakota East and West, largely because parents whose children would attend the southernmost school pressured the district's board, not wanting the school to bear the negative cultural stigma of the designation "South." Billboards in southern Illinois had beckoned tourists to the state's infamous "Old Slave House" since the 1930s, but in 2000 they quickly came down when the state's Historic Preservation Agency at last acquired John Crenshaw's Hickory Hill with the contingency of its state-funded restoration as a historical site. The embarrassed Illinois state legislature quickly closed the house to the public. It remains closed, and with it the most glaring reminder of the "Land of Lincoln's" long-forgotten history of slavery. As travelers zoom west on Interstate 71-75 through downtown Cincinnati, the National Underground Railroad Freedom Center, the staid edifice to "Freedom National" for the north side of the Ohio River, stands sentry to Kentucky on its southern shore. Across the highway, the elevated sign announcing the corporate home of the Western and Southern Life Insurance Company, founded in 1888, offers another, less understood reminder of the transitory nature of American regions. That opacity only grows by traveling farther west. Crossing the Mississippi River at St. Louis, travelers cannot avoid the massive arch billed as the "Gateway to the West," while miles farther yet in Missouri on Interstate 70, nearing Kansas, they are greeted by signs advertising that they have entered "Little Dixie," the moniker for the state's former slaveholding center. Once in Kansas City, another western gateway and Missouri's Confederate capital since its postwar political renascence in the 1880s, they will find joined, unlike in Cincinnati or just west on the Kansas prairie, the West and South in a nonsectional embrace.

More than a century ago, in 1893 a young historian spoke at a professional conference in Chicago, the capital of the emergent Middle West and the site of the World's Columbian Exposition. Frederick Jackson Turner offered an emphatic rejoinder to census-based claims that America's western expansion was dead. So long as boundaries between civilization and savagery existed, there would be an advancing American frontier, as there had been since the nation's earliest settlement. As his career would bear out, Turner's western "problem" was reconciling two interrelated yet warring themes: how the democratic frontier experience shaped American character, and how geographic—meaning cultural—sectionalism influenced political, social, and economic modalities throughout the nation's history. In both of Turner's themes, the West was "a phase of social organization...a form of society rather than an area."[17]

For the self-professed western historian, born in Wisconsin and trained at Johns Hopkins University in Baltimore, Maryland, in a former border slave state astride the famed Mason-Dixon Line, Turner there saw for the first time the complexities of regions when measured against established sectional narratives. He would wrestle with them his entire career, seeking to understand the transitive nature of the American frontier. At the turn of the twentieth century, the former western borderland had been replaced, or would soon be, by binate organizing principles known as North and South (and their variants above the rivers, the urbanized Middle West and ruralized Midwest), tangling his efforts to expand his frontier thesis into a sweeping sectional interpretation of the history of American civilization. After moving to Harvard, he struggled to complete his big book, largely because he sought by formal politics and other distinguishing data to sectionalize the diverse antebellum cultures and politics of his home region. His essays did not anticipate that it had taken a civil war to accomplish this, and even then not fully. In Cambridge, Massachusetts, the politics of region surrounding the war's semicentennial had rendered him among his northern colleagues a determinist, a "western sectionalist," and an essayist whose work was, ironically, "provincial." He was—like Clement L. Vallandigham, who embraced these phrases before the war came—a man without a country. Unable to conquer this academic frontier between civilization and savagery or to reconcile his amorphous concept of region in a sectionalized America, Turner left, bound for the newest western frontier, California, where he would spend the rest of his career and life. Left far behind was a border, no longer between East and West, but rather between North and South.[18]

Politics are destiny: high and low, urban and rural, economic, social, cultural, aesthetic, racial. Among the bitter fruits of the Civil War and its aftermath in the former middle border region was a struggle for ownership of new definitions of places and peoples that masked successive, unreconciled political conflicts, before, during, and after the war. The border that now defined them was completed only after the cool political culture of sectional moderation was replaced with the angry cultural politics of region. The former white man's country, which had long assimilated slavery and freedom into a western consensus, was vanquished by antagonistic cultures of slavery and abolition under new regional names: southern, northern, and midwestern.

Loss as much as victory thus defined the new regionalism on both sides of the rivers. Less overwhelmed by outside forces than driven by internal conflicts framed against competing organizing principles known as sections, the West, a place of multiplicities imagined as individual and national possibilities, was pushed on rather than being been won or lost. In its place there would be two regions, two core communities created by exclusivist politics that imagined as much as they had experienced the war. The national confluence once represented as the West was remade as South and North, the great divide symbolized by the former region's now-wide rivers.[19]

Change starts at the margins, but it is completed in the middle.

ABBREVIATIONS

AAS	American Antiquarian Society, Worcester, Massachusetts
AHR	*American Historical Review*
ALPL	Abraham Lincoln Presidential Library, Springfield, Illinois
AMA	American Missionary Association Archives, 1839–1882, 261 microfilm reels, Amistad Research Center, New Orleans, Louisiana
BDAC	James L. Harrison, ed., *Biographical Dictionary of the American Congress, 1774–1949* (Washington, D.C.: United States Government Printing Office, 1950)
Born in Slavery	*Born in Slavery: Slave Narratives from the Federal Writers' Project, 1936–1938* (Washington, D.C.: Manuscript and Prints and Photographs Division, Library of Congress, http://memory.loc.gov/ammem/snhtml/snhome.html)
CGCAC	Cape Girardeau County Archives Center, Jackson, Missouri
CHSL	Cincinnati Historical Society Library, Cincinnati Museum Center, Cincinnati, Ohio
CWAL	Roy P. Basler, ed., *The Collected Works of Abraham Lincoln*, 11 vols. (Springfield, Ill.: The Abraham Lincoln Association, 1953)
CWH	*Civil War History*
Duke	Special Collections, William R. Perkins Library, Duke University, Durham, North Carolina
EWT	Reuben Gold Thwaites, ed., *Early Western Travels, 1748–1846*, 30 vols. (Cleveland: Arthur H. Clark, 1904)
FHQ	*Filson [Club] History Quarterly*
FHS	Filson Historical Society, Louisville, Kentucky
Huntington	Henry E. Huntington Library and Art Gallery, San Marino, California
IHSL	Indiana Historical Society Library, Indianapolis
IMH	*Indiana Magazine of History*
IHSLR	Illinois Historical Survey and Lincoln Room, University Library, University of Illinois, Urbana-Champaign
IU	Lilly Library, Indiana University, Bloomington, Indiana
JAH	*Journal of American History*
JALA	*Journal of the Abraham Lincoln Association*
JCWE	*Journal of the Civil War Era*
JIH	*Journal of Illinois History*
JISHS	*Journal of the Illinois State Historical Society*
JSH	*Journal of Southern History*
KDLA	Kentucky Department of Libraries and Archives, Frankfort

Abbreviations

Ky. Laws	*Acts of the General Assembly of the Commonwealth of Kentucky* (Lexington, Frankfort: State Printer et al., 1792–1925)
KsHS	Kansas Historical Society, Topeka
KHS	Special Collections and Manuscripts, Kentucky Historical Society, Frankfort
Lincoln Papers	Abraham Lincoln Papers, Ser. 1—General Correspondence, 1833–1916, Library of Congress, Washington, D.C.
LC	Library of Congress, Washington, D.C.
MHR	*Missouri Historical Review*
MHS	Missouri Historical Society, St. Louis, Missouri
MSA	Missouri State Archives, Jefferson City, Missouri
MVHR	*Mississippi Valley Historical Review*
NARA	National Archives and Records Administration, Washington, D.C.
OHS	Ohio Historical Society, Columbus
OR	*War of the Rebellion: Official Records of the Union and Confederate Armies*, 4 ser., 128 vols. (Washington D.C.: United States Government Printing Office, 1881–1901)
OVH	*Ohio Valley History*
Provost I	*Union Provost Marshals' File of Papers Relating to Individual Citizens,* Record Group 109: War Department Collection of Confederate Records, File M345, 299 microfilm reels, NARA
Provost II	*Union Provost Marshals' File of Papers Relating to Two or More Citizens,* Record Group 109: War Department Collection of Confederate Records, File M416, 94 microfilm reels, NARA
Register	*Register of the Kentucky Historical Society*
RG 393	Records of the U.S. Army Continental Commands, 1821–1920, Record Group 393, NARA
SEMO	Special Collections and Archives, Southeast Missouri State University, Cape Girardeau, Missouri
UNC	Southern Historical Collections, Wilson Library, University of North Carolina, Chapel Hill
SHSM	Joint Collection/Western Historical Manuscript Collections, University of Missouri-State Historical Society of Missouri, Ellis Library, University of Missouri, Columbia, Missouri
SIU	Special Collections/Morris Library, Southern Illinois University, Carbondale
UK	Manuscripts and Special Collections, Margaret I. King Library, University of Kentucky, Lexington
UMSL	St. Louis Mercantile Library, Special Collections, University of Missouri at St. Louis
WHQ	*Western Historical Quarterly*
WKU	Manuscripts and Special Collections, Kentucky Library, Western Kentucky University, Bowling Green
WRHS	Western Reserve Historical Society, Cleveland, Ohio

NOTES

"There Is a West"

1. *Cincinnati Daily Enquirer*, January 27, 1860; [Frankfort] *Tri-Weekly Kentucky Yeoman*, January 28, 1860; [Frankfort] *Daily Kentucky Yeoman*, February 1, 1860; *Louisville Journal*, January 27, 1860; George H. Porter, *Ohio Politics During the Civil War Period* (New York: Columbia University, 1911), 30–32; *Report of the Excursion Made by the Executive and Legislatures of the States of Kentucky and Tennessee, to the State of Ohio, on the 26th, 27th, and 28th Jan., 1860: On the Invitation of the Governor and Legislature of Ohio, and the Citizens of Cincinnati* (Cincinnati: R. Clarke, 1860), 1–5, 17, passim. The descriptions of events in the following paragraphs are drawn largely from these sources.
2. Lowell H. Harrison and James C. Klotter, *A New History of Kentucky* (Lexington: University Press of Kentucky, 1997), 132.
3. [Cincinnati, Ohio] *The Daily Times*, April 26, 1861; Timothy Max Jenness, "Tentative Relations: Secession and War in the Central Ohio River Valley, 1859–1862" (Ph.D. dissertation, University of Tennessee, Knoxville, 2011), 1–4.
4. *Report of the Excursion*, 1–5.
5. BDAC, 1196; Emma Lou Thornbrough, *Indiana in the Civil War, 1850–1880* (Indianapolis: Indiana Historical Society, 1965), 40, 41, 75–76.
6. W. Anthony to Jesse W. Kincheloe, February 16, 1860, Kinchloe-Eskridge Families Papers, Mss. A K51, folder 2, FHS; [Nashville, Tenn.] *Union American*, February 1, 1860.
7. Stanley Harrold, *Border War: Fighting over Slavery before the Civil War* (Chapel Hill: University of North Carolina Press, 2010), 72, 82–93.
8. Hyn Hur, "Radical Antislavery and Personal Liberty Laws in Antebellum Ohio, 1803–1857" (Ph.D. dissertation, University of Wisconsin, Madison, 2012), 74–116; Nicole Etcheson, *Bleeding Kansas: Contested Liberty in the Civil War Era* (Lawrence: University Press of Kansas, 2004), 69; T. H. Gladstone, *The Englishman in Kansas* (New York: Miller, 1857), 14.

Introduction

1. Robert Penn Warren, *Legacy of the Civil War: Meditations on the Centennial* (New York: Random House, 1961; reprint Lincoln: University of Nebraska Press, 1998), 4.
2. Robert Penn Warren, *Jefferson Davis Gets His Citizenship Back* (Lexington: University Press of Kentucky, 1980), 1–7, 10, 15.
3. Ernest Renan, "What Is a Nation?," trans. Martin Hom, in Homi K. Bhabha, ed., *Nation and Narration* (London: Routledge, 1990), 19; David W. Blight, *Race and Reunion: The Civil War in American Memory* (Cambridge, Mass.: Belknap Press of Harvard University Press, 2001), 4 passim.

4. John Shelton Reed, *Southerners: The Social Psychology of Sectionalism* (Chapel Hill: University of North Carolina Press, 1983), 15–25, 56–69; Reed, *One South: An Ethnic Approach to Regional Culture* (Baton Rouge: Louisiana State University Press, 1982), 3–8 passim.
5. David L. Smiley, "The Quest for the Central Theme in Southern History," *South Atlantic Quarterly* 71 (Summer 1972): 307; Barbara J. Fields, "Dysplacement and Southern History," *JSH* 82 (February 2016), 15; Caroline E. Janney, *Remembering the Civil War: Reunion and the Limits of Reconciliation* (Chapel Hill: University of North Carolina Press, 2013), 5, 27–28. For exceptions, see especially Edward L. Ayers, *In the Presence of Mine Enemies: The Civil War in the Heart of America, 1859–1863* (New York: W. W. Norton, 2003); William W. Freehling, *The South vs. the South: How Anti-Confederate Southerners Shaped the Course of the Civil War* (New York: Oxford University Press, 2001); Adam Arenson, *The Great Heart of the Republic: St. Louis and the Cultural Civil War* (Cambridge, Mass.: Harvard University Press, 2011); Aaron Astor, *Rebels on the Border: Civil War, Emancipation, and the Reconstruction of Kentucky and Missouri* (Baton Rouge: Louisiana State University Press, 2012); and Nicole Etcheson, *A Generation at War: The Civil War Era in a Northern Community* (Lawrence: University Press of Kansas, 2011).
6. For the "Lower North," see Eric Foner, *Free Soil, Free Labor, Free Men: The Ideology of the Republican Party before the Civil War* (New York: Oxford University Press, 1970); and William W. Freehling, *The Road to Disunion*, 2 vols. (New York: Oxford University Press, 1990, 2007). For a recent triumviratist narrative, see James H. Bissland, *Blood, Tears, and Glory: How Ohioans Won the Civil War* (Wilmington, Ohio: Orange Frazier Press, 2007).
7. David M. Potter, "The Historian's Use of Nationalism and Vice Versa," in *The South and the Sectional Crisis* (Baton Rouge: Louisiana State University, 1968), 51.
8. Paula Baker, "The Domestication of Politics: Women and American Political Society, 1780–1920," *AHR* 89 (June 1984): 620–47; Peter J. Parish, "An Exception to Most of the Rules: American Nationalism in the Nineteenth Century," *Prologue* 27 (Fall 1995): 227; Jens Brockmeier, "Remembering and Forgetting: Narrative as Cultural Memory," *Culture and Psychology* 8 (2002): 15–43; Drew Gilpin Faust, *The Creation of Confederate Nationalism: Ideology and Identity in the Civil War South* (Baton Rouge: Louisiana State University Press, 1990), 15.
9. Message to Congress in Special Session, July 4, 1861, in *CWAL*, 4:438.
10. Edward L. Ayers, "The South, the West, and the Rest," *WHQ* 25 (Winter 1994): 473–76; Patricia Nelson Limerick, "Region and Reason," in Edward L. Ayers, Patricia Nelson Limerick, Stephen Nissenbaum, and Peter S. Onuf, eds., *All Over the Map: Rethinking American Regions* (Baltimore: Johns Hopkins University Press, 1996), 83–84.
11. Abraham Lincoln to James C. Conkling, August 26, 1863, in *CWAL*, 6:406–10.
12. Ibid.; François Furstenberg, "The Significance of the Trans-Appalachian Frontier in Atlantic History," *AHR* 113 (June 2008): 647–77 passim.

White Salt, Black Servitude

1. John W. Allen, *Legends and Lore of Southern Illinois* (Carbondale: Southern Illinois University, 1963), 41–42; Robert P. Howard, *Illinois: A History of the Prairie State* (Grand Rapids, Mich.: William B. Eerdmans, 1972), 163. The origins of the terms "Egypt" and "Little Egypt" are still debated.
2. John Bradbury, *Travels in the Interior of America in the Years 1809, 1810 and 1811* (London: Sherwood, Neely, and Jones, 1819), in *EWT*, 5:204–11; [Lorenzo Dow], *History of Cosmopolite, or the Four Volumes of Lorenzo Dow's Journal*, ed. Peggy Dow (Wheeling, Va.: Joshua Martin, 1848), 344–46; [Cincinnati, Ohio] *Liberty Hall*, December 16, 1811; John Reynolds, *My Own Times, Embracing Also, a History of My Life* (Belleville, Ill.: B. H. Perryman and H. L. Davison, 1855), 125; John Willis Allen, "The Romance of the Old Slave House" (typescript), 1–8, John Willis Allen Papers, Mss. 76-3-F1, box 39, SIU; William E. Foley, *A History of Missouri, Vol. 1: 1673–1820* (Columbia: University of Missouri Press, 1971), 36–37, 95, 136, 151, 191–92.
3. Foley, *History of Missouri*, 170–71; Tom Kanon, "'Scared from Their Sins for a Season': The Religious Ramifications of the New Madrid Earthquakes, 1811–1812," *OVH* 5 (Summer

Notes to Pages 16–20

2005): 21–38; "Memorandum of Remarkable Events by Samuel Swan McClelland," in J. P. MacLean, ed., *Shakers of Ohio: Fugitive Papers Concerning the Shakers of Ohio, with Unpublished Manuscripts* (Columbus: F. J. Heer Printing, 1907), 282–88; Stephen Aron, *American Confluence: The Missouri Frontier from Borderland to Border State* (Bloomington and Indianapolis: Indiana University Press, 2006), 149–50; Judy Magee, *Cavern of Crime* (Smithland, Ky.: The Livingston Ledger, 1973), 50; Howard, *Illinois*, 80; Fortescue Cuming, *Sketches of a Tour to the Western Country* (Pittsburgh: Cramer, Spear, and Eichbaum, 1810), in *EWT*, 22:270–71. Some thirty thousand square miles were affected by tremors that lasted more than a year.

4. Howard, *Illinois*, 84–85; Cuming, *Sketches of a Tour to the Western Country*.
5. Richard M. Phillips, "This Is the House That Salt Built," *Illiniwek* 10 (May–June 1972): 18–20; Barthelemi Tardiveau, "Memorandum on Business Arrangements between J. Holker and B. Tardiveau" (typescript), undated [ca. 1783], Mss. VF 3692, CHSL.
6. Magee, *Cavern of Crime*, 50–51; Howard, *Illinois*, 106–7; James Hall, *Letters from the West: Containing Sketches of Scenery, Manners, and Customs; and Anecdotes Connected with the First Settlements of the Western Sections of the United States* (London: Henry Colburn, 1828), in Paul M. Angle, ed., *Prairie State: Impressions of Illinois, 1673–1967* (Chicago: University of Chicago Press, 1968), 92; Seventh, Ninth, and Tenth U.S. Censuses, 1850, 1870, 1880, Population Schedule, Gallatin County, Illinois, NARA; Phillips, "This Is the House That Salt Built," 18–20.
7. Phillips, "This Is the House That Salt Built," 20–21; Hall, *Letters from the West*, in Angle, ed., *Prairie State*, 92–93; Howard, *Illinois*, 132–33; George W. Smith, "The Salines of Southern Illinois," *Transactions of the Illinois State Historical Library* 9 (1904): 245–58; Jacob W. Myers, "History of the Gallatin County Salines," *JISHS* 14 (April–July 1921): 337–50; Howard, *Illinois*, 103–4, 19–20; Hall, *Letters from the West*, in Angle, ed., *Prairie State*, 93; Tardiveau, "Memorandum on Business Arrangements."
8. Phillips, "This Is the House That Salt Built," 21–22; Howard, *Illinois*, 193–209.
9. Phillips, "This Is the House That Salt Built," 21–22; "Registry of Slaves and Servants, 1830, Gallatin County, Illinois" (typescript), John Willis Allen Papers, Mss. 76-3-F1, box 39, SIU; J. H. C. Ellis to Shawneetown Postmaster, December 26, 1843, and Henry Eddy, A. G. S. Wight, and George Leviston to Thomas Ford, December 8, 1846, both in Eddy Manuscript Collection, ISHLR.
10. Phillips, "This Is the House That Salt Built," 21–22; "Registry of Servants and Slaves, Kept at Shawneetown, Ill., from 1839–1849," John Willis Allen Papers, Mss. 76-3-Fl, box 39, SIU.
11. Phillips, "This Is the House That Salt Built," 21–22; Allen, *Legends and Lore*, 246–48; [Shawneetown] *Illinois Republican*, March 25, April 3, 8, 16, 1842.
12. [Shawneetown] *Illinois Republican*, April 3, 8, 16, 1842; Phillips, "This Is the House That Salt Built," 23–24; James A. Rose, "The Regulators and Flatheads in Southern Illinois," in *Transactions of the Illinois State Historical Library for the Year 1906* (Springfield: Illinois State Historical Society, 1906), 111, 114–16; Richard Maxwell Brown, *The South Carolina Regulators* (Cambridge, Mass.: Harvard University Press, 1963), passim; Jon Musgrave, "History Comes Out of Hiding Atop Hickory Hill," *Springhouse Magazine* (December 1996), http://www.illinoishistory.com/osharticle.html (accessed October 7, 2013).
13. Howard, *Illinois*, 189–91; N. Dwight Harris, *The History of Negro Servitude in Illinois and the Slavery Agitation in That State* (Chicago: A. C. McClurg, 1904), 116–21; Darrel E. Bigham, *On Jordan's Banks: Emancipation and Its Aftermath in the Ohio River Valley* (Lexington: University Press of Kentucky, 2006), 36. In 1850 John Crenshaw was the last leaseholder in the former Illinois salt reserve. The manuscript census for 1850 lists him as having in his household three black and mulatto members with his surname, while his three neighboring households contained a total of sixteen African Americans of various ages and sexes (mostly males of working age whose occupations were listed simply as "laborer") and at least eight different surnames, born variously in South Carolina, Virginia, Tennessee, Kentucky, and Illinois. He continued to make salt even after the state of Illinois sold the balance of the saline lands at public auction in 1852. Crenshaw died on December 4, 1871.
14. Seventh U.S. Census, 1850, Population Schedule, Gallatin County, Illinois, NARA.

Chapter 1: White Flows the River: Freedom and Unfreedom in the Early National West

1. D. W. Meinig, *The Shaping of America*, 2 vols. (New Haven, Conn.: Yale University Press, 1993), 1:52–53; C[harles] F[enno] Hoffman, *A Winter in the Far West*, 2 vols. (London: Richard Bentley, 1835), 2:128. For an interpretation of the Ohio valley as a borderland, see Jeremy Adelman and Stephen Aron, "From Borderlands to Borders: Empires, Nation-States, and the Peoples in Between in North American History," *AHR* 104 (June 1999): 814–41.
2. Elizabeth A. Perkins, *Border Life: Experience and Memory in the Revolutionary Ohio Valley* (Chapel Hill and London: University of North Carolina Press, 1998), 7–19, 160; Adam Rankin, *A Review of the Noted Revival in Kentucky: Commenced in the Year of Our Lord, 1801* (Pittsburgh: John Israel, 1802), 5; Evarts B. Greene and Virginia D. Carrington, *American Population before the Federal Census of 1790* (New York: Columbia University Press, 1932), 192; Harrison and Klotter, *New History of Kentucky*, 6, 48–49; Steven A. Channing, *Kentucky: A Bicentennial History* (New York: W. W. Norton, 1977), 28, 58–61.
3. Perkins, *Border Life*, 28–31; John Alden, *The First South* (Baton Rouge: Louisiana State University Press, 1961), 4–9; Everett Dick, *The Dixie Frontier: A Social History of the Southern Frontier from the First Transmontane Beginnings to the Civil War* (New York: Alfred A. Knopf, 1948), passim; Richard Lyle Power, *Planting Corn Belt Culture: The Impress of the Upland Southerner and Yankee in the Old Northwest* (Indianapolis: Indiana Historical Society, 1953), 1–2; John Parsons, *A Tour Through Indiana in 1840*, ed. Kate Milner Rabb (New York: Robert M. McBride, 1920), 1–2, 14–16, 23, 32–33, 79, 86–87, 114–15, 133–34, 140, 379, 364–65; William Conrad, *The Journal of Elder William Conrad: Pioneer Preacher*, ed. Lloyd W. Franks (Lexington: R F Publishing, 1976), 61–65. James Shortridge claims that the term "Middle West," which probably originated in Ohio in the 1820s, was largely unused until the 1880s, when it was revived as a reference to the rural, farming culture of central Plains states like Kansas and Nebraska. Federal census compendia in 1860 separate "Middle States," meaning Atlantic seaboard states Delaware, New Jersey, Maryland, and Virginia, from "Western States," including middle border states as well as Michigan, Wisconsin, Minnesota, and Iowa, as geographical groupings. James R. Shortridge, *The Middle West: Its Meaning in American Culture* (Lawrence: University Press of Kansas, 1989), 16–17; [Joseph C. G. Kennedy], *Manufactures of the United States in 1860: Compiled from the Original Returns of the Eighth Census* (Washington, D. C.: Government Printing Office, 1865), passim; Joseph C. G. Kennedy, *Agriculture of the United States in 1860: Compiled from the Original Returns of the Eighth Census* (Washington, D. C.: Government Printing Office, 1864), passim.
4. George W. Ogden, *Letters from the West, Comprising a Tour through the Western Country, and a Residence of Two Summers in the States of Ohio and Kentucky* (New Bedford, Mass.: Melcher and Bros., 1823), in *EWT*, 19:33–36; Hoffman, *A Winter in the Far West*, 2:134–35, 141, 144–48; Frederick Law Olmsted, *A Journey Through Texas: Or, A Saddle-Trip on the Southwestern Frontier* (New York and London: Dix, Edwards and Co., and S. Low, Son and Co., 1857), 24–25; Power, *Planting Corn Belt Culture*, 1, 82–85, 92–135. On the clash of regional folkways on the middle border, see also Henry Clyde Hubbart, *The Older Middle West, 1840–1880* (New York: Russell and Russell, 1963).
5. Nicole Etcheson, *The Emerging Midwest: Upland Southerners and the Political Culture of the Old Northwest, 1787–1861* (Bloomington: Indiana University Press, 1996), 3–5; *Home Missionary* 17 (December 1844): 187; [Franklin] *Missouri Intelligencer*, March 4, 1823; William L. Andrews et al., eds., *The Literature of the American South* (New York: W. W. Norton, 1986), 160–61, 254–57.
6. Henry Nash Smith, *Virgin Land: The American West as Symbol and Myth* (Cambridge, Mass.: Harvard University Press, 1950), 54–55; John Mack Faragher, *Daniel Boone: The Life and Legend of an American Pioneer* (New York: Henry Holt, 1992), 301; Ogden, *Letters from the West*, in *EWT*, 19:29; John Stillman Wright, *Letters from the West: Or a Caution to Emigrants* (Salem, N.Y.: Dodd and Stevenson, 1819; reprint Ann Arbor, Mich.: University Microforms, 1966), 34; Charles H. Titus, *Into the Old Northwest: Journeys with Charles H. Titus, 1841–1846*, ed. George P. Clark (East Lansing: Michigan State University, 1994), 47.

7. Power, *Planting Corn Belt Culture*, vii; W[illiam] Faux, *Memorable Days in America: Being a Journal of a Tour to the United States Principally Undertaken to Ascertain, by Positive Evidence, the Condition and Probable Prospects of British Emigrants; Including Accounts of Mr. Birkbeck's Settlement in the Illinois* (London: W. Simpkin and R. Marshall, 1823), in EWT, 9:282–83; Randy J. Mills, "'I Wish the World to Look Upon Them as My Murderers': A Story of Cultural Violence on the Ohio Valley Frontier," *OVH* 1 (Fall 2001): 26.
8. Andro Linklater, *Measuring America: How the United States Was Shaped by the Greatest Land Sale in History* (New York and London: Penguin, 2002), 39–41; Alfred J. Wright, "Ohio Town Patterns," *Geographical Review* 27 (October 1937): 616–17; David Hackett Fischer and James C. Kelly, *Bound Away: Virginia and the Westward Movement* (Charlottesville and London: University Press of Virginia, 2000), 253–55.
9. Etcheson, *The Emerging Midwest*, 3; James H. Madison, *The Indiana Way: A State History* (Bloomington and Indianapolis: Indiana University Press/Indiana Historical Society, 1986), 62; Douglas K. Meyer, *Making the Heartland Quilt: A Geographic History of Settlement and Migration in Early-Nineteenth Century Illinois* (Carbondale and Edwardsville: Southern Illinois University Press, 2000), 136–68, 288–95; Hubert G. H. Wilhelm, *The Origin and Distribution of Settlement Groups: Ohio, 1850* (Athens, Ohio: printed by author, 1982), 25, 30–31, 57–58; Henry Clyde, "Pro-Southern Influences in the Free West 1840–1865," *MVHR* 20 (June 1933): 48; Seventh U.S. Census, 1850, Population Schedule, Indiana, Illinois, Kentucky, Ohio, NARA. The sample of counties includes Alexander, Gallatin, and Williamson in Illinois, and Brown, Scott, and Switzerland in Indiana. The rank order of non-Illinois-born immigrants to Illinois drawn in 1850 is New York, 23,054; Kentucky, 20,066; Ohio, 17,069; Pennsylvania, 13,451; Tennessee, 12,079. The rank order of non-Ohio immigrants drawn from the 1850 population census is Pennsylvania, 190,396; Virginia, 83,300; New York, 75,442; Maryland, 34,775; New Jersey, 21,768.
10. Report of Attendance of Old Settlers by Counties at Union Fair Association, Centralia, Illinois, October 1, 1872, Old Settlers' Association File, Mss. SC 309, ALPL; *Centralia [Ill.] Sentinel*, August 18, 1864; Joseph C. G. Kennedy, *Population of the United States in 1860: Compiled from the Original Returns of the Eighth Census* (Washington, D.C.: Government Printing Office, 1864), 104–5. The four counties in the Old Settlers enumeration were Clinton, Jefferson, Marion, and Washington.
11. Howard, *Illinois*, 471; Fischer and Kelly, *Bound Away*, 255.
12. Power, *Planting Corn Belt Culture*, 26; William B. Sappington to Erasmus D. Sappington, November 14, 1830, John S. Sappington Papers, Mss. 1027, box 1, folder 18, SHSM; Allen, *Legends and Lore of Southern Illinois*, 119–20; Madison, *The Indiana Way*, 58–60; E. Merton Coulter, *The Civil War and Readjustment in Kentucky* (Chapel Hill: University of North Carolina Press, 1926; reprint Gloucester, Mass.: Peter Smith, 1966), 13–14.
13. John A. Jakle, *Images of the Ohio Valley: A Historical Geography of Travel, 1740–1860* (New York: Oxford University Press, 1977), 16; Wright, *Letters from the West*, 34, 67; Hoffman, *A Winter in the Far West*, 2:135; Daniel Drake, *Pioneer Life in Kentucky, 1785–1800* (New York: Henry Schuman, 1948), 93, 179–80, 207; Harry Toulmin, *The Western Country in 1793: Reports on Kentucky and Virginia by Harry Toulmin*, ed. Marion Tinling and Godfrey Davies (San Marino, Calif.: Henry E. Huntington Library, 1948), 68; Frances Trollope, *Domestic Manners of the Americans* (London: Whittaker, Treacher, 1832), 1:28–29.
14. Arthur C. Boggess, *The Settlement of Illinois, 1778–1830* (Chicago: Chicago Historical Society, 1908), 12–13; Harris, *History of Negro Servitude in Illinois*, 1–5; James Simeone, *Democracy and Slavery in Frontier Illinois: The Bottomland Republic* (DeKalb: Northern Illinois University Press, 2000), 19; Daniel H. Usner Jr., *Indians, Settlers, and Slaves in a Frontier Exchange Economy: The Lower Mississippi Valley Before 1783* (Chapel Hill: University of North Carolina Press, 1992), 14, 41–43; Andrew R. L. Cayton, *Frontier Indiana* (Bloomington: Indiana University Press, 1996), 50–52. For the fullest study of Indian slavery in early America, see Alan Gallay, *The Indian Slave Trade: The Rise of the English Empire in the American South, 1670–1717* (New Haven, Conn.: Yale University Press, 2002).
15. William E. Foley, *The Genesis of Missouri: From Wilderness Outpost to Statehood* (Columbia and London: University of Missouri Press, 1989), 15; Harris, *History of Negro Servitude in*

Illinois, 1–5; Simeone, *Democracy and Slavery in Frontier Illinois*, 19; Cayton, *Frontier Indiana*, 50; Emma Lou Thornbrough, *The Negro in Indiana Before 1900* (Indianapolis: Indiana Historical Bureau, 1985; reprint Bloomington and Indianapolis: Indiana University Press, 1993), 1–15; James Neal Primm, *Lion of the Valley: St. Louis, Missouri* (Boulder, Colo.: Pruett Publishing, 1981), 6, 23–26; Aron, *American Confluence*, 48–49; Richard C. Wade, *The Urban Frontier: Pioneer Life in Early Pittsburgh, Cincinnati, Lexington, Louisville, and St. Louis* (Cambridge, Mass.: Harvard University Press, 1959; reprint Chicago: University of Chicago Press, 1964), 3–7.

16. Patrick Griffin, *American Leviathan: Empire, Nation, and Revolutionary Frontier* (New York: Hill and Wang, 2007), 97–123; Stephen Aron, *How the West Was Lost: The Transformation of Kentucky from Daniel Boone to Henry Clay* (Baltimore and London: Johns Hopkins University Press, 1996), 24–25, 56; Karolyn E. Smardz, "'There We Were in Darkness,— Here We Are in Light': Kentucky Slaves and the Promised Land," in Craig T. Friend, ed., *The Buzzel About Kentuck: Settling the Promised Land* (Lexington: University Press of Kentucky, 1999), 245; Allan Kulikoff, "Uprooted Peoples: Black Migrants in the Age of the American Revolution, 1790–1820," in Ira Berlin and Ronald Hoffman, eds., *Slavery and Freedom in the Age of the American Revolution* (Urbana and Champaign: University of Illinois Press, 1986), 149; Malcolm J. Rohrbaugh, *The Trans-Appalachian Frontier: People, Societies, and Institutions* (New York: Oxford University Press, 1978; reprint Belmont, Calif.: Wadsworth Publishing, 1990), 13–22.

17. Peter S. Onuf, *Jefferson's Empire: The Language of American Nationhood* (Charlottesville: University Press of Virginia, 2000), 53–79; Drew R. McCoy, *The Elusive Republic: Political Economy in Jeffersonian America* (New York: W. W. Norton, 1980), 121–56; Stephen Middleton, *The Black Laws: Race and the Legal Process in Early Ohio* (Athens: Ohio University Press, 2005), 11–13. For the transference of republican values to the western country, see also Andrew R. L. Cayton, *The Frontier Republic: Ideology and Politics in the Ohio Country, 1780–1825* (Kent, Ohio: Kent State University Press, 1997); and Gregory H. Nobles, *American Frontiers: Cultural Encounters and Continental Conquest* (New York: Hill and Wang, 1997). In 1809 the Illinois Territory separated from the Indiana Territory, formed in 1800.

18. Eugene H. Berwanger, *The Frontier Against Slavery: Western Anti-Negro Prejudice and the Slavery Extension Controversy* (Urbana: University of Illinois Press, 1967), 9; Suzanne Cooper Guasco, "'The Deadly Influence of Negro Capitalists': Southern Yeomen and Resistance to the Expansion of Slavery in Illinois," *CWH* 47 (March 2001): 11; Thornbrough, *Negro in Indiana*, 6–13; Cayton, *Frontier Indiana*, 187–91.

19. Thornbrough, *Negro in Indiana*, 12–20.

20. Berwanger, *Frontier Against Slavery*, 10; Cayton, *Frontier Indiana*, 192.

21. Madison, *The Indiana Way*, 7–10, 50–54; Faux, *Memorable Days in America*, in *EWT*, 9:300; Thornbrough, *Negro in Indiana*, 13–16 (emphasis added), 26–28.

22. Guasco, "'Deadly Influence of Negro Capitalists,'" 11; Last Will and Testament of Shadrach Bond, April 7, 1832, Shadrach Bond Papers, Mss. SC 148, ALPL; Paul Finkelman, *Slavery and the Founders: Race and Liberty in the Age of Jefferson* (London: M. E. Sharpe, 1996), 74–79; Harris, *Negro Servitude in Illinois*, 6–15.

23. James E. Davis, *Frontier Illinois* (Bloomington: Indiana University Press, 1998), 117; Harris, *History of Negro Servitude in Illinois*, 10–15; Indenture of Caleb by Robert Chesney, 1815, Jesse J. Ricks Collection, Mss. 1274–1903, ALPL; John W. Allen, "Slavery and Negro Servitude in Pope County, Illinois," in Clyde C. Walton, ed., *An Illinois Reader* (DeKalb: Northern Illinois University Press, 1970), 102–12; Morris Birkbeck and George Flower, *History of the English Settlement in Edwards County, Illinois, Founded in 1817 and 1818* (Chicago: Fergus Publishing, 1882), 199.

24. Cayton, *Frontier Republic*, 57–58; Charles Thomas Hickok, *The Negro in Ohio 1802–1870* (Cleveland: Williams Publishing and Electric, 1896; reprint New York: AMS Press, 1975), 15–42; Middleton, *Black Laws*, 23–25; Donald J. Ratcliffe, *Party Spirit in a Frontier Republic: Democratic Politics in Ohio, 1793–1820* (Columbus: Ohio State University Press, 1998), 231.

25. Mary Alice Mairose, "Thomas Worthington and the Quest for Statehood and Gentility," in Warren Van Tine and Michael Pierce, eds., *Builders of Ohio: A Biographical History* (Columbus: Ohio State University Press, 2003), 65; "An Act to Regulate Black and Mulatto Persons," *Ohio Acts* 2 (1803), *Ohio Acts* 4 (1806); Paul Finkelman, *An Imperfect Union: Slavery, Federalism, and Comity* (Chapel Hill: University of North Carolina Press, 1981), 3–19, 87–92; Helen M. Thurston, "The 1802 Constitutional Convention and Status of the Negro," *Ohio History* 81 (Winter 1972): 15–37; Raymond Pelan, "Slavery in the Old Northwest," *State Historical Society of Wisconsin Proceedings* (Madison: State Historical Society of Wisconsin, 1906), 255–56; James A. Rodabaugh, "The Negro in Ohio," *Journal of Negro History* 31 (January 1946): 13; Charles Ray Wilson, "The Negro in Early Ohio," *Ohio History* 39 (July 1930): 713–78 passim. An 1804 statute committed local officials to recovering fugitives, but the legislature did little otherwise to clarify the legal status of slaves temporarily in Ohio. The fugitive slave provisions of Ohio's constitution were repealed on April 1, 1807.
26. Cayton, *Frontier Republic*, 57–58; Emil Pocock, "Slavery and Freedom in the Early Republic: Robert Patterson's Slaves in Kentucky and Ohio, 1804–1819," *OVH* 6 (Spring 2006): 3–4; Hickok, *Negro in Ohio*, 36–39.
27. Pocock, "Slavery and Freedom," 5–23; Paul Finkelman, "Evading the Ordinance: The Persistence of Bondage in Indiana and Illinois," *Journal of the Early Republic* 9 (Spring 1989): 21–51; Thornbrough, *Negro in Indiana*, 17–20; Peter S. Onuf, *Statehood and Union: A History of the Northwest Ordinance* (Bloomington: Indiana University Press, 1987), 109–32; Finkelman, *Imperfect Union*, 87–92, 155–78; Stephen Middleton, "The Fugitive Slave Issue in Southwest Ohio: Unreported Cases," *Old Northwest* 14 (Winter 1988–89): 285–310; Harrold, *Border War*, 65.
28. Suzanne Cooper Guasco, "Confronting Democracy: Edward Coles and the Cultivation of Authority in the Young Nation" (Ph.D. dissertation, College of William and Mary in Virginia, 2004), 102, 164, 211–19; Howard, *Illinois*, 134–35.
29. Allen, *Legends and Lore of Southern Illinois*, 119–20; Guasco, "'Deadly Influence of Negro Capitalists'," 7–21; [William N. Blane], *An Excursion Through the United States and Canada During the Years 1822–1823 by an English Gentleman* (London: Baldwin, Cradock, and Joy, 1824), 172; Howard, *Illinois*, 134–35; Harris, *Negro Servitude in Illinois*, 34–39.
30. Guasco, "'Deadly Influence of Negro Capitalists,'" 7–21, 26; Jensen, *Illinois*, 29; Harris, *History of Negro Servitude in Illinois*, 34–39.
31. Howard, *Illinois*, 134.
32. Guasco, "'Deadly Influence of Negro Capitalists,'" 9, 29.
33. Arthur Zilversmit, *The First Emancipation: The Abolition of Slavery in the North* (Chicago: University of Chicago Press, 1967), 109–38, 208–22; Gary B. Nash and Jean R. Soderlund, *Freedom by Degree: Emancipation in Pennsylvania and Its Aftermath* (New York: Oxford University Press, 1991), 99–113; Joanne Pope Melish, *Disowning Slavery: Gradual Emancipation and "Race" in New England, 1780–1860* (Ithaca, N.Y., and London: Cornell University Press, 1998), 69–79; David Brion Davis, "American Slavery and the American Revolution," in Berlin and Hoffman, eds., *Slavery and Freedom in the Age of the Revolution*, 277–78; Leon F. Litwack, *North of Slavery: The Negro in the Free States, 1790–1860* (Chicago and London: University of Chicago Press, 1961), 3–15; Fergus M. Bordewich, *Bound for Canaan: The Underground Railroad* (New York: Amistad Press, 2005), 112; William Henry Harrison to James Henry, May 10, 1806, William Henry Harrison Papers, Mss. M0364, box 1, folder 11, IHSL. For the best study of slavery in New Jersey, see Graham Russell Hodges, *Slavery, Freedom, and Culture Among Early American Workers* (Armonk, N.Y.: M. E. Sharpe, 1998).
34. Ira Berlin, *Slaves Without Masters: The Free Negro in the Antebellum South* (New York: Pantheon, 1974; reprint New York: Oxford University Press, 1981), 15–50, 138–39n2; Christopher Phillips, *Freedom's Port: The African American Community of Baltimore, 1790–1860* (Urbana and London: The University of Illinois Press, 1997), 35–56; T. Stephen Whitman, *The Price of Freedom: Slavery and Manumission in Baltimore and Early National Maryland* (Lexington: University Press of Kentucky, 1997), 93–118; Jonathan D. Martin,

Divided Mastery: Slave Hiring in the American South (Cambridge, Mass.: Harvard University Press, 2004), 39.

35. Morris Birkbeck, *Letters from Illinois* (Philadelphia: M. Carey and Son, 1818; reprint New York: Da Capo Press, 1970), 1–22; Charles Boewe, *Prairie Albion: An English Settlement in Pioneer Illinois* (Carbondale: Southern Illinois University Press, 1962), 7–8, 15–16, 258–59, 260–67; Richard Flower, *Letters from Lexington and the Illinois, Containing a Brief Account of the English Settlement in the Latter Territory, and a Refutation of the Misrepresentations of Mr. Cobbett* (London: J. Ridgway, 1819), in *EWT*, 10:98; [Blane], *Excursion Through the United States and Canada*, 171–72; "Speech on Conciliation with the Colonies," March 22, 1775, in [Edmund Burke], *The Works of the Right Honourable Edmund Burke*, 6 vols. (London: Henry G. Bohn, 1854–56), 1:464–71. Of the 288 residents of Albion who cast ballots, 135 voted for the convention.
36. John D. Barnhart, "Sources of the Southern Migration into the Old Northwest," *MVHR* 22 (June 1935): 57; "A Pioneer Looks Back: Lecture Delivered by Braxton Parrish in Benton," August 3, 1874 (transcript), Mss. VFM 18, SIU.
37. Birkbeck, *Letters from Illinois*, 20–21; Faux, *Memorable Days in America*, in *EWT*, 9:199.
38. Sixth U.S. Census, 1840, Slave Schedule, Illinois, NARA; Certificate of Freedom of Louis Bienvenue, May 13, 1850, Sidney Breese Papers, Mss. SC 165, ALPL; William Oliver, *Eight Months in Illinois, with Information to Immigrants* (Newcastle upon Tyne: W. A. Mitchell, 1843; reprint Carbondale: Southern Illinois University Press, 2002), 32–33.
39. Oliver, *Eight Months in Illinois*, 29; Reuben E. McDaniel to Delia Richerson McDaniel (typescript), April 28, May 3, 1836, April 20, 1839, McDaniel Family Papers, Mss. 2628, folder 1, pp. 9–10, SHSM; Eighth U.S. Census, 1850, Population and Slave Schedules, Saline County, Missouri, NARA; [Springfield] *Illinois State Journal*, February 15, 1853, quoted in Berwanger, *Frontier Against Slavery*, 28; Jane to Annie M. Cooper, July 21, 1863, Cooper-Phillips Family Papers, Mss. 66M37, UK.
40. Faux, *Memorable Days in America*, in *EWT*, 9:253–54; Harris, *History of Negro Servitude in Illinois*, 4–5; Henry T. Duncan Sr. to H. T. Duncan Jr., May 18, 1857, Duncan Family Papers, Mss. 71M38, UK; Seventh U.S. Census, 1860, Population Schedule, Fayette County, Kentucky, NARA. In *Jarrot v. Jarrot*, issued in December 1845, the Illinois Supreme Court ruled that indentured servants and French-owned slaves were free.
41. Guasco, "'Deadly Influence of Negro Capitalists,'" 22–26; Berwanger, *Frontier Against Slavery*, 11.
42. Birkbeck and Flower, *History of the English Settlement*, 163–73.
43. Nicholas Brice to Joseph Kent, December 11, 1827, reprinted in *Genius of Universal Emancipation*, March 1, 1828; Joe William Trotter Jr., *River Jordan: African American Urban Life in the Ohio Valley* (Lexington: University Press of Kentucky, 1998), 24–25. For a discussion of term slavery, see Phillips, *Freedom's Port*, 30–56.
44. Freehling, *Road to Disunion*, 1:186; Litwack, *North of Slavery*, 34–38; Trotter, *River Jordan*, 24–26; Clipping, *Cincinnati* [Ohio] *Daily Enquirer*, February 5, 1905, Edwin Henderson, Historical Sketches, Scrapbook, Mss. qXH496, CHS; Harrold, *Border War*, 65–66; Stephen A. Vincent, *Southern Seed, Northern Soil: African-American Farm Communities in the Midwest, 1785–1900* (Bloomington and Indianapolis: Indiana University Press, 1999), 29; Aron, *American Confluence*, 216–17; Juliet E. K. Walker, "The Legal Status of Free Blacks in Early Kentucky, 1792–1825," *FHQ* 57 (October 1983): 382–95; Perry McCandless, *A History of Missouri, Vol. II: 1820–1860* (Columbia: University of Missouri Press, 1971, 2000), 18–21.
45. Henry R. Reynolds Journal, 1839–1840, Mss. 686 (hereafter cited as Reynolds Journal), CHSL, 1–62 passim; "An Act to Encorporate the Baltimore City Iron Company," *Laws of Maryland* (Annapolis: William McNeir, 1847), 611:306; Alan M. Wilner, *The Maryland Board of Public Works: A History* (Annapolis: Hall of Records Commission, 1984; reprint Annapolis: Hall of Records Commission, 2001), 126; Seventh U.S. Census, 1850, Population Schedule, Baltimore City, Maryland, NARA; Phillips, *Freedom's Port*, 13–29; Barbara Jeanne Fields, *Slavery and Freedom on the Middle Ground: Maryland During the Nineteenth Century* (New Haven, Conn.: Yale University Press, 1985), 25–53; T. Stephen Whitman, *Price of Freedom*, 8–32; Berlin, *Slaves Without Masters*, 396–97.

North of Slavery, West of Abolition

1. Wade, *Urban Frontier*, 22–25; Charles Cist, *Cincinnati in 1841: Its Early Annals and Future Prospects* (Cincinnati: printed by author, 1841), 35.
2. Steven J. Ross, *Workers On the Edge: Work, Leisure, and Politics in Industrializing Cincinnati, 1788–1890* (New York: Columbia University Press, 1985), 173; Charles Lyell, *A Second Visit to North America* (London: John Murray, 1855), 2:290–91.
3. Bruce Levine, *The Spirit of 1848: German Immigrants, Labor Conflict, and the Coming of the Civil War* (Urbana: University of Illinois Press, 1992), 186–87; James Bergquist, "The Political Attitudes of the German Immigrant in Illinois, 1848–1860" (Ph.D. dissertation, Northwestern University, 1966), 11–12. My thanks to Zach Garrison for sharing his research on German communities on the middle border.
4. William W. Hinshaw et al., eds., *Encyclopedia of American Quaker Genealogy* (Ann Arbor, Mich.: Edwards Bros., Printers, 1946), 4:624, 5:905, and 6:311.
5. R. Griffith to Elwood Fisher, April 23, 1850, and Card for Charleston, Cincinnati and Louisville Rail Road Company Barbeque, August 9, 1838, both in Greve-Fisher Collection, Mss. M-257, UMSL; *The Cincinnati Directory Advertiser, for 1834* (Cincinnati: Deming, 1834), 61; J. H. Woodruff, *City Directory for the Years 1836-7* (Cincinnati: Woodruff, 1837), 57; Henry A. Ford and Kate B. Ford, *History of Cincinnati* (Cleveland: W. W. Williams, 1881), 219; Thomas S. Berry, *Western Prices Before 1861* (Cambridge, Mass.: Harvard University Press, 1943), 18–19, 532; Cist, *Cincinnati in 1841*, 49; William Alexander Mabry, "Ante-bellum Cincinnati and Its Southern Trade," in David Kelly Jackson, ed., *American Studies* (Durham, NC: Duke University Press, 1940), 82–83; E. Merton Coulter, "Effects of Secession upon the Commerce of the Mississippi Valley," *MVHR* 3 (December 1916): 284–85; Charles Ray Wilson, "Cincinnati, a Southern Outpost in 1860–61," *MVHR* 24 (March 1938): 473–82; *Portrait and Biographical Album of Greene and Clark Counties, Ohio* (Chicago: Chapman Bros., 1890), 441–44.
6. Charles Theodore Greve, *The Centennial History of Cincinnati and Representative Citizens* (Chicago: Biographical Publishing, 1904), 1:794; Stephen Gutgesell, ed., *Guide to Ohio Newspapers, 1793–1973: Union Bibliography of Ohio Newspapers Available in Ohio Libraries* (Columbus: Ohio Historical Society, 1974), 57; Bernard E. McClellan, "Cincinnati's Response to Abolitionism, 1835–1845" (M.A. thesis, University of Cincinnati, 1961), 105; Nikki M. Taylor, *Frontiers of Freedom: Cincinnati's Black Community, 1802–1868* (Athens: Ohio University Press, 2005), 34–35; Julie A. Mujic, "A Border Community's Unfulfilled Appeals: The Rise and Fall of the 1840s Anti-Abolitionist Movement in Cincinnati," *OVH* 7 (Summer 2007): 53, 56–57; Winifred Gregory, ed., *American Newspapers 1821–1936* (New York: Bibliographic Society of America, 1937; reprint New York: Kraus Reprint Corp., 1967), 228–36; Lewis A. Leonard, ed., *Greater Cincinnati and Its People: A History* (New York: Lewis Historical Publishing, 1927), 2:567; *Cincinnati Advertiser and Ohio Phoenix*, July 27, 1836; Cist, *Cincinnati in 1841*, 93; *Obituary of General Robert T. Lytle* ([Cincinnati]: Dawson and Fisher, [1840]), passim; *Cincinnati Gazette*, July 23 and August 4, 1836.
7. David Henry Shaffer, *The Cincinnati, Covington, Newport, and Fulton Directory, for 1840* (Cincinnati: J. B. And R. P. Donogh, 1840), 37, 179; Charles Cist, ed., *The Cincinnati Directory, for 1842* (Cincinnati: E. Morgan, 1842), 172; Charles Cist, ed., *The Cincinnati Directory, for 1843* (Cincinnati: R. P. Brooks, 1843), 119; *The Cincinnati Directory for the Year 1844* (Cincinnati: R. P. Brooks, 1844), 14; *Robinson and Jones' Cincinnati Directory, for 1846* (Cincinnati: Robinson and Jones, 1846), 163; J. W. Ewing to Elwood Fisher, October 1, 1842, Greve-Fisher Collection, M-257, UMSL; [Elwood Fisher et al.], *Letter to the Secretary of the Treasury, on the Effect of the Tariff of 1842: On the Agricultural and Other Interests of the West, by a Committee of the Democratic Convention of Hamilton County, Ohio* (Cincinnati: Democratic Party [Hamilton County, Ohio], 1845), 1–21; Mujic, "Unfulfilled Appeals," 58–60; McClellan, "Cincinnati's Response to Abolitionism," 66–69; [Cincinnati, Ohio] *The Philanthropist*, January 29, 1839; *Cincinnati* [Ohio] *Gazette*, October 5, 1839; *A Debate on Slavery; Held in the City of Cincinnati, on the First, Second, Third, and Sixth Days of October, 1845, Upon the Question: Is Slave-holding in Itself Sinful, and the Relation Between Master and Slave, a Sinful Relation?* (Cincinnati: William H. Moore, 1846), passim; Elizabeth Fox-Genovese

and Eugene D. Genovese, *Slavery in White and Black: Class and Race in the Southern Slaveholders' New World Order* (Cambridge: Cambridge University Press, 2008), 37. In these debates, held variously in Lexington and Cincinnati, Cincinnati Presbyterian minister Nathan L. Rice, a proslavery Kentucky native, contended with noted antislavery ministers Jonathan Blanchard and Alexander Campbell. Henry Clay moderated the Lexington debate.

8. [Fisher et al.], *Letter to the Secretary of the Treasury, on the Effect of the Tariff of 1842*, 6, 9; *Cincinnati* [Ohio] *Daily Enquirer*, January 17, 1849; Elwood Fisher, *Lecture on the North and the South: Delivered Before the Young Men's Mercantile Library Association, of Cincinnati, Ohio, January 16, 1849* (Washington: John T. Towers, 1849), 14, 18–21; Fox-Genovese and Genovese, *Slavery in White and Black*, 54–55, 142–43, 244–45; Chauncey S. Boucher, "In Re That Aggressive Slavocracy," *MVHR* 8 (June–September 1921), 26n11, 36n34, 40n41, 49n58.

9. Fisher, *Lecture on the North and the South*, 32.

10. John Hope Franklin, "The North, the South, and the American Revolution," *JAH* 62 (June 1975): 9; George William Bagby, "Editor's Table," *Southern Literary Messenger* 33 (September–October 1862): 585; [Daniel R. Goodloe], *The South and the North: A Reply to a Lecture on the North and the South, by Ellwood [sic] Fisher, Delivered Before the Young Men's Mercantile Library Association of Cincinnati, January 16, 1849, by a Carolinian* (Washington, D.C.: Buell and Blanchard, 1849), 3–4; D. J. M., "Review of *Industrial Exchanges and Social Remedies, with a Consideration of Taxation*, by David Parish Barhydt, *The Southern Quarterly Review* 15 (July 1849): 460–61; Edward B. Bryan, *The Rightful Remedy: Addressed to the Slaveholders of the South* (Charleston, S.C.: Walker and James, 1850), 46, 74; John F. H. Claiborne, *Life and Correspondence of John A. Quitman, Governor of the State of Mississippi* (New York: Harper and Bros., 1860), 174–76; Josiah Priest, *Bible Defence of Slavery* (Glasgow, Ky.: W. S. Brown, 1852), 485; *DeBow's Review, Agricultural, Commercial, Industrial Progress and Resources* 22 (June 1857): 623–30; 23 (August–October 1857): 194–203, 266–82, 377–85; [James Henry Hammond], *The North and the South: A Review of the Lecture on the Same Subject, Delivered by Mr. Elwood Fisher, Before the Young Men's Mercantile Association of Cincinnati, Ohio* (Charleston, S.C.: J. S. Burges, 1849); W[ilia]m. H. Holcombe, "A Separate Nationality, or the Africanization of the South," *Southern Literary Messenger* 32 (February 1861): 85; Jan C. Dawson, "The Puritan and the Cavalier: The South's Perception of Contrasting Traditions," *JSH* 44 (November 1978): 599.

11. "Speech, Delivered in the House of Representatives of the United States, Feb. 3, 1849," in [Horace Mann], *Slavery: Letters and Speeches, by Rep. Horace Mann* (Boston: B. B. Mussey, 1853), 136; *BDAC*, 1499; *Sacramento Transcript*, June 26, 1850; Stanley C. Harrold Jr., "The Southern Strategy of the Liberty Party," *Ohio History* 87 (Winter 1978): 34.

12. Foner, *Free Soil*, 105; McClellan, "Cincinnati's Response to Abolitionism," 87; *The Southern Press*, June 19, 1850; Joseph G. Rayback, *Free Soil: The Election of 1848* (Lexington: University of Kentucky Press, 1970), 103–6; *Richmond Enquirer*, August 7, 1849; [Washington, D.C.] *Daily National Intelligencer*, August 28, 1849; *New York Daily-Times*, August 11, 1852; Eighth and Ninth U.S. Censuses, 1850 and 1860, Population Schedule, District of Columbia, NARA.

Chapter 2: Babel: Changed Persistence on Slavery's Borderland

1. Lyman Beecher, *Autobiography, Correspondence, Etc., of Lyman Beecher, D.D. Ed.*, ed. Charles Beecher (New York: Harper, 1864–1865), 2:444–45. For the fullest history of slavery in the middle border region, see Matthew Salafia, *Slavery's Borderland: Freedom and Bondage Along the Ohio River* (Philadelphia: University of Pennsylvania Press, 2013).

2. Aron, *How the West Was Lost*, 124–25; Glyndon G. VanDeusen, *The Jacksonian Era, 1828–1848* (New York: Harper and Bros., 1959), 96.

3. Wade, *Urban Frontier*, 129–57; Merrill D. Peterson, *The Great Triumvirate: Webster, Clay, and Calhoun* (New York: Oxford University Press, 1987), 6–11, 487–89; Elbert Hubbard,

Little Journeys to the Homes of American Statesmen (Chicago: Wm. H. Wise and Co., 1916), 3:218–20; *BDAC*, 986–87.
4. Russell L. Gerlach, "Population Origins in Rural Missouri," *MHR* 71 (October 1976): 5–15; Coulter, *Civil War and Readjustment in Kentucky*, 13; Robert M. Crisler, "Republican Areas in Missouri," *MHR* 42 (July 1948): 291; Seventh U. S. Census, 1850, Population Schedule, Boone, Callaway, Clay, Cooper, Howard, Lafayette, and Saline counties, Missouri, NARA; Rufus Babcock, ed., *Forty Years of Pioneer Life: Memoir of John Mason Peck, D. D.* (Philadelphia: American Baptist Publication Society, 1864), 146; Foley, *History of Missouri, Vol. 1: 1673–1820*, 238–39; Federal Writers' Project, *Missouri: A Guide to the "Show Me" State* (New York: Duell, Sloan and Pearce, 1941; reprint University Press of Kansas, 1986), 226–27; R. Douglas Hurt, *Agriculture and Slavery in Missouri's Little Dixie* (Columbia: University of Missouri Press, 1992), 8.
5. Joyce Appleby, "Commercial Farming and the 'Agrarian Myth' in the Early Republic," *JAH* 68 (March 1982): 835–36, 844–45; [Fayette] *Missouri Intelligencer and Boon's Lick Advertiser*, November 2, 1826, quoted in Hurt, *Agriculture and Slavery in Little Dixie*, 52; Kennedy, *Population of the United States in 1860*; [Kennedy,] *Manufactures of the United States in 1860*; Kennedy, *Agriculture of the United States in 1860*. The sample includes 174 counties, including 21 in southern Ohio, 27 in southern Indiana, 38 in southern Illinois, and 88 in Kentucky (thus exclusive of those counties in the southeastern part of the state). All population, manufacturing, and agricultural totals for these counties are included in the sample.
6. T[imothy] H. Breen, *Tobacco Culture: The Mentality of the Great Tidewater Planters on the Eve of Revolution* (Princeton, N.J.: Princeton University Press, 1985), 47–58; Hurt, *Agriculture and Slavery in Little Dixie*, 80–81, 99; Lewis C. Gray, *History of Agriculture in the Southern United States to 1860* (Washington, D.C.: Carnegie Institution, 1933), 2:759, 765, 821, 1038; Harold Tallant, *Evil Necessity: Slavery and the Political Culture in Antebellum Kentucky* (Lexington: University Press of Kentucky, 2003), 9; Joseph J. Mersman, *The Whiskey Merchant's Diary: An Urban Life in the Emerging Midwest*, ed. Linda A. Fisher (Athens: Ohio University Press, 2007), 165; James F. Hopkins, *A History of the Hemp Industry in Kentucky* (Lexington: University Press of Kentucky, 1951), 5–12; D. Lee, "Cotton Culture in the United States," *The Cultivator* 12 (November 1864): 348–49; *Centralia* [Ill.] *Sentinel*, November 19, 1863.
7. Michael Cassity, *Defending a Way of Life: An American Community in the Nineteenth Century* (Albany: State University of New York Press, 1989), 24–25; Ralph A. Wooster, *Politicians, Planters and Plain Folk: Courthouse and Statehouse in the Upper South, 1850–1860* (Knoxville: University of Tennessee Press, 1969), 63, 114–17, 168; Robert M. Ireland, *The County Courts in Antebellum Kentucky* (Lexington: University Press of Kentucky, 1972), 13; James Oakes, *Slavery and Freedom: An Interpretation of the Old South* (New York: Alfred A. Knopf, 1990), 144; Frederic A. Culmer, "Selling Mules Down South in 1835," *MHR* 24 (July 1930): 540; Freehling, *Road to Disunion*, 1:17–18, 34–35 and passim; W[ill] T. Hart to Susan Grigsby, July 5, 1861, Grigsby Family Papers, Mss. A/G857, folder 171, FHS.
8. Douglass C. North, *The Economic Growth of the United States, 1790–1860* (New York: Prentice Hall, 1961; reprint New York: W. W. Norton, 1966), 135; Berry, *Western Prices Before 1861*, 156 (second quote); Gray, *History of Southern Agriculture to 1860*, 2:765–66, 876; Channing, *Kentucky*, 50–51; Wade, *The Urban Frontier*, 99, 253–54; Gregory, *American Newspapers*, 228–36; Parish, "Daniel Webster, New England, and the West," *JAH* 54 (December 1967): 526; Kim M. Gruenwald, *River of Enterprise: The Commercial Origins of Regional Identity in the Ohio Valley, 1790–1850* (Bloomington and Indianapolis: Indiana University Press, 2002), 44–54, 117 and passim; [Eliza R.] Steele, *A Summer Journey in the West* (New York: John S. Taylor, 1841), 249; W[illiam] H. Venable, *The Beginnings of Literary Culture in the Ohio Valley* (Cincinnati: Robert Clarke, 1891), 436; William Davis Gallagher, *Facts and Conditions of Progress in the North-West* (Cincinnati: H. W. Derby, 1850), 167.
9. Charles Sellers, *The Market Economy: Jacksonian America, 1815–1846* (New York: Oxford University Press, 1991), 164–71.
10. George Rogers Taylor, *The Transportation Revolution, 1815–1860* (New York: Harper and Row, 1968), 26, 47, 79; Aron, *How the West Was Lost*, 133–36; Patricia Ann Hoskins, "'The

Old First Is with the South': The Civil War, Reconstruction, and Memory in the Jackson Purchase Region of Kentucky" (Ph.D. dissertation, Auburn University, 2008), 60; Darrel E. Bigham, *Towns and Villages of the Lower Ohio* (Lexington: University Press of Kentucky, 1998), 44–97; Stuart Seely Sprague, "Town Making in the Era of Good Feelings: Kentucky, 1814-1820," *Register* 72 (October 1974), 337–41; Paul B. Trescott, "The Louisville and Portland Canal Company, 1825–1874," *MVHR* 44 (March 1958): 686; Kentucky River Steamboat Advertisements, 1845–1850, Mss. VF 1208, CHSL; Wade, *Urban Frontier*, 129–57; Clark, *Pleasant Hill in the Civil War*, 4; Harrison and Klotter, *New History of Kentucky*, 125–32.

11. Harry N. Schieber, "Internal Improvements and Economic Change in Ohio, 1820–1860" (Ph.D. dissertation, Cornell University, 1962), 532–35.

12. Taylor, *Transportation Revolution*, 79; North, *Economic Growth of the United*, 253–54; Wright, "Ohio Town Patterns," 622–23.

13. Richard K. Vedder and Lowell E. Gallaway, "Migration and the Old Northwest," in David C. Klingaman and Richard K. Vedder, eds., *Essays in Nineteenth-Century Economic History: The Old Northwest* (Athens: Ohio University Press, 1975), 161; Howard W. Beers, *Growth of Population in Kentucky, 1860–1940* (Lexington: Kentucky Agricultural Experiment Station, 1942), 2, 21–24; McCandless, *History of Missouri*, 37.

14. North, *Economic Growth of the United States*, 257; Howard, *Illinois*, 148–52; Walter Havighurst, *Ohio: A Bicentennial History* (New York: W. W. Norton, 1976), 87.

15. Schieber, "Internal Improvements and Economic Change in Ohio," 532–35; *Ohio State Journal*, April 6, 1854, quoted in Foner, *Free Soil*, 14.

16. *Niles' Weekly Register*, August 9, 1834, quoted in Jon Gjerde, *The Minds of the West: Ethnocultural Evolution in the Rural Middle West, 1830–1917* (Chapel Hill and London: University of North Carolina Press, 1997), 26, 88–93; Stewart H. Holbrook, *The Yankee Exodus: An Account of Migration from New England* (New York: Macmillan, 1950), 136; Oliver, *Eight Months in Illinois*, 29; Havighurst, *Ohio*, 93; Howard, *Illinois*, 152; Richard J. Jensen, *Illinois: A Bicentennial History* (New York: W. W. Norton, 1977), 48–49; Howard H. Peckham, *Indiana: A Bicentennial History* (New York: W. W. Norton, 1978), 68–69; Elfreda Lang, "Ohioans in Northern Indiana before 1850," *IMH* 49 (December 1953): 398–99; Kenneth M. Stampp, *Indiana Politics During the Civil War* (Bloomington: Indiana University Press, 1949; reprint 1978), 2.

17. Parish, "An Exception to Most of the Rules," 228; Kennedy, *Population of the United States in 1860*, 288–98; Phillip Shaw Paludan, *"A People's Contest": The Union and Civil War, 1861–1865* (New York: Harper and Row, 1988), 10–15.

18. North, *Economic Growth of the United States*, 258; Richard Wade, *Slavery in the Cities: The South 1820–1860* (New York: Oxford University Press, 1964), 3–7, 15–16, 326–27; Ross, *Workers On the Edge*, 72; Warner L. Underwood Diary (typescript), June 16, 1850 entry, Underwood Collection, Mss. 58, ser. 2, box 1, folder 3, WKU; Seventh and Ninth U.S. Censuses, 1840 and 1860, Population Schedule, Vanderburgh, Floyd, and Jefferson Counties, Indiana; Montgomery County, Ohio; Fayette, Kenton, and Campbell Counties, Kentucky, NARA; Alexander I. Burckin, "The Formation and Growth of an Urban Middle Class: Power and Conflict in Louisville, Kentucky, 1828–1861" (Ph.D. dissertation, University of California–Irvine, 1993), 637–67; Wade, *Urban Frontier*, 202; Primm, *Lion of the Valley*, 149–50, 201–10; Louis S. Gerteis, *Civil War St. Louis* (Lawrence: University Press of Kansas, 2001), 40–41; Jeffry S. Adler, *Yankee Merchants and the Making of the Urban West: The Rise and Fall of Antebellum St. Louis* (Cambridge and New York: Cambridge University Press, 1991), 89–90.

19. Ray Allen Billington, *Protestant Crusade, 1800–1860: A Study of the Origins of American Nativism* (New York: Macmillan, 1938; reprint New York: Quadrangle Books, 1964), 322–44; McCandless, *History of Missouri*, 40–41; J. D. B. DeBow, ed., *The Seventh Census of the United States: 1850* (Washington, D.C.: Robert Armstrong, Public Printer, 1853), 663; Burckin, "Formation and Growth of an Urban Middle Class," 105–8, 637–67; Bruce Levine, "Community Divided: German Immigrants, Social Class, and Political Conflict in Antebellum Cincinnati," in Henry Shapiro and Jonathan Sarna, eds., *Ethnic Diversity and Civic Identity: Patterns of Conflict and Cohesion in Cincinnati since 1820* (Urbana and

Chicago: University of Illinois Press, 1992), 50, 69; McCandless, *History of Missouri*, 35, 38–41; Gottfried Duden, *Report on a Journey to the Western States of North America, and a Residence of Several Years on the Missouri (During the Years 1824, '25, '26, and 1827), Dealing with the Question of Emigration and Excess Population*, in Selwyn K. Troen and Glen E. Holt, eds., *St. Louis* (New York and London: New Viewpoints, 1977), 66–68, 74; Paul C. Nagel, *Missouri: A Bicentennial History* (New York: W. W. Norton, 1977), 95–99; Mersman, *Whiskey Merchant's Diary*, 181–209 and passim.
20. oss, *Workers On the Edge*, 173; Lyell, *Second Visit to North America*, 2:290–91; Joseph Michael White, "Religion and Community: Cincinnati Germans, 1814–1870" (Ph.D. dissertation, University of Notre Dame, 1980), 159–60; Harrison and Klotter, *New History of Kentucky*, 221; Levine, "Community Divided," 46–93 passim. Census figures derived from http://www.census.gov/population/www/documentation/twps0029/twps0029.html, table 21.
21. Eric Foner, *The Fiery Trial: Abraham Lincoln and American Slavery* (New York: W. W. Norton, 2010), 33–36; Berry, *Western Prices Before 1861*, 11–14; Harry N. Scheiber, *Ohio Canal Era: A Case Study of Government and the Economy, 1820–1861* (Athens: Ohio University Press, 1987), 4–5, 15–16, 88–113; Taylor, *Transportation Revolution*, 15–31, 45–48, 74–79; Freehling, *Road to Disunion*, 1:340–41; Sherry K. Jelsma, "A Dose of Slangwhang and Hard Cider: Charles S. Todd and the Harrison Campaign of 1840," *OVH* 8 (Summer 2008): 3–8; Etcheson, *Emerging Midwest*, 12–13.
22. Channing, *Kentucky*, 81–82; Etcheson, *Emerging Midwest*, 66. On the moral dimension of Whig orthodoxy, see Daniel Walker Howe, *The Political Culture of the American Whigs* (Chicago: University of Chicago Press, 1980).
23. Richard F. Nation, *At Home in the Hoosier Hills: Agriculture, Politics, and Religion in Southern Indiana, 1810–1870* (Bloomington: Indiana University Press, 2005), 128–85 passim; Etcheson, *Emerging Midwest*, 37–38.
24. Richard J. Jensen, *Illinois: A Bicentennial History* (New York: W. W. Norton, 1977), 44–46; Howard K. Beale, ed., *The Diary of Edward Bates 1859–1866* (Washington, D.C.: American Historical Association, 1933; reprint New York: Da Capo Press, 1971), 421–22.
25. Jensen, *Illinois*, 43–48; Howard, *Illinois*, 207–12; David Herbert Donald, *Lincoln* (New York: Simon and Schuster, 1995), 60–64; Channing, *Kentucky*, 77–89; Rogers, *Transportation Revolution*, 47; McCandless, *History of Missouri*, 34; Wade, *Urban Frontier*, 277–79, 316; David Thelen, *Paths of Resistance: Tradition and Dignity in Industrializing Missouri* (New York: Oxford University Press, 1986), 12–13; Nagel, *Missouri*, 66–67.
26. Daniel P. Glenn, "Losing the Market Revolution: Lebanon, Ohio, and the Economic Transformation of Warren County, 1820–1850," *OVH* 5 (Winter 2005): 25; Mujic, "Unfulfilled Appeals," 54–55; Peterson, *Great Triumvirate*, 66–67; Sellers, *Market Revolution*, 167–70.
27. Jensen, *Illinois*, 45–46; Stephen G. Carroll, "Thomas Corwin and the Agonies of the Whig Party" (Ph.D. dissertation, University of Colorado, 1970), 24–68 passim; McCandless, *History of Missouri*, 92–95; John Ray Cable, *The Bank of the State of Missouri* (New York: Longmans, Green, 1923), 56; W. Stephen Belko, *The Invincible Duff Green: Whig of the West* (Columbia: University of Missouri Press, 2006), 143–57; Michael F. Holt, *The Rise and Fall of the American Whig Party* (New York: Oxford University Press, 1999), 50, 75, 141, 216–17; Arthur C. Cole, *The Whig Party in the South* (Washington, D.C.: American Historical Association, 1914), 43–62, 115, 133.
28. Stanley W. Campbell, *The Slave Catchers: Enforcement of the Fugitive Slave Law, 1850–1860* (New York: W. W. Norton, 1972), 6; Hanford Dozier Stafford, "Slavery in a Border City: Louisville 1790–1860" (Ph.D. dissertation, University of Kentucky, 1982), 108; John Hope Franklin and Loren Schweninger, *Runaway Slaves: Rebels on the Plantation* (New York: Oxford University Press, 1999), 19; J. Blaine Hudson, *Fugitive Slaves and the Underground Railroad in the Kentucky Borderland* (Jefferson, N.C.: McFarland, 2002), 156. The benchmark study of the Underground Railroad is Wilbur H. Siebert, *The Underground Railroad: From Slavery to Freedom* (New York: Macmillan, 1898; reprint New York: Arno Press, 1968). For recent studies, see Larry Gara, *The Liberty Line: The Legend of the Underground Railroad* (Lexington: University Press of Kentucky, 1961); and Keith Griffler, *Front Line of*

Freedom: African Americans and the Forging of the Underground Railroad in the Ohio Valley (Lexington: University Press of Kentucky, 2004).

29. James Brewer Stewart, *Holy Warriors: The Abolitionists and American Slavery* (New York: Hill and Wang, 1976), 112; Foner, *Free Soil*, 73; Ratcliffe, *Party Spirit in a Frontier Republic*, 232.

30. William D. Gallagher, "The Question of Slavery in the South," *Hesperian* 1 (September 1838): 415–16; Lewis Perry and Matthew C. Sherman, "'What Disturbed the Unitarian Church in This Very City?': Alton, the Slavery Conflict, and Western Unitarianism," *CWH* 54 (March 2008): 29–34; [St. Louis] *Western Journal and Civilian* 8 (1852), 226, quoted in Fox-Genovese and Genovese, *Slavery in White and Black*, 98.

31. Tallant, *Evil Necessity*, 27; Madison, *The Indiana Way*, 107; Thornbrough, *Indiana in the Civil War Era*, 16–21; Donald, *Lincoln*, 137; Richard N. Current, "The Friend of Freedom," in Kenneth M. Stampp and Leon F. Litwack, eds., *Reconstruction: An Anthology of Revisionist Writings* (Baton Rouge and London: Louisiana State University Press, 1969), 29; Foner, *Fiery Trial*, 14–24, 58; McClellan, "Cincinnati's Response to Abolitionism," 60–63.

32. Tallant, *Evil Necessity*, 30–31; E[dward] S. Abdy, *Journal of a Residence and Tour in the United States of North America, from April, 1833 to October, 1834* (London: John Murray, 1835; reprint New York: Negro Universities Press, 1969), 3:38; Litwack, *North of Slavery*, 254–55; Lowell H. Harrison, *The Antislavery Movement in Kentucky* (Lexington: University Press of Kentucky, 1978), 31; Berwanger, *Frontier Against Slavery*, 51–59; Harrison and Klotter, *New History of Kentucky*, 176; Stephen E. Maizlish, *The Triumph of Sectionalism: The Transformation of Ohio Politics, 1844–1856* (Kent, Ohio: Kent State University Press, 1983), 110–11.

33. Griffler, *Front Line of Freedom*, 21–23; Trotter, *River Jordan*, 33; Thornbrough, *Indiana in the Civil War Era*, 17, 23–24; Thornbrough, *The Negro in Indiana*, 80n43 (emphasis in original); P[hilip] J. Staudenraus, *The African Colonization Movement, 1816–1865* (New York: Columbia University Press, 1961), 1–3; Litwack, *North of Slavery*, 20–21. On free blacks in the free states, see also Leonard P. Curry, *The Free Black in Urban America 1800–1850: The Shadow of the Dream* (Chicago: University of Chicago Press, 1981), 249–51; James Brewer Stewart, "Modernizing 'Difference': The Political Meaning of Color in the Free States, 1776–1840," in Michael A. Morrison and James Brewer Stewart, eds., *Race and the Early Republic: Racial Consciousness and Nation Building in the Early Republic* (Lanham, Md.: Rowman and Littlefield, 2002), 75–94, 113–34; Berwanger, *Frontier Against Slavery*, 7–59; Melish, *Disowning Slavery*, 261–74.

34. Lacy K. Ford, *Deliver Us from Evil: The Slavery Question in the Old South* (New York: Oxford University Press, 2009), 38–40; McCandless, *History of Missouri*, 61–63; Nagel, *Missouri*, 93; Harrison, *Antislavery Movement in Kentucky*, 18–21; Harrison and Klotter, *New History of Kentucky*, 174–76; Louis Filler, *The Crusade Against Slavery, 1830–1860* (New York: Harper and Row, 1960), 78–79, 80–81; Merton Dillon, *The Abolitionists: The Growth of a Dissenting Minority* (New York: W. W. Norton, 1979), 93–98; Benjamin Merkel, "The Abolition Aspects of Missouri's Antislavery Controversy, 1819–1865," *MHR* 44 (April 1950): 240, 242–46; *Journal of the House of Representatives of the State of Missouri, Eleventh General Assembly, First Session, 1841–1842* (Jefferson City: James Lusk, 1842), 30.

35. Christine Heyrman, *Southern Cross: The Making of the Bible Belt* (New York: Alfred A. Knopf, 1997), 17, 24, 68–69, 138–39, 155–56; Harrison, *Antislavery Movement in Kentucky*, 22–28; Jacob F. Lee, "Between Two Fires: Cassius M. Clay, Slavery, and Antislavery in the Kentucky Borderlands," *OVH* 6 (Fall 2006): 54–57, 60–63; Cassius M. Clay to N. M. Gordon, April 21, 1845, Gordon Family Papers, Mss. 51M40, box 4, UK; Freehling, *Road to Disunion*, 1:464–72; Tallant, *Evil Necessity*, 116–23; clipping, *True American—Extra*, August 15, 1845, Cassius M. Clay Papers, Mss. 56M89, UK; Fredrika Bremer, *The Homes of the New World: Impressions of America* (New York: Harper and Brothers, 1853), 1:106–7; Victor B. Howard, *The Evangelical War Against Slavery and Caste: The Life and Times of John G. Fee* (Selinsgrove, Pa.: Susquehanna University Press, 1996), 81–133 passim. For the most complete biography of Clay, see David L. Smiley, *The Lion of White Hall: The Life of Cassius M. Clay* (Madison: University of Wisconsin Press, 1962).

36. Ratcliffe, *Party Spirit in a Frontier Republic*, 231–33; 145–51; Gruenwald, *River of Enterprise*, 142–50; Guasco, "Confronting Democracy," 113–14, 134–51, 301–4; Howard, *Illinois*, 137–38.
37. Edward C. Smith, *The Borderland in the Civil War* (New York: Macmillan, 1927), 37–39; Merton L. Dillon, *Benjamin Lundy and the Struggle for Negro Freedom* (Urbana: University of Illinois Press, 1966), 87–103 and passim; Ratcliffe, *Party Spirit in a Frontier Republic*, 231; Harrison, *Antislavery Movement in Kentucky*, 28–29; Stanley Harrold, *The Rise of Aggressive Abolitionism: Addresses to the Slaves* (Lexington: University Press of Kentucky, 2004), 84; Robert K. Wallace, "J. P. Ball's 1853 Daguerrotype of Cincinnati Abolitionists Harwood, Brisbane, and Coffin," *The Daguerreian Society Quarterly* 26 (July–September 2014): 16–17; *Cincinnati* [Ohio] *Daily Enquirer*, August 25, 2015; William Davis Gallagher to William Henry Venable, August 13, 1881, Dolores Cameron Venable Memorial Collection, Mss. 127, box 6, folder 1, OHS.
38. Peter Cartwright, *Autobiography of Peter Cartwright, the Backwoods Preacher*, ed. W[illiam] P[eter] Strickland (New York: Carlton and Porter, 1857), 128–29, 363–65; Foner, *Fiery Trial*, 6, 35; Albert Barnes, *The Church and Slavery* (Philadelphia: Parry and McMillan, 1857), 56; Smith, *Borderland in the Civil War*, 33; C. C. Goen, "Broken Churches, Broken Nation: Regional Religion and North-South Alienation in Antebellum America," *Church History* 52 (March 1983): 21–35; McClellan, "Cincinnati's Response to Abolitionism," 72; Gamaliel Bailey to James G. Birney, May 24, 1838, in Dwight L. Dumond, ed., *Letters of James Gillespie Birney, 1831–1857* (Gloucester, Mass.: Peter Smith, 1966), 1:456–57; Perry and Sherman, "'What Disturbed the Unitarian Church?'" 29–34. At the 1844 conference, delegates suspended one of the church's five bishops, James O. Andrew, who had acquired slaves through marriage, until he freed his slaves. A few days later dissidents drafted a Plan of Separation, which permitted the annual conferences in slaveholding states to separate from the Methodist Episcopal Church, and in May 1845 delegates from the slave states met in Louisville to organize the Methodist Episcopal Church, South.
39. Etcheson, *Emerging Midwest*, 110–11; Harrold, *Border War*, 69; Foner, *Fiery Trial*, 22–24; Levi Coffin, *Reminiscences of Levi Coffin, the Reputed President of the Underground Railroad* (Cincinnati: Western Tract Society, 1876), iii; Parsons, *A Tour Through Indiana*, 114–15, 132; John P. Parker, *His Promised Land: The Autobiography of John P. Parker, Former Slave and Conductor on the Underground Railroad*, ed. Stuart Seely Sprague (New York: W. W. Norton, 1996), 71, 87, 122–26 and passim; Keith Griffler, "Beyond the Quest for the 'Real Eliza Harris': Fugitive Slave Women in the Ohio Valley," *OVH* 3 (Summer 2003): 3–7.
40. Samuel Galloway to John A. Trimble, January 12, 1837, John A. Trimble Papers, OHS; Edward Beecher, Narrative of Riots at Alton (New York: E. P. Dutton, 1965), v–xxix.
41. Beecher, *Autobiography, Correspondence, of Lyman Beecher*, 2:323; Lyman Beecher, *A Plea for the West* (Cincinnati: Truman and Smith, 1835), 12, 17–18, 20, 24–25, 41 and passim; Billington, *Protestant Crusade*, 182.
42. Robert H. Abzug, *Passionate Liberator: Theodore Dwight Weld and the Dilemma of Reform* (New York: Oxford University Press, 1980), 60–88; Donald M. Scott, "Abolition as a Sacred Vocation," in Lewis Perry and Michael Fellman, eds., *Antislavery Reconsidered: New Perspectives on the Abolitionists* (Baton Rouge: Louisiana State University Press, 1979), 70–73; Theodore Weld to Lewis Tappan, March 18, 1834, in Gilbert H. Barnes and Dwight L. Dumond, eds., *Letters of Theodore Dwight Weld, Angelina Grimké Weld, and Sarah Grimké* (New York: D. Appleton-Century, 1934), 1:132–35.
43. Charles L. Zorbaugh, "From Lane to Oberlin—An Exodus Extraordinary," *Proceedings of the Ohio Presbyterian Historical Society* 2 (1940): 38–40; James Hall, "Education and Slavery," *Western Monthly Magazine* 17 (May 1834): 266–73; Dillon, *The Abolitionists*, 61–64; Stewart, *Holy Warriors*, 56–59; Litwack, *North of Slavery*, 93–103; Fred G. Gosman, "Opposition to Abolition in Cincinnati, 1835–1840" (M.A. thesis, Kent State University, 1972), 23; Minutes of Executive Committee of the Board of Directors, Regarding the Anti-Slavery Society, August 1834, and Resolution No. 6, August 20, 1834, both in Lane Theological Seminary Records, Presbyterian Historical Society, Philadelphia, Pennsylvania; Ronald G. Walters, *The Antislavery Appeal: American Abolitionism After 1830* (New York: W. W. Norton, 1978), 37–40; Filler, *Crusade Against Slavery*, 66–69; Etcheson, *Emerging*

Midwest, 112–13; Seventh U.S. Census, 1850, Population Schedule, Franklin County, Ohio, NARA; Beecher, *Autobiography, Correspondence*, 2:331.

44. Stacey M. Robertson, *Hearts Beating for Liberty: Women Abolitionists in the Old Northwest* (Chapel Hill: University of North Carolina, 2010), 13, 19–20 and passim.
45. Tallant, *Evil Necessity*, 19–22; Betty Fladeland, *James Gillespie Birney: Slaveholder to Abolitionist* (Ithaca, NY: Cornell University Press, 1955), 88–89; Stanley Harrold, *The Abolitionists and the South, 1831–1861* (Lexington: University Press of Kentucky, 1995), 28–39; "James G. Birney's Anti-Slavery Activities in Cincinnati 1835–1837," *Bulletin of the Historical and Philosophical Society of Cincinnati* 9 (October 1951), 253–58; [Cincinnati] *The Gazette*, January 22, August 1–4, 1836; [Cincinnati] *The Philanthropist*, January 29, July 15, 29, 1836; Charles Edward Stowe, *Life of Harriet Beecher Stowe: Compiled from Her Letters By Her Son* (Charleston, SC: BiblioBazaar, 2006), 78; McClellan, "Cincinnati's Response to Abolitionism," 16–43; Trotter, *River Jordan*, 35; Etcheson, *Emerging Midwest*, 110–11.
46. McCandless, *History of Missouri*, 61–63; Nagel, *Missouri*, 93; Filler, *Crusade Against Slavery*, 78–79, 80–81; Dillon, *The Abolitionists*, 93–98; Merkel, "Abolition Aspects of Missouri's Antislavery Controversy," 240, 242–46; BDAC, 1478; Foner, *Fiery Trial*, 22–24, 88–89; Beecher, *Narrative of Riots at Alton*, 60–66; Merton L. Dillon, *Elijah P. Lovejoy, Abolitionist Editor* (Urbana: University of Illinois Press, 1961), passim; Howard, *Illinois*, 184–89; *Dedication of the Lovejoy Monument, Alton, Illinois, November 8th, 1897* (Alton, Ill.: Cha[rle]s Holden, [1897]), passim.
47. Foner, *Fiery Trial*, 24, 45; *Cincinnati Post and Anti-Abolitionist*, February 5, 24, March 5, 12, 1842; *Cincinnati Whig*, February 5, 26, 1839; Middleton, *Black Laws*, 195–200; Finkelman, *An Imperfect Union*, 157–78; George W. Julian, *The Life of Joshua R. Giddings* (Chicago: A. C. McClurg, 1892), 424–25; Quinten R. Skrabec, *William McGuffey: Mentor to American History* (New York: Algora Publishing, 2009), 75–88, 156; Paul D. Carrington, "Teaching Law in the Antebellum Northwest," *University of Toledo Law Review* 23 (Fall 1991): 11–16. My thanks to Leah Wickett for the source on McGuffey.
48. McClellan, "Cincinnati's Response to Abolitionism," 90.
49. Lyell, *Second Visit to the United States*, 285; Berwanger, *Frontier Against Slavery*, 30–51; Harrison, *Antislavery Movement in Kentucky*, 56–60; McCandless, *History of Missouri*, 61–63; Mujic, "Unfulfilled Appeals," 55; Middleton, *Black Laws*, 148–56; Stampp, *Indiana Politics During the Civil War*, 9.
50. Litwack, *North of Slavery*, 70–74, 93–94, 100, 114–16, 121–22, 151; [Gallipolis, Ohio] *Gallia Courier*, December 22, 1852; Berwanger, *Frontier Against Slavery*, 34.
51. Matthew Salafia, "Searching for Slavery: Fugitive Slaves in the Ohio River Valley Borderland, 1830–1860," *OVH* 8 (Winter 2008): 44.
52. John Malvin, *North into Freedom: The Autobiography of John Malvin, Free Negro, 1795–1880* (1879; Cleveland: Press of the Western Reserve University, 1966), 39; Amelia M. Murray, *Letters from the United States, Cuba and Canada* (New York: G. P. Putnam, 1856), 1:327–28; Gara, *Liberty Line*, 150; [Cincinnati, Ohio] *The Philanthropist*, October 8, 1838; March 24, November 11, 1840; May 12, 1841. For free black kidnapping, see Carol Wilson, *Freedom at Risk: The Kidnapping of Free Blacks in America, 1780–1865* (Lexington: University Press of Kentucky, 1994).
53. J. Blaine Hudson, "In Pursuit of Freedom: Slave Law and Emancipation in Antebellum Louisville and Jefferson County, Kentucky," *FCHQ* 76 (Summer 2002): 287–325 passim; Thomas C. Buchanan, "Levees of Hope: African American Steamboat Workers, Cities and Slave Escapes on the Antebellum Mississippi," *Journal of Urban History* 30 (March 2004), 363–64, 366–67 and passim; and Buchanan, "Rascals on the Antebellum Mississippi: African American Steamboat Workers and the St. Louis Hanging of 1841," *Journal of Social History* 34 (Summer 2001): 798–99; Harrold, *Border War*, 40; Freehling, *South vs. the South*, 27; Alexander I. Burckin, "'A Spirit of Perseverance': Free African Americans in Late Antebellum Louisville," *FCHQ* 70 (January 1996): 64–74; Hudson, *Fugitive Slaves*, 14–17. See also Buchanan, *Black Life on the Mississippi: Slaves, Free Blacks, and the Western Steamboat World* (Chapel Hill: The University of North Carolina Press, 2004).
54. Griffler, *Front Line of Freedom*, 16–20; Harrold, *Border War*, 57–63; Maximilian [Alexander Philipp Wied-Neuwied, Prince of Wied], *Travels in the Interior of North America*, trans.

H. Evans Lloyd (London: Ackerman, 1843), in Thwaites, *Early Western Travels*, 22:152–53, 201; Jon Musgrave, "History Comes Out of Hiding Atop Hickory Hill," *Springhouse Magazine* (December1996), http://www.illinoishistory.com/osharticle.html (accessed October 7, 2013); Ira Berlin, *Generations of Captivity: A History of African-American Slaves* (Cambridge, Mass.: Belknap Press of Harvard University Press, 2003), 161.

55. Josiah Henson, *The Life of Josiah Henson, Formerly a Slave, Now an Inhabitant of Canada, as Narrated by Himself* (Boston: Arthur D. Phelps, 1849; reprint Bedford, Mass.: Applewood Books, 2002), 30–34.
56. Elisha Winfield Green, *Life of the Rev. Elisha W. Green, One of the Founders of the Kentucky Normal and Theological Institute—Now the State University at Louisville... and Over Thirty Years Pastor of the Colored Baptist Churches of Maysville and Paris, Written by Himself* (Maysville, Ky.: The Republican Printing Office, 1888), 5–7, 12–15; Lewis Garrard Clarke, *Narrative of the Sufferings of Lewis Clarke, During a Captivity of More than Twenty-Five Years, Among the Algerines of Kentucky, One of the So Called Christian States of North America* (Boston: David H. Ela, Printer, 1845), 15.
57. Clarke, *Narrative of the Sufferings of Lewis Clarke*, 30–38; Hudson, *Fugitive Slaves and the Underground Railroad*, 55–58, 156; Gara, *Liberty Line*, 19; Harrold, *Border War*, 62–63; William Wells Brown, *Narrative of William W. Brown, an American Slave, Written by Himself* (London: C. Gilpin, 1849), 30.
58. Ann Clymer Bigelow, "Antebellum Ohio's Black Barbers in the Political Vanguard," *OVH* 11 (Summer 2011): 30–31.
59. Michael Tadman, *Speculators and Slaves: Masters, Traders, and Slaves in the Old South* (Madison: University of Wisconsin Press, 1989), 301–2; J. W. Loguen, *Rev. J. W. Loguen, as a Slave and as a Freeman: A Narrative of Real Life* (Syracuse, N.Y.: J. G. K. Truair, 1859), 302–19; Hudson, *Fugitive Slaves*, 14; Oakes, *Slavery and Freedom*, 151; Harrold, *Border War*, 40–41; Freehling, *Road to Disunion*, 1:23–24.
60. Griffler, *Front Line of Freedom*, 35; Taylor, *Frontiers of Freedom*, 25–26; Berlin, *Generations of Captivity*, 196–209; Litwack, *North of Slavery*, 73, 100, 160, 168–70, 279; Nicole Etcheson, "Good Men and Notorious Rogues: Vigilantism in Massac County, Illinois, 1846–1850," in Michael A. Bellesiles, ed., *Lethal Imagination: Violence and Brutality in American History* (New York: New York University Press, 1999), 152, 157, 160.

Vox Populi

1. William Barclay Napton Journals (typescript), 78–79, 84, William Barclay Napton Papers, box 4, MHS (hereafter cited as Napton Journals). For an edited version of Napton's journals, see Christopher Phillips and Jason L. Pendleton, eds., *The Union on Trial: The Political Journals of Judge William Barclay Napton, 1829–1883* (Columbia: University of Missouri Press, 2005).
2. Hopkins, *History of the Hemp Industry in Kentucky*, 204; Don E. Fehrenbacher, "Kansas, Republicanism, and the Rise of the Republican Party," in *The Sectional Crisis and Southern Constitutionalism* (Baton Rouge: Louisiana State University Press, 1980), 53–56; Etcheson, *Bleeding Kansas*, 30; William L. Barney, *Road to Secession: A New Perspective on the Old South* (New York: Praeger, 1972), 6–17; William J. Cooper Jr., *Liberty and Slavery: Southern Politics to 1860* (New York: Alfred A. Knopf, 1983), 260; Napton Journals, 50–51.
3. William B. Napton to C[laiborne] F. Jackson, October 3, 1857, Miscellaneous Manuscripts, Mss. 1879, SHSM.
4. C[laiborne] F. Jackson to David R. Atchison, January 18, 1854, and Atchison to Col. J[efferson] Davis, September 24, 1854, both in David Rice Atchison Papers, Mss. 71, folder 4, SHSM; Napton Journals (typescript), 150.
5. Atchison to Col. J[efferson] Davis, September 24, 1854, in David Rice Atchison Papers, Mss. 71, folder 4, SHSM; William B. Napton et al., *Address to the People of the United States, Together with the Proceedings and Resolutions of the Pro-Slavery Convention of Missouri, Held at Lexington, July, 1855* (St. Louis: Missouri Republican, 1855), 6, 7–8.
6. William B. Napton to Melinda Napton, March 9, [1855], William Barclay Napton Papers, box 1, MHS.

7. Hurt, *Agriculture and Slavery in Little Dixie*, 283–88; *Glasgow Weekly Times*, July 26, 1855; [Liberty, Mo.] *Weekly Tribune*, July 20, 27, 1855; William E. Parrish, *David Rice Atchison, Border Politician* (Columbia: University of Missouri Press, 1961), 175–76; *Missouri Statesman*, June 8, 1849.
8. James Shannon, *An Address Delivered Before the Pro-Slavery Convention of the State of Missouri, Held in Lexington, July 13, 1855, on Domestic Slavery, as Examined in the Light of Scripture of Natural Rights, of Civil Government, and the Constitutional Power of Congress* (St. Louis: [*Missouri*] Republican Book and Job Office, 1855), 10, 32; Parrish, *David Rice Atchison*, 175–76; Napton to Melinda Napton, July 13, [1855] William Barclay Napton Papers, box 1, MHS; [Columbia] *Missouri Statesman*, August 3, 1855.
9. Robert W. Frizzell, "Southern Identity in Nineteenth-Century Missouri: Little Dixie's Slave-Majority Areas and the Transition to Midwestern Farming," *MHR* 99 (April 2005): 241–43; Etcheson, *Bleeding Kansas*, 30.
10. [Liberty, Mo.] *Weekly Tribune*, July 20, 1855. Lawyers and judges comprised 15 percent of the delegation; physicians and merchant traders each constituted slightly less than 9 percent each. About 4 percent held low-level government positions, including county clerks, land registers, receivers of public moneys, and public auditors.
11. Bruce Levine, *Half Slave and Half Free: The Roots of Civil War* (New York: Hill and Wang, 1992), 38–39; Barney, *Road to Secession*, 3–48 passim; John Hebron Moore, *The Emergence of the Cotton Kingdom in the Old Southwest: Mississippi, 1770–1860* (Baton Rouge: Louisiana State University Press, 1988), 128–29; Hopkins, *History of the Hemp Industry in Kentucky*, 109–11.
12. Hurt, *Agriculture and Slavery in Little Dixie*, 226; McCandless, *History of Missouri*, 21, 57–59; Marion B. Lucas, *History of Blacks in Kentucky: From Slavery to Segregation, 1760–1891* (Frankfort: Kentucky Historical Society, 1992), 84–100, 101–7; Hurt, *Agriculture and Slavery in Little Dixie*, 215–44; Diane Mutti Burke, *On Slavery's Border: Missouri's Small Slaveholding Households, 1815–1865* (Athens: University of Georgia Press, 2010), 107–19 and passim.
13. Of the 239 delegates that the correspondents for the *Tribune* and the *Glasgow Times* reported variably as having been in attendance at the convention, 194 are identifiable. Of them, thirty (15.5 percent) owned twenty or more slaves; another 36 (18.6 percent) owned between ten and nineteen slaves. Seventh and Eighth U.S. Censuses, 1850 and 1860, Population and Slave Schedules, Andrew, Benton, Boone, Caldwell, Carroll, Cass, Chariton, Clay, Clinton, Cole, Cooper, Daviess, Henry, Howard, Jackson, Johnson, Lafayette, Linn, Livingston, Morgan, Pettis, Platte, Randolph, Ray, St. Louis, and Saline Counties, Missouri, NARA.
14. McCandless, *History of Missouri*, 242, 251–52, 268, 279, 281–82.

Chapter 3: The Ten-Year War: Sectional Politics in a Dividing Region

1. George Caleb Bingham to James S. Rollins, February 1, 1861, in [George Bingham], in Lynn Wolf Gentzler and Roger E. Robinson, eds., *"But I Forget That I Am a Painter and Not a Politician": The Letters of George Caleb Bingham* (Columbia: State Historical Society of Missouri, 2011), 131–33; Civil War Reminiscences of Leeland Hathaway, 1893–94, Hathaway Papers, Mss. M-20 (microfilm), UK; original in Leeland Hathaway Recollections, Mss. 2954, UNC; McCandless, *History of Missouri*, 270; Etcheson, *Emerging Midwest*, 108; Power, *Planting Corn Belt Culture*, 7.
2. Jonathan H. Earle, *Jacksonian Antislavery and the Politics of Free Soil, 1824–1854* (Chapel Hill: University of North Carolina Press, 2004), 5–7 and passim; Carroll, "Thomas Corwin and the Agonies of the Whig Party," 101–2; Thornbrough, *Indiana in the Civil War Era*, 41; Michael A. Morrison, *Slavery and the American West: The Eclipse of Manifest Destiny and the Coming of the Civil War* (Chapel Hill: University of North Carolina Press, 1997), 35–36.
3. Thornbrough, *Indiana in the Civil War Era*, 26–27; *BDAC*, 1915.
4. Douglas A. Gamble, "Joshua Giddings and the Ohio Abolitionists: A Study in Radical Politics," *Ohio History* 88 (Winter 1979): 42; Morrison, *Slavery in the American West*,

79–81; Tallant, *Evil Necessity*, 70–71; Donald, *Lincoln*, 134–43; Robert W. Johannsen, ed., *The Lincoln-Douglas Debates of 1858* (New York: Oxford University Press, 1965), 4; Johannsen, *To the Halls of the Montezumas: The Mexican War in the American Imagination* (New York: Oxford University Press, 1985), 214–18, 270–79; Perry and Sherman, "'What Disturbed the Unitarian Church?'" 8; Carroll, "Thomas Corwin and the Agonies of the Whig Party," 26–35.
5. Maizlish, *Triumph of Sectionalism*, 106–11; Thornbrough, *Indiana in the Civil War Era*, 26–27.
6. Rayback, *Free Soil*, 92–94; Thornbrough, *Indiana in the Civil War Era*, 27; John Niven, *Salmon P. Chase: A Biography* (New York: Oxford University Press, 1995), 29–70, 124–46; Maizlish, *Triumph of Sectionalism*, 106–11.
7. Berlin, *Slaves Without Masters*, 136, 396–403; Wade, *Slavery in the Cities*, 38–54, 325–27; Hurt, *Agriculture and Slavery in Little Dixie*, 219; Harrison and Klotter, *New History of Kentucky*, 168.
8. Gray, *History of Agriculture in the Southern U.S.*, 2:482; Coulter, *Civil War and Readjustment in Kentucky*, 7–8.
9. Gray, *History of Agriculture in the Southern U.S.*, 2:219, 482; Hurt, *Agriculture and Slavery in Little Dixie*, 219; Harrison and Klotter, *A New History of Kentucky*, 168; Coulter, *Civil War and Readjustment in Kentucky*, 7–8; Ira Berlin et al., eds., *Freedom: A Documentary History of Emancipation, 1861–1867*, ser. 1, vol. 1, *The Destruction of Slavery* (Cambridge and New York: Cambridge University Press, 1982), 493.
10. Hurt, *Agriculture and Slavery in Little Dixie*, 219–20, 307–8; Frizzell, "Southern Identity in Nineteenth-Century Missouri, 241–42; *Compendium of the Inhabitants of the United States in 1840*, 88–89; Fifth and Sixth U.S. Censuses, 1830 and 1840, Population Schedules, Boone, Callaway, Chariton, Clay, Cooper, Howard, Lafayette, and Saline Counties, Missouri, NARA; Gray, *History of Agriculture in the Southern U.S.*, 2:482; Berlin, *Slaves Without Masters*, 396–403; Wade, *Slavery in the Cities*, 325–27.
11. Berlin, *Slaves Without Masters*, 136–37, 396–403; Gary W. Gallagher, *The Union War* (Cambridge, Mass.: Harvard University Press, 2011), 42–43; Berlin et al., *Freedom: A Documentary History of Emancipation, 1861–1867*, ser. 1, vol. 2, *The Wartime Genesis of Free Labor* (Cambridge and New York: Cambridge University Press, 1993), 626; McCandless, *History of Missouri*, 21, 57–59; Lucas, *History of Blacks in Kentucky*, 106–17. In 1860, African American populations in Ohio, Indiana, and Illinois were 1.6 percent, .85 percent, and .45 percent, respectively.
12. William Nisbet Chambers, *Old Bullion Benton: Senator from the New West* (Boston: Little, Brown and Company, 1956), 273–76; William M. Meigs, *Life of Thomas Hart Benton* (Philadelphia: J. B. Lippincott, 1904; reprint New York: Da Capo Press, 1970), 346–48; McCandless, *History of Missouri*, 233; Resolutions of the General Assembly of the State of Missouri on the Annexation of Texas to the United States, Capitol Fire Documents, 1806–1957, microfilm reel CFD-121, folder 11065: Thirteenth Gen. Assembly (1844–1845), House Resolutions (1844–45), MSA; Elbert B. Smith, *Magnificent Missourian: The Life of Thomas Hart Benton* (Philadelphia: J. B. Lippincott, 1958), 188–89, 200 (emphasis in original); Parrish, *David Rice Atchison*, 45; Christopher Phillips, *Missouri's Confederate: Claiborne Fox Jackson and the Creation of Southern Identity in the Border West* (Columbia: University of Missouri Press, 2000), 156–80.
13. Tallant, *Evil Necessity*, 18–19, 129, 145–48, 155; Freehling, *Road to Disunion*, 1:466–68; Jennifer Cole, "'For the Sake of the Songs of the Men Made Free': James Speed and the Emancipationists' Dilemma in Nineteenth-century Kentucky," *Ohio Valley History* 4 (Winter 2004): 31–35; Clement Eaton, "Minutes and Resolutions of an Emancipation Meeting in Kentucky in 1849," *JSH* 14 (November 1948): 541–45; Harrison, *Antislavery Movement in Kentucky*, 55–57, 83–83; S. S. Nicholas et al., *Slave Emancipation in Kentucky* (Louisville: Corresponding and Executive Committee on Emancipation, [1849]), 7; Harrison and Klotter, *New History of Kentucky*, 117–21; Richard Sutton, *Report of the Debates and Proceedings of the Convention for the Revision of the Constitution of the State of Kentucky* (Frankfort: A. G. Hodges, 1849), 118; Hopkins, *History of Hemp in Kentucky*, 29–30. For a thorough discussion of state emancipations in the eastern and middle states, see Zilversmit, *First Emancipation*, esp. 109–200.

14. Warner L. Underwood Diary (typescript), February 11, 1849 entry, Underwood Collection, Mss. 58, ser. 2, box 1, folder 3, WKU; Lowell H. Harrison, *Lincoln of Kentucky* (Lexington: University Press of Kentucky, 2000), 113.
15. Harrold, *Border War*, 138–58; Holman Hamilton, *Prologue to Conflict: The Crisis and Compromise of 1850* (New York: W. W. Norton, 1966), 21, 54, 59, 95–97, 168–69; Freehling, *Road to Disunion*, 1:502–5; Levine, *Half Slave and Half Free*, 186–90; Gara, *Liberty Line*, 141–42; Litwack, *North of Slavery*, 248–54; Ann Hagedorn, *Beyond the River: The Untold Story of the Heroes of the Underground Railroad* (New York: Simon and Schuster, 2004), 238–39, 243.
16. Hamilton, *Prologue to Conflict*, 92–95, 166–67; Thornbrough, *Indiana in the Civil War Era*, 42; Jeptha Carrigus to John G. Davis, February 25, 1854, John G. Davis Papers, Mss. M0082, box 1, folder 9, IHSL; Chambers, *Old Bullion Benton*, 359–62; *Congressional Globe*, 31st Cong., 1st Sess., 492, 640–43, 652–55, 702–14, 747–59.
17. Mary Logan, *Reminiscences of the Civil War and Reconstruction* (Carbondale: Southern Illinois University Press, 1970), 41–42.
18. Gamble, "Joshua Giddings and the Ohio Abolitionists," 46; *Journal of the House of Representatives of the United States, 1850–1851* (Washington, D.C.: House of Representatives, 1850–51), 31st Cong., 2nd Sess., 38, 56, 67, 69, 77, 83–84, 87–88, 100, 117, 122–23, 133, 142–43, 158, 164, 166–67, 193, 205, 222, 225; Harrold, *Border War*, 148–49; B. White to Thomas Corwin, September 30, 1850, Thomas Corwin Papers, Mss. 297, OHS.
19. David M. Potter, *The Impending Crisis, 1848–1861* (New York: Harper and Row, 1976), 158–77; Freehling, *Road to Disunion*, 1:546–49, 552; Foner, *Free Soil*, 155–56; Roy F. Nichols, "The Kansas-Nebraska Act: A Century of Historiography," *MVHR* 43 (September 1956): 204–5; Yonatan Eyal, "With His Eyes Open: Stephen A. Douglas and the Kansas-Nebraska Disaster of 1854," *JISHS* 91 (Winter 1998): 212–13; William L. Barney, *Road to Secession: A New Perspective on the Old South* (New York: Praeger, 1972), 6–17; James A. Rawley, *Race and Politics: "Bleeding Kansas" and the Coming of the Civil War* (Philadelphia: J. B. Lippincott, 1969; reprint Lincoln: University of Nebraska Press, 1979), 70.
20. Etcheson, *Emerging Midwest*, 108–13, 120–21 (italics in original); Yonatan Eyal, *The Young America Movement and the Transformation of the Democratic Party, 1828–1861* (Cambridge: Cambridge University Press, 2007), 9–12 and passim; *BDAC*, 1636; Donald, *Lincoln*, 183; John Hough James to George Reber, July 2, 1855, James Family Papers, Mss. 258, OHS.
21. Levine, *Half Slave and Half Free*, 194–95; Eulogy on Henry Clay, July 6, 1852, and Speech at Peoria, Illinois, October 16, 1854, both in *CWAL*, 2:130–32, 255; Eyal, *Young America Movement*, 186–94; Sean Wilentz, "Slavery, Antislavery, and Jacksonian Democracy," in Melvyn Stokes and Stephen Conway, eds., *The Market Revolution in America: Social, Political, and Religious Expressions, 1800–1880* (Charlottesville: University Press of Virginia, 1996), 202–23 passim; David Herbert Donald, *Charles Sumner and the Coming of the Civil War* (New York: Alfred A. Knopf, 1960), 252; *Congressional Globe*, 33rd Cong., 1st Sess., p. 281; Levine, *Spirit of 1848*, 192; Salmon P. Chase to E. S. Hamlin, January 22, 1854, in *Annual Report of the American Historical Association for the Year 1902 in Two Volumes: Sixth Report of Historic Manuscripts Commission; with Diary and Correspondence of Salmon P. Chase* (Washington, D.C.: Government Printing Office, 1903), 2:254–56; Foner, *Free Soil*, 48; Donald, *Lincoln*, 167–69.
22. Foner, *Free Soil*, 73, 126–28; Donald, *Lincoln*, 169–71; Frank L. Klement, *The Limits of Dissent: Clement L. Vallandigham and the Civil War* (Lexington: University Press of Kentucky, 1970), 13–14; Etcheson, *Emerging Midwest*, 123; Levine, *Half Slave and Half Free*, 193; Frank Towers, *The Urban South and the Coming of the Civil War* (Charlottesville: University of Virginia Press, 2004), 85–86; J[ames] S. Rollins to George R. Smith, January 30, 1856, General George R. Smith Papers, MHS; Carroll, "Thomas Corwin and the Agonies of the Whig Party," 224–28.
23. Madison, *Indiana Way*, 194; Foner, *Free Soil*, 73, 127, 198; Mark E. Neely Jr., *The Last Best Hope of Earth: Abraham Lincoln and the Promise of America* (Cambridge, Mass.: Harvard University Press, 1995), 39; Thornbrough, *Indiana in the Civil War Era*, 83; A. Bowen to John G. Davis, February 14, 1858, John G. Davis Papers, Mss. M0082, box 2, folder 16, IHSL; Levine, *Spirit of 1848*, 192–93; Etcheson, *Emerging Midwest*, 131–32; Carroll,

"Thomas Corwin and the Agonies of the Whig Party," 224–26; Maizlish, *Triumph of Sectionalism*, 185, 193, 211.
24. Foner, *Free Soil*, 128–31, 198; Foner, *Fiery Trial*, 82; Burckin, "Formation and Growth of an Urban Middle Class," 496; Carroll, "Thomas Corwin and the Agonies of the Whig Party," 257; Towers, *Urban South*, 117, 120; Mark Alan Neels, "'We Shall Be Literally 'Sold to the Dutch': Nativist Suppression of German Radicals in Antebellum St. Louis, 1852–1861," *The Confluence* 1 (Fall 2009): 23–26. My thanks to David Wolfford for sharing his research on the 1856 Cincinnati convention.
25. Foner, *Free Soil*, 198, 210–11; *BDAC*, 1391–92.
26. Maizlish, *Triumph of Sectionalism*, 236; Etcheson, *Emerging Midwest*, 114–15.
27. David Herbert Donald, *Lincoln's Herndon: A Biography* (New York: Alfred A. Knopf, 1948), 120–21; Donald, *Lincoln*, 211–13; Foner, *Fiery Trial*, 81, 73–75; William B. Napton to C[laiborne] F. Jackson, October 3, 1857, Miscellaneous Manuscripts, Mss. 1879, SHSM.
28. Donald, *Lincoln's Herndon: A Biography* (New York: Alfred A. Knopf, 1948), 120; Donald, *Lincoln*, 211; Foner, *Fiery Trial*, 75 (italics in original), 83–84; Foner, *Free Soil*, 48–51; Howard, *Illinois*, 290.
29. Michael Fellman, *Inside War: The Guerrilla Conflict in Missouri during the American Civil War* (New York: Oxford University Press, 1989), 6–7; *Appendix to the Congressional Globe*, 34th Cong., 1st sess., 465; [Columbia] *Missouri Statesman*, March 9, 1849.
30. James S. Rollins to My Dear Son, November 14, 1858, James S. Rollins Papers, Mss. 1026, box 2, folder 55, SHSM; [Columbia] *Missouri Statesman*, March 9, 1849; *Appendix to the Congressional Globe*, 33rd Cong., 1st sess., 301; Norma L. Peterson, *Freedom and Franchise: The Political Career of B. Gratz Brown* (Columbia: University of Missouri Press, 1965), 74; Thelma Jennings, *The Nashville Convention: Southern Movement for Unity, 1848–1851* (Memphis, Tenn.: Memphis State University Press, 1980), 87–211 passim; Parrish, *David Rice Atchison*, 101. Italics in Atchison's quote are mine.
31. Fehrenbacher, "Kansas, Republicanism, and the Rise of the Republican Party," 53–56; William E. Gienapp, "The Crime Against Sumner: The Caning of Charles Sumner and the Rise of the Republican Party," *Civil War History* 25 (September 1979): 238–45; Floyd C. Shoemaker, "Missouri's Proslavery Fight for Kansas, 1854–1855," *MHR* 48 (April 1954): 232; J[ames] H. Buckner to Thomas Buckner, August 2, 1856, Buckner Family Papers, Mss. A/B925, folder 19, FHS; Morrison, *Slavery and the American West*, 165–67; Gunja SenGupta, *For God and Mammon: Evangelicals and Entrepreneurs, Masters and Slaves in Territorial Kansas, 1854–1860* (Athens: University of Georgia Press, 1996), 118; J[ohn] J. Lowry to M[eredith] M. Marmaduke, September 8, 1848, Sappington Family Papers, box 5, MHS; Napton Journals, 50–51, MHS.
32. Etcheson, *Bleeding Kansas*, 32–34, 94–96; Phillip S. Paludan, "The American Civil War Considered as a Crisis of Law and Order," *AHR* 77 (October 1972): 1013–34; Nicole Etcheson, "The Goose Question: The Proslavery Party in Territorial Kansas and the 'Crisis in Law and Order,'" in Jonathan Earle and Diane Mutti Burke, eds., *Bleeding Kansas, Bleeding Missouri: The Long Civil War on the Western Border* (Lawrence: University Press of Kansas, 2013), 47–63; Bill Cecil-Fronsman, "'Death to All Yankees and Traitors in Kansas': The *Squatter Sovereign* and the Defense of Slavery in Kansas," *Kansas History* 16 (Spring 1993): 25; [Atchison, Kans.] *Squatter Sovereign*, October 16, March 6, February 13, 1855; William Walker to David R. Atchison, July 6, 1854, and C[laiborne] F. Jackson to David R. Atchison, January 18, 1854, both in David Rice Atchison Papers, Mss. 71, folder 4, SHSM; Atchison to Jefferson Davis, September 24, 1854, Jefferson Davis Papers, Duke; Shoemaker, "Missouri's Proslavery Fight for Kansas," 226–27.
33. Parrish, *David Rice Atchison*, 162–68; Napton Journals, 208.
34. William Walker to David R. Atchison, July 6, 1854, David Rice Atchison Papers, Mss. 71, folder 4, SHSM; Shoemaker, "Missouri's Proslavery Fight for Kansas," 230–34; Elmer LeRoy Craik, "Southern Interest in Territorial Kansas, 1854–1858," *Kansas Historical Collections* 15 (1919–1921): 376–95 passim; James C. Malin, "The Proslavery Background of the Kansas Struggle," *MVHR* 10 (December 1923): 285–305 passim; SenGupta, *For God and Mammon*, 116–18; Hurt, *Agriculture and Slavery in Little Dixie*, 281, 290; [Jefferson City, Mo.] *Jefferson Inquirer*, July 21, 1860; Jay Monaghan, *Civil War on the*

Western Border, 1854–1865 (Boston: Little, Brown, 1955; reprint Lincoln: University of Nebraska Press, 1984), 19–20, 147; Glasgow [Mo.] *Weekly Times,* June 14, 1855, October 19, 1854, March 15, 1855.

35. Morrison, *Slavery in the American West,* 160–61, 169–78; Glasgow [Mo.] *Weekly Times,* June 14, 28, 1855; [Atchison, Kans.] *Squatter Sovereign,* February 20, March 6, May 29, October 16, 1855; Cecil-Fronsman, "'Death to All Yankees and Traitors in Kansas,'" 25–29.

36. William E. Smith, *The Francis Preston Blair Family in Politics* (New York: Macmillan, 1933; reprint New York: Da Capo Press, 1969), 1:203; Foner, *Free Soil,* 55–56, 63; Gari Carter, ed., *Troubled State: Civil War Journals of Franklin Archibald Dick* (Kirksville, Mo.: Truman State University Press, 2008), 42.

37. Harry L. Watson, "Conflict and Collaboration: Yeomen, Slaveholders, and Politics in the Antebellum South," *Social History* 10 (October 1985): 295–96; Stephen C. LeSueur, *The 1838 Mormon War in Missouri* (Columbia: University of Missouri Press, 1990), 57–58; [Jackson Co., Mo.] *Southern Democrat,* September 14, 1850; *Appendix to the Congressional Globe,* 34th Cong., 1st sess., 465, 1303; Napton Journals, folder 1, 78–79.

38. Chambers, *Old Bullion Benton,* 276; David Rice Atchison to W. Y. Slack, W[illia]m Hudgins, and Others, November 19, 1850, in [St. Louis] *Missouri Republican,* January 7, 1851, reprinted in *MHR* 31 (July 1937): 443–44; Parrish, *David Rice Atchison,* 74; [Jefferson City, Mo.] *Jefferson Inquirer,* February 12, 1853.

39. Glasgow [Mo.] *Weekly Times,* March 29, 1855; David Rice Atchison to W. Y. Slack, W[illia]m. Hudgins, and Others, November 19, 1850, in [St. Louis] *Missouri Republican,* January 7, 1851, reprinted in *MHR* 31 (July 1937): 443–44; Napton Journals, 92–93.

40. Thomas L. Snead, *The Fight for Missouri from the Election of Lincoln to the Death of Lyon* (New York: Charles Scribner's Sons, 1886), 13; [Jefferson City, Mo.] *Jefferson Inquirer,* February 5, 12, 1853; Peterson, *Freedom and Franchise,* 28–29.

41. [Jefferson City, Mo.] *Jefferson Inquirer,* December 5, 1857.

42. *New York Times,* October 3, 1854.

43. Burton Milward, *A History of the Lexington Cemetery* (Lexington: Lexington Cemetery Association, 1989), 40–55; J. Winston Coleman, *Last Days, Death, and Funeral of Henry Clay, with Some Remarks on the Clay Monument in the Lexington Cemetery* (Lexington: Winburn Press, 1951), 3–30; A. H. Carrier, *Monument to the Memory of Henry Clay* (Philadelphia: D. Rulison, 1859), 129–30; *Report of the Ceremonies on the Fourth of July 1857, at the Laying of the Corner Stone of a National Monument, to Be Erected near Lexington, Kentucky, to the Memory of Henry Clay: Together with the Oration Delivered on the Occasion by the Rev. Robert J. Breckinridge* ([Cincinnati]: published by the Clay Monument Association, 1857), passim; Clay Monument Association, *Articles for the Government of the Clay Monument Association* (Lexington: The *Observer and Reporter* Office, 1852), passim; card, [New Orleans] Clay Monumental Association, February 20, 1860, Grigsby Family Papers, Mss. A/G857, folder 166, FHS; Peterson, *Great Triumvirate,* 488–89; [Henry Clay], "On Slavery and Abolition. At Richmond, Indiana, October 1, 1842," in Daniel Mallory, ed., *The Life and Speeches of Henry Clay* [2 vols.] (Hartford, Conn.: Silas and Andrus and Son, 1855), 2:595–600; David S. Heidler and Jeanne T. Heidler, *Henry Clay: The Essential American* (New York: Random House, 2010), 372–74.

44. Harrison and Klotter, *New History of Kentucky,* 183; Harrison, *Antislavery Movement in Kentucky,* 83–84; Hoskins, "The Old First Is with the South," 52; Journal of Ellen Kenton McGaughey Wallace, 1849–1865 (typescript), December 3, 1856–January 14, 1857 entries, Wallace-Starling Family Diaries, Mss. 96M07, KHS; Tallant, *Evil Necessity,* 167; Herbert Aptheker, *American Negro Slave Revolts* (New York: Columbia University Press, 1943), 350–58; H[enry] T. Duncan Sr. to H[enry] T. Duncan Jr., April 7, 1858, Duncan Family Papers, Mss. 71M38, UK; Harrold, *Border War,* 183–85.

45. Stephen I. Rockenbach, "'War Upon Our Border': War and Society in Two Ohio Valley Communities, 1861–1865" (Ph.D. dissertation, The University of Cincinnati, 2005), 10–16; Harrold, *Border War,* 179–82; Governor's Correspondence File—Military Correspondence, 1859–1862, folders 95–96, KDLA; Phillip T. Tucker, "'Ho, for Kansas': The Southwest Expedition of 1860," *MHR* 86 (October 1991): 22–36 passim; Jeremy Neely, *The Border*

Between Them: Violence and Reconciliation on the Kansas-Missouri Line (Columbia: University of Missouri Press, 2007), 93–94.
46. Michael P. Johnson, *Toward a Patriarchal Republic: The Secession of Georgia* (Baton Rouge: Louisiana State University Press, 1977), 43–47, 85–101; McCandless, *History of Missouri*, 277–78; Harrison, *Lincoln of Kentucky*, 114; Smith, *Borderland in the Civil War*, 65; Johannsen, *Lincoln-Douglas Debates*, 10–12; Howard, *Illinois*, 294; Fragment of a Speech, [May 18, 1858], in *CWAL*, 2:452; Perry and Sherman, "'What Disturbed the Unitarian Church in This Very City?,'" 5–6.
47. Donald, *Lincoln*, 199–201, 212; Foner, *Fiery Trial*, 74–78, 103, 129–31. See also James Oakes, *Freedom National: The Destruction of Slavery in the United States, 1861–1865* (New York: W. W. Norton, 2012). Oakes's argument for a Republican consensus in pursuit of emancipation nearly since the party's founding largely understates western Republicans'— including Lincoln's—persistent racial conservatism and moderate slavery politics before and during the early years of the war.
48. Lincoln to Joshua F. Speed, August 24, 1855; Speech at Ottawa, August 21, 1858; and Speech at New Haven, Connecticut, March 6, 1860, all in *CWAL*, 2:320–21, 4:16, 24, 3:16.
49. Johannsen, ed., *Lincoln-Douglas Debates*, 8–9, 44–45, 95–100, 132–33, 150–51, 152, 157–58, 195; Full Debate with Stephen A. Douglas at Ottawa, Illinois, August 21, 1858, *CWAL*, 3:8–9; George M. Fredrickson, "A Man but Not a Brother: Abraham Lincoln and Racial Equality," *JSH* 41 (February 1975): 39–58 passim; Howard, *Illinois*, 294; Harrison, *Lincoln of Kentucky*, 100–106.
50. Foner, *Fiery Trial*, 113–17; Speech at Columbus, Ohio, September 16, 1859, and Speech at Cincinnati, Ohio, September 17, 1859, both in *CWAL*, 3:401–2, 452–54; [Georgetown] *The Southern Ohio Argus*, October 6, 1859; Harold Holzer, *Lincoln at Cooper Union: The Speech That Made Abraham Lincoln President* (New York: Simon and Schuster, 2006), 16, 39–40; Gary Ecelbarger, *The Great Comeback: How Abraham Lincoln Beat the Odds to Win the 1860 Republican Nomination* (New York: Macmillan, 2008), 66–76. Published nationally, Lincoln's Cincinnati speech garnered his invitation to address Republicans at New York's Cooper Institute the following February.
51. *Kentucky Statesman*, November 22, 1859; *Tri-Weekly Kentucky Yeoman*, November 24, 1859; [Paris, Ky.] *Western Citizen*, November 11, 1859; Astor, *Rebels on the Border*, 70; Harrold, *Border War*, 183–85; Harrison and Klotter, *New History of Kentucky*, 183; Speech at Elwood, Kansas, December 1, 1859; Second Speech at Leavenworth, Kansas, December 5, 1859; and Address at Cooper Institute, February 27, 1860, all in *CWAL*, 3:496, 502–3, 538–42.
52. Harrison, *Antislavery Movement in Kentucky*, 64–66; W[illiam] S. Bailey, *A Short Sketch of Our Troubles in the Anti-Slavery Cause* (Newport: Office of the Daily and Weekly News, 1858), 1; Eighth and Ninth U.S. Censuses, 1850 and 1860, Population Schedule, Campbell County, Kentucky, NARA; William S. Bailey to S. S. Jocelyn, February 15, 1853, September 24, October 18, December 11, 1856; January 12, 21, 1857; John G. Fee to S. S. Jocelyn, February 15, July 15, 1853; William S. Bailey to S. S. Jocelyn, February 16, 1860; Rebecca Bailey to Lewis Tappan, May 29, 1862, all in microfilm reels 68–69, Kentucky, AMA; Anne H. Richardson, *Little Laura, the Kentucky Abolitionist, to the Young Friends of the Slave* (Newcastle: Thomas Pigg, 1859); *The Free South*, October 1, 1858, August 13, 1860; *Revised Statutes of Kentucky, 1859–1860* (Cincinnati: R. H. Stanton, 1860), 1:119.
53. George H. Porter, *Ohio Politics During the Civil War Period* (New York: Columbia University, 1911), 128–32; *Congressional Globe*, 36th Cong., 1st Sess., 73, and Appendix, 42–47; Klement, *Limits of Dissent*, 25–26; Jennifer L. Weber, *Copperheads: The Rise and Fall of Lincoln's Opponents in the* North (New York: Oxford University Press, 2006), 27.
54. Abraham Lincoln to John J. Crittenden, November 4, 1858, in *CWAL*, 3:335–36; Harrison, *Lincoln of Kentucky*, 107; *BDAC*, 265–69; Mark A. Plummer, *Lincoln's Rail-Splitter: Governor Richard L. Oglesby* (Urbana: University of Illinois Press, 2001), 58; Maizlish, *Triumph of Sectionalism*, 236; Porter, *Ohio Politics During the Civil War Period*, 26–29; Thornbrough, *Indiana in the Civil War Era*, 80–83; Smith, *Borderland in the Civil War*, 52; Peterson, *Freedom and Franchise*, 83–85; Parrish, *Frank Blair*, 72–73; Robert W. Goebel, "Casualty of War: The Governorship of Beriah Magoffin, 1859–1862" (M.A. thesis,

University of Louisville, 2005), 32–35; Harrison and Klotter, *New History of Kentucky*, 124; *Journal of the Senate of the Commonwealth of Kentucky 1859–1860* (Frankfort: Yeoman Office, 1860), 30–40; Lowell H. Harrison, "Governor Magoffin and the Secession Crisis," *Register* 72 (April 1974): 94–97.
55. Joel K. Lyle Daily Diary, 1860, November 6, 1860, January 1, 1861, Lyle Family Papers, Mss. 62M49, UK; Absalom Yarbrough Johnson Diaries, 1860–1864, (4 vols.) Mss. A/J67b, vol. 1, November 5 [6], 1860 entry, FHS. Voting totals and percentages in the election in the border slave states were: Delaware—3,815 for Lincoln, 12,224 for other candidates, or 31.2 percent; Kentucky—1,364 for Lincoln, 143,703 for other candidates, or. 95 percent; Maryland—2,294 for Lincoln, 89,848 for other candidates, or 11.5 percent; and Missouri—17,028 for Lincoln, 148,490 for other candidates, or 11.5 percent. William E. Gienapp, "Abraham Lincoln and the Border States," *JALA* 13 (1992): 22.
56. Annie Leslie McCarroll Starling Journal, 1860–1932, November 8, 1860 entry, Wallace-Starling Family Diaries, Mss. 96M07, KHS; [Elizabeth Pendleton Hardin], *The Private War of Lizzie Hardin: A Kentucky Confederate Girl's Diary of the Civil War in Kentucky, Virginia, Tennessee, Alabama, and Georgia*, ed. G. Glenn Clift (Frankfort: Kentucky Historical Society, 1963), 3; George Quigley Langstaff Jr., ed., *The Life and Times of Quintus Quincy Quigley, 1828–1910: His Personal Journals, 1859–1908* (Brentwood, Tenn.: Tallant Group, 1999), 57; Jasper B. Shannon and Ruth McQuown, *Presidential Politics in Kentucky, 1824–1948: A Compilation of Election Statistics and an Analysis of Political Behavior* (Lexington: University Press of Kentucky, 1950), 32–36; John Hunt Morgan to Thomas H. Morgan, November 17, 1860, and Thomas H. Morgan to Mrs. H[enrietta] H. Morgan, November 1860, both in Hunt-Morgan Family Papers, Mss. 63M202, box 15, folder 4, UK; Mildred Ann Bullitt to Thomas Bullitt, November 6, 1860, Bullitt-Chenoweth Family Papers, Mss. A/B937a, folder 298, FHS.
57. [Cincinnati] *The Daily Press*, December 17, 1860; [Cincinnati] *The Rail Splitter*, October 27, 1860; BDAC, 2050; Susan Terrell Scrogin to Henry H. Haviland, December 6, 1860, Scrogin-Haviland Collection, Mss. 2001 SC20, KHS; *Cincinnati* [Ohio] *Daily Enquirer*, August 21, 1860; Harrison and Klotter, *New History of Kentucky*, 184; William C. Davis, *Breckinridge—Statesman, Soldier, Symbol* (Baton Rouge: Louisiana State University Press, 1974), 242–43. For a map of county-by-county returns in the 1860 election, see Wilbur E. Garrett, ed., *Historical Atlas of the United States* (Washington, D.C.: National Geographic Society, 1988), 123.
58. Mildred Ann Bullitt to Thomas Bullitt, October 23, 1860, folder 298; Dr. Henry Bullitt to Sallie P. Bullitt, February 5, 1858, folder 115; Mildred Ann Bullitt to Thomas Bullitt, January 2, 1861, folder 299, and Mildred Ann Bullitt to Thomas Bullitt, February 186[1], folder 298; Mildred Ann Bullitt to Thomas Bullitt, January 18, 1861, folder 299, all in Bullitt-Chenoweth Family Papers, Mss. A/B937a, FHS.
59. *Cincinnati* [Ohio] *Daily Enquirer*, November 4, 1860; [Cincinnati] *The Daily Press*, November 23, 1860; Charles R. Wilson, "Cincinnati's Reputation During the Civil War," *JSH* 2 (November 1936): 472; Marshall L. DeRosa, ed., *The Politics of Dissolution: The Quest for a National Identity and the American Civil War* (New Brunswick, N.J.: Transaction Publishers, 1998), 115–16, 134; Elliot Jaspin, *Buried in the Bitter Waters: The Hidden History of Racial Cleansing in America* (New York: Basic Books, 2007), 23.
60. Asa Ransom Washburne to Lucius Washburne, January 2, 29, 1861, and Joseph M. Chrisman Lucius Washburne, January 29, 1861, all in Washburne Family Papers, Mss. 2971, box 1, folder 1, SHSM; [Cincinnati] *The Daily Press*, December 18, 1860; Etcheson, *Emerging Midwest*, 132–33; Absalom Yarbrough Johnson Diaries, 1860–1864, August 23, 1860 entry, Mss. A/J67b, vol. 1, FHS; S[imon] B. Buckner to Beriah Magoffin, March 8, 1861, Simon B. Buckner File, Mss. SC204, ALPL; Porter, *Ohio Politics During the Civil War Period*, 72.
61. Smith, *Borderland in the Civil War*, 133–39; Porter, *Ohio Politics During the Civil War Period*, 40–42, 49–55, 58–60, 69.
62. John A. Trimble to Jack Trimble, January 12, February 18, 22, March 7, 1861, John A. Trimble Papers, Mss. 249, box 10, folder 2, OHS; Silas Ford to Robert Neil, June 25, 1861, Robert Neil Family Papers, Mss. 259, OHS; Charles Buford Sr. to Charles Buford Jr., November 5, 1860, Charles Buford Papers, LC; [Cincinnati] *The Daily Press*, December 12,

1860; Stampp, *Indiana Politics During the Civil War*, 56; *BDAC*, 1031, 1707; Arthur C. Cole, *The Centennial History of Illinois: The Era of the Civil War, 1848–1870* (Springfield: Illinois Centennial Commission, 1919), 254–55, 261; Eighth U.S. Census, 1860, Population Schedule, LaSalle County, Illinois, NARA; Smith, *Borderland in the Civil War*, 133–39; Hugh Anderson to James M. Williams, October 27, 1860, in Christine Dee, ed., *Ohio's War: The Civil War in Documents* (Athens: Ohio University Press, 2006), 48; Dr. H. Wigand to Joseph Holt, January 24, 1861, Joseph Holt Papers, General Correspondence and Related Material (Bound), 1817–1894 (hereinafter cited as Holt Papers), book 26, LC.

63. Smith, *Borderland in the Civil War*, 133–39; *The Ripley Bee*, March 7, 1861; Plummer, *Lincoln's Rail-Splitter*, 62; Etcheson, *Emerging Midwest*, 128–30; Stampp, *Indiana Politics During the Civil War*, 26, 50, 54–60; Richard Yates and Catherine Yates Pickering, *Richard Yates: Civil War Governor*, ed. John H. Krenkel (Danville, Ill.: Interstate Printers and Publishers, 1966), 154; [Cincinnati] *The Israelite*, March 22, 1861; [Dayton] *Daily Empire*, March 26, 1861.

64. Donald, *Lincoln*, 162–63, 171–72; Coulter, *Civil War and Readjustment in Kentucky*, 32–33, 36; G. Robertson to J[ohn] J. Crittenden, December 16, 1860, Jones Family Papers, Mss. A/J78, folder 1, FHS; [Cincinnati] *The Israelite*, January 4, 1861; John O. Preston Jr. to William Preston, May 20, 1861, Wickliffe-Preston Family Papers, Mss. 63M349, box 54, UK; John Curd to Mr. Cornell, January 26, 1861, John Curd Letter, Mss. C/C, FHS; Garrett Davis to John A. Trimble, January 14, 1861, John A. Trimble Papers, Mss. 249, box 2, folder 2, OHS; Stampp, *Indiana Politics During the Civil War*, 55–56.

65. *Journal of the House of Representatives of the Commonwealth of Kentucky, 1861–1863* (Frankfort: *Yeoman* Office, 1863), 11–19; Harrison and Klotter, *New History of Kentucky*, 186–87; Beriah Magoffin to Stephen F. Hale, December 28, 1860, *OR*, ser. 4, vol. 1, 14; Goebel, "Casualty of War," 58–63; [St. Louis] *Daily Missouri Republican*, April 30, 1861; Coulter, *Civil War and Readjustment*, 81–110; Harrison, *Civil War in Kentucky*, 1–14.

66. William B. Napton to Melinda Napton, December 16, 1860, William Barclay Napton Papers, box 2, MHS; William E. Parrish, *A History of Missouri, Vol. III: 1860–1875* (Columbia: University of Missouri Press, 1973), 1; Buel Leopard and Floyd Shoemaker, eds., *The Messages and Proclamations of the Governors of the State of Missouri* (Columbia: State Historical Society of Missouri, 1922), 3:333; Nagel, *Missouri*, 128; Snead, *Fight for Missouri*, 13–25; *Missouri Statesman*, January 18, 1861; William E. Parrish, *Turbulent Partnership: Missouri and the Union 1861–1865* (Columbia: University of Missouri Press, 1963), 6–7; Lyon, "Jackson and the Secession Crisis," 431–32; Joseph A. Igel Jr., "A Rhetorical Evaluation of Claiborne Fox Jackson's Speeches on Slavery and States' Rights: 1847–1861" (M.A. thesis, Southwest Missouri State University, 1984), 25–27; Draft of C. F. Jackson's Inaugural Address to the General Assembly of Missouri, undated [December 30, 1860], John S. Sappington Papers, Mss. 1027, box 1, folder 7, SHSM; *Jefferson Inquirer*, January 5, 1861; Lyon, "Jackson and the Secession Crisis," 433; Sara Lee Sale, "Governor Claiborne Fox Jackson and His Role in the Secession Movement in Missouri" (M.A. thesis, Central Missouri State University, 1979), 13–15.

67. *Congressional Globe*, 36th Cong., 2nd Sess., 1236, 1263–64, 1283–85, 1397–1403; R. Alton Lee, "The Corwin Amendment in the Secession Crisis," *Ohio Historical Quarterly* 70 (January 1961): 1–26 passim; *BDAC*, 265–69, 1021.

68. William B. Napton to Melinda Napton, July 15 [1860], box 1a, William Barclay Napton Papers, MHS; Phillips and Pendleton, *Union on Trial*, 161.

House of Cards

1. Diary of Johanna Louisa "Josie" (Underwood) Nazro, December 10, 1860, February 3, 1861 entries, Johanna Louisa (Underwood) Nazro Collection, Mss. SC 1709, ser. 2, box 1, WKU (hereafter cited as Nazro Diary); Gilbert Gordon to Neal M. Gordon, March 14, 1862, Gordon Family Papers, Mss. 51M40, box 4, UK. The typescript, which includes the first half of the Nazro Diary, is published as Nancy Disher Baird, ed., *Josie Underwood's Civil War Diary* (Lexington: University Press of Kentucky, 2009). The original second volume

of the diary, recently discovered, is located in the Johanna Louisa (Underwood) Nazro Collection, Mss. SC 1709, WKU.
2. Nazro Diary, February 5, 1861 entry; Elizabeth Cox Underwood to Joseph R. Underwood, February 15, 1850, and Warner L. Underwood Diary, undated 1849 entry, both in Underwood Collection, Mss. 58, ser. 2, box 1, folders 7, 3, WKU; *BDAC*, 1942–43.
3. Nazro Diary, February 25, April 15–17, May 5, 8, 1861 entries; Proclamation Calling Militia and Convening Congress, in *CWAL*, 4:332; Coulter, *Civil War and Readjustment in Kentucky*, 38.
4. Nazro Diary, January 8, February 5, March 20, April 17, 1861, March 1, 1862 entries.
5. Nazro Diary, February 5, 1861 entry.
6. Nazro Diary, February 10, 25, 28, March 10, April 5, 20, June 20, August 1, September 15, 1861 entries.
7. Nazro Diary, March 25–April 17, 1861 entries.
8. Samuel Haycraft Journal (typescript), 1 vol., June 30, 1861 entry, p. 22, Mss. A/H414, FHS; Steven E. Woodworth, "'The Indeterminate Quantities': Jefferson Davis, Leonidas Polk, and the End of Kentucky Neutrality, September 1861," *CWH* 38 (December 1992): 389–97; Harrison and Klotter, *New History of Kentucky*, 191–92; James Lee McDonough, *War in Kentucky: From Shiloh to Perryville* (Knoxville: University of Tennessee Press, 1994), 62–65; William C. Davis, *The Orphan Brigade: The Kentucky Confederates Who Couldn't Go Home* (Baton Rouge: Louisiana State University Press, 1980), 13; A[lbert] T. Bledsoe to William T. Withers, July 31, 1861, and Albert Sidney Johnston to Jefferson Davis, September 16, 1861, both in *OR*, ser. 1, vol. 4, 193–94, 378; [Nancy Moore], *The Journal of Eldress Nancy, Kept at the South Union, Kentucky, Shaker Colony, August 15, 1861–September 4, 1864*, ed. Mary Julia Neal (Nashville: The Parthenon Press, 1963), 3; Lowell H. Harrison, *The Civil War in Kentucky* (Lexington: University Press of Kentucky, 1975), 11. Following the August 5 election, the Kentucky House held a 76-24 unionist majority and a 27-11 margin in the state senate.
9. Nazro Diary, September 25–October 16, November 8, 30, 1861 entries; Phil Gottschalk, *In Deadly Earnest: The History of the First Missouri Brigade, C.S.A.* (Columbia: Missouri River Press, 1991), 79–81; Josephine Wells Covington to My Dear Father, March 2, 1862, Josephine (Wells) Covington Letters, Mss. SC236, WKU.
10. Nazro Diary, September 20, 30, November 20, December 10, 19, 1861 entries; Josephine Wells Covington to My Dear Father, March 2, 1862, Josephine (Wells) Covington Letters, SC236, WKU; Operations in Kentucky and Tennessee, July 1–November 19, 1861, and Isham G. Harris to L[ucius] P. Walker, May 25, 1861, both in *OR*, ser. 1, vol. 4, 176; vol. 52, pt. 2, 109.
11. Nazro Diary, December 27, 1861–January 10, 1862 entries.
12. Nazro Diary, March 1, 1862 entry.
13. Nazro Diary, January 22–March 1, 1862 entries.
14. Nazro Diary, March 1, 1862 entry; Mary E. Van Meter Diary, February 10–13, 1862 entries, Mss. 54M98 (microfilm), UK; Journal of Ellen Kenton McGaughey Wallace, 1849–1865 (typescript), February 6–17, 1862 entries, Wallace-Starling Family Diaries, Mss. 96M07, KHS; Josephine Wells Covington to My Dear Father, March 2, 1862, Josephine (Wells) Covington Letters, SC236, WKU.
15. Nazro Diary, March 1, 1862 entry; Josephine Wells Covington to My Dear Father, March 2, 1862, Josephine (Wells) Covington Letters, SC236, WKU; Mary E. Van Meter Diary, February 10–13, 1862 entries, Mss. 54M98 (microfilm), UK.
16. Nazro Diary, March 1–April 25, 1862 entries; Gilbert Gordon to Neal M. Gordon, March 14, 1862, Gordon Family Papers, Mss. 51M40, box 4, UK.

Chapter 4: No North—No South—No East—No West: The Fiction of the Wartime Middle Ground

1. Parrish, *History of Missouri*, 6–7; Parrish, *Turbulent Partnership*, 8–9; Snead, *Fight for Missouri*, 53–59; Dozier Lewis to Searles L. Davis, March 8, 1861, Davis-Lewis Family

Papers, Mss. C/D, FHS; Thomas J. C. Fagg to James O. Broadhead, February 8, 1861, James O. Broadhead Papers, MHS; Sale, "Governor Claiborne Fox Jackson," 16–18; Robert E. Shalhope, *Sterling Price: Portrait of a Southerner* (Columbia: University of Missouri Press, 1971), 148–51; W[ill] T. Hart to Susan Preston Shelby Grigsby, January 12, May 6, 1861, both in Grigsby Family Papers, Mss. A/G857, folder 168, FHS.
2. R. M. Fairleigh to Dr. Galt Booth, May 8, 1861, Beall-Booth Family Papers, Mss. A/B365, folder 189, FHS.
3. Johnson, *Toward a Patriarchal Republic*, 46–52; Charles B. Dew, *Apostles of Disunion: Southern Secession Commissioners and the Causes of the Civil War* (Charlottesville: University Press of Virginia, 2001), 51–57, 78, 90–103 and passim; *Journal of the House of Representatives of the State of Missouri, Twenty-first General Assembly, First Session, 1860–1861* (Jefferson City: State Printer, 1861), 87–88; Sale, "Governor Claiborne Fox Jackson," 14–15; Thomas J. C. Fagg to James O. Broadhead, February 8, 1861, James O. Broadhead Papers, MHS; R. A. Cind to Cal[vin C.] Morgan, November 29, 1860, Hunt-Morgan Family Papers, Mss. 63M202, box 15, folder 5, UK; C. F. Mitchell to Abraham Lincoln, January 27, 1861, Abraham Lincoln Papers, ser. 1—General Correspondence, 1833–1916, LC. Alabamian Stephen F. Hale visited Frankfort in late December 1860. Alabamian William Cooper and Mississippian Daniel R. Russell, as well as Georgian Luther J. Glenn, traveled to Jefferson City in December 1860 and January and March 1861, respectively.
4. John O. Preston Jr. to William Preston, May 20, 1861, Wickliffe-Preston Family Papers, Mss. 63M349, box 54, UK; Abiel Leonard to James S. Rollins, January 17, 1861, James S. Rollins Papers, Mss. 1026, box 3, folder 72, SHSM; Joseph M. Chrisman to Dear Sir [Lucius Washburne], January 29, 1861, Washburne Family Papers, Mss. 2971, box 1, folder 1, SHSM; Hurt, *Agriculture and Slavery in Little Dixie*, 297–98; Daniel W. Crofts, *Reluctant Confederates: Upper South Unionists in the Secession Crisis* (Chapel Hill: University of North Carolina Press, 1989), 104–22; Weber, *Copperheads*, 18–20; William Garrett Piston and Richard W. Hatcher III, *Wilson's Creek: The Second Battle of the Civil War and the Men Who Fought It* (Chapel Hill: University of North Carolina Press, 2000), 27.
5. Carl Degler, *The Other South: Southern Dissenters in the Nineteenth Century* (New York: Harper and Row, 1974), 116; *Calhoun County* [Ill.] *Weekly Union*, January 11, 1861.
6. J. M. Harlan to Joseph Holt, March 11, 1861, and R. S. Holt to Holt, January 10, 1861, Holt Papers, books 26 and 28, LC; Linda Przybyszewski, *The Republic According to John Marshall Harlan* (Chapel Hill: University of North Carolina Press, 1999), 20–23, 34–37; *Cincinnati* [Ohio] *Daily Enquirer*, March 24, 1861; Resolutions of Citizens of Mead[e] Co., Ky., January 19, 1861, Haycraft Family Papers, Mss. 69M690 (microfilm), UK.
7. Crofts, *Reluctant Confederates*, 130–42; Walter H. Ryle, *Missouri: Union or Secession* (Nashville: George Peabody College for Teachers, 1931), 71–72, 155; Hurt, *Agriculture and Slavery in Little Dixie*, 298–99; S[almon] B. Axtell to L. Kerr, April 5, 1861, Vertical File A, WRHS.
8. James M. McPherson, *Battle Cry of Freedom: The Civil War Era* (New York: Oxford University Press, 1988), 257; Chandra Manning, *What This Cruel War Was Over: Soldiers, Slavery, and the Civil War* (New York: Alfred A. Knopf, 2007), 26–27; Porter, *Ohio Politics During the Civil War*, 67–69; Harrison and Klotter, *New History of Kentucky*, 185–86; Smith, *Borderland in the Civil War*, 91–94; Goebel, "Casualty of War," 66–67; Diary of Thomas Walker Bullitt, vol. 1 (1857–1862, 1893), March 4, 1861 entry, Bullitt Family Papers, Mss. 3549, box 7, folder 99, UNC; Coulter, *Civil War and Readjustment in Kentucky*, 28–29.
9. Parrish, *History of Missouri*, 6; Parrish, *Turbulent Partnership*, 9–14; William Roed, "Secessionist Strength in Missouri," *MHR* 72 (July 1978): 419–21; Snead, *Fight for Missouri*, 66–67; [St. Louis] *Daily Missouri Democrat*, February 20, 1861; *Proceedings of the Missouri State Convention, Held at Jefferson City and St. Louis, March, 1861–June, 1863* (St. Louis: George Knapp, 1861–1863), 11–20.
10. [Platte City, Mo.] *The Weekly Tenth Legion*, March 30, 1861; *Proceedings of the Missouri State Convention*, 34–37, 46–49, 55–57, 58, 217–30, 237–45; Smith, *Francis Preston Blair Family*, 2:2, 26–29; Parrish, *Turbulent Partnership*, 10–14; William H. Lyon, "Claiborne Fox Jackson and the Secession Crisis in Missouri," *MHR* 58 (July 1964): 433.

11. Frank Moore, ed., *The Rebellion Record: A Diary of American Events* (New York: G. P. Putnam, 1861–1868; reprint New York: Arno Press, 1977), 1:74; M. H. Cooper to Samuel Haycraft, January 21, 1861, Haycraft Family Papers, Mss. 69M690 (microfilm), UK; Joseph Holt, *Letter from the Hon. Joseph Holt upon the Policy of the General Government, the Pending Revolution, Its Objects, Its Probable Results If Successful, and the Duty of Kentucky in the Crisis* (Louisville: Bradley and Gilbert, 1861); S. D. Brice et al. to Holt, June 22, 1861; Thornton F. Marshall to Holt, July 5, 1861; and R. H. Hanson et al. to Holt, July 15, 1861, all in Holt Papers, books 27–30, LC. Subsequent editions include Holt, *Letter from the Hon. Joseph Holt, upon the Policy of the General Government, the Pending Revolution, Its Objects, Its Probable Results If Successful, and the Duty of Kentucky in the Crisis* (Washington, D.C.: H. Polinkhorn, 1861); and Holt, *The Fallacy of Neutrality: An Address by the Hon. Joseph Holt, to the People of Kentucky, Delivered at Louisville, July 13th, 1861; Also a Letter to J. F. Speed, Esq.* (New York: J. G. Gregory, 1861). The original letter, Joseph Holt to J[oshua] F. Speed, Esq., May 31, 1861, is in the Speed Family, Miscellaneous Papers, Mss. C/S, FHS.
12. Elizabeth D. Leonard, *Lincoln's Forgotten Ally: Judge Advocate General Joseph Holt of Kentucky* (Chapel Hill: University of North Carolina Press, 2010), 113–57; Coulter, *Civil War and Readjustment in Kentucky*, 93–97.
13. Roger J. Bartman, "Joseph Holt and Kentucky in the Civil War," *FCHQ* 40 (April 1966), 105–22 passim; Harrison, *Lincoln of Kentucky*, 145–46; Jacob F. Lee, ed., "An Honorable Position: Joseph Holt's Letter to Joshua F. Speed on Neutrality and Secession in Kentucky, May 1861," *OVH* 7 (Winter 2007): 32–37.
14. *Kentucky House Journal, 1861–63*, 153–57; Goebel, "Casualty of War," 70–71; John C. Breckinridge to William Preston, March 13, 1861, Wickliffe-Preston Family Papers, Mss. 63M349, box 54, UK; Smith, *Borderland in the Civil War*, 106–7; Coulter, *Civil War and Readjustment in Kentucky*, 29–30, 35–37; Harrison and Klotter, *New History of Kentucky*, 186–89.
15. McPherson, *Battle Cry of Freedom*, 294; William Conrad, *The Journal of Elder William Conrad: Pioneer Preacher*, ed. Lloyd W. Franks (Lexington: R F Publishing, 1976), 76.
16. Moore, ed., *Rebellion Record*, 1:75; Coulter, *Civil War and Readjustment in Kentucky*, 35–36; A. M. Brown to Samuel Haycraft, January 18, 19, 1861, Haycraft Family Papers, Mss. 69M690 (microfilm), UK.
17. Jane Stuart Woolsey to a Friend in Paris, May 10, 1861, in Henry Steele Commager, ed., *The Blue and the Gray* (Indianapolis: Bobbs-Merrill, 1973), 1:47–48; Paludan, *"A People's Contest"*, 3–11, 14–27; James M. McPherson, *For Cause and Comrades: Why Men Fought in the Civil War* (New York: Oxford University Press, 1997), 16–17; W. W. Parmenter to My Dear Mother, April 22, 1861, in Christine Dee, ed., *Ohio's War: The Civil War in Documents* (Athens: Ohio University Press, 20060, 52; Jacob D. Cox, "War Preparations in the North," in Robert Underwood Johnson and Howard L. Conard, eds. *Battles and Leaders of the Civil War*, 4 vols. (New York: Thomas Yoseloff, 1956), 1:85–87; McPherson, *Battle Cry of Freedom*, 274–75; Bruce Catton, *This Hallowed Ground: The Story of the Union Side of the Civil War* (Garden City, N.J.: Doubleday, 1956), 21; S[almon] B. Axtell to L. Kerr, April 5, 1861, Vertical File A, WRHS; Smith, *Borderland in the Civil War*, 184.
18. Smith, *Borderland in the Civil War*, 149; Amanda Landrum Wilson Diary, April 13–22, 1861 entries, Mss. zW746 RMV, CHSL; Thornbrough, *Indiana in the Civil War Era*, 106; Rachel Sherman Thorndike, ed., *The Sherman Letters: Correspondence Between General and Senator Sherman from 1837 to 1891* (New York: Charles Scribner's Sons, 1894), 110; Henry H. Haviland to Susan Terrill Scrogin, April 25, 1861, Scrogin-Haviland Collection, Mss. 2001SC20, folder 6, KHS; Jacob P. Dunn to Oliver P. Aiken, May 6, 1861, Oliver Perry Aiken Papers, Mss. SC7, IHSL; *Hannibal [Mo.] Daily Messenger*, September 4, 1861; William B. Fletcher, "The Civil War Journal of William B. Fletcher," *IMH* 57 (March 1961): 49; Robert W. Kirkham to Richard Yates, April 15, 1861, in Yates and Pickering, *Richard Yates*, 154–55; Porter, *Ohio Politics in the Civil War Era*, 73–74; Cox, "War Preparations in the North," 86–87; *Cincinnati [Ohio] Daily Commercial*, February 13, 1861; *Cincinnati Daily Gazette*, February 16, 1861; Daniel J. Ryan, "Lincoln and Ohio," *Ohio Archeological and Historical Quarterly* 32 (January 1923): 151–57; Diaries and Letters of Rutherford Birchard Hayes (hereafter cited as Rutherford B. Hayes Diaries), vol. 2, January 27,

February 13–15, April 15, May 15, 1861 entries (transcript, pp. 4–6, 8, 17), Manuscript Division, Rutherford B. Hayes Presidential Center, Fremont, Ohio.

19. "Sarah Patience" (unpublished manuscript, typescript), Martha W. Dorsey Papers, Mss. SC510, folder 2, pp. 47–49, IHSL; John A. Trimble to Jack Trimble, June 24, 1861, John A. Trimble Papers, Mss. 249, box 10, folder 2, OHS; Thornbrough, *Indiana in the Civil War Era*, 100, 103; Theodore F. Upson, *With Sherman to the Sea: The Civil War Letters and Diaries and Reminiscences of Theodore F. Upson*, ed. Oscar Winther (Bloomington: Indiana University Press, 1958), 10; Cox, "War Preparations in the North," 86–87; John R. McBride to Lucas F. Smith, August 5, 1861, John Randolph McBride Papers, Mss. SC1005, IHSL; Howard, *Illinois*, 304.

20. Porter, *Ohio Politics During the Civil War Period*, 51–52, 55–57, 71–72, 75–78, 84–91; Richard H. Abbott, *Ohio's War Governors* (Columbus: Ohio State University Press, 1962), 13–21. Tod won by 55,223 votes of 358,791 votes cast, and carried even the Western Reserve counties.

21. Porter, *Ohio Politics During the Civil War*, 75–78; *Cincinnati [Ohio] Daily Enquirer*, June 9, 1861; Henry H. Haviland to Susan Terrell Scrogin, April 25, 1861, folder 6, Scrogin-Haviland Collection, Mss. 2001 SC20, KHS; John A. Trimble to Dear Brother, March 7, 1861; Trimble to Jack Trimble, May 4, 1861, both in John A. Trimble Papers, Mss. 249, box 10, folder 2, OHS; [Cincinnati, Ohio] *The Daily Times*, April 16, 1861; [Cincinnati, Ohio] *Catholic Telegraph and Advocate*, April 27, 1861; Jacob P. Dunn to Oliver P. Aiken, May 6, 1861, Oliver Perry Aiken Papers, Mss. SC7, IHSL; Rutherford B. Hayes Diaries, vol. 2, April 25, 1861 entry (transcript p. 12), Manuscript Division, Rutherford B. Hayes Presidential Center, Fremont, Ohio.

22. Etcheson, *Emerging Midwest*, 136; "Journal of Events Leading to the Civil War by J. P. Mann" (typescript), undated, Mann Family Papers, Coll. 111, box 5, SIU; Herman R. Lantz, *A Community in Search of Itself: A Case Study of Cairo, Illinois* (Carbondale: Southern Illinois University Press, 1972), 24–25; Cole, *Centennial History of Illinois*, 253; Christopher K. Hays, "Way Down in Egypt Land: Community and Conflict in Cairo, Illinois, 1850–1930" (Ph.D. dissertation, University of Missouri-Columbia, 1996), 122–23; Steven E. Woodworth, *Nothing but Victory: The Army of the Tennessee, 1861–1865* (New York: Alfred A. Knopf, 2005), 22; *Cairo* [Ill.] *City Weekly Gazette*, March 28, April 25, 1861; William A. Pitkin, "When Cairo was Saved for the Union," *JISHS* 51 (Autumn 1958): 287; *New York Times*, May 11, 1861; Ulysses S. Grant to Julia Grant, May 21, 1861, in John Y. Simon, ed., *The Papers of Ulysses S. Grant* (Carbondale: Southern Illinois University Press, 1967–), 2:33; Daniel E. Sutherland, *A Savage Conflict: The Decisive Role of Guerrillas in the American Civil War* (Chapel Hill: University of North Carolina Press, 2009), 38–39; *Cairo* [Ill.] *Evening Citizen and Bulletin*, April 24, 1861; John A. Trimble to Jack Trimble, June 24, 1861, John A. Trimble Papers, Mss. 249, box 10, folder 2, OHS; Victor Hicken, *Illinois in the Civil War* (Urbana: University of Illinois Press, 1966), 13; Ed Gleeson, *Illinois Rebels* (Carmel, Ind.: Guild Press of Indiana, 1996), 1–8 and passim; Howard, *Illinois*, 309.

23. Civil War Diary of John Preston Mann (transcription, vol. 6), February 22–23, 1862 entries, and Alfred M. Mann to J[ohn] P. Mann, March 20, 1862, both in Mann Family Papers, Coll. 111, SIU; James Pickett Jones, *"Black Jack": John A. Logan and Southern Illinois in the Civil War Era* (Carbondale: Southern Illinois University Press, 1995), xiii–xiv; *Cairo City Weekly Gazette*, April 25, 1861; Daniel Harmon Brush, *Growing Up in Southern Illinois*, ed. Milo Milton Quaife (Madison: University of Wisconsin Press, 1944), 119; [Springfield, Ill.] *Illinois State Journal*, June 5, 6, 10, 11, 1861; *Jonesboro* [Ill.] *Gazette*, June 29, 1861; John S. Tarkington to Marion Trust Co., August 5, 1905, Churchman Family Papers, Mss. M53, IHSL; Hicken, *Illinois in the Civil War*, 5; Thornbrough, *Indiana in the Civil War Era*, 124; Richard E. Nation and Stephen E. Towne, eds., *Indiana's War: The Civil War in Documents* (Athens: Ohio University Press, 2009), 48–49.

24. Hicken, *Illinois in the Civil War*, 2, 13; Thornbrough, *Indiana in the Civil War Era*, 170, 395; Woodworth, *Nothing but Victory*, 7–8; John A. Trimble to Jack Trimble, May 4, 1861, John A. Trimble Papers, Mss. 249, box 10, folder 2, OHS; Civil War Diary of John Preston Mann (transcription, vol. 6), February 22–23, 1862 entries, Mann Family Papers, Coll. 111, SIU.

25. Invitation, "Mass Meeting and Pic-nic," August 30, 1861, Wickliffe-Preston Family Papers, Mss. 63M349, box 54, UK; Journal of Ellen Kenton McGaughey Wallace, 1849–1865 (typescript), April 19, 1862 entry, Wallace-Starling Family Diaries, Mss. 96M07, KHS; Stephen Barker to Dear William, April 28, 1861, Stephen Barker Letter, Mss. C/B, FHS; Thomas M. Allen to John Allen Gano, May 9, 28, 1861, John Allen Gano Family Papers, Mss. 6S, box 1, folder 38, SHSM; [Platte City, Mo.] *The Weekly Tenth Legion*, March 30, 1861; S. D. Brice and J. L. Gilmore to Joseph Holt, June 22, 1861, Holt Papers, book 29, LC.

26. Langstaff, *Life and Times of Quigley*, 69; Bevie W. Cain to James M. Davis, May 22, October 24, 1861, Bevie Cain Letters, Mss. SC2251, WKU; Sutherland, *A Savage Conflict*, 32.

27. Journal of Ellen Kenton McGaughey Wallace, 1849–1865 (typescript), September 23, 1861 entry, Wallace-Starling Family Diaries, Mss. 96M07, KHS; Harrison, *Civil War in Kentucky*, 14–15; Frank Steel to Cyrus Boys Trimble, June 16, July 21, October 10, 1861, John A. Trimble Papers, Mss. 249, box 10, folder 2, OHS; Woodworth, *Nothing but Victory*, 7; Ulysses S. Grant, *Personal Memoirs of U. S. Grant* (New York: Da Capo Press, 1982), 132; Kentucky Volunteer Infantry Roster, Mss. VF 1195, CHSL; Minutes of the Citizens' Home Guard of West Covington, Kentucky (typescript), June 22, 24, 1861 entries, Mss. fC581 RFM, CHSL; Samuel Gill to Lorenzo Thomas, January 17, 1862; Chester Harding to H[amilton] R. Gamble, January 1, 1862; and J[udah] P. Benjamin to Jefferson Davis, February 1862, all in *OR*, ser. 3, vol. 1, 796–97, 801; ser. 4, vol. 1, 962–63. By the end of 1861, 29,203 Kentuckians had enlisted for federal service (or 69.5 percent of the state's 42,000 quota), while 7,950 had enlisted in Confederate service. Some 32,821 Missourians were in federal ranks (with another 6,185 in state militia), while some 3,200 served for the Confederacy. For Missouri's various enlisted units, see *Missouri Troops in Service During the Civil War* (Washington, D.C.: Government Printing Office, 1902).

28. Langstaff, *Life and Times of Quigley*, 69; Hannibal [Mo.] *Daily Messenger*, November 5, 1861; Lizzie J. S____ to Anonymous, February 24, 1863, Hunt-Morgan Family Papers, Mss. 63M202, box 16, folder 9, UK; Records of Georgetown College, 1859–1887 (Faculty Minutes Book), November 21, 1860, January 5, February 4, March 13, April 23, September 2, 1861 entries, pp. 9–13, and Kentucky Baptist Education Society, Proceedings of the Board of Trustees, 1837–1866, June 26, 1860 entry, pp. 146–9, both at C. J. and Frances Lyons Bolton Special Collections and Archives, Ensor Learning Resource Center, Georgetown College, Georgetown, Kentucky; Hul-cee M. Acton, *History of the Tau Theta Kappa Society of Georgetown College* (Georgetown, Ky.: Tau Theta Kappa Society, 1918), 34–37; William Moody Pratt Diaries, vol. 2, June 12, 1862 entry, Mss. 46M79, UK; Jon G. Taylor to Robert Neil, August 15, September 21, 1863, Robert Neil Family Papers, Mss. 259, OHS.

29. McPherson, *Battle Cry of Freedom*, 284; Sutherland, *A Savage Conflict*, 26–27, 41; Walter A. Schroeder, *Missouri Water Atlas* (Jefferson City: Missouri Department of Natural Resources, 1982), 2; Coulter, *Civil War and Readjustment in Kentucky*, 38; [Charleston, Mo.] *The Courier*, May 3, 1861; [Thomas W. Parsons], *Incidents and Experiences in the Life of Thomas W. Parsons, from 1826 to 1900*, ed. Frank Furlong Mathias (Lexington: University Press of Kentucky, 1975), 74–75; Hoskins, "The First Is with the South," 94–96; R. W. Woolley to William Preston, undated, Wickliffe-Preston Family Papers, Mss. 63M349, box 54, UK; Resolutions for Polk County, March 17, 1861, John F. Snyder Papers, box 2, MHS.

30. [Parsons], *Incidents and Experiences*, 116; *Congressional Globe*, 37th Cong., 2nd Sess., 2297; C. F. Mitchell to Abraham Lincoln, January 27, 1861, Lincoln Papers; Lunsford Yandell Jr. to Dear Sally and Father, April 22, 1861, Yandell Family Papers, Mss. A/Y21a, FHS; William B. Napton to Melinda Napton, April 19, 1861, both in William Barclay Napton Papers, box 2, MHS.

31. Weber, *Copperheads*, 21–22; Isaac Shelby Jr. to Wife, [n.d.], January 16, May 1, 1861, all in Darbishire Family Papers, Mss. 62M68, Correspondence 1751–1882, UK; Langstaff, *Life and Times of Quigley*, 62; Nazro Diary, December 12, 1860–January 27, 1861 entries.

32. Nazro Diary, January 28, 1861 entry.

33. Faust, *Creation of Confederate Nationalism*, 7–21; Williamson Dixon Ward Civil War Journal, October 27, 1861 entry, Mss. SC627, WKU; Rev. T. A. Hoyt to Pat Joyes, October 28, 1862, Joyes Family Papers, Mss. A/J89b, folder 18, FHS; McPherson, *For Cause and Comrades*, 104–6; Columbia *Missouri Statesman*, April 15, 1861.

34. Anne Sarah Rubin, *A Shattered Nation: The Rise and Fall of the Confederacy, 1861–1868* (Chapel Hill: University of North Carolina Press, 2007), 14–19; Benjamin Helm Bristow to Dear Hage, February 22, 1862, Mrs. James M. Gill and Miss Mary Gill Collection of Bristow Papers, Mss. 64M578 (microfilm), UK; Ettie Scott to Susan Preston Shelby Grigsby, May [1862], Grigsby Family Papers, Mss. A/G857, folder 172, FHS; John J. Crittenden to George B. Crittenden, April 30, 1861, John J. Crittenden Papers, Mss. C/C, FHS; W. E. Hobson to Jack Harding, August 20, 1861, John Harding Collection, Mss. A/H263, folder 4, FHS.
35. "Sermon Delivered in the Lexington Presbyterian Church," June 3, 1862, p. 12, Lyle Family Papers, Mss. 62M49, box 1848–1872, UK; G. L. Chaney to H[enry] T. Duncan Jr., September 22, 1861, Duncan Family Papers, Mss. 71M38, UK.
36. Newspaper Clipping, January 31, 1861, Lyle Family Papers, Mss. 62M49, box 1848–1872, UK; [Hardin], *Private War of Lizzie Hardin*, 3–4.
37. G. L. Chaney to H[enry] T. Duncan Jr., September 22, 1861, Duncan Family Papers, Mss. 71M38, UK; Cora Owens Hume Journal (typescript), June 1, 1865, November 2, 1864 entries, vol. 2, pp. 119, 37, Mss. A/H921 Vault C, FHS.
38. William Preston to My Dear Son and Daughters, April 3, 1862, Johnston Family Papers, Mss. A/J72j, folder 9, FHS.
39. John F. Bradbury Jr., ed., "Union or Disunion: The Letters of Allen B. Johnson," *Newsletter of the Phelps County Historical Society* 6 (June 1987): 3–5, 16, 22, 25; Frank Steel to Cyrus Boys Trimble, October 10, 1861, John A. Trimble Papers, Mss. 249, box 10, folder 2, OHS; [J. P. Caldwell], *A Northern Confederate at Johnson's Island Prison: The Civil War Diaries of James Park Caldwell*, ed. George H. Jones (Jefferson, N.C.: McFarland, 2010), 14–20.
40. Thomas Speed, *The Union Cause in Kentucky, 1860–1865* (New York: G. P. Putnam's Sons, 1907), 47; Broadhead, "St. Louis during the War," James O. Broadhead Papers, MHS; Draft of the 1858 Militia Bill, Missouri Militia Collection, MHS; John McElroy, *The Struggle for Missouri* (Washington, D.C.: National Tribune Company, 1909), 62–63; Snead, *Fight for Missouri*, 148–49; Christopher Phillips, *Damned Yankee: The Life of General Nathaniel Lyon* (Columbia: University of Missouri Press, 1990; reprint Baton Rouge: Louisiana State University Press, 1996), 176; [St. Louis] *Daily Missouri Republican*, April 27, 1861; [Columbia] *Missouri Statesman*, May 3, 1861; Jackson to Hon. David Walker, April 19, 1861, Governor's Papers: Claiborne Fox Jackson, General Correspondence, 1861, box 1, folder 3, MSA; C[laiborne] F. Jackson to Jefferson Davis, April 17, 1861, Jefferson Davis Letters, box 1, Duke; Davis to Jackson, April 23, 1861, in Robert J. Rombauer, *The Union Cause in St. Louis* (St. Louis: Nixon-Jones Printing, 1909), 212–13; Jackson to Davis, April 28, 1861, *OR*, ser. 1, vol. 1, 689; Basil W. Duke, *Reminiscences of General Basil W. Duke, C.S.A.* (Garden City, N.Y.: Doubleday, Page, 1911), 44–50; James Peckham, *General Nathaniel Lyon and Missouri in 1861* (New York: American News Company, 1866), 158–59, 286–87, 301. On Jackson's secession strategy in Missouri's secession crisis, see Christopher Phillips, "Calculated Confederate: Claiborne Fox Jackson and the Strategy for Secession in Missouri," *MHR* 94 (July 2000): 389–414.
41. B. F. Massey to J. F. Snyder, April 26, 29, 1861, both in John F. Snyder Papers, box 2, MHS; Phillips, *Damned Yankee*, 159–65; Anderson, *Border City During the Civil War*, 88–9; William E. Parrish, *Frank Blair: Lincoln's Conservative* (Columbia: University of Missouri Press, 1998), 99–101; W. Turner to anonymous [David R. Atchison], May 3, 1861, David Rice Atchison Papers, Mss. 71, folder 10, SHSM; Draft of the 1858 Militia Bill, Missouri Militia Collection, MHS; Parrish, *History of Missouri*, 12–13.
42. Coulter, *Civil War and Readjustment in Kentucky*, 38–44; Beriah Magoffin to Stephen F. Hale, December 28, 1860; Blanton Duncan to L[eroy] P. Walker, March 29, 1861; W[illia]m Preston Johnston to Walker, April 26, 1861; and Garret Davis to G[eorge] B. McClellan, April [June] 8, 1861, all in *OR*, ser. 4, vol. 1, 12; ser. 1, vol. 52, pt. 1, 31–32; pt. 2, 71–72; ser. 1, vol. 2, 677–78; Richard Stone Jr., *A Brittle Sword: The Kentucky Militia, 1776–1912* (Lexington: University Press of Kentucky, 1977), 61–68; Smith, *Borderland in the Civil War*, 155–56, 269–71; Isham G. Harris to Beriah Magoffin, August 4, 1861, Isham Green Harris Papers, LC; Beriah Magoffin to Dr. John M. Johnson, May 24, 1861, and Magoffin to Harris, August 12, 1861, both in Beriah Magoffin Letters, LC; Harrison, *Civil War in*

Kentucky, 11–12; Davis, *Orphan Brigade*, 13–16; Albert D. Kirwan, *John J. Crittenden: The Struggle for the Union* (Lexington: University of Kentucky Press, 1962), 433–34; S. H. S. Fishback to Susan Preston Shelby Grigsby, July 8, 1861, Grigsby Family Papers, Mss. A/G857, folder 171, FHS; Robert E. Corlew, *Tennessee: A Short History* (Knoxville: University of Tennessee Press, 1989), 291–97; Goebel, "Casualty of War," 83–86; Richard Collins, *History of Kentucky* (Louisville: John P. Morton, 1874), 87–88; Harrison and Klotter, *New History of Kentucky*, 187; Berry F. Craig, "The Jackson Purchase Considers Secession: The 1861 Mayfield Convention," *Register* 99 (Autumn 2001): 344–53; Hoskins, "The First Is with the South," 80–91.

43. Freehling, *South vs. the South*, 52–53; Sutherland, *A Savage Conflict*, 38; Moore, *Rebellion Record*, 1:91, 377–78; William Moody Pratt Diaries, May 20, 1861 entry, Mss. 46M79, vol. 2, UK; Stampp, *And the War Came*, 74–81, 99–105; Elizabeth D. Leonard, "One Kentuckian's Hard Choice: Joseph Holt and Abraham Lincoln," *Register* 106 (Summer–Autumn 2008): 373–408 passim; Robert S. Holt to Joseph Holt, November 9, 20, 1860, Holt Papers, book 26, LC; Harrison, *Civil War in Kentucky*, 9–10; William Preston Johnston to William Preston, April 23, 1861, Wickliffe-Preston Family Papers, Mss. 63M349, box 54, UK; [Danville] *Weekly Kentucky Tribune*, April 12, 1861; Snead, *Fight for Missouri*, 94–95; [St. Louis] *Daily Missouri Democrat*, January 9, 1861; Anderson, *Border City during the Civil War*, 71; Peckham, *Lyon and Missouri*, 69–71, 93–95; Gerteis, *Civil War St. Louis*, 90–91; Arthur Roy Kirkpatrick, "Missouri on the Eve of the Civil War," *MHR* 55 (January 1961): 108; Smith, *Borderland in the Civil War*, 148–49; Parrish, *Frank Blair*, 90–95; Alice E. Cayton to Alexander Badger, May 12, 1861, Badger Papers, MHS; J. P. Lancaster to J. O. Broadhead, May 9, 1861, James O. Broadhead Papers, box 1, MHS.

44. Phillips, *Damned Yankee*, 192–99; Snead, *Fight for Missouri*, 172–74; [St. Louis] *Daily Missouri Democrat*, May 13, 1861; Peckham, *Lyon and Missouri*, 165–76; Kirkpatrick, "Missouri in the Early Months of the Civil War," 240; G. W. to Dear Bro[.], May 9, 1861, Camp Jackson Papers, MHS; Unsigned to Dear Sister, May 20, 1861, Civil War Collection, box 1, MHS; Parrish, *History of Missouri*, 14–17; J. Proctor Knott to My Dear Mother, May 13, 1861, Knott Collection, Mss. 53, box 1, folder 2, WKU; Charles Gibson to Thomas T. Gantt, May 13, 1861, Charles Gibson Papers, MHS; Alice E. Cayton to Alexander Badger, May 12, 1861, Badger Papers, MHS; Mark M. Krug, ed., *Mrs. Hill's Journal: Civil War Reminiscences, by Sarah Jane Full Hill* (Chicago: R. R. Donnelly and Sons, 1980), 13–18.

45. Coulter, *Civil War and Readjustment in Kentucky*, 81–82; S. B. Axtell to L. Kerr, April 5, 1861, Vertical File A, WRHS; Doc. 243, Addresses of the Convention of the Border States, in Moore, *Rebellion Record*, 1:91, 350–56; Charlton Morgan to Mrs. Henrietta H. Morgan, July 24, 1861, Hunt-Morgan Family Papers, Mss. 63M202, box 15, folder 9, UK. The delegates were John J. Crittenden, James Guthrie, R. K. Williams, Charles S. Morehead, Archibald Dixon, Francis M. Bristow, Joshua F. Bell, Charles A. Wickliffe, G. W. Dunlap, James F. Robinson, John B. Huston, and Robert Richardson, from Kentucky; Hamilton R. Gamble, William A. Hall, John B. Henderson, and William G. Pomeroy from Missouri; and John Caldwell from Tennessee.

46. Absalom Yarbrough Johnson Diaries, 1860–1864, 4 vols., Mss. A/J67b, April 17–August 27, 1861 entries; FHS; Harrison, *Civil War in Kentucky*, 10; Smith, *Borderland in the Civil War*, 271–72; William Moody Pratt Diaries, May 20, 1861 entry, Mss. 46M79, vol. 2, UK; Memorial of W. Dennison, Rich'd Yates, and O. P. Morton, May 24, 1861; Garret Davis to G[eorge] B. McClellan, April [June] 8, 1861; General Orders No. 27, May 28, 1861; and [Winfield Scott], Remarks on a Memorial Signed by Their Excellencies the Governors of Ohio, Illinois, and Indiana, and Handed to Me Yesterday by the Second of These High Functionaries, May 29, 1861, all in *OR*, ser. 1, vol. 52, pt. 1, 146–47; vol. 2, 677–68; vol. 52, pt. 1, 147–48; Coulter, *Civil War and Readjustment in Kentucky*, 100.

47. Thomas Speed, *The Union Regiments of Kentucky* (Louisville: Courier-Journal Job Print, 1897), 20–22; Absalom Yarbrough Johnson Diaries, 1860–1864, 4 vols., Mss. A/J67b, August 24–October 5, 1861 entries; FHS; Petition of Gallatin County [Kentucky] Home Guards, June 8, 1861, Charles Whittlesey Papers, Mss. 3196, WRHS; William C. Harris, *Lincoln and the Border States: Preserving the Union* (Lawrence: University Press of Kansas, 2011), 94; Harrison and Klotter, *New History of Kentucky*, 192; Gerald J. Prokopowicz,

All for the Regiment: The Army of the Ohio, 1861-1862 (Chapel Hill: University of North Carolina Press, 2001), 12-13; Abraham Lincoln to Beriah Magoffin, August 24, 1861, in *CWAL*, 4:497; Clement Eaton, *A History of the Southern Confederacy* (New York: Macmillan, 1956), 34-35. As part of Nelson's orders, he was instructed to "muster into the service, or designate some suitable person so to do, in Southeast Kentucky, three regiments of infantry.... All of the regiments aforesaid will be raised for service in East and West Tennessee and adjacent counties and in East Kentucky." L[orenzo] Thomas to William Nelson, July 1, 1861, *OR*, ser. 1, vol. 4, 251-52.

48. Snead, *Fight for Missouri*, 173-81; Peckham, *Lyon and Missouri*, 167-68; Shalhope, *Sterling Price*, 158-59; Albert Castel, *General Sterling Price and the Civil War in the West* (Baton Rouge: Louisiana State University Press, 1968), 14; Phillips, *Damned Yankee*, 243; Parrish, *History of Missouri*, 17.

49. J. D. and B. P. McKown to Son, May 29, 1861, John D. McKown Papers, Mss. 2335, SHSM; *Liberty* [Mo.] *Tribune*, September 13, 1861; "Reminiscences of Patrick Ahern," undated, Mrs. Jesse P. Henry Papers, MHS; William Carr Lane to Sterling Price, June 3, 1861, William Carr Lane Papers, box 8, MHS; D. C. Hunter to John F. Snyder, May 24, 1861, John F. Snyder Papers, box 2, MHS; Unsigned to Dear Sister, May 20, 1861, and H. S. Turner to Dear General, July 15, 1861, both in Civil War Collection, box 1, MHS; A. P. Richardson to J. O. Broadhead, May 20, 1861, and J. P. Lancaster to Broadhead, May 9, 1861, both in James O. Broadhead Papers, box 1, MHS; *Congressional Globe*, 37th Cong., 2nd Sess., 2297; Bradbury, "Union or Disunion," 29-30, 30n1, 31-34.

50. Memoirs of M. Jeff Thompson, Meriwether Jeff Thompson Papers, Mss. 1030, folder 2, 13-14, 17-19, SHSM; Parrish, *History of Missouri*, 16, 20; Kirkpatrick, "Missouri in the Early Months of the Civil War," 258-61; Robert E. Miller, "'One of the Ruling Class'— Thomas Caute Reynolds: Second Confederate Governor of Missouri," *MHR* 80 (July 1986): 425-34; Sterling Price and William S. Harney to the People of the State of Missouri, May 21, 1861, *OR*, ser. 1, vol. 3, 374-75; Gerald Cannon, "The Harney-Price Agreement," *Civil War Times Illustrated* 23 (December 1984): 42; Phillips, *Damned Yankee*, 206-9, 211-14; Parrish, *Frank Blair*, 104-8; J[ames] O. Broadhead to Montgomery Blair, May 22, 1861, and Broadhead to Edwin Draper, May 21, 1861, both in James O. Broadhead Papers, box 1, MHS; Peckham, *Lyon and Missouri*, 159, 247-52; Montgomery Blair, "Missouri's Unionists in War," in Peter Cozzins, ed., *Battles and Leaders of the Civil War*, vol. 5 (Urbana: University of Illinois Press, 2002), 77; [St. Louis] *Daily Missouri Democrat*, July 2, 1861; Snead, *Fight for Missouri*, 199-206; Governor's Proclamation, June 12, 1861, Claiborne Fox Jackson File, Mss. 2447, folder 1, SHSM; *Boonville* [Mo.] *Observer Extra*, June 12, 1861; Reynolds, "General Sterling Price and the Confederacy," unpublished manuscript, pp. 18-44, and Reynolds to Jefferson Davis, January 20, November 13, 1880, all in Thomas C. Reynolds Papers, MHS; Diary of Thomas C. Reynolds, 1862-1866, Thomas Caute Reynolds Papers, LC. Thomas Snead's famous 1886 account of Lyon's peroration ("I would see you, and you, and you, and you, and you, and every man, woman, and child in the State, dead and buried") is likely less accurate than the *Daily Missouri Democrat* eyewitness account, published three weeks after the meeting.

51. Telegrams, C. F. Jackson to J. F. Snyder, June 13, 1861 (mismarked as July 13), John F. Snyder Collection, box 2, MHS; Albert Cotsworth to Kate Draper, October 8, 1934, Draper-McClurg Family Papers, Mss. 3069, folder 80, microfilm reel 4, SHSM; George R. Taylor to Col. Ward, August 3, 1861, General George R. Taylor Collection, MHS; Snead, *Fight for Missouri*, 206-9, 212-16, 231-34; Phillips, *Damned Yankee*, 215-18; Arthur Roy Kirkpatrick, "The Admission of Missouri to the Confederacy," *MHR* 55 (July 1961): 366-70; Kirkpatrick, "Missouri's Secessionist Government, 1861-1865," *MHR* 45 (January 1951): 127-37; Kirkpatrick, "Missouri in the Early Months of the Civil War," *MHR* 55 (April 1961): 259-66; McElroy, *Struggle for Missouri*, 123-25; [St. Louis] *Daily Missouri Democrat*, June 17, 1861, in Peckham, *Lyon and Missouri*, 260-63; Thomas W. Knox, *Camp-Fire and Cotton Field: Southern Adventure in Time of War* (Philadelphia: Jones Brothers and Co., 1865), 40-44, Parrish, *History of Missouri*, 24; Nathaniel Lyon to George B. McClellan, 30 June 1861, *OR*, ser. 3, vol. 1, 12-14; Paul Rorvig, "A Significant Skirmish: The Battle of Boonville," *MHR* 86 (January 1992): 127-48; Shalhope, *Sterling Price*, 166-70.

The term "Governor in the Saddle" was an epithet deriding Jackson's futile efforts to maintain authority while in exile.

52. [Columbia] *Missouri Statesman*, June 28, August 2, 16, 1861; [Jefferson City, Mo.] *Jefferson Inquirer*, June 16, 1861; Parrish, *Turbulent Partnership*, 35–47; Dennis K. Boman, *Lincoln's Resolute Unionist: Hamilton Gamble—Dred Scott Dissenter and Missouri's Civil War Governor* (Baton Rouge: Louisiana State University Press, 2006), 112–15 and passim; *Proceedings of the Missouri State Convention*, 5–18; Jefferson Davis to C. F. Jackson, June 5, 1861, *OR*, ser. 1, vol. 53, 707.

53. William Garrett Piston, "'Springfield Is a Vast Hospital': The Dead and Wounded at the Battle of Wilson's Creek," *MHR* 93 (July 1999): 347–55; Reynolds, "General Price and the Confederacy," 47; T. C. Reynolds to Jefferson Davis, November 13, 1880, Thomas C. Reynolds Papers, MHS; Parrish, *David Rice Atchison*, 216–17; Phillips, *Damned Yankee*, 240–64; Lowndes Henry Davis to Mary B. Hall, June 28, 1861, Civil War Papers, MHS. See also Piston and Hatcher, *Wilson's Creek*.

54. Coulter, *Civil War and Readjustment in Kentucky*, 98–99; Smith, *Borderland in the Civil War*, 271–72; Harrison and Klotter, *New History of Kentucky*, 192; George B. McClellan to E[dward] D. Townsend, and McClellan to Simon B. Buckner, both June 11, 1861, and Garret Davis to G[eorge] B. McClellan, April [June] 8, 1861, all in *OR*, ser. 1, vol. 2, 674–75, 677–78; Gienapp, "Lincoln and the Border States," 16–17.

55. Sutherland, *A Savage Conflict*, 39; Woodworth, *Nothing but Victory*, 32, 42; Hoskins, "The First Is with the South," 104–23; S. B. Buckner to Beriah Magoffin, June 15, 1861, Simon B. Buckner File, SC204, ALPL; U. S. Grant to Speaker House of Representatives, Frankfort, Ky., September 5, 1861; G[ustav] Waagner to Grant, September 8, 1861; Grant to John C. Fremont, September 10, 1861; and Garret Davis to G[eorge] B. McClellan, April [June] 8, 1861, all in *OR*, ser. 1, vol. 3, 166–68; vol. 2, 677–78; Smith, *Borderland in the Civil War*, 273–77; Harrison, *Civil War in Kentucky*, 11–13; J. Proctor Knott to My Dear Mother, August 1, 1861, Knott Collection, Mss. 53, box 1, folder 2, WKU; Parrish, *Turbulent Partnership*, 33–47, 77–79, 86.

56. George C. Taylor et al. to L[eonidas] Polk, September 5, 1861; John M. Johnston to Polk and reply, September 9, 1861; Proclamation to the Citizens of Paducah, September 6, 1861; Memorandum, August 4, 1861, in Extract, Embracing the "First Period," from Maj. Gen. George B. McClellan's Report of the Operations of the Army of the Potomac from July 27, 1861, to November 9, 1862, all in *OR*, ser. 1, vol. 4, 181–85, 179–88 passim; vol. 52, pt. 1, 109; vol. 5, 5–8; William Howard Russell, *My Diary North and South* (London: Bradbury and Evans, 1863), 53–57; S[imon] B. Buckner to Beriah Magoffin, June 15, 1861, Simon B. Buckner File, Mss. SC204, ALPL; Langstaff, *Life and Times of Quigley*, 71; [Memphis, Tenn.] *Daily Appeal*, September 18, 1861, quoted in Hoskins, "The First Is with the South," 116; McFeely, *Grant*, 90–93; Nathaniel Cheairs Hughes Jr., *The Battle of Belmont: Grant Strikes South* (Chapel Hill: University of North Carolina Press, 1991), 4–5. In addition to Fort Prentiss and Mound City in Illinois, federal troops occupied Forts Payne and Holt on the Kentucky side of the Ohio and Mississippi and Bird's Point on the Missouri side of the Mississippi. See William H. Githens to Dear Wife, February 22, 1862, William H. Githens Letter, Mss. SC1364, WKU. About the postwar South, Gregory P. Downs has convincingly argued against the long-standing idea "that a country cannot occupy its own territory." See Downs, *After Appomattox: Military Occupation and the Ends of War* (Cambridge, Mass.: Harvard University Press, 2015), 6–7 and passim.

57. William F. Swindler, "The Southern Press in Missouri, 1861–1864," *MHR* 35 (April 1941): 399; Kirkpatrick, "Admission of Missouri to the Confederacy," 377–85; An Act to Aid the State of Missouri, August 20, 1861; Ben McCulloch to J[udah] P. Benjamin, October 14, 1861; C[laiborne] F. Jackson to Jefferson Davis, October 21, 1861; Jackson to Davis, August 13, November 5, 1861, all in *OR*, ser. 4, vol. 1, 576–77; ser. 3, 718–19; ser. 53, 725, 754–55; Parrish, *Turbulent Partnership*, 34–35; Lincoln to Gamble, October 19, 1863, in *CWAL*, 6:526–27.

58. Parrish, *David Rice Atchison*, 219–20; Missouri, General Assembly (Confederate), Journal, 1861, passim, Mss. C2502, SHSM; [Columbia] *Missouri Statesman*, November 15, 22, 1861, January 31, 1862; *Charleston* [S.C.] *Mercury*, November 25, 1861; *Journal of the*

Senate, Extra Session of the Rebel Legislature, Called Together by a Proclamation of C. F. Jackson, Begun and Held at the Town of Neosho, Newton County, Missouri on the Twenty-first Day of October, Eighteen Hundred and Sixty-One (Jefferson City, Mo.: Emory S. Foster, 1865–1866), 3–4, 7–9, 12–13, 19, 34–38, 40–41; An Act Declaring the Political Ties Heretofore Existing Between the State of Missouri and the United States of America, Dissolved, October 28, 1861, and C[laiborne] F. Jackson to the Speaker of the House of Representatives, November 8, 1861, both in Missouri Confederate Archives, 1861, Mss. 2722, folder 1, SHSM; Jackson to Jefferson Davis, November 5, 1861, and An Act Admitting Missouri to the Confederacy, November 28, 1861, both in *OR*, ser. 1, vol. 53, 754–55, 758. The Senate *Journal* suggests lingering absences and attempts to bring members to Neosho, but the evidence is inconclusive. The House *Journal*, recently discovered in the collections of the State Historical Society of Missouri, casts doubt on such assertions of quorum. Complete from the beginning of the session to the end, the handwritten document never reports a roll call vote, so there is no authentication of a quorum. Missouri's delegation to the Confederate Congress was composed of John B. Clark and R. L. Y. Peyton, senators; and William M. Cooke, Thomas A. Harris, Casper W. Bell, Aaron H. Conrow, George G. Vest, Thomas W. Freeman, and John Hyer, representatives.

59. Proceedings of the Convention Held at Russellville, November 18, 19, and 20, 1861; Constitution of the Provisional Government of Kentucky, November 20, 1861; and George W. Johnson to Jefferson Davis, November 21, 1861, all in *OR*, ser. 4, vol. 1, 741–45; Eighth U.S. Census, 1860, Population and Slave Schedules, Scott County, Kentucky, NARA; Davis, *Orphan Brigade*, 62–64; Coulter, *Civil War and Readjustment in Kentucky*, 137–39; Smith, *Borderland in the Civil War*, 356–59; Harrison and Klotter, *New History of Kentucky*, 192–94; Harrison, *Civil War in Kentucky*, 20–23.

60. Abraham Lincoln to Orville H. Browning, September 22, 1861, in *CWAL*, 4:533; *BDAC*, 904.

61. Donald, *Lincoln*, 149–50; William H. Townsend, *Lincoln and the Bluegrass: Slavery and Civil War in Kentucky* (Lexington: University of Kentucky Press, 1955), 354; Mark E. Neely Jr., *The Fate of Liberty: Abraham Lincoln and Civil Liberties* (New York: Oxford University Press, 1991), 32–34, 49–50. For an interpretation of Lincoln's insistence upon restraint in the federal army's handling of southern civilians, see Burrus M. Carnahan, *Lincoln on Trial: Southern Civilians and the Law of War* (Lexington: University Press of Kentucky, 2010). For a fuller interpretation of Lincoln's harder strategy in these states, see Christopher Phillips, "Lincoln's Grasp of War: Hard War and the Politics of Neutrality and Slavery in the Western Border Slave States, 1861–62," *JCWE* 3 (June 2013): 184–210.

62. John W. Hamilton to Dear Brother and Sister, July 1, 1861, John Watts Hamilton Papers, Mss. SC676, folder 2, IHSL; Harris, *Lincoln and the Border States*, 35; [Cincinnati, Ohio] *Daily Commercial*, February 13, 1861; Speech from the Balcony of the Bates House at Indianapolis, Indiana, February 11, 1861, Remarks at Lawrenceburg, Indiana, February 12, 1861, and Speech at Cincinnati, Ohio, February 12, 1861, First Inaugural Address—Final Text, March 4, 1861, all in *CWAL*, 4:194–201, 262–71.

63. Mark Grimsley, *The Hard Hand of War: Union Military Policy toward Southern Civilians, 1861–1865* (Cambridge and New York: Cambridge University Press, 1995), 35; Donald, *Lincoln*, 332; McPherson, *Battle Cry of Freedom*, 284–90; Lorenzo Thomas to Nathaniel Lyon, April 30, 1861, and I. M. Forbes to Seth C. Hawley, November 16, 1861, both in *OR*, ser. 1, vol. 1, 675; ser. 2, vol. 1, 658; Neely, *Fate of Liberty*, 14–18.

64. Thurlow Weed to Abraham Lincoln, January 10, 1861, Lincoln Papers; James Russell Lowell, "Pickens-and-stealin's Rebellion (1861)," in *The Works of James Russell Lowell*, vol. 5 (Boston and New York: Houghton, Mifflin, 1871), 86, 89; Gienapp, "Lincoln and the Border States," 23. Gienapp was the first to criticize scholars who have devoted nearly exclusive attention to secession and gradual emancipation in border states, only to ignore them in terms of the evolving war effort. Gienapp claims that Lincoln's policies in the border states need to be evaluated against military objectives rather than simply against the question of secession.

65. Message to Congress in Special Session, July 4, 1861; Abraham Lincoln to Beriah Magoffin, August 24, 1861; Lincoln to Orville H. Browning, September 22, 1861; and Lincoln to

Reverdy Johnson, July 26, 1862, all in *CWAL*, 4:426–28, 497, 531–33; 5:343; William Preston Johnston to William Preston, December 28, 1860, Wickliffe-Preston Family Papers, Mss. 63M349, box 54, UK.

66. James M. McPherson, *Tried by War: Abraham Lincoln as Commander in Chief* (New York: Penguin Press, 2008), 30–33; David Herbert Donald, *Lincoln Reconsidered: Essays on the Civil War Era* (New York: Alfred A. Knopf, 19650, 128; Bruce Tap, "Amateurs at War: Abraham Lincoln and the Committee on the Conduct of the War," *JALA* 23 (Summer 2002): 1–18; Grimsley, *Hard Hand of War*, 38; H. S. Turner to Dear General, July 15, 1861, Civil War Collection, MHS; Robert Anderson to Abraham Lincoln, September 16, 1861, and Joshua F. Speed to Lincoln, October 7, 1861, both in Lincoln Papers. McPherson argues that Lincoln was more "hands-off" in Kentucky than in other border slave states. Although most accounts attribute Anderson's resignation to ill health, the general, who was eager to put troops under arms but reluctant to implement Lincoln's wishes to distribute rifles to Kentucky's unionists, "seemed grieved that [he] had to surrender his command... [but] agreed that it was necessary and gracefully yielded." A native Philadelphian, McClellan had lived in Cincinnati for a number of years immediately prior to the war.

67. L[orenzo] Thomas to W[illiam] S. Harney, May 27, 1861, and reply, June 5, 1861; Sterling Price to Harney, May 29, 1861, all in *OR*, ser. 1, vol. 3, 376, 383, 380–81; Daniel E. Sutherland, "Abraham Lincoln, John Pope, and the Origins of Total War," *Journal of Military History* 56 (October 1992): 577–79. Sutherland has argued that in Missouri, Lincoln "certainly had not encouraged or endorsed coercive policies aimed at civilians." Yet neither did he specifically countermand directives that did so.

68. Nathaniel P. Banks to William H. Seward, July 9, 1861, Lincoln Papers; Grimsley, *Hard Hand of War*, 4, 29, 35, 48–49; Stephen V. Ash, *When the Yankees Came: Conflict and Chaos in the Occupied South, 1861–1865* (Chapel Hill: University of North Carolina Press, 1995), 25–27; General Orders No. 34, September 13, 1863, in *Missouri Troops in Service During the Civil War*, 179; U[lysses] S. Grant to Richard J. Oglesby, November 20, 1861, *OR*, ser. 1, vol. 8, 369–70; E. Hyatt to C[harles] Whittlesey, December 31, 1861, and reply, January 1, 1862, Charles Whittlesey Papers, Mss. 3196 (microfilm), WRHS.

69. Grimsley, *Hard Hand of War*, 37; A. Barnett to Henry W. Halleck, February 5, 1862, and William Crawford to Halleck, January 5, 1862, both in RG 393, pt. 1, ser. 2593: Letters Received, Department of the Missouri, 1862–1867, box 2, NARA.

70. Sutherland, *A Savage Conflict*, 61; Thomas Ewing Jr. to Abraham Lincoln, June 27, 1863, Lincoln Papers; Ian Michael Spurgeon, *Man of Douglas, Man of Lincoln: The Political Odyssey of James Henry Lane* (Columbia: University of Missouri Press, 2008), 18–38, 41, 94–95; Albert Castel, *A Frontier State at War: Kansas, 1861–1865* (Ithaca, N.Y.: Cornell University Press, 1959; reprint Lawrence: Kansas Heritage Press, 1992), 42–43, 48–55; *Athens* [Ohio] *Messenger*, October 24, 1861; *Clinton* [Mo.] *Advocate*, August 3, 1876; *Carrollton* [Mo.] *Democrat*, August 25, 1876; Abraham Lincoln to Simon Cameron, June 20, 1861; J[ames] H. Lane to John C. Fremont, September 24, 1861; Lane to W[illiam] E. Prince, August 25, 1861; and Lane to S[amuel] S. Sturgis, October 3, 1861, all in *OR*, ser. 3, vol. 1, 282; ser. 1, vol. 3, 196, 505–6, 455, 516.

71. Sutherland, *A Savage Conflict*, 16–17; Samuel R. Curtis, "Report on Operations of Iowa Troops in Missouri in June, 1861," in Charles Aldrich, ed., *The Annals of Iowa: A Historical Quarterly*, 3rd ser. (Des Moines: Historical Department of Iowa, 1907–1908), 8:358–61; *Clinton* [Mo.] *Advocate*, August 3, 1876; *Carrollton* [Mo.] *Democrat*, August 25, 1876. Curtis's report, dated June 27, 1861, was not included in *OR*.

72. Montgomery Blair to Abraham Lincoln, May 16, 1861, Lincoln Papers; William T. Sherman, *Memoirs of General William T. Sherman*, 2 vols. (New York: Appleton, 1875; reprint New York: Da Capo Press, 1984), 1:210–14, 229, 266–67, 277–78.

73. Stathis N. Kalyvas, "The Ontology of 'Political Violence': Action and Identity in Civil Wars," *Perspectives on Politics* 1 (2003): 475–94; *Cape Girardeau* [Mo.] *Eagle* [Union Series], May 5, 1862, SEMO; Stephen A. Hurlbut to Joseph Story, July 22, 1861, Record Group 133: Adjutant General Records, Home Guards (Adair County, Walmuthsville Company), Orders, MSA; Memorandum, August 4, 1861; J. T. K. Hayward to John C. Fremont, August 10, 1861; John Edwards to S[amuel] J. Kirkwood, July 31, 1861;

Notes to Pages 151–154   377

Correspondence, Orders, and Returns Relating to Operations in Missouri, Arkansas, Kansas, the Indian Territory, and Department of the Northwest, from January 1 to December 31, 1863; Notice, July 21, 1861; General Order No. 3, July 31, 1861; Report and Order of Brig. Gen. John Pope, U.S. Army, August 17, 19, 1861; General Orders No. 5, 7, and 11, July 10–23, 1862; and J. T. K. Hayward to John C. Fremont, August 10, 12, 1861, all in *OR*, ser. 1, vol. 5, 6; vol. 3, 434, 412–13 404, 418, 135; vol. 22, pt. 2, 109–10; vol, 12, pt. 2, 50–52; ser. 2, vol. 1, 204–6; Grimsley, *Hard Hand of War*, 38; Wallace J. Schutz and Walter N. Trenerry, *Abandoned by Lincoln: A Military Biography of General John Pope* (Urbana: University of Illinois Press, 1990), 66–69; Peter Cozzins and Robert I. Girardi, eds., *The Military Memoirs of John Pope* (Chapel Hill: University of North Carolina Press, 1998), 16–26; Neely, *Fate of Liberty*, 128–29; LeeAnn Whites, "'Corresponding with the Enemy': Mobilizing the Relational Field of Battle in St. Louis," in Whites and Alecia P. Long, eds., *Occupied Women: Gender, Military Occupation, and the American Civil War* (Baton Rouge: Louisiana State University Press, 2009), 106.

74. Lowell, "Pickens-and-stealin's Rebellion (1861)," 86; Grimsley, *Hard Hand of War*, 1–6, 23, 35–36; Ephram J. Wilson to Odon Guitar, July 27, 1863, Odon Guitar Papers, Mss. C0882, SHSM; Gienapp, "Lincoln and the Border States," 36–37; Walter D. Kamphoefner and Wolfgang Helbich, eds., *Germans in the Civil War: The Letters They Wrote Home* (Chapel Hill: University of North Carolina Press, 2006), 347–53; Sutherland, *A Savage Conflict*, 61; *Annual Report of the Adjutant General of Missouri for the Year Ending December 31, 1863* (Jefferson City, Mo.: State Printer, 1864), 97–98; *Journal of the Senate of the State of Missouri, at the Adjourned Session of the Twenty-second General Assembly* (Jefferson City, Mo.: J. P. Ament, 1863), 656; *Cape Girardeau* [Mo.] *Eagle* [Union Series], May 6, 1862, SEMO; Fellman, *Inside War*, 13–15, 161; Thomas E. Wilson to Joseph Holt, May 5, 8, 1861, both in Holt Papers, book 27, LC.

75. Williamson Dixon Ward Civil War Journal, October 25, 1861 entry, Mss. SC627, WKU; Norman G. Markham to My Dear Eunice, October 25, 1862, and Markham to Dear Wife and Boy, February 3, March 20, 1863, N. G. Markham Papers, Mss. A/M345, folder 1, FHS.

76. [Hillsboro] *The Illinois Free Press*, April 4, 1861; Watson Goodrich to Alvin C. Woolfolk, November 26, 1861, Watson Goodrich Letters, Mss. C/G, FHS; Daniel M. Davis to Dear Father, September 22, 1862, Daniel M. Davis Letters, Microfilm 48, SIU; Daniel Berry to Mary B. Crebs, November 30, 1862, Daniel Berry Letters, Misc. Vol. 53, SIU; [Sullivan, Ind.] *The Stars and Stripes*, December 26, 1861; [Fredricktown, Mo.] *The Advance Guard*, August 28, 1861; Eli Thayer to Abraham Lincoln, October 12, 1861, Lincoln Papers.

77. Winfred A. Harbison, "Lincoln and Indiana Republicans, 1861–1862," *IMH* 33 (September 1937): 278, 295; Ash, *When the Yankees Came*, 50–53; Gerteis, *Civil War St. Louis*, 174–75; Neely, *Fate of Liberty*, 36, 39; General Orders No. 8, November 26, 1861, and General Orders No. 13, December 4, 1861, and Halleck to Charles Whittlesey, January 2, 1862, all in *OR*, ser. 1, vol. 8, 380–81, 405–6, 481; Geo[rge] D. Blakey to J[eremiah] T. Boyle, November 28, 1862, RG 393, pt. 1, ser. 2173: Letters Received, Department of Kentucky, 1862–1869, box 1, NARA; P. H. Watson to George W. Morgan, May 11, 1862, *OR*, ser. 1, vol. 10, pt. 2, 182. Ash refers to conciliation generally by the term "rosewater policy," but does not ascribe the term's origin. The term predated Lincoln's use in 1862, when he wrote to a Louisianan who protested the troops' hard treatment of civilians, asking whether he would rather they prosecute the war "with elder-stalk squirts, charged with rose-water." [Terre Haute, Ind.] *Wabash Express*, July 14, 1862; Abraham Lincoln to Cuthbert Bullitt, July 28, 1862, in *CWAL*, 5:346.

78. W[illiam] G. Eliot to Hamilton R. Gamble, December 1, 1862, *OR*, ser. 1, vol. 32, pt. 1, 801–3; John Preston Jr., May 20, 1861, Wickliffe-Preston Family Papers, Mss. 63M349, box 54, UK; H. and O. Wilson to H[enry] W. Halleck, February 5, 1862, RG 393, pt. 1, ser. 2593: Letters Received, Department of the Missouri, 1862–1867, box 3, NARA; Carter, *Troubled State*, 22.

79. W. James Morgan to Henry W. Halleck, December 24, 1861, *OR*, ser. 2, vol. 1, 238; General Orders No. 13a, February 26, 1862, *OR*, ser. 1, vol. 7, 669–70; Grimsley, *Hard Hand of War*, 64–65; *Harper's Weekly*, May 10, 1862, p. 289.

80. Hicken, *Illinois in the Civil War*, 81; [Joseph Cowgill Maple], "Incidents of the Campaign of 1861 in Southeast Missouri" (hereafter cited as Maple Diary), pp. 8–9, CGCAC; Ettie Scott to Susan Grigsby, August 3, 1862, Grigsby Family Papers, Mss. A/G857, folder 173, FHS; James Frank Fee to Brother Junius Fee, January 26, 1862, James Frank Fee Letters, SC567, folder 1, IHSL; Regimental (11th Illinois Infantry) Orders No. 7, May 10, 1861, Wallace-Dickey Family Papers, ALPL; Parrish, *History of Missouri*, 66–70; McPherson, *Battle Cry of Freedom*, 784–85; Grimsley, *Hard Hand of War*, 190–204; Halleck to Lorenzo Thomas, January 18, 1862, OR, ser. 1, vol. 8, 503.
81. John H. Tilford Diary, September 5, 1862 entry, Mss. A/T572, vol. 1, FHS; Allen to Eliza, April 5, 1862, Mss. VFM 802, OHS; Paulina H. Stratton Diary (typescript), October 12, 1862 entry, Paulina H. Stratton Papers, Mss. C0842, SHSM; John A. Higgins to Nancy Higgins, October 19, 1861, John A. Higgins Papers, Mss. SC1918, folder 1, ALPL.
82. Ormsby M. Mitchel to Joseph Ripley, August 16, 1861, Mitchel to Dear Ned [Edwin W. Mitchel], October 1, 15, November 3, 1861, Lovell H. Rousseau to J[ames] B. Fry, August 7, 1862, all in Ormsby M. Mitchel Papers, Mss. M679, box 1, folder 1, CHSL; P. C. Headley, *The Patriot Boy; or, The Life and Career of Major-General Ormsby M. Mitchel* (New York: William H. Appleton, 1865), 166–67; Freehling, *South vs. the South*, 102; Hoskins, "The First Is with the South," 146; Civil War Diary of John Preston Mann (transcription, vol. 6), March 15, 1862 entry, Mann Family Papers, Coll. 111, SIU; Sutherland, *A Savage Conflict*, 103–6; Findings of "Buell Commission" and accompanying documents, 1862–1872, OR, ser. 1, vol. 16, pt. 1, 7–67 passim.
83. Edward F. Noyes to R. H. Stephenson, September 21, 1861, Nathaniel Wright Family Papers, LC; O. D. Williams to Samuel R. Curtis, December 4, 1862, RG 393, pt. 1, ser. 2593: Letters Received, Department of the Missouri, 1862–1867, box 7, NARA; J[ohn] Preston Mann to Nancy Mann, April 2, 1862, Mann Family Papers, Coll. 111, box 1, SIU; David T. Statham to Dear Brother, November 16, 1861, David T. Statham Papers, Mss. 688, OHS; James E. Love to Dear Molly, October 10, 1861, James Edwin Love Papers, box 1, MHS. The Galt House meeting occurred on October 11, 1861.
84. Ash, *When the Yankees Came*, 29–30; General Orders No. 46, February 22, 1862, OR, ser. 1, vol. 8, 563–64; Sutherland, *A Savage Conflict*, 18–19.
85. H[enry] W. Halleck to George B. McClellan, December 19, 1861, and endorsement, December 27, 1861, Halleck to McClellan, January 14, 1862, Halleck to Lorenzo Thomas, and endorsement, January 18, 1862, and J[ohn] M. Schofield to J. C. Kelton, January 2, 1862, all in OR, ser. 1, vol. 8, 449–50, 502–3, 507; Carter, *Troubled State*, 41.
86. William Moody Pratt Diaries, October 2, 1862 entry, vol. 3, Mss. 46M79, UK; James H. Goodnow to Dear Nancy, August 29, 1862, James H. Goodnow Papers, LC; D. Warren Lambert, "The Decisive Battle of Richmond, Kentucky," in Kent Masterson Brown, ed., *The Civil War in Kentucky: Battle for the Bluegrass* (Mason City, Iowa: Savas Publishing Company, 2000), 109–28; Berlin et al., *Freedom: Destruction of Slavery*, 498.
87. Edwin Smith to Maria Smith, October 14, 1862, Smith Family Papers, CHSL.
88. J. T. K. Hayward to John C. Fremont, August 10, 1861, OR, ser. 1, vol. 3, 434; "Sermon Delivered in the Lexington Presbyterian Church," June 3, 1862, p. 12, Lyle Family Papers, Mss. 62M49, box 1848–72, UK; [Hardin], *Private War of Lizzie Hardin*, 51.
89. [Hardin], *Private War of Lizzie Hardin*, 48, 59; Mary A. Crebs to My Own Dear Husband [Daniel Crebs], November 16, 1863, Mary A. Berry [Crebs] Letters, Misc. Vol. 88, SIU; T. Harry Williams, "Voters in Blue: The Citizen Soldiers of the Civil War," *MVHR* 31 (September 1944): 199; Martha M. Jones to My Dear Father, December 21, 1862, Jones Family Papers, Mss. A/J78, folder 1, FHS; Henry Chenoweth to Thomas W. Bullitt, March 1, 1862, and Thomas Bullitt to Mildred Ann Bullitt, March 23, 1864, both in Bullitt-Chenoweth Family Papers, Mss. A/B937a, folders 300, 301, FHS; T[homas] A. Hoyt to Pat Joyes, October 28, 1862, Joyes Family Papers, Mss. A/J89b, folder 19, FHS; Luke Edward Harlow, "From Border South to Solid South: Religion, Race, and the Making of Confederate Kentucky, 1830–1880" (Ph.D. dissertation, Rice University, 2009), 133–36; Cora Owens Hume Journal (typescript), June 1, 1865 entry, vol. 2, p. 119, Mss. A/H921 Vault C [3 vols.], FHS.

90. Smith, *Borderland in the Civil War*, 305–6; William L. Burton, *Melting Pot Soldiers: The Union's Ethnic Regiments* (Ames: Iowa State University Press, 1988; reprint New York: Fordham University Press, 1998), 79, 80–84, 92–93, 104, 135–38, 202–3, 205; Henry W. Halleck to George B. McClellan, January 14, 1862, OR, ser. 1, vol. 8, 502; William L. Shea and Earl J. Hess, *Pea Ridge: Civil War Campaign in the West* (Chapel Hill: University of North Carolina Press, 1992), 14; Joseph R. Reinhart, ed., *Two Germans in the Civil War: The Diary of John Daeuble and the Letters of Gottfried Rentschler, 6th Kentucky Volunteer Infantry* (Knoxville: University of Tennessee Press, 2004), xxvii–xxviii, 68; Samuel Haycraft Journal, 1849–1873, January 4, 1862 entry, Mss. A/H414, FHS; Ettie Scott to Susan Grigsby, August 3, 1862, Grigsby Family Papers, Mss. A/G857, folder 173, FHS; Carl Theodore Schwartz Journal, 1854–1871, October 25, 1862 entry, Mss. A/S399, FHS; Elvira A. W. Scott Diary (typescript), Mss. 1053, folder 4, pp. 104–6, SHSM; Maple Diary, pp. 17–21, CGCAC.

91. [Parsons], *Incidents and Experiences*, 87–89, 114; Petition of Thomas H. Smith et al., September 1, 1864, and affidavits, RG 393, pt. 1, ser. 2229: Correspondence, Affidavits, Oaths Regarding Civilians Charged with Disloyalty, Department of Kentucky, box 1, NARA; *Great Union Meeting, Philadelphia December 7, 1859* (Philadelphia: Crissy and Markley, 1859), 1–4; J. Matthew Gallman, *Mastering Wartime: A Social History of Philadelphia During the Civil War* (Cambridge: Cambridge University Press, 1990; reprint Philadelphia: University of Pennsylvania Press, 2000), 4–5; Typescript, "Some Recollections of the War," by Thomas W. Bullitt, August 29, 1907, Bullitt-Chenoweth Family Papers, Mss. A/B937a, folder 330, FHS; Diary of Thomas Walker Bullitt, vol. 1 (1857–1862, 1893), entries January 5, February 10, 12, 16, May 12, June 15, 1859, March 4, 1861; vol. 2 (July 1861), entries July 17, 21, 1861, both in Bullitt Family Papers, Mss. 3549, box 7, folders 99–100, UNC; Rev. T. A. Hoyt, to Pat Joyes, October 28, 1862, Joyes Family Papers, Mss. A/J89b, folder 18, FHS. Parsons and his home guard unit used the ploy more than once to trick unsuspecting southern sympathizers into revealing their political sentiments.

92. Joseph S. Stern Jr., "The Suspension Bridge: They Said It Couldn't Be Built," *Cincinnati Historical Society Bulletin* 23 (October 1965), 210–28; John Clubbe, *Cincinnati Observed: Architecture and History* (Columbus: Ohio State University Press, 1992), 174–75; Don Heinrich Tolzmann, *The John A. Roebling Suspension Bridge on the Ohio River* (Cincinnati: University of Cincinnati, 1998), 1–8.

The Gates of Zion

1. Pleasant Hill, Kentucky, ca. 1804–1879: Diary, church records, social compact, correspondence and writings, church orders, and laws and ordinances, Shakertown at Pleasant Hill Collection, 1805–1920, Mss. 1M87M31, microfilm reel 2, UK (hereafter cited as Pleasant Hill Journal, UK); South Union, Kentucky, 1830–1869: Church orders, diary, journal, poem, and other writings, microfilm reels 2–3, LC; South Union, Kentucky: Family Journal (hereafter cited as South Union Journal); December 31, 1861 entry and passim, Shakers of South Union, Kentucky Collection, 1800–1916, WKU; Tom Kanon, "Seduced, Bewildered, and Lost: Anti-Shakerism on the Early Nineteenth-Century Frontier," *OVH* (Summer 2007): 2–3, 7–8 and passim; [Moore], *Journal of Eldress Nancy*, viii. Shaker communities also existed in Ohio at North Union, Watervliet, Union Village, and White Water, and in Indiana at West Union.

2. Clark, *Pleasant Hill in the Civil War*, 20.

3. Pleasant Hill Journal, UK, September 6, 1861 entry; Journal of Events kept by James L. Ballance, Deacon of the East Family, April 1, 1860 to December 21, 1866, January 5, 1861 entry, Shakers, Pleasant Hill, Kentucky, Collection Mss. BA/S 527, vol. 12, FHS (hereafter cited as Pleasant Hill Journal, FHS); Julia Neal, *The Kentucky Shakers* (Lexington: University Press of Kentucky, 1982), 1–11, 18–19; Clark, *Pleasant Hill in the Civil War*, 7–18; Thomas D. Clark and F. Gerald Ham, *Pleasant Hill and Its Shakers* (Harrodsburg, Ky.: Pleasant Hill Press, 1983), 1–3; [Moore], *Journal of Eldress Nancy*, 8, 27.

4. Pleasant Hill Journal, UK, January 4, August 1, December 31, 1861 entries; Pleasant Hill Journal, FHS, December 31, 1861 entry.
5. Pleasant Hill Journal, UK, January 4, August 1, December 31, 1861 entries; Pleasant Hill Journal, FHS, December 31, 1861 entry.
6. Pleasant Hill Journal, UK, January 4–December 31, 1861, August 10, 1862 entries; Pleasant Hill Journal, FHS, January 4, September 26, November 28, 1861 entries; Lillian Schlissel, ed., *Conscience in America* (New York: Dutton, 1968), 58. In 1864 Congress abolished commutation fees except for conscientious objectors, thus categorizing for the first time religious objectors to war service. The law did not exclude objectors from being drafted into the military, but required that they "be considered non-combatants." Lincoln made it policy, assigning noncombatants to duty in hospitals or freedpeople's schools.
7. [Moore], *Journal of Eldress Nancy*, 8, 14–29, 37, 62, 67; "History of South Union, Ky., No. 9 [January 15, 1862]," *Manifesto (1884–1899)* 24 (July 1894): 149–51; Pleasant Hill Journal, UK, September 25, 1861 entry.
8. [Moore], *Journal of Eldress Nancy*, 12, 18, 20–23, 25, 31, 54; A[lbert] Sidney Johnston to Hon. J[udah] P. Benjamin, January 5, 1862, OR, ser. 1, vol. 7, 820–22.
9. [Moore], *Journal of Eldress Nancy*, 31–36.
10. Pleasant Hill Journal, UK, December 31, 1861–August 17, 29, 1862 entries; Pleasant Hill Journal, FHS, December 12, 1861, April 5, 8, 1862 entries; December 31, 1861; Harrison, *Civil War in Kentucky*, 33–46, 80–82; Lowell H. Harrison, ed., *Kentucky's Governors* (Lexington: University Press of Kentucky, 2004), 89–90.
11. Pleasant Hill Journal, UK, July 12–October 6, 15, 1862 entries; Ash, *When the Yankees Came*, 77–92.
12. Pleasant Hill Journal, UK, September 3–October 25, 1862 entries; Harrison, *Civil War in Kentucky*, 42–46; Clark, *Pleasant Hill in the Civil War*, 7–18, 35–54. For the best study of the battle of Perryville, see Kenneth W. Noe, *Perryville: This Grand Havoc of Battle* (Lexington: University Press of Kentucky, 2001).
13. Pleasant Hill Journal, UK, October 12, 1862 entry.
14. Pleasant Hill Journal, UK, November 16, 27, 1862 entry; McPherson, *Battle Cry of Freedom*, 492–94; Anita Sanchez, *Mr. Lincoln's Chair: The Shakers and Their Quest for Peace* (Granville, Ohio: McDonald and Woodward, 2009), 110–24 and passim; Iver Bernstein, *The New York City Draft Riots: Their Significance for American Society and Politics in the Age of the Civil War* (New York: Oxford University Press, 1990), 7, 289n14. Militia drafts in Wisconsin, Maryland, Indiana, and Ohio in 1862 resulted in localized resistance.
15. [Moore], *Journal of Eldress Nancy*, 77–90; Pleasant Hill Journal, UK, December 25–31, 1862 entries; Clark, *Pleasant Hill in the Civil War*, 57–59.

Chapter 5: Netherworld of War: Civilians, Soldiers, and the Dominion of War

1. Carter, *Troubled State*, 41.
2. Sutherland, *A Savage Conflict*, 61; Greenville [Ill.] *Advocate*, March 10, 1864; Harrisburg [Ill.] *Chronicle*, April 4, 1863; Krug, *Mrs. Hill's Journal*, 97–115.
3. Woodworth, *Nothing but Victory*, 202–4; Conrad, *Journal of Elder William Conrad*, 81–82; Ronald D. Smith, *Thomas Ewing Jr.: Frontier Lawyer and Civil War General* (Columbia: University of Missouri Press, 2008), 158; Carter, *Troubled State*, 41.
4. [Hardin], *Private War of Lizzie Hardin*, 58; "Sarah Patience" [unpublished manuscript, typescript], 51, Martha W. Dorsey Papers, Mss. SC510, folder 2, IHSL. For the most thorough discussion of the rebel grapevine, see Jason Phillips, "The Grape Vine Telegraph: Rumors and Confederate Persistence," *JSH* 72 (November 2006): 753–88.
5. Scott Nelson and Carol Sheriff, *A People at War: Civilians and Soldiers in America's Civil War, 1854–1877* (New York: Oxford University Press, 2008), 106–10; Drew Gilpin Faust, *This Republic of Suffering: Death and the American Civil War* (New York: Vintage Books, 2008), 61–68; Georgia Cryer to Sister, April 12, 1862, Cooper-Phillips Family Papers, Mss. 66M37, UK; Nazro Diary, July 29, 1862 entry, WKU.

Notes to Pages 172–175   381

6. Julian S. Rumsey to Henry W. Halleck, February 24, 1862; F[ranklin] A. Dick to Francis P. Blair, March 5, 1862; and Halleck to Richard Yates, March 15, 1862, all in *OR*, ser. 2, vol. 3, 315, 379–80; Whites, "'Corresponding with the Enemy,'" in Whites and Long, eds., *Occupied Women*, 107–8; Neely, *Fate of Liberty*, 128–29; Nancy Mann to J[ohn] Preston Mann, February 20, 1862, Mann Family Papers, Coll. 111, box 1, SIU.
7. Parrish, *David Rice Atchison*, 220–21; Anna Hunt to Henrietta H. Morgan, undated, Hunt-Morgan Family Papers, Mss. 63M202, box 15, folder 10, UK; Civil War Diary of John Preston Mann (typescript, vol. 6), March 26, 1862 entry, Mann Family Papers, Coll. 111, SIU; Mary E. Van Meter Diary, February 10, 1862–February 25, 1863 entries, Mss. 54M98 (microfilm), UK; Eighth U.S. Census, 1860, Population Schedule, Warren County, Kentucky.
8. Woodworth, *Nothing but Victory*, 72–73; Civil War Diary of John Preston Mann (typescript, vol. 6), March 15, 1862 entry, and Petition, J. H. Clendenin and Others to A. J. Walters, June 8, 1861, both in Mann Family Papers, Coll. 111, box 5, SIU; *Cincinnati* [Ohio] *Daily Enquirer*, November 21, 1861.
9. Civil War Diary of John Preston Mann (typescript, vol. 6), March 26, 1862, Mann Family Papers, Coll. 111, SIU; Henry Harris to Neal M. Gordon, July 16, 1862, Gordon Family Papers, Mss. 51M40, box 4, UK; J. T. K. Hayward to John C. Fremont, August 10, 1861, *OR*, ser. 1, vol. 3, 434.
10. Eben Perry Sturges to Dear Folks, January 26, 1862, Sturges Family Papers, Mss. 539, OHS; Nancy C. Mann to J[ohn] P. Mann, September 16, 1862, December 14, 1863, May 24, June 3, 1864, all in Mann Family Papers, Coll. 111, boxes 1–2, SIU; Philip B. Swing to Horatio G. Wright, September 30, 1862, RG 393, pt. 1, ser. 3514: Letters Received, Department of the Ohio, box 2, NARA; T. E. Pickett to Cyrus Boys Trimble, October 1861, November 22, 1862, John A. Trimble Papers, Mss. 249, box 10, folder 3, OHS; Frances Dallam Peter to Arthur, May 7, 1864, Evans Papers, Mss. 72M15, box 7, UK; Maria [Holyoke] to My Dear Mother and Sister, August 18, 1861, Holyoke Family Papers—Davie Collection, Mss. C/H, FHS; Ash, *When the Yankees Came*, 81; "My Memories" (unpublished manuscript, typescript), ca. 1921, pp. 6–20, J. Milton Pitts Papers, Mss. SC1207, IHSL; John F. Bradbury Jr., "'Buckwheat Cake Philanthropy': Refugees and the Union Army in the Ozarks," *Arkansas Historical Quarterly* 57 (Autumn 1998): 237–38; Diane Mutti Burke, "Scattered People: The Long History of Forced Eviction in the Kansas-Missouri Borderlands," in Adam Arenson, ed., *Civil War Wests: Testing the Limits of the United States*, (Berkeley: University of California Press, 2015), 78–82.
11. *Centralia* [Ill.] *Sentinel*, July 14, 1864; Mrs. Alfred Clapp to The Commanding General of the District of Saint Louis, undated [1864], RG 393, pt. 1, ser. 2593: Letters Received, Department of the Missouri, box 15, NARA; Circular, Rooms of the Cincinnati Refugee Relief Commission, December 18, 1864; L. von Kadowitz to C. H. Potter, December 10, 1864; and Thomas G. Odiorne to Potter, October 18, 1864, all in RG 393, pt. 1, ser. 3349: Letters Received, Northern Department, boxes 2–3, NARA.
12. Lizzie M. Ridgway to H[enry] T. Duncan Jr., October 20, 1861, Duncan Family Papers, Mss. 71M38, UK; Ellen Sudduth to Anna Cooper, May 28, [1862], Cooper-Phillips Family Papers, Mss. 66M37, UK; Mary Louisa Reed to George J. Reed, January 22, [1862], Reed Family of Indiana and Kentucky Papers, LC.
13. Harmony Baptist Church Record Book, 1855–1902, August 4, 1861–January [26], 1862 entries, Mss. 46M141, UK; Records of the Particular Baptist Church, Williamstown, Kentucky, 1826–1919, Mss. M798 (microfilm), January 26–June 27, 1861 entries, UK; Jerusalem Baptist Church Records, October 1860–June 1863 entries, Mss. 63M485 (microfilm0, UK; Record of the Board of Trustees of the Public Schools of New Albany, Indiana (microfilm), June 6, 1861, July 16, 1862, January 7, 1865 entries, IHSL; Langstaff, *Life and Times of Quigley*, 76; Transcription of County Court Records, 1835–1868, folders 4653–4725, U.S. Works Projects Administration, Historical Records Survey, Missouri, 1935–1942, Mss. 3551, SHSM; "History of South Union, Ky., No. 12 [February 13, 1862]," *Manifesto (1884–1899)* 24 (October 1894): 221–25; J[ohn] Preston Mann to Nancy Mann, October 27, 1861, Mann Family Papers, Coll. 111, box 1, SIU.

14. "An Army Wife's Forty Years in the Service, 1862–1902" (unpublished manuscript, typescript), p. 12, Elizabeth J. Reynolds Burt Papers, LC; [Hardin], *Private War of Lizzie Hardin*, 57–59; Euphrasia Pettus to Sister, May 20, 1861, Pettus Family Papers, MHS; Mary E. Van Meter Diary, February 25, 1863 entry, Mss. 54M98 (microfilm), UK; Journal of Ellen Kenton McGaughey Wallace, 1849–1865 (transcription), February 7, 1862 entry, Wallace-Starling Family Diaries, Mss. 96M07, KHS; "Sarah Patience" (unpublished manuscript, typescript), Martha W. Dorsey Papers, Mss. SC510, folder 2, pp. 49, IHSL; Nazro Diary, August 1, 1861, April 20, August 2–September 1, 1862 entries, WKU.

15. Alfred M. Mann to J[ohn] P. Mann, June 2, 1862; Nancy C. Mann to J[ohn] P. Mann, undated [1861], both in Mann Family Papers, Coll. 111, box 1, SIU; [Frances Dallam Peter], *A Union Woman in Civil War Kentucky: The Diary of Frances Peter*, ed. John David Smith and William J. Cooper Jr. (Lexington: University Press of Kentucky, 2000), xix–xx, 163.

16. Conrad, *Journal of Elder William Conrad*, 55; Mark A. Noll, *The Civil War as a Theological Crisis* (Chapel Hill: University of North Carolina Press, 2006), 1, 125–55; George M. Fredrickson, "The Coming of the Lord: The Northern Protestant Clergy and the Civil War Crisis," in Randall M. Miller, Harry S. Stout, and Charles Reagan Wilson, eds., *Religion and the American Civil War* (New York: Oxford University Press, 1998), 118; Henry Ward Beecher, *Addresses in America and England, from 1850 to 1885, on Slavery, the Civil War, and the Development of Civil Liberty in the United States*, ed. John R. Howard (New York: Fords, Howard, and Hulbert, 1887), 297. See also Edward Needles Wright, *Conscientious Objectors in the Civil War* (Philadelphia: University of Pennsylvania Press, 1931).

17. Bryon C. Andreasen, "'As Good a Right to Pray': Copperhead Christians on the Northern Civil War Home Front" (Ph.D. dissertation, University of Illinois, Urbana-Champaign, 1998), 33–36, 48–62, 174; *Centralia [Ill.] Sentinel*, February 25, 1864; David Christy, *Pulpit Politics; or, Ecclesiastical Legislation on Slavery, in Its Disturbing Influences on the American Union* (Cincinnati: Faran and McLean, 1862), vi and passim; *Cincinnati [Ohio] Daily Enquirer*, November 26, 1862, April 19, 1863; Newspaper Clipping, January 30, 1864, Lyle Family Papers, Mss. 62M49, box 1848–1872, UK; *Salem [Ill.] Advocate*, March 3, 1864; [Columbus, Ohio] *Crisis*, June 25, 1862.

18. Thomas Prickett to Matilda Prickett, February 23, 1863, Thomas Prickett Papers, Mss. SC1222, IHSL; Andreasen, "As Good a Right to Pray," 85, 428; Joel H. Silbey, *A Respectable Minority: The Democratic Party in the Civil War Era, 1860–1868* (New York: W. W. Norton, 1977), 8.

19. Andreasen, "As Good a Right to Pray," 123–24; Newspaper Clippings, 1860–1864; J[oel] K. Lyle to John A. Lyle, October 17, 1862; Tract, "Major Sanderson," undated; "Sermon Delivered in the Lexington Presbyterian Church," June 3, 1862, pp. 12–24, 29–29, all in Lyle Family Papers, Mss. 62M49, box 1848–1872, UK; Bevie W. Cain to James M. Davis, November 6, 1864, Bevie Cain Letters, Mss. SC2251, WKU.

20. [Louisville, Ky.] *The True Presbyterian*, April 17, 1862; Gerteis, *Civil War St. Louis*, 184–85. See also Samuel Brown McPheeters, *Memoir of Rev. Samuel B. McPheeters*, ed. John S. Grasty (St. Louis and Louisville: Southwestern Book and Publishing Co. and Davidson Bros. and Co., 1871).

21. Mag Dudley to Neal M. Gordon and Family, April 27, 1862, and Gilbert Gordon to Gordon, November 31, 1866, both in Gordon Family Papers, Mss. 51M40, box 4, UK; Andreasen, "As Good a Right to Pray," 123–74 passim; *Cincinnati [Ohio] Daily Enquirer*, January 8, 25, March 18, July 15, 1863, June 8, 1864.

22. Andreasen, "As Good a Right to Pray," 87–111, 143; *Harrisburg [Ill.] Chronicle*, June 27, 1863; Gilbert Gordon to Neal M. Gordon, February 5, 1862; Alexander Young to Mr. Gordon, September 22, 1864, both in Gordon Family Papers, Mss. 51M40, box 4, UK; Jean A. Baker, *Affairs of Party: The Political Culture of Northern Democrats in the Mid-Nineteenth Century* (Ithaca, N.Y.: Cornell University Press, 1983), 169–73; Silbey, *Respectable Minority*, 72–75.

23. William Moody Pratt Diaries, June 22, 1862 entry, and List of Sermons Preached, 1860–1862, both in vol. 2; October 2, 1862, May 9, 1864, January 7–8, 23, February 6, 1865 entries, all in vol. 3, Mss. 46M79, UK.

24. Henry H. Haviland to Susan Terrill Scrogin, August 4, 1861, Scrogin-Haviland Collection, Mss. 2001SC20, folder 6, KHS; S[usan] H. S. Fishback to Susan Grigsby, July 8, 1861, Grigsby Family Papers, Mss. A/G857, folder 171, FHS; Elvira A. W. Scott Diary (typescript), Mss. 1053, folder 4, pp. 116-31, SHSM; Maple Diary, pp. 36-42, CGCAC.

25. Amy Murrell Taylor, *The Divided Family in Civil War America* (Chapel Hill: University of North Carolina Press, 2006), 36-37, 44-45; Marriage Records File (1815-1865), Daviess County Clerk Records, unprocessed collection, KDLA; Annie Leslie McCarroll Starling Journal, 1860-1932, December 20, 28, 1861 entries, Wallace-Starling Family Diaries, Mss. 96M07, KHS; [Peter], *Union Woman in Civil War Kentucky*, xx-xxiii, 33, 53; Benjamin Forsythe Buckner to Dear Helen, June 3, September 25, December 15, 19, 1861, August 10, 1862, all in Benjamin Forsythe Buckner Papers, 1785-1918, Mss. 48M39, UK; Eighth U.S. Census, 1860, Population and Slave Schedules, Clark County, Kentucky, NARA; Susan Terrill Scrogin to Henry H. Haviland, July 15, 1861, Scrogin-Haviland Collection, Mss. 2001SC20, folder 6, KHS.

26. Michael Fellman, *Citizen Sherman: A Life of William Tecumseh Sherman* (New York: Random House, 1995), 85-88, 91-99; Sherman, *Memoirs of General Sherman*, 1: 170-74; John F. Marszalek, *Sherman: A Soldier's Passion for Order* (New York: The Free Press, 1993), 142-46, 157-63; W[illiam] T. Sherman to Ellen Sherman, August 19, September 18, 25, October 3, 20, 1861, William T. Sherman Family Papers (microfilm), reel 2, LC; Maria [Holyoke] to My Dear Mother and Sister, August 18, 1861, Holyoke Family Papers—Davie Collection, Mss. C/H, FHS; Harrison, *Civil War in Kentucky*, 15; Simon Cameron to Abraham Lincoln, October 16, 1861, *OR*, ser. 1, vol. 4, 308. In November 1861 Don Carlos Buell replaced Sherman in Louisville.

27. Barton Bates to Edward Bates, undated [July-August 1861], Bates Family Papers, MHS; J. Proctor Knott to My Dear Mother, August 1, 1861, Knott Collection, Mss. 53, box 1, folder 2, WKU; Harrison, *Kentucky's Governors*, 115-16.

28. J. B. Bowman and J. L. Smedley to J[eremiah] T. Boyle, November 10, 1862, RG 393, Pt. 1, Ser. 2173: Letters Received, Department of Kentucky, 1862-1869, box 1, NARA; *New York Times*, June 22, 1862; *Kentucky Opinions, Containing the Unreported Opinions of the Court of Appeals* (Lexington: Central Law Book, 1906), 1:101-4; Lewis D. Asper, "The Long and Unhappy History of Loyalty Testing in Maryland," *American Journal of Legal History* 13 (April 1969): 106; Joseph A. Ranney, *In the Wake of Slavery: Civil War, Civil Rights, and the Reconstruction of Southern Law* (Westport, Conn.: Greenwood Publishing Group, 2006), 35-41; Thomas S. Crutcher File, August 16, 1864, Mss. C/C, FHS; Parrish, *History of Missouri*, 42-44; Boman, *Lincoln's Resolute Unionist*, 121, 133-36, 172; H[enry] W. Halleck to George B. McClellan, December 19, 1861; Special Orders No. 13, August 30, 1861; and General Orders No. 1, November 25, 1861, all in *OR*, ser. 1, vol. 8, 448-49; ser. 2, vol. 1, 220-21; ser. 1, vol. 8, 369-70; *Hannibal [Mo.] Daily Messenger*, October 30, 1861; Gerteis, *Civil War St. Louis*, 129-31; Parrish, *Turbulent Partnership*, 78-80; Coulter, *Civil War and Readjustment*, 139-44; Bettie Terrell to Susan Grigsby, July 29, 1862, Grigsby Family Papers, Mss. A/G857, folder 173, FHS; *Congressional Globe*, 37th Cong., 2nd Sess., pt. 1 (1861-1862), 891-92. In December 1861 the Kentucky legislature also expelled U.S. representative Henry C. Burnett, who was a member of the provisional government.

29. Coulter, *Civil War and Readjustment*, 151-53; [Conrad], *Journal of Elder William Conrad*, 76-77; Ettie Scott to Susan Grigsby, August 3, 1862, Grigsby Family Papers, Mss. A/G857, folder 173, FHS; [Hardin], *Private War of Lizzie Hardin*, 63; L. C. Turner to J[eremiah] T. Boyle, November 2, 1862, and Isaac R. Gray to Boyle, November 17, 1862, both in RG 393, pt. 1, ser. 2173: Letters Received, Department of Kentucky, 1862-1869, box 1, NARA; William B. Sipes to Horatio G. Wright, December 18, 1862, and enclosures, RG 393, pt. 1, ser. 3514: Letters Received, Department of the Ohio, box 2, NARA; R. A. Curd to Cal Morgan, June 22, 1862, Hunt-Morgan Family Papers, Mss. 63M202, box 15, folder 9, UK; Smith, *Borderland in the Civil War*, 372; Coulter, *Civil War and Readjustment*, 153; General Orders No. 49, October 26, 1862, *OR*, ser. 1, vol. 16, pt. 2, 646.

30. George Caleb Bingham to Ja[me]s S. Rollins and Wi[llia]m A. Hall, February 12, 1862, in C. B. Rollins, ed., "Letters of George Caleb Bingham to James M. Rollins—Part V, Letters: January 22, 1862-November 21, 1871," *MHR* 33 (October 1938): 53-54.

31. David Bailey to Hamilton R. Gamble, January 13, 1862, RG 133: Adjutant General Missouri Volunteers, 27th Regiment Infantry, Regimental Correspondence—Miscellaneous, box 1, MSA.
32. Judkin Browning, "'I Am Not So Patriotic as I Was Once': The Effects of Military Occupation on the Occupying Soldiers during the Civil War," *CWH* 55 (June 2009): 219–20; L. C. Turner to J[eremiah] T. Boyle, November 2, 1862, RG 393, pt. 1, ser. 2173: Letters Received, Department of Kentucky, 1862–1869; box 1, NARA; Henry W. Halleck to Hon. T[homas] Ewing, January 1, 1862, *OR*, ser. 1, vol. 8, 475.
33. M. Jeff Thompson to Jefferson Davis, July 2, 1861; Proclamation, "To all peaceably-disposed citizens of the State of Missouri, greeting," November 1, 5, 1861; and Paul Ravesies to W. H. Hardee, November 23, 1861; An Act to authorize the President of the Confederate States to grant commissions to raise volunteer regiments and battalions composed of persons who are or have been residents of the States of Kentucky, Missouri, Maryland, and Delaware, August 8, 1861, all in *OR*, ser. 1, vol. 3, 601–2, 563–64; vol. 7, 697; ser. 4, vol. 1, 536; Daniel W. Hamilton, "The Confederate Sequestration Act," *CWH* 52 (December 2006): 373–75, 383; Ash, *When the Yankees Came*, 25–27.
34. Ash, *When the Yankees Came*, 44–45, 84; Fellman, *Inside War*, 40; H[enry] W. Halleck to George B. McClellan, December 19, 1861, *OR*, ser. 1, vol. 8, 448–49. The term "dominion system" is my own construction.
35. William H. Blair, *With Malice Toward Some: Treason and Loyalty in the Civil War Era* (Chapel Hill: University of North Carolina Press, 2014), 100–159 passim; Report of Capt. Nelson Cole, May 16, 1861, *OR*, ser. 1, vol. 3, 10–11; Martha M. Jones to My Dear Father [W. S. Buford], December 21, 1862, Jones Family Papers, Mss. A/J78, folder 1, FHS; Coulter, *Civil War and Readjustment in Kentucky*, 80; Clinton W. Terry, "'Let Commerce Follow the Flag': Trade and Loyalty to the Union in the Ohio Valley," *OVH* 1 (Spring 2001): 7 (emphasis in original).
36. Robert Winn to Dear Sister, December 31, 1861, Winn-Cook Family Papers, Mss. A/W776, box 1, folder 1, FHS; Maple Diary, pp. 4–6, CGCAC; David T. Statham to Dear Brother, November 16, 1861, David T. Statham Papers, Mss. 688, OHS; John A. Martin to Dear Sister, December 31, 1861, Josephine B. Martin Papers, KsHS; Samuel Ayres to L. Langdon, February 17, 1862, Samuel Ayres Collection, KsHS; T. J. Stiles, *Jesse James: Last Rebel of the Civil War* (New York: Alfred A. Knopf, 2002), 75–76; Fellman, *Inside War*, 76–77, 281n108.
37. Scout Through Saline County, Missouri, December 14, 1861, *OR*, ser. 1, vol. 8, 34–36; "Biographical Sketch of Robert Field, Saline County, Missouri," in *Plat Book of Saline County, Missouri* (Philadelphia: North West Publishing, 1876), 42; *History of Saline County, Missouri* (St. Louis: Missouri Historical, 1881), 628–29; Daniel O'Flaherty, *General Jo Shelby: Undefeated Rebel* (Chapel Hill: University of North Carolina Press, 1954, 2000), 95–96. On April 28, 1862, Jefferson Davis reluctantly signed his war department's Partisan Ranger Act. In July Maj. Gen. Thomas C. Hindman published his "Confederate Partisan Act in Missouri." Together the two initiatives authorized the organization of and military structure for irregular partisan bands. Hindman's order instructed such outfits "to cut off Federal pickets, scouts, foraging parties and trains and to kill pilots and others on gunboats and transports, attacking them day and night and using the greatest vigor in their movements." Parrish, *History of Missouri*, 51; Fellman, *Inside War*, 98–99.
38. E. Hyatt to Charles Whittlesey, December 30, 31, 1861, C. H. McElroy to Whittlesey, January 2, 1862, John N. Cossells to Whittlesey, January 14, 1862, and various notes on arrests, dated December 28, 1861–January 1, 1862, all in Charles Whittlesey Papers, Mss. 3196 (microfilm), WRHS.
39. McPherson, *For Cause and Comrades*, 3–13 and passim; Proclamation, "To all peaceably-disposed citizens,"563–64; Ettie Scott to Susan Grigsby, August 3, 1862, Grigsby Family Papers, Mss. A G857, folder 173, FHS; Williamson Dixon Ward Civil War Journal, October 12, 1861 entry, Mss. SC627, WKU; J[ohn] M. Schofield to E[dwin] M. Stanton, May 16, 1862, *OR*, ser. 1, vol. 13, 386; Elvira A. W. Scott Diary (typescript), Mss. 1053, folder 4, pp. 116–31, SHSM; Samuel S. Hildebrand, *The Autobiography of Sam S. Hildebrand: The Renowned Missouri Bushwhacker*, comp. James W. Evans and Abraham Wendell Keith (Jefferson City, Mo.: State Times Printing House, 1870), 47.

40. Smith, *Borderland in the Civil War*, 367–68; William Crawford to H[enry] W. Halleck, January 5, 1862, RG 393, pt. 1, ser. 2593: Letters Received, Department of the Missouri, 1862–1867, box 2, NARA; Elvira A. W. Scott Diary (typescript), Mss. 1053, folder 4, p. 99, SHSM; Abraham Lincoln to Samuel R. Curtis, January 5, 1863, and H[enry] W. Halleck to George B. McClellan, December 19, 1861, both in *OR*, ser. 1, vol. 22, pt. 2, 17–18; vol. 8, 448–49.

41. General Orders No. 5, October 7, 1861; William T. Sherman to W. T. Ward, November 2, 1861; and J. T. K. Hayward to John C. Fremont, August 10, 1861, and all in *OR*, ser. 1, vol. 4, 296, 327; vol. 3, 434; Harrison, *Kentucky's Governors*, 75–77; Coulter, *Civil War and Readjustment*, 148; Smith, *Borderland in the Civil War*, 372; R. A. Curd to Cal Morgan, June 22, 1862, Hunt-Morgan Family Papers, Mss. 63M202, box 15, folder 9, UK; Neely, *Fate of Liberty*, 44–46, 128–33. One historian has found 130 individuals arrested by federal authorities in Maryland, including one woman, between March 1861 and March 1862. Jessica Ann Cannon, "Lincoln's Divided Backyard: Maryland in the Civil War Era" (Ph.D. dissertation, Rice University, 2009), 114–17.

42. Ash, *When the Yankees Came*, 122–23; Elvira A. W. Scott Diary, Mss. 1053, p. 144, SHSM; Minutes of the Harrodsburg Trustees, 1786–1875, Mss. 66M622 (microfilm), October 2, December 9, 1861 entries, UK; Deposition of David Daniel, M. Morris, February 21, 1862, RG 393, part 1, ser. 2173: Letters Received, Department of Kentucky, 1862–1869, box 3, NARA.

43. Adam I. P. Smith, *No Party Now: Politics in the Civil War North* (New York: Oxford University Press, 2006), 194n17; Loyalty Oath Collection and Finding Aid, 1861–1868, Andrew County Civil War Collection, box CW1, files 1–16, and box CW2, files 1–8, MSA; F. D. Dickinson to Dear Aunt, May 15, 1863, F. D. Dickinson Letter, Mss. C/D, FHS; Oath of Allegiance, May 19, 1862, William Johnson Stone Papers, Mss. 54M131 (microfilm), UK; J. Howard McHenry to Lt. Col. Chesebrough, February 21, 1863, Hunt-Morgan Family Papers, Mss. 63M202, box 16, folder 9, UK; James W. McHenry to Albert Sidney Johnston, October 10, 1861, *OR*, ser. 1, vol. 4, 442–43; Bettie Terrell to Susan Grigsby, July 29, 1862, Grigsby Family Papers, Mss. A/G857, folder 173, FHS; Margaret W. Preston to William Preston, July 28, August 17, 1864, all in Wickliffe-Preston Family Papers, Mss. 63M349, box 48.1, UK.

44. M. A. Shelby to Susan Grigsby, July 26, [1863], Grigsby Family Papers, Mss. A/G857, folder 179, FHS; John S. Morton to Pat [Joyes], July 26, 1862, Joyes Family Papers, Mss. A/J89b, folder 18, FHS; Samuel W. Pruitt to Dear Bettie, April 20, 1863, Samuel W. Pruitt Letters, Mss. C/P, FHS; James Prentiss to John B. Bruner, September 12, 1861, John B. Bruner Papers, Mss. A/B894, folder 17, FHS; C. H. McElroy to Charles Whittlesey, January 2, 1862, Charles Whittlesey Papers, Mss. 3196, WRHS.

45. Carole Emberton, "Reconstructing Loyalty: Love, Fear, and Power in the Postwar South," in Paul A. Cimbala and Randall M. Miller, eds., *The Great Task Remaining Before Us: Reconstruction As America's Continuing Civil War* (New York: Fordham University Press, 2010), 173–74; Printed Oath of Allegiance, August 16, 1864, Thomas S. Crutcher File, Mss. C/C, FHS; Oath of Allegiance of Samuel Jones Denton, Mss. C/D, FHS; Maple Diary, 7, 12, CGCAC; Bettie Morton to Pat [Joyes], July 21, 1862, Joyes Family Papers, Mss. A/J89b, folder 18, FHS; Barton Bates to Edward Bates, September 8, 1861, Bates Family Papers, MHS; Coulter, *Civil War and Readjustment*, 151; Grimsley, *Hard Hand of War*, 38. On loyalty oaths during the Civil War, see Harold M. Hyman, *Era of the Oath: Northern Loyalty Tests During the Civil War and Reconstruction* (New York: Octagon Books, 1954) and *To Try Men's Souls: Loyalty Tests in American History* (Berkeley: University of California Press, 1959).

46. Fanny Gunn to John and Thomas Gunn, August 16, 1862, Gunn Family Papers, Mss. 73M28, UK; [Peter], *A Union Woman in Civil War Kentucky*, 65; W. L. Gibson to S. G. Hicks, November 19, 1863, both in RG 393, pt. 1, ser. 2173: Letters Received, Department of Kentucky, 1862–1869, box 1, NARA; O. D. Williams to Samuel R. Curtis, December 4, 1862, RG 393, pt.1, ser. 2593: Letters Received, Department of the Missouri, 1862–1867, box 7, NARA; Richard S. Brownlee, *Gray Ghosts of the Confederacy: Guerrilla Warfare in the West, 1861–1865* (Baton Rouge: Louisiana State University Press, 1958), 164–67; Parrish,

History of Missouri, 67; Bond of R. B. Steele, November 15, 1862, and W. L. Gibson to S. G. Hicks, November 19, 1863, both in RG 393, pt. 1, ser. 2173: Letters Received, Department of Kentucky, 1862–1869, box 1, NARA.

47. Isaac R. Gray to J[eremiah] T. Boyle, November 17, 1862, RG 393, pt. 1, ser. 2173: Letters Received, Department of Kentucky, 1862–1869, box 1, NARA; Elvira A. W. Scott Diary (typescript), Mss. 1053, p. 155, SHSM; Abraham Lincoln to Samuel R. Curtis, January 2, 1863, in *CWAL*, 6:33–34.

48. Samuel Haycraft Journal, 1849–1873, June 17, 1862 entry, Mss. A/H414, FHS; R. A. Curd to Cal Morgan, June 22, 1862, Hunt-Morgan Family Papers, Mss. 63M202, box 15, folder 9, UK; Thomas B[oston] Gordon to Neal M. Gordon, August 12, 1862, Gordon Family Papers, Mss. 51M40, box 4, UK; Ettie Scott to Susan Grigsby, August 3, 1862, Grigsby Family Papers, Mss. A/G857, folder 173, FHS; Elvira A. W. Scott Diary (typescript), Mss. 1053, pp. 118–31, SHSM.

49. W. Wayne Smith, "An Experiment in Counterinsurgency: The Assessment of Confederate Sympathizers in Missouri," *JSH* 35 (August 1969): 361–62; Notice and General Orders No. 3, both dated July 31, 1861, and John Pope to Stephen Hurlbut, August 17, 1861, all in *OR*, ser. 2, vol. 1, 189–90, 195–96, 211–12; John W. Foster to J[eremiah] T. Boyle, January 6, 1863, RG 393, pt. 1, ser. 3514: Letters Received, Department of the Ohio, box 3, NARA.

50. Smith, "Experiment in Counterinsurgency," 363–67, 368–72; Gerteis, *Civil War St. Louis*, 174–77; Whites, *Gender Matters*, 51–56; General Orders No. 24, December 12, 1861; General Orders No. 16, December 20, 1861; General Orders No. 3, June 23, 1862; General Orders No. 3, July 2, 1862; Special Orders No. 3, September 29, 1862; Special Orders No. 4, September 30, 1862; General Orders No. 2, October 1, 1862; General Orders No. 3, October 2, 1862; Special Orders No. 37, November 17, 1862; J[eremiah] T. Boyle to H[oratio] G. Wright, November 14, 1862; Henry Dent to Boyle, November 14, 1862, and responses, November 19–20, 1862; W[illiam] G. Eliot to H[amilton] R. Gamble and endorsements [by Gamble and Samuel R. Curtis], December 1, 1862; and John M. Schofield to James S. Thomas, December 5, 1862, all in *OR*, ser. 1, vol. 8, 431–32, 452; vol. 13, 446, 459, 691, 693, 700–702, 704–5, 800; vol. 30, pt. 2, 51, 95–96; vol. 22, pt. 1, 801–3, 810–12.

51. J. Preston Mann to Nancy Mann, April 3, 1862, box 1, Mann Family Papers, Mss. 111, SIU; Grimsley, *Hard Hand of War*, 38; James F. Robinson to Dear Sir, October 8, 1862; W. A. Allbrecht to J. A. Duble, September 27, 1862; William B. Sipes to Gordon Granger, October 17, 1862; and John W. Foster to J[eremiah] T. Boyle, January 6, 1863, all in RG 393, pt. 1, ser. 3514: Letters Received, Department of the Ohio, boxes 1–3, NARA; Boyle to Capt. King, November 14, 1862; Leonidas Metcalfe to Boyle, December 14, 1862; B[enjamin] H. Bristow to S. D. Bruce, December 21, 1864, all in RG 393, pt. 1, ser. 2173: Letters Received, Department of Kentucky, box 1, NARA.

52. Lincoln to Samuel R. Curtis, December 10, 1862; Lincoln to John R. Underwood and Henry Grider, October 26, 1864; and Lincoln to Stephen G. Burbridge, October 27, 1864, all in *CWAL*, 5:127, 548; 6: 87; 8:77–78; Hamilton R. Gamble to Lincoln, December 31, 1862, Lincoln Papers; Abraham Lincoln to Jeremiah T. Boyle, February 1, 1863, Letters of Asa Strain and B. H. Bradshaw, November 1862, both in Strain, Asa, File, microfilm reel 259, Provost I; Thomas B. Fairleigh to A. C. Semple, August 26, 1863, with endorsements and enclosures; Edward R. S. Canby to Ambrose E. Burnside, November 21, 1863; E. D. Townsend to S[tephen] G. Burbridge, November 26, 1864, and endorsement; J. Bates Dickson to Daniel J. Dill, and Dickson to Samuel Matlack, both dated February 16, 1865, all in *OR*, ser. 1, vol. 30, pt. 3, 180–83; vol. 31, pt. 3, 221; vol. 52, pt. 1, 663–64; vol. 49, pt. 1, 733–34; Smith, "Experiment in Counterinsurgency," 363, 373–75; Fellman, *Inside War*, 95.

53. Loyalty Oath Collection and Finding Aid, 1861–1868, Andrew County Civil War Collection, box CW1, files 1–16, and box CW2, files 1–8, MSA; Gerteis, *Civil War St. Louis*, 131–32, 169–70, 173–74; Ettie Scott to Susan Preston Shelby Grigsby, May [1862], Grigsby Family Papers, Mss. A/G857, folder 172, FHS; *Gallipolis* [Ohio] *Journal*, August 29, 1861; Langstaff, *Life and Times of Quigley*, 81; [Hardin], *Private War of Lizzie Hardin*, 66, 74; Neely, *Fate of Liberty*, 44; Boman, *Lincoln's Resolute Unionist*, 150–55; Harrison and

Klotter, *New History of Kentucky*, 206; [Paris, Ky.] *The True Kentuckian*, November 10, 1869; *Hannibal* [Mo.] *Daily Messenger*, September 4, 1861.
54. James W. Goodrich, ed., "The Civil War Letters of Bethiah Pyalt McKown," *MHR* 67 (January, April 1973): 237; [Peter], *Union Woman in Civil War Kentucky*, 4–5, 21–29.
55. Burckin, "Formation and Growth of an Urban Middle Class," 525; James O. Broadhead, "St. Louis in the Early Days of the War," unpublished manuscript, James O. Broadhead Papers, MHS; Peckham, *Lyon and Missouri*, 202; E. Polk Johnson, *A History of Kentucky and Kentuckians* (Louisville: Lewis Publishing, 1912), 2:848–49; *Louisville Past and Present* (Louisville: John P. Morton, 1875), 263; Preston D. Graham Jr., *A Kingdom Not of This World: Stuart Robinson's Struggle to Distinguish the Sacred from the Secular during the Civil War* (Macon: Mercer University Press, 2002), 6 and passim; [Louisville] *The True Presbyterian*, April 17, 1862; A. C. Semper to [Stephen G.] Burbridge, August 9, 1864, RG 393, pt. 1, ser. 2173: Letters Received, Department of Kentucky, box 4, NARA; Lewis George Vander Velde, *The Presbyterian Churches and the Federal Union, 1861–1869* (Cambridge, Mass.: Harvard College, 1932), 167–77; Reed W. Smith, *Samuel Medary and the Crisis: Testing the Limits of Press Freedom* (Columbus: Ohio State University Press, 1995), 12; Commission Proceedings against Edmund J. Ellis, February 25–26, 1862, *OR*, ser. 2, vol. 1, 453–57; Neely, *Fate of Liberty*, 44; Harbaugh, Howard F. File, microfilm reel 118, and Abeel, D. K. File, September 17, 1863, microfilm reel 1, both in Provost I; [Hillsboro, Ill.] *Montgomery County Herald*, December 4, 1863; *Marion* [Ill.] *Record*, July 24, 1863; [Lexington] *The Kentucky Loyalist*, July 11, 1863; *Cape Girardeau* [Mo.] *Eagle* [Union Series], July 16, 1862; Stephen E. Towne, "Killing the Serpent Speedily: Governor Morton, General Hascall, and the Suppression of the Democratic Press in Indiana, 1863," *CWH* 52 (March 2006): 61–62; [Fredricktown, Mo.] *The Advance Guard*, August 28, 1861.
56. Neely, *Fate of Liberty*, 32–44; Gerteis, *Civil War St. Louis*, 131–34, 173–75; Proceedings and Findings of St. Louis Military Commission, 1863, RG 393, pt. 1, ser. 2620: General Orders, Department of the Missouri, 1862–1864, vol. 2, NARA.
57. Coulter, *Civil War and Readjustment in Kentucky*, 57–61; Gerteis, *Civil War St. Louis*, 236–42. For the most thorough assessment of the federal naval blockade and its effects on the Confederate war effort, see David G. Surdam, *Northern Naval Superiority and the Economics of the American Civil War* (Columbia: University of South Carolina Press, 2001).
58. Coulter, *Civil War and Readjustment in Kentucky*, 62–67; Whitelaw Reid, *Ohio in the War*, 2 vols. (New York: Moore, Wilsatch, and Baldwin, 1868), 1:39–40; E. D. Townsend to Commanding Officer Illinois Volunteers, May 2, 1861, *OR*, ser. 1, vol. 52, pt. 1, 137; Lantz, *Community in Search of Itself*, 23–24.
59. Coulter, *Civil War and Readjustment in Kentucky*, 67–72, 76–78; Proclamation, April 19, 1861, and U[lysses] S. Grant to Chauncey McKeever, October 1, 1861, both in *OR*, ser. 3, vol. 2, 31; ser. 1, vol. 3, 511; E. Merton Coulter, "Commercial Intercourse with the Confederacy in the Mississippi Valley, 1861–1865," *MVHR* 4 (March 1919): 377–82; Neely, *Fate of Liberty*, 33–34; General Orders No. 5, October 1, 1862, *OR*, ser. 1, vol. 13, 698–700; Thomas E. Wilson to Joseph Holt, May 5, 1861, both in Holt Papers, book 27, LC.
60. General Orders No. 10, March 28, 1862, *OR*, ser. 1, vol. 8, 834; Coulter, "Commercial Intercourse," 382n15; Salmon P. Chase to William P. Millen, July 4, 1863, Record Group 56—Department of the Treasury Records, Part 56, Ser. 40: Letters Sent Related to Restricted Commercial Intercourse, box 60, book 13 entry 3/6, pp. 321, 362–64, NARA; Ross Jekyll to Bernard G. Farrar, May 7, 1863, Provost I, microfilm reel 199, NARA; E. W. Bradley to Gen. [J. M.] Judah, April 13, 1863, and Thomas M. Redd to D. G. Barnitz, January 25, 1865, both in RG 393, pt. 1, ser. 2173: Letters Received, Department of Kentucky, 1862–1869, boxes 1, 5, NARA. Cities with boards of trade operating in them included Pittsburgh, Wheeling, Mayville, Cincinnati, Madison, Lawrenceburg, Louisville, New Albany, Evansville, Paducah, Cairo, Quincy, St. Louis, Hickman, Cadiz, Hopkinsville, Bowling Green, Catlettsburg, and Rolla. By August 2, 1861, the Confederacy had banned the trade of cotton, tobacco, sugar, rice, molasses, and naval stores with the United States. On January 5, 1865, Stephen E. Burbridge banned boards of trade in his department owing to corruption.

61. [Paris, Ky.] *The Western Citizen*, March 7, 1862; J. M. Judah to A. C. Semple, April 18, 1863; Charles B. Colton to J[eremiah] T. Boyle, December 22, 1862; William P. Millen to S[tephen] G. Burbridge, October 27, 1864; S. Meredith to J. Bates Dickson, February 7, 1865; all in RG 393, pt. 1, ser. 2173: Letters Received, Department of Kentucky, 1862–1869, boxes 1, 4, 5, NARA; *Centralia* [Ill.] *Sentinel*, February 11, March 31, 1864.
62. J. M. Judah to A. C. Semple, April 18, 1863, and enclosures; J. P. Jackson to J. Bates Dickson, August 20, 1864; Thomas M. Redd to William P. Millen, October 3, 1864, all in RG 393, pt. 1, ser. 2173: Letters Received, Department of Kentucky, 1862–1869, boxes 1, 4, NARA; *Cincinnati* [Ohio] *Daily Enquirer*, September 4, 1861; [Conrad], *Journal of Elder William Conrad*, 81–82; Steven V. Ash, "Civil War Exodus: The Jews and Grant's General Orders 11," in Jeffery S. Gurock, ed., *American Jewish History: Anti-Semitism in America* (New York: Routledge Press, 1998), 135–55.
63. Terry, "'Let Commerce Follow the Flag,'" 7; Salmon P. Chase to William P. Millen, May 29, 1861, Record Group 56—Department of the Treasury Records, Part 56, Ser. 40: Letters Sent Related to Restricted Commercial Intercourse, box 60, book 11, pp. 16–17; [Conrad], *Journal of Elder William Conrad*, 81; Harrison, *Civil War in Kentucky*, 99–100; J. H. Hammond to J. Bates Dickson, September 3, 1864, RG 393, pt. 1, ser. 2173: Letters Received, Department of Kentucky, 1862–1869, box 4, NARA.
64. Joseph C. Butler, W[illia]m McCreary, and Geo[rge] H. Thurston to Edwin M. Stanton, all March 26, 1862, in *OR*, ser. 3, vol. 1, 950–51; Hoskins, "The First Is with the South," 150–54; Terry, "Let Commerce Follow the Flag," 1–3, 7–9; Charles B. Colton to J[eremiah] T. Boyle, December 22, 1862, RG 393, pt. 1, ser. 2173: Letters Received, Department of Kentucky, 1862–1869, box 1, NARA; Coulter, *Civil War and Readjustment*, 80n142. Chase included the phrase in his 1861 annual report on government finances.
65. Edward Dicey, *Spectator of America*, ed. Herbert Mitgang (Chicago: Quadrangle, 1971; reprint Athens: University of Georgia Press, 1989), 175–81; Contract, Rule and Bro. to Alexander Jeffrey, July 21, 1862, and Jeffrey to Rosa V. J. Jeffrey, January 6, 7, 1863, all in Rosa V. J. Jeffrey Papers, Mss. A/J46r, folder 83, FHS.
66. Bernard G. Farrar to Major Hunt, March 8, 1862, and General Orders No. 34, December 26, 1861, both in *OR*, ser. 2, vol. 1, 173–74; ser. 1, vol. 8, 468; [St. Joseph, Mo.] *The Weekly Herald*, April 17, 1862.
67. James M. McPherson, *War on the Waters: The Union and Confederate Navies, 1861–1865* (Chapel Hill: University of North Carolina Press, 2012), 72–82; McPherson, *Battle Cry of Freedom*, 414–22, 436; Neely, *Fate of Liberty*, 77; Nazro Diary, April 15, 25, August 20, 1862 entries, WKU.
68. McPherson, *Battle Cry of Freedom*, 511–22; Harrison, *Civil War in Kentucky*, 33–42; William C. Davis and Meredith L. Swentor, eds., *Bluegrass Confederate: The Headquarters Diary of Edward O. Guerrant* (Baton Rouge: Louisiana State University Press, 1999), 143; Stephen I. Rockenbach, "A Border City at War: Louisville and the 1862 Confederate Invasion of Kentucky," *OVH* 3 (Winter 2003): 37–38.
69. William Moody Pratt Diaries, undated [November 1862] entry, vol. 3, Mss. 46M79, UK.
70. Harrison, *Civil War in Kentucky*, 40–42; Noe, *Perryville*, 32–40; Brian D. McKnight, "Hope and Humiliation: Humphrey Marshall, the Mountaineers, and the Confederacy's Last Chance in Eastern Kentucky," *OVH* 5 (Fall 2005): 8–9; Harrison, *Civil War in Kentucky*, 42–56; [Peter], *Union Woman in Civil War Kentucky*, 77.
71. John F. Jefferson Diary, June 1–November 1, 1862 entries, vol. 6, John F. Jefferson Papers, Mss. A/J45, FHS; Noe, *Perryville*, 80–81, 344–46 and passim; Lizzie J. S____ to Anonymous, February 24, 1863, Hunt-Morgan Family Papers, Mss. 63M202, box 16, folder 9, UK.
72. Rockenbach, "Border City at War," 36–37; Coulter, *Civil War and Readjustment*, 165–68; Humphrey Marshall to Alexander Stephens, February 22–23, 1862, Edward O. Guerrant Papers, 1861–1867, Mss. C/Ga, FHS; Noe, *Perryville*, 26, 128–30; Braxton Bragg to Samuel Cooper, September 25, 1862, and John Pegram to John S. Scott, August 24, 1862, both in *OR*, ser. 1, vol. 16, pt. 2, 876, 778; Berlin et al., *Freedom: Destruction of Slavery*, 498; Braxton Bragg to Samuel Cooper, September 25, 1862, *OR*, ser. 1, vol. 16, pt. 2, 876.
73. E. Kirby Smith to Braxton Bragg, August 24, 1862, *OR*, vol. 16, pt. 2, 775–76; Davis and Swentor, *Bluegrass Confederate*, 158.

74. Braxton Bragg to Samuel Cooper, September 25, 1862, *OR*, ser. 1, vol. 16, pt. 2, 876; Davis, *Breckinridge*, 325–29; Noe, *Perryville*, 105; Proclamation of E. Kirby Smith, [1862], Frost Family Papers, Mss. C/F, FHS; Broadside, "The Inaugural Address of the Provisional Governor of Kentucky!," KHS. See also Brian D. McKnight, *Contested Borderland: The Civil War in Appalachian Kentucky and Virginia* (Lexington: University Press of Kentucky, 2006).
75. Coulter, *Civil War and Readjustment*, 168–69; Berlin et al., *Freedom: Destruction of Slavery*, 499; J[ohn] W. Calvert to E. M. Davis, February 20, 1863, J. W. Calvert Letter, Mss. C/C, FHS; W[ill] T. Hart to Susan Grigsby, September 25, 1862, Grigsby Family Papers, Mss. A/G857, folder 173, FHS.
76. McPherson, *Battle Cry of Freedom*, 513–14; [Lexington, Ky.] *The Mail Bag*, March 28, 1864; [Hardin], *Private War of Lizzie Hardin*, 82–87, 92.
77. Jack Hurst, *Nathan Bedford Forrest: A Biography* (New York: Vintage Books, 1994), 77; [Hardin], *Private War of Lizzie Hardin*, 81–82; Mary E. Van Meter Diary, August 10, 1862 entry, Mss. 54M98 (microfilm), UK.
78. [Hardin], *Private War of Lizzie Hardin*, 81, 93–94; [Peter], *Union Woman in Civil War Kentucky*, 30; Samuel Haycraft Journal, 1849–1873 (typescript), October 20, December 27, 1862 entries, p. 27, Haycraft Family Papers, 1792–1870, Mss. A/H414, FHS; Krug, *Mrs. Hill's Journal*, 130–33.
79. Alice Todd Field Diary, September 6, 1862 entry (typescript), p. 38, Mss. M368, UK; [Hardin], *Private War of Lizzie Hardin*, 89, 83, 94; J. M. McFerren to Susan Grigsby, January 17, 1863, Grigsby Family Papers, Mss. A/G857, folder 176, FHS; Journal of Ellen Kenton McGaughey Wallace, 1849–1865 (transcription), October 28, 1862 entry, Wallace-Starling Family Diaries, Mss. 96M07, KHS; Davis and Swentor, *Bluegrass Confederate*, 169; Fanny Gunn to John and Thomas Gunn, August 16, 1862, Gunn Family Papers, Mss. 73M28, UK.
80. Freehling, *South vs. the South*, 68–73; Nagel, *Missouri*, 129. See also Richard Nelson, *Lincoln's Loyalists: Union Soldiers from the Confederacy* (Boston: Northeastern University Press, 1992; reprint New York: Oxford University Press, 1994).
81. Mary E. Van Meter Diary, December 2, 1862–February 25, 1863 entries, Mss. 54M98 (microfilm), UK.

War of Another Kind

1. David Hackett Fischer, *Albion's Seed: Four British Folkways in America* (New York: Oxford University Press, 1990), 605–32.
2. Cannel, or "candle," coal was used widely for domestic lighting owing to its especially bright flame, easy lighting, and little ash residue.
3. Robert Winn to Martha Winn, December 4, 1861, November 22, January 15, undated [ca. April 1862], July 2, 1862, all in Winn-Cook Family Papers, Mss. A/W776, box 1, folders 1–2, FHS; Burton, *Melting Pot Soldiers*, 104.
4. Winn to Martha Winn, May 22, 1862, undated [ca. August 12, 1862], August 17, 1862, all in Winn-Cook Family Papers, Mss. A/W776, box 1, folder 2, FHS.
5. Winn to Martha Winn, April 12–October 28, 1862, all in Winn-Cook Family Papers, Mss. A/W776, box 1, folder 2, FHS; Noe, *Perryville*, 214, 236–37, 304, 377.
6. Noe, *Perryville*, 491–92; Sutherland, "Abraham Lincoln, John Pope," 572. On March 3, 1863, the Militia Act was supplanted by the nation's first Conscription Act, which required the registration of all eligible, nonexempt men and authorized the procedure and infrastructure for a draft when necessary. Beyond exemptions for aliens and those with physical and mental disabilities, all eligible males between the ages of twenty and forty-five were divided into two classes: single men from twenty to forty-five and married men from twenty to thirty-five constituted the first class, and married men from thirty-five to forty-five constituted the second class. Men in Class II were to be drafted only when Class I was exhausted. Robert E. Sterling, "Civil War Draft Resistance in Illinois," *JISHS* 64 (Autumn 1971): 250.
7. Winn to Martha Winn, June 15, July 25, August 17, 1862, January 12, 1863, all in Winn-Cook Family Papers, Mss. A/W776, box 1, folders 2–3, FHS; Smith, *No Party Now*, 99;

Notes to Pages 208–213

John Hope Franklin, *Reconstruction: After the Civil War* (Chicago: University of Chicago Press, 1961), 20; Silvana R. Siddali, *From Property to Person: Slavery and the Confiscation Acts, 1861–1862* (Baton Rouge: Louisiana State University Press, 2005), 141; *BDAC*, 278; Preliminary Emancipation Proclamation, September 22, 1863, in *CWAL*, 5:435.

8. Winn to Martha Winn, July 25, 1862, in Winn-Cook Family Papers, Mss. A/W776, box 1, folder 2, FHS; McPherson, *Battle Cry of Freedom*, 500–501; U.S., *Statutes at Large, Treaties, and Proclamations of the United States of America* (Boston: Little and Brown, 1863), 12:589–92.

9. Winn to Martha Winn, June 15, July 25, August 17, 1862, January 12, 1863, all in Winn-Cook Family Papers, Mss. A/W776, box 1, folders 2–3, FHS; Berlin et al., *Freedom: Destruction of Slavery*, 26–27; Smith, *No Party Now*, 99; Franklin, *Reconstruction*, 20; Siddali, *From Property to Person*, 141; *BDAC*, 278; Preliminary Emancipation Proclamation, September 22, 1863, in *CWAL*, 5:435.

10. Winn to Martha Winn, Aug 17, 1862, August 8, 1863, Winn-Cook Family Papers, Mss. A/W776, folders 2–3, FHS.

11. Benjamin F. Buckner to Dear Helen, September 25, December 15, 1861, Benjamin Forsythe Buckner Papers, 1785–1918, Mss. 48M39, UK; Seventh, Eighth, Ninth, and Tenth U.S. Censuses, 1850–1870, Population and Slave Schedules, Clark County, Kentucky, NARA; *BDAC*, 911–12; Patrick A. Lewis, "'All Men of Decency Ought to Quit the Army': Benjamin F. Buckner, Manhood, and Proslavery Unionism in Kentucky," *Register* 107 (Fall 2009): 513–49.

12. Buckner to Dear See also Lewis, *For Slavery and Union: Benjamin Buckner and Kentucky Loyalties in the Civil War* (Lexington: University Press of Kentucky, 2015). Helen, November 5, 1862, in Benjamin Forsythe Buckner Papers, 1785–1918, Mss. 48M39, UK; James M. McPherson, *Crossroads of Freedom: Antietam* (New York: Oxford University Press, 2002), 146–47; Proclamation Suspending the Writ of Habeas Corpus, September 24, 1862, in *CWAL*, 5:436–37.

13. Buckner to Dear Helen, November 5, 1862, Benjamin Forsythe Buckner Papers, 1785–1918, Mss. 48M39, UK.

14. Buckner to Dear Helen, November 5, December 2, 1862, February 1, 1863, Benjamin Forsythe Buckner Papers, 1785–1918, Mss. 48M39, UK.

15. Buckner to Dear Helen, November 5, December 2, 1862, February 1, 1863, Benjamin Forsythe Buckner Papers, 1785–1918, Mss. 48M39, UK.

Chapter 6: Bitter Harvest: Emancipation and the Politics of Loyalty

1. E[ugene] F. Ware, *The Lyon Campaign in Missouri* (Topeka, Ks.: Crane, 1907), 113–14; Piston and Hatcher, *Wilson's Creek*, 51; Ira Berlin, Barbara J. Fields, Steven F. Miller, Joseph P. Reidy, and Leslie S. Rowland, eds., *Free at Last: A Documentary History of Slavery, Freedom, and the Civil War* (New York: The Free Press, 1992), 107. For the fullest argument for the war being fought principally to restore the Union, see Gallagher, *The Union War*.

2. [Georgetown] *The Southern Ohio Argus*, October 6, 1859; *Cincinnati* [Ohio] *Daily Enquirer*, August 21, 1860; [Cincinnati] *The Free Nation*, February 9, 1861; S[almon] B. Axtell to L. Kerr, April 5 [25?], 1861, Vertical File A, WRHS.

3. Gerteis, *Civil War St. Louis*, 177, 261–62; Thomas T. Gantt to William S. Harney, and response, May 14, 1861, both in *OR*, ser. 1, vol. 3, 372–73; Kamphoefner and Helbich, eds., *Germans in the Civil War*, 372–74; J[oshua] F. Speed to Joseph Holt, September 7, 1861, Holt Papers, book 30, LC.

4. McPherson, *Battle Cry of Freedom*, 496; *Congressional Globe*, 37th Cong., 1st Sess., 186–94, 261–62; Resolution adopted by the House of Representatives, special session, July 9, 1861, *OR*, ser. 2, vol. 1, 759; Siddali, *From Property to Person*, 58–59, 66–67; *Speech of Hon. William Allen of Ohio, on Confiscation and Emancipation. Delivered in the House of Representatives of the United States, April 24, 1862* (Washington, D.C.: McGill, Witherow, 1862), 5; Davis, *Breckinridge*, 168–71; DeRosa, *Politics of Dissolution*, 22–26; Siddali, *From Property to Person*, 76–77; William S. Harney to Thomas T. Gantt, May 14, 1861, *OR*, ser. 1, vol. 3, 372–73; Victor B. Howard, *Black Liberation in Kentucky: Emancipation and Freedom*,

1862–1884 (Lexington: University Press of Kentucky, 1983), 9; Harrison, *Lincoln of Kentucky*, 224–25; Gerteis, *Civil War St. Louis*, 263; Resolution adopted by the House of Representatives, special session, July 9, 1861, *OR*, ser. 2, vol. 1, 759; Louis S. Gerteis, *From Contraband to Freedman: Federal Policy Toward Southern Blacks, 1861–1865* (Westport, Conn.: Greenwood Press, 1973), 15–18. McPherson has found that eleven of twelve northern senators chaired committees, and New England–born men representing other states held five of eleven remaining chairmanships.

5. Proclamation of J[ohn] C. Fremont, August 30, 1861, *OR*, ser. 1, vol. 3, 466–67.
6. Abraham Lincoln to John C. Fremont, September 2, 1861, in *CWAL*, 4:506–7n1–2; E. C. Hurst to Abraham Lincoln, September 19, 1861, Lincoln Papers; A Kentuckian [John A. Trimble] to Anonymous, September 20, 1861, John A. Trimble Papers, Mss. 249, box 10, folder 3, OHS; Harrison, *Lincoln of Kentucky*, 224–25; Howard, *Black Liberation in Kentucky*, 6–7; John B. Helm to S[amuel] Haycraft, October 7, 1864, Haycraft Family Papers, Mss. 69M690 (microfilm), UK; Absalom Yarbrough Johnson Diaries, 1860–1864, August 31, 1861 entry, Mss. A/J67b, vol. 1, FHS; Jennifer Cole, "'For the Sake of the Songs of the Men Made Free': James Speed and the Emancipationists' Dilemma in Nineteenth-century Kentucky," *OVH* 4 (Winter 2004): 36–37; Joshua Speed to Joseph Holt, September 7, 1861, Holt Papers, book 30, LC; Abraham Lincoln to John C. Frémont, September 2, 1861; Lincoln to Orville H. Browning, September 22, 1861, both in *CWAL*, 4:506–7n1–2, 531–33; John B. Helm to Samuel Haycraft, October 7, 1864, Haycraft Family Papers, Mss. 69M690 (microfilm), UK; Joseph Holt to Lincoln, September 12, 1861, and Robert Anderson to Lincoln, September 13, 1861, both in Moore, *Rebellion Record*, 3:126–27; Parrish, *Turbulent Partnership*, 60–63; *Hannibal* [Mo.] *Daily Messenger*, September 21, 1861; Berlin et al., *Freedom: Destruction of Slavery*, 396–99, 496–97.
7. Siddali, *From Property to Person*, 101–102; *Cincinnati* [Ohio] *Daily Enquirer*, September 17, 1861; J[ohua] F. Speed to Joseph Holt, September 7, 1861, Holt Papers, book 27, LC; Thornbrough, *Indiana in the Civil War Era*, 111–12; Harbison, "Lincoln and Indiana Republicans," 288–89; Hardin Edwards to George Edwards, December 28, 1861, George Edwards Papers, Mss. SC532, folder 1, IHSL.
8. J[oshua] F. Speed to Joseph Holt, September 7, 1861, Holt Papers, book 27, LC; Speed to Lincoln, September 3, 1861, Lincoln Papers, LC; Lincoln to Orville H. Browning, September 22, 1861, in *CWAL*, 4:531–33; [Orville H. Browning], *The Diary of Orville Hickman Browning 1850–1864*, ed. Theodore Calvin Pease and James G. Randall (Springfield: Illinois State Historical Library, 1927), 541–62; *Speech of Hon. O. H. Browning of Illinois, on the Confiscation Bill, Delivered in the Senate of the United States, April 29, 1862* (Washington, D.C.: L. Towers, 1862), passim; Neely, *Fate of Liberty*, 34–35; McPherson, *Battle Cry of Freedom*, 354, 496; George W. Julian, *Personal Recollections, 1840–1872* (Chicago: Jansen, McClurg, 1884), 222–23; Siddali, *From Property to Person*, 96–98, 101–102; [Cincinnati] *The Free Nation*, December 7, 1861. Lincoln removed Frémont on November 2 and replaced him with David Hunter, a known supporter of abolition and hard-liner then stationed in Kansas. Six months later Hunter issued an emancipation proclamation in the coastal sea islands, which Lincoln would similarly revoke. Lincoln to David Hunter, September 9, 1861, in *CWAL*, 4:513.
9. Siddali, *From Property to Person*, 120–21; *BDAC*, 273–76; Thornbrough, *Indiana in the Civil War Era*, 115–16; Stephen B. Oates, *To Purge This Land with Blood: A Biography of John Brown* (New York: Harper and Row, 1970), 168–69; Nation and Towne, *Indiana's War*, 53–55; Phillips and Pendleton, *Union on Trial*, 73n99.
10. Howard, *Black Liberation in Kentucky*, 186n6; Annual Message to Congress, December 3, 1861, in *CWAL*, 5:48–49; Journal of Ellen Kenton McGaughey Wallace, 1849–1865 (transcript), December 15, 1861 entry, Wallace-Starling Family Diaries, Mss. 96M07, KHS; Beale, *Diary of Edward Bates*, 232, 241; Parrish, *Frank Blair*, 146–47; Siddali, *From Property to Person*, 131; Smith, *Borderland in the Civil War*, 377–78; Foner, *Fiery Trial*, 181–82; Donald, *Lincoln*, 347; Message to Congress, March 6, 1862, in *CWAL*, 5:144–46; Draft of Bill for Compensated Emancipation in Delaware, November 1861, Lincoln Papers; John A. Munroe, *History of Delaware* (Newark: University of Delaware Press, 2006), 238–40. Lincoln's favored plan called for a payment of $400 per slave freed to be

paid over twenty annual installments, by government bonds yielding 6 percent, but emancipation would not become universal until 1893.

11. James M. Vanice to Charles Whittlesey, January 1, 1862, Charles Whittlesey Papers, Mss. 3196 (microfilm), WRHS; Seventh and Eighth U.S. Censuses, 1850–1860, Population Schedule, Gallatin and Jefferson Counties, Kentucky, NARA.

12. Howard, *Black Liberation in Kentucky*, 10–11; *Congressional Globe*, 37th Cong., 2nd Sess., 1826–1828, 2297–98, 2270, 1780; Harrison, *Lincoln of Kentucky*, 228–29.

13. McPherson, *Battle Cry of Freedom*, 498–99; Boman, *Lincoln's Resolute Unionist*, 163–64, 167–69; U.S., *Statutes at Large, Treaties, and Proclamations of the United States of America* (Boston: Little and Brown, 1863), 12:354; Donald, *Lincoln*, 347–48; *Congressional Globe*, 37th Cong., 2nd Sess., 1826–1828, 2297–98; Howard, *Black Liberation in Kentucky*, 10–11.

14. McPherson, *Battle Cry of Freedom*, 498–99; *Speech of Hon. William Allen of Ohio, on Confiscation and Emancipation. Delivered in the House of Representatives of the United States, April 24, 1862* (Washington, D.C.: McGill, Witherow, 1862), 6; *Cincinnati* [Ohio] *Daily Enquirer*, March 24–25, 1862; Clinton W. Terry, "'The Most Commercial of People': Cincinnati, the Civil War, and the Rise of Commercial Capitalism, 1861–1865" (Ph.D. dissertation, University of Cincinnati, 2002), 76–77; Wilson, "Cincinnati's Reputation," 476–77; [Cincinnati, Ohio] *Daily Commercial*, April 5, 1862; Harrison, *Lincoln of Kentucky*, 230; Robert Tracy McKenzie, "Contesting Secession: Parson Brownlow and the Rhetoric of Proslavery Unionism, 1860–1861," *CWH* 48 (December 2002): 294–309.

15. Castel, *Frontier State at War*, 45–46, 50, 55–56; H[enry] W. Halleck to D[avid] Hunter, February 13, 1862; and J[ames]. H. Lane to S[amuel]. D. Sturgis, October 3, 1861, both in *OR*, ser. 1, vol. 8, 554–55; vol. 3, 516; *Congressional Globe*, 37th Cong., 1st Sess., 187; Burton J. Williams, "Quantrill's Raid on Lawrence: A Question of Complicity," *Kansas Historical Quarterly* 34 (Summer 1968): 145; Ben McCulloch to S[amuel] Cooper, November 19, 1861, *OR*, ser. 1, vol. 3, 742–43; Berlin et al., *Freedom: Destruction of Slavery*, 401.

16. A[lexander] M. McCook to William T. Sherman, November 5, 1861, *OR*, ser. 1, vol. 4, 337; Coulter, *Civil War and Readjustment*, 157; Parrish, *History of Missouri*, 88; Maple Diary, pp. 22–23, CGCAC; Edward Wilkins to Daniel Farris, October 4, 1861; and W. H. Parish to John A. McClernand, October 19, 1861, both in John A. McClernand Papers, box 4, ALPL; Eighth U.S. Census, 1860, Population and Slave Schedules, Mississippi County, Missouri, NARA; Matthew E. Stanley, "'Purely Military Matters': John A. McClernand and Civil Liberties in Cairo, Illinois, in 1861," *OVH* 8 (Spring 2008): 23–42 passim; Jones, *"Black Jack"*, 104; Resolution adopted by the House of Representatives, special session, July 9, 1861, *OR*, ser. 2, vol. 1, 759; Special Order No. 1023, October 12, 1861; William H. Parrish to John A. McClernand, October 16, 1861; and John A. McClernand to U[lysses] S. Grant, September 17, 1861; all in John A. McClernand Papers, box 5, ALPL.

17. *Hannibal* [Mo.] *Daily Messenger*, October 3, 1861; Berlin et al., *Freedom: Destruction of Slavery*, 403–4; Benjamin Gratz Brown, *Emancipation as a State Policy: Letter of B. Gratz Brown to the "Palmyra Courier"* (n.P.: s.n., 1862), 8–9; Leslie Schwalm, "'Overrun with Free Negroes': Emancipation and Wartime Migration in the Upper Midwest," *CWH* 50 (June 2004): 154–55.

18. Gerteis, *Civil War St. Louis*, 262–63; Berlin et al., *Freedom: Destruction of Slavery*, 399; Parrish, *History of Missouri*, 88; Henry W. Halleck to L[eonard] F. Ross, January 14, 1862; General Orders No. 14, February 26, 1862, and George B. McClellan to D[on] C[arlos] Buell, November 7, 1861, all in *OR*, ser. 1, vol. 8, 825–26; vol. 7, 668; vol. 4, 342.

19. Henry W. Halleck to L[eonard] F. Ross, January 14, 1862, *OR*, ser. 1, vol. 8, 825–26.

20. William T. Sherman to Col. [John B.] Turchin, October 15, 1861, and Organization of the Third Division, Army of the Ohio, March 31, 1862, both in *OR*, ser. 1, vol. 4, 307; vol. 10, pt. 2, 85; Berlin et al., *Freedom: Destruction of Slavery*, 497–98.

21. *The Cause and Cure of Our National Troubles* (Washington, D.C.: Scammel, 1862), 3–4; *Speech of Hon. J. A. Wright, of Indiana, on the Bill to Confiscate the Property and Free the Slaves of Rebels, Delivered in the Senate of the United States, April 30, 1862* (Washington, D. C.: *Congressional Globe*, 1862), 5–6; James G. Randall and David Donald, *The Civil War and Reconstruction* (Lexington, Mass.: D. C. Heath, 1969), 234–42; *Congressional Globe*, 37th

Cong., 2nd Sess., 1631–46; Donald, *Lincoln*, 362–64; Proclamation Revoking General Hunter's Order of Military Emancipation of May 9, 1863, May 19, 1863; Appeal to Border State Representatives to Favor Compensated Emancipation, July 12, 1862; and To the Senate and House of Representatives, July 14, 1862, all in *CWAL*, 5:222–24, 317–19, 324–25; Donald, *Lincoln*, 363–64; Siddali, *From Property to Person*, 132; Harrison, *Lincoln of Kentucky*, 231–32; Border State Congressmen to Abraham Lincoln, July 14, 1862, Lincoln Papers. On July 15, a day after the majority response, seven border-staters sent a minority reply supportive of Lincoln's appeal. Among them were John W. Noell of Missouri, Samuel L. Casey of Kentucky, and George P. Fisher of Delaware. A day later, Tennessean Horace Maynard sent an individual pledge of support for Lincoln's plan.

22. U.S., *Statutes at Large*, 12:589–92; Weber, *Copperheads*, 50–54; Annual Message to Congress, December 3, 1861, in *CWAL*, 5:49; *Warren* [Ohio] *Constitution*, August 5, 1862, in Dee, *Ohio's War*, 81–82, 131–32.
23. Lincoln to the Senate and House of Representatives, July 17, 1862; Lincoln to Horace Greeley, August 22, 1862; and Lincoln to Albert G. Hodges, April 4, 1864, all in *CWAL*, 5:328–29, 389n2; 7:282; McPherson, *Battle Cry of Freedom*, 500.
24. Emancipation Proclamation—First Draft, July 22, 1862, in *CWAL*, 5:336–38; Nazro Diary, July 20, 1862 entry, WKU; John Hope Franklin, *The Emancipation Proclamation* (New York: Anchor Books, 1965), 41; John G. Nicolay and John Hay, *Abraham Lincoln: A History* (Chicago: Century, 1890), 6:127; McPherson, *Battle Cry of Freedom*, 501–5; [Centerville] *Indiana True Republican*, January 2, 1862; Donald, *Lincoln*, 364–66; Howard, *Black Liberation in Kentucky*, 30–31.
25. Memorandum on Recruiting Negroes, July 22, 1862, and Lincoln to Horace Greeley, August 22, 1862, both in *CWAL*, 5:338, 388–89; Donald, *Lincoln*, 366–67.
26. Parrish, *History of Missouri*, 99–101; H. S. Lipscomb to W. S. Harney, August 9, 1861, in Berlin et al., *Freedom: Destruction of Slavery*, 414–15; Berlin, et al., *Freedom: Wartime Genesis of Free Labor*, 557; Fellman, *Inside War*, 66; Castel, *Frontier State at War*, 90–91, 92–94; C. P. Buckingham to James H. Lane, July 22, 1862; Lane to Edwin M. Stanton, August 5, 1862, Stanton to Lane, August 23, 1862, all in *OR*, ser. 3, vol. 2, 294–95, 312–14, 444–45, 959; Dudley Taylor Cornish, *The Sable Arm: Negro Troops in the Union Army, 1861–1865* (1956; reprint Lawrence: University of Kansas Press, 1987), 59, 66, 78; Castel, *Frontier State at War*, 90–94; Moore, *Rebellion Record*, 6:52–54; "Skirmish at Island Mound, Mo., Report of Maj. Richard G. Ward, First Kansas Colored Infantry," *OR*, ser. 1, vol. 53, 456–58.
27. Call for 300,000 Volunteers, July 1, 1862; Emancipation Proclamation—First Draft, July 22, 1862; Preliminary Emancipation Proclamation, September 22, 1862; Preliminary Draft of Final Emancipation Proclamation, [December 30, 1862]; and To Erastus Corning and Others, [June 12] 1863, all in *CWAL*, 5:296–97, 336–38, 433–36; 6:23–26, 260–63; Donald, *Lincoln*, 373–76; McPherson, *Battle Cry of Freedom*, 491–92, 557–60, 598–99.
28. John P. Mann to Anonymous, December 18, 1862, and Mann to Nancy Mann, December 23, 1862, Mann Family Papers, Coll. 111, box 1, SIU; Rhonda M. Kohl, "'This Godforsaken Town': Death and Disease at Helena, Arkansas, 1862–63," *CWH* 50 (June 2004): 117–18, 123–27; Beale, *Diary of Edward Bates*, 279; Noe, *Perryville*, 334–37, 342–43; in Mann Family Papers, Coll. 111, box 1, SIU.
29. McPherson, *Battle Cry of Freedom*, 561–62; Smith, *No Party Now*, 58; Weber, *Copperheads*, 69; V. Jacques Voegeli, *Free But Not Equal: The Midwest and the Negro* (Chicago: University of Chicago Press, 1967), 61–63; Parrish, *History of Missouri*, 89–90; Harrison and Klotter, *New History of Kentucky*, 178–79; Cole, "For the Sake of the Songs," 38–39; *Cincinnati* [Ohio] *Daily Enquirer*, October 17, 1862; M. Dinsmore to Dear Bro, November 4, 1862, John C. Dinsmore Papers, Mss. SC405, ALPL. Overall, Democrats increased their congressional number by thirty-four seats.
30. Weber, *Copperheads*, 18–19; Peter J. Parish, *The North, the Nation, and the Era of the Civil War* (New York: Fordham University Press, 2003), 132–43; [Anonymous], *For Peace, and Peaceable Separation: Citizen's Democratic Address to the People of the State of Ohio, and the People of the Several States of the West and North* (Cincinnati: printed by author, 1863), 11.

31. Andreasen, "'As Good a Right to Pray,'" 44–45; Smith, *No Party Now*, 41–42; Klement, *Limits of Dissent*, 75–79, 111–12, 183; Clement L. Vallandigham, *The Great Civil War in America: Speech of Hon. Clement Laird Vallandigham, of Ohio, Delivered in the House of Representatives, January 14, 1863* (Washington, D. C.: L. Towers, 1863), passim; Henry D. Jordan, "Daniel Wolsey Voorhees," *MVHR* 6 (March 1920): 536–38; Wilson, "Cincinnati's Reputation," 476–79; Terry, "'The Most Commercial of People',"71–94; Porter, *Ohio Politics During the Civil War Period*, 90–91, 108–9; Schwalm, "'Overrun with Free Negroes'," 146–47, 172–73; Voegeli, *Free But Not Equal*, 62–64; Harbison, "Lincoln and Indiana Republicans," 301–2; Eugene H. Roseboom, "Southern Ohio and the Union in 1863," *MVHR* 39 (June 1952): 32; Williams, "Voters in Blue," 189; Thornbrough, *Indiana in the Civil War Era*, 152, 175; Stampp, *Indiana Politics During the Civil War*, 159–60; Smith, *Borderland in the Civil War*, 317–19.

32. Stampp, *Indiana Politics during the Civil War*, 74–99, 156–57; Voegeli, *Free But Not Equal*, 62, 79, 86; Julian, *Personal Recollections*, 223; Harbison, "Lincoln and Indiana Republicans," 300–301; Smith, *Borderland in the Civil War*, 313–15, 324–28, 333; Klement, *Limits of Dissent*, 106; O[liver] M. Dickerson, *The Illinois Constitutional Convention of 1862* (Urbana: University [of Illinois] Press, 1905), 48–54, McPherson, *Battle Cry of Freedom*, 598; Call for 300,000 Volunteers, July 1, 1862; To Erastus Corning and Others, [June 12] 1863, all in *CWAL*, 5:296–97; 6:266; Yates and Pickering, *Richard Yates*, 173–82; Weber, *Copperheads*, 48–51; Howard, *Illinois*, 307–11; Bruce S. Allardice, "'Illinois Is Rotten with Traitors!': The Republican Defeat in the 1862 State Election," *JISHS* 104 (Spring 2011): 97–114 passim; Richard L. Kiper, *General John Alexander McClernand: Politician in Uniform* (Kent, Ohio: Kent State University Press, 1999), 22. In Illinois's Senate, Democrats outnumbered Republicans 13–12, and 54–32 in the House.

33. *Cincinnati* [Ohio] *Daily Enquirer*, April 11, 1862; McPherson, *Battle Cry of Freedom*, 591–92; Terry, "The Most Commercial of People," 80–94; Taylor, *Frontiers of Freedom*, 180–82; Frank L. Klement, "Sound and Fury: Civil War Dissent in the Cincinnati Area," *Cincinnati Historical Society Bulletin* 35 (Summer 1977): 100; *Defiance Democrat*, July 26, 1862, in Dee, *Ohio's War*, 79–81; [New Albany, Ind.] *Daily Ledger*, July 22, 29, October 20, November 10, 1862; [Cincinnati] *Catholic Telegraph and Advocate*, July 23, 30, 1862; *Cincinnati* [Ohio] *Daily Enquirer*, April 18, September 26, 1862; Wilson, "Cincinnati's Reputation," 476; David Tod to Geo[rge] B. Wright, September 9, 1862, David Tod Papers, LC; Thornbrough, *The Negro in Indiana Before 1900*, 185–91; Rockenbach, "'War Upon Our Border,'" 131–35; Bigham, *On Jordan's Banks*, 91–92.

34. Voegeli, *Free But Not Equal*, 62; Weber, *Copperheads*, 48–49; McPherson, *Battle Cry of Freedom*, 506–8; Smith, *No Party Now*, 68–75; E[dwin] M. Stanton to N. B. Buford, April 21, 1863, Jacob Ammen Papers, ALPL; Buford to Stanton, April 25, 1863; *OR*, ser. 2, vol. 5, 521–22.

35. E. J. Wickersham to Samuel R. Curtis, October 12, 1862, RG 393, pt. 1, ser. 2593: Letters Received, Department of the Missouri, 1862–67, box 7, NARA; Schwalm, "'Overrun with Free Negroes'," 145; Smith, *No Party Now*, 54–56; Lot Abraham to Maggie Abraham, January 25, 1865, Lot Abraham Letters, Mss. C/A, FHS; Nancy C. Mann to J[ohn] P. Mann, July 7, 1863, Mann Family Papers, Coll. 111, box 2, SIU; E[dwin] M. Stanton to N. B. Buford, April 21, 1863, and J. F. Dunn to Jacob Ammen, April 25, 1863, both in Jacob Ammen Papers, ALPL; Emily Wiley to Ben Wiley, April 9, 1863, John Willis Allen Papers, Mss. 76-3-F1, box 11, SIU; Daniel Dinsmore to Dear Brother, September 4, 1862; James Dinsmore to John C. Dinsmore, October 11, 1862; and M. Dinsmore to Dear Bro, November 4, 1862, all in John C. Dinsmore Papers, Mss. SC405, ALPL; Robert Smith to Richard Yates, October 13, 1862, Lincoln Papers; *BDAC*, 1833; Voegeli, *Free But Not Equal*, 18, 60–61; McPherson, *Battle Cry of Freedom*, 507–508; *Congressional Globe*, 37th Cong., 2nd Sess., 944; *Belleville* [Ill.] *Advocate*, December 4, 1863.

36. James E. Moss to Jacob Ammen, April 24, 1863; and Hannah Throne to Jacob Ammen, May 23, 1863, both in Jacob Ammen Papers, ALPL; Civil War Diary of John Preston Mann (typescript, vol. 6), March 8, 1862 entry, Mann Family Papers, Mss. 111, SIU; Anonymous to Annie M. Cooper, July 21, 1863, Cooper-Phillips Family Papers, Mss. 66M37, UK; [William McKnight], *Do They Miss Me at Home? The Civil War Letters of William McKnight,*

Seventh Ohio Volunteer Cavalry, ed. Donald C. Maness and H. Jason Combs (Athens: Ohio University Press, 2010), 80.

37. Hugh Campbell to Joseph Holt, September 26, 1862, and T[heodore] S. Bell to Joseph Holt, December 22, 1862, both in Holt Papers, book 34 (July 4–October 11, 1862) and 36 (December 11–31, 1862), LC; Journal of Ellen Kenton McGaughey Wallace, 1849–1865 (typescript), August 4, December 25, 1863 entries, Wallace-Starling Family Diaries, Mss. 96M07, KHS; Charles Jones to His Excellency Abraham Lincoln, March 24, 1863, in Berlin et al., *Freedom: Destruction of Slavery*, 452, 399–405; Berlin, et al., *Freedom: Wartime Genesis of Free Labor*, 457–58, 553–58; Parrish, *History of Missouri*, 87–97.

38. Bevie W. Cain to James M. Davis, January 10, 1863, Bevie Cain Letters, Mss. SC2251, WKU; Journal of Ellen Kenton McGaughey Wallace, 1849–1865 (typescript), April 10, 1856–October 28, 1862 entries, Wallace-Starling Family Diaries, Mss. 96M07, KHS.

39. Mary E. Van Meter Diary, February 25, 1863, Mss. 54M98 (microfilm), UK; Coulter, *Civil War and Readjustment*, 173–76; Cole, "'For the Sake of the Songs,'" 37–38; Berlin et al., *Freedom,Destruction of Slavery*; 259, 292, 403–4, 412; Berlin, et al., *Freedom: Wartime Genesis of Free Labor*, 553–54; Virgil C. Blum, "The Political and Military Activities of the German Element in St. Louis, 1859–1861," *MHR* 42 (January 1948): 103–29; Parrish, *Turbulent Partnership*, 123–41; Boman, *Lincoln's Resolute Unionist*, 163–74; 163–206; General Orders No. 35, December 24, 1863, *OR*, ser. 1, vol. 22, pt. 1, 868–71; William E. Parrish, *Missouri under Radical Rule, 1865–1870* (Columbia: University of Missouri Press, 1965), 3–4, 14–19.

40. Marvin R. Cain, *Lincoln's Attorney General: Edward Bates of Missouri* (Columbia: University of Missouri Press, 1965), 139–51, 193–99, 212–38; Beale, *Diary of Edward Bates*, 321–35, 350, 373–75, 393–94, 421–22, 431–32.

41. Foner, *Free Soil*, 186–93; Foner, *Fiery Trial*, 136–37; *Evansville* [Ind.] *Daily Journal*, May 25, June 1, 1860; *Harrisburg* [Ill.] *Chronicle*, November 28, 1863.

42. Parrish, *History of Missouri*, 107–8; *Centralia* [Ill.] *Sentinel*, January 14, 1864; Newspaper Clipping, January 31, 1861, Lyle Family Papers, Mss. 62M49, box 1848–1872, UK.

43. McPherson, *Battle Cry of Freedom*, 560; Richard Yates to Abraham Lincoln, July 11, 1862, Richard Yates Papers, Mss. SC421, ALPL; Weber, *Copperheads*, 48; Smith, *No Party Now*, 59–63, 101–2.

44. Smith, *No Party Now*, 68–75; Melinda Lawson, "'A Profound National Devotion': The Civil War Union Leagues and the Construction of a New National Patriotism," *CWH* 48 (December 2002): 338–44; Paludan, *"A People's Contest"*, 237–38; *Centralia* [Ill.] *Sentinel*, December 3, 1863; *Grayville* [Ill.] *Independent*, April 10, 1863. See also Melinda Lawson, *Patriot Fires: Forging a New American Nationalism in the Civil War North* (Lawrence: University Press of Kansas, 2002); and Clement M. Silvestro, *Rally Round the Flag: The Union Leagues in the Civil War* (Lansing: Historical Society of Michigan, 1966).

45. Bernstein, *New York City Draft Riots*, 3–5, 129–30; Lucy Fletcher Kellogg Memoir (transcript), 1–13 and passim, AAS; Joyce Appleby, ed., *Recollections of the Early Republic: Selected Autobiographies* (Boston: Northeastern University Press, 1997), 145–58; Virginia Barden and Lois Barris, eds., "1828 Jamestown Census—The City of Jamestown, New York," *The Chautauqua Genealogist* 13 (Spring 1992): 11–13; Fourth and Seventh U.S. Censuses, 1820 and 1850, Population Schedule, Chautauqua County, New York, NARA; Eighth and Ninth U.S. Censuses, 1860 and 1870, Population Schedule, Randolph and Marion Counties, Illinois, NARA; Edmund J. James, *A Bibliography of Newspapers Published in Illinois Prior to 1860* (Springfield, Ill.: Phillips Bros., 1899), 17–18; Frank William Scott, *Newspapers and Periodicals of Illinois, 1814–1879* (Urbana, Ill.: printed by author, 1910), 47; Nancy Mann to J. Preston Mann, May 26, 1863, box 2, Mann Family Papers, Coll. 111, SIU; *Centralia* [Ill.] *Sentinel*, May 28, July 16, 1863; Ella Lonn, *Desertion During the Civil War* (1928; reprint Lincoln: University of Nebraska Press, 1998), 204; Howard, *Illinois*, 314n17; James M. Forrester to J. P. Sanderson, May 28, 1864, *OR*, ser. 2, vol. 7, 277–80.

46. Foner, *Fiery Trial*, 20–21; Smith, *Borderland in the Civil War*, 324–27; Weber, *Copperheads*, 48–49; Hicken, *Illinois in the Civil War*, 139–41; Howard, *Illinois*, 314–15; Smith, *No Party Now*, 98–101; *Centralia* [Ill.] *Sentinel*, August 6, 1863; Bentley Hamilton, "The Union League: Its Origin and Achievements in the Civil War," *Transactions of the Illinois State*

Historical Society 28 (1921): 110–15; Frank L. Klement, *Dark Lanterns: Secret Political Societies, Conspiracies, and Treason Trials in the Civil War* (Baton Rouge: Louisiana State University Press, 1984), 36–39; Arthur C. Cole, *The Era of the Civil War, 1848–1870* (Chicago: A. C. McClurg, 1922), 301; James B. Boyd to David T. Statham, July 19, 1863, David T. Statham Papers, Mss. 688, OHS; *Grayville* [Ill.] *Independent*, April 10, 1863; Beale, *Diary of Edward Bates*, 321–22, 292.

47. Parish, "The North, the Nation, and the Southern Response," 132–43; John McCardell, *The Idea of a Southern Nation: Southern Nationalists and Southern Nationalism, 1830–1860* (New York: W. W. Norton, 1979), 2–9 and passim; John A. Trimble to Jack Trimble, June 23, 1861, John A. Trimble Papers, Mss. 249, box 10, folder 2, OHS; Smith, *No Party Now*, 86; Langstaff, *Life and Times of Quigley*, 74; T. F. Blakeman to Jack Harding, May 16, 1862, John Harding Collection, Mss. A/H263, folder 5, FHS; Phillips and Pendleton, *Union on Trial*, 208.

48. Smith, *Borderland in the Civil War*, 317; Parish, "The North, the Nation, and the Southern Response," 130; Potter, "Historians' Use of Nationalism," 48–49; McPherson, *Battle Cry of Freedom*, 450–53; Rev. T[homas] A. Hoyt to Pat Joyes, February 2, 1863, Joyes Family Papers, Mss. A/J89b, folder 19, FHS. For the most thorough discussion of wartime initiatives and the consolidation of federal power, see Richard Franklin Bensel, *Yankee Leviathan: The Origins of Central State Authority in America, 1859–1877* (Cambridge: Cambridge University Press, 1990).

49. Kamphoefner and Helbich, *Germans in the Civil War*, 352–55; Potter, "Historians' Use of Nationalism," 66; John W. McKerley, "Citizens and Strangers: The Politics of Race in Missouri from Slavery to the Era of Jim Crow" (Ph.D. dissertation, University of Iowa, 2008), 71; Smith, *No Party Now*, 85–86.

50. Centralia [Ill.] *Sentinel*, February 11, 1864, August 20, 1863; Charles H. Coleman, "The Use of the Term 'Copperhead' during the Civil War," *MVHR* 25 (September 1938): 263–64; Jaspin, *Buried in the Bitter Waters*, 23; [West Union, Ohio] *The Scion*, September 19, 1862; [Cincinnati, Ohio] *The Free Nation*, December 7, 1861; [Anonymous], *For Peace, and Peaceable Separation*, iii–iv, 10; Cincinnati [Ohio] *Daily Enquirer*, March 18, 1863.

51. McPherson, *For Cause and Comrades*, 117–30; Gallagher, *Union War*, 76–118; N[orman] G. Markham to My Dear Eunice and Willie, February 6, 1863, N. G. Markham Papers, Mss. A/M345, folder 2, FHS; Reinhart, *Two Germans in the Civil War*, 68; *Grayville* [Ill.] *Independent*, April 10, 1863; William P. Hurtley to Mr. and Mrs. Thomas T. Hurtley, September 22, 1863, Union Soldiers' Letters, 1861–1865, Mss. C/U, FHS; Hardin Edwards to George Edwards, December 28, [1862], George Edwards Papers, Mss. SC532, folder 1, IHSL; Broadside, "To the Happy Land of Union," item BSVG301256, Duke.

52. Plummer, *Lincoln's Rail-Splitter*, 83; Jac[ob] H. Stokes to Lyman Trumbull, November 17, 1862, Lyman Trumbull Papers, LC; Donald Allendorf, *Long Road to Liberty: The Odyssey of a German Regiment in the Yankee Army—The 15th Missouri Volunteer Infantry* (Kent, Ohio: Kent State University Press, 2006), 53; McPherson, *For Cause and Comrades*, 128–9; McPherson, *Battle Cry of Freedom*, 560; Williams, "Voters in Blue," 201; *Chicago Times*, February 2, 1863, quoted in George E. Parks, "'The Long Winter': Being a Factual Narrative of One Story of the 'Unusual' 109th Regiment Volunteer Infantry of State of Illinois 1862–1863," unpublished paper, pp. 19, 24–27, in John Willis Allen Papers, Mss. 76-3-F1, box 25, SIU; Daniel Lafayette Thomas to John Q. A. Thomas, February 17, 1863, Daniel Lafayette Thomas Papers, Mss. SC1445, IHSL; Edwin A. Loosley to Wife Ann, February 8, 1863, Edwin A. Loosley Papers, Coll. 2, SIU. Chandra Manning misinterprets Williams's argument about Democratic editors' propagandizing anti-emancipation desertions in southern Illinois regiments. Manning, *What This Cruel War Was Over*, 257n14.

53. McPherson, *For Cause and Comrades*, 119–28; Manning, *What This Cruel War Was Over*, 86–97; Siddali, *Missouri's War*, 113–14; Weber, *Copperheads*, 60, 78–79; Daniel Lafayette Thomas to John Q. A. Thomas, February 17, 1863, Daniel Lafayette Thomas Papers, Mss. SC1445, IndHS; [William McKnight], *Do They Miss Me at Home? The Civil War Letters of William McKnight, Seventh Ohio Volunteer Cavalry*, ed. Donald C. Maness and H. Jason Combs (Athens: Ohio University Press, 2010), 92; Orville T. Chamberlain to Family, May 31, April 12, 1863, Joseph W. and Orville T. Chamberlain Papers, Mss. M44, IndHS;

Grayville [Ill.] *Independent*, April 10, 1863; Maria [Holyoke] to My Dear Mother and Sister, August 18, 1861, Holyoke Family Papers—Davie Collection, Mss. C/H, FHS; Alfred Pirtle to Dear Sister, September 8, 1863, Albert Pirtle Papers, Mss. A/P672, folder 78, FHS.

54. William F. Wickersham to Dear Father, February 6, 1863, Wickersham Family Papers, 1861–1877 (typescript), 45–46, Mss. SC560, WKU; C. C. Gilbert to Jeremiah T. Boyle, December 21, 1862, RG 393, pt. 1, ser. 3514: Letters Received, Department of the Ohio, box 1, NARA; [Parsons], *Incidents and Experiences*, 127; [McKnight], *Do They Miss Me at Home?*, 72; Smith, *No Party Now*, 93–95; McPherson, *For Cause and Comrades*, 122; Samuel Haycraft Journal, September 27, 1863 entry, Mss. A/H414, FHS; Howard, *Black Liberation in Kentucky*, 32–34; Siddali, *Missouri's War*, 201–2; B[enjamin] S[mith] Jones to Lemuel Jones, March 9, 1864, Union Soldiers' Letters, 1861–1865, Mss. C/U, FHS.

55. Howard, *Black Liberation in Kentucky*, 32–34; Thomas M. Gunn to Mother, December 3, 1862, Gunn Family Papers, Mss. 73M28, UK; Berlin et al., *Freedom: Destruction of Slavery*, 505–6; John Harrington to Dear Jennie, January 19, May 9, 1863, John T. Harrington Letters, Mss. 97SC130, KHS.

56. Orlando Brown Sr. to Orlando Brown Jr. March 3, 1863, Orlando Brown Papers, Mss. A/B879, folder 25, FHS; Benjamin F. Buckner to Dear Helen [Martin], December 2, 1862, Benjamin Forsythe Buckner Papers, 1785–1918, Mss. 48M39, UK; Przybyszewski, *Republic According to Harlan*, 35–37; J[ohn] M. Harlan to James Garfield, March 2, 1863, John Marshall Harlan Papers, microfilm reel 2: General Correspondence, LC; *New Albany* [Ind.] *Ledger*, October 4, 1864.

57. Williams, "Voters in Blue," 189–91, 196–97, 203; General Orders No. 13a, February 26, 1862, *OR*, ser. 1, vol. 7, 669–70; Grimsley, *Hard Hand of War*, 64–65; *Harper's Weekly*, May 10, 1862, 289; Ormsby M. Mitchel to Joseph Ripley, August 16, 1861, Mitchel to Dear Ned [Edwin W. Mitchel], October 1, 15, November 3, 1861, Lovell H. Rousseau to J[ames] B. Fry, August 7, 1862, all in Ormsby M. Mitchel Papers, Mss. M679, box 1, folder 1, CHSL; James B. Fry, *Military Miscellanies* (New York: Brentano's, 1889), 486–505; John H. Tilford Diary, Mss. A/T572, September 29, 1862 entry, vol. 1 (August 27–November 30, 1862), FHS; P. C. Headley, *The Patriot Boy; or, The Life and Career of Major-General Ormsby M. Mitchel* (New York: William H. Appleton, 1865), 166–67; McPherson, *Battle Cry of Freedom*, 364; Transcript from Phonographic Notes of the Buell Court of Inquiry, December 13, 1862, *OR*, ser. 1, vol. 16, pt. 1, 130–49; Brooks D. Simpson, *Let Us Have Peace: Ulysses S. Grant and the Politics of War and Reconstruction, 1861–1868* (Chapel Hill: University of North Carolina Press, 1991), 6–7; Alexander K. McClure, *Lincoln and Men of War-Times: Some Personal Recollections of War and Politics During the Lincoln Administration* (Philadelphia: Times Publishing Co., 1892), 196–98; Ayers, *In the Presence of Mine Enemies*, 13, 48–49.

58. Charles Royster, *The Destructive War: William Tecumseh Sherman, Stonewall Jackson, and the Americans* (New York: Alfred A. Knopf, 1991), passim; [St. Louis] *Daily Missouri Republican*, August 28, 1863; William L. Barney, *Flawed Victory: A New Perspective on the Civil War* (New York: Praeger, 1975), 27–28.

59. Stathis N. Kalyvas, "The Ontology of 'Political Violence': Action and Identity in Civil Wars," *Perspectives on Politics* 1 (2003): 479, 482, 485 and passim; Richard Cobb, *Reactions to the French Revolution* (New York: Oxford University Press, 1972), 56, 90; Ash, *When the Yankees Came*, 41–49; Kenneth W. Noe, "Who Were the Bushwhackers? Age, Class, Kin, and Western Virginia's Confederate Guerrillas, 1861–1862," *CWH* 49 (March 2003): 5–25.

The Art of Retaliation

1. Nancy Rash, *The Painting and Politics of George Caleb Bingham* (New Haven, Conn.: Yale University Press, 1991), 5, 15–20, 59–63, 157–71, 176–83, 186–87; Fern Helen Rusk, *George Caleb Bingham, The Missouri Artist* (Jefferson City, Mo.: Hugh Stephens, 1917), 77–82; Michael Dickey, *Arrow Rock: Crossroads of the Missouri Frontier* (Arrow Rock, Mo.: Friends of Arrow Rock, 2004), 76, 136–37, 184–87.

2. Joan Stack, "Toward an Emancipationist Interpretation of George Caleb Bingham's *General Order No. 11*: The Reception History of the Painting and the Remembered Civil War in Missouri," *MHR* 107 (July 2013): 205; George Caleb Bingham to James Shannon, January 18, 25, February 8, 1856, and Bingham to James S. Rollins, June 2, 1856, January 9, December 9, 1860, in [Bingham], *"But I Forget That I Am a Painter",* 152–231.
3. Bingham to Rollins, January 9, 1860, February 2, March 6, May 16, June 29, 1861, in [Bingham], *"But I Forget That I Am a Painter,"* 217–20, 241–43, 246–50, 253–57; Paul C. Nagel, *George Caleb Bingham: Missouri's Famed Painter and Forgotten Politician* (Columbia: University of Missouri Press, 2005), 1–16, 100–102, 104; *Missouri Troops in Service During the Civil War*, 222–23; Parrish, *Turbulent Partnership*, 85–86; Stiles, *Jesse James*, 68, 75–76; Christopher Phillips, *The Making of a Southerner: William Barclay Napton's Private Civil War* (Columbia: University of Missouri Press, 2008), 62.
4. George Caleb Bingham to Ja[me]s S. Rollins and W[illia]m A. Hall, January 22, February 12, 1862, in Rollins, ed., "Letters of Bingham to Rollins—Part V, Letters: January 22, 1862–November 21, 1871," 47, 52, 56, 59; Rash, *Painting and Politics of Bingham*, 177–83, 188; Bingham to H[amilton] R. Gamble, June 8, 1863, Hamilton R. Gamble Papers, folder 10, MHS; Bingham to John M. Schofield, June 4, 1863, Correspondence: Letters Received, ser. 1, 1861–1875, John McAllister Schofield Papers, box 2, folder B4–30, LC.
5. George C. Bingham to John M. Schofield, June 4, 1863, Correspondence: Letters Received, ser. 1, 1861–1875, John McAllister Schofield Papers, box 2, folder B4–30, LC; Duane Schultz, *Quantrill's War: The Life and Times of William Clarke Quantrill, 1837–1865* (New York: Macmillan, 1997), 141–42; Castel, *Frontier State at War*, 125–26.
6. Albert E. Castel, *William Clarke Quantrill: His Life and Times* (Norman: University of Oklahoma Press, 1999), 123–43; Schultz, *Quantrill's War*, 141; Fellman, *Inside War*, 140–41; Stiles, *Jesse James*, 94–95; Smith, *Thomas Ewing Jr.*, 197–98.
7. Smith, *Thomas Ewing Jr.*, 20–21, 32, 68–69, 186–89, 191; Thomas Ewing Jr. to John M. Schofield, June 23, 1863, Correspondence: Letters Received, ser. 1, 1861–1868, John McAllister Schofield Papers, box 4, folder E1–20, LC; H. B. Bouton to A[bram] Comingo, August 11, 1863, and Comingo to Willard P. Hall, August 17, 1863, both in RG 393, pt. 1, ser. 2593: Letters Received, Department of the Missouri, box 8, NARA; Thomas Goodrich, *Bloody Dawn: The Story of the Lawrence Massacre* (Kent, Ohio: Kent State University Press, 1992), 140; John M. Schofield, *Forty-six Years in the Army* (New York: Century, 1897), 68–70; Beale, *Diary of Edward Bates*, 332; Thomas Ewing Sr. to Abraham Lincoln, June 27, 1863, Lincoln Papers; Schofield to Lincoln, August 28, 1863, *OR*, ser. 1, vol. 22, pt. 2, 482–84; Castel, *Frontier State at War*, 112.
8. Smith, *Thomas Ewing Jr.*, 198–99; LeeAnn Whites, *Gender Matters: Civil War, Reconstruction, and the Making of the New South* (New York: Palgrave Macmillan, 2005), 6, 45–64 and passim; Whites, "Forty Shirts and a Wagonload of Wheat: Women, the Domestic Supply Line, and the Civil War on the Western Border," *JCWE* 1 (March 2011): 56–57, 63–67; Burke, "Scattered People," 82–85; Marszalek, *Sherman*, 194–95; Abraham Lincoln to Hon. H. T. Blow, C. D. Drake, and Others, May 15, 1863, in *CWAL*, 6:218; William E. Connelly, *Quantrill and the Border Wars* (Cedar Rapids, Iowa.: Torch Press, 1910), 417–18; Thomas Ewing Jr. to C. W. Marsh, August 3, 1863; William H. Wherry to Ewing, August 14, 1863; Ewing to John M. Schofield, August 25, 1863; and Report of Brig. Gen. Thomas Ewing Jr., U.S. Army, August 31, 1863, all in *OR*, ser. 1, vol. 22, pt. 2, 428–29, 450–51, 281, 472–73, 579–85; Lincoln to John M. Schofield, August 27, 1863, and Lincoln to Charles D. Drake and Others, Committee, October 5, 1863, both in in *CWAL*, 6:415, 8:500; Carnahan, *Lincoln on Trial*, 65–66.
9. Albert Castel, "Order No. 11 and the Civil War on the Border," in *Winning and Losing in the Civil War: Essays and Stories* (Columbia: University of South Carolina Press, 1996), 53; *New York Evening Post*, August 23, 1863; *New York Times*, August 24, 1863; [St. Louis] *Tri-Weekly Missouri Democrat*, September 2, 1863; Schofield, *Forty-six Years in the Army*, 80; A[bel] C. Wilder and J[ames] H. Lane to Abraham Lincoln (telegram), August 26, 1863, Lincoln Papers, LC; J[ohn] M. Schofield to Thomas Ewing, August 25, 1863, *OR*, ser. 1, vol. 22, pt. 2, 471–72.

Notes to Pages 239–242   399

10. Ewing to J. B. Fry, December 28, 1863, and Report of Brig. Gen. Thomas Ewing Jr., U.S. Army, August 31, 1863, both in OR, ser. 1, vol. 22, pt. 2, 472–73, 753; Stiles, *Jesse James*, 96.
11. Smith, *Thomas Ewing Jr.*, 199–203; Castel, "Order No. 11 and the Civil War on the Border," 55–56; Charles R. Mink, "General Orders No. 11: The Forced Evacuation of Civilians During the Civil War," *Foreign Affairs* 34 (December 1970): 132–33; Neely, *The Border Between Them*, 122–25; E[gbert] B. Brown to O. D. Greene, March 1, 1864, RG 393, pt. 1, ser. 2593: Letters Received, Department of the Missouri, box 12, NARA.
12. Newspaper Clipping, "A SCORCHER—Gen. Bingham on Order No. 11," undated [1876], Garland Carr Broadhead Scrapbook, Mss. 1000, pp. 68–69, SHSM; Recollection of Frances Fitzhugh George, Oak Grove, Jackson Co., Mo., March 1, 1897, written to A. J. Adair (typescript), pp. 3–4, B. James George Sr. Collection, Mss. 3564, box 1, folder 7, SHSM; E[gbert] B. Brown to O. D. Greene, March 1, 1864, RG 393, pt. 1, ser. 2593: Letters Received, Department of the Missouri, box 12, NARA; *Liberty* [Mo.] *Tribune*, September 11, 1863; [St. Louis] *Daily Missouri Republican*, September 2, 1863.
13. Stiles, *Jesse James*, 96; [Kansas City, Mo.] *Western Journal of Commerce*, September 19, 1863, January 23, 1864; George Miller, *Missouri's Memorable Decade, 1860–1870* (Columbia, Mo.: E. W. Stephens, 1898), 36; Vivian K. McLarty, ed., "The Civil War Letters of Colonel Bazel F. Lazear," *MHR* 44 (April–July 1950), 390; vol. 45 (October 1950), 390; Diary of Events in Department of Missouri 1863, September 8, 1863 entry, and Egbert B. Brown to Schofield, August 28, 1863, Correspondence: Letters Received, ser. 1, 1861–1875, folder B32–52, both in John McAllister Schofield Papers, boxes 1–2, LC; Brownlee, *Gray Ghosts of the Confederacy*, 126; Mink, "General Orders No. 11," 132–33, 134–35; Smith, *Thomas Ewing Jr.*, 203; Thomas Ewing Jr. to Thomas Ewing Sr., August 28, 1863; General Order No. 11 memorandum, undated; and Wyllis Ransom to Thomas Ewing Jr., May 30, 1871, folder B32–52, all in Ewing Family Papers: General Correspondence, boxes 17, 212, LC; McLarty, "Civil War Letters," 390; Neely, *The Border Between Them*, 124; George Caleb Bingham to J[ames] S. Rollins, December 21, 1862, in Rollins, "Letters of George Caleb Bingham to Rollins—Part V, Letters: January 22, 1862–November 21, 1871," 62; [Lachlan A.] Maclean to William C. Quantrill, November 2, 1863, OR, ser. 1, vol. 53, 908.
14. Rash, *Painting and Politics of Bingham*, 189–91; Nagel, *Bingham*, 112.
15. Report of Col. W. C. Quantrill, October 13, 1863; Samuel R. Curtis to Citizens of Kansas City, March 4, 1864; and Thomas Ewing Jr. to H. M. Hiller, October 27, 1864, both in OR, ser. 1, vol. 22, pt. 1, 700; vol. 34, pt. 2, 500–501; and vol. 41, pt. 4, 275–76.

Chapter 7: Shadow Wars: The Crucible of Social Violence

1. Cora Owens Hume Journal (typescript), April 5, 1863 entry, vol. 1, pp. 38–39; September 10, 11, 12, October 11, 13, 15, 1864 entries, vol. 2, pp. 16–19, 28–30, Mss. A/H921 Vault C, FHS; William E. Connelly and E. Merton Coulter, *History of Kentucky* (Chicago: American Historical Society, 1922), vol. 5, 36; *Centralia* [Ill.] *Sentinel*, December 3, 1863; "Sarah Patience" (unpublished manuscript, typescript), Martha W. Dorsey Papers, Mss. SC510, folder 2, pp. 48–49, IHSL.
2. Kalyvas, "Ontology of 'Political Violence,'" 475; David Kilcullen, *The Accidental Guerrilla: Fighting Small Wars in the Midst of a Big One* (New York: Oxford University Press, 2009), 4–5. In Missouri home guards were consolidated into the state militia beginning in December 1861. In Kentucky home guards continued to serve largely as county militias throughout the war. [War Department, Record and Pension Office,] *Organization and Status of Missouri Troops (Union and Confederate) in Service during the Civil War* (Washington, D.C.: Government Printing Office, 1902), 146–52.
3. James C. Scott, *Weapons of the Weak: Everyday Forms of Peasant Resistance* (New Haven, Conn.: Yale University Press, 1985), xvi; Kalyvas, "Ontology of 'Political Violence'," 482–83; Fellman, *Inside War*, 23; Daniel E. Sutherland, *Guerrillas, Unionists, and Violence on the Confederate Home Front* (Fayetteville: University of Arkansas Press, 1999), 3; M. Todd White to W. and E. Hardeman, May 23, 1864, Hardeman Family Papers, Mss.

A/H159, folder 6, FHS. For a comparative study of military violence as an instrument for building politicized communities, see Isabel V. Hull, *Absolute Destruction: Military Culture and the Practices of War in Imperial Germany* (Ithaca, N.Y.: Cornell University Press, 2006).

4. [Richmond, Ind.] *The Broad Axe of Freedom*, February 13, 1864; Elvira A. W. Scott Diary (typescript), July 23, 1863 entry, folder 8, p. 212, SHSM; James E. Potter, *Standing Firmly by the Flag: Nebraska Territory and the Civil War, 1861–1867* (Lincoln, Ne.: Bison Books, 2013), 15–28; Robert R. Mackey, *The Uncivil War: Irregular Warfare in the Upper South, 1861–1865* (Norman: University of Oklahoma Press, 2004), 205–206; Daniel E. Sutherland, "Guerrilla Warfare, Democracy, and the Fate of the Confederacy," *JSH* 68 (May 2002): 281–83, 287–88; Sutherland, *A Savage Conflict*, 10–11, 16–17, 38–40, 100–101; Gienapp, "Lincoln and the Border States," 25; Cicero Maxwell to To Whom It May Concern, May 6, 1863, and Affidavit of Jacob S. Cave, March 31, 1865, both in RG 393, pt. 1, ser. 2229: Correspondence, Affidavits, and Oaths Regarding Civilians Charged with Disloyalty, Department of Kentucky, box 1, NARA; "Sarah Patience" (unpublished manuscript, typescript), Martha W. Dorsey Papers, Mss. SC510, folder 2, pp. 47–49, IHSL; Oliver P. Morton to Joseph Hooker, January 11, 1865, RG 393, pt. 1, ser. 3349: Letters Received, Northern Department, box 2, NARA; H. Smith to J. J. Key, September 2, 1862, RG 393, pt. 1, ser. 3514: Letters Received, Department of the Ohio, box 2, NARA; *Pomeroy [Ohio] Weekly Telegraph*, May 26, 1864; Nancy C. Mann to J[ohn] Preston Mann, November 19, 1863, Mann Family Papers, Coll. 111, box 2, SIU; Sallie Hendricks to Abram W Hendricks, September 12, 1862, Abram W. Hendricks Papers, Mss. SC733, IHSL; *Hannibal [Mo.] Daily Messenger*, September 4, 1861; Thomas G. Morrow to [Stephen G.] Burbridge, October 3, 1864, RG 393, pt. 1, ser. 2173: Letters Received, Department of Kentucky, box 4, NARA.

5. Sutherland, *A Savage Conflict*, 122–52, 154; James B. Martin, "Black Flag over the Bluegrass: Guerrilla Warfare in Kentucky, 1863–1865," *Register* 86 (Autumn 1988): 368–70 [352–75]; Benjamin Franklin Cooling, *Forts Henry and Donelson: The Key to the Confederate Heartland* (Knoxville: University of Tennessee Press, 1987), 205–10; Sallie Hendricks to Abram W. Hendricks, September 12, 1862, Abram W. Hendricks Papers, Mss. SC733, IHSL; John Raymer to Orlando Brown, June 3, 1862, Orlando Brown Papers, Mss. A/B879, folder 38a, FHS; C. D. Bradley to Jeremiah T. Boyle, November 9, 1862, RG 393, pt. 1, ser. 3514: Letters Received, Department of the Ohio, box 1, NARA; Don Bowen, "Guerrilla Warfare in Western Missouri, 1862–1865: Historical Extensions of the Relative Deprivation Hypothesis," *Comparative Studies in Society and History* 19 (July 1977): 30; John Pope to Cyrus Bussey, August 10, 1861, and Pope to John C. Kelton, August 4, 1861, both in *OR*, ser. 1, vol. 3, 435–36, 427; Grant, *Personal Memoirs*, 132. U. S. Grant to W. E. McMackin, August 12, 1861, in *OR*, ser. 1, vol. 3, 438–39; Bruce Nichols, *Guerrilla Warfare in Civil War Missouri, 1862* (Jefferson, N.C.: McFarland, 2004), 34–38; Ash, *When the Yankees Came*, 76–107; Stiles, *Jesse James*, 85–87; *Missouri Troops in Service During the Civil War*, 82–84; Boman, *Lincoln's Resolute Unionist*, 222–23; Elvira A. W. Scott Diary, Mss. 1053, p. 144, SHSM; Thomas Ewing to C. W. Marsh, August 3, 1863, *OR*, ser. 1, vol. 22, pt. 2, 428–29; Neely, *The Border Between Them*, 108–9; Bradbury, "'Buckwheat Cake Philanthropy,'" 241–43, 248–49; Current, *Lincoln's Loyalists*, 153–54; [Parsons], *Incidents and Experiences*, 94–95, 121, 139; Gordon Granger to Jeremiah T. Boyle, November 28, 1862, and John W. Foster to Boyle, November 28, 1862, both in RG 393, pt. 1, ser. 2173: Letters Received, Department of Kentucky, 1862–1869, box 1, NARA; J[ohn] M. Schofield to Abraham Lincoln, August 28, 1863, *OR*, ser. 1, vol. 22, pt. 2, 482–84. After the Partisan Ranger Act instilled a "bitter mood of retaliation... in the military policies of both North and South, beginning in the summer of 1862," Sutherland suggested the accretion of guerrilla warfare in Kentucky in the spring of 1863.

6. Statement of Thomas Burris, August 16, 1864, RG 393, pt. 1, ser. 2229: Correspondence, Affidavits, and Oaths Regarding Civilians Charged with Disloyalty, Department of Kentucky, box 2, NARA; James M. Fidler to James M. Fry, June 20, 1864; R. G. Samuel, December 15, 1862; William Mattingly, September 10 [1864], all in RG 393, pt. 1, ser. 2137: Letters Received, Department of Kentucky, boxes 1, 3, 4, NARA; Phil[ander] B. Price, January 18, 1864, Hunt-Morgan Family Papers, Mss. 63M202, box 17, folder 1, UK; Cora Owens Hume Journal (typescript), September 15, 1864 entry, vol. 2, pp. 20–22, Mss. A/H921 Vault C, FHS; Notations of Military Commission Hearing of Jacob Snowden,

undated [May 1863], RG 393, pt. 1, ser. 2620: General Orders, Department of the Missouri, 1862–1864, 2:19–21, NARA; Hoskins, "The First Is with the South," 58.

7. Yancey Wilson to James B. Meriwether, March 24, 1865, and enclosures, RG 393, pt. 1, ser. 2229: Correspondence, Affidavits, and Oaths Regarding Civilians Charged with Disloyalty, Department of Kentucky, box 2, NARA; Elvira A. W. Scott Diary (typescript), folder 4, p. 144, SHSM; J[ohn] M. Schofield to Abraham Lincoln, August 28, 1863, OR, ser. 1, vol. 22, pt. 2, 482–84; Boman, *Lincoln's Resolute Unionist*, 176–77; Coulter, *Civil War and Readjustment*, 189–94; Abraham Lincoln to Green Adams, January 7, 1863, in *CWAL*, 6:42; O. F. Miner to A. M. Stout, February 9, 1865, OR, ser. 3, vol. 4, 1188; Sterling, "Civil War Draft Resistance in Illinois," 248–49; Peter Levine, "Draft Evasion in the North during the Civil War, 1863–1865," *JAH* 67 (March 1981): 819, 825n19; Fellman, *Inside War*, 26–31; Le Roy Fitch to David D. Porter, June 11, 1864, OR, ser. 1, vol. 39, pt. 2, 102; General Order No. 2, August 8, 1864, Edward Henry Hobson Papers, Mss. 51M41, UK. Although in August 1864 the Confederate War Department ordered mandatory enlistment in western Kentucky for all men between the ages of seventeen and forty-five and conscription for those who evaded, far more would in fact become guerrillas than Confederates. The 1866 Kentucky adjutant general's report lists 12,486 individuals who served in the Kentucky militia system during the Civil War. This figure includes all soldiers called to duty in Kentucky in 1861 by Robert Anderson, those who continued service in the Kentucky State Guard (1861–1864), and those 4,519 men who served in the ten Kentucky Active Militia Battalions (also called Kentucky State Troops Proper) from 1864 to 1866. This total does not include 114 regiments of the Kentucky Enrolled Militia authorized by the Militia Act of 1860 (with 800–1,100 men authorized to fill in each regiment, but whose totals are unrecorded), or the various home guard units, county and municipal, which historian Lowell Harrison has estimated as having exceeded 10,000. Aggregation of men who served in Missouri's various militias is even less easily determined. Although Missouri State Militia (MSM) enrollment was capped at 10,000, it actually exceeded 13,000 in 1862 before being reduced by disbanding and consolidating some regiments. Later, some MSM units were opened to recruiters for the federal volunteers. By September 1862 more than twenty Enrolled Missouri Militia (EMM) regiments had been formed in the city and county of St. Louis, representing approximately seventeen thousand men. By the end of 1862 sixty-nine regiments, three battalions, and fifty-eight independent companies had been organized, with a total of 52,056 officers and enlisted men; ultimately eighty-five regiments, sixteen battalions, and thirty-three independent companies were organized. The 1864 Missouri adjutant general's report includes monthly aggregates of active EMM units, with the peak coming in October at 24,164 and the low in the previous May at 339. The median figure for active militia during these months is 2,448. As in Kentucky, these figures likely do not include home guards, Six-Months' Militia; Provisional Enrolled Missouri Militia (PEMM); Provisional Companies of Enrolled Missouri Militia (PCEMM), which were organized within townships and counties; or other independent companies and battalions. Any listing of enrollment assumes the risk of overcounting because men, and their enrollment figures, transferred from organization to organization. (For example, the provisional versions of the EMM, especially the PEMM, were often the same men who had enrolled in the original EMM.) General Order No. 2, August 8, 1864, David. L. Thornton Papers, Mss. 61M256, box 1, UK; [War Department, Record and Pension Office], *Organization and Status of Missouri Troops*, 53; *Annual Report of the Adjutant General of Missouri for 1864* (Jefferson City: W. A. Curry, 1865), 38; Harrison, *Civil War in Kentucky*, 95.

8. McPherson, *Battle Cry of Freedom*, 602–6; Weber, *Copperheads*, 88; Potter, *Standing Firmly by the Flag*, 105–107; Andrew William Fialka, "Controlled Chaos: Spatiotemporal Patterns within Missouri's Irregular War," in Joseph M. Beilein Jr. and Matthew C. Hulbert, eds., *The Civil War Guerrilla: Unfolding the Black Flag in History and Myth*, (Lexington: University Press of Kentucky, 2014), 43–70 passim; Elvira A. W. Scott Diary (typescript), folder 8, p. 214, SHSM; Cora Owens Hume Journal (typescript), September 4, 1864 entry, vol. 2, p. 13, Mss. A/H921 Vault C, FHS; "Enrollment of Disloyal men or those who have sympathized with the Rebellion between the ages of 18 and 45 years," and "Enrollment of Disloyal men and those who have sympathized with the Rebellion over the age of 45 years

living in Andrew County," both in Andrew County Civil War Document Collection, box CW2, file 15, MSA; Henry Asbury to H. H. Dean, January 11, 1865, RG 393, pt. 1, ser. 3349: Letters Received, Northern Department, boxes 1-2, NARA; Anonymous to Dear Wick, March 28, 1865, Wickliffe-Preston Family Papers, Mss. 63M349, box 56, UK.

9. Parrish, *Turbulent Partnership*, 91-94; Stiles, *Jesse James*, 84; Elvira A. W. Scott Diary, Mss. 1053, folder 5, pp. 138-39, folder 8, pp. 214-15.

10. Special Orders No. 10, September 29, 1861, in *OR*, ser. 2, vol. 1, 284; Fellman, *Inside War*, 252-53; Samuel S. Hildebrand, *Autobiography of Samuel S. Hildebrand: The Renowned Missouri "Bushwacker" and Unconquerable Rob Roy of America; Being His Complete Confession, Recently Made to the Writers and Carefully Compiled by James W. Evans and A. Wendell Keith, Together with All the Facts Connected with His Early History* (Jefferson City, Mo.: State Times Book and Job Printing House, 1870; reprint Woodbridge, Conn.: Research Publications, 1985), 27-28, 35, 37, 41-51; Kirby Ross, "James O. Broadhead: Ardent Unionist, Unrepentant Slaveholder," 173, http://www.civilwarstlouis.com/History2/broadheadprofile.htm (accessed January 14, 2010); T. Coleman Younger, *The Story of Cole Younger by Himself: Being an Autobiography of the Missouri Guerrilla Captain and Outlaw* (Chicago: Henneberry Company, 1903), 4-5; Neely, *The Border Between Them*, 108-9.

11. Mark W. Geiger, *Financial Fraud and Guerrilla Violence in Missouri's Civil War, 1861-1865* (New Haven, Conn.: Yale University Press, 2010), passim; Geiger, "Indebtedness and the Origins of Guerrilla Warfare in Civil War Missouri," *JSH* 75 (February 2009): 49-82; Bowen, "Guerrilla War in Western Missouri," 43-51; Neely, *Border between Them*, 108-10; Elvira A. W. Scott Diary (typescript), folder 4, pp. 94-99, SHSM. The sample in Bowen's study is a group of 194 identified guerrillas who lived in or near Jackson County, Missouri.

12. J[eremiah] T. Boyle to W. P. Anderson, November 10, 1863, RG 393, pt. 1, ser. 3514: Letters Received, Department of the Ohio, box 3, NARA; Reid Mitchell, *The Vacant Chair: The Northern Soldier Leaves Home* (New York: Oxford University Press, 1993), 33-34; [St. Louis] *Daily Missouri Republican*, September 2, 1863; Correspondence, Orders, and Returns Relating to Operations in Missouri, Arkansas, Kansas, the Indian Territory, and Department of the Northwest, from January 1 to December 31, 1863, *OR*, ser. 1, vol. 22, pt. 2, 109-10; *Journal of the Senate of the State of Missouri, at the Adjourned Session of the Twenty-second General Assembly* (Jefferson City, Mo.: J. P. Ament, 1863), 656; J. H. Collins to William S. Rosecrans, February 10, 1864, RG 393, pt. 1, ser. 2593: Letters Received, Department of the Missouri, box 12, NARA; General Orders No. 32, December 22, 1861, *OR*, ser. 1, vol. 8, 463-64; Stiles, *Jesse James*, 74-75; *Daily Missouri Republican*, November 10, 1861, in Silvana R. Siddali, *Missouri's War: The Civil War in Documents* (Athens: Ohio University Press, 2009), 82.

13. [Lexington, Ky.] *The National Unionist*, November 11, 1864; James A. Ramage, *Rebel Raider: The Life of General John Hunt Morgan* (Lexington: University Press of Kentucky, 1986), 6; *Missouri Republican*, August 25, 28, 1863; Sutherland, "Guerrilla Warfare, Democracy, and the Fate of the Confederacy," 267-69; South Union Journal, January 29, 1863 entry, WKU; Elvira A. W. Scott Diary (typescript), folder 4, pp. 94-99, folder 7, 197, folder 8, 212-16, SHSM; [Hardin], *Private War of Lizzie Hardin*, 75, 89; Sutherland, *A Savage Conflict*, 167-70; Scott J. Lucas, "'Indignities, Wrongs, and Outrages': Military and Guerrilla Incursions on Kentucky's Civil War Home Front," *FHQ* 73 (October 1999): 367-69; Martin, "Black Flag over the Bluegrass," 370-75. On Morgan's Raid, see Ramage, *Rebel Raider*, 147-79. See also Lester V. Horwitz, *The Longest Raid of the Civil War* (Cincinnati: Farmcourt Publishing, 1999).

14. Report of Brig. Gen. John M. Schofield, U.S. Army, of Operations in Missouri and Northwestern Arkansas, April 10-November 20, 1862, *OR*, ser. 1, vol. 13, 12; [War Department, Record and Pension Office,] *Organization and Status of Missouri Troops in the Civil War*, 53; "Sarah Patience" (unpublished manuscript, typescript), p. 54, Martha W. Dorsey Papers, Mss. SC510, folder 2, IHSL; Elvira A. W. Scott Diary, Mss. 1053, folder 5, pp. 138-39, folder 8, pp. 214-15, SHSM; [Frankfort, Ky.] *Tri-weekly Commonwealth*, March 25, 1863, March 16, 1864; Stephen V. Ash, *Middle Tennessee Society Transformed, 1860-1870: War and Peace in the Upper South* (Baton Rouge: Louisiana State University Press, 1988), 148-51; Sutherland, "Guerrilla Warfare, Democracy, and the Fate of the

Confederacy," 271–72, 284–85; Fellman, *Inside War*, 153–55; Phillips, *Making of a Southerner*, 99; W. Randolph to Stephen G. Burbridge, December 1, 1864, Stephen Gano Burbridge Correspondence, Mss. C/B, FHS; Nichols, *Guerrilla Warfare in Civil War Missouri*, 43–44; Nazro Diary, August 2, September 22, October 23, 1864 entries, WKU. To pay for EMM enlistments, in March 1863 the Missouri General Assembly authorized Gamble to issue $1 million of "Union Military" bonds, payable in twelve months at 6 percent interest, and when that proved insufficient authorized another $1.5 million the following November.

15. General Orders No. 1, January 1, 1862, *OR*, ser. 1, vol. 8, 475–76; "Diary of Events in Department of Missouri, 1863," August 26, 1863 entry, John McAllister Schofield Papers, box 1, LC; Milo T. Haswell to Ambrose E. Burnside, May 19, 1863, RG 393, pt. 1, ser. 3514: Letters Received, Department of the Ohio, box 3, NARA; J. B. Meriwether to G. M. Bascom, March 11, 1865, and E. B. Burnett to Provost Marshall, Louisville, March 11, 1865, both in RG 393, pt. 1, ser. 2229: Correspondence, Affidavits, and Oaths Regarding Civilians Charged with Disloyalty, Department of Kentucky, box 1, NARA; Sutherland, *A Savage Conflict*, 59–63; General Orders No. 1, January 1, 1862, and General Orders No. 32, December 22, 1861, both in *OR*, ser. 1, vol. 8, 476–78; ser. 2, vol. 1, 237; Stiles, *Jesse James*, 86–88.

16. Th[eophilus] H. Holmes to Samuel R. Curtis, October 11, 1862, and J[ohn] M. Schofield to Colonel [John] McNeil, June 12, 1862, both in *OR*, ser. 1, vol. 8, 726–28; vol. 13, 427; Joseph A. Mudd, *With Porter in Northeast Missouri* (Washington, D.C.: National Publishing, 1909), 299–310; Scott E. Sallee, "Porter's Campaign in Northeast Missouri, 1862, Including the Palmyra Massacre," *Blue and Gray* 17 (February 2000): 6–20, 44–51; William E. Parrish, "'The Palmyra Massacre': A Tragedy of Guerrilla Warfare," *Journal of Confederate History* 1 (Fall 1988): 259–72; Daniel Berry to Mary B. Crebs, November 28, 1862, Daniel Berry Letters, Misc. Vol. 53, SIU. Curtis claimed in a subsequent letter to Holmes that he had no knowledge of the Palmyra execution until afterward and regarded it as "a kind of police resentment...by an indignant and outraged community." Curtis to Holmes, December 24, 1862, *OR*, ser. 1, vol. 22, pt. 2, 860–61.

17. Fellman, *Inside War*, 82–84; Henry W. Halleck to Francis Lieber, August 6, 1862, and response [undated], both in *OR*, ser. 3, vol. 2, 301–309; Sutherland, *A Savage Conflict*, 126–29; Grimsley, *The Hard Hand of War*, 11–13; John Fabian Witt, *Lincoln's Code: The Laws of War in American History* (New York: The Free Press, 2012), 170–249 passim; Matthew J. Mancini, "Francis Lieber, Slavery, and the 'Genesis' of the Laws of War," *JSH* 77 (May 2011): 326–39; [Francis W. Lieber,] *No Party Now But All for Our Country* (Philadelphia: Crissy and Markley, Printers, 1863), 3–5, 10–12; Burrus M. Carnahan, "Lincoln, Lieber and the Laws of War: The Origins and Limits of the Principle of Military Necessity," *American Journal of International Law* 92 (April 1998): 213–15; Sutherland, "Guerrilla Warfare, Democracy, and the Fate of the Confederacy," 288; Smith, *No Party Now*, 3.

18. Searching these terms in the digitized version of *OR* volumes, the contents of which were themselves culled from the original War Department records (and thus are not complete), and narrowing the search to reports specific to commands located or events occurring in Missouri and Kentucky yields 64 individual reports dated on or before July 18, 1862, the date Lincoln issued his initial call for three hundred thousand additional troops. By contrast, 358 such reports dated thereafter are contained in the volumes. A similar search of the term "bushwhacker" yielded 4 reports prior to the implementation of the draft and 121 after it. Using only the term "guerrilla," 17 percent of its usage appears in the reports prior to July 18, 1862, as compared with. 3 percent for the term "bushwhacker." This sampling is of course limited, suggestive of the resources committed by federal military authorities in these states by way of individual reports about irregulars rather than the breadth of their activities.

19. Fellman, *Inside War*, 82; *Annual Report of the Adjutant General of Missouri for 1864*, 38; John N. Edwards, *Shelby and His Men* (Cincinnati: Miami Printing and Publishing, 1867), 197. Quantification from the provost marshal files for Missouri is based on the Missouri State Archives's complete indexing of extant Missouri cases in 394 microfilm reels of Record Group 109, War Department Collection of Confederate Records, housed at NARA,

organized as *Union Provost Marshals' File of Papers Relating to Individual Citizens* (300 microfilm reels, dated 1861–1866) and *Union Provost Marshals' File of Papers Relating to Two or More Civilians* (94 microfilm reels, dated 1861–1867). These records were assembled in the U.S. War Department from documents that were extracted from the files of the Union Army provost marshals and from other records of army territorial commands. This sampling derives from the online database index compiled by the staff of the Missouri State Archives, which began in 2000 and concluded in 2009. Staffers included 66,129 case files originating in the state of Missouri, drawn from 378 reels of both of the NARA collections, and thus are included in this sampling. See http://www.sos.mo.gov/archives/provost/history.asp#projects (accessed December 3, 2009).

20. Sutherland, *A Savage Conflict*, 152; Nelson McDowell to Hamilton R. Gamble, August 3, 1862, Record Group 3.16: Records of Hamilton Rowan Gamble, box 1B, folder 9, MSA; J[eremiah] T. Boyle to E[dward] M. Stanton, August 21, 1862, *OR*, ser. 3, vol. 2, 431; Samuel Haycraft Journal (typescript), 1 vol., October 10, 20, 1862 entries, pp. 26–27, Mss. A/H414, FHS; Lucas, "'Indignities, Wrongs, and Outrages,'" 357; A[aron] Harding to Dear Jack, November 16, 1862, and Sallie A. Harding to John and Samuel Harding, December 4, 1862, both in John Harding Collection, Mss. A/H263, folder 6, FHS; Marian M. Ohman, *Encyclopedia of Missouri Courthouses* (Columbia: Curators of the University of Missouri, 1981), passim. Three Missouri courthouses were destroyed or damaged by federal troops or state militia, while another nine were damaged by occupation. Only two were in the western part of the state, where the guerrilla war was perhaps most vicious, but also where garrisons in county seats were larger.

21. Manning, *What This Cruel War Was Over*, 1; "History of South Union, Ky., No. 16 [November 28, 1862]," *Manifesto (1884–1899)* 25 (February 1895): 25–28; Nazro Diary, February 18, 1863 entry, WKU; Joseph A. Eppstein to J[ohn] M. Schofield, March 16, 1862, Provost, microfilm reel 269, NARA; Fellman, *Inside War*, 137–38, 161–62; Lucas, "'Indignities, Wrongs, and Outrages,'" 358–59; Benjamin F. Loan to Samuel R. Curtis, January 27, 1863, *OR*, ser. 1, vol. 22, pt. 2, 80; W. Anthony to Judge Jesse W. Kincheloe, December 3, 1862, Kinchloe-Eskridge Families Papers, Mss. A/K51, folder 2, FHS; *New York Times*, November 8, 1863; Hiram Carver to J[eremiah] T. Boyle, December 22, 1862; Leonidas Metcalfe to Boyle, December 14, 1862, and James M. Fidler to J[ames] B. Fry, June 10, 1864, all in RG 393, pt. 1, ser. 2173: Letters Received, Department of Kentucky, boxes 1, 3, NARA; *Speech of Hon. George H. Yeaman, of Kentucky, on the President's Proclamation, Delivered in the House of Representatives, December 18, 1962* (Baltimore: John Murphy, 1863), 17.

22. Parrish, *History of Missouri*, 54–55; Stiles, *Jesse James*, 85, 98; George R. Todd to Thomas J. Bartholomew, February 2, 1863, in George R. Todd et al., file 3899, microfilm reel M416, Provost II; Speed S. Fry to Lewis Richmond, May 9, 1863, RG 393, pt. 1, ser. 3514: Letters Received, Department of the Ohio, box 3, NARA; D. Little to J[eremiah] T. Boyle, December 20, 1862, RG 393, pt. 1, ser. 2173: Letters Received, Department of Kentucky, box 1, NARA; Parrish, *Turbulent Partnership*, 94–97; Stiles, *Jesse James*, 87–90; Macon [Mo.] *Weekly Argus*, January 31, 1866; Preston Filbert, *The Half Not Told: The Civil War in a Frontier Town* (Mechanicsburg, Pa.: Stackpole Books, 2001), 116–21; Special Orders, No. 255, September 18, 1863, *OR*, ser. 1, vol. 22, pt. 2, 542–43; [War Department, Record and Pension Office,] *Organization and Status of Missouri Troops in the Civil War*, 82–86, 230; Petition of John Osborne et al., February 26, 1864, RG 393, pt. 1, ser. 2593: Letters Received, Department of the Missouri, box 14, NARA. Missouri raised eleven regiments of PEMM. On September 18, 1863, the 10th and 11th Provisional Regiments mutinied and were disbanded by Special Order No. 255 on November 1, 1863. The PEMM was formally disbanded by act of legislature on March 12, 1865. The term "Paw Paw Militia" has been attributed to the brushy bottoms of the region where guerrillas commonly hid out.

23. Fellman, *Inside War*, 31–32; Bowen, "Guerrilla War in Western Missouri," 47; Lucas, "'Indignities, Wrongs, and Outrages,'" 370; Elvira A. W. Scott Diary (typescript), folder 6, pp. 163–65, SHSM; Berlin et al., *Freedom: Destruction of Slavery*, 407; Kalyvas, "Ontology of 'Political Violence,'" 481.

24. *Centralia* [Ill.] *Sentinel*, June 30, 1864; Elvira A. W. Scott Diary (typescript), folder 8, pp. 209, 212, 221–23, SHSM; Frances Dallam Peter to Arthur, May 7, 1864, Evans Papers, Mss. 72M15, box 7, UK; M. Todd White to W. and E. Hardeman, May 23, 1864, Hardeman Family Papers, Mss. A H159, folder 6, FHS.
25. St. Joseph [Mo.] *The Weekly Herald*, April 17, 1862; Kamphoefner and Helbich, *Germans in the Civil War*, 353; Berlin et al., *Freedom: Destruction of Slavery*, 505; Howard, *Black Liberation in Kentucky*, 14–15; Lucas, *History of Blacks in Kentucky*, 149; Elvira A. W. Scott Diary (typescript), folder 6, pp. 177–78; Bowen, "Guerrilla War in Western Missouri," 47n27; R. C. Vaughan to Edward Bates, August 28, 1863, *OR*, ser. 1, vol. 22, pt. 2, 484–85.
26. Berlin et al., *Freedom: Destruction of Slavery*, 403–5, 505–6; Hoskins, "The First Is with the South," 146; James B. Woollard to Anonymous, February 2, June 3, 1863, James B. Woollard Papers, ALPL; Jasper N. Barry to Dear Affectionate Brother, October 24, 1862, John C. Dinsmore Papers, Mss. SC 405, ALPL; Berlin et al., *Freedom: Wartime Genesis of Free Labor*, 628–31, 642–43; Howard, *Black Liberation in Kentucky*, 18–25; Elvira A. W. Scott Diary (typescript), pp. 226–27, Mss. 1053, SHSM; Lot Abraham to Maggie Abraham, February 23, 1864, January 25, 1865, both in Lot Abraham Letters, Mss. C/A, FHS.
27. Faust, *This Republic of Suffering*, 54; Mary Gunn to Thomas M. Gunn, n.d. [1862], Gunn Family Papers, Mss. 73M28, UK; [St. Joseph, Mo.] *The Weekly Herald*, April 17, 1862; Berlin et al., *Freedom: Destruction of Slavery*, 407.
28. Berlin et al., *Freedom: Destruction of Slavery*, 411–12, 510; Coulter, *Civil War and Readjustment*, 176; J. N. Stiles to Isaac Clark, October 14, 1863, and contract, Isaac Clark Letters, Mss. A/C593a4, FHS; Isaac Sturgeon to J[ohn] M. Schofield, May 23, 1863, and Washington Graves et al. to J. H. Sturgeon, August 31, 1863, both in RG 393, pt. 1, ser. 2593: Letters Received, Department of the Missouri, box 11, NARA; General Orders No. 25, February 26, 1864, *OR*, ser. 1, vol. 32, pt. 2, 479; C. Maxwell to [Stephen G.] Burbridge, September 11, 1864, RG 393, pt. 1, ser. 2173: Letters Received, Department of Kentucky, box 4, NARA; Stiles, *Jesse James*, 85; Newspaper Clipping, Isaac D. Snedecor to Mr. Editor, April 10, 1863, and J. Wendall Keiter to Thomas Armstrong, March 19, 1863, both in microfilm reel 73, file 19533, Provost II. Schofield was goaded into issuing a ban, but he softened it after moderates pressured him to allow loyal masters to sell slave and women and men unfit for military duty out of state, with the slaves' consent. Opposition soon ensued, and in March 1864 Schofield forbade all further removals of slaves from the state. William G. Eliot to Schofield, June 20, November 9, 1863, Correspondence: Letters Received, ser. 1, 1861–1868, John McAllister Schofield Papers, box 4, folder E1–20, LC.
29. Siddali, *Missouri's War*, 190–93; [Weston, Mo.] *Platte County Sentinel*, May 14, 1863; *Cincinnati Weekly Gazette*, July 30, 1862; Berlin et al., *Freedom: Destruction of Slavery*, 403–4; Parrish, *Turbulent Partnership*, 127–28, 223–24n54; [Charles D. Drake], *Immediate Emancipation in Missouri: Speech of Charles D. Drake, Delivered in the Missouri State Convention, June 16th, 1863* (St. Louis: s.n., 1863), 1–10; Charles D. Drake, *Union and Anti-Slavery Speeches, Delivered during the Rebellion by Charles D. Drake* (Cincinnati: Applegate, 1864), 106–7, 341; [St. Louis] *Daily Missouri Democrat*, September 4, 1863; John Hay, *Lincoln and the Civil War in the Diaries and Letters of John Hay*, ed. Tyler Dennett (New York: Dodd, Mead, 1939; reprint New York: Da Capo Press, 1988), 108; Beale, *Diary of Edward Bates*, 333; Michael Fellman, "Emancipation in Missouri," *Missouri Historical Review* 83 (October 1988): 50–56; Parrish, *History of Missouri*, 102–18.
30. Coulter, *Civil War and Readjustment*, 158–60, 170–79; Ettie Scott to Susan Preston Shelby Grigsby, undated [1862–1863], Grigsby Family Papers, Mss. A/G857, folder 184, FHS; Lucas, *History of Blacks in Kentucky*, 152; Berlin et al., *Freedom: Destruction of Slavery*, 503–4, 505–7, 520; Berlin et al., *Freedom: Wartime Genesis of Free Labor* 549, 631; Howard, *Black Liberation in Kentucky*, 20–25; Lucas, *History of Blacks in Kentucky*, 152; M[arcellus] Mundy to A. C. Semple, April 4, 1863, RG 393, Part I, Ser. 2173: Letters Received, Department of Kentucky box 1, NARA; General Orders No. 53, April 28, 1863, *OR*, ser. 1, vol. 23, pt. 2, 287; Howard, *Black Liberation in Kentucky*, 35–38, 45–55; Smith, *Borderland in the Civil War*, 375; Hoskins, "The First Is with the South," 159–63; General Orders No. 120, July 31, [1863], *OR*, ser. 1, vol. 23, pt. 2, 572; John Marshall Harlan to M. M. Benton, July 21, 1863, RG 393, pt. 1, ser. 3514: Letters Received, Department of the Ohio, box 3,

NARA; Lucy Craig Woolfolk Diary, August 4, 1863 entry, Mss. M580 (microfilm), UK; [Parsons], *Incidents and Experiences*, 189–90n37; Gienapp, "Lincoln and the Border States," 36; James Michael Rhyne, "Rehearsal for Redemption: The Politics of Post-Emancipation Violence in Kentucky's Bluegrass Region" (Ph.D. dissertation, University of Cincinnati, 2006), 49. Missouri's gradual emancipation ordinance stipulated that slaves over the age of forty would remain slaves for life, while those under twelve would remain servants until they reached the age of twenty-three, allowing the peculiar institution to exist legally in the state until nearly 1900.

31. W[illia]m M. Wherry to Thomas Ewing Jr., August 14, 1863, *OR*, ser. 1, vol. 22, pt. 2, 450; John W. Blassingame, "The Recruitment of Colored Troops in Kentucky, Maryland and Missouri, 1863–1865," *The Historian* 29 (August 1967): 535–56; Gienapp, "Lincoln and the Border States," 36–37; General Orders No. 329, October 3, 1863, and General Orders No. 135, November 15, 1863, both in *OR*, ser. 3, vol. 3, 861, 215; Kamphoefner and Helbich *Germans in the Civil War*, 355; R. D. Mussey to W. H. Sidell, April 29, 1864, RG 393, pt. 1, ser. 2173: Letters Received, Department of Kentucky, box 3, NARA; Paulina H. Stratton Diary (typescript), December 7, 1863–April 3, 1864 entries, Paulina H. Stratton Papers, Mss. C0842, SHSM.

32. Henry Clay Bruce, *The New Man: Twenty-Nine Years a Slave, Twenty-Nine Years a Free Man, Recollections of H. C. Bruce* (York, Penn.: P. Anstadt and Sons, 1895); Berlin et al., *Freedom: Destruction of Slavery*, 406. White federal enlistments among age-eligible males were, in Missouri, 100,767 of 270,695, or 37.2 percent; and in Kentucky, 52,057 of 213,973, or 24.3 percent. These totals do not include enlistments in state and county militias or home guards. Kennedy, *Population of the United States in 1860*, 592–95; Frederick H. Dyer, *A Compendium of the War of the Rebellion* (Des Moines, Iowa: Dyer Publishing, 1908), 11; http://www.civilwar.net/pages/troops_furnished_losses.html (accessed November 25, 2010).

33. Siddali, *Missouri's War*, 211–13; John W. Blassingame, "The Recruitment of Negro Troops in Missouri During the Civil War," *MHR* 58 (April 1964): 326–38; Thornbrough, *Negro in Indiana*, 197–200; W. H. Sidell to S[tephen] G. Burbridge, February 18, 19, 1865, and Petition of W. L. Carpenter et al. to John M. Palmer, May 25, 1865, all in RG 393, pt. 1, ser. 2173: Letters Received, Department of Kentucky, 1862–69, box 5, NARA; H. S. Bennett to E[dwin] M. Stanton, July 4, 1864; George M. Maxwell to Samuel P. Heintzelman, July 15, 1864; William C. Griers, August 25, 1864; John W. Skiles to C. H. Potter, August 18, 1864; J. N. Barber to Joseph Hooker, June 1, 1865, all in RG 393, pt. 1, ser. 3349: Letters Received, Northern Department, boxes 1–3, NARA; Rush G. Leanning to James H. Ford, February 14, 1864; William A. Pile to Henry T. Blow, February 26, 1864; and Gustavus St. Gem to C. W. Marsh, March 30, 1864, all in RG 393, pt. 1, ser. 2593: Letters Received, Department of the Missouri, boxes 12, 14–15, NARA; L[ydia] H. H. Montague to Rev. Mr. [S. S.] Jocelyn, July 28, 1864, No. 73564, Missouri, microfilm reel 1, AMA.

34. Blassingame, "Recruitment of Colored Troops in Kentucky," 534; Fellman, *Inside War*, 70; W. A. Pollion to Dr. Martine, December 28, 1863, and Charles Jones to His Excellency Abraham Lincoln, March 24, 1863, both in Berlin et al., *Freedom: Destruction of Slavery*, 476–79, 450–53; Elvira A. W. Scott Diary (typescript), pp. 226–27, Mss. 1053, SHSM.

35. John Schofield to Abraham Lincoln, August 28, 1863, *OR*, pt. 1, vol. 22, 482–84; "Diary of Events in Department of Missouri, 1863," August 26, 1863 entry, John McAllister Schofield Papers, box 1, LC; Parrish, *Turbulent Partnership*, 98; Elvira A. W. Scott Diary (typescript), folders 8, 4, pp. 212–14, 97–98, Mss. 1053, SHSM; [Parsons], *Incidents and Experiences*, 134; "Statement of the names, ages and appearance of the bodies found in the Mississippi River, at Compromise Tennessee, after being murdered by negroes, from Island No. 10 on Tuesday, August 4, '63," August 8, 1863, microfilm reel 22, Provost II; Court Martial Case File of Jim Webb, William Ray, and Lewis Stevenson, Case No. MM813, RG 153: Records of the Office of the Judge Advocate General (Army), box 953, NARA.

36. Robert Winn to Dear Sister, February 25, 1864, Winn-Cook Family Papers, Mss. A/W776, box 1, folder 5, FHS; Lucas, *History of Blacks in Kentucky*, 153; Berlin et al., *Freedom: Wartime Genesis of Free Labor*, 549, 631; Howard, *Black Liberation in Kentucky*, 20–25, 45–47, 50–51; James Guthrie to Genl [Jeremiah T.] Boyle, March 2, 1863, RG 393, Pt. I, Ser. 2173: Letters Received, Department of Kentucky, box 1, NARA. Boyle allowed owners

to hire out their impressed slaves for wages to military or railroad contractors. He exempted owners of one male slave between eighteen and forty-five years of age and limited impressments from owners of four or more working-aged males to no more than one-third of their eligible bondmen.

37. Howard, *Black Liberation in Kentucky*, 45–55; Boman, *Lincoln's Resolute Unionist*, 220–22; Berlin et al., *Freedom: Destruction of Slavery*, 505–11; Berlin et al., *Freedom: Wartime Genesis of Free Labor*, 630–34; L[orenzo] Thomas to E[dwin] M. Stanton, December 13, 1864, *OR*, ser. 3, vol. 4, 995.

38. F. A. Richardson to A. G. Hobson, August 7, 1864; Lorenzo Thomas to Edwin M. Stanton, July 3, 1864; William H. Sidell to [Stephen G.] Burbridge, April 18, 1864; Walter S. Babcock to Col. Andrews, October 27, 1864; and Geo[rge] W. Hite to Lincoln, July 5, 1864, all in RG 393, pt. 1, ser. 2173: Letters Received, Department of Kentucky, boxes 3–4, NARA; A. J. Ewing to Margaret W. Preston, January 8, 1865, Wickliffe-Preston Family Papers, Mss. 63M349, box 56, UK; Journal of Ellen Kenton McGaughey Wallace, 1849–1865 (typescript), February 17–April 24, July 25, 1864 entries, Wallace-Starling Family Diaries, Mss. 96M07, KHS; Claim of Compensation for Enlisted Slave and accompanying forms, [1866], Slaughter Family Papers, Mss. A/S631g, folder 14, FHS; Berlin, et al., *Freedom: Destruction of Slavery*, 410, 511–12; J[oseph] Holt to E[dwin] M. Stanton, August 5, 1864, *OR*, ser. 3, vol. 4, 577–79; Robert Winn to Dear Sister, February 25, 1864, Winn-Cook Family Papers, Mss. A/W776, box 1, folder 5, FHS; *Weekly Bryan* [Ohio] *Democrat*, December 3, 1863; Rhyne, "Rehearsal for Redemption," 71; Lucas, *History of Blacks in Kentucky*, 153; Claims [Book] for Compensation, Owners of Slaves Who Were Enlisted in Federal Army [1864], Edward Henry Hobson Papers, Mss. 51M41, UK.

39. Coulter, *Civil War and Readjustment*, 177–78; J[ames] M. Fidler to Stephen G. Burbridge, June 19, 1864; Fidler to J[ames] B. Fry, June 10, 1864; and William H. Sidell to Fry, June 25, 1864; Circular, May 27, 1864; Lorenzo Thomas to Edwin M. Stanton, July 3, 1864; George P. Webster, July 14, 1864, all in RG 393, pt. 1, ser. 2173: Letters Received, Department of Kentucky, boxes 3–4, NARA; Thomas O'Reilly to William S. Rosecrans, February 12, 1864, RG 393, pt. 1, ser. 2593: Letters Received, Department of the Missouri, box 14, NARA; Thomas E. Bramlette to Abraham Lincoln, October 19, 1863; Edwin M. Stanton to Abraham Lincoln, February 8, 1864, both in Lincoln Papers; Hoskins, "The First Is with the South," 167–77; Bramlette to Stephen G. Burbridge, March 14, 1864, Stephen Gano Burbridge Correspondence, Mss. C/B, FHS; Gienapp, "Lincoln and the Border States," 39; Abraham Lincoln to the Cincinnati *Gazette*, August 5, 1863; Lincoln to Mary Todd Lincoln, August 8, 1863; Lincoln to Green Adams, August 22, 1863, all in *CWAL*, 6:366, 371–72, 401–2; Berlin et al., *Freedom: Destruction of Slavery*, 511–12, 409–12. Missouri's USCT regiments were the 18th, 62nd, 65th, 67th, and 68th.

40. Coulter, *Civil War and Readjustment*, 152; Petition of D. R. Harrington et al., February 9, 1864, RG 393, pt. 1, ser. 2593: Letters Received, Department of the Missouri, box 14, NARA; Anne E. Marshall, *Creating a Confederate Kentucky: The Lost Cause and Civil War Memory in a Border State* (Chapel Hill: University of North Carolina Press, 2010), 26–30; Howard, *Black Liberation in Kentucky*, 56–59, 63–64; *Nashville* [Tenn.] *Dispatch*, May 31, 1864; Sutherland, *A Savage Conflict*, 221; Richard A. Sears, *Camp Nelson, Kentucky: A Civil War History* (Lexington: University Press of Kentucky, 2002), 58–59, 83–86; Marion B. Lucas, "Camp Nelson, Kentucky during the Civil War: Cradle of Liberty or Refugee Death Camp?" *FHQ* 63 (October 1989): 439–445; Affidavit of John Clark, February 15, 1864; J[ames] M. Fidler to S[tephen] G. Burbridge, June 19, 1864; Fidler to J[ames] B. Fry, June 10, 1864; William H. Sidell to Fry, June 25, 1864; Sidell to J. Bates Dickson, May 27, 1864; Circular, May 27, 1864; A. G. Hobson to Fry, August 11, 1864, all in RG 393, pt. 1, ser. 2173: Letters Received, Department of Kentucky, box 4, NARA; Burbridge to S[amuel] P. Heintzelman, July 26, 1864; R[ichard] J. Oglesby to Joseph Hooker, January 16, 1865; and Lorenzo Thomas to Hooker, January 20, 1865, all in RG 393, pt. 1, ser. 3349: Letters Received, Northern Department, boxes 1, 3, NARA; [Conrad], *Journal of Elder William Conrad*, 97; Mark A. Lause, *Race and Radicalism in the Union Army* (Urbana: University of Illinois Press, 2009), 93, 112; Cornish, *Sable Arm*, 176–77; Derek W. Frisby, "'Remember Fort Pillow!': Politics, Atrocity Propaganda, and the Evolution of Hard War," in Gregory

J. W. Urwin, ed., *Black Flag Over Dixie: Racial Atrocities and Reprisals in the Civil War* (Carbondale: Southern Illinois University Press, 2005), 108n22.

41. Michael Fellman, "Emancipation in Missouri," *MHR* 83 (October 1988): 50; Rhyne, "Rehearsal for Redemption," 71, 89; Berlin et al., *Freedom: Destruction of Slavery*, 511–12, 409–12; Anonymous to Annie Cooper, April 5, [1864], Cooper-Phillips Family Papers, Mss. 66M37, UK; Siddali, *Missouri's War*, 156, 168, 213–14; George Candee to George Whipple, June 14, 24, July 11, 1864, Doc. Nos. 73530, 73540, 73555; L[ydia] H. H. Montague to Rev. Mr. Streby, June 20, 1864, Doc. No. 73533; Montague to Rev. Mr. Jocelyn, September 7, 1864, Doc. No. 73593, all in AMA, Missouri, microfilm reel 1; Joe M. Richardson, "The American Missionary Association and Black Education in Civil War Missouri," *MHR* 69 (July 1975): 437–43; Elijah Buchanan et al. to Alfred Pleasanton, July 16, 1864, RG 393, pt. 1, ser. 2593: Letters Received, Department of the Missouri, box 12, NARA; J. P. Jackson to J. Bates Dickson, August 20, 1864, RG 393, pt. 1, ser. 2173: Letters Received, Department of Kentucky, box 4, NARA; Sutherland, *A Savage Conflict*, 210–13; [Parsons], *Incidents and Experiences*, 121, 140–41; Caroline Preston to William Preston, June 26, 1864, and Mary O. Preston to William Preston, June 27, 1864, both in Wickliffe-Preston Family Papers, Mss. 63M349, box 48.1, UK; Howard, *Black Liberation in Kentucky*, 26–27; Berlin et al., *Freedom: Wartime Genesis of Free Labor*, 628–31, 642–43; Wilson Bromly and Others to Abraham Lincoln, December 7, 1864, RG 393, pt. 1, ser. 2173: Letters Received, Department of Kentucky, box 4, NARA; Affidavits of Charles Smith, S. W. Abbott, and Erwin Bell, December 14–15, 1864, and Affidavit of U. S. Goodwin, December 8, 1864, all in RG 393, pt. 1, ser. 2229: Correspondence, Affidavits, and Oaths Regarding Civilians Charged with Disloyalty, Department of Kentucky, box 1, NARA.

42. Sutherland, *A Savage Conflict*, 210–13, 220–26; W[illiam] S. Rosecrans to H[enry] W. Halleck, February 17, 1863, and response, February 18, 1863; General Orders No. 31, February 24, 1863; General Orders No. 175, March [July] 28, 1863, all in *OR*, ser. 1, vol. 23, pt. 2, 75, 84, 184–5; Thomas E. Bramlette to Abraham Lincoln, December 17, 1863; Bland Ballard to Lincoln, January 14, 1864; E. W. Hawkins et al. to Lincoln, June 5, 1864, all in Lincoln Papers; Stephen G. Burbridge to Uncle Harry, October 29, 1862; J[onathan] R. Bailey to Burbridge, January 21, 1864; Bramlette to Burbridge, March 14, 1864, all in Stephen Gano Burbridge Correspondence, Mss. C/B, FHS; Rhyne, "Rehearsal for Redemption," 80–81; J[oseph] Holt to Burbridge, October 1, 1864, John Scott Papers, Mss. 62M301, UK; James D. Hardin to the President of the United States, October 17, 1864; F. A. Richardson to A. G. Hobson, August 7, 1864, both in RG 393, pt. 1, ser. 2173: Letters Received, Department of Kentucky, box 4, NARA; Hoskins, "The First Is with the South," 202–3, 208–10; Lincoln to Edwin M. Stanton, June 18, 1864, in *CWAL*, 7:400.

43. Sutherland, *A Savage Conflict*, 210–13, 220–26; Stephen E. Jones to T. B. Fairleigh, November 29, 1864, RG 393, pt. 1, ser. 2229: Correspondence, Affidavits, and Oaths Regarding Civilians Charged with Disloyalty, Department of Kentucky, box 2, NARA; Broadside, "Public Meeting!! Order No. 107," July 28, 1864, and William A. Scott et al. to Rosecrans, undated [July 1864], both in RG 393, pt. 1, ser. 2593: Letters Received, Department of the Missouri, box 15, NARA; [Parsons], *Incidents and Experiences*, 139; Hoskins, "The First Is with the South," 182–220; Proclamation of Amnesty and Reconstruction, December 8, 1863, in *CWAL*, 7:53–56; McPherson, *Battle Cry of Freedom*, 698–99; Henry Plessner to J. C. Grier, October 24, 1864, and Affidavit of J. T. Brannon, October 18, 1864, both in RG 393, pt. 1, ser. 2229: Correspondence, Affidavits, and Oaths Regarding Civilians Charged with Disloyalty, Department of Kentucky, box 2, NARA; [Stephen G.] Burbridge to Joseph Holt, September 9, 1864; R. R. Bush to Burbridge, November 14, 1864; and C. M. Pennell to [John M.] Palmer, March 13. 1865, all in RG 393, pt. 1, ser. 2173: Letters Received, Department of Kentucky, boxes 3–5, NARA; [Lexington, Ky.] *The National Unionist*, November 8, 1864; J. Bates Dickson to N. C. McLean, November 2, 1864, *OR*, ser. 1, vol. 39, pt. 2, 612; Howard, *Black Liberation in Kentucky*, 7; General Order No. 2, August 8, 1864, David. L. Thornton Papers, Mss. 61M256, box 1, UK.

44. J[oseph] Holt to Burbridge, August 18, 1864, and enclosures; William Alexander to T[homas] B. Fairleigh, June 16, 1864; General Orders No. 16, August 13, 1864, all in RG 393, pt. 1, ser. 2173: Letters Received, Department of Kentucky, box 3, NARA; Holt to

E[dward] M. Stanton, August 5, 1864, *OR*, ser. 3, vol. 4, 577–78; H. A. Koehler to Wife, August 19, 1864, River Hutchings-Koehler Family Papers, Mss. M152, box 2, folder 1, IHSL; Journal of Ellen Kenton McGaughey Wallace, 1849–1865 (typescript), October 8, 1864, January 10, 1865 entries, Wallace-Starling Family Diaries, Mss. 96M07, KHS; Rhyne, "Rehearsal for Redemption," 72–73; Cora Owens Hume Journal (typescript), November 5, 1864 entry, vol. 2, p. 39, Mss. A/H921 Vault C, FHS; J. Proctor Knott to My Dear Mollie, November 21, 1864, Knott Collection, Mss. 53, box 1, folder 2, WKU; E. H. Ludington to Edwin M. Stanton, December 7, 1864, *OR*, ser. 1, vol. 45, pt. 2, 93–94; William H. Eany to Samuel P. Heintzelman, July 4, 1864, RG 393, pt. 1, ser. 3349: Letters Received, Northern Department, box 2, NARA.

45. D. P. Henderson to Stephen G. Burbridge, May 13, 1864, and T. S. Bell to Burbridge, May 16, 1864, both in Stephen Gano Burbridge Correspondence, Mss. C/B, FHS; J. Hawthorn et al. to Burbridge, July 17, 1864, RG 393, pt. 1, ser. 2173: Letters Received, Department of Kentucky, box 4, NARA; Rhyne, "Rehearsal for Redemption," 83, 89; John Helm to Samuel Haycraft, May 9, 1864, Haycraft Family Papers, Mss. 69M690 (microfilm), UK; Journal of Ellen Kenton McGaughey Wallace, 1849–1865 (typescript), December 11–18, 1864 entries; Annie Leslie McCarroll Starling Journal, 1860–1932, December 14, 17, 1864 entries, both in Wallace-Starling Family Diaries, Mss. 96M07, KHS; Johanna L. Underwood Diary, August 2, September 22, October 23, 1864, entries, Johanna Louisa (Underwood) Nazro Collection, Mss. SC1709, WKU. Cora Owens Hume Journal (typescript), October 23, 1864 entry, vol. 2, p. 33, Mss. A/H921 Vault C, FHS.

46. Paulina H. Stratton Diary (typescript), October 2, 1864 entry, Paulina H. Stratton Papers, Mss. C0842, SHSM. Historian Paula Baker broke new ground in American women's history by expanding the long-held notions of domesticity beyond the household and into the political realm and redefining politics as "any action, formal or informal, taken to affect the course of behavior of the government or the community." In the past two decades especially, gender has become an essential scholarly category of analysis of the American Civil War. On southern women, see LeeAnn Whites, *The Civil War as a Crisis in Gender: Augusta, Georgia, 1860–1890* (Athens: University of Georgia Press, 1995); George C. Rable, *Civil Wars: Women and the Crisis of Southern Nationalism* (Urbana: University of Illinois Press, 1989); Drew Gilpin Faust, *Mothers of Invention: Women of the Slaveholding South in the American Civil War* (Chapel Hill: University of North Carolina Press, 1996). Also see Catherine Clinton and Nina Silber, eds., *Divided Houses: Gender and the Civil War* (New York: Oxford University Press, 1992); Laura F. Edwards, *Scarlett Doesn't Live Here Anymore: Southern Women in the Civil War Era* (Urbana: University of Illinois Press, 2000). On northern women, see especially Elizabeth D. Leonard, *Yankee Women: Gender Battles in the Civil War* (New York: W. W. Norton, 1994); and Silber, *Daughters of the Union: Northern Women Fight the Civil War* (Cambridge, Mass.: Harvard University Press, 2005).

47. Whites, "Forty Shirts and a Wagonload of Wheat," 56–57; [Conrad], *Journal of Elder William Conrad*, 82; General Orders No. 38, April 13, 1863, *OR*, ser. 1, vol. 23, pt. 2, 237; Taylor, *Divided Family in Civil War America*, 112–16; Whites, "Corresponding with the Enemy," and Kristen L. Streater, "'She-Rebels' on the Supply Line: Gender Conventions in Civil War Kentucky," both in Whites and Long, eds., *Occupied Women*, 4–7, 98–100, 103–11; "Sarah Patience" (unpublished manuscript, typescript), Martha W. Dorsey Papers, Mss. SC510, folder 2, pp. 59–60, IHSL; *Pomeroy* [Ohio] *Weekly Telegraph*, May 26, 1864. On Kentucky's Confederate women, see also Kristen L. Streater, "'Not Much a Friend to Traiters No Matter How Beautiful': The Union Military and Confederate Women in Civil War Kentucky," in Kent T. Dollar, Larry Howard Whiteaker, and W. Calvin Dickinson, eds., *Sister States, Enemy States: The Civil War in Kentucky and Tennessee* (Lexington: University Press of Kentucky, 2009), 245–63; Notations of Military Commission Hearing of Laidee J. and Augusta Bagwell, February 3, 1863, RG 393, pt. 1, ser. 2620: General Orders, Department of the Missouri, 1862–1864, 2:2–4, NARA. The cited RG 393 volume consists mainly of military commissions and courts martial held in St. Louis, the largest portion of them being civilian cases heard before military commissions.

48. Coulter, *Civil War and Readjustment in Kentucky*, 152; [Hardin], *Private War of Lizzie Hardin*, 157; *Cincinnati* [Ohio] *Daily Enquirer*, May 30, 1863; Caroline Preston to William

Preston, undated [1864], and Margaret W. Preston to William Preston, July 28, August 17, 1864, all in Wickliffe-Preston Family Papers, Mss. 63M349, box 48.1, UK; Lucas, "'Indignities, Wrongs, and Outrages,'" 361.

49. E. W. Woodward to Samuel P. Heintzelman, March 15, 1864, RG 393, pt. 1, ser. 3349: Letters Received, Northern Department, box 3, NARA; Ella [Pirtle] to My Dearest Friend, October 5, 1862, Holyoke Family Letters, Mss. C/H, FHS; Cora Owens Hume Journal (typescript), January 23, 24, February 14, April 5, 30, May 10, July 4, 1863, May 10, 1864 entries, vol. 1, pp. 3, 4, 20–25, 39, 45, 49–50, 67–68, 143–44; August 8, 1864, October 4, 23, 1864 entries, vol. 2, pp. 5, 26–27, 32–33, Mss. A/H921 Vault C, FHS; Ettie Scott to Susan Preston Shelby Grigsby, August 3, 1862; W. Voorhies to Grigsby, July 17, 1864, both in Grigsby Family Papers, Mss. A/G857, folders 173, 180, FHS.

50. Fellman, *Inside War*, 195, 228; Cora Owens Hume Journal (typescript), January 24, 1863 entry, vol. 1, p. 4, Mss. A/H921 Vault C, FHS; Streater, "'She-Rebels' on the Supply Line," 88–99; [Lexington, Ky.] *The National Unionist*, November 11, 1864; [Hardin], *Private War of Lizzie Hardin*, 153; Elvira A. W. Scott Diary (typescript), folder 4, pp. 116–20, SHSM.

51. Stiles, *Jesse James*, 85; Euphrasia Pettus to Sister, May 20, 1861, Pettus Family Papers, MHS; Krug, *Mrs. Hill's Journal*, 191–93; Notations of Military Commission Hearing of Laidee J. and Augusta Bagwell, February 3, 1863, RG 393, Pt. I, Ser. 2620: General Orders, Department of the Missouri, 1862–64, vol. 2, pp. 2–4, NARA.

52. "Sarah Patience" (unpublished manuscript, typescript), Martha W. Dorsey Papers, Mss. SC510, folder 2, pp. 58–59, IHSL; Mary E. Van Meter Diary, February 25, 1863 entry, Mss. 54M98 (microfilm), UK.

53. F. A. Richardson to A. G. Hobson, August 7, 1864, RG 393, pt. 1, ser. 2173: Letters Received, Department of Kentucky, box 4, NARA; Frances Dallam Peter to Arthur and Hugh, April 23, 1864, Evans Papers, Mss. 72M15, box 7, UK; Ettie Scott to Susan Preston Shelby Grigsby, May [1862], Grigsby Family Papers, Mss. A/G857, folder 172, FHS; Harrison and Klotter, *New History of Kentucky*, 209; Cora Owens Hume Journal (typescript), August 11, September 23, 1864 entries, vol. 2, pp. 6–7, 23, Mss. A/H921 Vault C, FHS; [Hardin], *Private War of Lizzie Hardin*, 57.

54. Krug, *Mrs. Hill's Journal*, 21; Maria Holyoke to My Dear Sister, September 8, [1861], Holyoke Family Letters, Mss. C/H, FHS; "Sarah Patience" (unpublished manuscript, typescript), 50–51, Martha W. Dorsey Papers, SC510, folder 2, IHSL; Cora Owens Hume Journal, January 30, 1863 entry, Mss. A/H921, Vault C, vol. 1, p. 9, FHS; Peter Bardaglio, "On the Border: White Children and the Politics of War in Maryland," in Joan Cashin, ed., *The War Was You and Me: Civilians in the American Civil War* (Princeton, N.J.: Princeton University Press, 2002), 313–31; Krug, *Mrs. Hill's Journal*, 20–21; Nazro Diary, March 10, 1861 entry, WKU; Mary Louisa Reed to George J. Reed, March 2, 1862, Reed Family of Indiana and Kentucky Papers, LC; [Hardin], *Private War of Lizzie Hardin*, 74, 81, 93–94. For the most thorough source on children's experiences during the Civil War, see James Marten, *The Children's Civil War* (Chapel Hill: University of North Carolina Press, 1998).

55. [Conrad], *Journal of Elder William Conrad*, 93; Mary E. Tolle to A. M. Tolle, June 29, 1862, Tolle Family Letters, Mss. C/T, FHS; W[ill]. T. Hart to Susan Grigsby, January 15, 1863, Grigsby Family Papers, Mss. A/G857, folders 173–75, FHS; Samuel Matlack et al. to [Stephen G.] Burbridge, February 4, 1865, and S. Meredith to J. Bates Dickson, February 7, 1865, both in RG 393, pt. 1, ser. 2173: Letters Received, Department of Kentucky, box 5, NARA; Minutes of the Harrodsburg [Kentucky] Trustees, 1786–1875, Mss. 66M622 (microfilm), November 28, 1863, UK.

56. Faust, *This Republic of Suffering*, 6–10; Sean A. Scott, "'Earth Has No Sorrow That Heaven Cannot Cure': Northern Civilian Perspectives on Death and Eternity During the Civil War," *Journal of Social History* 41 (Summer 2008): 846–47; J. Warren Grigsby to Susan Preston Shelby Grigsby, August 7, 1862; S. H. S. Fishback to Susan Grigsby, October 2, 1862; Kate A. Pawling to Grigsby, October 19, 1862; Mary B. Scott to Dear Rebecca, October 23, 1862; S. H. S. Fishback to Grigsby, November 4, 1862; Jane Drummond to Grigsby, November 5, 1862; Travel Passes from J. T. Boyle to Grigsby, November 2, 12, 1862; Gertie Tevis to Grigsby, November 30, 1862; W. B. Nold to Grigsby, December 8, 1862; J. H. Irvin to Grigsby, December 2, 17, 1862; W[ill] T. Hart to Grigsby, February 27,

July 24, September 25, November 17, December 21, 27, 1862, January 15, 1863; Willis True to Grigsby, January 11, 1863; J. M. McFerren to Grigsby, January 17, 22, 1863; M. D. Gibson to Grigsby, January 1863; J[ohn] Warren Grigsby to Grigsby, February 11, 1863; J. H. Bell to Grigsby, April 15, 1863; Ambrose E. Burnside to Grigsby, undated [April 20, 1863]; Joseph Wheeler to William B. Hazen, with endorsements, June 9, 1863; Pass by William S. Rosecrans to Grigsby, June 19, 1863; John Mason Brown to Capt. W. P. Anderson, October 21, 1863, all in Grigsby Family Papers, Mss. A/G857, folders 173–80, FHS; Margaret W. Preston to Susan Hepburn, February 16, 1863, Preston Family Papers—Davie Collection, Mss. A/P937d, folder 35, FHS.

57. Peter Bardaglio, "The Children of Jubilee: African American Childhood in Wartime," in Clinton and Silber, eds., *Divided Houses*, 213–29; Berlin et al., *Freedom: Destruction of Slavery*, 608; R. H. Earnest to S[tephen] G. Burbridge, undated [August 1864]; J. H. Grider to J. M. Wilkins, August 1864; Cadwallader Curry to Abraham Lincoln, December 5, 1864; A. Read to Col. Carey, April 20, 1865, all in RG 393, pt. 1, ser. 2173: Letters Received, Department of Kentucky, boxes 3–5, NARA; William A. Pile to William S. Rosecrans, February 23, 1864, RG 393, pt. 1, ser. 2593: Letters Received, Department of the Missouri, box 14, NARA; Berlin et al., *Freedom: Wartime Genesis of Free Labor*, 680–85; Bigham, *On Jordan's Banks*, 76–79; Sears, *Camp Nelson*, 126–29.

58. [Cincinnati, Ohio] *The Rail Splitter*, October 17, 1860.

59. Weber, *Copperheads*, 7–9, 25, 243n35, 246n23–26; Lucien J. Barnes to C. W. Marsh, August 25, 1863, Correspondence: Letters Received, ser. 1, 1861–1875, John McAllister Schofield Papers, box 2, folder B32–52, LC; [Sullivan, Ind.] *The Stars and Stripes*, January 30, 1862. Frank Klement contended that Copperheadism's threat, whether political or paramilitary, was exaggerated by opportunistic Republicans, while Weber argues for "the danger [Copperhead] organizations posed to the government." More recently, Nicole Etcheson has largely agreed with Weber's interpretation in her study of the war in one Indiana county. See Klement, *Copperheads in the Middle West*, and Etcheson, *A Generation at War*, 100–117, 148–54, 172.

60. Alonzo Eaton to Jacob Ammen, August 2, 1863, Jacob Ammen Papers, ALPL; Oliver C. Haskell Diary, June 24, 1863 entry, Mss. SC707, folder 1, IHSL.

61. Michael F. Holt, "An Elusive Synthesis: Northern Politics during the Civil War," in James M. McPherson and William J. Cooper Jr., eds., *Writing the Civil War: The Quest to Understand* (Columbia: University of South Carolina Press, 1998), 112–13; Robert Churchill, "Liberty, Conscription, and a Party Divided: The Sons of Liberty Conspiracy, 1863–1864," *Prologue Quarterly* 30 (Winter 1998): 295–303; *Centralia* [Ill.] *Sentinel*, July 23, 1863.

62. Henry B. Carrington to [Samuel] P. Heintzelman, March 26, 1864, RG 393, pt. 1, ser. 3349: Letters Received, Northern Department, box 1, NARA; McPherson, *Battle Cry of Freedom*, 450–53; Weber, *Copperheads*, 17–19; *Centralia* [Ill.] *Sentinel*, July 16, 1863.

63. *Centralia* [Ill.] *Sentinel*, February 11, 1864; Andreasen, "As Good a Right to Pray," 4, 10n8, 162; Weber, *Copperheads*, 3; Grapeland [Will T. Hart] to Susan Preston Shelby Grigsby, February 23, 1863, Grigsby Family Papers, Mss. A/G857, folder 180, FHS; *Centralia* [Ill.] *Sentinel*, July 16, 30, August 20, 1863.

64. Hannah Throne to Jacob J. Ammen, May 23, 1863, Jacob Ammen Papers, ALPL; Klement, *Limits of Dissent*, 106; McPherson, *Battle Cry of Freedom*, 598; Call for 300,000 Volunteers, July 1, 1862, in *CWAL*, 5:296–97; Smith, *Borderland in the Civil War*, 319–22, 332–43; Nation and Towne, *Indiana's War*, 125–27; Robert B. Hanna to Dear Wife, January 29, 1863, Robert B. Hanna Family Papers, Mss. M129, IHSL; Yates and Pickering, *Richard Yates*, 173–82; D[avid] L. Phillips to William A. Seward, December 1861, quoted in Jasper William Cross, "Divided Loyalties in Southern Illinois During the Civil War" (Ph.D. dissertation, University of Illinois at Urbana-Champaign, 1939), 24, 118; Scott Owen Reed, "Military Arrests of Lawyers in Illinois during the Civil War," *Western Illinois Regional Studies* 6 (Fall 1983): 5–22 passim; Order Authorizing Arrests of Persons Discouraging Enlistments, August 8, 1862, *OR*, ser. 3, vol. 2, 321; D[ennis] A. Mahony, *The Prisoner of State* (New York: Carleton, 1863), 359–64; John A. Marshall, *American Bastille: A History of the Illegal Arrests and Imprisonment of American Citizens During the Late Civil War* (Philadelphia: T. W. Hartley, 1869), 301, 359–64, 394; Stampp, *Indiana Politics During the Civil War*, 158–85; To Erastus Corning and Others, [June 12] 1863, in *CWAL*, 6:266.

65. [Vienna, Ill.] *The Union Courier*, April 4, 1863.
66. Weber, *Copperheads*, 26–27; Smith, *No Party Now*, 71–72; Frank L. Klement, *The Copperheads in the Middle West* (Chicago: University of Chicago Press, 1960), 179; Anonymous to Annie Cooper, April 28, [1861], Cooper-Phillips Family Papers, Mss. 66M37, UK; Nancy Mann to J[ohn] Preston Mann, February 11, 1862, Mann Family Papers, Coll. 111, box 1, SIU; Robert J. Price to Dear Father, October 16, 1861, Robert J. Price Letters, Mss. SC1221, folder 2, IHSL.
67. James F. Lee to Brother Junius Fee, October 15, 1861, James Frank Fee Letters, Mss. SC567, folder 1, IHSL; "The Civil War and Activities in Union County: As related by E. R. Jinnette, late of Oakland, California; formerly of Union County, Illinois," unpublished interview (typescript), John Willis Allen Papers, Mss. 76-3-F1, box 25, SIU; Nancy Mann to J[ohn] Preston Mann, February 11, 1862, Mann Family Papers, Coll. 111, box 1, SIU.
68. Gallman, *Mastering Wartime*, 133–44; Jeanie Attie, "Warwork and the Crisis of Domesticity in the North," in Clinton and Silber, eds., *Divided Houses*, 247–59; Nation and Towne, *Indiana's War*, 88; *Centralia* [Ill.] *Sentinel*, February 25, June 30, August 25, October 6, 1864; *Pomeroy* [Ohio] *Weekly Telegraph*, May 26, 1864; Nancy C. Mann to J. Preston Mann, August 30, 1862, Mann Family Papers, Coll. 111, box 1, SIU.
69. *Centralia* [Ill.] *Sentinel*, December 3, 1863; [Hillsboro, Ill.] *Montgomery County Herald*, December 4, 1863; Scott, *Newspapers and Periodicals of Illinois*, 230; Nancy C. Mann to J[ohn] P. Mann, July 7, September 16, 1863, Mann Family Papers, Coll. 111, box 2, SIU; Weber, *Copperheads*, 128; William R. Stuckey to Dear Wife, July 28, 1863, William Roberts Stuckey Papers, Mss. M269, IHSL; Bevie W. Cain to James M. Davis, November 6, 1864, Bevie R. Cain Letters, Mss. SC2251, WKU; J. O. Guthrie to N. H. McLean, March 7, 1863, RG 393, pt. 1, ser. 3514: Letters Received, Department of the Ohio, box 3, NARA.
70. Weber, *Copperheads*, 66, 128, 141, 165; Klement, *Limits of Dissent*, 163; David B. Sachsman, S. Kittrell Rushing, and Roy Morris, *Words at War: The Civil War and American Journalism* (West Lafayette, Ind.: Purdue University Press, 2008), 184–85; Jean Baker, *Affairs of Party: The Political Culture of Northern Democrats in the Mid-Nineteenth Century* (Ithaca, N.Y.: Cornell University Press, 1983), 152–54; John A. Trimble to Robert Breckinridge, September 26, 1861, John A. Trimble Papers, Mss. 249, box 10, folder 3, OHS; Eben Perry Sturges to Dear Folks, November 17, 1862, Sturges Family Papers, Mss. 539, OHS; Howard, *Illinois*, 313–4; James E. Moss to Jacob Ammen, April 24, 1863, Jacob Ammen Papers, ALPL; George R. Clarke to George A. Thomas, September 14, 1863, RG 393, pt. 1, ser. 3514: Letters Received, Department of the Ohio, box 3, NARA; T. C. Smithton to William S. Rosecrans, July 24, 1864, RG 393, pt. 1, ser. 3349: Letters Received, Northern Department, box 2, NARA; Stampp, *Indiana Politics During the War*, 164–65; Klement, *The Copperheads in the Middle West*, 19; *Salem* [Ind.] *Union Advocate*, June 2, 1864; *Eaton* [Ohio] *Weekly Register*, August 7, 1862; C[harles] A. Dana to J. Bates Dickson, April 29, 1864, RG 393, Pt. 1, Ser. 2173: Letters Received, Department of Kentucky, 1862–1869, box 3, NARA.
71. Nation and Towne, *Indiana's War*, 179–80, 184–8; Coulter, *Civil War and Readjustment*, 185; *Centralia* [Ill.] *Sentinel*, July 30, 1863; Sterling, "Civil War Draft Resistance in Illinois," 252; A. J. Davis to D[avid] L. Phillips, February 23, 1862, *OR*, ser. 2, vol. 2, 242–44; Daniel L. Thomas, June 18, 1863, Daniel Lafayette Thomas Papers, Mss. SC1445, IHSL; Anthony Miller to Sam Beck, April 26, 1863; Jacob Ammen to Samuel R. Curtis, April 18, 1863; A[nson] Babcock to Ammen, April 23, 1863; N[apoleon] B. Buford to [Alexander S.] Asboth, April 27, 1863; Anthony Miller to Sam Beck, April 26, 1863; James J. Langdon to Ammen, April 27, 1863; C. T. Hotchkiss to Ammen, May 7, 1863; James Lovett to Ammen, May 15, 1863; J. M. Kelly to J. K. Dubois, May 22, 1863; GCW to Ammen, June 9, 1863, all in Jacob Ammen Papers, ALPL; M. L. Deal to Henry R. Strong, September 27, 1864, Henry R. Strong Papers, Mss. SC1423, folder 1, IHSL; Nancy C. Mann to J[ohn] Preston Mann, January 9, 1863, Mann Family Papers, Coll. 111, box 2, SIU.
72. D. S. Brown to J[ames] A. Wilcox, September 28, 1864, and Benjamin F. Cory to James A. Wilcox, October 7, 1864, RG 393, pt. 1., ser. 3349: Letters Received, Northern Department, boxes 1, 3, NARA; Smith, *No Party Now*, 89; Affidavit, March 21, 1863; J. F. Dunn to Jacob Ammen, April 25, 1863; R. U. Mallory and S. G. Nesbitt to Ammen, May

Notes to Pages 275–276   413

19, 1863; N[apoleon] B. Buford to [Alexander S.] Asboth, April 27, 1863, all in Jacob Ammen Papers, ALPL; Ammen to L. Richards, July 23, 1863, RG 393, pt. 1, ser. 3514: Letters Received, Department of the Ohio, box 2, NARA; Sterling, "Civil War Draft Resistance in Illinois," 255–58; Nation and Towne, *Indiana's War*, 167–69.
73. Weber, *Copperheads*, 90, 153–54; Sterling, "Civil War Draft Resistance in Illinois," 251, 258, 261; Roster of Enlisted Men from Liberty Precinct, Randolph Co, Illinois, January 18, 1865, Mann Family Papers, Coll. 111, box 2, SIU; Robert E. Sterling, "Draft Resistance in the Middle West" (Ph.D. dissertation, Northern Illinois University, 1974), 163; [Vienna, Ill.] *The Union Courier*, April 4, 1863; W[illiam] D. Dulaney to Robert L. Dulaney, December 20, 1863, Robert L. Dulaney Papers, Mss. SC428, ALPL; Joan E. Cashin, "Deserters, Civilians, and Draft Resistance in the North," in Cashin, *The War Was You and Me*, 263–64; D[avid] L. Phillips to William A. Seward, December 1861, quoted in Cross, "Divided Loyalties in Southern Illinois," 118; George R. Clarke to Jacob Ammen, September 2, 1863, Jacob Ammen Papers, ALPL; Journal of Ellen Kenton McGaughey Wallace, 1849–1865 (typescript), September 29, 1864 entry, Wallace-Starling Family Diaries, Mss. 96M07, KHS; Levine, "Draft Evasion in the North during the Civil War," 816–34. Congress repealed commutation in July 1864, so substitution was the only legal means of evading drafts. Approximate white federal enlistments among age-eligible males were Illinois: 257,281 of 436,719, or 58.9 percent; and Indiana: 194,826 of 313,607, or 62.1 percent. Both ranked above the three free states with the largest aggregate federal enlistment totals: New York, Pennsylvania, and Ohio. I derived these percentages by cross-referencing the federal enlistment totals against the census totals for white males aged fifteen to forty-nine (which groupings approximate most closely the mandated enrollment ages of eighteen to forty-five) and then subtracted the overlapping numbers in the aggregate upper and lower age groups to reduce to the closest estimate of individuals in those age groups. Kennedy, *Population of the United States in 1860*, 592–95; Dyer, *Compendium of the War of the Rebellion*, 11; http://www.civil-war.net/pages/troops_furnished_losses.html (accessed November 25, 2010).
74. Nancy C. Mann to J[ohn] Preston Mann, August 1, 1862, Mann Family Papers, Coll. 111, box 1, SIU; "The Civil War and Activities in Union County: As related by E. R. Jinnette, late of Oakland, California; formerly of Union County, Illinois," unpublished interview (typescript), John Willis Allen Papers, Mss. 76-3-F1, box 25, SIU; Mary A. Crebs to My Own Dear Husband [Daniel Crebs], August 21, 1864, Mary A. Berry [Crebs] Letters, Misc. Vol. 88, SIU.
75. Sterling, "Civil War Draft Resistance in Illinois," 252; Affidavit of Joseph B. Rowland, February 11, 1865, John Scott Papers, Mss. 62M301 (microfilm), UK; R. U. Mallory and S. G. Nesbitt to Ammen, May 19, 1863; N[apoleon] B. Buford to [Alexander S.] Asboth, April 27, 1863; James E. Moss to Jacob Ammen, April 24, 1863, all in Jacob Ammen Papers, ALPL; Sterling, "Civil War Draft Resistance in Illinois," 265–66; Klement, *Dark Lanterns*, 36–39; *Centralia* [Ill.] *Sentinel*, August 18, 1864; [Springfield] *Illinois State Journal*, February 8, 1864; T. C. Smithton to William S. Rosecrans, July 24, 1864, RG 393, pt. 1. ser. 3349: Letters Received, Northern Department, box 2, NARA. The Conscription Act required enrollment squads to present enrolled men to provost marshals.
76. Wayne County List of Sympathizers, August 1863, Merton W. Grill Papers, Mss. M120, box 1, folder 1, IHSL; Sterling, "Civil War Draft Resistance in Illinois," 256–57; Emily Wiley to Ben Wiley, April 5, 1863, John Willis Allen Papers, Mss. 76-3-Fl, SIU; Thomas Alexander Genealogy, Mss. SC9, IHSL; *Cincinnati* [Ohio] *Daily Enquirer*, April 8, 1865.
77. Thomas Sakmyster, "A Visit to the Shaker Village of White Water in 1881," *Communal Societies* 32 (2012): 75–76; Halbert E. Paine to C. H. Potter, August 21, 1864, RG 393, pt. 1, ser. 3349: Letters Received, Northern Department, boxes 1–2, NARA; Nancy C. Mann to J. Preston Mann, March 13, 1863, Mann Family Papers, Coll. 111, box 2, SIU; J. W. Blackburn et al. to Samuel Heintzelman, July 8, 1864, RG 393, pt. 1, ser. 3349: Letters Received, Northern Department, box 1, NARA; E. S. Jones to [Milo S.] Hascall, April 3, 1863; J. A. Poller to Ambrose E. Burnside, April 7, 1863; Thomas J. McKean to H. Z. Curtis, April 8, 1863; L. Nowland to Jacob Ammen, April 23, 1863; W. Scott Ketchum to Jacob Ammen, April 10, 1863; Alonzo Eaton to Ammen, April 17, 1863; S[amuel] R.

Curtis to Ammen, April 21, 1863; J. C. Scott et al. to Ambrose E. Burnside, April 23, 1863; D. P. Dyer to Curtis, May 8, 1863; Affidavit of James Lovett, May 15, 1863; Joshua Ricketts to Ammen, May 18, 1863; "G. C. W." to Ammen, June 9, 1863, all in Jacob Ammen Papers, ALPL; J. W. Finnie to S. E. Jones, January 19, 1865, RG 393, pt. 1, ser. 2173: Letters Received, Department of Kentucky, 1862–1869, box 5, NARA.

78. *Hamilton* [Ohio] *Telegraph*, undated [January 1865]; *Pomeroy* [Ohio] *Weekly Telegraph*, May 26, 1864; Thomas A. Cobb to Dear Father, May 12, 1863, Thomas A. Cobb Letters, Mss. SC251, IHSL; Taylor, *Divided Family in Civil War America*, 108–109; Statement of Frank Howe, August 15, 1864, RG 393, pt. 1, ser. 2229: Correspondence, Affidavits, Oaths Regarding Civilians Charged with Disloyalty, Department of Kentucky, box 1, NARA; Jon G. Taylor to Robert Neil, September 21, 1863, Robert Neil Family Papers, Mss. 259, OHS.

79. J. F. Dunn to Jacob Ammen, April 25, 1863, and Campbell Young to Ammen, June 4, 1863, both in Jacob Ammen Papers, ALPL; Alfred M. Mozley to My Dear Uncle, August 4, 1863, Alfred M. Mozley Letters, Mss. VFM 1642, SIU; Charles W. Starr to W. C. Starr, May 3, 1863, W. C. Starr Papers, Mss. SC1400, folder 4, IHSL.

80. Nation and Towne, *Indiana's War*, 177; *Carbondale* [Ill.] *Times*, quoted in [Springfield, Ill.] *Illinois State Register*, December 7, 1861; Oliver C. Haskell Diary, February 9, 1863 entry, Mss. SC707, folder 1, IHSL; J[ohn] Preston Mann to Nancy C. Mann, November 17, 1861; Nancy C. Mann to J. Preston Mann, February 11, August 1, 1862, all in Mann Family Papers, Coll. 111, box 1, SIU; Henry Carrington to C. H. Potter, July 15, 1864, RG 393, pt. 1, ser. 3349: Letters Received, Northern Department, box 1, NARA.

81. Whites, *Gender Matters*, 26–27, 43–46, 68–69; Eaton [Ohio] *Democratic Press*, June 25, 1863, in Dee, *Ohio's War*, 152–53; J. M. Kelly to J. K. Dubois, May 22, 1863, Jacob Ammen Papers, ALPL.

82. William Houghton to Walter Houghton, July 26, 1862, William Houghton Papers, Mss. M147, box 1, folder 5, IHSL; Cross, "Divided Loyalties in Southern Illinois," 134–43; Nation and Towne, *Indiana's War*, 177–78, 185–88; Mary A. Crebs to My Own Dear Husband, July 11, August 14, 1864, Mary A. Berry [Crebs] Letters, Misc. Vol. 88, SIU; Nancy C. Mann to J[ohn] Preston Mann, July 7, March 13, September 16, and undated, 1863, January 25, 1864, Mann Family Papers, Coll. 111, boxes 1–2, SIU; Mary A. Crebs to My Own Dear Husband [Daniel Crebs], November 16, 1863, Mary A. Berry [Crebs] Letters, Misc. Vol. 88, SIU; Leo D. Sirrania to Friend Monroe, November 22, 1863, Amos C. Weaver Papers, Mss. SC1545, folder 2, IHSL; Jeptha V. King to Dear Uncle, February 7, 1863, Jeptha King Letters, Mss. SC916, IHSL.

83. Daniel L. Thomas, June 18, 1863, Daniel Lafayette Thomas Papers, Mss. SC1445, IHSL; *Corydon* [Ind.] *Weekly Democrat*, July 14, 1863.

84. [Cincinnati, Ohio] *American Republic*, December 6, 1863; Weber, *Copperheads*, 114–16; Paludan, *A People's Contest*, 154–56; Harrison and Klotter, *New History of Kentucky*, 207; Parrish, *History of Missouri*, 77–81; Charles Calahan to Samuel B. Heintzelman, May 29, 1864, and W. H. Riley to James B. Fry, September 28, 1864, both in RG 393, pt. 1., ser. 3349: Letters Received, Northern Department, box 1, NARA; *Centralia* [Ill.] *Sentinel*, June 4, 1863, February 11, March 24, 31, April 7, 21, 28, May 5, 12, 19, July 14, 1864. For an edited version of Fletcher's articles, see Christopher Phillips, "Travels in Egypt: Eyewitness to the Civil War in Illinois's 'Butternut' Region," *OVH* 8 (Summer 2008): 23–47.

85. Jaspin, *Buried in the Bitter Waters*, 16–29; Bigham, *On Jordan's Banks*, 92–93, 94–95.

86. Sidney Kaplan, "The Miscegenation Issue in the Election of 1864," *Journal of Negro History* 34 (July 1949): 274–343 passim; Smith, *No Party Now*, 117–30; McPherson, *Battle Cry of Freedom*, 789–91; [McConnelsville, Ohio] *Valley Democrat*, May 25, 1864; [McKnight], *Do They Miss Me at Home?*, 72; McArthur [Ohio] *Register*, June 2, 1864.

87. [Parsons], *Incidents and Experiences*, 98–99; Anthony Miller to Sam Beck, April 26, 1863; G. C. W. to Jacob Ammen, June 9, 1863; B. Pilkington to N[apoleon]. B. Buford, June 16, 1863; J. W. Woodruff to S. R. Holmes, July 15, 1864, all in Jacob Ammen Papers, ALPL; Mary A. Berry to My Own Dear Husband [Daniel Berry], July 11, August 14, October 2, November 10, 1864, Mary A. Berry [Crebs] Letters, Misc. Vol. 88, SIU; M. D. White to Lazarus Noble, June 23, 1863, in Nation and Towne, *Indiana's War*, 173; [Newport, Ky.]

The Free South, October 26, 1864; Hicken, *Illinois in the Civil War*, 263; *Centralia* [Ill.] *Sentinel*, June 30, August 18, 1864; Sampson, "Pretty Damned Warm Times," 111 and passim; Henry Carrington to Carroll H. Potter, March 30, 1864, and Hiram Sandford to Samuel B. Heintzelman, September 6, 1864, both in RG 393, pt. 1., ser. 3349: Letters Received, Northern Department, boxes 1–2, NARA; Stephen E. Towne, "'Such Conduct Must Be Put Down,': The Military Arrest of Judge Charles H. Constable during the Civil War," *Journal of Illinois History* 9 (June 2006): 57; Cole, *Era of the Civil War*, 307–8.

88. Weber, *Copperheads*, 196–200; "Memorandum Concerning His Probable Failure of Re-election," *CWAL*, 7:514–15n1; *Executive Documents. Messages and Annual Reports for 1864 made to the 56th General Assembly of Ohio* (Columbus: State Printer, 1865), 679; *Proceedings and Resolutions of the Indiana Soldiers in the "Department of the Cumberland." To the Indiana Legislature* (Indianapolis: Indianapolis Journal, 1863), 3 and passim; Circulars, October 7, 27, 1864, and S. A. Lathrop to C. H. Potter, November 11, 1864, all in RG 393, pt. 1, ser. 2249: Letters Received, Northern Department, boxes 1–2, NARA; Fred Previts, "Battlefield Ballots: The 1864 Presidential Election," *Timeline* 26 (October–December 2009): 38–54 passim; *Centralia* [Ill.] *Sentinel*, October 13, 20, 1864.

89. Mark A. Lause, *Price's Lost Campaign: The 1864 Invasion of Missouri* (Columbia: University of Missouri Press, 2011), 17, 37, 57, 69.

90. Lause, *Price's Lost Campaign*, 116, 124–26, 135, 140, 179, 185; Kyle S. Sinisi, *The Last Hurrah: Sterling Price's Missouri Expedition of 1864* (Lanham, Md.: Rowman and Littlefield, 2015), 272–89.

91. Weber, *Copperheads*, 196–200; Smith, *No Party Now*, 95–100; John Cook to C. H. Potter, November 8, 1864, RG 393, pt. 1, ser. 2249: Letters Received, Northern Department, box 1, NARA; James M. McPherson, *Ordeal by Fire* (New York: Knopf, 1982), 457–58; Dixon Wecter, "The Soldier and the Ballot," *Huntington Library Quarterly* 7 (August 1944): 397–400; Benjamin P. Thomas and Harold M. Hyman, *Stanton: The Life and Times of Lincoln's Secretary of War* (New York: Alfred A. Knopf, 1962), 331–34; Howard, *Illinois*, 305–12; Moses, *Illinois, Historical and Statistical*, 2:1208–11; Cole, *Centennial History of Illinois*, 261–327; *BDAC*, 273–74, 277, 282–83, 286, 291–92, 295.

92. McPherson, *Battle Cry of Freedom*, 756–58, 784–88; Gienapp, "Lincoln and the Border States," 19–20; John B. Helm to Samuel Haycraft, October 7, 1864, Haycraft Family Papers, Mss. 69M690 (microfilm), UK; John B. Helm to Samuel Haycraft, October 7, 1864, Haycraft Family Papers, Mss. 69M690 (microfilm), UK; James D. Hardin to the President of the United States, October 17, 1864; RG 393, pt. 1, ser. 2173: Letters Received, Department of Kentucky, box 4, NARA.

93. Second Inaugural Address, March 4, 1865, and Abraham Lincoln to Thomas C. Fletcher, February 20, 1865, and response, both in *CWAL*, 8:332–33, 294, 297, 308, 319–20n1; Stiles, *Jesse James*, 175; Coulter, *Civil War and Readjustment*, 286.

94. Merrill D. Peterson, *Lincoln in American Memory* (New York: Oxford University Press, 1994), 14–22; *Athens* [Ohio] *Messenger*, April 21, 1865; *Delaware* [Ohio] *Gazette*, April 21, 1865; [West Union, Ohio] *The Scion*, April 21, 1865; Jones, *"Black Jack"*, 264.

A River Between Them

1. *The Ripley* [Ohio] *Bee*, July 12, 1876; *Cincinnati* [Ohio] *Daily Enquirer*, July 9, 10, 12, 1876; *Cincinnati* [Ohio] *Commercial*, July 9, 12, 14, 1876; *Cincinnati* [Ohio] *Daily Gazette*, July 10, 1876; Ninth U.S. Census, 1870, Population Schedule, Kenton County, Kentucky, and Clermont County, Ohio. The account of the incident in this and following paragraphs is taken from these newspaper sources.
2. Ninth U.S. Census, 1870, Population Schedules, Clermont County, Ohio.
3. Seventh and Eighth U.S. Censuses, 1850 and 1860, Population Schedule, Calloway and Kenton County, Kentucky.
4. Cheryl Crowell, *New Richmond: Images of America* (Charleston, SC: Arcadia Publishing, 2012), 40; Bethany Richter Pollitt, "The Antislavery Movement in Clermont County" (M.A. thesis, Wright State University, 2012), 54.

5. Z. S. Stroube to Horatio G. Wright, September 29, 1862, and William B. Sipes to Horatio G. Wright, December 18, 1862, and enclosures, all in RG 393, pt. 1, ser. 3514: Letters Received, Department of the Ohio, box 2, NARA; Eric Foner, *Reconstruction: America's Unfinished Revolution, 1863-1877* (New York: Harper and Row, 1988), 571-73.

Chapter 8: Southern Cross, North Star: The Politics of Irreconciliation

1. Rhyne, "Rehearsal for Redemption," 13-17; Downs, *After Appomattox*, 4-6.
2. Fellman, "Emancipation in Missouri," 50-56; Clinton B. Fisk to James E. Yeatman, March 25, 1865, *OR*, ser. 1, vol. 48, pt. 1, 1257.
3. Foner, *Reconstruction*, 37-50; Beale, *Diary of Edward Bates*, 271; Parrish, *History of Missouri*, 102-18; Parrish, *Missouri Under Radical Rule*, 3-4, 14-19; Jessica Ann Cannon, "Lincoln's Divided Backyard: Maryland in the Civil War Era" (Ph.D. dissertation, Rice University, 2009), 236.
4. Geiger, *Financial Fraud*, 132; Foner, *Reconstruction*, 42; McKerley, "Citizens and Strangers," 79-85; Peterson, *Freedom and Franchise*, 106-34; Clinton B. Fisk to Abraham Lincoln, October 24, 1863, Correspondence: Letters Received, ser. 1, 1861-1875, John McAllister Schofield Papers, box 4, folder F1-20, LC; Parrish, *History of Missouri*, 116-26.
5. Coulter, *Civil War and Readjustment*, 274-76, 285-86; Parrish, *History of Missouri*, 147-69; Gilbert Gordon to Neal M. Gordon, July 12, 1865, Gordon Family Papers, Mss. 51M40, box 4, UK; [Hardin], *Private War of Lizzie Hardin*, 280; F. F. Dobory to E. B. Harlan, August 23, 1865; Edmund Bartlett to [John M.] Palmer, August 30, 1865; James G. Haswell to Palmer, May 10, 1865; and James M. Fidler to Harlan, September 27, 1865, all in RG 393, pt. 1, ser. 2173: Letters Received, Department of Kentucky, 1862-69, box 5, NARA. On Confederados, see Cyrus B. Dawsey and James M. Dawsey, eds., *The Confederados: Old South Immigrants in Brazil* (Tuscaloosa: University of Alabama Press, 1995) and Eugene C. Harter, *The Lost Colony of the Confederacy* (Oxford: University Press of Mississippi, 1985).
6. Coulter, *Civil War and Readjustment*, 259-70, 289; William Moody Pratt Diaries, July 8, 1867 entry, vol. 2, Mss. 46M79, UK; Orlando Brown Sr. to Orlando Brown Jr., December 20, 1865, Orlando Brown Papers, Mss. A/B879, folder 25, FHS; [Elizabethtown, Ky.] Severn's Valley Baptist Church Minutes, 1788-1884, July 26, 1866 entry, Mss. M117 (microfilm), UK; Bigham, *On Jordan's Banks*, 78-79, 98-100; Patrick A. Lewis, "The Democratic Partisan Militia and the Black Peril: The Kentucky Militia, Racial Violence, and the Fifteenth Amendment, 1870-1873," *CWH* 56 (June 2010): 152; Siddali, *Missouri's War*, 232-36; McKerley, "Citizens and Strangers," 85-100; Gary R. Kremer, *James Milton Turner and the Promise of America: The Public Life of a Post-Civil War Black Leader* (Columbia: University of Missouri Press, 1991), 18-20.
7. John M. Palmer to Dear Wife, March 19, September 26, October 23, 1865, all in John M. Palmer Papers, ALPL; John McAuley Palmer, *Personal Recollections of John M. Palmer: The Story of an Earnest Life* (Cincinnati: The Robert Clarke, 1901), 223-43; Bigham, *On Jordan's Banks*, 77; Coulter, *Civil War and Readjustment*, 260-61; Harrison, *Civil War in Kentucky*, 78-79; Rhyne, "Rehearsal for Redemption," 98-99, 101-2; John M. Palmer to Dear Wife, October 10, December 3, 1865; Palmer to John Mayo Palmer, October 10, 1865, all in John M. Palmer Papers, ALPL; Resolution No. 25, March 11, 1865; W. J. Gage to Palmer, April 25, 1865; James R. Fry to Palmer, June 1, 1865; Philip Hayes to James S. Brisbin, July 27, 1865, all in RG 393, pt. 1, ser. 2173: Letters Received, Department of Kentucky, 1862-1869, box 5, NARA; David C. Phillips to W. K. White, August 25, 1865, D. C. Phillips Letter, KHS. The War Department suspended all enlistment of black troops on June 1, 1865. Phillips is the author's direct paternal ancestor.
8. Rhyne, "Rehearsal for Redemption," 9-10, 107-16; George C. Wright, *Racial Violence in Kentucky, 1865-1940: Lynchings, Mob Rule, and "Legal Lynchings"* (Baton Rouge: Louisiana State University Press, 1990), 2; Minutes of the Harrodsburg [Kentucky] Trustees, 1786-1875, August 26, 28, 1865 entries, Mss. 66M622 (microfilm), UK; John Helm to Samuel Haycraft, January 16, 1868, Haycraft Family Papers, Mss. 69M690 (microfilm), UK; R. D. Baker to [John M.] Palmer, March 2, 1865; A. H. Bowen to Palmer, September 25, 1865;

Notes to Pages 295–297   417

Henry Sommers to W. F. Drum, November 4, 1867; Jonas R. King to Drum, January 20, June 13, 1867, October 13, 1868; W. R. Maize to Drum, October 18, 1868; J. W. Caldwell to George H. Thomas, June 16, 1868; J. W. Crawford to Drum, September 4, 1868, all in RG 393, pt. 1, ser. 2173: Letters Received, Department of Kentucky, boxes 5–6, NARA; *Madison* [Ind.] *Courier*, October 18, 1865.

9. Harrison, *Civil War in Kentucky*, 78; Coulter, *Civil War and Readjustment*, 213–14, 258–59, 264–70; F. F. Dobory to E. B. Harlan, August 23, 1865, and J. R. Bailey, T. C. Calvert, et al., June 12, 1865, both in RG 393, pt. 1, ser. 2173: Letters Received, Department of Kentucky, 1862–69, box 5, NARA; Marshall, *Creating a Confederate Kentucky*, 35; [Parsons], *Incidents and Experiences*, 143–44.

10. A. W. Blair to D. S. Goodloe, August 8, 1865; J. J. Miller to Anonymous, July 7, 1865; J. R. Bailey, T. C. Calvert, et al. to W. S. Babcock, June 12, 1865; and James M. Fidler to E. B. Harlan, September 27, 1865, all in RG 393, pt. 1, ser. 2173: Letters Received, Department of Kentucky, 1862–1869, box 5, NARA; David C. Phillips to W. K. White, August 25, 1865, D. C. Phillips Letter, KHS; James M. Fidler to E. B. Harlan, September 27, 1865; J. J. Miller to Anonymous, July 7, 1865; A. W. Blair to D. S. Goodloe, August 8, 1865; J. R. Bailey, T. C. Calvert, et al. to W. S. Babcock, June 12, 1865; L. Hussey to N. P. Forster, August 7, 1865; John H. King to [John M.] Palmer, August 19, 1865; H. S. Park to Palmer, August 8, 1865; A. N. Davis to Palmer, August 8, 1865; Isaac Heaton to Palmer, July 21, 1865; A. W. Blair to D. S. Goodloe, August 8, 1865; J[ames] M. Fidler to John M. Palmer, October 25, 1865; Fidler to W[illiam] H. Sidell, October 26, 1865; Fidler to S. G. Gray, October 20, 1865, all in RG 393, pt. 1, ser. 2173: Letters Received, Department of Kentucky, 1862–1869, box 5, NARA; Wright, *Racial Violence in Kentucky*, 20–22; Marshall, *Creating a Confederate Kentucky*, 38–39, 48–49.

11. Astor, *Rebels on the Border*, 188–94; R. D. Baker to [John M.] Palmer, March 2, 1865; J. A. Murray to N. S. Andrews, October 30, 1865; J. W. Read to E. B. Harlan, July 31, 1865; A. W. Blair to D. S. Goodloe, August 8, 1865; D. S. Goodloe to Palmer, August 10, 1865; Ira Delano to Palmer, September 29, 1865; M. D. Rodocker to John M. Palmer, August 12, 1865; A. Smith to Anonymous, December 29, 1865; Samuel Martin to Charles F. Johnson, July 11, 1867, and enclosures, July 11, 1867; C. T. Delling to Abraham Lincoln, February 13, 1865; J. W. Crawford to William F. Drum, April 27, 1868, all in RG 393, pt. I, ser. 2173: Letters Received, Department of Kentucky, 1862–1869, boxes 5–6, NARA; Affidavit of James Edwards, July 3, 1865, RG 393, pt. 1, ser. 2229: Correspondence, Affidavits, and Oaths Regarding Civilians Charged with Disloyalty, Department of Kentucky, box 1, NARA; Aaron Astor, "The Lexington *Weekly Caucasian*: White Supremacist Political Discourse in post-Civil War Western Missouri," in Jonathan H. Earle and Diane Mutti Burke, eds., *Bleeding Kansas, Bleeding Missouri: The Long Civil War on the Western Border* (Lawrence: University Press of Kansas, 2013), 189–203; Lewis, "The Democratic Partisan Militia and the Black Peril," 151; *Born in Slavery*, vol. 12, *Ohio Narratives*, 21.

12. M. L. Rice to F. H. Burbower, May 29, 1865; Petition of G. A. Armstrong et al., May 17, 1865; D. S. Goodloe to Palmer, August 25, 1865; C. M. Pennell to Palmer, March 13, 1865; William Falck to Drum, November 14, 1868, all in RG 393, pt. 1, ser. 2173: Letters Received, Department of Kentucky, boxes 5–6, NARA; Marshall, *Creating a Confederate Kentucky*, 66, 71–2; Langstaff, *Life and Times of Quigley*, 81; *Madison* [Ind.] *Courier*, October 18, 1865; Parrish, *History of Missouri*, 151–55; *Boonville* [Mo.] *Eagle*, October 21, 1865; Lewis, "The Democratic Partisan Militia and the Black Peril," 146–47; John M. Palmer to J. D. Cole, August 4, 1865; J. R. Bailey, T. C. Calvert, et al. to W. S. Babcock, June 12, 1865; Report of W. H. Beebe, August 11, 1865; Charles Chase, James M. Ogden, W. C. Simpson to Brisban, June 5, 1865; M. Norton to W. F. Drum, March 18, 1867; J. W. Cardwell to William H. Edelin, November 11, 1867; Petition of James S. McHatton et al., undated, all in RG 393, pt. 1, ser. 2173: Letters Received, Department of Kentucky, 1862–1869, boxes 5–6, NARA; George Hancock to William Preston, October 26, 1865, Wickliffe-Preston Family Papers, box 56, UK; Circular, "To All Who Were Rebels, Traitors, Sympathizers and Their Friends During the War," undated, Civil War Collection, MHS; [Union, Mo.] *Franklin County Progress*, March 10, 1866; Castel, *General Sterling Price*, 272–85; Robert Winn to Dear Sister, March 10, 1866, Winn-Cook Papers, Mss. A/W776, box 2, folder 13, FHS.

13. Wright, *Racial Violence in Kentucky*, 20-21 and passim; [Cape Girardeau, Mo.] *Southeast Radical*, March 9, 1866; Report of the Proceedings of Judge Lynch at or near Lebanon, Kentucky, December 14, 1866; T. E. Hall to E. M. Harlan, June 4, 1865; G. W. Gwin to [John M.] Palmer, July 7, 1865; F. B. Hancock to Palmer, July 12, 1865, and W. Davenport to John M. Palmer, September 8, 1865; J. W. Crawford to William F. Drum, April 27, 1868; James D. Beatis to Capt. Phil, June 25, 1865; R. C. Howard to W. F. Drum, April 17, 1868; Jonas R. King to Drum, October 13, 1868, all in RG 393, pt. 1, ser. 2173: Letters Received, Department of Kentucky, boxes 5-6, NARA; Astor, *Rebels on the Border*, 2-3; Marshall, *Creating a Confederate Kentucky*, 34, 55-66; [Parsons], *Incidents and Experiences*, 143-46; Parrish, *History of Missouri*, 152-54; McKerley, "Citizens and Strangers," 99; *Born in Slavery: Slave Narratives from the Federal Writers' Project, 1936-1938*, vol. 7, *Kentucky Narratives*, p. 93; Rhyne, "Rehearsal for Redemption," 108-9, 115, 162-89; [Little Rock] *Daily Arkansas Gazette*, July 29, 1873; Stiles, *Jesse James*, 179-81; William Moody Pratt Diaries, April 10, 1865 entry, vol. 3, Mss. 46M79, UK; Coulter, *Civil War and Readjustment in Kentucky*, 268, 286; W. A. Low, "The Freedmen's Bureau in the Border States," in Richard O. Curry, ed., *Radicalism, Racism, and Party Realignment: The Border States during Reconstruction* (Baltimore: Johns Hopkins University Press, 1969), 254-56; Bigham, *On Jordan's Banks*, 105-106.

14. Will L. Dulaney to Robert L. Dulaney, undated [1865], Robert L. Dulaney Papers, Mss. SC 428, ALPL; Rhyne, "Rehearsal for Redemption," 162-89; Marshall, *Creating a Confederate Kentucky*, 63-64, 65-67; Przybyszewski, *Republic According to Harlan*, 39-41; R. D. Baker to [John M.] Palmer, March 2, 1865; J. A. Murray to N. S. Andrews, October 30, 1865; A. W. Blair to D. S. Goodloe, August 8, 1865; J. R. Bailey, T. C. Calvert, et al. to W. S. Babcock, June 12, 1865; J. S. Catten to Ben[jamin] P. Runkle, September 4, 1868; Alfred S. Hough to George W. Thomas, June 16, 1868, all in RG 393, pt. 1, ser. 2173: Letters Received, Department of Kentucky, boxes 5-6, NARA.

15. Petroleum V. Nasby [David Ross Locke], *The Nasby Letters, Being the Original Nasby Letters as Written During His Lifetime* (Toledo: Toledo Blade, 1893), 3-30, 36.

16. Jon Grinspan, "'Sorrowfully Amusing': The Popular Comedy of the Civil War," *JCWE* (September 2011): 313-20, 328-29; Havighurst, *Ohio*, 102-3; John Killits, *Toledo and Lucas, Ohio, 1623-1923* (Toledo: S. J. Clarke Publishing, 1923), 2:491.

17. Nasby [Locke], *Nasby Letters*, 5-9, 44-46; Petroleum V. Nasby [David Ross Locke], *Ekkoes from Kentucky* (Boston: Lee and Shepard, 1868), 13-20, 230-37, 247, 251-52, 261, 271-81, 288-96 and passim; Marshall, *Creating a Confederate Kentucky*, 49-50.

18. Robert Gilmore, "Ozarks Editors: Guardians and Gadflies—Politicians and Promoters—Preachers and Teachers," *Ozarks Watch* 7 (Summer 1993): 10; Astor, *Rebels on the Border*, 183; Coulter, *Civil War and Readjustment in Kentucky*, 287-311; Marshall, *Creating a Confederate Kentucky*, 48-49. The *Unterrified Democrat* is among the longest-running newspapers published in Missouri.

19. Astor, "Lexington *Weekly Caucasian*," 19-20; Owensboro [Ky.] *Monitor*, May 1, 1867; [Chillicothe, Ohio] *Scioto Gazette*, May 7, 1867; Lewis Saum, "Donan and the *Caucasian*," *MHR* 63 (July 1969): 419-50; James S. Hughes, "Lexington, Missouri, and the Aftermath of Slavery, 1861-1870," *MHR* 75 (October 1980): 51-63; [Lexington, Mo.] *Weekly Caucasian*, June 27, 1866; D. S. Goodloe to Palmer, August 25, 1865, RG 393, pt. 1, ser. 2173: Letters Received, Department of Kentucky, box 5, NARA; [St. Joseph] *Missouri Vindicator*, May 23, 1868.

20. Woodward, *Reunion and Reaction*, 245; [Newport, Ky.] *The Free South*, February 1, 1865; Parrish, *History of Missouri*, 93, 234-57, 258-59; Peterson, *Freedom and Franchise*, 130-44, 226-31; *Appendix to the Congressional Globe*, 38th Cong., 1st Sess., 48-49; Parrish, *Frank Blair*, 231-45; Parrish, *Missouri Under Radical Rule*, 288-326; Stiles, *Jesse James*, 202-3.

21. Peterson, *Freedom and Franchise*, 189; Lawrence O. Christensen and Gary R. Kremer, *A History of Missouri*, vol. 4, *1875 to 1919* (Columbia: University of Missouri Press, 1997), 1-3; Parrish, *History of Missouri*, 43n, 48, 290-92; Parrish, *Missouri under Radical Rule*, 324-26; Phillips, *Missouri's Confederate*, 288-91.

22. M. Jeff Thompson to George D. Prentice, June 16, 1867, Meriwether Jeff Thompson Papers, Mss. 1030, folder 1, SHSM; Thomas C. Reynolds to Jefferson Davis, November 13, 1880,

Notes to Pages 302–306   419

Thomas C. Reynolds Papers, MHS; Parrish, *Missouri Under Radical Rule*, 324–25; Christensen and Kremer, *History of Missouri*, 16–17.

23. W. Sherman Jackson, "Emancipation, Negrophobia, and Civil War Politics in Ohio," *Journal of Negro History* 65 (July 1980): 253–58; Voegeli, *Free But Not Equal*, 169–70; Bigham, *On Jordan's Banks*, 78–79, 98–100; First Baptist Church (Paris, Ky.) Minutes, 1818–1945, August 1, 1863, August 1, 1865, August 14, 1866 entries, pp. 56, 66, Mss. 78M812 (microfilm), UK; *Cincinnati* [Ohio] *Daily Enquirer*, March 9, 1865; [Cincinnati, Ohio] *Colored Citizen*, May 19, 1866; [Cincinnati, Ohio] *Catholic Telegraph*, June 28, 1865. Between 1860 and 1870, the black populations of Illinois, Indiana, and Ohio increased 277 percent, 115 percent, and 72 percent, respectively.

24. Jackson, "Emancipation, Negrophobia, and Civil War Politics in Ohio," 251; J. E. Cornelius to B. F. Smith, August 8, 1865; Richard J. Oglesby to E. O. C. Ord, August 25, 1865; Samuel C. Gold to O. H. Hart, November 14, 1865; and James Runcie et al. to Ord, September 6, 1865, all in RG 393, pt. 1, ser. 3349: Letters Received, Northern Department, box 4, NARA; Nation and Towne, *Indiana's War*, 204–206; *Connersville* [Ind.] *Weekly Times*, October 26, 1865; Daniel Berry to Mary A. Berry, May 15, 1865, in [Daniel Berry], *Letters Written by Dr. Daniel Berry to Mary Crebs Berry During the Civil War*, ed. Harriet B. Vaught (Carmi, Ill.: By the author, 1976), 282; [Cincinnati, Ohio] *Colored Citizen*, May 19, 1866.

25. [Chillicothe, Ohio] *Scioto Gazette*, May 14, 1867; *Madison* [Ind.] *Courier*, October 18, 1865; Marshall, *Creating a Confederate Kentucky*, 117–22; Steven Hahn, *A Nation Under Our Feet: Black Political Struggles in the Rural South from Slavery to the Great Migration* (Cambridge, Mass.: Belknap Press, 2003), 118.

26. William Dudley Foulke, *Life of Oliver P. Morton: Including His Important Speeches*, 2 vols. (Indianapolis and Kansas City: Bowen-Merrill, 1899), 1: 467–78; A. James Fuller, *Oliver P. Morton and the Politics of the Civil War and Reconstruction* (Kent, Ohio: Kent State University Press, 2016), ch. 8; Mark Wahlgren Summers, *The Ordeal of the Reunion: A New History of Reconstruction* (Chapel Hill: University of North Carolina Press, 2014), 17–25 and passim. My thanks to Jim Fuller for sharing his research on Morton.

27. Stanley P. Hirshson, *Farewell to the Bloody Shirt: Northern Republicans and the Southern Negro, 1877–1893* (Bloomington: Indiana University Press, 1962; reprint Chicago: Quadrangle Books, 1968), 22–33.

28. Gallagher, *Union War*, 23–24; Stephen Budiansky, *The Bloody Shirt: Terror After the Civil War* (New York: Plume, 2009), 2–3; Mark A. Summers, *Rum, Romanism, and Rebellion: The Making of a President, 1884* (Chapel Hill: University of North Carolina Press, 2000), 40–44.

29. Howard, *Illinois*, 327–28; Jones, *"Black Jack"*, 269; [Society of the Army of the Tennessee], *Report of the Proceedings of the Society of the Army of the Tennessee at the First Annual Meeting Held at Cincinnati, Ohio, November 14th and 15th 1866* (Cincinnati: The Society, 1866–1867), passim; Anne Sarah Rubin, "'An Organization of Dudes': The Society of the Army of the Tennessee Remembers Sherman's March" (paper presented at the Organization of American Historians Annual Meeting, Houston, Texas, March 23, 2011), with permission of the author; Mary R. Dearing, *Veterans in Politics: The Story of the G.A.R.* (Westport, Ct.: Greenwood Press, 1974), 70, 80–112; Neely, *Border Between Them*, 242; David W. Blight, *Race and Reunion: The Civil War in American Memory* (Cambridge, Mass.: Belknap Press of Harvard University Press, 2001), 65–72; Tim Pinnick, "African American Veterans in the Grand Army of the Republic," NGS Magazine 35 (July–September 2009): 28–32; Thornbrough, *Indiana in the Civil War Era*, 234–35.

30. Heather Cox Richardson, *The Death of Reconstruction: Race, Labor, and Politics in the Post–Civil War North, 1865–1901* (Cambridge, Mass.: Harvard University Press, 2001), xv; Summers, *Rum, Romanism, and Rebellion*, 42; [Chillicothe, Ohio] *Scioto Gazette*, March 26, April 16, May 7, 1867; Jensen, *Illinois*, 71.

31. Stewart McConnell, *Glorious Contentment: The Grand Army of the Republic, 1865–1900* (Chapel Hill: University of North Carolina Press, 1992), 11–12; Jones, *"Black Jack"*, 257–59; Jensen, *Illinois*, 71–73; Nation and Towne, *Indiana's War*, 212–13; [Evansville, Ind.] *Daily Courier*, November 14, 1865; *Xenia* [Ohio] *Torch-Light*, January 2, 1867; *Ripley* [Ohio] *Bee*, March 6, 1867; [Ripley, Ohio] *Independent Press*, March 6, 1868; *Dayton*

[Ohio] *Daily Journal*, April 1, 1870; [Hamilton, Ohio] *Daily Telegraph*, June 1, 8, 1865; [Golconda, Ill.] *Pope County Transcript*, December 26, 1865.

32. Foner, *Reconstruction*, 264–65, 471; Eric L. McKitrick, *Andrew Johnson and Reconstruction* (New York: Oxford University Press, 1960), 428–38, 443–47; Hans L. Trefousse, *Andrew Johnson: A Biography* (New York: W. W. Norton, 1989), 262–67; Petroleum V. Nasby [David R. Locke], *Swingin Round the Cirkle; or Andy's Trip to the West Together with a Life of Its Hero* (New York: American News Corp., 1866), 207; David A. Rosenberger, "Ohio Press Reaction to Andrew Johnson's 'Swing Around the Circle'—1866" (M.A. thesis, Ohio State University, 1947), 58–61, 63–70; Broeck N. Oder, "Andrew Johnson and the 1866 Illinois Election," *JISHS* 73 (Autumn 1980): 189–94, 195–99; Voegeli, *Free But Not Equal*, 168–69; [Cincinnati, Ohio] *Colored Citizen*, May 19, 1866; David Donald, *The Politics of Reconstruction, 1863–1867* (Baton Rouge: Louisiana State University Press, 1965), 42–45; Thornbrough, *Indiana in the Civil War Era*, 227, 237–38.

33. Marshall, *Creating a Confederate Kentucky*, 93–94; Parrish, *History of Missouri*, 147–69; Dee, *Ohio's War*, 196–97.

34. Harris L. Dante, "Western Attitudes and Reconstruction Policies in Illinois, 1865–1872," *JISHS* 49 (Summer 1956): 160n31; *Congressional Globe*, 41st Cong., 1st Sess., 401; Thornbrough, *Indiana in the Civil War Era*, 229–31; *Cincinnati* [Ohio] *Daily Enquirer*, March 9, 1865; Dee, *Ohio's War*, 196–97; Litwack, *North of Slavery*, 72, 74–93; Robert R. Dykstra and Harlan Hahn, "Northern Voters and Negro Suffrage: The Case of Iowa, 1868," *Public Opinion Quarterly* 32 (Summer 1968): 203; Blight, *Race and Reunion*, 171–72; Barbara A. Gannon, *The Won Cause: Black and White Comradeship in the Grand Army of the Republic*. Chapel Hill: University of North Carolina Press, 2011), 2–6 and passim; Stuart McConnell, "Who Joined the Grand Army? Three Case Studies in the Construction of Union Veteranhood, 1866–1900," in Maris Vinoskis, ed., *Toward a Social History of the American Civil War: Exploratory Essays* (Cambridge: Cambridge University Press, 1990), 170; Pinnick, "African Americans and the Grand Army of the Republic in Illinois" (paper presented at the Annual Conference on Illinois History, Springfield, Illinois, October 13, 2006), 2–3, 6; *New York Times*, March 4, 1892; "Black List," 1887, McCook Post [G.A.R., Leesville, Mo.] Collection, Mss. R375, State Historical Society of Missouri, Research Center-Rolla; Register of Soldiers for GAR Reunion at Salt River, Shelby County, Missouri, August 1895, Shelby County [Mo.] Historical Society, Shelbina, Mo.; Dee, *Ohio's War*, 196–97; Matthew E. Stanley, "'Between Two Fires': War and Reunion in Middle America, 1860–1920" (Ph.D. dissertation, University of Cincinnati, 2013), 229–302 passim.

35. Foner, *Reconstruction*, 315, 446–49, 455; Thornbrough, *Indiana in the Civil War Era*, 242–44; [Macon, Ga.] *Weekly Georgia Telegraph*, March 26, 1869; Havighurst, *Ohio*, 102.

36. *St. Louis* [Mo.] *Globe-Democrat*, August 25, September 6, 7, 1875, February 12, August 11, 1877, August 7, 1880; [Little Rock, Ark.] *Daily Arkansas Gazette*, July 14, 1872; Thornbrough, *Negro in Indiana*, 231–57, 277–78; W. Fitzhugh Brundage, *Lynching in the New South: Georgia and Virginia, 1880–1930* (Urbana: University of Illinois Press, 1993), 19–27; Howard, *Illinois*, 328; *Born in Slavery*, vol. 12, Ohio Narratives, 36; William F. Holmes, "Whitecapping: Agrarian Violence in Mississippi, 1902-1906," *JSH* 35 (May 1969): 165–69; Thornbrough, *Indiana in the Civil War Era*, 242–44, 271–73; *Ripley* [Ohio] *Bee*, March 6, 1867; *Washington* [Ind.] *Weekly Gazette*, December 26, 1868; Madelein Noble, "The White Caps of Harrison and Crawford Counties, Indiana" (Ph.D. dissertation, University of Michigan, 1972), 11–29; Bryan D. Palmer, "Discordant Music: Charivaris and Whitecapping in Nineteenth-Century North America," in Chris McCormick and Len Green, eds., *Crime and Deviance in Canada: Historical Perspectives* (Toronto: Canadian Scholars Press, 2005), 40–44; Richard Maxwell Brown, *The Strain of Violence: Historical Studies of American Violence and Vigilantism* (New York: Oxford University Press, 2002), 71–73; *Galveston* [Tex.] *Daily News*, September 10, 1875; *Boston* [Mass.] *Daily Advertiser*, August 18, 25, 1875; Paul M. Angle, *Bloody Williamson: A Chapter in American Lawlessness* (New York: Alfred A. Knopf, 1969), 72–88.

37. William Gillette, *The Right to Vote: Politics and the Passage of the Fifteenth Amendment* (Baltimore: Johns Hopkins University Press, 1965), esp. ch. 5; Lewis, "Democratic Partisan Militia and the Black Peril," 145–46, 149–50, 152–53; Astor, *Rebels on the Border*, 239–40.

38. James M. McPherson, "Grant or Greeley? The Abolitionist Dilemma in the Election of 1872," *AHR* 71 (October 1965): 43–44, 48–51, 58–59.
39. Matthew T. Downey, "Horace Greeley and the Politicians: The Liberal Republican Convention in 1872," *JAH* 53 (March 1967): 727–33, 740, 750; Kristen L. Anderson, "German Americans, African Americans, and the Republican Party in St. Louis, 1865–1872," *Journal of American Ethnic History* 28 (Fall 2008): 41–46; John G. Sproat, *"The Best Men": Liberal Reformers in the Gilded Age* (New York: Oxford University Press, 1968), 12–13, 76–85; Yonatan Eyal, "Charles Eliot Norton, E. L. Godkin, and the Liberal Republicans of 1872," *American Nineteenth Century History* 2 (Spring 2001): 56–58; *Cleveland* [Ohio] *Daily Herald*, June 14, 1872; *Milwaukee* [Wis.] *Sentinel*, April 12, 1872, April 19, 1873; Parrish, *History of Missouri*, 234–59; Peterson, *Freedom and Franchise*, 130–44, 226–31; Parrish, *Frank Blair*, 231–45; Parrish, *Missouri Under Radical Rule*, 288–326.
40. Grinspan, "'Sorrowfully Amusing,'" 315–17, 326–28; Henry Nash Smith, *Virgin Land: The American West as Symbol and Myth* (Cambridge, Mass.: Harvard University Press, 1950), 151–52.
41. John R. Neff, *Honoring the Civil War Dead: Commemoration and the Problem of Reconciliation* (Lawrence: University Press of Kansas, 2005), 7–10; Kyle S. Sinisi, *Sacred Debts: State Civil War Claims and American Federalism, 1861–1880* (New York: Fordham University Press, 2003), 34–36, 58; Marshall, *Creating a Confederate Kentucky*, 67–71; [Chillicothe, Ohio] *Scioto Gazette*, May 21, 1867; Anonymous to Dear Wick, March 28, 1865, Wickliffe-Preston Family Papers, Mss. 63M349, box 56, UK.
42. Marshall, *Creating a Confederate Kentucky*, 103–10; Neff, *Honoring the Civil War Dead*, 244–45; W. Fitzhugh Brundage, *The Southern Past: A Clash of Race and Memory* (Cambridge, Mass.: Belknap Press of Harvard University Press, 2005), 14–15.
43. [Springfield, Mo.] *Missouri Weekly Patriot*, September 14, 1865; [Chillicothe, Ohio] *Scioto Gazette*, April 2, 1867; *Salem* [Ohio] *Democrat*, July 5, 1876; Sarah Richards, ed., *Civil War Sites: The Official Guide to Battlefields, Monuments, and More* (Guilford, Conn.: Globe Pequot Press, 2003), 286.
44. Dee, *Ohio's War*, 202–206.
45. [Dayton, Ohio] *Daily Democrat*, October 4, 1876.
46. Blight, *Race and Reunion*, 147; Marshall, *Creating a Confederate Kentucky*, 95; M. H. Carson to D. Howard Smith, December 11, 1866, and George B. Hodge to William Preston, November 23, 1866, both in Wickliffe-Preston Family Papers, Mss. 63M349, box 56, UK; Astor, *Rebels on the Border*, 194–95. See also George B. Hodge, *Sketch of the First Kentucky Brigade by Its Adjutant General, G. B. Hodge* (Frankfort, Ky.: Major and Johnston, 1874).
47. Gaines M. Foster, *Ghosts of the Confederacy: Defeat, the Lost Cause, and the Emergence of the New South* (New York: Oxford University Press, 1987), 4–5, 22–26; Astor, *Rebels on the Border*, 194–201; Blight, *Race and Reunion*, 258–60; W[illiam] J. Stone to Mrs. R. F. Clinton, February 20, 1865, William Johnson Stone Papers, Mss. 54M131 (microfilm), UK.
48. Gary Robert Matthews, *Basil Wilson Duke, CSA: The Right Man in the Right Place* (Lexington: University Press of Kentucky, 2005), 208–20; Basil Wilson Duke, *History of Morgan's Cavalry* (Cincinnati: Miami Printing and Publishing, 1867), 7–17; John Newman Edwards, *Shelby and His Men, or the War in the West* (Cincinnati: Miami Printing and Publishing, 1867), 10; Astor, *Rebels on the Border*, 196–97; Foster, *Ghosts of the Confederacy*, 49; Stiles, *Jesse James*, 207–26.
49. Matthew C. Hulbert, "Constructing Guerrilla Memory: John Newman Edwards and Missouri's Irregular Lost Cause," *JCWE* 2 (March 2012): 58–65; Fellman, *Inside War*, 249–51; Stiles, *Jesse James*, 209–20, 288–91; Hildebrand, *Autobiography of Samuel S. Hildebrand*, passim; John N[ewman] Edwards, *Noted Guerrillas, or the Warfare on the Border* (St. Louis: Bryan, Brand, 1877), passim.
50. *David Bowles vs. Joseph S. Fant*, 1869, box 14, folder 42 (microfilm reel C60385), Circuit Court Records, St. Charles County, Missouri, MSA; William F. Leftwich, *Martyrdom in Missouri: A History of Religious Proscription, the Seizure of Churches, and the Persecution of Ministers of the Gospel, in the State of Missouri during the Late Civil War, and under the "Test Oath" of the New Constitution* (St. Louis: Southwestern Book and Publishing, 1870), 1:131–32; Rash, *Paintings and Politics of Bingham*, 209–13; Clipping, "A SCORCHER—Gen.

Bingham on Order No. 11," undated [1876], pp. 68–69, Garland Carr Broadhead Scrapbook, Mss. 1000, SHSM.
51. Karen Cox, *Dixie's Daughters: The United Daughters of the Confederacy and the Preservation of Confederate Culture* (Gainesville: University Press of Florida, 2003), 15–16.
52. Brundage, *Southern Past*, 19–21; Card, Atlanta Association for the Reinterment of the Kentucky Confederate Dead, May 7, 1866, Emilie Todd Helm Collection, Mss. 85M01, box 1: Correspondence, 1861–1868, KHS; Stephen Berry, *House of Abraham: Lincoln and the Todds, A Family Divided by War* (Boston: Houghton Mifflin, 2007), 151, 191; Cox, *Dixie's Daughters*, 1.
53. Stiles, *Jesse James*, 102–103; William H. Gregg, "A Little Dab of History Without Embellishment," pp. 88–89, unpublished manuscript (microfilm, 1906), Mss. C1113, SHSM; Marshall, *Creating a Confederate Kentucky*, 87; "Missouri Monuments," Center for Civil War Research, University of Mississippi, Oxford, http://civilwarcenter.olemiss.edu/monuments%20mo.html (accessed July 12, 2011). Marshall misstates the erection date of the Thompson and Powell Martyr Monument at St. Joseph, Kentucky, as 1864. It was erected in 1880.
54. Brundage, *Southern Past*, 15–27; Blight, *Race and Reunion*, 274–87; Mary Poppenheim, *The History of the United Daughters of the Confederacy* (Raleigh, NC: Edwards and Broughton, 1956), 2–3; Marshall, *Creating a Confederate Kentucky*, 156, 160–67; Organizational Sketch, n.d., United Daughters of the Confederacy, Missouri Division, Mss. C3188, box 1, SHSM; *Proceedings of the Twenty-third Annual Convention of the Missouri Division United Daughters of the Confederacy, Held in Sedalia, Missouri, October 19, 20, 21, 1920* (n.p.: s.n.), 11, 23.
55. Marshall, *Creating a Confederate Kentucky*, 157–60; Astor, *Rebels on the Border*, 194–97; *Organization of Camps of the United Confederate Veterans* (New Orleans: J. G. Hauser, 1910), 27; Thomas D. Osborne Civil War Scrapbook, Mss. 98SC201, KHS.
56. Organization Sketch, Missouri Confederate Home, Higginsville, Records, 1897–1944 (microfilm), Mss. C0066, SHSM; R. B. Rosenburg, *Living Monuments: Confederate Soldiers' Homes in the New South* (Chapel Hill: University of North Carolina Press, 1993), 140; *History of the Confederate Home*, Confederate Memorial State Historic Site Collection, comp. Bernard C. Hunt (Higginsville, Mo.: Confederate Memorial State Historic Site, 1936), 2; Francis Eloise Vaughn, "Confederate Veterans Home, Chapel and UDC Cemetery," *UDC: The United Daughters of the Confederacy Magazine* 57 (June/July 1994): 10; Stacy D. Hisle-Chaudri, "A Landscape of Collective Memory: The Confederate Memorial State Historic Site, Higginsville, Mo." (M.A. thesis, Central Missouri State University, 2013), 67–101 passim; Register of Inmates in Home, 1902–1908, Kentucky Confederate Veterans' Home Collection (unprocessed), box 3, KHS; *Rules and Regulations for the Government of the Kentucky Confederate Home at Pewee Valley, Kentucky* (Louisville: Courier-Journal Job Printing, 1922), passim; Clipping, *Oldham Era*, November 3, 1922, United Daughters of the Confederacy Records, Mss. 2005M13, box 1, KHS; Marshall, *Creating a Confederate Kentucky*, 144, 164.
57. Daniel S. Margolies, *Henry Watterson and the New South: The Politics of Empire, Free Trade, and Globalization* (Lexington: University Press of Kentucky, 2006), 17–27; Foster, *Ghosts of the Confederacy*, 80–81; Marshall, *Creating a Confederate Kentucky*, 50–54, 68–71, 98–99.
58. Margolies, *Henry Watterson and the New South*, 28–44; Marshall, *Creating a Confederate Kentucky*, 51–54, 97–99; Cobb, *Away Down South*, 65; Blight, *Race and Reunion*, 263, 281–82; Paul M. Gaston, *The New South Creed: A Study in Southern Mythmaking* (New York: Alfred A. Knopf, 1970), 48–53, 85, 92–96.
59. Robert Hunt, *The Good Men Who Won the War: Army of the Cumberland Veterans and Emancipation Memory* (Tuscaloosa: University of Alabama Press, 2010), 5, 74 and passim; Stanley, "'Between Two Fires,'" 237–40; John A. Logan, *The Great Conspiracy: Its Origins and History* (New York: A. R. Hart, 1886), 1–2, 12.
60. [Louisville, Ky.] *Courier-Journal*, April 22, 28, 1885; *The Sixty-Third Birthday of Ulysses S. Grant* (Louisville, Ky.: *Courier-Journal*, 1885); Robert B. Symon Jr., "Louisville's Lost National Holiday: Sectional Reconciliation and the Ulysses S. Grant 1885 Birthday Celebration," *OVH* 8 (Fall 2008): 40–45; Joan Waugh, *U. S. Grant: American Hero,*

American Myth (Chapel Hill: University of North Carolina Press, 2009), 218–22; Marshall, *Creating a Confederate Kentucky*, 179–81.
61. Marshall, *Creating a Confederate Kentucky*, 103–10.
62. *Roster of the Department of Missouri, Grand Army of the Republic, and Its Auxiliaries* (Kansas City: Western Veteran, 1895), passim; *St. Louis Republican*, July 8, 1887; *Chicago* [Ill.] *Inter-ocean*, July 8, 1887; *Chicago* [Ind.] *Herald*, July 9, 1887; Galveston [Tex.] *News*, July 8, 1887; [Cincinnati, Ohio] *Commercial Gazette*, July 10, 1887; *New York Times*, June 13, July 8, 1887.
63. Circular, Women's Confederate Monument Association of Kentucky, Scrapbooks of Albert Sidney Johnston Chapter, No. 120, Louisville, United Daughters of the Confederacy Records, Mss. 2005M13, ser. 3: Kentucky Chapters, 1892–1999, box 30, KHS; Marshall, *Creating a Confederate Kentucky*, 155.
64. *Confederate Home Messenger*, March 1910, United Daughters of the Confederacy Records, Mss. 2005M13, box 41, KHS; David W. Blight, *Beyond the Battlefield: Race, Memory, and the American Civil War* (Amherst: University of Massachusetts Press, 2002), 178; Matthew E. Stanley, "'No More Shall the Winding Rivers Be Red': Civil War Commemoration and Regional Identity in Evansville, Indiana, 1887–1899" (paper presented at Great Lakes Regional History Conference, October 9, 2010, Grand Valley State University, Grand Rapids, Michigan), with permission of the author; Marshall, *Creating a Confederate Kentucky*, 156–57; Phillips, *Making of a Southerner*, 108. By one contemporary estimate, some twenty-four Blue-Gray reunions were held between 1881 and 1887.
65. Castel, *William Clarke Quantrill*, 231–33; Jeremy Neely, "The Quantrill Men Reunions: The Missouri-Kansas Border War, Fifty Years On," in Earle and Burke, *Bleeding Kansas, Bleeding Missouri*, 243–57; Stiles, *Jesse James*, 363–67. For the fullest study of the reunions, see Donald R. Hale, *The William Clarke Quantrill Men Reunions, 1898–1929* (Independence, Mo.: Blue and Grey Book Shoppe, 2001).
66. Marshall, *Creating a Confederate Kentucky*, 123–30, 133–45; Blight, *Race and Reunion*, 211; Silber, *Romance of Reunion*, 39–65, 105–23; Speed, *Union Cause in Kentucky*, passim.
67. List of Indigent Ex-Confederate Soldiers Enrolled under the Confederate Pension Act, 1929, Confederate Home Correspondence, box 82 (unprocessed), Adjutant General Records, Record Group 133, MSA; "An Act Granting Pension to Indigent and Disabled Confederate Soldiers, and the Widows of Confederate Soldiers," in *Acts of the General Assembly of the Commonwealth of Kentucky* (Frankfort: Kentucky State Journal Publishing Company, 1912), 1:187; Alicia Simpson, *Index of Confederate Pension Applications, Commonwealth of Kentucky* (Frankfort: Division of Archives and Records Management, Department of Library and Archives, 1978), 1–2; Brian Craig Miller, "Filling the Empty Sleeves: Southern States Respond to the Crisis of Amputation" (paper presented at the Organization of American Historians Annual Conference, March 19, 2011), with permission of the author.
68. Warren, *Jefferson Davis Gets His Citizenship Back*, 15, 22–23; Jefferson Davis to R. W. Downer, December 5, 1885, October 6, 21, November 14, 1886, all in Jefferson Davis Papers, Mss. 97SC194, KHS; Leaflet, *Our Monument: An Account of the Obelisk Being Erected to Jefferson Davis at Fairview, Ky., His Birthplace: Told by Gen. Bennett H. Young in His Address to the United Daughters of the Confederacy, in Convention at Chattanooga, Tenn., November 15, 1897*, and "Statement of the Condition of the Jefferson Davis Monument at Fairview, Ky.," November 1, 1918, both in Mrs. Thomas D. Osborne Scrapbook, United Daughters of the Confederacy Records, Mss. 2005M13, box 30, KHS; Marshall, *Creating a Confederate Kentucky*, 175–77.
69. *Abraham Lincoln Birthplace Memorial Building Historic Structure Report* (Atlanta: Cultural Resources, Southeast Region, National Park Service, 2001), 1–4, and passim; Marshall, *Creating a Confederate Kentucky*, 175–77.
70. *Acts of the General Assembly of the Commonwealth of Kentucky* (Frankfort: State Journal, 1912), 1:220–21; *Acts of the General Assembly of the Commonwealth of Kentucky* (Frankfort: State Journal, 1914), 1:514–16; Leaflet, *Our Monument: An Account of the Obelisk Being Erected to Jefferson Davis at Fairview, Ky., His Birthplace: Told by Gen. Bennett H. Young in His Address to the United Daughters of the Confederacy, in Convention at Chattanooga, Tenn.,*

November 15, 1897; Bennett H. Young to D. D. Halyburton, May 4, 1917; and Map of Proposed Jefferson Davis Highway, undated, all in Mrs. Thomas D. Osborne Scrapbook, United Daughters of the Confederacy Records, Mss. 2005M13, box 30, KHS.
71. Marshall, *Creating a Confederate Kentucky*, 183; Warren, *Jefferson Davis Gets His Citizenship Back*, 95–96.

Rally Round the Flags

1. [Louisville, Ky.] *Courier-Journal*, May 31, 1923.
2. Ibid.; Marshall, *Creating a Confederate Kentucky*, 181–82.

Conclusion

1. Foster, *Ghosts of the Confederacy*, 48–50; David Thelen, "Memory and American History," *JAH* 75 (March 1989): 1119; James C. Cobb, *Away Down South: A History of Southern Identity* (New York: Oxford University Press, 2005), 64; Brundage, *Southern Past*, 8–10.
2. Phillips, *Making of a Southerner*, 113–17; Daniel Joseph Conoyer, "Missouri's Little Dixie: A Geographical Delineation" (Ph.D. dissertation, Saint Louis University, 1973), 1–3, 224–314 passim; Crisler, "Missouri's Little Dixie," 130–39; John H. Fenton, *Politics in the Border States* (New Orleans: Hauser Press, 1957), 156–57. A Kansas City newspaperman in 1941 traced the term to the congressional candidacy of John B. Hale, who popularized it as a description for the Boon's Lick counties while campaigning in the Second Congressional District in 1887. In a speech at Paris, Hale reputedly referred to the solid Democratic counties as the "Little Dixie of [the] Missouri Democracy," regaling its residents about their traditional allegiance to the party. Fenton found that all but two of the traditional Boon's Lick counties voted solidly Democratic between 1872 and 1952.
3. Phillips, *Making of a Southerner*, 113–17. For a full discussion of victimization as a central facet of southern identity, see Paul Quigley, *Shifting Grounds: Nationalism and the American South, 1848–1865* (New York: Oxford University Press, 2012).
4. Hector Hillenmeyer to Gentlemen, March 13, 1864, Hillenmeyer Family Papers, Mss. 59M306 (microfilm), UK; Speech of Leeland Hathaway, Capt. CSA, to United Daughters of the Confederacy, Lexington, undated [1890]; and "Civil War Reminiscences of Leeland Hathaway, Capt. CSA," undated [1893–1894], both in Leeland Hathaway Papers, Mss. M20 (microfilm), UK; Ethan S. Rafuse, "'Far More Than a Romantic Adventure': The American Civil War in Harry Truman's History and Memory," *MHR* 104 (October 2009): 3–7.
5. Anne E. Marshall, "The 1906 *Uncle Tom's Cabin* Law and the Politics of Race and Memory in Early-Twentieth-Century Kentucky," *JCWE* 1 (September 2011): 368–93 passim; *Chicago InterOcean*, April 19, 1878, April 23, 1881; *Atchison* [Kans.] *Globe*, March 20, 1880, May 6, 1881.
6. Marshall, "The 1906 *Uncle Tom's Cabin* Law," 378–88; *Journal of the Regular Session of the House of Representatives of the Commonwealth of Kentucky* (Louisville: George G. Fetter, 1906), 568–69; Roger A. Burns-Watson, "*The Birth of A Nation* and the Death of a Board: Race, Politics and Film Censorship in Ohio, 1913–1921" (M.A. thesis, University of Cincinnati, 2001), 3–25.
7. Thomas W. Bullitt, *My Life at Oxmoor: Life on a Farm in Kentucky Before the War* (Louisville: J. P. Morton, 1911), passim; Thomas W. Bullitt to Thomas Halsey, July 25, 1898, and Scott Bullitt to William M. Bullitt, July 21, 1898, both in Bullitt Family Papers, folders 936 and 634, FHS; Foster, *Ghosts of the Confederacy*, 4–8, 80, 86, 90–91.
8. Cobb, *Away Down South*, 54–61; C. Vann Woodward, *The Burden of Southern History* (Baton Rouge: Louisiana State University, 1960; reprint New York: Mentor Books, 1969), 27.
9. Abraham Lincoln to Samuel Haycraft, June 4, 1860, in *CWAL*, 4:69–70; E. H. Haycraft to Samuel Haycraft, August 7, 1868, Haycraft Family Papers, Mss. 69M690 (microfilm), UK; Marshall, *Creating a Confederate Kentucky*, 107–10. Searches of digitized newspaper databases, including the *New York Times*, the *Chicago Tribune*, *Early American Newspapers*,

Illinois Digital Newspaper Collection, 1831–2011, Hoosier State Chronicles, 1840–1922, The Godfrey Library's Nineteenth-century Newspapers, The Kentuckiana Digital Library, 1787–2012, and the *Cleveland Press, 1878–1982*, offer consistent evidence that the term "Middle West" came into use mainly in the 1880s and was used nearly exclusively in urban newspapers in the former western free states.

10. Wilbur Henry Siebert, *The Underground Railroad: From Slavery to Freedom* (New York: Macmillan, 1898), passim; Gara, *Liberty Line*, 166–70; Eric Foner, *Gateway to Freedom: The Hidden History of the Underground Railroad* (New York: W. W. Norton, 2015), 12–15. Although he mentions the work of Siebert and Gara, Foner's study focuses nearly exclusively on the Underground Railroad in New York City and states east of the Appalachians.
11. In 2010 an Ohio legislative committee voted to replace Allen's statue with one of Thomas A. Edison.
12. Blight, *Race and Reunion*, 231–37; James H. Madison, "Civil War Memories and 'Pardnership Forgittin', 1865–1913," *IMH* 99 (September 2003): 198–99.
13. Shortridge, *The Middle West*, 1–26; Jaspin, *Buried in the Bitter Waters*, 31–52; Charles E. Delgadillo, "'A Pretty Weedy Flower': William Allen White, Midwestern Liberalism, and the 1920s Culture War," *Kansas History: A Journal of the Central Plains* 35 (Autumn 2012): 186–202 passim.
14. Reuben Gold Thwaites, *Afloat on the Ohio*, republished as *On the Storied Ohio* (Chicago: A. C. McClurg, 1903; reprint New York: Arno Press, Inc., 1975), 89, 157–58, 185 and passim; Rohrbaugh, *The Trans-Appalachian Frontier*, 122; Archer Butler Hulbert, *The Ohio River: A Course of Empire* (New York and London: G. P. Putnam's Sons, 1906), 322; James M. Miller, *The Genesis of Western Culture: The Upper Ohio Valley, 1800–1825* (Columbus: Ohio State Archeological and Historical Society, 1938; reprint New York: Da Capo Press, 1969), 28.
15. Cobb, *Away Down South*, 45; Mark Twain, "The Private History of a Campaign That Failed," *Century Magazine* (1885), in Teacher, ed., Mark Twain [Samuel L. Clemens], *The Unabridged Mark Twain*, ed. Lawrence Teacher, 2 vols. (Philadelphia: Running Press, 1979), 1:1193, 1202; Absalom C. Grimes, "Campaigning with Mark Twain," in David Rachels, ed., *Mark Twain's Civil War* (Lexington: University Press of Kentucky, 2007), 111–28; Joe B. Fulton, *The Reconstruction of Mark Twain: How a Confederate Bushwhacker Became the Lincoln of Our Literature* (Baton Rouge: Louisiana State University Press, 2010), 44–49, 93, 125 and passim.
16. Victor Fischer, "Huck Finn Reviewed: The Reception of *Huckleberry* Finn in the United States, 1885–1897," *American Literary Realism* 16 (Spring 1983): 1–57 passim; James D. Drake, "A Divide to Heal the Union: The Creation of the Continental Divide," *Pacific Historical Review* 84 (November 2015): 410–12, 435–41, 447; Ari Kelman, *A Misplaced Massacre: Struggling Over Sand Creek in American Memory* (Cambridge, Mass.: Harvard University Press, 2013), passim; P[hilip] H. Sheridan to General W[illiam] T. Sherman, July 6, 1875, Special File of Letters Received, War Department, Military Division of the Missouri, 1866–1891, Mss. M1495, microfilm reel 11, NARA, quoted in Elliott West, "Reconstructing Race," *WHQ* 34 (Spring 2003): 15.
17. Frederick Jackson Turner, "The Problem of the West," *Atlantic Monthly* (September 1896): 289–90; Richard Jensen, "On Modernizing Frederick Jackson Turner: The Historiography of Regionalism," *WHQ* 11 (July 1980): 307–22; Turner, "Geographic Sectionalism in American History," *Annals of the American Association of Geographers* 16 (1926): 85–93.
18. John E. Miller, "Frederick Jackson Turner and the Dream of Regional History," *Middle West Review* 1 (Fall 2014): 1–8; Turner, "The Problem of the West," 289–97; Wilbur R. Jacobs, "Turner's Methodology: Multiple Working Hypothesis or Ruling Theory?" *JAH* 54 (March 1968): 858. See also Turner, *The Significance of Sections in American History* (New York: Henry Holt, 1932), and M[erle] E. Curti, "The Section and Frontier in American History: The Methodological Concepts of Frederick Jackson Turner," in S. A. Rice, ed., *Methods in Social Science: A Case Book* (Chicago: University of Chicago Press, 1931), passim. Published posthumously, Turner's book, a collection of essays, would win the Pulitzer Prize for History in 1933.
19. Ayers et al., *All Over the Map*, 4–10.

BIBLIOGRAPHY

Primary Sources

MANUSCRIPT COLLECTIONS

Abraham Lincoln Presidential Library, Springfield, Illinois
    Jacob Ammen Papers
    Shadrach Bond Papers, Mss. SC148
    Sidney Breese Papers, Mss. SC165
    Simon B. Buckner File, Mss. SC204
    John C. Dinsmore Papers, Mss. SC405
    Robert L. Dulaney Papers, Mss. SC428
    John A. Higgins Papers, Mss. SC1918
    John A. McClernand Papers, 1823–1919
    Old Settlers' Association File, Mss. SC309
    Jesse J. Ricks Collection, Mss. 1274–1903
    Wallace-Dickey Family Papers
    James B. Woollard Papers
American Antiquarian Society, Worcester, Massachusetts
    Lucy Fletcher Kellogg Memoir (transcript)
Amistad Research Center, New Orleans, Louisiana
    American Missionary Association Archives, 1839–1882. 261 microfilm reels
Cape Girardeau County Archives Center, Jackson, Missouri
    Joseph Cowgill Maple Memoir, "Incidents of the Campaign of 1861 in Southeast Missouri" (transcript)
Cincinnati Historical Society Library, Cincinnati Museum Center, Cincinnati, Ohio
    Barthelemi Tardiveau Memorandum, Mss. VF 3692
    Edwin Henderson, Historical Sketches, Scrapbook, Mss. qXH496
    Kentucky River Steamboat Advertisements, 1845–1850, Mss. VF 1208
    Kentucky Volunteer Infantry Roster, Mss. VF 1195
    Minutes of the Citizens' Home Guard of West Covington, Kentucky (typescript), Mss. fC581 RFM
    Ormsby M. Mitchel Papers, Mss. M679
    Smith Family Papers, Mss qS655
    Amanda Landrum Wilson Diary, Mss. zW746 RMV
Duke University, Special Collections, William R. Perkins Library, Durham, North Carolina
    Jefferson Davis Papers
    Missouri Volunteer Militia Papers, 1860–1865
    M. J. Solomons Scrapbook, 1861–1863

Filson Historical Society, Louisville, Kentucky
　　Lot Abraham Letters, Mss. C/A
　　Stephen Barker Letter, Mss. C/B
　　Orlando Brown Papers, Mss. A/B879
　　John B. Bruner Papers, Mss. A/B894
　　Buckner Family Papers, Mss. A/B925
　　Bullitt-Chenoweth Family Papers, Mss. A/B937a
　　Stephen Gano Burbridge Correspondence, Mss. C/B
　　J. W. Calvert Letter, Mss. C/C
　　Isaac Clark Letters, Mss. A/C593a4
　　John J. Crittenden Papers, Mss. C/C
　　Thomas S. Crutcher File, Mss. C/C
　　John Curd Letter, Mss. C/C
　　Davis-Lewis Family Papers, Mss. C/D
　　F. D. Dickinson Letter, Mss. C/D
　　Watson Goodrich Letters, Mss. C/G
　　Grigsby Family Papers, Mss. A/G857
　　Edward O. Guerrant Papers, 1861–1867, Mss. C/Ga
　　Hardeman Family Papers, Mss. A/H159
　　John Harding Collection, Mss. A/H263
　　Samuel Haycraft Miscellaneous Papers, 1792–1870, Mss. A/H414
　　Holyoke Family PapersCDavie Collection, Mss. C/H
　　Cora Owens Hume Journal (transcript), Mss. A/H921, Vault C., 3 vols.
　　John F. Jefferson Papers, Mss. A/J45
　　Rosa V. J. Jeffrey Papers, Mss. A/J46r
　　Jones Family Papers, Mss. A/J78
　　Joyes Family Papers, Mss. A/J89b
　　Kinchloe-Eskridge Families Papers, Mss. A K51
　　N[orman] G. Markham Papers, Mss. A/M345
　　Oath of Allegiance of Samuel Jones Denton, Mss. C/D
　　Albert Pirtle Papers, Mss. A/P672
　　Samuel W. Pruitt Letters, Mss. C/P
　　Shakers, Pleasant Hill, Kentucky, Collection, Mss. BA/S 527
　　Slaughter Family Papers, Mss. A/S631g
　　Speed Family, Miscellaneous Papers, Mss. C/S
　　John H. Tilford Diary, Mss. A/T572. 2 vols.
　　Tolle Family Letters, Mss. C/T
　　Union Soldiers Letters, 1861–1865, Mss. C/U
　　Yandell Family Papers, Mss. A/Y21a, FHS
　　Absalom Yarbrough Johnson Diaries, 1860–1864, 2 vols., Mss. A/J67b
Georgetown College, Frances Lyons Bolton Special Collections and Archives, Ensor Learning Resource Center, Georgetown, Kentucky
　　Kentucky Baptist Education Society, Proceedings of the Board of Trustees, 1837–1866
　　Records of Georgetown College, 1859–1887, Faculty Minutes Book
Henry E. Huntington Library and Art Gallery, San Marino, California
　　EG Box 30
Illinois Historical Survey and Lincoln Room, University Library, University of Illinois, Urbana-Champaign.
　　Eddy Manuscript Collection
Indiana Historical Society Library, Indianapolis
　　Oliver Perry Aiken Papers, Mss. SC7
　　Thomas Alexander Genealogy, Mss. SC9
　　Joseph W. and Orville T. Chamberlain Papers, Mss. M44

Churchman Family Papers, Mss. M53
Thomas A. Cobb Letters, Mss. SC251
John G. Davis Papers, Mss. M0082
Martha W. Dorsey Papers, Mss. SC510
John Dowling Papers, Mss. M87
George Edwards Papers, Mss. SC532
James Frank Fee Letters, SC567
V. W. Hale Personal File, Mss. SC669
John Watts Hamilton Papers, Mss. SC676
Robert B. Hanna Family Papers, Mss. M129
William Henry Harrison Papers, Mss. M0364
Oliver C. Haskell Diary, Mss. SC707
Abram W. Hendricks Papers, Mss. SC733
William Houghton Papers, Mss. M147
River Hutchings-Koehler Family Papers, Mss. M152
James Ireland Family Papers, Mss. M169
Jeptha King Letters, Mss. SC916
John Randolph McBride Papers, Mss. SC1005
J. Milton Pitts Papers, Mss. SC1207
Robert J. Price Letters, Mss. SC1221
Thomas Prickett Papers, Mss. SC1222
Record of the Board of Trustees of the Public Schools of New Albany, Indiana (microfilm)
W. C. Starr Papers, Mss. SC1400
Henry R. Strong Papers, Mss. SC1423
Daniel Lafayette Thomas Papers, Mss. SC1445
Amos C. Weaver Papers, Mss. SC1545
Kansas State Historical Society, Topeka, Kansas
   Samuel Ayres Collection
   Josephine B. Martin Papers
Kentucky Department of Libraries and Archives, Frankfort
   Daviess County Clerk Records
   Governor's Correspondence File—Military Correspondence, 1859–1862
   Kentucky Historical Society, Special Collections and Manuscripts, Frankfort, Kentucky
   John T. Harrington Letters, Mss. 97SC130
   Emilie Todd Helm Collection, Mss. 85M01
   Kentucky Confederate Veterans' Home Collection (unprocessed)
   Scrogin-Haviland Collection, Mss. 2001SC20
   South Union, Kentucky, 1830–1869, church orders, diary, journal, poem, and other writings (microfilm)
   United Daughters of the Confederacy Records, Mss. 2005M13, Series 3: Kentucky Chapters, 1892–1999
   Wallace-Starling Family Diaries, Mss. 96M07
Library of Congress, Washington, D.C.
   Elizabeth J. Reynolds Burt Papers
   James H. Goodnow Papers
   John Marshall Harlan Papers (microfilm)
   Isham Green Harris Papers
   Joseph Holt Papers, General Correspondence and Related Material (Bound), 1817–1894
   Abraham Lincoln Papers, Ser. 1—General Correspondence, 1833–1916
   Beriah Magoffin Letters
   Reed Family of Indiana and Kentucky Papers
   Thomas Caute Reynolds Papers (microfilm)
   John M. Schofield Papers

William T. Sherman Family Papers (microfilm)
David Tod Papers
Lyman Trumbull Papers
Missouri Historical Society, St. Louis, Missouri
    Badger Collection
    Bates Family Papers
    James O. Broadhead Papers
    Camp Jackson Papers
    Circulars
    Civil War Collection
    Charles Gibson Papers
    Julius J. Goldberg Collection
    Willard P. Hall Papers
    Mrs. Jesse P. Henry Papers
    William Carr Lane Papers
    James Edwin Love Papers
    Missouri Militia Collection
    William Barclay Napton Papers
    Pettus Family Papers
    Thomas C. Reynolds Papers
    Sappington Family Papers
    General George R. Smith Papers
    John F. Snyder Collection
    George R. Taylor Collection
Missouri State Archives, Jefferson City, Missouri
    Adjutant General Records, Record Group 133
    Andrew County Civil War Collection
    Capitol Fire Documents, 1806–1957 (microfilm)
    Governors' Papers, Record Group 3: John C. Edwards Papers, Claiborne Fox Jackson Papers, Hancock Jackson Papers, Sterling Price Papers, Thomas Reynolds Papers
Ohio Historical Society, Columbus, Ohio
    Thomas Corwin Papers, Mss. 297
    James Family Papers, Mss. 258
    Robert Neil Family Papers, Mss. 259
    David T. Statham Papers, Mss. 688
    Sturges Family Papers, Mss. 539
    John A. Trimble Papers, Mss. 249
    Dolores Cameron Venable Memorial Collection, Mss. 127
National Archives and Records Administration, Washington, D.C.
    Record Group 56: Department of the Treasury Records
    Part 56, Ser. 40: Letters Sent Related to Restricted Commercial Intercourse
    Record Group 109: War Department Collection of Confederate Records
    Union Provost Marshals' File of Papers Relating to Individual Citizens, Mss. M345. 299 microfilm reels
    Union Provost Marshals' File of Papers Relating to Two or More Citizens, File M416. 94 microfilm reels
    Record Group 153: Records of the Office of the Judge Advocate General (Army)
    Register of the Records of the Proceedings of the U. S. Army General Courts-Martial, 1809–1890. Mss. M1105. 8 microfilm reels
    Record Group 393: Records of the U.S. Army Continental Commands, 1821–1920
    Part 1, Series 2229: Correspondence, Affidavits, Oaths Regarding Civilians Charged with Disloyalty, Department of Kentucky. 2 boxes
    Part 1, Series 2620: General Orders, Department of the Missouri, 1862–1864. 5 vols.

Part 1, Series 2173: Letters Received, Department of Kentucky, 1862–1869. 5 boxes
    Part 1, Series 2593: Letters Received, Department of the Missouri, 1862–1867. 20 boxes
    Part 1, Series 3514: Letters Received, Department of the Ohio, 1863–1866. 8 boxes
    Part 1, Series 3349: Letters Received, Northern Department, 1864–1865. 3 boxes
Presbyterian Historical Society, Philadelphia, Pennsylvania
    Lane Theological Seminary Records
Rutherford B. Hayes Presidential Center, Manuscript Division, Fremont, Ohio
    Diaries and Letters of Rutherford Birchard Hayes
St. Louis Mercantile Library, Special Collections, University of Missouri at St. Louis
    Greve-Fisher Collection, Mss. M-257
Shelby County Historical Society, Shelbina, Missouri
    Register of Soldiers for G.A.R. Reunion at Salt River, Shelby County, Missouri, August 1895
Southeast Missouri State University, Special Collections and Archives, Cape Girardeau, Missouri
    Joseph Cowgill Maple manuscript, "Incidents of the Campaign of 1861 in Southeast Missouri"
Southern Historical Collections, Wilson Library, University of North Carolina, Chapel Hill
    Bullitt Family Papers, Mss. 3549
    Leeland Hathaway Recollections, Mss. 2954
    South Union Shaker Records, 1769–1893, Mss. 1854 (microfilm)
Southern Illinois University, Special Collections, Morris Library, Carbondale, Illinois
    John Willis Allen Papers, Mss. 76-3-F1
    Daniel Berry Letters, Misc. Vol. 53
    Mary A. Berry [Crebs] Letters, Misc. Vol. 88
    Daniel M. Davis Letters, Microfilm 48
    Edwin A. Loosley Papers, Coll. 2
    Mann Family Papers, Coll. 111
    Alfred M. Mozley Letters, Mss. VFM 1642
    "A Pioneer Looks Back: Lecture Delivered by Braxton Parrish in Benton," Mss. VFM 18
State Historical Society of Missouri, Research Center, Rolla, Missouri
    McCook Post [G.A.R., Leesville, Mo.] Collection, Mss. R375
University of Kentucky, Special Collections and Archives, Margaret I. King Library, Lexington, Kentucky
    Benjamin Forsythe Buckner Papers, 1785–1918, Mss. 48M39
    Cassius M. Clay Papers, Mss. 56M89
    Cooper-Phillips Family Papers, Mss. 66M37
    Darbishire Family Papers, Mss. 62M68
    Duncan Family Papers, Mss. 71M38
    Evans Papers, Mss. 72M15
    Alice Todd Field Diary, Mss. M368
    First Baptist Church (Paris, Ky.) Minutes, 1818–1945, Mss. 78M812 (microfilm)
    Gibson-Humphreys Family Papers, Mss. 61M140
    Mrs. James M. Gill and Miss Mary Gill Collection of Bristow Papers, Mss. 64M578 (microfilm)
    Gordon Family Papers, Mss. 51M40
    Gunn Family Papers, Mss. 73M28
    Lizzie Hardin Diary, Mss. 55M181 (microfilm)
    Harmony Baptist Church Record Book, 1855–1902, Mss. 46M141
    Leeland Hathaway Papers, Mss. M20 (microfilm)
    Haycraft Family Papers, Mss. 69M690 (microfilm)
    Edward Henry Hobson Papers, Mss. 51M41
    Hillenmeyer Family Papers, Mss. 59M306 (microfilm)
    Hunt-Morgan Family Papers, Mss. 63M202
    Jerusalem Baptist Church Records, October 1860–June 1863 entries, Mss. 63M485 (microfilm)
    Lyle Family Papers, Mss. 62M49
    Minutes of the Harrodsburg Trustees, 1786–1875, Mss. 66M622 (microfilm)

William Moody Pratt Diaries, Mss. 46M79. 5 vols.
Records of the Particular Baptist Church, Williamstown, Kentucky, 1826–1919, Mss. M798 (microfilm)
John Scott Papers, Mss. 62M301
[Elizabethtown, Kentucky] Severn's Valley Baptist Church Minutes, 1788–1884, Mss. M117 (microfilm)
Shakertown at Pleasant Hill Collection, 1805–1920, Mss. 1M87M31 (microfilm)
Smith Family Papers, 1858–1955, Mss. 1M64M142
William Johnson Stone Papers, Mss. 54M131 (microfilm)
David. L. Thornton Papers, Mss. 61M256
Mary E. Van Meter Diary, Mss. 54M98 (microfilm)
Wickliffe-Preston Family Papers, Mss. 63M349
Lucy Craig Woolfolk Diary, Mss. M580 (microfilm)

University of Missouri, Western Historical Manuscripts Collection, Joint Collection—State Historical Society of Missouri/University of Missouri, Ellis Library, Columbia
David Rice Atchison Papers, Mss. 71
Bingham Family Papers, Mss. 998
William C. Breckenridge Papers, Mss. 1036 (microfilm)
Garland Carr Broadhead Scrapbook, Mss. 1000
Charles D. Drake Autobiography, Mss. 1003
Draper-McClurg Family Papers, Mss. 3069
John Allen Gano Family Papers, Mss. 65
B. James George, Sr., Collection, Mss. 3564
William H. Gregg Manuscript, Mss. C1113 (microfilm)
Odon Guitar Papers, Mss. C0882
Isaac Hockaday Letters, Mss. 2728
Ira B. Hyde Papers, Mss. 2406
Claiborne Fox Jackson File, Mss. 2447
Claiborne Fox Jackson Letters, Mss. 1789
Lucy Wortham James Collection, Mss. 1
Lilian Kingsbury Collection, Mss. 3724
Abiel Leonard Collection, Mss. 1013
John D. McKown Papers, Mss. 2335
McDaniel Family Papers, Mss. 2628
Miscellaneous Manuscripts, Mss. 1879
Missouri, General Assembly (Confederate), Journal, 1861, Mss. C2502
Missouri Confederate Archives, 1861, Mss. 2722
Missouri Confederate Home, Higginsville, Records, 1897–1944, Mss. C0066 (microfilm)
Bryan Obear Collection, Mss. 1387
William M. Paxton Papers, Mss. 1025
George Pohlman Collection, Mss. 3476
A. W. Reese, Recollections of the Civil War, 1870, Mss. 3627. 2 microfilm reels
Herbert F. Rice Papers, Mss. 2903
James S. Rollins Papers, Mss. 1026
John S. Sappington Papers, Mss. 1027
John Sappington Family Papers, Mss. 2889
Elvira A. W. Scott Diary (typescript), Mss. 1053
Frederick Starr Jr., Papers, Mss. 2073
Paulina H. Stratton Papers, Mss. C0842
Meriwether Jeff Thompson Papers, Mss. 1030
United Daughters of the Confederacy, Missouri Division, Records Mss. C3188
U.S. Works Projects Administration, Historical Records Survey, Missouri, 1935–1942, Mss. 3551

Washburne Family Papers, Mss. 2971
Marie Oliver Watkins Papers, Mss. 2689
Western Kentucky University, Manuscripts and Special Collections, Kentucky Library, Bowling Green, Kentucky
Bevie R. Cain Letters, Mss. SC2251
Josephine (Wells) Covington Letters, Mss. SC236
William H. Githens Letter, Mss. SC1364
Knott Collection, Mss. 53
Johanna Louisa (Underwood) Nazro Collection, Mss. SC1709
Shakers of South Union, Kentucky Collection, 1800–1916, Mss. 63
Underwood Collection, Mss. 58
Williamson Dixon Ward Civil War Journal, Mss. SC627
Wickersham Family Papers, 1861–1877, Mss. SC560
Western Reserve Historical Society, Cleveland, Ohio
S[almon]. B. Axtell Letter, Vertical File A
Charles Whittlesey Papers, Mss. 3196 (microfilm)

PRINTED GOVERNMENT DOCUMENTS

Acts of the General Assembly of the Commonwealth of Kentucky. 2 vols. Frankfort: Kentucky State Journal Publishing Company, 1912.
Acts of the General Assembly of the Commonwealth of Kentucky. 2 vols. Frankfort: The State Journal, 1914.
Annual Report of the Adjutant General of Missouri for 1864. Jefferson City: W. A. Curry, 1865.
Annual Report of the Adjutant General of Missouri for the Year Ending December 31, 1863. Jefferson City: State Printer, 1864.
Appendix to the Congressional Globe. 33rd Cong., 1st Sess. Washington, D.C.: Office of the Globe, 1855.
Appendix to the Congressional Globe. 38th Cong., 1st Sess.. Washington, D.C.: Office of the Globe, 1860.
Compendium of the Enumeration of the Inhabitants and Statistics of the United States in 1840. Washington, D.C.: Thomas Allen, 1841.
Congressional Globe. 46 vols. Washington, D.C.: Blair and Rives, 1834–1873.
DeBow, J. D. B., ed. The Seventh Census of the United States: 1850. Washington, D.C.: Robert Armstrong, Public Printer, 1853.
Fifth Census; or, Enumeration of the Inhabitants of the United States—1830. Washington, D.C.: Duff Green, 1832.
Journal and Proceedings of the Missouri State Convention, March 1861. St. Louis: George Knapp and Co., Printers and Binders, 1861.
Journal of the House of Representatives of the Commonwealth of Kentucky, 1861–1863. Frankfort: Yeoman Office, 1863.
Journal of the House of Representatives of the State of Missouri, Eleventh General Assembly, First Session, 1841–1842. Jefferson City: James Lusk, 1842.
Journal of the House of Representatives of the State of Missouri, Twenty-first General Assembly, First Session, 1860–1861. Jefferson City: State Printer, 1861.
Journal of the House of Representatives of the United States, 1850–1851. Washington, D.C.: House of Representatives, 1850–1851.
Journal of the Regular Session of the House of Representatives of the Commonwealth of Kentucky. Louisville: George G. Fetter, 1906.
Journal of the Senate, Extra Session of the Rebel Legislature, Called Together by a Proclamation of C. F. Jackson, Begun and Held at the Town of Neosho, Newton County, Missouri on the Twenty-first Day of October, Eighteen Hundred and Sixty-One. Jefferson City, Mo.: Emory S. Foster, 1865–1866.
Journal of the Senate of the Commonwealth of Kentucky 1859–1860. Frankfort: Yeoman Office, 1860.

Journal of the Senate of the State of Missouri, at the Adjourned Session of the Twenty-second General Assembly. Jefferson City: J. P. Ament, 1863.
Kennedy, Joseph C. G. *Agriculture of the United States in 1860: Compiled from the Original Returns of the Eighth Census*. Washington, D.C.: Government Printing Office, 1864.
Kennedy, Joseph C. G. *Manufactures of the United States in 1860: Compiled from the Original Returns of the Eighth Census*. Washington, D.C.: Government Printing Office, 1865
Kennedy, Joseph C. G. *Population of the United States in 1860: Compiled from the Original Returns of the Eighth Census*. Washington, D.C.: Government Printing Office, 1864.
Laws of the State of Missouri, Passed at the Called Session of the Twenty-first General Assembly, Begun and Held at the City of Jefferson, on Thursday, May 2, 1861. Jefferson City: J. P. Ament, 1861.
Proceedings of the Missouri State Convention, Held at Jefferson City and St. Louis, March, 1861–June, 1863. St. Louis: George Knapp, 1861–1863.
Revised Statutes of Kentucky, 1859–1860. 2 vols. Cincinnati: R. H. Stanton, 1860.
Terrell, W[illiam] H. H. *Indiana in the War of the Rebellion: Report of the Adjutant General*. Indianapolis: State Printer, 1869; reprint Indianapolis: Indiana Historical Society, 1960.
United States. *Statutes at Large, Treaties, and Proclamations of the United States of America*. Vol. 12. Boston: Little and Brown, 1863.
The War of the Rebellion: A Compilation of the Official Records of the Union and Confederate Armies. 4 series, 128 vols. Washington, D.C: War Department, 1881–1901.

NEWSPAPERS AND PERIODICALS

[Fredricktown, Mo.] *The Advance Guard*
[Little Rock, Ark.] *Arkansas Patriot*
Athens [Ohio] *Messenger*
Belleville [Ill.] *Advocate*
[Fayette, Mo.] *Boon's Lick Times*
Boonville [Mo.] *Eagle*
Boonville [Mo.] *Observer Extra*
Boston [Mass.] *Daily Advertiser*
[Richmond, Ind.] *The Broad Axe of Freedom*
Cairo [Ill.] *City Weekly Gazette*
Cairo [Ill.] *Evening Citizen and Bulletin*
Calhoun County [Ill.] *Weekly Union*
Cape Girardeau [Mo.] *Eagle* [Union Series]
Carbondale [Ill.] *Times*
Carrollton [Mo.] *Democrat*
[Cincinnati, Ohio] *Catholic Telegraph and Advocate*
Centralia [Ill.] *Sentinel*
Charleston [S.C.] *Mercury*
Chicago [Ill.] *Inter-ocean*
Chicago [Ill.] *Herald*
Cincinnati [Ohio] *Advertiser and Ohio Phoenix*
[Cincinnati, Ohio] *American Republic*
Cincinnati [Ohio] *Daily Commercial*
Cincinnati [Ohio] *Daily Enquirer*
Cincinnati [Ohio] *Daily Gazette*
Cincinnati [Ohio] *Post and Anti-Abolitionist*
Cincinnati [Ohio] *Weekly Gazette*
Cleveland [Ohio] *Daily Herald*
Clinton [Mo.] *Advocate*
[Cincinnati, Ohio] *Colored Citizen*
Columbia [Mo.] *Missouri-Herald*
Columbia [Mo.] *Patriot*

[Charleston, Mo.] *The Courier*
[Louisville, Ky.] *Courier-Journal*
Corydon [Ind.] *Weekly Democrat*
[Columbus, Ohio] *The Crisis*
[Little Rock, Ark.] *Daily Arkansas Gazette*
[Evansville, Ind.] *Daily Courier*
[Dayton, Ohio] *Daily Democrat*
[Frankfort, Ky.] *Daily Kentucky Yeoman*
[New Albany, Ind.] *Daily Ledger*
[St. Louis] *Daily Missouri Democrat*
[St. Louis] *Daily Missouri Republican*
[Washington, D.C.] *Daily National Intelligencer*
[Hamilton, Ohio] *Daily Telegraph*
[Cincinnati, Ohio] *The Daily Times*
Dayton [Ohio] *Daily Journal*
[New Orleans, La.] *De Bow's Review*
Delaware [Ohio] *Gazette*
Eaton [Ohio] *Weekly Register*
Evansville [Ind.] *Daily Journal*
[Union, Mo.] *Franklin County Progress*
[Cincinnati, Ohio] *The Free Nation*
[Newport, Ky.] *The Free South*
[Gallipolis, Ohio] *Gallia Courier*
Galveston [Tex.] *Daily News*
Genius of Universal Emancipation
Glasgow [Mo.] *Weekly Times*
Grayville [Ill.] *Independent*
Greenville [Ill.] *Advocate*
Hannibal [Mo.] *Daily Messenger*
Hamilton [Ohio] *Telegraph*
[New York] *Harper's Weekly*
Harrisburg [Ill.] *Chronicle*
[Hillsboro] *The Illinois Free Press*
[Shawneetown] *Illinois Republican*
[Springfield] *Illinois State Journal*
[Ripley, Ohio] *Independent Press*
[Centerville] *Indiana True Republican*
[Cincinnati, Ohio] *The Israelite*
[Jefferson City, Mo.] *Jefferson Inquirer*
Jonesboro [Ill.] *Gazette*
[Lexington] *The Kentucky Loyalist*
[Frankfort] *Kentucky Statesman*
[Cincinnati, Ohio] *Liberty Hall*
Liberty [Mo.] *Tribune*
Louisville [Ky.] *Journal*Macon [Mo.] *Weekly Argus*
Madison [Ind.] *Courier*
[Lexington, Ky.] *The Mail Bag*
Marion [Ill.] *Record*
McArthur [Ohio] *Register*
Milwaukee [Wis.] *Sentinel*
[Fayette] *Missouri Democrat*
[St. Louis] *Missouri Gazette*
[Franklin] *Missouri Intelligencer*

[Fayette] *Missouri Intelligencer and Boon's Lick Advertiser*
[Columbia] *Missouri Statesman*
[St. Joseph] *Missouri Vindicator*
[Springfield] *Missouri Weekly Patriot*
[Columbia] *Missourian*
[Hillsboro, Ill.] *Montgomery County Herald*
Nashville [Tenn.] *Dispatch*
[Lexington, Ky.] *The National Unionist*
New York Daily-Times
New York Evening Post Owensboro [Ky.] *Monitor*
Philadelphia [Pa.] *Inquirer*
[Cincinnati, Ohio] *The Philanthropist*
[Weston, Mo.] *Platte County Sentinel*
Pomeroy [Ohio] *Weekly Telegraph*
[Golconda, Ill.] *Pope County Transcript*
[Cincinnati, Ohio] *The Rail Splitter*
Richmond [Va.] *Enquirer*
The Ripley [Ohio] *Bee*
Sacramento [Calif.] *Transcript*
Saint Louis [Mo.] *Daily Union* Salem [Ill.] *Advocate*
Salem [Ind.] *Union Advocate*
Salem [Ohio] *Democrat*
[West Union, Ohio] *The Scion*
[Chillicothe, Ohio] *Scioto Gazette*
[Cape Girardeau, Mo.] *Southeast Radical*
[Cape Girardeau, Mo.] *Southern Democrat*
[Georgetown] *The Southern Ohio Argus*
[Washington, D.C.] *The Southern Press*
[Atchison, Kans.] *Squatter Sovereign*
St. Louis [Mo.] *Globe-Democrat*
St. Louis Republican
[Sullivan, Ind.] *The Stars and Stripes*
[Frankfort, Ky.] *Tri-Weekly Kentucky Yeoman*
[Louisville, Ky.] *The True Presbyterian*
[Nashville, Tenn.] *Union American*
[Vienna, Ill.] *The Union Courier*
[McConnelsville, Ohio] *Valley Democrat*
[Terre Haute, Ind.] *Wabash Express*
Warren [Ohio] *Constitution*
Washington [Ind.] *Weekly Gazette*
Weekly Bryan [Ohio] *Democrat*
[Lexington, Mo.] *Weekly Caucasian*
[Macon] *Weekly Georgia Telegraph*
[St. Joseph, Mo.] *The Weekly Herald*
[Danville] *Weekly Kentucky Tribune*
[Platte City, Mo.] *The Weekly Tenth Legion*
[Paris, Ky.] *The Western Citizen*
[Kansas City, Mo.] *Western Journal of Commerce*
Xenia [Ohio] *Torch-Light*

CITY AND COUNTY HISTORIES

Cist, Charles. *Cincinnati in 1841: Its Early Annals and Future Prospects*. Cincinnati: printed by author, 1841.

Ford, Henry A., and Kate B. Ford. *History of Cincinnati*. Cleveland: W. W. Williams, 1881.
Greve, Charles Theodore. *The Centennial History of Cincinnati and Representative Citizens*. 2 vols. Chicago: Biographical Publishing, 1904.
History of Howard and Chariton Counties, Missouri, Written and Compiled from the Most Official Authentic and Private Sources, Including a History of Its Townships, Towns and Villages. St. Louis: National Historical Company, 1883.
History of Saline County, Missouri, Carefully Written and Compiled from the Most Authentic Official and Private Sources, Including a History of its Townships, Cities, Towns and Villages. St. Louis: Missouri Historical Company, 1881.
Killits, John. *Toledo and Lucas, Ohio, 1623–1923*. 2 vols. Toledo: S. J. Clarke Publishing, 1923.
Leonard, Lewis A., ed. *Greater Cincinnati and Its People: A History*. 4 vols. New York: Lewis Historical Publishing, 1927.
Louisville Past and Present. Louisville: John P. Morton, 1875.
Napton, William B. *Past and Present of Saline County, Missouri*. Indianapolis: B. F. Bowen, 1910.
Portrait and Biographical Album of Greene and Clark Counties, Ohio. Chicago: Chapman Bros., 1890.
Scharf, J. Thomas. *History of St. Louis City and County*. Philadelphia: Louis H. Everts and Co., 1883.

PRINTED PRIMARY MATERIALS

Abdy, E[dward] S. *Journal of a Residence and Tour in the United States of North America, from April, 1833 to October, 1834*. 3 vols. London: John Murray, 1835; reprint New York: Negro Universities Press, 1969.
Acton, Hul-cee M. *History of the Tau Theta Kappa Society of Georgetown College*. Georgetown, Ky.: Tau Theta Kappa Society, 1918.
Anderson, Galusha. *A Border City during the Civil War*. Boston: Little, Brown, 1908.
Andrews, William L., et al., eds. *The Literature of the American South*. New York: W. W. Norton, 1986.
Annual Report of the American Historical Association for the Year 1902 in Two Volumes: Sixth Report of Historic Manuscripts Commission; with Diary and Correspondence of Salmon P. Chase. 2 vols. Washington, D.C.: Government Printing Office, 1903.
[Anonymous]. *For Peace, and Peaceable Separation: Citizen's Democratic Address to the People of the State of Ohio, and the People of the Several States of the West and North*. Cincinnati: printed by author, 1863.
[Anonymous, "D. J. M."] Review of *Industrial Exchanges and Social Remedies, with a Consideration of Taxation*, by David Parish Barhydt. *Southern Quarterly Review* 15 (July 1849): 449–60.
Bagby, George William. "Editor's Table." *Southern Literary Messenger* 33 (September–October 1862): 581–91.
Bailey, W[illiam]. S. *A Short Sketch of Our Troubles in the Anti-Slavery Cause*. Newport, Ky.: Office of the *Daily and Weekly News*, 1858.
Barnes, Albert. *The Church and Slavery*. Philadelphia: Parry and McMillan, 1857.
Barnes, Gilbert H., and Dwight L. Dumond, eds. *Letters of Theodore Dwight Weld, Angelina Grimké Weld, and Sarah Grimké*. 2 vols. New York: D. Appleton-Century, 1934.
Basler, Roy F., ed. *The Collected Works of Abraham Lincoln*. 9 vols. Springfield, Ill.: The Abraham Lincoln Association, 1953; reprint New Brunswick, N.J.: Rutgers University Press, 1988.
Bates, Edward. *The Diary of Edward Bates 1859–1866*, ed. Howard K. Beale. Washington, D.C.: American Historical Association, 1933; reprint New York: Da Capo Press, 1971.
Beecher, Edward. *Narrative of Riots at Alton*. New York: E. P. Dutton, 1965.
Beecher, Henry Ward. *Addresses in America and England, from 1850 to 1885, on Slavery, the Civil War, and the Development of Civil Liberty in the United States*, ed. John R. Howard. New York: Fords, Howard, and Hulbert, 1887.
Beecher, Lyman. *Autobiography, Correspondence, Etc., of Lyman Beecher, D.D.Ed.*, ed. Charles Beecher. 2 vols. New York: Harper, 1864–1865.
Beecher, Lyman. *A Plea for the West*. Cincinnati: Truman and Smith, 1835.
[Berry, Daniel]. *Letters Written by Dr. Daniel Berry to Mary Crebs Berry During the Civil War*, ed. Harriet B. Vaught. Carmi, Ill.: [s.n.], 1976.

[Bingham, George Caleb]. *"But I Forget That I Am a Painter and Not a Politician": The Letters of George Caleb Bingham*, ed. Lynn Wolf Gentzler and Roger E. Robinson. Columbia: State Historical Society of Missouri, 2011.
Birkbeck, Morris. *Letters from Illinois*. Philadelphia: M. Carey and Son, 1818; reprint New York: DaCapo Press, 1970.
Birkbeck, Morris, and George Flower. *History of the English Settlement in Edwards County, Illinois, Founded in 1817 and 1818*. Chicago: Fergus Publishing, 1882.
[Birney, James G.] *Letters of James Gillespie Birney, 1831–1857*, ed. Dwight L. Dumond. 2 vols. Gloucester, Mass.: Peter Smith, 1966.
[Blane, William N.] *An Excursion Through the United States and Canada During the Years 1822–1823 by an English Gentleman*. London: Baldwin, Cradock, and Joy, 1824.
Bradbury, John. *Travels in the Interior of America in the Years 1809, 1810 and 1811*. London: Sherwood, Neely, and Jones, 1819.
Bradbury, John F., Jr., ed. "The Civil War Letters of Moses Jasper Bradford, Phelps County Confederate and One of the 'Immortal 600.'" *Newsletter of the Phelps County Historical Society* 19 (April 1999): 2–22.
Bradbury, John F., Jr. ed. "Union or Disunion: The Letters of Allen B. Johnson." *Newsletter of the Phelps County Historical Society* 6 (June 1987): 3–34.
[Breckinridge, Robert J.] *Discourse of Robert J. Breckinridge, Jan. 4, 1861*. Cincinnati: Faran and McLean, 1861.
Bremer, Fredrika. *The Homes of the New World: Impressions of America*. 2 vols. New York: Harper and Brothers, 1853.
Brown, Benjamin Gratz. *Emancipation as a State Policy: Letter of B. Gratz Brown to the "Palmyra Courier"*. N.p.: s.n., 1862.
Brown, William Wells. *Narrative of William W. Brown, an American Slave, Written by Himself*. London: C. Gilpin, 1849.
[Browning, Orville H.] *The Diary of Orville Hickman Browning 1850–1864*, ed. Theodore Calvin Pease and James G. Randall. Springfield: Illinois State Historical Library, 1927.
Bruce, Henry Clay. *The New Man: Twenty-Nine Years a Slave. Twenty-Nine Years a Free Man; Recollections of H. C. Bruce*. York, Pa.: P. Anstadt and Sons, 1895.
Brush, Daniel Harmon. *Growing Up in Southern Illinois*, ed. Milo Milton Quaife. Madison: University of Wisconsin Press, 1944.
Bryan, Edward B. *The Rightful Remedy: Addressed to the Slaveholders of the South*. Charleston, S.C.: Walker and James, 1850.
Bullitt, Thomas W. *My Life at Oxmoor: Life on a Farm in Kentucky Before the War*. Louisville: J. P. Morton, 1911.
[Caldwell, J. P.] *A Northern Confederate at Johnson's Island Prison: The Civil War Diaries of James Park Caldwell*, ed. George H. Jones. Jefferson, N.C.: McFarland, 2010.
Carrier, A. H. *Monument to the Memory of Henry Clay*. Philadelphia: D. Rulison, 1859.
Carter, Gari. *Troubled State: Civil War Journals of Franklin Archibald Dick*. Kirksville, Mo.: Truman State University Press, 2008.
Cartwright, Peter. *Autobiography of Peter Cartwright, the Backwoods Preacher*, ed. W[illiam]. P[eter]. Strickland. New York: Carlton and Porter, 1857.
Christy, David. *Pulpit Politics; or, Ecclesiastical Legislation on Slavery, in Its Disturbing Influences on the American Union*. Cincinnati: Faran and McLean, 1862.
The Cincinnati Directory for the Year 1844. Cincinnati: R. P. Brooks, 1844.
The Cincinnati Directory Advertiser, for 1834. Cincinnati: Deming, 1834.
Cist, Charles, ed. *The Cincinnati Directory, for 1842*. Cincinnati: E. Morgan, 1842.
Cist, Charles, ed. *The Cincinnati Directory, for 1843*. Cincinnati: R. P. Brooks, 1843.
Claiborne, John F. H. *Life and Correspondence of John A. Quitman, Governor of the State of Mississippi*. New York: Harper and Bros., 1860.
Clarke, Lewis Garrard. *Narrative of the Sufferings of Lewis Clarke, During a Captivity of More Than Twenty-Five Years, Among the Algerines of Kentucky, One of the So Called Christian States of North America*. Boston: David H. Ela, Printer, 1845.

[Clay, Henry]. *The Life and Speeches of Henry Clay*, ed. Daniel Mallory. 2 vols. Hartford, Conn.: Silas and Andrus and Son, 1855.
Clay Monument Association. *Articles for the Government of the Clay Monument Association*. Lexington: The *Observer and Reporter* Office, 1852.
Coffin, Levi. *Reminiscences of Levi Coffin, the Reputed President of the Underground Railroad*. Cincinnati: Western Tract Society, 1876.
Collins, Richard. *History of Kentucky*. Louisville: John P. Morton, 1874.
Commager, Henry Steele, ed. *The Blue and the Gray*. 2 vols. Indianapolis: Bobbs-Merrill, 1973.
Connelly, William E. *Quantrill and the Border Wars*. Cedar Rapids, Iowa: Torch Press, 1910.
Conrad, William. *The Journal of Elder William Conrad: Pioneer Preacher*, ed. Lloyd W. Franks. Lexington: R F Publishing, 1976.
Cozzins, Peter, ed. *Battles and Leaders of the Civil War*. Vol. 5. Urbana: University of Illinois Press, 2002.
Cuming, Fortescue. *Sketches of a Tour to the Western Country*. Pittsburgh: Cramer, Spear, and Eichbaum, 1810.
Curtis, Samuel R. "Report on Operations of Iowa Troops in Missouri in June, 1861," in *The Annals of Iowa: A Historical Quarterly*, ed. Charles Aldrich, 8:358–61. 3rd ser. Des Moines: Historical Department of Iowa, 1907–1908.
"David Rice Atchison Letter." *Missouri Historical Review* 31 (July 1937): 443–44.
[Davis, William]. *The Civil War Journal of Billy Davis*, ed. Richard Skidmore. Greencastle, Ind.: Nugget Publishers, 1989.
A Debate on Slavery; Held in the City of Cincinnati, on the First, Second, Third, and Sixth Days of October, 1845, Upon the Question: Is Slave-holding in Itself Sinful, and the Relation Between Master and Slave, a Sinful Relation? Cincinnati: William H. Moore, 1846.
Dedication of the Lovejoy Monument, Alton, Illinois, November 8th, 1897. Alton, Ill.: Cha[rle]s Holden, [1897].
Dee, Christine, ed. *Ohio's War: The Civil War in Documents*. Athens: Ohio University Press, 2006.
Dicey, Edward. *Spectator of America*, ed. Herbert Mitgang. Chicago: Quadrangle Books, 1971; reprint Athens: University of Georgia Press, 1989.
Dow, Lorenzo. *History of Cosmopolite, or the Four Volumes of Lorenzo Dow's Journal*, ed. Peggy Dow. Wheeling, Va.: Joshua Martin, 1848.
[Drake, Charles D.] *Immediate Emancipation in Missouri: Speech of Charles D. Drake, Delivered in the Missouri State Convention, June 16th, 1863*. St. Louis: [s.n.], 1863.
[Drake, Charles D.] *Union and Anti-Slavery Speeches, Delivered during the Rebellion by Charles D. Drake*. Cincinnati: Applegate, 1864.
Drake, Daniel. *Pioneer Life in Kentucky, 1785–1800*. New York: Henry Schuman, 1948.
Duden, Gottfried. *Report of a Journey to the Western States of North America, and a Residence of Several Years on the Missouri (During the Years 1824, '25, '26, and 1827), Dealing with the Question of Emigration and Excess Population*, ed. James W. Goodrich and Wayne N. Senner. Columbia: University of Missouri Press, 1980.
Duke, Basil W[ilson]. *History of Morgan's Cavalry*. Cincinnati: Miami Printing and Publishing, 1867.
Duke, Basil W[ilson]. *Reminiscences of General Basil W. Duke, C.S.A.* Garden City, N.Y.: Doubleday, Page, 1911.
Edwards, John N[ewman]. *Noted Guerrillas, or the Warfare on the Border*. St. Louis: Bryan, Brand, 1877.
Edwards, John N[ewman]. *Shelby and His Men, or the War in the West*. Cincinnati: Miami Printing and Publishing, 1867.
Executive Documents: Messages and Annual Reports for 1864 Made to the 56th General Assembly of Ohio. Columbus: State Printer, 1865.
Faux, W[illiam]. *Memorable Days in America: Being a Journal of a Tour to the United States Principally Undertaken to Ascertain, by Positive Evidence, the Condition and Probable Prospects of British Emigrants; Including Accounts of Mr. Birkbeck's Settlement in the Illinois*. London: W. Simpkin and R. Marshall, 1823.

Fisher, Elwood. *Lecture on the North and the South: Delivered Before the Young Men's Mercantile Library Association, of Cincinnati, Ohio, January 16, 1849.* Washington, D.C.: John T. Towers, 1849.

Fletcher, William B. "The Civil War Journal of William B. Fletcher." *Indiana Magazine of History* 57 (March 1961): 41–76.

Flint, Timothy. *Recollections of the Last Ten Years.* Boston: Cummings, Hilliard, 1826.

Flower, Richard. *Letters from Lexington and the Illinois, Containing a Brief Account of the English Settlement in the Latter Territory, and a Refutation of the Misrepresentations of Mr. Cobbett.* London: J. Ridgway, 1819.

"Fragments of the Broadhead Collection." *Glimpses of the Past* 2 (March 1935): 49–51.

Fry, James B. *Military Miscellanies.* New York: Brentano's, 1889.

Gallagher, William Davis. *Facts and Conditions of Progress in the North-West.* Cincinnati: H. W. Derby, 1850.

Gallagher, William Davis. "The Question of Slavery in the South." *Hesperian* 1 (September 1838): 415–16.

Gladstone, T. H. *The Englishman in Kansas.* New York: Miller, 1857.

[Goodloe, Daniel R.] *The South and the North: A Reply to a Lecture on the North and the South, by Ellwood [sic] Fisher, Delivered Before the Young Men's Mercantile Library Association of Cincinnati, January 16, 1849, by a Carolinian.* Washington, D.C.: Buell and Blanchard, 1849.

Goodrich, James W., ed. "The Civil War Letters of Bethiah Pyalt McKown." *Missouri Historical Review* 67 (January, April 1973): 227–52, 351–70.

Grant, Ulysses S. *The Papers of Ulysses S. Grant,* ed. John Y. Simon. 28 vols. Carbondale: Southern Illinois University Press, 1967.

Grant, Ulysses S. *Personal Memoirs of U. S. Grant.* New York: Da Capo Press, 1982.

Great Union Meeting, Philadelphia December 7, 1859. Philadelphia: Crissy and Markley, 1859.

Green, Elisha Winfield. *Life of the Rev. Elisha W. Green, One of the Founders of the Kentucky Normal and Theological Institute Now the State University at Louisville... and Over Thirty Years Pastor of the Colored Baptist Churches of Maysville and Paris, Written by Himself.* Maysville, Ky.: The Republican Printing Office, 1888.

Grimes, Absalom C. "Campaigning with Mark Twain," in *Mark Twain's Civil War,* ed. David Rachels, 111–28. Lexington: University Press of Kentucky, 2007.

[Guerrant, Edward O.] *Bluegrass Confederate: The Headquarters Diary of Edward O. Guerrant,* ed. William C. Davis and Meredith L. Swentor. Baton Rouge: Louisiana State University Press, 1999.

Hall, James. "Education and Slavery." *Western Monthly Magazine* 17 (May 1834): 266–73.

Hall, James. *Letters from the West: Containing Sketches of Scenery, Manners, and Customs; and Anecdotes Connected with the First Settlements of the Western Sections of the United States.* London: Henry Colburn, 1828.

[Hammond, James Henry]. *The North and the South: A Review of the Lecture on the Same Subject, Delivered by Mr. Elwood Fisher, Before the Young Men's Mercantile Association of Cincinnati, Ohio.* Charleston, S.C.: J. S. Burges, 1849.

Hay, John. *Lincoln and the Civil War in the Diaries and Letters of John Hay,* ed. Tyler Dennett. New York: Dodd, Mead, 1939; reprint New York: Da Capo Press, 1988.

[Hardin, Elizabeth Pendleton]. *The Private War of Lizzie Hardin: A Kentucky Confederate Girl's Diary of the Civil War in Kentucky, Virginia, Tennessee, Alabama, and Georgia,* ed. G. Glenn Clift. Frankfort: Kentucky Historical Society, 1962.

Headley, P. C. *The Patriot Boy; or, The Life and Career of Major-General Ormsby M. Mitchel.* New York: William H. Appleton, 1865.

Henson, Josiah. *The Life of Josiah Henson, Formerly a Slave, Now an Inhabitant of Canada, as Narrated by Himself.* Boston: Arthur D. Phelps, 1849; reprint Bedford, Mass.: Applewood Books, 2002.

Hildebrand, Samuel S. *Autobiography of Samuel S. Hildebrand: The Renowned Missouri "Bushwacker" and Unconquerable Rob Roy of America; Being His Complete Confession, Recently Made to the*

Writers and Carefully Compiled by James W. Evans and A. Wendell Keith, Together with All the Facts Connected with His Early History. Jefferson City: State Times Book and Job Printing House, 1870; reprint Woodbridge, Conn.: Research Publications, 1985.

[Hill, Sarah Jane Full]. *Mrs. Hill's Journal: Civil War Reminiscences, by Sarah Jane Full Hill,* ed. Mark M. Krug. Chicago: R. R. Donnelly, 1980.

"History of South Union, Ky." *Manifesto (1884–1899)* 24 (April–December 1894): 77–81, 101–4, 125–27, 149–51, 173–76, 197–99, 221–25, 245–48, 269–71; 25 (January–April 1895): 3–5, 25–28, 49–52, 73–77.

Hodge, George B. *Sketch of the First Kentucky Brigade by Its Adjutant General, G. B. Hodge.* Frankfort, Ky.: Major and Johnston, 1874.

Hoffman, C[harles]. F[enno]. *A Winter in the Far West.* 2 vols. London: Richard Bentley, 1835.

Holcombe, W[illiam]. H. "A Separate Nationality, or the Africanization of the South." *Southern Literary Messenger* 32 (February 1861): 81–88.

Holt, Joseph. *Letter from the Hon. Joseph Holt upon the Policy of the General Government, the Pending Revolution, Its Objects, Its Probable Results If Successful, and the Duty of Kentucky in the Crisis.* Louisville: Bradley and Gilbert, 1861.

Johnson, E. Polk. *A History of Kentucky and Kentuckians.* 2 vols. Louisville: Lewis Publishing, 1912.

Johnson, Robert Underwood, and Howard L. Conard, eds. *Battles and Leaders of the Civil War.* 4 vols. New York: Thomas Yoseloff, 1956.

Julian, George W. *The Cause and Cure of Our National Troubles.* Washington, D.C.: Scammel, 1862.

Julian, George W. *The Life of Joshua R. Giddings.* Chicago: A. C. McClurg, 1892.

Julian, George W. *Personal Recollections, 1840–1872.* Chicago: Jansen, McClurg, 1884.

King, Edward. "The Great South: Some Notes on Missouri; The Heart of the Republic." *Scribner's Monthly* 8 (July 1874): 264–69.

Knox, Thomas W. *Camp-Fire and Cotton Field: Southern Adventure in Time of War.* Philadelphia: Jones Brothers, 1865.

Korn, Bertram W. *American Jewry and the Civil War.* Philadelphia: The Jewish Publication Society of America, 1951.

Langstaff, George Quigley, Jr., ed. *The Life and Times of Quintus Quincy Quigley, 1828–1910: His Personal Journals, 1859–1908.* Brentwood, Tenn.: Tallant Group, 1999.

Lee, D. "Cotton Culture in the United States." *The Cultivator* 12 (November 1864): 348–49.

Lee, Jacob F., ed. "An Honorable Position: Joseph Holt's Letter to Joshua F. Speed on Neutrality and Secession in Kentucky, May 1861." *Ohio Valley History* 7 (Winter 2007): 32–55.

Leftwich, W[illiam]. M. *Martyrdom in Missouri: A History of Religious Proscription, the Seizure of Churches, and the Persecution of Ministers of the Gospel, in the State of Missouri during the Late Civil War, and under the "Test Oath" of the New Constitution.* 2 vols. St. Louis: S. W. Book and Publishing, 1870.

Leopard, Buel, and Floyd Shoemaker, eds. *The Messages and Proclamations of the Governors of the State of Missouri.* 4 vols. Columbia: State Historical Society of Missouri, 1922.

Letter to the Secretary of the Treasury, on the Effect of the Tariff of 1842: On the Agricultural and Other Interests of the West, by a Committee of the Democratic Convention of Hamilton County, Ohio. Cincinnati: Democratic Party [Hamilton County, Ohio], 1845.

[Lieber, Francis W.] *No Party Now But All for Our Country.* Philadelphia: Crissy and Markley, Printers, 1863.

Lilienthal, Max. *Max Lilienthal: American Rabbi—Life and Writings,* ed. David Philipson. New York: Bloch Publishing, 1915.

Logan, John A. *The Great Conspiracy: Its Origins and History.* New York: A. R. Hart, 1886.

Logan, Mary. *Reminiscences of the Civil War and Reconstruction.* Carbondale: Southern Illinois University Press, 1970.

Loguen, J. W. *Rev. J. W. Loguen, as a Slave and as a Freeman: A Narrative of Real Life.* Syracuse, N.Y.: J. G. K. Truair, 1859.

Lowell, James Russell. *The Works of James Russell Lowell.* 5 vols. Boston and New York: Houghton, Mifflin, 1871.

Lyell, Charles. *A Second Visit to North America*. 2 vols. London: John Murray, 1855.
Lyell, Charles. *Travels in North America, Canada, and Nova Scotia*. 2 vols. London: John Murray, 1855.
MacLean, J. P., ed., *Shakers of Ohio: Fugitive Papers Concerning the Shakers of Ohio, with Unpublished Manuscripts*. Columbus: F. J. Heer Printing, 1907.
Mahony, D[ennis]. A. *The Prisoner of State*. New York: Carleton, 1863.
Malvin, John. *North into Freedom: The Autobiography of John Malvin, Free Negro, 1795–1880*. Cleveland: Press of the Western Reserve University, 1966.
[Mann, Horace]. *Slavery: Letters and Speeches, by Rep. Horace Mann*. Boston: B. B. Mussey, 1853.
Marshall, John A. *American Bastille: A History of the Illegal Arrests and Imprisonment of American Citizens During the Late Civil War*. Philadelphia: T. W. Hartley, 1869.
Maximilian [Alexander Philipp Wied-Neuwied, Prince of Wied]. *Travels in the Interior of North America*, trans. H. Evans Lloyd. London: Ackerman, 1843.
McClure, Alexander K. *Lincoln and Men of War-Times: Some Personal Recollections of War and Politics During the Lincoln Administration*. Philadelphia: Times Publishing, 1892.
McElroy, John. *The Struggle for Missouri*. Washington, D.C.: National Tribune Company, 1909.
[McKnight, William]. *Do They Miss Me at Home? The Civil War Letters of William McKnight, Seventh Ohio Volunteer Cavalry*, ed. Donald C. Maness and H. Jason Combs. Athens: Ohio University Press, 2010.
McLarty, Vivian K. ed. "The Civil War Letters of Colonel Bazel F. Lazear." *Missouri Historical Review* 44 (April–July 1950): 254–73, 387–401; 45 (October 1950): 47–63.
McPheeters, Samuel Brown. *Memoir of Rev. Samuel B. McPheeters*, ed. John S. Grasty. St. Louis and Louisville: Southwestern Book and Publishing and Davidson Bros., 1871.
Mersman, Joseph J. *The Whiskey Merchant's Diary: An Urban Life in the Emerging Midwest*, ed. Linda A. Fisher. Athens: Ohio University Press, 2007.
Miller, George. *Missouri's Memorable Decade, 1860–1870*. Columbia, Mo.: E. W. Stephens, 1898.
Missouri Troops in Service During the Civil War. Washington, D.C.: Government Printing Office, 1902.
Moore, Frank, ed. *The Rebellion Record: A Diary of American Events*. 12 vols. New York: G. P. Putnam, 1861–1868; reprint New York: Arno Press, 1977.
[Moore, Nancy]. *The Journal of Eldress Nancy, Kept at the South Union, Kentucky, Shaker Colony, August 15, 1861-September 4, 1864*, ed. Mary Julia Neal. Nashville, Tenn.: Parthenon Press, 1963.
Moses, John. *Illinois, Historical and Statistical*. 2 vols. Chicago: Fergus Print, 1895.
Mudd, Joseph A. *With Porter in Northeast Missouri*. Washington, D.C.: National Publishing, 1909.
Murray, Amelia M. *Letters from the United States, Cuba and Canada*. 2 vols. New York: G. P. Putnam, 1856.
Napton, William Barclay. *The Union on Trial: The Political Journals of Judge William Barclay Napton, 1829–1883*, ed. Christopher Phillips and Jason L. Pendleton. Columbia: University of Missouri Press, 2005.
Napton, William Barclay, et al. *Address to the People of the United States, Together with the Proceedings and Resolutions of the Pro-Slavery Convention of Missouri, Held at Lexington, July, 1855*. St. Louis: *Missouri Republican*, 1855.
Nasby, Petroleum V. [David R. Locke]. *Ekkoes from Kentucky*. Boston: Lee and Shepherd, 1868.
Nasby, Petroleum V. [David R. Locke]. *The Nasby Letters, Being the Original Nasby Letters as Written During His Lifetime*. Toledo, Oh.: Toledo Blade, 1893.
Nasby, Petroleum V. [David R. Locke]. *Swingin Round the Cirkle, or Andy's Trip to the West Together with a Life of Its Hero*. New York: American News Corp., 1866.
Nation, Richard E., and Stephen E. Towne, eds. *Indiana's War: The Civil War in Documents*. Athens: Ohio University Press, 2009.
Nicholas, S. S., et al. *Slave Emancipation in Kentucky*. Louisville: Corresponding and Executive Committee on Emancipation, [1849].
Nicolay, John G., and John Hay. *Abraham Lincoln: A History*. 8 vols. Chicago: Century, 1890.

Obituary of General Robert T. Lytle. Cincinnati: Dawson and Fisher, [1840].
Ogden, George W. *Letters from the West, Comprising a Tour through the Western Country, and a Residence of Two Summers in the States of Ohio and Kentucky.* New Bedford, Mass.: Melcher and Bros., 1823.
Oliver, William. *Eight Months in Illinois, with Information to Immigrants.* Newcastle upon Tyne: W. A. Mitchell, 1843; reprint Carbondale: Southern Illinois University Press, 2002.
Olmsted, Frederick Law. *A Journey Through Texas; or, A Saddle-Trip on the Southwestern Frontier.* New York and London: Dix, Edwards and S. Low, 1857.
Organization of Camps of the United Confederate Veterans. New Orleans: J. G. Hauser, 1910.
Palmer, John McAuley. *Personal Recollections of John M. Palmer: The Story of an Earnest Life.* Cincinnati: Robert Clarke, 1901.
Parsons, John. *A Tour Through Indiana in 1840*, ed. Kate Milner Rabb. New York: Robert M. McBride, 1920.
[Parsons, Thomas W.] *Incidents and Experiences in the Life of Thomas W. Parsons, from 1826 to 1900*, ed. Frank Furlong Mathias. Lexington: University Press of Kentucky, 1975.
Peckham, James. *General Nathaniel Lyon and Missouri in 1861.* New York: American News, 1866.
[Peter, Frances Dallam]. *A Union Woman in Civil War Kentucky: The Diary of Frances Peter*, ed. John David Smith and William J. Cooper Jr. Lexington: University Press of Kentucky, 2000.
Plat Book of Saline County, Missouri. Philadelphia: North West Publishing, 1876.
[Polk, Jefferson J.] *Autobiography of Dr. J. J. Polk.* Louisville: John P. Morton, 1867.
[Pope, John]. *The Military Memoirs of John Pope*, ed. Peter Cozzins and Robert I. Girardi. Chapel Hill: University of North Carolina Press, 1998.
Priest, Josiah. *Bible Defence of Slavery.* Glasgow, Ky.: W. S. Brown, 1852.
Proceedings and Resolutions of the Indiana Soldiers in the "Department of the Cumberland": To the Indiana Legislature. Indianapolis: Indianapolis Journal, 1863.
Proceedings of the Twenty-third Annual Convention of the Missouri Division United Daughters of the Confederacy, Held in Sedalia, Missouri, October 19, 20, 21, 1920. N.p.: s.n., [1920–1921].
Rankin, Adam. *A Review of the Noted Revival in Kentucky: Commenced in the Year of Our Lord, 1801.* Pittsburgh: John Israel, 1802.
Reid, Whitelaw. *Ohio in the War.* 2 vols. New York: Moore, Wilsatch, and Baldwin, 1868.
Reinhart, Joseph R., ed. *Two Germans in the Civil War: The Diary of John Daeuble and the Letters of Gottfried Rentschler, 6th Kentucky Volunteer Infantry.* Knoxville: University of Tennessee Press, 2004.
Report of the Ceremonies on the Fourth of July 1857, at the Laying of the Corner Stone of a National Monument, to Be Erected near Lexington, Kentucky, to the Memory of Henry Clay: Together with the Oration Delivered on the Occasion by the Rev. Robert J. Breckinridge. [Cincinnati]: Clay Monument Association, 1857.
Report of the Excursion Made by the Executive and Legislatures of the States of Kentucky and Tennessee, to the State of Ohio, on the 26th, 27th, and 28th Jan., 1860: On the Invitation of the Governor and Legislature of Ohio, and the Citizens of Cincinnati. Cincinnati: R. Clarke and Co., 1860.
Reynolds, John. *My Own Times, Embracing Also, a History of My Life.* Belleville, Ill.: B. H. Perryman and H. L. Davison, 1855.
Richardson, Anne H. *Little Laura, the Kentucky Abolitionist, to the Young Friends of the Slave.* Newcastle, UK: Thomas Pigg, 1859.
Robinson and Jones' Cincinnati Directory, for 1846. Cincinnati: Robinson and Jones, 1846.
Rollins, C. B., ed. "Letters of George Caleb Bingham to James M. Rollins." *Missouri Historical Review* 32 (October 1937–July 1938): 3–34, 164–202, 340–77, 484–522; 33 (October 1938–July 1939): 45–78, 203–29, 349–84, 499–526.
Rombauer, Robert J. *The Union Cause in St. Louis in 1861.* St. Louis: Nixon-Jones Printing Co., 1909.
Roster of the Department of Missouri, Grand Army of the Republic, and Its Auxiliaries. Kansas City, Mo.: Western Veteran, 1895.
Rowan, Steven C., and James Neal Primm, eds. *Germans for a Free Missouri: Translations from the St. Louis Radical Press, 1857–1862.* Columbia: University of Missouri Press, 1983.

Rules and Regulations for the Government of the Kentucky Confederate Home at Pewee Valley, Kentucky. Louisville: Courier-Journal Job Printing, 1922.

Russell, William Howard. *My Diary North and South.* London: Bradbury and Evans, 1863.

Sakmyster, Thomas, ed. "A Visit to the Shaker Village of White Water in 1881." *Communal Societies* 32, no. 1 (2012): 57–81.

Schofield, John M. *Forty-six Years in the Army.* New York: Century, 1897.

Shaffer, David Henry. *The Cincinnati, Covington, Newport, and Fulton Directory, for 1840.* Cincinnati: J. B. and R. P. Donogh, 1840.

Shannon, James. *An Address Delivered Before the Pro-Slavery Convention of the State of Missouri, Held in Lexington, July 13, 1855, on Domestic Slavery, as Examined in the Light of Scripture, of Natural Rights, of Civil Government, and the Constitutional Power of Congress.* St. Louis: [Missouri] Republican Book and Job Office, 1855.

Sherman, William T. *Memoirs of General William T. Sherman.* 2 vols. New York: Appleton, 1875; reprint New York: Da Capo Press, 1984.

Siddali, Silvana R. *Missouri's War: The Civil War in Documents.* Athens: Ohio University Press, 2009.

Siebert, Wilbur Henry. *The Underground Railroad: From Slavery to Freedom.* New York: Macmillan, 1898; reprint New York: Arno Press, 1968.

The Sixty-Third Birthday of Ulysses S. Grant. Louisville: *Courier-Journal*, 1885.

Snead, Thomas L. *The Fight for Missouri from the Election of Lincoln to the Death of Lyon.* New York: Charles Scribner's Sons, 1886.

[Society of the Army of the Cumberland]. *Fifteenth Reunion, Society of the Army of the Cumberland, October 1883.* Cincinnati: Robert Clarke and Co., Printers, 1884.

[Society of the Army of the Cumberland]. *First Annual Report, Society of the Army of the Cumberland, February, 1868.* Cincinnati: Robert Clarke and Co. Printers, 1868.

[Society of the Army of the Tennessee]. *Report of the Proceedings of the Society of the Army of the Tennessee at the First Annual Meeting Held at Cincinnati, Ohio, November 14th and 15th 1866.* Cincinnati: The Society, 1866–1867.

[Society of the Army of the Tennessee]. *Report of the Proceedings of the Society of the Army of the Tennessee at the Sixth Annual Meeting Held at Madison, Wisconsin, July 3rd and 4th, 1872.* Cincinnati: The Society, 1872.

Speech of Hon. George H. Yeaman, of Kentucky, on the President's Proclamation, Delivered in the House of Representatives, December 18, 1962. Baltimore: John Murphy, 1863.

Speech of Hon. J. A. Wright, of Indiana, on the Bill to Confiscate the Property and Free the Slaves of Rebels, Delivered in the Senate of the United States, April 30, 1862. Washington, D.C.: Congressional Globe, 1862.

Speech of Hon. O. H. Browning of Illinois, on the Confiscation Bill, Delivered in the Senate of the United States, April 29, 1862. Washington, D.C.: L. Towers, 1862.

Speech of Hon. William Allen of Ohio, on Confiscation and Emancipation, Delivered in the House of Representatives of the United States, April 24, 1862. Washington, D.C.: McGill, Witherow, 1862.

Speed, Thomas. *The Union Cause in Kentucky, 1860–1865.* New York: G. P. Putnam's Sons, 1907.

Speed, Thomas. *The Union Regiments of Kentucky.* Louisville: Courier-Journal Job Print, 1897.

Steele, [Eliza R.] *A Summer Journey in the West.* New York: John S. Taylor, 1841.

Stowe, Charles Edward. *Life of Harriet Beecher Stowe: Compiled from Her Letters by Her Son.* Charleston, S.C.: BiblioBazaar, 2006.

Sutton, Richard. *Report of the Convention of the Constitution of Kentucky.* Frankfort, Ky.: A. G. Hodges, 1850.

Switzler, William F. *Illustrated History of Missouri from 1541 to 1877.* 5 vols. St. Louis: C. R. Barns, 1879.

[Thompson, Meriwether J.] *The Civil War Reminiscences of General M. Jeff Thompson*, ed. Donal J. Stanton, Goodwin F. Berquist, and Paul C. Bowers. Dayton: Morningside House, 1988.

Thorndike, Rachel Sherman, ed. *The Sherman Letters: Correspondence Between General and Senator Sherman from 1837 to 1891.* New York: Charles Scribner's Sons, 1894.

Thwaites, Reuben Gold, ed. *Early Western Travels, 1748-1846*. 30 vols. Cleveland: Arthur H. Clark, 1904.
Titus, Charles H. *Into the Old Northwest: Journeys with Charles H. Titus, 1841-1846*, ed. George P. Clark. East Lansing: Michigan State University, 1994.
Tocqueville, Alexis de. *Democracy in America*, ed. Phillips Bradley. 2 vols. New York: Alfred A. Knopf, 1948; reprint New York: Alfred A. Knopf, 1997.
Toulmin, Harry. *The Western Country in 1793: Reports on Kentucky and Virginia by Harry Toulmin*, ed. Marion Tinling and Godfrey Davies. San Marino, Calif.: Henry E. Huntington Library, 1948.
Trollope, Frances. *Domestic Manners of the Americans*. 2 vols. London: Whittaker, Treacher, 1832.
[Underwood, Johanna Louisa]. *Josie Underwood's Civil War Diary*, ed. Nancy Disher Baird. Lexington: University Press of Kentucky, 2009.
Upson, Theodore F. *With Sherman to the Sea: The Civil War Letters and Diaries and Reminiscences of Theodore F. Upson*, ed. Oscar Winther. Bloomington: Indiana University Press, 1958.
Vallandigham, Clement L. *The Great Civil War in America: Speech of Hon. Clement Laird Vallandigham, of Ohio, Delivered in the House of Representatives, January 14, 1863*. Washington, D.C.: L. Towers, 1863.
Venable, W[illiam] H. *The Beginnings of Literary Culture in the Ohio Valley*. Cincinnati: Robert Clarke, 1891.
[War Department, Record and Pension Office]. *Organization and Status of Missouri Troops (Union and Confederate) in Service During the Civil War*. Washington, D.C.: Government Printing Office, 1902.
Ware, E[ugene] F. *The Lyon Campaign in Missouri*. Topeka, Kans.: Crane, 1907.
Woodruff, J. H. *City Directory for the Years 1836-7*. Cincinnati: Woodruff, 1837.
Woodward, Ashbel. *Life of General Nathaniel Lyon*. Hartford, Conn.: Case, Lockwood, 1862.
Wright, John Stillman. *Letters from the West; or a Caution to Emigrants*. Salem, N.Y.: Dodd and Stevenson, 1819; reprint Ann Arbor, Mich.: University Microforms, 1966.
Yates, Richard, and Catherine Yates Pickering. *Richard Yates: Civil War Governor*, ed. John H. Krenkel. Danville, Ill.: Interstate Printers and Publishers, 1966.
Young, Chester Raymond, ed. *Westward into Kentucky: The Narrative of Daniel Trabue*. Lexington: University Press of Kentucky, 1981.
Younger, T. Coleman. *The Story of Cole Younger by Himself: Being an Autobiography of the Missouri Guerrilla Captain and Outlaw*. Chicago: Henneberry Company, 1903.

Secondary Sources

THESES, DISSERTATIONS, UNPUBLISHED PAPERS, AND MANUSCRIPTS

Andreasen, Bryon C. "'As Good a Right to Pray': Copperhead Christians on the Northern Civil War Home Front." Ph.D. dissertation, University of Illinois, Urbana-Champaign, 1998.
Bergquist, James. "The Political Attitudes of the German Immigrant in Illinois, 1848-1860." Ph.D. dissertation, Northwestern University, 1966.
Bierbaum, Milton E. "The Rhetoric of Union or Disunion in Missouri, 1844-1861." Ph.D. dissertation, University of Missouri-Columbia, 1965.
Burckin, Alexander I. "The Formation and Growth of an Urban Middle Class: Power and Conflict in Louisville, Kentucky, 1828-1861." Ph.D. dissertation, University of California-Irvine, 1993.
Cannon, Jessica Ann. "Lincoln's Divided Backyard: Maryland in the Civil War Era." Ph.D. dissertation, Rice University, 2009.
Carroll, Stephen G. "Thomas Corwin and the Agonies of the Whig Party." Ph.D. dissertation, University of Colorado, 1970.
Conoyer, Daniel Joseph. "Missouri's Little Dixie: A Geographical Delineation." Ph.D. dissertation, Saint Louis University, 1973.
Craig, Douglas L. "An Examination of the Reasons for Missouri's Decision Not to Secede in 1860." M.A. thesis, University of Missouri-Kansas City, 1969.

Cross, Jasper William. "Divided Loyalties in Southern Illinois During the Civil War." Ph.D. dissertation, University of Illinois at Urbana-Champaign, 1939.

Garrison, Zachary S. "*Im Abendlande*: German American Liberalism and the Civil War in the Border West, 1830–1877." Ph.D. dissertation, University of Cincinnati, 2015.

Goebel, Robert W. "Casualty of War: The Governorship of Beriah Magoffin, 1859–1862." M.A. thesis, University of Louisville, 2005.

Gosman, Fred G. "Opposition to Abolition in Cincinnati, 1835–1840." M.A. thesis, Kent State University, 1972.

Guasco, Suzanne Cooper. "Confronting Democracy: Edward Coles and the Cultivation of Authority in the Young Nation." Ph.D. dissertation, College of William and Mary in Virginia, 2004.

Harlow, Luke Edward. "From Border South to Solid South: Religion, Race, and the Making of Confederate Kentucky, 1830–1880." Ph.D. dissertation, Rice University, 2009.

Hays, Christopher K. "Way Down in Egypt Land: Community and Conflict in Cairo, Illinois, 1850–1930." Ph.D. dissertation, University of Missouri-Columbia, 1996.

Hoskins, Patricia Ann. "'The Old First is with the South': The Civil War, Reconstruction, and Memory in the Jackson Purchase Region of Kentucky." Ph.D. dissertation, Auburn University, 2008.

Hur, Hyn. "Radical Antislavery and Personal Liberty Laws in Antebellum Ohio, 1803–1857." Ph.D. dissertation, University of Wisconsin, Madison, 2012.

Jenness, Timothy Max. "Tentative Relations: Secession and War in the Central Ohio River Valley, 1859–1862." Ph.D. dissertation, University of Tennessee, Knoxville, 2011.

McClellan, Bernard E. "Cincinnati's Response to Abolitionism, 1835–1845." M.A. thesis, University of Cincinnati, 1961.

McKerley, John W. "Citizens and Strangers: The Politics of Race in Missouri from Slavery to the Era of Jim Crow." Ph.D. dissertation, University of Iowa, 2008.

Miller, Brian Craig. "Filling the Empty Sleeves: Southern States Respond to the Crisis of Amputation." Paper presented at the Organization of American Historians Annual Conference, March 19, 2011.

Noble, Madelein. "The White Caps of Harrison and Crawford Counties, Indiana." Ph.D. dissertation, University of Michigan, 1972.

Pinnick, Tim. "African Americans and the Grand Army of the Republic in Illinois." Paper presented at the Annual Conference on Illinois History, Springfield, Illinois, October 13, 2006.

Rhyne, James Michael. "Rehearsal for Redemption: The Politics of Post-Emancipation Violence in Kentucky's Bluegrass Region." Ph.D. dissertation, University of Cincinnati, 2006.

Rockenbach, Stephen I. "'War Upon Our Border': War and Society in Two Ohio Valley Communities, 1861–1865." Ph.D. dissertation, University of Cincinnati, 2005.

Rosenberger, David A. "Ohio Press Reaction to Andrew Johnson's 'Swing Around the Circle'— 1866." M.A. thesis, Ohio State University, 1947.

Rubin, Anne Sarah. "'An Organization of Dudes': The Society of the Army of the Tennessee Remembers Sherman's March." Paper presented at the Organization of American Historians Annual Meeting, Houston, Texas, March 23, 2011.

Sale, Sara Lee. "Governor Claiborne Fox Jackson and His Role in the Secession Movement in Missouri." M.A. thesis, Central Missouri State University, 1979.

Schieber, Harry N. "Internal Improvements and Economic Change in Ohio, 1820–1860." Ph.D. dissertation, Cornell University, 1962.

Stafford, Hanford Dozier. "Slavery in a Border City: Louisville 1790–1860." Ph.D. dissertation, University of Kentucky, 1982.

Stanley, Matthew E. "'Between Two Fires:' War and Reunion in Middle America, 1860–1920." Ph.D. dissertation, University of Cincinnati, 2013.

Stanley, Matthew E. "'No More Shall the Winding Rivers Be Red': Civil War Commemoration and Regional Identity in Evansville, Indiana, 1887–1899." Paper presented at Great Lakes Regional History Conference, Grand Valley State University, Grand Rapids, Michigan, October 9, 2010.

Sterling, Robert E. "Draft Resistance in the Middle West." Ph.D. dissertation, Northern Illinois University, 1974.
Terry, Clinton W. "'The Most Commercial of People': Cincinnati, the Civil War, and the Rise of Commercial Capitalism, 1861–1865." Ph.D. dissertation, University of Cincinnati, 2002.
White, Joseph Michael. "Religion and Community: Cincinnati Germans, 1814–1870." Ph.D. dissertation, University of Notre Dame, 1980.

REFERENCE WORKS

Blunt, Roy D., Jr., ed. *Historical Listing of the Missouri Legislature.* Jefferson City: Secretary of State/Missouri State Archives, 1988.
Christensen, Lawrence O., William E. Foley, Gary R. Kremer, and Kenneth H. Winn, eds. *Dictionary of Missouri Biography.* Columbia: University of Missouri Press, 1999.
Clark, Thomas D., ed. *Historical Maps of Kentucky.* Lexington: University Press of Kentucky, 1979.
Current, Richard N., ed. *Encyclopedia of the Confederacy.* 4 vols. New York: Simon and Schuster, 1993.
Dyer, Frederick H. *A Compendium of the War of the Rebellion.* Des Moines: Dyer Publishing Company, 1908.
Faust, Patricia L., ed. *Historical Times Illustrated Encyclopedia of the Civil War.* New York: Harper, Row, 1986.
Garrett, Wilbur E., ed. *Historical Atlas of the United States.* Washington, D.C.: National Geographic Society, 1988.
Gregory, Winifred, ed. *American Newspapers 1821–1936.* New York: Bibliographic Society of America, 1937; reprint New York: Kraus Reprint Corp., 1967.
Gutgesell, Stephen, ed. *Guide to Ohio Newspapers, 1793–1973: Union Bibliography of Ohio Newspapers Available in Ohio Libraries.* Columbus: Ohio Historical Society, 1974.
Harrison, James L., ed. *Biographical Dictionary of the American Congress, 1774–1949.* Washington, D.C.: United States Government Printing Office, 1950.
Hinshaw, William W., et al., eds. *Encyclopedia of American Quaker Genealogy.* Ann Arbor, Mich.: Edwards Bros., 1946.
James, Edmund J. *A Bibliography of Newspapers Published in Illinois Prior to 1860.* Springfield, Ill.: Phillips Bros., 1899.
Johnson, Allen, and Dumas Malone, eds. *The Dictionary of American Biography.* 20 vols. New York: Charles Scribner's Sons, 1937–1943.
Kleber, John E., ed. *The Encyclopedia of Louisville.* Lexington: University Press of Kentucky, 2001.
Kleber, John E., ed. *The Kentucky Encyclopedia.* Lexington: University Press of Kentucky, 1992.
Leonard, Lewis A., ed., *Greater Cincinnati and Its People: A History.* 4 vols. New York: Lewis Historical Publishing, 1927.
Ohman, Marian M. *Encyclopedia of Missouri Courthouses.* Columbia: Curators of the University of Missouri, 1981.
Richards, Sarah, ed. *Civil War Sites: The Official Guide to Battlefields, Monuments, and More.* Guilford, Conn.: Globe Pequot Press, 2003.
Schroeder, Walter A. *Missouri Water Atlas.* Jefferson City: Missouri Department of Natural Resources, 1982.
Scott, Frank William. *Newspapers and Periodicals of Illinois, 1814–1879.* Urbana, Ill: printed by author, 1910.
Simpson, Alicia, ed. *Index of Confederate Pension Applications, Commonwealth of Kentucky.* Frankfort: Division of Archives and Records Management, Department of Library and Archives, 1978.
Warner, Ezra J. *Generals in Blue: Lives of the Union Commanders.* Baton Rouge: Louisiana State University Press, 1964.
Warner, Ezra J. *Generals in Gray: Lives of the Confederate Commanders.* Baton Rouge: Louisiana State University Press, 1959.

INTERNET SOURCES

"Missouri Monuments." Center for Civil War Research, University of Mississippi, Oxford. http://civilwarcenter.olemiss.edu/monuments%20mo.html (accessed July 12, 2011).

Musgrave, Jon. "History Comes Out of Hiding Atop Hickory Hill." *Springhouse Magazine* (December 1996). http://www.illinoishistory.com/osharticle.html (accessed October 7, 2013).

Ross, Kirby. "James O. Broadhead: Ardent Unionist, Unrepentant Slaveholder." http://www.civilwarstlouis.com/History2/broadheadprofile.htm (accessed January 14, 2010).

https://s1.sos.mo.gov/records/archives/archivesdb/provost/ (accessed December 2015).

http://www.civil-war.net/pages/troops_furnished_losses.html (accessed December 2015).

ARTICLES AND ESSAYS

Adelman, Jeremy, and Stephen Aron. "From Borderlands to Borders: Empires, Nation-States, and the Peoples in Between in North American History." *American Historical Review* 104 (June 1999): 814–41.

Adler, Jeffrey S. "Yankee Colonizers and the Making of Antebellum St. Louis." *Gateway Heritage* 12 (Winter 1992): 4–21.

Allardice, Bruce S. "'Illinois Is Rotten with Traitors!': The Republican Defeat in the 1862 State Election." *Journal of Illinois State Historical Society* 104 (Spring 2011): 97–114.

Allen, John W. "Slavery and Negro Servitude in Pope County, Illinois," in *An Illinois Reader*, ed. Clyde C. Walton, 102–12. DeKalb: Northern Illinois University Press, 1970.

Anderson, Kristen L. "German Americans, African Americans, and the Republican Party in St. Louis, 1865-1872." *Journal of American Ethnic History* 28 (Fall 2008): 34–51.

Appleby, Joyce. "Commercial Farming and the 'Agrarian Myth' in the Early Republic." *Journal of American History* 68 (March 1982): 833–849.

Ash, Steven V. "Civil War Exodus: The Jews and Grant's General Orders 11," in *American Jewish History: Anti-Semitism in America*, ed. Jeffery S. Gurock, 135–55. New York: Routledge Press, 1998.

Asper, Lewis D. "The Long and Unhappy History of Loyalty Testing in Maryland." *American Journal of Legal History* 13 (April 1969): 97–109.

Attie, Jeanie. "Warwork and the Crisis of Domesticity in the North," in *Divided Houses: Gender and the Civil War*, ed. Catherine Clinton and Nina L. Silber, 247–59. New York: Oxford University Press, 1992.

Ayers, Edward L. "The South, the West, and the Rest." *Western Historical Quarterly* 25 (Winter 1994): 473–76.

Baker, Paula. "The Domestication of Politics: Women and American Political Society, 1780–1920." *American Historical Review* 89 (June 1984): 620–47.

Bardaglio, Peter. "The Children of Jubilee: African American Childhood in Wartime," in *Divided Houses: Gender and the Civil War*, ed. Catherine Clinton and Nina L. Silber, 213–29. New York: Oxford University Press, 1992.

Bardaglio, Peter. "On the Border: White Children and the Politics of War in Maryland," in *The War Was You and Me: Civilians in the American Civil War*, ed. Joan E. Cashin, 313–31. Princeton, N.J.: Princeton University Press, 2002.

Barden, Virginia, and Lois Barris, eds. "1828 Jamestown Census—The City of Jamestown, New York." *Chautauqua Genealogist* 13 (Spring 1992): 11–13.

Bartman, Roger J. "Joseph Holt and Kentucky in the Civil War." *Filson Club History Quarterly* 40 (April 1966): 105–22.

Barnhart, John D. "Sources of the Southern Migration into the Old Northwest." *Mississippi Valley Historical Review* 22 (June 1935): 49–62.

Bigelow, Ann Clymer. "Antebellum Ohio's Black Barbers in the Political Vanguard." *Ohio Valley History* 11 (Summer 2011): 26–39.

Blum, Virgil C. "The Political and Military Activities of the German Element in St. Louis, 1859–1861." *Missouri Historical Review* 42 (January 1948): 103–29.

Boucher, Chauncey S. "*In Re* That Aggressive Slavocracy." *Mississippi Valley Historical Review* 8 (June–September 1921): 13–79.
Bowen, Don. "Guerrilla Warfare in Western Missouri, 1862–1865: Historical Extensions of the Relative Deprivation Hypothesis." *Comparative Studies in Society and History* 19 (July 1977): 30–51.
Bradbury, John F., Jr. "'Buckwheat Cake Philanthropy': Refugees and the Union Army in the Ozarks." *Arkansas Historical Quarterly* 57 (Autumn 1998): 233–54.
Brockmeier, Jens. "Remembering and Forgetting: Narrative as Cultural Memory." *Culture and Psychology* 8 (2002): 15–43.
Browning, Judkin. "'I Am Not So Patriotic as I Was Once': The Effects of Military Occupation on the Occupying Soldiers during the Civil War." *Civil War History* 55 (June 2009): 217–43.
Buchanan, Thomas C. "Levees of Hope: African American Steamboat Workers, Cities and Slave Escapes on the Antebellum Mississippi." *Journal of Urban History* 30 (March 2004): 360–77.
Buchanan, Thomas C. "Rascals on the Antebellum Mississippi: African American Steamboat Workers and the St. Louis Hanging of 1841." *Journal of Social History* 34 (Summer 2001): 797–816.
Burckin, Alexander I. "'A Spirit of Perseverance': Free African Americans in Late Antebellum Louisville." *Filson Club History Quarterly* 70 (January 1996): 61–81.
Cannon, Gerald. "The Harney-Price Agreement." *Civil War Times Illustrated* 23 (December 1984): 40–45.
Carnahan, Burrus M. "Lincoln, Lieber and the Laws of War: The Origins and Limits of the Principle of Military Necessity." *American Journal of International Law* 92 (April 1998): 213–31.
Cashin, Joan E. "Deserters, Civilians, and Draft Resistance in the North," in *The War Was You and Me: Civilians in the American Civil War*, ed. Joan E. Cashin, 262–85. Princeton, N.J.: Princeton University Press, 2002.
Castel, Albert. "Order No. 11 and the Civil War on the Border." *Missouri Historical Quarterly* 57 (July 1963): 357–68.
Cecil-Fronsman, Bill. "'Death to All Yankees and Traitors in Kansas': The *Squatter Sovereign* and the Defense of Slavery in Kansas." *Kansas History* 16 (Spring 1993): 22–33.
Churchill, Robert. "Liberty, Conscription, and a Party Divided: The Sons of Liberty Conspiracy, 1863–1864." *Prologue Quarterly* 30 (Winter 1998): 295–303.
Clyde, Henry. "Pro-Southern Influences in the Free West 1840–1865." *Mississippi Valley Historical Review* 20 (June 1933): 45–62.
Cole, Jennifer. "'For the Sake of the Songs of the Men Made Free': James Speed and the Emancipationists' Dilemma in Nineteenth-century Kentucky." *Ohio Valley History* 4 (Winter 2004): 27–48.
Coleman, Charles H. "The Use of the Term 'Copperhead' During the Civil War." *Mississippi Valley Historical Review* 25 (September 1938): 263–64.
Coulter, E. Merton. "Commercial Intercourse with the Confederacy in the Mississippi Valley, 1861–1865." *Mississippi Valley Historical Review* 4 (March 1919): 377–95.
Coulter, E. Merton. "Effects of Secession upon the Commerce of the Mississippi Valley." *Mississippi Valley Historical Review* 3 (December 1916): 275–300.
Covington, James W. "The Camp Jackson Affair, 1861." *Missouri Historical Review* 55 (April 1961): 197–212.
Craig, Berry F. "The Jackson Purchase Considers Secession: The 1861 Mayfield Convention." *Register of the Kentucky Historical Society* 99 (Autumn 2001): 339–61.
Craik, Elmer LeRoy. "Southern Interest in Territorial Kansas, 1854–1858." *Kansas Historical Collections* 15 (1919–1921): 376–95.
Crisler, Robert M. "Missouri's Little Dixie." *Missouri Historical Review* 42 (January 1948): 130–39.
Crisler, Robert M. "Republican Areas in Missouri." *Missouri Historical Review* 42 (July 1948): 299–309.
Culmer, Frederic A. "Abiel Leonard." *Missouri Historical Review* 28 (October 1933): 17–37.

Culmer, Frederic A. "Selling Mules Down South in 1835." *Missouri Historical Review* 24 (July 1930): 537–49.
Current, Richard N. "The Friend of Freedom," in *Reconstruction: An Anthology of Revisionist Writings*, ed. Kenneth M. Stampp and Leon F. Litwack, 241–63. Baton Rouge and London: Louisiana State University Press, 1969.
Dante, Harris L. "Western Attitudes and Reconstruction Policies in Illinois, 1865–1872." *Journal of the Illinois State Historical Society* 49 (Summer 1956): 149–62.
Davis, David Brion. "American Slavery and the American Revolution," in *Slavery and Freedom in the Age of the Revolution*, ed. Ira Berlin and Ronald Hoffman, 262–80. Urbana and Champaign: University of Illinois Press, 1986.
Davis, David Brion. "Some Themes of Counter-Subversion: An Analysis of Anti-Masonic, Anti-Catholic, and Anti-Mormon Literature." *Mississippi Valley Historical Review* 47 (September 1960): 205–24.
Davis, Stephen. "Empty Eyes, Marble Hand: The Confederate Monument and the South." *Journal of Popular Culture* 16 (Winter 1982): 2–19.
Dawson, Jan C. "The Puritan and the Cavalier: The South's Perception of Contrasting Traditions." *Journal of Southern History* 44 (November 1978): 597–614.
DeArmond, Fred. "Reconstruction in Missouri." *Missouri Historical Review* 41 (April 1967): 365–71.
Delgadillo, Charles E. " 'A Pretty Weedy Flower': William Allen White, Midwestern Liberalism, and the 1920s Culture War." *Kansas History: A Journal of the Central Plains* 35 (Autumn 2012): 186–202.
Downey, Matthew T. "Horace Greeley and the Politicians: The Liberal Republican Convention in 1872." *Journal of American History* 53 (March 1967): 727–50.
Dyer, Thomas G. " 'A Most Unexampled Exhibition of Madness and Brutality': Judge Lynch in Saline County, Missouri, 1859." *Missouri Historical Review* 89 (April and July 1995): 269–89, 367–83.
Dykstra, Robert R., and Harlan Hahn. "Northern Voters and Negro Suffrage: The Case of Iowa, 1868." *Public Opinion Quarterly* 32 (Summer 1968): 202–15.
Eaton, Clement. "Minutes and Resolutions of an Emancipation Meeting in Kentucky in 1849." *JSH* 14 (November 1948): 541–45.
Eaton, Miles W. "The Development and Later Decline of the Hemp Industry in Missouri." *Missouri Historical Review* 43 (July 1949): 344–59.
Emberton, Carole. "Reconstructing Loyalty: Love, Fear, and Power in the Postwar South," in *The Great Task Remaining Before Us: Reconstruction as America's Continuing Civil War*, ed. Paul A. Cimbala and Randall M. Miller, 173–82. New York: Fordham University Press, 2010.
Etcheson, Nicole. "Good Men and Notorious Rogues: Vigilantism in Massac County, Illinois, 1846–1850," in *Lethal Imagination: Violence and Brutality in American History*, ed. Michael A. Bellesiles, 149–69. New York: New York University Press, 1999.
Eyal, Yonatan. "Charles Eliot Norton, E. L. Godkin, and the Liberal Republicans of 1872." *American Nineteenth Century History* 2 (Spring 2001): 53–74.
Eyal, Yonatan. "With His Eyes Open: Stephen A. Douglas and the Kansas-Nebraska Disaster of 1854." *Journal of the Illinois State Historical Society* 91 (Winter 1998): 175–217.
Fehrenbacher, Don E. "Kansas, Republicanism, and the Rise of the Republican Party, 1854–1856," in *The Sectional Crisis and Southern Constitutionalism*, 45–80. Baton Rouge: Louisiana State University Press, 1995.
Fellman, Michael. "Emancipation in Missouri." *Missouri Historical Review* 83 (October 1988): 36–56.
Fields, Barbara J. "Dysplacement and Southern History." *Journal of Southern History* 82 (February 2016): 7–26.
Finkelman, Paul. "Evading the Ordinance: The Persistence of Bondage in Indiana and Illinois." *Journal of the Early Republic* 9 (Spring 1989): 21–51.
Fischer, Victor. "Huck Finn Reviewed: The Reception of *Huckleberry Finn* in the United States, 1885–1897." *American Literary Realism* 16 (Spring 1983): 1–57.
Franklin, John Hope. "The North, the South, and the American Revolution." *Journal of American History* 62 (June 1975): 5–23.

Fredrickson, George M. "The Coming of the Lord: The Northern Protestant Clergy and the Civil War Crisis," in *Religion and the American Civil War*, ed. Randall M. Miller, Harry S. Stout, and Charles Reagan Wilson, 110–30. New York: Oxford University Press, 1998.

Fredrickson, George M. "A Man but Not a Brother: Abraham Lincoln and Racial Equality." *Journal of Southern History* 41 (February 1975): 39–58.

Frisby, Derek W. "'Remember Fort Pillow!': Politics, Atrocity Propaganda, and the Evolution of Hard War," in *Black Flag Over Dixie: Racial Atrocities and Reprisals in the Civil War*, ed. Gregory J. W. Urwin, 104–31. Carbondale: Southern Illinois University Press, 2005.

Frizzell, Robert W. "Southern Identity in Nineteenth-Century Missouri: Little Dixie's Slave-Majority Areas and the Transition to Midwestern Farming." *Missouri Historical Review* 99 (April 2005): 238–60.

Furstenberg, François. "The Significance of the Trans-Appalachian Frontier in Atlantic History." *American Historical Review* 113 (June 2008): 647–77.

Gamble, Douglas A. "Joshua Giddings and the Ohio Abolitionists: A Study in Radical Politics." *Ohio History* 88 (Winter 1979): 37–56.

Geertz, Clifford. "Thick Description: Toward an Interpretive Theory of Culture," in *The Interpretation of Cultures: Selected Essays*, 3–30. New York: Basic Books, 1975.

Geiger, Mark W. "Indebtedness and the Origins of Guerrilla Warfare in Civil War Missouri." *Journal of Southern History* 75 (February 2009): 49–82.

Gerlach, Russell L. "Population Origins in Rural Missouri." *Missouri Historical Review* 71 (October 1976): 5–15.

Gienapp, William E. "Abraham Lincoln and the Border States." *Journal of the Abraham Lincoln Association* 13 (1992): 1–46.

Gienapp, William E. "The Crime Against Sumner: The Caning of Charles Sumner and the Rise of the Republican Party." *Civil War History* 25 (September 1979): 218–45.

Gilmore, Robert. "Ozarks Editors: Guardians and Gadflies—Politicians and Promoters—Preachers and Teachers." *Ozarks Watch* 7 (Summer 1993): 8–13.

Glenn, Daniel P. "Losing the Market Revolution: Lebanon, Ohio, and the Economic Transformation of Warren County, 1820–1850." *Ohio Valley History* 5 (Winter 2005): 23–46.

Goen, C. C. "Broken Churches, Broken Nation: Regional Religion and North-South Alienation in Antebellum America." *Church History* 52 (March 1983): 21–35.

Gorn, Elliot. "Gouge and Bite, Pull Hair and Scratch: The Significance of Fighting in the Southern Backcountry." *American Historical Review* 90 (February 1985): 18–32.

Grinspan, John. "'Sorrowfully Amusing': The Popular Comedy of the Civil War." *Journal of the Civil War Era* (September 2011): 313–38.

Guasco, Suzanne Cooper. "'The Deadly Influence of Negro Capitalists': Southern Yeomen and Resistance to the Expansion of Slavery in Illinois." *Civil War History* 47 (March 2001): 7–29.

Hamilton, Bentley. "The Union League: Its Origin and Achievements in the Civil War." *Transactions of the Illinois State Historical Society* 28 (1921): 110–15.

Hamilton, Daniel W. "The Confederate Sequestration Act." *Civil War History* 52 (December 2006): 373–405.

Harbison, Winfred A. "Lincoln and Indiana Republicans, 1861–1862." *Indiana Magazine of History* 33 (September 1937): 277–303.

Harrison, Lowell H. "Governor Magoffin and the Secession Crisis." *Register of the Kentucky Historical Society* 72 (April 1974): 91–110.

Harrold, Stanley C., Jr. "The Southern Strategy of the Liberty Party." *Ohio History* 87 (Winter 1978): 21–36.

Harvey, Charles M. "Missouri from 1849 to 1861." *Missouri Historical Review* 2 (October 1907): 23–40.

Holmes, William F. "Whitecapping: Agrarian Violence in Mississippi, 1902-1906." *Journal of Southern History* 35 (May 1969): 165–85.

Holt, Michael F. "An Elusive Synthesis: Northern Politics during the Civil War," in *Writing the Civil War: The Quest to Understand*, ed. James M. McPherson and William J. Cooper, Jr., 112–34. Columbia: University of South Carolina Press, 1998.

Hudson, J. Blaine. "In Pursuit of Freedom: Slave Law and Emancipation in Antebellum Louisville and Jefferson County, Kentucky." *Filson Club History Quarterly* 76 (Summer 2002): 287–325.

Hughes, James S. "Lexington, Missouri, and the Aftermath of Slavery, 1861–1870." *Missouri Historical Review* 75 (October 1980): 51–63.

Hulbert, Matthew C. "Constructing Guerrilla Memory: John Newman Edwards and Missouri's Irregular Lost Cause." *Journal of the Civil War Era* 2 (March 2012): 58–81.

"James G. Birney's Anti-Slavery Activities in Cincinnati 1835–1837." *Bulletin of the Historical and Philosophical Society of Cincinnati* 9 (October 1951): 252–65.

Jackson, W. Sherman. "Emancipation, Negrophobia, and Civil War Politics in Ohio." *Journal of Negro History* 65 (July 1980): 250–60.

Jelsma, Sherry K. "A Dose of Slangwhang and Hard Cider: Charles S. Todd and the Harrison Campaign of 1840." *Ohio Valley History* 8 (Summer 2008): 1–22.

Jordan, Henry D. "Daniel Wolsey Voorhees." *Mississippi Valley Historical Review* 6 (March 1920): 532–55.

Kalyvas, Stathis N. "The Ontology of 'Political Violence': Action and Identity in Civil Wars." *Perspectives on Politics* 1 (2003): 475–94.

Kanon, Tom. "'Scared from Their Sins for a Season': The Religious Ramifications of the New Madrid Earthquakes, 1811–1812." *Ohio Valley History* 5 (Summer 2005): 21–38.

Kanon, Tom. "Seduced, Bewildered, and Lost: Anti-Shakerism on the Early Nineteenth-Century Frontier." *Ohio Valley History* 7 (Summer 2007): 1–30.

Kaplan, Sidney. "The Miscegenation Issue in the Election of 1864." *Journal of Negro History* 34 (July 1949): 274–343.

Kirkpatrick, Arthur Roy. "The Admission of Missouri to the Confederacy." *Missouri Historical Review* 55 (July 1961): 366–86.

Kirkpatrick, Arthur Roy. "Missouri in the Early Months of the Civil War." *Missouri Historical Review* 55 (April 1961): 235–66.

Kirkpatrick, Arthur Roy. "Missouri on the Eve of the Civil War." *Missouri Historical Review* 55 (January 1961): 99–108.

Kirkpatrick, Arthur Roy. "Missouri's Secessionist Government, 1861–1865." *Missouri Historical Review* 45 (January 1951): 124–37.

Klement, Frank L. "Sound and Fury: Civil War Dissent in the Cincinnati Area." *Cincinnati Historical Society Bulletin* 35 (Summer 1977): 98–114.

Kohl, Martha. "Enforcing a Vision of Community: The Role of the Test Oath in Missouri's Reconstruction." *Civil War History* 40 (December 1994): 292–307.

Kohl, Rhonda M. "'This Godforsaken Town': Death and Disease at Helena, Arkansas, 1862–63." *Civil War History* 50 (June 2004): 109–44.

Kulikoff, Allan. "Uprooted Peoples: Black Migrants in the Age of the American Revolution, 1790–1820," in *Slavery and Freedom in the Age of the American Revolution*, ed. Ira Berlin and Ronald Hoffman, 143–71. Urbana and Champaign: University of Illinois Press, 1986.

Lambert, D. Warren. "The Decisive Battle of Richmond, Kentucky," in *The Civil War in Kentucky: Battle for the Bluegrass*, ed. Kent Masterson Brown, 109–28. Mason City, Iowa: Savas Publishing Company, 2000.

Lang, Elfreda. "Ohioans in Northern Indiana before 1850." *Indiana Magazine of History* 49 (December 1953): 391–404.

Laughlin, Sceva B. "Missouri Politics During the Civil War." *Missouri Historical Review* 23 (April and July 1929): 400–426, 583–618; 24 (October 1929 and January 1930): 87–113, 261–84.

Lawson, Melinda. "'A Profound National Devotion': The Civil War Union Leagues and the Construction of a New National Patriotism." *Civil War History* 48 (December 2002): 338–62.

Lee, Jacob F. "Between Two Fires: Cassius M. Clay, Slavery, and Antislavery in the Kentucky Borderlands." *Ohio Valley History* 6 (Fall 2006): 50–70.

Lee, R. Alton. "The Corwin Amendment in the Secession Crisis." *Ohio Historical Quarterly* 70 (January 1961): 1–26.

Leonard, Elizabeth D. "One Kentuckian's Hard Choice: Joseph Holt and Abraham Lincoln." *Register of the Kentucky Historical Society* 106 (Summer–Autumn 2008): 373–408.

Levine, Bruce. "Community Divided: German Immigrants, Social Class, and Political Conflict in Antebellum Cincinnati," in *Ethnic Diversity and Civic Identity: Patterns of Conflict and Cohesion in Cincinnati since 1820*, ed. Henry Shapiro and Jonathan Sarna, 46–93. Urbana and Chicago: University of Illinois Press, 1992.

Levine, Peter. "Draft Evasion in the North during the Civil War, 1863–1865." *Journal of American History* 67 (March 1981): 816–34.

Lewis, Patrick A. "'All Men of Decency Ought to Quit the Army': Benjamin F. Buckner, Manhood, and Proslavery Unionism in Kentucky." *Register of the Kentucky Historical Society* 107 (Fall 2009): 513–49.

Lewis, Patrick A. "The Democratic Partisan Militia and the Black Peril: The Kentucky Militia, Racial Violence, and the Fifteenth Amendment, 1870–1873." *Civil War History* 56 (June 2010): 145–74.

Low, W. A. "The Freedmen's Bureau in the Border States," in *Radicalism, Racism, and Party Realignment: The Border States during Reconstruction*, ed. Richard O. Curry, ed. 245–64. Baltimore: Johns Hopkins University Press, 1969.

Lucas, Marion B. "Camp Nelson, Kentucky during the Civil War: Cradle of Liberty or Refugee Death Camp?" *Filson Club Historical Quarterly* 63 (October 1989): 439–45.

Lucas, Scott J. "'Indignities, Wrongs, and Outrages': Military and Guerrilla Incursions on Kentucky's Civil War Home Front." *Filson Historical Quarterly* 73 (October 1999): 355–79.

Lyon, William H. "Claiborne Fox Jackson and the Secession Crisis in Missouri." *Missouri Historical Review* 58 (July 1964): 422–41.

Mabry, William Alexander. "Ante-bellum Cincinnati and Its Southern Trade," in *American Studies*, ed. David Kelly Jackson, 82–83. Durham, N.C.: Duke University Press, 1940.

Madison, James H. "Civil War Memories and 'Pardnership Forgittin', 1865–1913." *Indiana Magazine of History* 99 (September 2003): 198–230.

Mairose, Mary Alice. "Thomas Worthington and the Quest for Statehood and Gentility," in *Builders of Ohio: A Biographical History*, ed. Warren Van Tine and Michael Pierce, 60–71. Columbus: Ohio State University Press, 2003.

Malin, James C. "The Proslavery Background of the Kansas Struggle." *Mississippi Valley Historical Review* 10 (December 1923): 285–305.

Mancini, Matthew J. "Francis Lieber, Slavery, and the 'Genesis' of the Laws of War." *Journal of Southern History* 77 (May 2011): 325–48.

Marshall, Anne E. "The 1906 *Uncle Tom's Cabin* Law and the Politics of Race and Memory in Early-Twentieth-Century Kentucky." *Journal of the Civil War Era* 1 (September 2011): 368–93.

Martin, James B. "Black Flag over the Bluegrass: Guerrilla Warfare in Kentucky, 1863–1865." *Register of the Kentucky Historical Society* 86 (Autumn 1988): 352–75.

McConnell, Stuart. "Who Joined the Grand Army? Three Case Studies in the Construction of Union Veteranhood, 1866–1900," in *Toward a Social History of the American Civil War: Exploratory Essays*, ed. Maris Vinoskis, 139–70. Cambridge: Cambridge University Press, 1990.

McKenzie, Robert Tracy. "Contesting Secession: Parson Brownlow and the Rhetoric of Proslavery Unionism, 1860–1861." *Civil War History* 48 (December 2002): 294–312.

McKnight, Brian D. "Hope and Humiliation: Humphrey Marshall, the Mountaineers, and the Confederacy's Last Chance in Eastern Kentucky." *Ohio Valley History* 5 (Fall 2005): 3–20.

McPherson, James M. "Grant or Greeley? The Abolitionist Dilemma in the Election of 1872." *American Historical Review* 71 (October 1965): 43–61.

Merkel, Benjamin. "The Abolition Aspects of Missouri's Antislavery Controversy 1819–1865." *Missouri Historical Review* 44 (April 1950): 232–53.

Merkel, Benjamin. "The Slavery Issue and the Political Decline of Thomas Hart Benton, 1846–1856." *Missouri Historical Review* 38 (July 1944): 388–407.

Middleton, Stephen. "The Fugitive Slave Issue in Southwest Ohio: Unreported Cases." *Old Northwest* 14 (Winter 1988–1989): 285–310.

Middleton, Stephen. "'One of the Ruling Class'—Thomas Caute Reynolds: Second Confederate Governor of Missouri." *Missouri Historical Review* 80 (July 1986): 422–48.

Middleton, Stephen. "Proud Confederate: Thomas Lowndes Snead of Missouri." *Missouri Historical Review* 79 (January 1985): 167–91.

Mills, Randy J. "'I Wish the World to Look Upon Them as My Murderers': A Story of Cultural Violence on the Ohio Valley Frontier." *Ohio Valley History* 1 (Fall 2001): 21–30.

Mink, Charles R. "General Orders No. 11: The Forced Evacuation of Civilians During the Civil War." *Foreign Affairs* 34 (December 1970): 132-36.

Mujic, Julie A. "A Border Community's Unfulfilled Appeals: The Rise and Fall of the 1840s Anti-Abolitionist Movement in Cincinnati." *Ohio Valley History* 7 (Summer 2007): 53–69.

Myers, Jacob W. "History of the Gallatin County Salines." *Journal of the Illinois State Historical Society* 14 (April–July 1921): 337–50.

Neels, Mark Alan. "'We Shall Be Literally 'Sold to the Dutch': Nativist Suppression of German Radicals in Antebellum St. Louis, 1852–1861." *The Confluence* 1 (Fall 2009): 22–29.

Neely, Mark E., Jr. "The Constitution and Civil Liberties Under Lincoln," in *Our Lincoln: New Perspectives on Lincoln and His World*, ed. Eric Foner, 37–60. New York: W. W. Norton, 2008.

Nichols, Roy F. "The Kansas-Nebraska Act: A Century of Historiography." *Mississippi Valley Historical Review* 43 (September 1956): 201–12.

Noe, Kenneth W. "Who Were the Bushwhackers? Age, Class, Kin, and Western Virginia's Confederate Guerrillas, 1861–1862." *Civil War History* 49 (March 2003): 5–25.

Oder, Broeck N. "Andrew Johnson and the 1866 Illinois Election." *Journal of the Illinois State Historical Society* 73 (Autumn 1980): 189–200.

Owsley, Frank L. "The Pattern of Migration and Settlement on the Southern Frontier." *Journal of Southern History* 11 (May 1945): 147–76.

Palmer, Bryan D. "Discordant Music: Charivaris and Whitecapping in Nineteenth-Century North America," in *Crime and Deviance in Canada: Historical Perspectives*, ed. Chris McCormick and Len Green, 40–44. Toronto: Canadian Scholars Press, 2005.

Parish, Peter J. "An Exception to Most of the Rules: American Nationalism in the Nineteenth Century." *Prologue* 27 (Fall 1995): 219–30.

Parish, Peter J. "Daniel Webster, New England, and the West." *Journal of American History* 54 (December 1967): 524–49.

Parrish, William E. "Fremont in Missouri." *Civil War Times Illustrated* 17 (April 1978): 4–10, 40–45.

Parrish, William E. "Jefferson Davis Comes to Missouri." *Missouri Historical Review* 57 (July 1963): 344–56.

Parrish, William E. "'The Palmyra Massacre': A Tragedy of Guerrilla Warfare." *Journal of Confederate History* 1 (Fall 1988): 259–72.

Parrish, William E. "Reconstruction Politics in Missouri," in *Radicalism, Racism, and Party Realignment: The Border States during Reconstruction*, edited by Richard O. Curry, 1–36. Baltimore: Johns Hopkins University Press, 1969.

Pelan, Raymond. "Slavery in the Old Northwest," in *State Historical Society of Wisconsin Proceedings*, 255–56. Madison: State Historical Society of Wisconsin, 1906.

Perry, Lewis, and Matthew C. Sherman. "'What Disturbed the Unitarian Church in This Very City?': Alton, the Slavery Conflict, and Western Unitarianism." *Civil War History* 54 (March 2008): 5–34.

Phillips, Christopher. "Lincoln's Grasp of War: Hard War and the Politics of Neutrality and Slavery in the Western Border Slave States, 1861–62." *Journal of the Civil War Era* 3 (June 2013): 184–210.

Phillips, Christopher. "Travels in Egypt: Eyewitness to the Civil War in Illinois's 'Butternut' Region." *Ohio Valley History* 8 (Summer 2008): 23–47.

Phillips, Richard M. "This Is the House That Salt Built." *Illiniwek* 10 (May–June 1972): 18–24.

Pinnick, Tim. "African American Veterans in the Grand Army of the Republic." *NGS Magazine* 35 (July–September 2009): 28–32.

Piston, William Garrett. "'Springfield Is a Vast Hospital': The Dead and Wounded at the Battle of Wilson's Creek." *Missouri Historical Review* 93 (July 1999): 345–66.

Pitkin, William A. "When Cairo Was Saved for the Union." *Journal of the Illinois State Historical Society* 51 (Autumn 1958): 284–305.

Pocock, Emil. "Slavery and Freedom in the Early Republic: Robert Patterson's Slaves in Kentucky and Ohio, 1804–1819." *Ohio Valley History* 6 (Spring 2006): 1–23.

Potter, David M. "The Historian's Use of Nationalism and Vice Versa," in *The South and the Sectional Crisis*, 34–83. Baton Rouge: Louisiana State University, 1968.

Previts, Fred. "Battlefield Ballots: The 1864 Presidential Election." *Timeline* 26 (October–December 2009): 38–54.

Rafuse, Ethan S. "'Far More than a Romantic Adventure': The American Civil War in Harry Truman's History and Memory." *Missouri Historical Review* 104 (October 2009): 1–20.

Reed, Scott Owen. "Military Arrests of Lawyers in Illinois during the Civil War." *Western Illinois Regional Studies* 6 (Fall 1983): 5–22.

Renan, Ernest. "What Is a Nation?," in *Nation and Narration*, ed. Homi K. Bhabha, 8–22. London: Routledge, 1990.

Richardson, Joe M. "The American Missionary Association and Black Education in Civil War Missouri." *Missouri Historical Review* 69 (July 1975): 433–48.

Rister, Carl Coke. "Carlota: A Confederate Colony in Mexico." *Journal of Southern History* 11 (February 1945): 33–50.

Rockenbach, Stephen I. "A Border City at War: Louisville and the 1862 Confederate Invasion of Kentucky." *Ohio Valley History* 3 (Winter 2003): 35–52.

Rodabaugh, James A. "The Negro in Ohio." *Journal of Negro History* 31 (January 1946): 9–29.

Roed, William. "Secessionist Strength in Missouri." *Missouri Historical Review* 72 (July 1978): 412–23.

Rorvig, Paul. "A Significant Skirmish: The Battle of Boonville." *Missouri Historical Review* 86 (January 1992): 127–48.

Rose, James A. "The Regulators and Flatheads in Southern Illinois," in *Transactions of the Illinois State Historical Library for the Year* 1906. Springfield: Illinois State Historical Society, 1906.

Roseboom, Eugene H. "Southern Ohio and the Union in 1863." *Mississippi Valley Historical Review* 39 (June 1952): 29–44.

Ryan, Daniel J. "Lincoln and Ohio." *Ohio Archeological and Historical Quarterly* 32 (January 1923): 151–57.

Ryle, Walter H. "Slavery and Party Realignment in Missouri in the State Election of 1856." *Missouri Historical Review* 39 (April 1945): 320–32.

Salafia, Matthew. "Searching for Slavery: Fugitive Slaves in the Ohio River Valley Borderland, 1830–1860." *Ohio Valley History* 8 (Winter 2008): 38–63.

Sallee, Scott E. "Porter's Campaign in Northeast Missouri, 1862, Including the Palmyra Massacre." *Blue and Gray* 17 (February 2000): 2–51.

Saum, Lewis. "Donan and the *Caucasian*." *Missouri Historical Review* 63 (July 1969): 419–50.

Schauinger, J. Herman, ed. "The Letters of Godlove S. Orth: Hoosier Whig." *Indiana Magazine of History* 39 (December 1943): 360–400.

Schwalm, Leslie Ann. "'Overrun with Free Negroes': Emancipation and Wartime Migration in the Upper Midwest." *Civil War History* 50 (June 2004): 145–74.

Scott, Donald M. "Abolition as a Sacred Vocation," in *Antislavery Reconsidered: New Perspectives on the Abolitionists*, ed. Lewis Perry and Michael Fellman, 51–74. Baton Rouge: Louisiana State University Press, 1979.

Scott, Sean A. "'Earth Has No Sorrow That Heaven Cannot Cure': Northern Civilian Perspectives on Death and Eternity During the Civil War." *Journal of Social History* 41 (Summer 2008): 843–66.

Shoemaker, Floyd C. "Missouri's Proslavery Fight for Kansas, 1854–1855." *Missouri Historical Review* 48 (April 1954 and July 1954): 221–36, 325–40; 49 (October 1954): 41–54.

Smiley, David L. "The Quest for the Central Theme in Southern History." *South Atlantic Quarterly* 71 (Summer 1972): 307–25.

Smith, George W. "The Salines of Southern Illinois." *Transactions of the Illinois State Historical Library* 9 (1904): 245–58.

Smith, Gerald L. "Slavery and Abolition in Kentucky: 'Patter-rollers' Were Everywhere," in *Bluegrass Renaissance: The History and Culture of Central Kentucky, 1792–1852*, ed. James C. Klotter and Daniel Rowland, 75–92. Lexington: University Press of Kentucky, 2012.

Smith, Paul S. "First Use of the Term 'Copperhead.'" *American Historical Review* 32 (July 1927): 799–800.

Smith, W. Wayne. "An Experiment in Counterinsurgency: The Assessment of Confederate Sympathizers in Missouri." *Journal of Southern History* 35 (August 1969): 361–80.

Snyder, John F. "The Democratic State Convention of Missouri in 1860." *Missouri Historical Review* 2 (January 1908): 112–22.

Sprague, Stuart Seely. "Town Making in the Era of Good Feelings: Kentucky, 1814–1820." *Register of the Kentucky Historical Society* 72 (October 1974): 337–41.

Stack, Joan. "Toward an Emancipationist Interpretation of George Caleb Bingham's *General Order No. 11*: The Reception History of the Painting and the Remembered Civil War in Missouri." *Missouri Historical Review* 107 (July 2013): 203–21.

Stanley, Matthew E. "'Purely Military Matters': John A. McClernand and Civil Liberties in Cairo, Illinois, in 1861." *Ohio Valley History* 8 (Spring 2008): 23–42.

Sterling, Robert E. "Civil War Draft Resistance in Illinois." *Journal of the Illinois State Historical Society* 64 (Autumn 1971): 244–66.

Stern, Joseph S., Jr. "The Suspension Bridge: They Said It Couldn't Be Built." *Cincinnati Historical Society Bulletin* 23 (October 1965): 210–28.

Stewart, James Brewer. "Modernizing 'Difference': The Political Meaning of Color in the Free States, 1776–1840," in *Race and the Early Republic: Racial Consciousness and Nation Building in the Early Republic*, ed. Michael A. Morrison and James Brewer Stewart, 75–134. Lanham, Md.: Rowman and Littlefield, 2002.

Streater, Kristen L. "'Not Much a Friend to Traiters No Matter How Beautiful': The Union Military and Confederate Women in Civil War Kentucky," in *Sister States, Enemy States: The Civil War in Kentucky and Tennessee*, ed. Kent T. Dollar, Larry Howard Whiteaker, and W. Calvin Dickinson, 245–63. Lexington: University Press of Kentucky, 2009.

Streater, Kristen L. "'She-Rebels' on the Supply Line: Gender Conventions in Civil War Kentucky," in *Occupied Women: Gender, Military Occupation, and the American Civil War*, ed. LeeAnn Whites and Alecia P. Long, 88–99. Baton Rouge: Louisiana State University Press, 2009.

Sutherland, Daniel E. "Abraham Lincoln, John Pope, and the Origins of Total War." *Journal of Military History* 56 (October 1992): 567–86.

Sutherland, Daniel E. "Guerrilla Warfare, Democracy, and the Fate of the Confederacy." *Journal of Southern History* 68 (May 2002): 259–92.

Swindler, William F. "The Southern Press in Missouri, 1861–1864." *Missouri Historical Review* 35 (April 1941): 373–99.

Symon, Robert B., Jr. "Louisville's Lost National Holiday: Sectional Reconciliation and the Ulysses S. Grant 1885 Birthday Celebration." *Ohio Valley History* 8 (Fall 2008): 40–61.

Tap, Bruce. "Amateurs at War: Abraham Lincoln and the Committee on the Conduct of the War." *Journal of the Abraham Lincoln Association* 23 (Summer 2002): 1–18.

Tasher, Lucy Lucile. "The *Missouri Democrat* and the Civil War." *Missouri Historical Review* 31 (July 1937): 402–19.

Temkin, Sefton D. "Isaac Mayer Wise and the Civil War," in *Jews and the Civil War: A Reader*, ed. Jonathan D. Sarna and Adam Mendelsohn, 161–80. New York: New York University Press, 2010.

Terry, Clinton W. "'Let Commerce Follow the Flag': Trade and Loyalty to the Union in the Ohio Valley." *Ohio Valley History* 1 (Spring 2001): 2–14.

Thelen, David. "Memory and American History." *Journal of American History* 75 (March 1989): 1117–29.

Thurston, Helen M. "The 1802 Constitutional Convention and Status of the Negro." *Ohio History* 81 (Winter 1972): 15–37.

Tindall, George B. "Mythology: A New Frontier in Southern History." In *The Idea of the South: Pursuit of a Central Theme*, ed. Frank E. Vandiver, 1–15. Chicago: University of Chicago Press, 1964.

Towne, Stephen E. "Killing the Serpent Speedily: Governor Morton, General Hascall, and the Suppression of the Democratic Press in Indiana, 1863." *Civil War History* 52 (March 2006): 41–65.

Towne, Stephen E. "'Such Conduct Must Be Put Down': The Military Arrest of Judge Charles H. Constable during the Civil War." *Journal of Illinois History* 9 (June 2006): 43–62.

Trescott, Paul B. "The Louisville and Portland Canal Company, 1825–1874." *Mississippi Valley Historical Review* 44 (March 1958): 686–708.

Tucker, Phillip T. "'Ho, for Kansas': The Southwest Expedition of 1860." *Missouri Historical Review* 86 (October 1991): 22–36.

Van Bolt, Roger H. "The Indiana Scene in the 1840's." *Indiana Magazine of History* 47 (December 1951): 333–56.

Vedder, Richard K., and Lowell E. Gallaway. "Migration and the Old Northwest," in *Essays in Nineteenth-Century Economic History: The Old Northwest*, ed. David C. Klingaman and Richard K. Vedder, 159–76. Athens: Ohio University Press, 1975.

Walker, Juliet E. K. "The Legal Status of Free Blacks in Early Kentucky, 1792–1825." *Filson Club History Quarterly* 57 (October 1983): 382–95.

Watson, Harry L. "Conflict and Collaboration: Yeomen, Slaveholders, and Politics in the Antebellum South." *Social History* 10 (October 1985): 273–98.

Wecter, Dixon. "The Soldier and the Ballot." *Huntington Library Quarterly* 7 (August 1944): 397–400.

West, Elliott. "Reconstructing Race." *Western Historical Quarterly* 34 (Spring 2003): 6–26.

Whites, LeeAnn. "'Corresponding with the Enemy': Mobilizing the Relational Field of Battle in St. Louis," in *Occupied Women: Gender, Military Occupation, and the American Civil War*, ed. LeeAnn Whites and Alecia P. Long, 103–16. Baton Rouge: Louisiana State University Press, 2009.

Whites, LeeAnn. "Forty Shirts and a Wagonload of Wheat: Women, the Domestic Supply Line, and the Civil War on the Western Border." *Journal of the Civil War Era* 1 (March 2011): 56–78.

Wilentz, Sean. "Slavery, Antislavery, and Jacksonian Democracy," in *The Market Revolution in America: Social, Political, and Religious Expressions, 1800–1880*, ed. Melvyn Stokes and Stephen Conway, 202–23. Charlottesville: University Press of Virginia, 1996.

Williams, Burton J. "Quantrill's Raid on Lawrence: A Question of Complicity." *Kansas Historical Quarterly* 34 (Summer 1968): 143–49.

Williams, T. Harry. "Voters in Blue: The Citizen Soldiers of the Civil War." *Mississippi Valley Historical Review* 31 (September 1944): 187–204.

Wilson, Charles Ray. "Cincinnati, a Southern Outpost in 1860–61." *Mississippi Valley Historical Review* 24 (March 1938): 473–82.

Wilson, Charles Ray. "Cincinnati's Reputation During the Civil War." *Journal of Southern History* 2 (November 1936): 468–79.

Wilson, Charles Ray. "The Negro in Early Ohio." *Ohio History* 39 (July 1930): 713–78.

Woodworth, Steven E. "'The Indeterminate Quantities': Jefferson Davis, Leonidas Polk, and the End of Kentucky Neutrality, September 1861." *Civil War History* 38 (December 1992): 388–400.

Wright, Alfred J. "Ohio Town Patterns." *Geographical Review* 27 (October 1937): 615–24.

Wurthman, Leonard B., Jr. "Frank Blair: Lincoln's Congressional Spokesman." *Missouri Historical Review* 64 (April 1970): 263–88.

Zorbaugh, Charles L. "From Lane to Oberlin—An Exodus Extraordinary," *Proceedings of the Ohio Presbyterian Historical Society* 2 (1940): 38–40.

BOOKS

Abbott, Richard H. *Ohio's War Governors*. Columbus: Ohio State University Press, 1962.

Abzug, Robert H. *Passionate Liberator: Theodore Dwight Weld and the Dilemma of Reform*. New York: Oxford University Press, 1980.

Adamson, Hans Christian. *Rebellion in Missouri, 1861: Nathaniel Lyon and His Army of the West*. Philadelphia and New York: Chilton, 1961.

Adler, Jeffrey S. *Yankee Merchants and the Making of the Urban West: The Rise and Fall of Antebellum St. Louis*. Cambridge and New York: Cambridge University Press, 1991.

Alden, John. *The First South*. Baton Rouge: Louisiana State University Press, 1961.
Allen, John W. *Legends and Lore of Southern Illinois*. Carbondale: Southern Illinois University Press, 1963.
Allendorf, Donald. *Long Road to Liberty: The Odyssey of a German Regiment in the Yankee Army—The 15th Missouri Volunteer Infantry*. Kent, Ohio: Kent State University Press, 2006.
Angle, Paul M. *Bloody Williamson: A Chapter in American Lawlessness*. New York: Alfred A. Knopf, 1969.
Angle, Paul M., ed. *Prairie State: Impressions of Illinois, 1673–1967*. Chicago: University of Chicago Press, 1968.
Appleby, Joyce, ed. *Recollections of the Early Republic: Selected Autobiographies*. Boston: Northeastern University Press, 1997.
Aptheker, Herbert. *American Negro Slave Revolts*. New York: Columbia University Press, 1943.
Arenson, Adam. *The Great Heart of the Republic: St. Louis and the Cultural Civil War*. Cambridge, Mass.: Harvard University Press, 2011.
Aron, Stephen. *American Confluence: The Missouri Frontier from Borderland to Border State*. Bloomington and Indianapolis: Indiana University Press, 2006.
Aron, Stephen. *How the West Was Lost: The Transformation of Kentucky from Daniel Boone to Henry Clay*. Baltimore: Johns Hopkins University Press, 1996.
Ash, Stephen V. *Middle Tennessee Society Transformed, 1860–1870: War and Peace in the Upper South*. Baton Rouge: Louisiana State University Press, 1988.
Ash, Stephen V. *When the Yankees Came: Conflict and Chaos in the Occupied South, 1861–1865*. Chapel Hill: University of North Carolina Press, 1995.
Astor, Aaron. *Rebels on the Border: Civil War, Emancipation, and the Reconstruction of Kentucky and Missouri*. Baton Rouge: Louisiana State University Press, 2012.
Ayers, Edward L. *In the Presence of Mine Enemies: The Civil War in the Heart of America, 1859–1863*. New York: W. W. Norton, 2003.
Ayers, Edward L. *Vengeance and Justice: Crime and Punishment in the 19th-Century American South*. New York: Oxford University Press, 1984.
Ayers, Edward L., Patricia Nelson Limerick, Stephen Nissenbaum, and Peter S. Onuf, eds. *All Over the Map: Rethinking American Regions*. Baltimore: Johns Hopkins University Press, 1996.
Baker, Jean A. *Affairs of Party: The Political Culture of Northern Democrats in the Mid-Nineteenth Century*. Ithaca, N.Y.: Cornell University Press, 1983.
Barney, William L. *Flawed Victory: A New Perspective on the Civil War*. New York: Praeger, 1975.
Barney, William L. *The Road to Secession: A New Perspective on the Old South*. New York: Praeger, 1972.
Beers, Howard W. *Growth of Population in Kentucky, 1860–1940*. Lexington: Kentucky Agricultural Experiment Station, 1942.
Beilein, Joseph M., Jr., and Matthew C. Hulbert, eds. *Unfolding the Black Flag: The Civil War Guerrilla in History and Myth*. Lexington: University Press of Kentucky, 2014.
Belko, W. Stephen. *The Invincible Duff Green: Whig of the West*. Columbia: University of Missouri Press, 2006.
Bell, David A. *The First Total War: Napoleon's Europe and the Birth of Warfare as We Know It*. Boston: Houghton Mifflin, 2007.
Bellesiles, Michael A., ed. *Lethal Imagination: Violence and Brutality in American History*. New York: New York University Press, 1999.
Berlin, Ira. *Generations of Captivity: A History of African-American Slaves*. Cambridge, Mass.: Belknap Press of Harvard University Press, 2003.
Berlin, Ira. *Many Thousands Gone: The First Two Centuries of Slavery in North America*. Cambridge, Mass.: Belknap Press of Harvard University Press, 1998.
Berlin, Ira. *Slaves without Masters: The Free Negro in the Antebellum South*. New York: Pantheon Books, 1974; reprint New York: Oxford University Press, 1981.
Berlin, Ira, Barbara J. Fields, Thavolia Glymph, Stephen F. Miller, Joseph P. Reidy, Leslie S. Rowland, and Julie Saville, eds. *Freedom: A Documentary History of Emancipation, 1861–1867*. 5 vols. Cambridge and New York: Cambridge University Press, 1982–1993.

Berlin, Ira, Barbara J. Fields, Steven F. Miller, Joseph P. Reidy, and Leslie S. Rowland, eds. *Free at Last: A Documentary History of Slavery, Freedom, and the Civil War*. New York: The Free Press, 1992.

Berlin, Ira, and Ronald Hoffman, eds. *Slavery and Freedom in the Age of the American Revolution*. Urbana and Champaign: University of Illinois Press, 1986.

Bernstein, Iver. *The New York City Draft Riots: Their Significance for American Society and Politics in the Age of the Civil War*. New York: Oxford University Press, 1990.

Berry, Stephen. *House of Abraham: Lincoln and the Todds, A Family Divided by War*. Boston: Houghton Mifflin, 2007.

Berry, Thomas S. *Western Prices before 1861: A Study of the Cincinnati Market*. Cambridge, Mass.: Harvard University Press, 1943.

Berwanger, Eugene H. *The Frontier against Slavery: Western Anti-Negro Prejudice and the Slavery Extension Controversy*. Urbana: University of Illinois Press, 1967.

Bensel, Richard Franklin. *Yankee Leviathan: The Origins of Central State Authority in America, 1859–1877*. Cambridge: Cambridge University Press, 1990.

Bigham, Darrel E. *On Jordan's Banks: Emancipation and Its Aftermath in the Ohio River Valley*. Lexington: University Press of Kentucky, 2006.

Bigham, Darrel E. *Towns and Villages of the Lower Ohio*. Lexington: University Press of Kentucky, 1998.

Billington, Ray Allen. *The Far Western Frontier, 1830–1860*. New York: Harper and Row, 1956.

Billington, Ray Allen. *The Protestant Crusade*. New York: Macmillan, 1938; reprint Chicago: Quadrangle Books, 1964.

Bissland, James H. *Blood, Tears, & Glory: How Ohioans Won the Civil War*. Wilmington, Ohio: Orange Frazier Press, 2007.

Blight, David W. *Race and Reunion: The Civil War in American Memory*. Cambridge, Mass.: Belknap Press of Harvard University Press, 2001.

Boewe, Charles. *Prairie Albion: An English Settlement in Pioneer Illinois*. Carbondale: Southern Illinois University Press, 1962.

Boggess, Arthur C. *The Settlement of Illinois, 1778–1830*. Chicago: Chicago Historical Society, 1908.

Bordewich, Fergus M. *Bound For Canaan: The Underground Railroad*. New York: Amistad Press, 2005.

Breen, T[imothy] H. *Tobacco Culture: The Mentality of the Great Tidewater Planters on the Eve of Revolution*. Princeton, N.J.: Princeton University Press, 1985.

Brown, Kent Masterson, ed. *The Civil War in Kentucky: Battle for the Bluegrass*. Mason City, Iowa: Savas Publishing, 2000.

Brown, Richard D. *Modernization: The Transformation of American Life, 1600–1865*. Prospect Heights, Ill.: Waveland Press, 1976.

Brown, Richard Maxwell. *The South Carolina Regulators*. Cambridge, Mass.: Harvard University Press, 1963.

Brown, Richard Maxwell. *The Strain of Violence: Historical Studies of American Violence and Vigilantism*. New York: Oxford University Press, 2002.

Brownlee, Richard S. *Gray Ghosts of the Confederacy: Guerrilla Warfare in the West, 1861–1865*. Baton Rouge: Louisiana State University Press, 1958.

Brundage, W. Fitzhugh. *Lynching in the New South: Georgia and Virginia, 1880–1930*. Urbana: University of Illinois Press, 1993.

Brundage, W. Fitzhugh. *The Southern Past: A Clash of Race and Memory*. Cambridge, Mass.: Belknap Press of Harvard University Press, 2005.

Buchanan, Thomas C. *Black Life on the Mississippi: Slaves, Free Blacks, and the Western Steamboat World*. Chapel Hill: University of North Carolina Press, 2004.

Budiansky, Stephen. *The Bloody Shirt: Terror After the Civil War*. New York: Plume, 2009.

Burke, Diane Mutti. *On Slavery's Border: Missouri's Small Slaveholding Households, 1815–1865*. Athens: University of Georgia Press, 2010.

Burton, William L. *Melting Pot Soldiers: The Union's Ethnic Regiments*. Ames: Iowa State University Press, 1988; reprint New York: Fordham University Press, 1998.

Cable, John Ray. *The Bank of the State of Missouri*. New York: Longmans, Green, 1923.
Cain, Marvin R. *Lincoln's Attorney General: Edward Bates of Missouri*. Columbia: University of Missouri Press, 1965.
Campbell, Stanley W. *The Slave Catchers: Enforcement of the Fugitive Slave Law, 1850–1860*. New York: W. W. Norton, 1972.
Carnahan, Burrus M. *Lincoln on Trial: Southern Civilians and the Law of War*. Lexington: University Press of Kentucky, 2010.
Catton, Bruce. *This Hallowed Ground: The Story of the Union Side of the Civil War*. Garden City, N.J.: Doubleday, 1956.
Cash, Wilbur J. *The Mind of the South*. New York: Alfred A. Knopf, 1941.
Cashin, Joan E., ed. *The War Was You and Me: Civilians in the American Civil War*. Princeton, N.J.: Princeton University Press, 2002.
Cassity, Michael. *Defending a Way of Life: An American Community in the Nineteenth Century*. Albany: State University of New York Press, 1989.
Castel, Albert. *A Frontier State at War: Kansas, 1861–1865*. Ithaca, N.Y.: Cornell University Press, 1959; reprint Lawrence: Kansas Heritage Press, 1992.
Castel, Albert. *General Sterling Price and the Civil War in the West*. Baton Rouge: Louisiana State University Press, 1968.
Castel, Albert. *William Clarke Quantrill: His Life and Times*. Norman: University of Oklahoma Press, 1999.
Castel, Albert. *Winning and Losing in the Civil War: Essays and Stories*. Columbia: University of South Carolina Press, 1996.
Cayton, Andrew R. L. *Frontier Indiana*. Bloomington: Indiana University Press, 1996.
Cayton, Andrew R. L. *The Frontier Republic: Ideology and Politics in the Ohio Country, 1780–1825*. Kent, Ohio: Kent State University Press, 1997.
Chambers, William Nisbet. *Old Bullion Benton: Senator from the New West*. Boston: Little, Brown, 1956.
Channing, Steven A. *Kentucky: A Bicentennial History*. New York: W. W. Norton, 1977.
Christensen, Lawrence O., and Gary R. Kremer. *A History of Missouri: Volume IV—1875 to 1919*. Columbia: University of Missouri Press, 1997.
Cimbala, Paul A., and Randall M. Miller, eds. *The Great Task Remaining Before Us: Reconstruction as America's Continuing Civil War*. New York: Fordham University Press, 2010.
Clark, Thomas D. *Frontier America: The Story of the Westward Movement*. New York: Charles Scribner's Sons, 1959.
Clark, Thomas D. *Pleasant Hill in the Civil War*. Lexington: Pleasant Hill Press, 1972.
Clark, Thomas D., and F. Gerald Ham. *Pleasant Hill and Its Shakers*. Harrodsburg, Ky.: Pleasant Hill Press, 1983.
Clinton, Catherine, and Nina L. Silber, eds. *Divided Houses: Gender and the Civil War*. New York: Oxford University Press, 1992.
Clubbe, John. *Cincinnati Observed: Architecture and History*. Columbus: Ohio State University Press, 1992.
Cobb, James C. *Away Down South: A History of Southern Identity*. New York: Oxford University Press, 2005.
Cobb, Richard. *Reactions to the French Revolution*. New York: Oxford University Press, 1972.
Cohen, Anthony P. *The Symbolic Construction of Community*. London and New York: Routledge, 1985.
Cole, Arthur C. *The Centennial History of Illinois: The Era of the Civil War, 1848–1870*. Springfield: Illinois Centennial Commission, 1919.
Cole, Arthur C. *The Era of the Civil War, 1848–1870*. Chicago: A. C. McClurg, 1922.
Cole, Arthur C. *The Whig Party in the South*. Washington, D.C.: American Historical Association, 1914.
Coleman, J. Winston. *Last Days, Death, and Funeral of Henry Clay, with Some Remarks on the Clay Monument in the Lexington Cemetery*. Lexington: Winburn Press, 1951.

Connelly, William E., and E. Merton Coulter. *History of Kentucky*. 5 vols. Chicago: American Historical Society, 1922.

Cooling, Benjamin Franklin. *Forts Henry and Donelson: The Key to the Confederate Heartland*. Knoxville: University of Tennessee Press, 1987.

Cooper, William J., Jr. *Liberty and Slavery: Southern Politics to 1860*. New York: Alfred A. Knopf, 1983.

Corlew, Robert E. *Tennessee: A Short History*. Knoxville: University of Tennessee Press, 1989.

Cornish, Dudley T. *The Sable Arm: Negro Troops in the Union Army, 1861–1865*. Ithaca, N.Y.: Cornell University Press, 1956.

Coulter, E. Merton. *The Civil War and Readjustment in Kentucky*. Chapel Hill: University of North Carolina Press, 1926; reprint Gloucester, Mass.: Peter Smith, 1966.

Cox, Karen. *Dixie's Daughters: The United Daughters of the Confederacy and the Preservation of Confederate Culture*. Gainesville: University of Florida Press, 2003.

Crofts, Daniel W. *Reluctant Confederates: Upper South Unionists in the Secession Crisis*. Chapel Hill: University of North Carolina Press, 1989.

Current, Richard Nelson. *Lincoln's Loyalists: Union Soldiers from the Confederacy*. Boston: Northeastern University Press, 1992; reprint New York: Oxford University Press, 1994.

Curry, Leonard P. *The Free Black in Urban America 1800–1850: The Shadow of the Dream*. Chicago: University of Chicago Press, 1981.

Curry, Richard O., ed. *Radicalism, Racism, and Party Realignment: The Border States during Reconstruction*. Baltimore: Johns Hopkins University Press, 1969.

Davis, James E. *Breckenridge: Statesman, Soldier, Symbol*. Baton Rouge: Louisiana State University Press, 1974.

Davis, James E. *Frontier Illinois*. Bloomington: Indiana University Press, 1998.

Davis, James E. *The Orphan Brigade: The Kentucky Confederates Who Couldn't Go Home*. Baton Rouge: Louisiana State University Press, 1980.

Dearing, Mary R. *Veterans in Politics: The Story of the G.A.R.* Westport, Conn.: Greenwood Press, 1974.

Degler, Carl. *The Other South: Southern Dissenters in the Nineteenth Century*. New York: Harper and Row, 1974.

DeRosa, Marshall L., ed. *The Politics of Dissolution: The Quest for a National Identity and the American Civil War*. New Brunswick, N.J.: Transaction Publishers, 1998.

Dew, Charles B. *Apostles of Disunion: Southern Secession Commissioners and the Causes of the Civil War*. Charlottesville: University Press of Virginia, 2001.

Dick, Everett. *The Dixie Frontier: A Social History of the Southern Frontier from the First Transmontane Beginnings to the Civil War*. New York: Alfred A. Knopf, 1948.

Dickerson, O[liver]. M. *The Illinois Constitutional Convention of 1862*. Urbana: University [of Illinois] Press, 1905.

Dickey, Michael. *Arrow Rock: Crossroads of the Missouri Frontier*. Arrow Rock, Mo.: Friends of Arrow Rock, 2004.

Dillon, Merton L. *The Abolitionists: The Growth of a Dissenting Minority*. DeKalb: Northern Illinois University Press, 1974; reprint New York: W. W. Norton, 1979.

Dillon, Merton L. *Benjamin Lundy and the Struggle for Negro Freedom*. Urbana: University of Illinois Press, 1966.

Dillon, Merton L. *Elijah P. Lovejoy, Abolitionist Editor*. Urbana: University of Illinois Press, 1961.

Dollar, Kent T., Larry Howard Whiteaker, and W. Calvin Dickinson, eds. *Sister States, Enemy States: The Civil War in Kentucky and Tennessee*. Lexington: University Press of Kentucky, 2009.

Donald, David Herbert. *Charles Sumner and the Coming of the Civil War*. New York: Alfred A. Knopf, 1960.

Donald, David Herbert. *Lincoln*. New York: Simon and Schuster, 1995.

Donald, David Herbert. *Lincoln Reconsidered: Essays on the Civil War Era*. New York: Alfred A. Knopf, 1965.

Donald, David Herbert. *Lincoln's Herndon: A Biography*. New York: Alfred A. Knopf, 1948.
Donald, David Herbert. *The Politics of Reconstruction, 1863-1867*. Baton Rouge: Louisiana State University Press, 1965.
Downs, Gregory P. *After Appomattox: Military Occupation and the Ends of War*. Cambridge, Mass.: Harvard University Press, 2015.
Earle, Jonathan H. *Jacksonian Antislavery and the Politics of Free Soil, 1824-1854*. Chapel Hill: University of North Carolina Press, 2004.
Earle, Jonathan H., and Diane Mutti Burke, eds. *Bleeding Kansas, Bleeding Missouri: The Long Civil War on the Western Border*. Lawrence: University Press of Kansas, 2013.
Eaton, Clement. *A History of the Southern Confederacy*. New York: Macmillan, 1956.
Ecelbarger, Gary. *The Great Comeback: How Abraham Lincoln Beat the Odds to Win the 1860 Republican Nomination*. New York: Macmillan, 2008.
Edwards, Laura F. *Scarlett Doesn't Live Here Anymore: Southern Women in the Civil War Era*. Urbana: University of Illinois Press, 2000.
Engle, Stephen D. *Don Carlos Buell: Most Promising of All*. Chapel Hill: University of North Carolina Press, 1999.
Etcheson, Nicole. *Bleeding Kansas: Contested Liberty in the Civil War Era*. Lawrence: University Press of Kansas, 2004.
Etcheson, Nicole. *The Emerging Midwest: Upland Southerners and the Political Culture of the Old Northwest, 1787-1861*. Bloomington: Indiana University Press, 1996.
Etcheson, Nicole. *A Generation at War: The Civil War Era in a Northern Community*. Lawrence: University Press of Kansas, 2010.
Eyal, Yonatan. *The Young America Movement and the Transformation of the Democratic Party, 1828-1861*. Cambridge, Mass.: Cambridge University Press, 2007.
Faragher, John Mack. *Daniel Boone: The Life and Legend of an American Pioneer*. New York: Henry Holt, 1992.
Faragher, John Mack. *Sugar Creek: Life on the Illinois Frontier*. New Haven, Conn.: Yale University Press, 1986.
Faust, Drew Gilpin. *The Creation of Confederate Nationalism: Ideology and Identity in the Civil War South*. Baton Rouge: Louisiana State University Press, 1988.
Faust, Drew Gilpin. *Mothers of Invention: Women of the Slaveholding South in the American Civil War*. Chapel Hill: University of North Carolina Press, 1996.
Faust, Drew Gilpin. *This Republic of Suffering: Death and the American Civil War*. New York: Vintage Books, 2008.
Federal Writers' Project. *Kentucky: A Guide to the Bluegrass State*. New York: Harcourt, Brace, 1939.
Federal Writers' Project. *Missouri: A Guide to the "Show Me" State*. New York: Duell, Sloan and Pearce, 1941; reprint University Press of Kansas, 1986.
Fehrenbacher, Don E. *The Sectional Crisis and Southern Constitutionalism*. Baton Rouge: Louisiana State University Press, 1995.
Fehrenbacher, Don E. *The South and Three Sectional Crises*. Baton Rouge: Louisiana State University Press, 1980.
Fellman, Michael. *Citizen Sherman: A Life of William Tecumseh Sherman*. New York: Random House, 1995.
Fellman, Michael. *Inside War: The Guerrilla Conflict in Missouri during the American Civil War*. New York: Oxford University Press, 1989.
Fenton, John H. *Politics in the Border States*. New Orleans: Hauser Press, 1957.
Filbert, Preston. *The Half Not Told: The Civil War in a Frontier Town*. Mechanicsburg, Pa.: Stackpole Books, 2001.
Filler, Louis. *The Crusade against Slavery, 1830-1860*. New York: Harper and Bros., 1960.
Finkelman, Paul. *An Imperfect Union: Slavery, Federalism, and Comity*. Chapel Hill: University of North Carolina Press, 1981.
Finkelman, Paul. *Slavery and the Founders: Race and Liberty in the Age of Jefferson*. London: M. E. Sharpe, 1996.

Fischer, David Hackett. *Albion's Seed: Four British Folkways in America*. New York: Oxford University Press, 1990.

Fischer, David Hackett, and James C. Kelly. *Bound Away: Virginia and the Westward Movement*. Charlottesville and London: University Press of Virginia, 2000.

Fladeland, Betty. *James Gillespie Birney: Slaveholder to Abolitionist*. Ithaca, N.Y.: Cornell University Press, 1955.

Foley, William E. *The Genesis of Missouri: From Wilderness Outpost to Statehood*. Columbia: University of Missouri Press, 1989.

Foley, William E. *A History of Missouri. Vol. 1: 1673–1820*. Columbia: University of Missouri Press, 1971.

Foner, Eric. *The Fiery Trial: Abraham Lincoln and American Slavery*. New York: W. W. Norton, 2010.

Foner, Eric. *Free Soil, Free Labor, Free Men: The Ideology of the Republican Party before the Civil War*. New York: Oxford University Press, 1970.

Foner, Eric, ed. *Our Lincoln: New Perspectives on Lincoln and His World*. New York: W. W. Norton, 2008.

Foner, Eric. *Reconstruction: America's Unfinished Revolution, 1863–1877*. New York: Harper and Row, 1988.

Ford, Lacy K. *Deliver Us from Evil: The Slavery Question in the Old South*. New York: Oxford University Press, 2009.

Ford, Lacy K. *The Roots of Southern Radicalism: The South Carolina Upcountry, 1800–1865*. New York: Oxford University Press, 1988.

Foster, Gaines M. *Ghosts of the Confederacy: Defeat, the Lost Cause, and the Emergence of the New South, 1865 to 1913*. New York: Oxford University Press, 1987.

Fox-Genovese, Elizabeth, and Eugene D. Genovese. *Slavery in White and Black: Class and Race in the Southern Slaveholders' New World Order*. Cambridge: Cambridge University Press, 2008.

Franklin, John Hope. *The Emancipation Proclamation*. New York: Anchor Books, 1965.

Franklin, John Hope. *Reconstruction: After the Civil War*. Chicago: University of Chicago Press, 1961.

Franklin, John Hope, and Loren Schweninger. *Runaway Slaves: Rebels on the Plantation*. New York: Oxford University Press, 1999.

Freehling, William W. *The Road to Disunion*. 2 vols. New York: Oxford University Press, 1990, 2007.

Freehling, William W. *The South vs. the South: How Anti-Confederate Southerners Shaped the Course of the Civil War*. New York: Oxford University Press, 2001.

Friend, Craig T., ed. *The Buzzel About Kentuck: Settling the Promised Land*. Lexington: University Press of Kentucky, 1999.

Fuller, A. James. *Oliver P. Morton and the Politics of the Civil War and Reconstruction*. Kent, Ohio: Kent State University Press, 2016.

Fulton, Joe B. *The Reconstruction of Mark Twain: How a Confederate Bushwhacker Became the Lincoln of Our Literature*. Baton Rouge: Louisiana State University Press, 2010.

Gallagher, Gary W. *The Union War*. Cambridge, Mass.: Harvard University Press, 2011.

Gallay, Alan. *The Indian Slave Trade: The Rise of the English Empire in the American South, 1670–1717*. New Haven, Conn.: Yale University Press, 2002.

Gallman, J. Matthew. *Mastering Wartime: A Social History of Philadelphia During the Civil War*. Cambridge: Cambridge University Press, 1990; reprint Philadelphia: University of Pennsylvania Press, 2000.

Gannon, Barbara A. *The Won Cause: Black and White Comradeship in the Grand Army of the Republic*. Chapel Hill: University of North Carolina Press, 2011.

Gara, Larry. *The Liberty Line: The Legend of the Underground Railroad*. Lexington: University Press of Kentucky, 1961.

Gaston, Paul M. *The New South Creed: A Study in Southern Mythmaking*. New York: Alfred A. Knopf, 1970.

Geiger, Mark W. *Financial Fraud and Guerrilla Violence in Missouri's Civil War, 1861–1865*. New Haven, Conn.: Yale University Press, 2010.

Gerteis, Louis S. *Civil War St. Louis*. Lawrence: University Press of Kansas, 2001.
Gerteis, Louis S. *From Contraband to Freedman: Federal Policy Toward Southern Blacks, 1861–1865*. Westport, Conn.: Greenwood Press, 1973.
Giglierano, Geoffrey J., and Deborah A. Overmyer. *The Bicentennial Guide to Greater Cincinnati: A Portrait of Two Hundred Years*. Cincinnati: Cincinnati Historical Society, 1988.
Gillette, William. *The Right to Vote: Politics and the Passage of the Fifteenth Amendment*. Baltimore: Johns Hopkins University Press, 1965.
Gjerde, Jon. *The Minds of the West: Ethnocultural Evolution in the Rural Middle West, 1830–1917*. Chapel Hill and London: University of North Carolina Press, 1997.
Gleeson, Ed. *Illinois Rebels*. Carmel: Guild Press of Indiana, 1996.
Goodrich, Thomas. *Bloody Dawn: The Story of the Lawrence Massacre*. Kent, Ohio: Kent State University Press, 1992.
Gottschalk, Phil. *In Deadly Earnest: The History of the First Missouri Brigade, C.S.A.* Columbia: Missouri River Press, 1991.
Graham, Preston D., Jr. *A Kingdom Not of This World: Stuart Robinson's Struggle to Distinguish the Sacred from the Secular during the Civil War*. Macon, Ga.: Mercer University Press, 2002.
Gray, Lewis C. *History of Agriculture in the Southern United States to 1860*. 2 vols. Washington, D.C.: Carnegie Institution of Washington, 1932; reprint Gloucester, Mass.: Peter Smith, 1958.
Greene, Evarts B., and Virginia D. Carrington. *American Population before the Federal Census of 1790*. New York: Columbia University Press, 1932.
Griffin, Patrick. *American Leviathan: Empire, Nation, and Revolutionary Frontier*. New York: Hill and Wang, 2007.
Griffler, Keith. *Front Line of Freedom: African Americans and the Forging of the Underground Railroad in the Ohio Valley*. Lexington: University Press of Kentucky, 2004.
Grimsley, Mark. *The Hard Hand of War: Union Military Policy toward Southern Civilians, 1861–1865*. Cambridge and New York: Cambridge University Press, 1995.
Gruenwald, Kim M. *River of Enterprise: The Commercial Origins of Regional Identity in the Ohio Valley, 1790–1850*. Bloomington and Indianapolis: Indiana University Press, 2002.
Gurock, Jeffery S. ed. *American Jewish History: Anti-Semitism in America*. New York: Routledge Press, 1998.
Hahn, Steven. *A Nation Under Our Feet: Black Political Struggles in the Rural South from Slavery to the Great Migration*. Cambridge, Mass.: Belknap Press of Harvard University Press, 2003.
Hale, Donald R. *The William Clarke Quantrill Men Reunions, 1898–1929*. Independence, Mo.: Blue and Grey Book Shoppe, 2001.
Hamilton, Daniel W. *The Limits of Sovereignty: Property Confiscation in the Union and Confederacy during the Civil War*. Chicago: University of Chicago Press, 2007.
Hamilton, Holman. *Prologue to Conflict: The Crisis and Compromise of 1850*. New York: W. W. Norton, 1966.
Harris, N. Dwight. *The History of Negro Servitude in Illinois and the Slavery Agitation in That State*. Chicago: A. C. McClurg, 1904.
Harris, William C. *Lincoln and the Border State: Preserving the Union*. Lawrence: University Press of Kansas, 2011.
Harrison, Lowell H. *The Antislavery Movement in Kentucky*. Lexington: University Press of Kentucky, 1978.
Harrison, Lowell H. *The Civil War in Kentucky*. Lexington: University Press of Kentucky, 1975.
Harrison, Lowell H., ed. *Kentucky's Governors*. Lexington: University Press of Kentucky, 2004.
Harrison, Lowell H. *Lincoln of Kentucky*. Lexington: University Press of Kentucky, 2000.
Harrison, Lowell H., and James C. Klotter. *A New History of Kentucky*. Lexington: University Press of Kentucky, 1997.
Harrold, Stanley. *Border War: Fighting over Slavery before the Civil War*. Chapel Hill: University of North Carolina Press, 2010.
Harrold, Stanley. *The Abolitionists and the South, 1831–1861*. Lexington: University Press of Kentucky, 1995.

Havighurst, Walter. *Ohio: A Bicentennial History*. New York: W. W. Norton, 1976.
Heidler, David S., and Jeanne T. Heidler. *Henry Clay: The Essential American*. New York: Random House, 2010.
Heyrman, Christine. *Southern Cross: The Making of the Bible Belt*. New York: Alfred A. Knopf, 1997.
Hicken, Victor. *Illinois in the Civil War*. Urbana: University of Illinois Press, 1966.
Hickok, Charles Thomas. *The Negro in Ohio 1802–1870*. Cleveland: Williams Publishing and Electric Co., 1896; reprint New York: AMS Press, 1975.
Hinze, David C., and Karen Farnham. *The Battle of Carthage: Border War in Southwest Missouri, July 5, 1861*. Campbell, Calif.: Savas Publishing, 1997.
Heineman, Kenneth J. *Civil War Dynasty: The Ewing Family of Ohio*. New York: New York University Press, 2012.
Hirshson, Stanley P. *Farewell to the Bloody Shirt: Northern Republicans and the Southern Negro, 1877–1893*. Bloomington: Indiana University Press, 1962; reprint Chicago: Quadrangle Books, 1968.
Hodges, Graham Russell. *Slavery, Freedom, and Culture Among Early American Workers*. Armonk, N.Y.: M. E. Sharpe, 1998.
Holbrook, Stewart H. *The Yankee Exodus: An Account of Migration from New England*. New York: Macmillan, 1950.
Holt, Michael F. *The Rise and Fall of the American Whig Party*. New York: Oxford University Press, 1999.
Holzer, Harold. *Lincoln at Cooper Union: The Speech That Made Abraham Lincoln President*. New York: Simon and Schuster, 2006.
Hopkins, James F. *A History of the Hemp Industry in Kentucky*. Lexington: University Press of Kentucky, 1951.
Horsman, Reginald. *Race and Manifest Destiny: The Origins of American Racial Anglo-Saxonism*. Cambridge, Mass.: Harvard University Press, 1981.
Horwitz, Lester V. *The Longest Raid of the Civil War*. Cincinnati: Farmcourt Publishing, 1999.
Howard, Robert P. *Illinois: A History of the Prairie State*. Grand Rapids, Mich.: William B. Eerdmans, 1972.
Howard, Victor B. *Black Liberation in Kentucky: Emancipation and Freedom, 1862–1884*. Lexington: University Press of Kentucky, 1983.
Howard, Victor B. *The Evangelical War Against Slavery and Caste: The Life and Times of John G. Fee*. Selinsgrove, Pa.: Susquehanna University Press, 1996.
Howe, Daniel Ward. *The Political Culture of the American Whigs*. Chicago: University of Chicago Press, 1980.
Hubbard, Elbert. *Little Journeys to the Homes of American Statesmen*. Chicago: Wm. H. Wise, 1916.
Hubbart, Henry Clyde. *The Older Middle West, 1840–1880*. New York: Russell and Russell, 1963.
Hudson, J. Blaine. *Fugitive Slaves and the Underground Railroad in the Kentucky Borderland*. Jefferson, N.C.: McFarland, 2002.
Hughes, Nathaniel Cheairs, Jr. *The Battle of Belmont: Grant Strikes South*. Chapel Hill: University of North Carolina Press, 1991.
Hull, Isabel V. *Absolute Destruction: Military Culture and the Practices of War in Imperial Germany*. Ithaca, N.Y.: Cornell University Press, 2006.
Hunt, Robert. *The Good Men Who Won the War: Army of the Cumberland Veterans and Emancipation Memory*. Tuscaloosa: University of Alabama Press, 2010.
Hurst, Jack. *Nathan Bedford Forrest: A Biography*. New York: Vintage Books, 1994.
Hurt, R. Douglas. *Agriculture and Slavery in Missouri's Little Dixie*. Columbia: University of Missouri Press, 1992.
Hyman, Harold M. *Era of the Oath: Northern Loyalty Tests During the Civil War and Reconstruction*. New York: Octagon Books, 1954.
Hyman, Harold M. *To Try Men's Souls: Loyalty Tests in American History*. Berkeley: University of California Press, 1959.
Ireland, Robert M. *The County Courts in Antebellum Kentucky*. Lexington: University Press of Kentucky, 1972.

Jakle, John A. *Images of the Ohio Valley: A Historical Geography of Travel, 1740–1860.* New York: Oxford University Press, 1977.
Janney, Caroline E. *Remembering the Civil War: Reunion and the Limits of Reconciliation.* Chapel Hill: University of North Carolina Press, 2013.
Jaspin, Elliot. *Buried in the Bitter Waters: The Hidden History of Racial Cleansing in America.* New York: Basic Books, 2007.
Jennings, Thelma. *The Nashville Convention: Southern Movement for Unity, 1848–1851.* Memphis, Tenn.: Memphis State University Press, 1980.
Jensen, Richard J. *Illinois: A Bicentennial History.* New York: W. W. Norton, 1977.
Johannsen, Robert W., ed. *The Lincoln-Douglas Debates.* New York: Oxford University Press, 1965.
Johannsen, Robert W. *To the Halls of the Montezumas: The Mexican War in the American Imagination.* New York: Oxford University Press, 1985.
Johnson, Michael P. *Toward a Patriarchal Republic: The Secession of Georgia.* Baton Rouge: Louisiana State University Press, 1977.
Jones, James Pickett. *"Black Jack": John A. Logan and Southern Illinois in the Civil War Era.* Carbondale: Southern Illinois University Press, 1995.
Kamphoefner, Walter D., and Wolfgang Helbich, eds. *Germans in the Civil War: The Letters They Wrote Home.* Chapel Hill: University of North Carolina Press, 2006.
Kilcullen, David. *The Accidental Guerrilla: Fighting Small Wars in the Midst of a Big One.* New York: Oxford University Press, 2009.
Kiper, Richard L. *General John Alexander McClernand: Politician in Uniform.* Kent, Ohio: Kent State University Press, 1999.
Kirwan, Albert D. *John J. Crittenden: The Struggle for the Union.* Lexington: University of Kentucky Press, 1962.
Klement, Frank L. *The Copperheads in the Middle West.* Chicago: University of Chicago Press, 1960.
Klement, Frank L. *Dark Lanterns: Secret Political Societies, Conspiracies, and Treason Trials in the Civil War.* Baton Rouge: Louisiana State University Press, 1984.
Klement, Frank L. *The Limits of Dissent: Clement L. Vallandigham and the Civil War.* Lexington: University Press of Kentucky, 1970.
Klingaman, David C., and Richard K. Vedder. *Essays in Nineteenth-Century Economic History: The Old Northwest.* Athens: Ohio University Press, 1975.
Klotter, James C. *The Breckinridges of Kentucky.* Lexington: University Press of Kentucky, 1986.
Klotter, James C., and Daniel Rowland, eds. *Bluegrass Renaissance: The History and Culture of Central Kentucky, 1792–1852.* Lexington: University Press of Kentucky, 2012.
Kremer, Gary R. *James Milton Turner and the Promise of America: The Public Life of a Post-Civil War Black Leader.* Columbia: University of Missouri Press, 1991.
Lantz, Herman R. *A Community in Search of Itself: A Case Study of Cairo, Illinois.* Carbondale: Southern Illinois University Press, 1972.
Lause, Mark A. *A Secret Society History of the Civil War.* Urbana: University of Illinois Press, 2011.
Lause, Mark A. *Price's Lost Campaign: The 1864 Invasion of Missouri.* Columbia: University of Missouri Press, 2011.
Lause, Mark A. *Race and Radicalism in the Union Army.* Urbana: University of Illinois Press, 2009.
Leonard, Elizabeth D. *Lincoln's Forgotten Ally: Judge Advocate General Joseph Holt of Kentucky.* Chapel Hill: University of North Carolina Press, 2011.
Leonard, Elizabeth D. *Yankee Women: Gender Battles in the Civil War.* New York: W. W. Norton, 1994.
LeSueur, Stephen C. *The 1838 Mormon War in Missouri.* Columbia: University of Missouri Press, 1990.
Levine, Bruce. *Half Slave and Half Free: The Roots of Civil War.* New York: Hill and Wang, 1992.
Levine, Bruce. *The Spirit of 1848: German Immigrants, Labor Conflict, and the Coming of the Civil War.* Urbana: University of Illinois Press, 1992.
Lewis, Patrick A. *For Slavery and Union: Benjamin Buckner and Kentucky Loyalties in the Civil War.* Lexington: University Press of Kentucky, 2015.

Limerick, Patricia Nelson. *The Legacy of Conquest: The Unbroken Past of the American West.* New York: W. W. Norton, 1987.
Linklater, Andro. *Measuring America: How the United States Was Shaped by the Greatest Land Sale in History.* New York and London: Penguin, 2002.
Litwack, Leon F. *North of Slavery: The Negro in the Free States, 1790–1860.* Chicago and London: University of Chicago Press, 1961.
Lonn, Ella. *Desertion During the Civil War.* Gloucester, Mass.: American Historical Association, 1928; reprint Lincoln: University of Nebraska Press, 1998.
Lucas, Marion B. *A History of Blacks in Kentucky. Vol. 1, From Slavery to Segregation, 1760–1891.* Frankfort: Kentucky Historical Society, 1992.
Mackey, Robert R. *The Uncivil War: Irregular Warfare in the Upper South, 1861–1865.* Norman: University of Oklahoma Press, 2004.
Madison, James H. *The Indiana Way: A State History.* Bloomington and Indianapolis: Indiana University Press/Indiana Historical Society, 1986.
Magee, Judy. *Cavern of Crime.* Smithland, Ky.: The Livingston Ledger, 1973.
Maizlish, Stephen E. *The Triumph of Sectionalism: The Transformation of Ohio Politics, 1844–1856.* Kent, Ohio: Kent State University Press, 1983.
Manning, Chandra. *What This Cruel War Was Over: Soldiers, Slavery, and the Civil War.* New York: Alfred A. Knopf, 2007.
Marcus, Jacob Rader. *The Americanization of Isaac Mayer Wise.* Cincinnati: printed by author, 1931.
Margolies, Daniel S. *Henry Watterson and the New South: The Politics of Empire, Free Trade, and Globalization.* Lexington: University Press of Kentucky, 2006.
Marshall, Anne E. *Creating a Confederate Kentucky: The Lost Cause and Civil War Memory in a Border State.* Chapel Hill: University of North Carolina Press, 2010.
Marszalek, John F. *Sherman: A Soldier's Passion for Order.* New York: The Free Press, 1993.
Marten, James. *The Children's Civil War.* Chapel Hill: University of North Carolina Press, 1998.
Martin, Jonathan D. *Divided Mastery: Slave Hiring in the American South.* Cambridge, Mass.: Harvard University Press, 2004.
Matthews, Gary Robert. *Basil Wilson Duke, CSA: The Right Man in the Right Place.* Lexington: University Press of Kentucky, 2005.
Shelby and His Men. Cincinnati: Miami Printing and Publishing Co., 1867.
McCandless, Perry. *A History of Missouri. Vol. II: 1820–1860.* Columbia: University of Missouri Press, 1972.
McCardell, John. *The Idea of a Southern Nation: Southern Nationalists and Southern Nationalism, 1830–1860.* New York: W. W. Norton, 1979.
McClure, Charles H. *Opposition in Missouri to Thomas Hart Benton.* Nashville: George Peabody College for Teachers, 1927.
McConnell, Stewart. *Glorious Contentment: The Grand Army of the Republic, 1865–1900.* Chapel Hill: University of North Carolina Press, 1992.
McCormick, Chris, and Len Green, eds. *Crime and Deviance in Canada: Historical Perspectives.* Toronto: Canadian Scholars Press, 2005.
McCormick, Richard P. *The Second American Party System: Party Formation in the Jacksonian Era.* Chapel Hill: University of North Carolina Press, 1966.
McCoy, Drew R. *The Elusive Republic: Political Economy in Jeffersonian America.* New York: W. W. Norton, 1980.
McDonough, James Lee. *War in Kentucky: From Shiloh to Perryville.* Knoxville: University of Tennessee Press, 1994.
McDougle, Ivan E. *Slavery in Kentucky, 1792–1865.* Lancaster, Pa.: Press of the New Era Printing Co., 1918.
McFeely, William S. *Grant: A Biography.* New York: W. W. Norton, 1981.
McKitrick, Eric L. *Andrew Johnson and Reconstruction.* New York: Oxford University Press, 1960.
McKnight, Brian D. *Contested Borderland: The Civil War in Appalachian Kentucky and Virginia.* Lexington: University Press of Kentucky, 2006.

McPherson, James M. *Battle Cry of Freedom: The Civil War Era.* New York: Oxford University Press, 1988.
McPherson, James M. *Crossroads of Freedom: Antietam.* New York: Oxford University Press, 2002.
McPherson, James M. *For Cause and Comrades: Why Men Fought in the Civil War.* New York: Oxford University Press, 1997.
McPherson, James M. *Ordeal by Fire.* New York: Knopf, 1982.
McPherson, James M. *Tried by War: Abraham Lincoln as Commander in Chief.* New York: Penguin Press, 2008.
McPherson, James M. *War on the Waters: The Union and Confederate Navies, 1861–1865.* Chapel Hill: University of North Carolina Press, 2012.
McPherson, James M., and William J. Cooper Jr., eds. *Writing the Civil War: The Quest to Understand.* Columbia: University of South Carolina Press, 1998.
Meigs, William M. *The Life of Thomas Hart Benton.* Philadelphia: J. B. Lippincott, 1904; reprint New York: DaCapo Press, 1970.
Meinig, D. W. *The Shaping of America.* 2 vols. New Haven, Conn.: Yale University Press, 1993.
Melish, Joanne Pope. *Disowning Slavery: Gradual Emancipation and "Race" in New England, 1780–1860.* Ithaca, N.Y., and London: Cornell University Press, 1998.
Mering, John Volmer. *The Whig Party in Missouri.* Columbia: University of Missouri Press, 1967.
Meyer, Douglas K. *Making the Heartland Quilt: A Geographic History of Settlement and Migration in Early-Nineteenth Century Illinois.* Carbondale and Edwardsville: Southern Illinois University Press, 2000.
Middleton, Stephen. *The Black Laws: Race and the Legal Process in Early Ohio.* Athens: Ohio University Press, 2005.
Miller, James M. *The Genesis of Western Culture: The Upper Ohio Valley, 1800–1825.* Columbus: Ohio State Archeological and Historical Society, 1938; reprint New York: Da Capo Press, 1969.
Milward, Burton. *A History of the Lexington Cemetery.* Lexington: Lexington Cemetery Association, 1989.
Mitchell, Reid. *The Vacant Chair: The Northern Soldier Leaves Home.* New York: Oxford University Press, 1993.
Monaghan, Jay. *Civil War on the Western Border, 1854–1865.* Boston: Little, Brown, 1955; reprint Lincoln: University of Nebraska Press, 1984.
Moore, Arthur K. *The Frontier Mind: A Cultural Analysis of the Kentucky Frontiersmen.* Lexington: University of Kentucky Press, 1957.
Moore, John Hebron. *The Emergence of the Cotton Kingdom in the Old Southwest: Mississippi, 1770–1860.* Baton Rouge: Louisiana State University Press, 1988.
Morris, Christopher. *Becoming Southern: The Evolution of a Way of Life, Warren County and Vicksburg, Mississippi, 1770–1860.* New York and Oxford: Oxford University Press, 1995.
Morrison, Michael A. *Slavery and the American West: The Eclipse of Manifest Destiny and the Coming of the Civil War.* Chapel Hill: University of North Carolina Press, 1997.
Morrison, Michael A., and James Brewer Stewart, eds. *Race and the Early Republic: Racial Consciousness and Nation Building in the Early Republic.* Lanham, Md.: Rowman and Littlefield, 2002.
Nagel, Paul C. *George Caleb Bingham: Missouri's Famed Painter and Forgotten Politician.* Columbia: University of Missouri Press, 2005.
Nagel, Paul C. *Missouri: A Bicentennial History.* New York: W. W. Norton, 1977.
Nash, Gary B., and Jean R. Soderlund. *Freedom by Degree: Emancipation in Pennsylvania and Its Aftermath.* New York: Oxford University Press, 1991.
Nation, Richard F. *At Home in the Hoosier Hills: Agriculture, Politics, and Religion in Southern Indiana, 1810–1870.* Bloomington: Indiana University Press, 2005.
Neal, Julia. *The Kentucky Shakers.* Lexington: University Press of Kentucky, 1982.
Neely, Jeremy. *The Border between Them: Violence and Reconciliation on the Kansas-Missouri Line.* Columbia: University of Missouri Press, 2007.

Neely, Mark E., Jr. *Abraham Lincoln and the Triumph of the Nation: Constitutional Conflict During the Civil War*. Chapel Hill: The University of North Carolina Press, 2011.
Neely, Mark E., Jr. *The Fate of Liberty: Abraham Lincoln and Civil Liberties*. New York: Oxford University Press, 1991.
Neely, Mark E., Jr. *The Last Best Hope of Earth: Abraham Lincoln and the Promise of America*. Cambridge, Mass.: Harvard University Press, 1995.
Neff, John R. *Honoring the Civil War Dead: Commemoration and the Problem of Reconciliation*. Lawrence: University Press of Kansas, 2005.
Nelson, Scott, and Carol Sheriff. *A People at War: Civilians and Soldiers in America's Civil War, 1854–1877*. New York: Oxford University Press, 2008.
Nichols, Bruce. *Guerrilla Warfare in Civil War Missouri. Vol. I, 1862*. Jefferson, N.C.: McFarland, 2004.
Nichols, Bruce. *Guerrilla Warfare in Civil War Missouri. Vol. II, 1863*. Jefferson, N.C.: McFarland, 2007.
Niven, John. *Salmon P. Chase: A Biography*. New York: Oxford University Press, 1995.
Nobles, Gregory H. *American Frontiers: Cultural Encounters and Continental Conquest*. New York: Hill and Wang, 1997.
Noe, Kenneth W. *Perryville: This Grand Havoc of Battle*. Lexington: University Press of Kentucky, 2001.
Noll, Mark A. *The Civil War as a Theological Crisis*. Chapel Hill: University of North Carolina Press, 2006.
North, Douglass C. *The Economic Growth of the United States, 1790–1860*. New York: Prentice Hall, 1961; reprint New York: W. W. Norton, 1966.
Oakes, James. *Slavery and Freedom: An Interpretation of the Old South*. New York: Alfred A. Knopf, 1990.
Oakes, James. *The Ruling Race: A History of American Slaveholders*. New York: Alfred A. Knopf, 1982.
Oates, Stephen B. *Confederate Cavalry West of the River*. Austin: University of Texas Press, 1961.
Oates, Stephen B. *To Purge This Land with Blood: A Biography of John Brown*. New York: Harper and Row, 1970.
O'Flaherty, Daniel. *General Jo Shelby: Undefeated Rebel*. Chapel Hill: University of North Carolina Press, 1954; reprint Chapel Hill: University of North Carolina Press, 2000.
Onuf, Peter S. *Jefferson's Empire: The Language of American Nationhood*. Charlottesville: University Press of Virginia, 2000.
Onuf, Peter S. *Statehood and Union: A History of the Northwest Ordinance*. Bloomington: Indiana University Press, 1987.
Paludan, Phillip Shaw. *"A People's Contest": The Union and Civil War, 1861–1865*. New York: Harper and Row, 1988.
Parish, Peter J. *The North, the Nation, and the Era of the Civil War*. New York: Fordham University Press, 2003.
Parrish, William E. *David Rice Atchison of Missouri—Border Politician*. Columbia: University of Missouri Press, 1961.
Parrish, William E. *Frank Blair: Lincoln's Conservative*. Columbia: University of Missouri Press, 1998.
Parrish, William E. *A History of Missouri. Vol. III, 1860–1875*. Columbia: University of Missouri Press, 1973.
Parrish, William E. *Missouri under Radical Rule, 1865–1870*. Columbia: University of Missouri Press, 1965.
Parrish, William E. *Turbulent Partnership: Missouri and the Union 1861–1865*. Columbia: University of Missouri Press, 1963.
Peckham, Howard H. *Indiana: A Bicentennial History*. New York: W. W. Norton, 1978.
Perkins, Elizabeth A. *Border Life: Experience and Memory in the Revolutionary Ohio Valley*. Chapel Hill and London: University of North Carolina Press, 1998.
Perry, Lewis, and Michael Fellman, eds. *Antislavery Reconsidered: New Perspectives on the Abolitionists*. Baton Rouge: Louisiana State University Press, 1979.

Peterson, Merrill D. *The Great Triumvirate: Webster, Clay, and Calhoun.* New York: Oxford University Press, 1987.
Peterson, Merrill D. *Lincoln in American Memory.* New York: Oxford University Press, 1994.
Peterson, Norma L. *Freedom and Franchise: The Political Career of B. Gratz Brown.* Columbia: University of Missouri Press, 1965.
Phillips, Christopher. *Damned Yankee: The Life of General Nathaniel Lyon.* Columbia: University of Missouri Press, 1990.
Phillips, Christopher. *Freedom's Port: The African American Community of Baltimore, 1790–1860.* Urbana: University of Illinois Press, 1997.
Phillips, Christopher. *The Making of a Southerner: William Barclay Napton's Private Civil War.* Columbia: University of Missouri Press, 2008.
Phillips, Christopher. *Missouri's Confederate: Claiborne Fox Jackson and the Creation of Southern Identity in the Border West.* Columbia: University of Missouri Press, 2000.
Phillips, Christopher and Jason L. Pendleton, eds. *The Union on Trial: The Political Journals of William Barclay Napton.* Columbia: University of Missouri Press, 2005.
Piston, William Garrett, and Richard W. Hatcher III. *Wilson's Creek: The Second Battle of the Civil War and the Men Who Fought It.* Chapel Hill: University of North Carolina Press, 2000.
Plummer, Mark A. *Lincoln's Rail-Splitter: Governor Richard L. Oglesby.* Urbana: University of Illinois Press, 2001.
Porter, George H. *Ohio Politics During the Civil War Period.* New York: Columbia University, 1911.
Potter, David M. *The Impending Crisis, 1848–1861.* New York: Harper and Row, 1976.
Potter, David M. *The South and the Sectional Conflict.* Baton Rouge: Louisiana State University Press, 1968.
Potter, James E. *Standing Firmly by the Flag: Nebraska Territory and the Civil War, 1861–1867.* Lincoln, Ne.: Bison Books, 2013.
Power, Richard Pyle. *Planting Corn Belt Culture: The Impress of the Upland Southerner and Yankee in the Old Northwest.* Indianapolis: Indiana Historical Society, 1953.
Primm, James Neal. *Lion of the Valley: St. Louis, Missouri.* Boulder, Colo.: Pruett Publishing Co., 1981.
Prokopowicz, Gerald J. *All for the Regiment: The Army of the Ohio, 1861–1862.* Chapel Hill: University of North Carolina Press, 2001.
Przybyszewski, Linda. *The Republic according to John Marshall Harlan.* Chapel Hill: University of North Carolina Press, 1999.
Rable, George C. *Civil Wars: Women and the Crisis of Southern Nationalism.* Urbana: University of Illinois Press, 1989.
Rachels, David, ed. *Mark Twain's Civil War.* Lexington: University Press of Kentucky, 2007.
Ramage, James A. *Rebel Raider: The Life of General John Hunt Morgan.* Lexington: University Press of Kentucky, 1986.
Randall, James G., and David Donald. *The Civil War and Reconstruction.* Lexington, Mass.: D. C. Heath, 1969.
Ranney, Joseph A. *In the Wake of Slavery: Civil War, Civil Rights, and the Reconstruction of Southern Law.* Westport, Conn.: Greenwood Publishing Group, 2006.
Rash, Nancy. *The Painting and Politics of George Caleb Bingham.* New Haven, Conn.: Yale University Press, 1991.
Ratcliffe, Donald J. *Party Spirit in a Frontier Republic: Democratic Politics in Ohio, 1793–1820.* Columbus: Ohio State University Press, 1998.
Rawley, James A. *Race and Politics: "Bleeding Kansas" and the Coming of the Civil War.* Philadelphia: J. B. Lippincott, 1969; reprint Lincoln: University of Nebraska Press, 1979.
Rayback, Joseph G. *Free Soil: The Election of 1848.* Lexington: University of Kentucky Press, 1970.
Reed, John Shelton. *One South: An Ethnic Approach to Regional Culture.* Baton Rouge: Louisiana State University Press, 1982.
Reed, John Shelton. *Southerners: The Social Psychology of Sectionalism.* Chapel Hill: University of North Carolina Press, 1983.

Richardson, Heather Cox. *The Death of Reconstruction: Race, Labor, and Politics in the Post-Civil War North, 1865-1901.* Cambridge, Mass.: Harvard University Press, 2001.

Risjord, Norman K. *The Old Republicans: Southern Conservatism in the Age of Jefferson.* New York: Columbia University Press, 1965.

Robertson, Stacey M. *Hearts Beating for Liberty: Women Abolitionists in the Old Northwest.* Chapel Hill: University of North Carolina, 2010.

Rohrbough, Malcolm J. *The Trans-Appalachian Frontier: People, Societies, and Institutions, 1775-1850.* New York: Oxford University Press, 1978; reprint Belmont, Calif.: Wadsworth Publishing, 1990.

Ross, Steven J. *Workers On the Edge: Work, Leisure, and Politics in Industrializing Cincinnati, 1788-1890.* New York: Columbia University Press, 1985.

Royster, Charles. *The Destructive War: William Tecumseh Sherman, Stonewall Jackson, and the Americans.* New York: Alfred A. Knopf, 1991.

Rubin, Anne Sarah. *A Shattered Nation: The Rise and Fall of the Confederacy, 1861-1868.* Chapel Hill: University of North Carolina Press, 2007.

Rusk, Fern Helen. *George Caleb Bingham, The Missouri Artist.* Jefferson City, Mo.: Hugh Stephens, 1917.

Ryle, Walter H. *Missouri: Union or Secession.* Nashville, Tenn.: George Peabody College for Teachers, 1931.

Sachsman, David B., S. Kittrell Rushing, and Roy Morris, eds. *Words at War: The Civil War and American Journalism.* West Lafayette, Ind.: Purdue University Press, 2008.

Salafia, Matthew. *Slavery's Borderland: Freedom and Bondage Along the Ohio River.* Philadelphia: University of Pennsylvania Press, 2013.

Sanchez, Anita. *Mr. Lincoln's Chair: The Shakers and Their Quest for Peace.* Granville, Ohio: McDonald and Woodward, 2009.

Sarna, Jonathan D., and Adam Mendelsohn, eds. *Jews and the Civil War: A Reader.* New York: New York University Press, 2010.

Sarris, Jonathan Dean. *A Separate Civil War: Communities in Conflict in the Appalachian South.* Charlottesville: University of Virginia Press, 2007.

Scheiber, Harry N. *Ohio Canal Era: A Case Study of Government and the Economy, 1820-1861.* Athens: Ohio University Press, 1987.

Schlesinger, Arthur M., Jr. *The Bitter Heritage: Vietnam and American Democracy 1941-1966.* Boston: Houghton Mifflin, 1967

Schlissel, Lillian, ed. *Conscience in America.* New York: Dutton, 1968.

Schultz, Duane. *Quantrill's War: The Life and Times of William Clarke Quantrill, 1837-1865.* New York: Macmillan, 1997.

Schutz, Wallace J., and Walter N. Trenerry. *Abandoned by Lincoln: A Military Biography of General John Pope.* Urbana: University of Illinois Press, 1990.

Scott, James C. *The Moral Economy of the Peasant.* New Haven, Conn.: Yale University Press, 1976.

Scott, James C. *Weapons of the Weak: Everyday Forms of Peasant Resistance.* New Haven, Conn.: Yale University Press, 1985.

Sears, Richard A. *Camp Nelson, Kentucky: A Civil War History.* Lexington: University Press of Kentucky, 2002.

Sellers, Charles. *The Market Economy: Jacksonian America, 1815-1846.* New York: Oxford University Press, 1991.

SenGupta, Gunja. *For God and Mammon: Evangelicals and Entrepreneurs, Masters and Slaves in Territorial Kansas, 1854-1860.* Athens: University of Georgia Press, 1996.

Shalhope, Robert E. *Sterling Price: Portrait of a Southerner.* Columbia: University of Missouri Press, 1971.

Shannon, Jasper B., and Ruth McQuown. *Presidential Politics in Kentucky, 1824-1948: A Compilation of Election Statistics and an Analysis of Political Behavior.* Lexington: University Press of Kentucky, 1950.

Shapiro, Henry, and Jonathan Sarna, eds. *Ethnic Diversity and Civic Identity: Patterns of Conflict and Cohesion in Cincinnati since 1820.* Urbana and Chicago: University of Illinois Press, 1992.

Shea, William L., and Earl J. Hess. *Pea Ridge: Civil War Campaign in the West.* Chapel Hill: University of North Carolina Press, 1995.
Shortridge, James R. *The Middle West: Its Meaning in American Culture.* Lawrence: University Press of Kansas, 1989.
Siddali, Silvana R. *From Property to Person: Slavery and the Confiscation Acts, 1861–1862.* Baton Rouge: Louisiana State University Press, 2005.
Silber, Nina L. *Daughters of the Union: Northern Women Fight the Civil War.* Cambridge, Mass.: Harvard University Press, 2005.
Silbey, Joel H. *A Respectable Minority: The Democratic Party in the Civil War Era, 1860–1868.* New York: W. W. Norton, 1977.
Silvestro, Clement M. *Rally Round the Flag: The Union Leagues in the Civil War.* Lansing: Historical Society of Michigan, 1966.
Simeone, James. *Democracy and Slavery in Frontier Illinois: The Bottomland Republic.* DeKalb: Northern Illinois University Press, 2000.
Simpson, Brooks D. *Let Us Have Peace: Ulysses S. Grant and the Politics of War and Reconstruction, 1861–1868.* Chapel Hill: University of North Carolina Press, 1991.
Sinisi, Kyle S. *The Last Hurrah: Sterling Price's Missouri Expedition of 1864.* Lanham, Md.: Rowman and Littlefield, 2015.
Sinisi, Kyle S. *Sacred Debts: State Civil War Claims and American Federalism, 1861–1880.* New York: Fordham University Press, 2003.
Smiley, David L. *The Lion of White Hall: The Life of Cassius M. Clay.* Madison: University of Wisconsin Press, 1962.
Smith, Adam I. P. *No Party Now: Politics in the Civil War North.* New York: Oxford University Press, 2006.
Smith, Edward Conrad. *The Borderland in the Civil War.* New York: Macmillan, 1927.
Smith, Elbert B. *Magnificent Missourian: The Life of Thomas Hart Benton.* Philadelphia: J. B. Lippincott, 1958.
Smith, Henry Nash. *Virgin Land: The American West as Symbol and Myth.* Cambridge, Mass.: Harvard University Press, 1950.
Smith, Reed W. *Samuel Medary and the Crisis: Testing the Limits of Press Freedom.* Columbus: Ohio State University Press, 1995.
Smith, Ronald D. *Thomas Ewing Jr.: Frontier Lawyer and Civil War General.* Columbia: University of Missouri Press, 2008.
Smith, William E. *The Francis Preston Blair Family in Politics.* 2 vols. New York: Macmillan, 1933; reprint New York: Da Capo Press, 1969.
Sproat, John G. *"The Best Men": Liberal Reformers in the Gilded Age.* New York: Oxford University Press, 1968.
Spurgeon, Ian Michael. *Man of Douglas Man of Lincoln: The Political Odyssey of James Henry Lane.* Columbia: University of Missouri Press, 2008.
Stampp, Kenneth M. *And the War Came: The North and the Secession Crisis, 1860–1861.* Chicago: University of Chicago Press, 1964.
Stampp, Kenneth M. *Indiana Politics During the Civil War.* Bloomington: Indiana University Press, 1949; reprint Bloomington: Indiana University Press, 1978.
Stampp, Kenneth M., and Leon F. Litwack, eds. *Reconstruction: An Anthology of Revisionist Writings.* Baton Rouge and London: Louisiana State University Press, 1969.
Staudenraus, P[hilip]. J. *The African Colonization Movement, 1816–1865.* New York: Columbia University Press, 1961.
Stewart, James Brewer. *Holy Warriors: The Abolitionists and American Slavery.* New York: Hill and Wang, 1976.
Stiles, T. J. *Jesse James: Last Rebel of the Civil War.* New York: Alfred A. Knopf, 2002.
Stokes, Melvyn, and Stephen Conway, eds. *The Market Revolution in America: Social, Political, and Religious Expressions, 1800–1880.* Charlottesville: University Press of Virginia, 1996.
Stone, Richard, Jr. *A Brittle Sword: The Kentucky Militia, 1776–1912.* Lexington: University Press of Kentucky, 1977.

Summers, Mark Wahlgren. *The Ordeal of the Reunion: A New History of Reconstruction*. Chapel Hill: University of North Carolina Press, 2014.

Summers, Mark Wahlgren. *Rum, Romanism, and Rebellion: The Making of a President, 1884*. Chapel Hill: University of North Carolina Press, 2000.

Surdam, David G. *Northern Naval Superiority and the Economics of the American Civil War*. Columbia: University of South Carolina Press, 2001.

Sutherland, Daniel E. *Guerrillas, Unionists, and Violence on the Confederate Home Front*. Fayetteville: University of Arkansas Press, 1999.

Sutherland, Daniel E. *A Savage Conflict: The Decisive Role of Guerrillas in the American Civil War*. Chapel Hill: University of North Carolina Press, 2009.

Tallant, Harold. *Evil Necessity: Slavery and the Political Culture in Antebellum Kentucky*. Lexington: University Press of Kentucky, 2003.

Taylor, George Rogers. *The Transportation Revolution, 1815–1860*. New York: Harper and Row, 1968.

Taylor, Nikki M. *Frontiers of Freedom: Cincinnati's Black Community, 1802–1868*. Athens: Ohio University Press, 2005.

Thelen, David. *Paths of Resistance: Tradition and Dignity in Industrializing Missouri*. New York and Oxford: Oxford University Press, 1986.

Thomas, Benjamin P., and Harold M. Hyman. *Stanton: The Life and Times of Lincoln's Secretary of War*. New York: Alfred A. Knopf, 1962.

Thornbrough, Emma Lou. *Indiana in the Civil War, 1850–1880*. Indianapolis: Indiana Historical Society, 1965.

Thornbrough, Emma Lou. *The Negro in Indiana Before 1900: A Study of a Minority*. Indianapolis: Indiana Historical Bureau, 1985; reprint Bloomington and Indianapolis: Indiana University Press, 1993.

Thwaites, Reuben Gold. *Afloat on the Ohio* [republished as *On the Storied Ohio*]. Chicago: A. C. McClurg, 1903; reprint New York: Arno Press, 1975.

Tise, Larry E. *Pro-Slavery: A History of the Defense of Slavery in America, 1701–1840*. Athens: University of Georgia Press, 1987.

Tolzmann, Don Heinrich. *The John A. Roebling Suspension Bridge on the Ohio River*. Cincinnati: University of Cincinnati, 1998.

Towers, Frank. *The Urban South and the Coming of the Civil War*. Charlottesville: University of Virginia Press, 2004.

Townsend, William H. *Lincoln and the Bluegrass: Slavery and Civil War in Kentucky*. Lexington: University of Kentucky Press, 1955.

Trefousse, Hans L. *Andrew Johnson: A Biography*. New York: W. W. Norton, 1989.

Trexler, Harrison A. *Slavery in Missouri 1804–1865*. Baltimore: Johns Hopkins University Press, 1914.

Troen, Selwyn K., and Glen E. Holt, eds. *St. Louis*. New York and London: New Viewpoints, 1977.

Trotter, Joe William, Jr. *River Jordan: African American Urban Life in the Ohio Valley*. Lexington: University Press of Kentucky, 1998.

Twombly, Albert E. *Little Dixie*. Columbia: University of Missouri Press, 1955.

Urwin, Gregory J. W., ed. *Black Flag Over Dixie: Racial Atrocities and Reprisals in the Civil War*. Carbondale: Southern Illinois University Press, 2005.

Usner, Daniel H., Jr. *Indians, Settlers, and Slaves in a Frontier Exchange Economy: The Lower Mississippi Valley Before 1783*. Chapel Hill: University of North Carolina Press, 1992.

Van Tine, Warren, and Michael Pierce, eds. *Builders of Ohio: A Biographical History*. Columbus: Ohio State University Press, 2003.

Vander Velde, Lewis George. *The Presbyterian Churches and the Federal Union, 1861–1869*. Cambridge, Mass.: Harvard College, 1932.

VanDeusen, Glyndon G. *The Jacksonian Era: 1828–1848*. New York: Harper and Row, 1959.

Vandiver, Frank E., ed. *The Idea of the South: Pursuit of a Central Theme*. Chicago: University of Chicago Press, 1964.

Vincent, Stephen A. *Southern Seed, Northern Soil: African-American Farm Communities in the Midwest, 1785–1900*. Bloomington and Indianapolis: Indiana University Press, 1999.

Vinoskis, Maris, ed. *Toward a Social History of the American Civil War: Exploratory Essays.* Cambridge: Cambridge University Press, 1990.
Voegeli, V. Jacques. *Free But Not Equal: The Midwest and the Negro.* Chicago: University of Chicago Press, 1967.
Vorenberg, Michael. *Final Freedom: The Civil War, the Abolition of Slavery, and the Thirteenth Amendment.* New York: Cambridge University Press, 2001.
Wade, Richard C. *Slavery in the Cities: The South, 1820–1860.* New York: Oxford University Press, 1964.
Wade, Richard C. *The Urban Frontier: Pioneer Life in Early Pittsburgh, Cincinnati, Lexington, Louisville, and St. Louis.* Chicago: University of Chicago Press, 1964.
Walters, Ronald G. *The Antislavery Appeal: American Abolitionism After 1830.* New York: W. W. Norton, 1978.
Walton, Clyde C., ed. *An Illinois Reader.* DeKalb: Northern Illinois University Press, 1970.
Warren, Robert Penn. *Jefferson Davis Gets His Citizenship Back.* Lexington: University Press of Kentucky, 1980.
Warren, Robert Penn. *Legacy of the Civil War: Meditations on the Centennial.* New York: Random House, 1961; reprint Lincoln: University of Nebraska Press, 1998.
Waugh, Joan. *U. S. Grant: American Hero, American Myth.* Chapel Hill: University of North Carolina Press, 2009.
Weber, Jennifer L. *Copperheads: The Rise and Fall of Lincoln's Opponents in the North.* New York: Oxford University Press, 2006.
Whites, LeeAnn. *The Civil War as a Crisis in Gender: Augusta, Georgia, 1860–1890.* Athens: University of Georgia Press, 1995.
Whites, LeeAnn. *Gender Matters: Civil War, Reconstruction, and the Making of the New South.* New York: Palgrave Macmillan, 2005.
Whites, LeeAnn, and Alecia P. Long, eds. *Occupied Women: Gender, Military Occupation, and the American Civil War.* Baton Rouge: Louisiana State University Press, 2009.
Whitman, T. Stephen. *The Price of Freedom: Slavery and Manumission in Baltimore and Early National Maryland.* Lexington: University Press of Kentucky, 1997.
Widener, Ralph W. *Confederate Monuments: Enduring Symbols of the South and the War Between the States.* Washington, D.C.: Andromeda Associates, 1982.
Wilhelm, Hubert G. H. *The Origin and Distribution of Settlement Groups: Ohio, 1850.* Athens, Ohio: printed by author, 1982.
Wilson, Carol. *Freedom at Risk: The Kidnapping of Free Blacks in America, 1780–1865.* Lexington: University Press of Kentucky, 1994.
Witt, John Fabian. *Lincoln's Code: The Laws of War in American History.* New York: The Free Press, 2012.
Woodward, C. Vann. *The Burden of Southern History.* Baton Rouge: Louisiana State University, 1960; reprint New York: Mentor Books, 1969.
Woodworth, Stephen E. *Nothing but Victory: The Army of the Tennessee, 1861–1865.* New York: Alfred A. Knopf, 2005.
Wooster, Ralph A. *Politicians, Planters and Plain Folk: Courthouse and Statehouse in the Upper South, 1850–1860.* Knoxville: University of Tennessee Press, 1969.
Wright, Edward Needles. *Conscientious Objectors in the Civil War.* Philadelphia: University of Pennsylvania Press, 1931.
Wright, Louis B. *Culture on the Moving Frontier.* Bloomington: Indiana University Press, 1955; reprint New York: Harper and Row, 1961.
Wyatt-Brown, Bertram. *Southern Honor: Ethics and Behavior in the Old South.* New York: Oxford University Press, 1982.
Wyman, Mark. *Immigrants in the Valley. Irish, Germans, and Americans in the Upper Mississippi Country, 1830–1860.* Chicago: Nelson-Hall, 1984.
Zilversmit, Arthur. *The First Emancipation: The Abolition of Slavery in the North.* Chicago: University of Chicago Press, 1967.

INDEX

A Plea for the West, 68; see also Beecher, Lyman
A True Picture of Abolition, see Lord, Nathan; see also Churches
Abbott, Amanda, 285–286
Abdy, Edward, 63
Abolition Intelligencer and Missionary Magazine (Shelbyville, Ky.), 66
Abolitionism/Abolitionists, 3, 48, 114, 289, 307, 313; African Americans as, 76; and Republican party, 91–92, 103–104, 106; "conservative," 68, 69; defined, xviii, federal officers as, 155–156, 253–254, 294; "Freedom National" mantra of, 102, 110, 228, 336; in American West, 11, 37, 44–45, 46–48, 50, 62–72, 89, 95, 96, 97, 98, 99–100, 100–105, 107, 115, 135, 208, 214, 228, 257; in western federal armies, 231, 254; ministers as, 3, 47, 63, 176, 289, see also Churches; opposition to, see Anti-abolitionism; see also Antislavery; Jayhawkers; Republican Party; Slavery; Southerners, politicized use of abolition/abolitionist
Abraham, Lot, 254
Adams, Charles Francis, 92
Advance Guard (Lexington, Ky.), *The*, 195
Adventures of Huckleberry Finn, 89, 335; see also Clemens, Samuel L.
Adventures of Tom Sawyer, The, 334; see also Clemens, Samuel L.
Advertiser (Cincinnati, Oh.), *The*, 46
African Americans, and abolition, 76, 178; and war memory, 303–304; as federal military laborers, 200; as informants, 191, 202; as federal military veterans, 294, 297–298; as federal soldiers, 22, 253–262, 267–268, 295–298; as freedpeople, 220, 221, 257, 289, 293, 294–298, 300, 302, 307, 319, 327; as wartime fugitives/refugees, 119, 216–221, 222–226, 253–262, 267–268, 296; children in wartime, 267–268; churches, 75, 189, 293–294; citizenship rights of, 293, 303–304; commemorative activities, 303–304, 307, 319, 327; Emancipation Day celebrations, 304; federal military enlistment, 12, 208, 211, 220–221, 253–262; free, 18, 20, 30–32, 33, 34, 41, 63, 65, 67, 70, 72–73, 74–77, 87, 107–108, 121, 289, see also Colonization/colonizationists, "Reverse underground railroad"; in Grand Army of the Republic, 307, 319, 327; in middle border free states, 41, 63–64, 72–77, 302; in middle border slave states, 72–77, 277; in North, 2; in West, 11, 29–32; postwar "colored conventions," 293; postwar relocation of, 293–294; racial views of westerners of, 207–209; racial violence against, 19–20, 77, 132, 208, 259–262, 280, 282, 294–298, 308–309; schools, 260, 297; wartime/postwar proscriptions against, 293–295; western GAR posts, 319; see also Middle Border, slavery in; Slavery; Slaves
Alabama, 38, 106, 253; commissioner to Kentucky from, 137; secession of, 108; towns/cities in, 55
Albion, 37; see also Birkbeck, Morris; Flower, George
Alexandria, Ky., 288, 290
Allen, William, 216; statue in U.S. Capitol, 333
Alton, Il., 71, 224, 280; camp of instruction at, 129; Lincoln-Douglas debate at, 100; prison camp at, 172
American Anti-Slavery Society, see Antislavery
"American Bottom," see Illinois; Mississippi River
American Colonization Society, 63, 70, 177; see also Colonization/colonizationists

American Missionary Association, 260
American party, 91; see also Immigration; "Know-Nothings;" Nativism
American Revolution, 28; and emancipation of slaves, 36–37; and southern identity, 133–134
"American System," 46, 50, 59, 60; see also Whig party, economic platform of; Clay, Henry
American Tract Society, 178
Amish, 120
Ammen, Jacob, 276, 277
Anderson, Robert, 126, 139, 147, 213
Anti-abolitionism/anti-abolitionists, 4, 46–48, 62–72, 78–82, 87–88, 99, 103–104, 216, 225; defined, xviii and wartime emancipation, 221–226; see also Abolitionism/Abolitionists
Antislavery, 35, 42–43, 75; defined, xvii–xviii; in American West, 37–39, 40–41, 62–66, 92, 100, 130; publications, 64, 65; societies, 46, 64–66, 67, 70, 71, 75, 89; see also West, American, antislavery influences in
Appalachian Mountains, xvii, 5, 7, 22, 52, 86, 87, 121, 307; British ban on westward migration, 28
Arkansas, 240, 282; and deserters/draft evaders, 244; as territory, 62; emancipation of slaves in, 292; federal occupation of, 199; fugitive slaves from, 221, 258; secession of, 136; state troops, 141; western migration to, 26
Armies, U.S., Colored Troops (USCT), 258, 259, 267; desertion from, 208, 209, 231, 232, 244, 247, 260, 264, 268, 274–275, 276, 281, 282, see also Dissent/dissenters; debates over slavery/emancipation among officers, 218–219, 220–221, 234; foreign-born troops, 160, 180, 207–208; proslavery influences in, 219, 231–234; see also Cumberland, Army of the; Kentucky; Kentucky, Army of; Middle Border; Military confiscation; Military conscription; Missouri; Ohio, Army of the; Potomac, Army of the; Tennessee, Army of the
Arrow Rock, Mo., 186, 236
Asher, Martin V., 247
Ashland, see Clay, Henry
Ashtabula (Oh.) *Sentinel*, 127
Assessments, 165, 192–194, 248; Confederate, 165; see also Dominion system; Loyalty/disloyalty; Military occupation
Astor, Aaron, 312
Atchison, David Rice, 79, 94, 95, 96, 97
"Athens of the West," see Lexington, Ky.
Athens, Oh., 71
Atlanta, Ga., 314, 319; Association for the Reinterment of the Kentucky Confederate Dead, 314

Atlantic seaboard, 50
Axtell, Salmon B., 122–123, 212

Bagwell, Augusta, 195–196
Bagwell, Laidee J., 195–196, 263, 265
Bailey, David, 184
Bailey, Gamaliel, 48, 66
Bailey, William Shields, 104
Balance, James, 166
Baltimore, Md., 42, 55, 66, 92, 337; African Americans in, 42; free blacks in, 42; GAR national encampment, 319; riot in 1861, 136; slavery/slaves in, 42
Banishment, Military, see Civilians
Bank of the United States, 61
Banks, Nathaniel, 147
Baptist Church/Baptists, 66, 175, 176, 190, 246, 294; African, 75, 294; Anti-slavery Society, 66; see also Churches
Barboursville, Ky., 200
Bardstown, Ky., 261, 336; wartime slave trade, 259
Barry, Jasper, 254
Batavia, Oh., 173–174
Bates, Barton, 182, 191
Bates, Edward, 182, 213, 229; as Lincoln's attorney general, 182, 220, 226–227; resigns, 227
Baton Rouge, La., federal arsenal in, 136, 138
Bax, Adam, 180
Baxter Springs, Ks., racial atrocity at, 240–241, 260
Beecher, Lyman, 68–69; see also Lane Theological Seminary
Bell, John, 105, 199, 236
Bell, Joshua F., 123
Belleville (Ill.) *Advocate*, 224
Belmont (Mo.), battle at, 143; see also Columbus, Ky.; Grant, Ulysses S.
Bennett, Mary E., 285–289
Benton, Ill., 275
Benton, Thomas Hart, 61, 87, 88, 92, 97, 111
Berea College (Ky.), 294
Berlin, Ira, 211
Bethel, Oh., 286
Bible View of Slavery, see Hopkins, John Henry: see also Churches
Bickley, George L., 269; see also Knights of the Golden Circle
Bingham, George Caleb, 83, 183, 236–240, 314; as U.S. congressman, 314; *Martial Law, or Order No. 11*, 314; Mo. state treasurer, 237; "War of Desolation, The," 240, 314; see also Ewing, Thomas, Jr.; Order No. 11
Bingham, Mary, 236
Bird, Stephen, 217
Birkbeck, Morris, 37, 40; see also Albion; "English prairie;" Flower, George

Index

Birney, James Gillespie, 45, 70, 72, 85; see also *Philanthropist, The*; Liberty party
Birney, William, 70
Birth of a Nation, The, 331; banned, 331; see also *Clansman, The*; Dixon, Thomas; Griffith, D. W.
Bishop, William, 151
Black Brigade, see African Americans, as federal military laborers
Black Hawk, 54; see also Illinois; Lincoln, Abraham
"Black Republicans," see Republican Party, abolitionist wing of
Black River (Ar.), 173
Blade (Toledo, Oh.), *The*, 299
Blair, Francis P., Jr. "Frank," 97, 105, 136–137, 138, 240, 301, 309; at Planters' House conference, 140
Blair, Montgomery, 136–137, 149, 220
Blight, David W., 6, 333
"Bloody shirt," 303; see also Democratic party, postwar politics; Military veterans, postwar politics; Republican party, postwar politics
Bloomington, Il., 91
Blue Springs, Mo., 320
"Bluegrass System," see Kentucky
Blundell, William C., 179
Boards of trade, 197–198; see also Middle Border; Military occupation; Trade permit system (federal)
Bond, Achsah, 31
Bond, Shadrach, 31, 32
Bonds, 184, 185, 191, 196, 197, 245, 263
Boone County (Mo.) *Standard*, suppressed, 195
Boone, Daniel, 24, 327
Boone County Herald (Columbia, Mo.), suppressed, 195
"Boon's Lick," see Missouri
Boonville (Mo.), 282; battle at, 141
Booth, John Wilkes, 283–284, 328
Border, District of the (federal), 238
Border South, 6–7, 331–332; see also South, American
Border State Convention of 1861, 138–139, 188
Border States, 146, 209; congressional delegation, 220–221; population of, 144
Boston, Ma., 16, 145; wartime riots in 1863 in, 13
Bowles, David, 314
Bowling Green, Ky., 114–119, 267; and Bragg's Confederate invasion of Ky., 201; Confederate military occupation of, 114–119, 142, 164–166, 197–198, 201, 225; federal military occupation of, 172, 201, 206, 225; marble, 323; southern sympathizers in, 265; trade restrictions in, 197
Boyle, Jeremiah T., 182, 193, 194, 219, 244, 258, 264; impressment of slaves by, 257–258; orders trade restrictions, 198

Bracht, F. G., 194
Bradley, James, 69
Bragg, Braxton, 166, 200; see also Kentucky, Confederate incursion into; Mississippi, Army of (Confederate)
Bramlette, Thomas E., 198, 256
Brazil, as locus for postwar Confederate expatriation, 293
Breckinridge, John C., as presidential candidate in 1860, 105, 106, 109, 121; expatriation, 293; expelled from U.S. Senate, 182, 214; heads Ky. secession convention, 144; in Confederate Congress, 182
Breckinridge, Robert J., 87, 99, 110
Bright, Jesse D., 84; expelled from U.S. Senate, 214
Brisbane, William H., 66
Bristow, Benjamin Helm, 134
Broadhead, James O., 137, 140
Brown, Benjamin Gratz, 98, 218, 309
Brown, John, 3; in Kansas, 322; raid of, 2, 11, 103–104, see also Harpers Ferry, Va.
Brown, Orlando, 233
Brown, William Wells, 75, 223
Browning, Orville H., 91, 144, 223
Brownlow, William G. "Parson," 216
Buchanan, James, 92, 112
Buckner, Benjamin F., 181, 209–210, 308–309
Buckner, James H., 94
Buckner, Simon B., 110, 137, 200, 209, 323; neutrality agreement with George B. McClellan, 141–142
Buell, Don Carlos, 147, 183, 208, 218, 234; and Bragg's Confederate invasion of Ky., 166, 200–201; and fugitive slaves, 218; inquiry of, 155–156; perception of by antislavery officers, 155; see also Perryville (Ky.), battle at
Bull Run, First, battle of, 213
Bullenhaar, Anton H., 212
Bullitt, Henry, 331
Bullitt, Mildred, 105, 106–107
Bullitt, Thomas W., 160–161, 331
Bullitt, William C., 88, 106, 107; Oxmoor as home of, 106, 161, 331
Bundy, Hezekiah S., 222
Burbridge, Stephen E., 260, 261, 315
Burgoo, 22
Burke, Edmund, 37
Burnett, Henry C., 213; expelled from U.S. House, 214; heads Ky. secession convention, 144; in Confederate Congress, 213, 243
Burns, John, 34
Burnside, Ambrose E., 267, 270
Burnt District, see Missouri; Order No. 11
Bushwhackers, see Guerrillas
Butler, Andrew P., 48

Butler, Benjamin F., 249; see also African Americans, as federal military laborers; Confiscation; Contrabands
Butler, Joseph C., 198
"Butternuts," 93, 128–129, 273, 280, 333–334; cultural prejudice against, 129
Byrd, Charles Willing, 33

Cadiz, Ky., 99
Cahokia, Il., 28
Cain, Bevie W., 130–131, 225
Cairo, Il., 43, 89, 128–129, 142, 143, 232; African American military enlistments, 258; camp of instruction at, 129, 154, 224; contraband camp at, 218, 258, 302; fugitive slaves in, 258; racial violence, 302; river trade interrupted at, 196, 267
Cairo (Il.) *Gazette*, 128
Calhoon, Ky., 251
Calhoun, John C., 47, 80, 105
California, 48, 109, 262
Calvert, John W., 202
Cambridge, Ma., 337
Camp Butler (Il.), prison camp at, 172; see also Springfield, Il.
Camp Chase (Oh.), prison camp at, 172, 183, 188, 190, 290; see also Columbus, Oh.
Camp [Henry] Clay (Oh.), 129; see also Ohio, federal military recruitment in
Camp Dennison (Oh.), 129; see also Ohio, federal military recruitment in
Camp Dick Robinson (Ky.), 139, 267; see also Kentucky, federal military recruitment in
Camp Douglas (Il.), prison camp at, 172; see also Chicago, Il.
Camp Jackson (Mo.), Confederate, riot at, see St. Louis, Mo.
Camp Jo Holt (In.), 139; see also Kentucky, federal military recruitment in
Camp Morton (In.), 129; prison camp at, 172; see also Indiana, federal military recruitment in; Indianapolis, In.
Camp Nelson (Ky.), 258; as African American enlistment site, 262; African American refugees, 268, 294; expulsion of African American civilians, 268
Campbell, Easter, 297–298
Campbell, Hugh, 225
Canada, 122, 161; as destination of fugitive slaves, 76–77, 89, 107; as destination for Confederate sympathizers, 245, 263, 265
Canals, 52–53; see also Illinois; Indiana; Kentucky; Missouri; Ohio
Cantrell, Tilman B., 275
Cape Girardeau, Mo., 96, 151, 217

Cape Girardeau (Mo.) *Eagle*, 195
Capitol, U.S., "Statuary Hall" in, 333
Carbondale, Il., 274
Carlinville, Il., 129
Carmi, Il., 279, 281
Carns, Abraham, 40
Carriage, Braxton, 37
Carthage (Mo.), battle at, 141
Cartwright, Peter, 66
Carver, Hiram, 251
Caseyville, Il., camp of instruction at, 129
Catholic Church/Catholics, 44; and dissent, 268
Cemeteries, 310
Centennial, national, 285, 291
Centralia, Il., 228
Centralia (Il.) *Sentinel*, 228
Centralia (Mo.), atrocity at, 260
Centre College (Ky.), 201; racial violence, 259–260
Centreville, In., 129
Chamberlain, Orville T., 232
Chaplin River (Ky.), 167, 201
Character and Influence of Abolitionism!, The, see VanDyke, Henry J.; see also Churches, slavery divisions
"Charcoals," see Missouri, "Radical"/Republican party
Charleston, Il., Lincoln-Douglas debate at, 101, 102–103; riot, 281
Charleston, Mo., home guard in, 132
Charleston, S.C., 48, 82, 126; St. Andrews Hall in, 82; slave population of, 86
Chase, Salmon P., 45, 63, 72, 85, 88–89, 90, 91, 109; as U.S. secretary of the treasury, 150, 185, 196, 213, 220; view of Abraham Lincoln, 145
Chattanooga, Tn., 319; smuggling to, 196
Chesapeake Bay, as source for western migration, 22; as region, 22, 37; tobacco production/culture in, 51
Chester, Il., 128, 273, 275, 277
Chicago, Il., 55, 90, 93, 132–133, 333, 337; and Democratic convention of 1864, 281; and Lincoln's funeral train, 284; wartime race riots in, 223
Children, wartime experiences of, 265–268; see also Women
Chillicothe, Oh., 25, 76, 303
Christy, David, 177
Churches/faiths, and slavery, 46, 47, 62–63, 66, 177; wartime social divisions, 175, 176–180; see also Baptist Church/Baptists; Catholic Church/Catholics; Communities of allegiance; Episcopal Church/Episcopalians; Jewry/Jews/Judaism; Methodist Church/Methodists;

Index

Presbyterian Church/Presbyterians; Unitarian Church/Unitarians

Cincinnati, Oh., 33, 53, 61, 67, 80, 127, 139, 171, 215, 306, 317, 327, 337; abolitionism/abolitionists in, 68–70, 71–72, 89, 104, 214, 216; African Americans in, 33, 41, 69, 70, 72, 73, 74, 75, 107–108, 302; and Bragg's Confederate invasion of Ky., 200; and "Confederate tradition," 313, 317; and Fugitive Slave Act, 89; and Lincoln's funeral train, 284; Anti-Abolition Society of, 71; Anti-Slavery Society, 46; Baptist Church in, 66; boatyards used to outfit gunboats, 127, 128; "Bucktown" in, 73; Catholic influences in, 58; Chamber of Commerce, 198; "College of Teachers" in, 72; commercial interests in, 45–46, 57, 66; Democratic party/conventions in, 92, 198, 309; dissent/dissenters in, 229, 268, 273, 276, 280, 309; draft evasion in, 275, 276, see also Military conscription; "Dublin" in, 223; earthquakes in 1812 felt at, 16; Eighth Ward in, 276; elections in, 72; federal military enlistments, 160; federal military veterans, 301; foreign-born population of, 44, 58, 59, 212, 224; fugitive slaves in, 75; GAR encampment, 320; German Americans in, 58, 92, 161, 212; headquarters of federal Department of the Ohio, 139, 142; Irish Americans in, 223; Jewish population of, 59, 108; Lane Theological Seminary in, 68–69, 70; Liberal Republicans, 309; Lincoln speeches in, 103; "Little Africa" in, 73; Lyceum, 45; manufacturing in, 57; National Underground Freedom Center in, 336; New England influence in, 44; Ohio River (Roebling) suspension bridge at, 161–162; Pike's Opera House in, 106, 216; Presbyterian Church/synod in, 46–47; population of, 57; proslavery influences in, 45–48, 66, 70, 71, 84, 106, 107–108, 124, 229; racial violence in, 69, 70, 72, 77, 124, 223, 302; refugees in, 174; relief commission in, 174; Republican party in, 91, 106, 198; response to war in, 126–127; river trade in, 45–46, 57, 66, 127, 128, 231; slave laborers in, 73, 74; slave ordinances in, 41; slavery politics in, 44–48, 64, 70, 77, 85, 90; trade restrictions, 198–199; "Union festival" in 1860 in, 1; wartime race riots in, 223; Western and Southern Life Insurance Co. in, 336; Young Men's Mercantile Library in, 47–48

Cincinnati (Oh.) Advertiser and Journal, 46
Cincinnati (Oh.) Gazette, 92
"Cincinnati Panorama of" 1848, 56–57

Cincinnati (Oh.) Post and Anti-Abolitionist, 46, 71
Circleville, Oh., 76, 273
Civil liberties, wartime violations of, 12, 13–14, 169, 185, 206, 208; see also Dominion system; Habeas corpus; Hard-line war; Loyalty/disloyalty; Military occupation
Civil War, American, 5; interpretations of, 5–6, 7–9, 13; reconciliation after, see Reconciliation; semicentennial of, 6, 323, 331, 332
Civilians, military banishment, 154, 178, 185, 188, 194, 195–196, 248, 261, 263, 264, 328, see also Martial Law; social relations in wartime, 175–199; as refugees, 172–175; see also Civil liberties; Dominion system; Habeas corpus; Hard-line war; Military occupation
Clansman, The, 330–331; see also *Birth of a Nation*; Dixon, Thomas
Clarke, Lewis, 75, 76
Clausewitz, Carl von, 299
Clay, Brutus, 294
Clay, Cassius M., 64–65, 87, 88, 90–91, 104, 220
Clay, Henry, 2, 46, 49–50, 52, 53, 59, 60, 61, 62, 87, 88, 91, 130, 188; Ashland as home of, 50; death of, 99; funeral train, 99, 284; grave monument of, 99, 100; see also "American System;" "Bluegrass System"
Clay, James, 188
Clemens, Samuel L., 23–24, 89, 334–335; and slavery, 334–335
Clermont (Oh.) Academy, 289; see also Parker, Daniel
Cleveland, Grover, 319
Cleveland, Oh., 54, 55, 108, 122, 333; and fugitive slaves, 77; GAR posts, 319
Cobb, James C., 331
Cockrell, Francis M., 301, 321
Coffin, Levi, 66, 67, 257
Coles, Edward, 34–35, 40, 65, 66; see also Illinois, slavery politics in
Collectivism, see Northern
Collins, Peter, 157, 159
Colonization/colonizationists, 11, 50, 63, 64–65, 114; and abolitionism, 68; and compensated emancipation, 216
Colored Citizen (Cincinnati, Oh.), *The*, 229, 302
Colored Women's Relief Corps, see African Americans, commemorative activities, in Grand Army of the Republic
Columbia, Ky., 189
Columbia, Mo., 80, 195
Columbus, Ky., 142, 143, 259; and Lincoln's funeral train, 284; contraband camp at, 218; federal forays to, 143; Iron Banks at, 142; occupied by Confederate troops, 116, 142; railroad terminus at, 142

Columbus, Oh., 1, 3, 54, 332; response to war in, 126
Commemorations, postwar, 310–327; see also Cemeteries; Lost Cause; Public monuments; Union Triumphant; Women
"Communities of allegiance," 12, 175–181, 235, 272–274, 275–282; defined, 170; see also Churches/faiths; Civilians, social relations in wartime; Dissent/dissenters; Exclusivism
Conciliation, as military policy, 146–157
"Confederados," 293
Confederacy, see Confederate States of America
Confederate States of America, 137; Army, 141, 199–205; Congress of, 141, 144, 196, 197, 301; federal armies in, 199; "first national flag" of, 116; military recruiting in Middle Border by, 164–165, 184; Partisan Ranger Act of, 186, 243; sends commissioners to Middle Border, 134; Sequestration Act, 184; slavery as basis for enlisting in army, 132; Western Military Department of, 137; see also Secession
"Confederate tradition," see Exclusivism; Kentucky; Middle Border; Missouri; Southern
Confedrit-X-Roads, see Nasby, Petroleum V.
Confiscation, see Military Confiscation
Congregational Church/Congregationalists, 23, 71
Congress, U.S., 22, 27, 29, 40, 50, 52, 84, 104–105, 112, 208; abolition of slavery in federal territories, 219; and Corwin Amendment, 112; and Crittenden Compromise, 109, 123; Article of War (1862) regarding fugitive slaves, 215; Dependent Pension Act (1890), 322; First Confiscation Act (1861), 129, 212–213, 214, 219; Fugitive Slave Act (1850), 11, 88–89, 107, 108, 125; Homestead Act, 222, 269; internal revenue act, 222, 269; ironclad oath, 208; Joint Committee on the Conduct of the War, 222; Kansas-Nebraska Act (1854), 11, 78, 90–91, 92, 94, 97; Land grant college act, 222, 269; legal tender act, 222; Militia Act, 208, 219, 220; national banking act, 222, see also Military conscription; Second Confiscation Act (1862), 208, 219–220, 226, 259; transcontinental railroad act, 222, 269; see also House, U.S.; Senate, U.S.
Connecticut, 23, 51; as source for western migration, 140, 147; emancipation of slaves in, 36
Conrad, William, 183
Conscientious objectors, 164; see also Amish; Mennonites; Quakers; Shakers
Conscription, see Military Conscription
Conservatism/conservatives, 11, 12; in West, 11, 12, 44, 60, 64, 68–69, 84, 93, 115, 309; as

anti-emancipation political designation, 12, 214, 222–223, 226–227; in Republican party, 227–232; racial foundation of, 12, 214, 221–222, 224, 227, 228, 300–302, 308, 309; see also Anti-abolitionism; Middle Border; Democratic Party, Conservative faction of; Emancipation; Republican party; Unionism/unionists; West, American, racial traditionalism in
Constitution, U.S., 2, 3, 55, 102; and slavery, 228; Tenth Amendment to, 102
Constitutional Union party, 105, 127
Continental Divide, as reconciliationist symbol, 335
Contraband goods, 185, 196–199, 263; see also Trade permit system (federal); Women
Contraband camps, 218, 254, 257–258; see also African Americans, as wartime fugitives
Contrabands, see African Americans; Middle Border, wartime erosion of slavery in; Emancipation; Slavery, wartime erosion of; Slaves, wartime emancipation of
Contract apprenticeship, 17–18; see Illinois; Indiana
"Conventionists," see Illinois, constitutional convention of 1824
Copperhead(s), 8, 211, 222, 227, 268–284; as western racial euphemism, 42, 227; see also Butternuts; Democratic party, Peace faction in; Dissent/dissenters
Corwin, Thomas, 84, 104; constitutional amendment protecting slavery, 112
Coulter, E. Merton, 331
Courier (Louisville, Ky.), 213; suppressed, 127
Courier (Madison, In.), The, 127
Courier-Journal (Louisville, Ky.), 320; see also Courier (Louisville, Ky.); Journal (Louisville, Ky.); Watterson, Henry
Covington, Ky., 106; federal military enlistments in, 131; foreign-born population of, 59; German Americans in, 58, 92; Ohio River (Roebling) suspension bridge at, 161, 162
Covington and Lexington Railroad (Ky.), 263
Cox, Jacob D., 126, 307
Cranor, Manlove, 247
Crawfordsville, In., 281
Cravens, James H., 108
Crenshaw, John Hart, 15–20, 21, 336; and "reverse underground railroad," 18–20; 16, 336; Hickory Hill as home, 33 see also Illinois, salt-making in; Salt; Slavery
Crenshaw, William, 16
Crèvecoeur, J. Hector St. Jean de, 22
Crisis (Columbus, Oh.), The, 273
Crittenden Compromise, see Congress, U.S.; Crittenden, John J.
Crittenden, John J., 109, 134; slavery compromise plan of, 109, 123

Cuba, 326; as locus for postwar Confederate expatriation, 293; San Juan Hill in, 327; see also Spanish-American War
Cumberland, Army of the (federal), 267; Society of, 304
Cumberland Gap, 22
Cumberland River, 52, 74, 86, 130, 142, 244; valley of, 17
Cumberland Road (Md.), 52
Cuming, Fortescue, 16
Curfews, 194; see also Martial Law
Curtis, Samuel R., 149, 156, 197, 226, 248, 250, 251, 282
Custer, George A., 290
Cynthiana (Ky.), 262; battle at/raid on, 166
Cypressville, Il., 18, 19

Daily Message (Cincinnati, Oh.), 66; see also Gallagher, William Davis
Daily Democrat (Dayton, Oh.), 311
Daily Enquirer (Cincinnati, Oh.), 73, 91, 107–108, 122, 223, 263, 273, 307
Daily Herald (Paducah, Ky.), suppressed, 195
Dallas, Tx., 323
Daniels, Edward, 151
Danville, Il., 270
Danville, Ky., 26, 131, 201, 231, 297; racial violence, 259–260, 295
Daughters of the Confederacy (Mo.) (DOC), 315; see also United Daughters of the Confederacy
Davis, David, 309
Davis, Garret, 27, 110, 124, 139, 142, 213, 294
Davis, Jefferson, 79, 115, 183, 201, 214, 224, 275, 301, 305, 308, 329; administration of, 143, 201–202; birthplace monument of, 323–326, 327, 331, see also Fairview, Ky., Kentucky, "Confederate tradition"; in; death, 323; highway system, 325; Home Association, 323, 325
Davis, Jefferson C., 234
Dayton, Oh., 33, 67, 170, 286, 305; "Union festival" in 1860 in, 1
DeBow, J(ames). D. B., 48, 62
DeBow's Review (New Orleans, La.), 48; see also DeBow, J(ames). D. B.
Declaration of Independence, 35, 102, 103; and slavery, 228
Deere, John, 55
Degler, Carl, 122
Delaware, 22; emancipation of slaves in, 37, 214–215; free blacks in, 87; neutrality stance of, 145; slave population of, 37; slavery in, 37, 85; Thirteenth Amendment rejected, 295; Union Party in, 214
Democracy, see Free labor ideology; Free-soil; Slavery, as democratic principle in West

"Democratic leagues," see Dissent/dissenters; Home guards
Democratic Party, 11, 13, 44, 57–59, 60–61, 80, 84–88, 90, 112, 142, 330; and election of 1862; and "New Departure," 309; and wartime emancipation, 12, 220–226, 268–284; antislavery wing of, 45, 85–88, 90, 106; convention of 1864, 281; free-soil faction of, 85, 90; in Congress, 214; Jacksonian influence on, 44; ministers as, 177–181, see also Churches/faiths; Peace faction of, 8, 13, 211, 222, 222, 227, 268–283, see also Copperheads; postwar politics, 299–301, 303–308, 309, 311, 318–325, see also "Bloody shirt"; proslavery/Conservative faction in, 12, 80, 87, 177, 213, 220, 222, 226, 309; War faction of, 127, 211, 222, 225, 227, 260, 276, 281–283; see also Delaware; Dissent/dissenters; Kentucky; Maryland; Missouri
Democratic Platform (Liberty, Mo.), 96
Demossville, Ky., 263
Dennison, William, 1, 127
Desertions/deserters, see Military Desertions
Desha, Joseph, 61
Detroit, Mi., 55
Dick, Franklin A., 96, 153, 157
Dickey, John M., 23
Dickinson, George H., 195
Disease, in wartime, 119; see also Hospitals
Dissent/dissenters, 8, 12–13, 13–14, 178–181, 268–284; class dimension of, 270; "Democratic leagues," 272, 280; ministers, 178–180, 187–188, 190, 216, 229, 246, 270, 313–314; opposition to military conscription/enrollment, 269, 275–276; opposition to wartime emancipation and, 222–223, 227–232, 269, 275–276; proslavery dimension, 298–299; racial dimension of, 13–14, 227–228, 268, 298–300; secret societies, 268, 275–276, 280; violence by, 273–274; see also "Communities of Allegiance;" Butternuts; Churches/faiths; Confiscation; Conscription; Copperheads; Democratic party; Emancipation; Exclusivism
District of Columbia, 310; compensated emancipation in, 216; free blacks in, 87
District of the Border, U.S., 238
"Dixie Frontier," 22; see also Middle border, migration to
Dixon, Archibald, 126
Dodge, Grenville M., 156
Dominion system, see Military occupation
Doniphan, Alexander, 80
Dorsey, Sally, 127, 176

Douglas, Stephen A., 11, 223; and Democratic party, 90–91, 92, 93; and Kansas-Nebraska Act, 90–91, 92; as candidate in 1860 election, 106, 110; death, 144; debates with Abraham Lincoln, 11, 100–103; encourages support for Lincoln administration, 126
Douglass, Frederick, 63, 303, 304
Draft, see Military Conscription
Drake, Charles D., 240, 255
Drake, Daniel, 27, 51
Dred Scott v. Sanford (1857), see Supreme Court, U.S.
Duden, Gottfried, 162
Duke, Basil W., 298, 313, 316, 319
Duncan, Henry T., 40, 134
Durham, Eng., 207

East, Nancy, 308
Edgar, John, 32
Editors, see Military arrests (federal); Newspapers, suppressions of
Edwards, John Newman, 313; see also Lost Cause, guerrillas/partisans
"Egypt," 15, 18; see also Illinois, southern counties in
Elections, of 1824, 61; of 1840, 72; of 1848, 85; of 1856, 92; of 1858, 105; of 1860, 11, 83, 105–108; of 1861, 214; of 1862, 12, 221–222, 223, 271; of 1864, 13, 280–283
Eliot, William Greenleaf, 63, 66, 153
Elizabethtown, Ky., 192
Elk Fork, Mo., 188
Elkhorn Tavern, Ar., battle at, 170; see also Pea Ridge
Elkhill, see Napton, William Barclay
Elliott, Robert, 245
Ellis, Edmund J., 195
Ellsworth, Elmer, 149
Emancipation of slaves, 9, 12, 50; as facet of regionalism, 10; as loyalty test, 226–228; by post-Revolution manumissions, 37, 41; First, 36–37; in Atlantic seaboard states, 36; opposition to, see Proslavery; western federal soldiers' opposition, 208–210, 232–234; see also African Americans; Middle Border, slavery in; Emancipation Proclamation; Lincoln, Abraham; Slavery, wartime erosion of; Thirteenth Amendment
Emancipation Proclamation, Preliminary, 12, 219–226, 227–232, 250; exemption of Border States from Final, 221, 225; federal soldiers' responses to, 208–210, 227, 231–234, 238; Final, 12, 13–14, 210, 228, 250; see also African Americans; Lincoln, Abraham; Slavery
Emancipationism/emancipationists, xviii, 11, 20, 33, 34–35, 36–37, 50, 72, 87–88; as postwar Republican trope, 293, 294, 295, 300, 303, 304, 305, 306, 307, 309, 311, 318, 327, 332, 333, 334
Emigrant Aid Societies, 79, 95; see also Kansas; New England
Eminence, Ky., 315; martyr monument at, 315
Empire (Dayton, Oh.), *The*, 273
Emporia, Ks., 334
"English prairie," 39; see also Albion; Birkbeck, Morris; Flower, George
Enlistment brokers (federal), 258
Enrolled Missouri Militia, 193, 251, 255; see also Missouri, state militia in; Provisional Enrolled Missouri Militia
Enrollment, see Military Conscription
Equality, Il., 18
Erie Canal, 52, 54
Evansville, In., 57, 280; Blue-Gray reunion, 320; German Americans in, 58, 106, 227; Republican party in, 106, 227; racial violence in, 223, 280, 302
Evansville (In.) *Journal*, 227
Everett, Edward, 50; and Constitutional Union party, 105
Ewing, Thomas, Jr., 238–239, 240, 241, 314; and General Orders No. 10, 238; and General Orders No. 11, 239, 240, 314, 321; and Price's Raid in 1864, 282; see also Lawrence, Ks.; Quantrill, William C.
Exclusion policy (federal), 217, 218; see also Halleck, Henry W.; Slaves, as wartime fugitives
"Exclusionists," see Illinois, constitutional convention of 1823 in, proslavery influences in
Exclusivism, defined, 9–10; academic, 334; as culture, 328–338; "Confederate tradition" in, 312–318, 328–332; literary/counter-narratives, 9–10, 13, 311–314, 322; and slavery, 334; as wartime politics, 9–10, 120, 235; Union Triumphant trope in, 303–304, 310, 311; see also Middle Border; Northern, Southern

Fagg, Thomas J. C., 121
Farrar, Bernard G., 199
Fairview, Ky., Jefferson Davis birthplace monument, 323–326
Faux, William, 24, 38, 39
Fee, John G., 65, 69, 99
Fields, Barbara J., 7
Findley, Oh., 299
Finney, Charles Grandison, 68, 307
Fifteenth Amendment, 307–309; see also Illinois; Indiana; Kentucky; Missouri; Ohio, Reconstruction
First Confiscation Act, see Military Confiscation, of slaves by federal armies

First World War, 326
Fisher, Elwood, 44–48, 49, 77, 80; see also Anti-abolitionists/abolitionism; Cincinnati, Oh.
Fisher, Samuel, 45
Fisher, George P., 214–215
Fitzpatrick, William, 286–287
"Flatheads," 77; see also Illinois, racial violence in; "Regulators"
Fletcher, John W., 228, 270
Fletcher, Thomas C., 283, 292; emancipation order of, 292
Flint, James, 62
Florida, secession of, 108
Flower, George, 32, 37; see also Albion; Birkbeck, Morris; "English prairie"
Floyd, John, 124
Foner, Eric, 7
Fontayne, Charles, 57
Ford's Theater, see Lincoln, Abraham, assassination; Washington, D.C.
Forrest, Nathan Bedford, 164; and Bragg's invasion of Ky., 200, 203; raids into Kentucky, 259
Fort Donelson (Tn.), battle at, 118, 165, 169, 199; as destination for fugitive slaves, 225
Fort Henry (Tn.), 134, 199; surrender of, 272
Fort Leavenworth (Ks.), 238
Fort Pillow (Tn.), racial atrocity at, 6, 241, 259
Fort Sumter, 116, 126, 132, 212, 271
Foster, Gaines M., 312; see also "Confederate tradition"
Foster, Stephen, 327, 336; see also "My Old Kentucky Home, Good Night"
Fourteenth Amendment, 306; see also Illinois; Indiana; Kentucky; Missouri; Ohio
Fourth of July, celebrations of, 76, 180, 276, 277, 278, 279, 293
Franklin, In., 229
Frankfort, Ky., 87, 99, 122, 138, 234, 300; and Bragg's Confederate invasion of Ky., 201, 202; Border State Convention in, 138–139, 188; Green Hill Cemetery, 327; racial atrocity near, 262
Fredrickstown, Mo., 152
Fredericksburg, Va., battle at, 271
Free blacks, see African Americans, free
Free labor ideology, 42, 47, 67, 78, 102
Free Nation (Cincinnati, Oh.), 214; see also Abolitionism/abolitionists
Free South (Newport, Ky.), The, 104; see also Anti-abolitionism; Bailey, William Shields
Free-soil, 83–84, 88, 90–91, 96; see also Antislavery; Slavery, politics of; West, American, slavery politics in
Free Soil party, 85, 88, 92
Freedmen's Bureau, 296, 306; violence against, 297; see also Middle Border; Kentucky; Maryland; Missouri, South, American, Reconstruction in
"Freedom National, Slavery Sectional," 102, 110, 229, 336; see also Abolitionism/abolitionists
Freehling, William W., 7
Freeport, Il., Lincoln-Douglas debate at, 102
Frémont, John C., 146; and contraband slaves, 217; as commander of the federal Department of the West, 142, 188, 213; as Republican party presidential candidate, 92; declares martial law in Mo., 213–214; emancipation proclamation in Mo., 213–214, 217; removed from command, 214
Frick, Karl Adolph, 230
Frost, Daniel M., 137
Fry, Speed S., 297
Fugitive Slave Act, see Congress, U.S.
Fugitive slaves, see Slaves

Gabbert, Forrest, 327
Galena, Il., 142
Galesburg, Il., 277
Gallagher, William Davis, 52, 62, 66
Gallatin County, Il., 16–20; racial violence in, 19–20; "Regulators" in, 19–20; see also Crenshaw, John Hart; Illinois, salt-making in; Salt
Galloway, Samuel, 68, 69
Gamble, Hamilton R., 141, 157, 237; and wartime emancipation, 226, 256; as Mo. provisional governor, 141, 225
Gantt, Thomas T., 212
Garfield, James G., 2, 304; statue in U.S. Capitol, 333
Garrigus, Jeptha, 89
Garrison, William Lloyd, 67
Garrisons, see Military Garrisons (federal)
Gazette (Cincinnati, Oh.), 308
General Orders No. 100 (federal), see Lieber, Francis W., "Code"; see also Guerrillas
General Orders No. 140 (federal), see Provost marshals
Genius of Universal Emancipation, 65; see also Antislavery; Lundy, Benjamin
Georgetown College (Ky.), 131
Georgia, 19, 48; as source for western migration, 22, 26–27, 30; secession of, 108; slave population of, 86; towns/cities in, 55
German Americans, 15, 44, 57, 90, 161, 230; and Democratic party, 92; and Liberal Republicans, 309; and Republican party, 106, 137, 225, 245; antipathy/violence toward by slaveholders/southerners, 118, 138, 140, 160, 188, 245, 255, 260, 312,

German Americans (*continued*)
  253–254, 255, 282; in federal armies, 160, 230; see also Cincinnati, Oh.; Immigration, foreign; Kentucky; "Know-Nothings;" Louisville, Ky.; Missouri; Nativism; St. Louis, Mo.
Gettysburg, Pa., 13; battle at, 13, 210; Lincoln's 1863 Address at, 13
"Gibraltar of the West," see Columbus, Ky., occupied by Confederate troops
Giddings, Joshua, 92
Gist, Samuel, 65
Glasgow, Mo., 186, 323
Goodloe, Robert, 48
"Goose question," see Missouri, controversy over Kansas in
Grand Army of the Republic (GAR), 304, 305, 307, 315; Ladies of, 304, see also Women, commemorative organizations; national encampments, 304, 319–320; see also Military veterans
Grand Detour, Il., 55
Granger, John, 18; see also Crenshaw, John Hart
Granger, Gordon, 218
Grant, Julia Dent, 142
Grant, Ulysses S., 7, 149, 196, 232, 276, 309; and "Great Triumvirate," 304; and Union Triumphant trope, 304; as president, 306, 310; death, 318; expulsion order of Jewish traders, 198; in Mo., 243; memoirs, 335; presidential administration, 309; occupies western Ky., 142, 198
"Great Debates" (1858), 11, 100–103; see also Lincoln, Abraham; Douglas, Stephen A.; Illinois
"Great Compromiser," see Clay, Henry
Great Lakes region, 54, 90
Greeley, Horace, 220
Green, Elisha W., 75
Green River (Ky.), 6, 168
Greeneville (Oh.), Treaty of, 25; see also Native Americans
Greensburg, In., 280
Greensburg, Ky., 250
Griffith, D. W., 331
Grigsby, John Warren, 267–268
Grigsby, Susan Shelby, 267–268
Guerrant, Edward O., 202
Guerrillas, 152, 168, 170, 237, 239, 243–253; counterinsurgency against, 261–262, 275–279; destruction of courthouses by, 250–251; executions of, 248–249, 261–262; postwar idealization of, 313; proslavery ideology of, 170, 249–250, 260–262; politicized violence of, 12, 13–14, 170, 197–198, 204–205, 250–251, 261–262, 282; racial violence of, 251, 259–262, 282, 296–298; Unionist, 252–253, 277–279, 298; see also Hard-line war; Kentucky; Military occupation; Missouri; Partisans
Guitar, Odon, 251
Gunn, Fanny, 191
Gunn, Thomas, 233

Habeas corpus, wartime suspension, 12, 211, 221; see also Civil Liberties; Dissent/dissenters; Lincoln, Abraham; Military occupation
Hadrian's Wall, 207
Hale, Edward Everett, 8; see also "Man Without a Country"
Hale, John P., 88
Hall, Willard P., 199
Halleck, Henry W., and guerrillas, 248, 249; as general-in-chief of U.S. armies, 249; as commander of Department of the West/Missouri, 152–153, 154, 156–157, 184, 192, 216, 218; as western army commander, 160; "exclusion policy" of, 218; orders capital punishment for Mo. guerrillas, 153
Hamburg, SC, 290
Hamilton, Oh., 305, 306
Hammond, Abraham A., 93
Hammond, James Henry, 48
Hannibal and St. Joseph Railroad (Mo.), 78, 149; see also Missouri, railroads in
Hannibal, Mo., 89, 131, 213, 217–218, 262; African Americans, 295
Hanson, Charles S., 210
Hard-line war, 144, 147–157, 211, 237, 253, 260–262, 311; and women, 262–268; defined, 11; see also Middle Border; Civil liberties; Conciliation; Kentucky; Missouri; Military occupation
Hardee, William J., 165
Hardin, Elizabeth Pendleton "Lizzie," 105–106, 134–135, 159, 176, 203, 205, 293; banished, 264, 293
Harding, Aaron, 250
Harlan, John Marshall, 122, 234, 297
Harney, William S., 20, 66; neutrality agreement with Sterling Price, 140, 142, 145; as commander of federal Department of the West, 137, 140, 145, 212
Harpers Ferry, Va., 2, 103; see also Brown, John, raid of
Harrington, John T., 232
Harrison, William Henry, 29, 30, 36–37
Harrod, James, 28
Harrodsburg, Ky., 106, 176; African Americans in, 294–295; and Bragg's Confederate invasion of Ky., 167–168, 203, 204; Board of Trustees, 189, 294–295
Hart, Will T., 121

Index

Harvard College/University, 135, 145, 333, 337
Hatch, George, 126
Hathaway, Leeland, 329–330
Hawes, Richard, 202, 209
Hawesville, Ky., 207
Haycraft, Samuel, 192, 332
Hayes, Rutherford B., 126–127
Hegel, Georg W., 161
Helena, Ar., contraband camp at, 218
Helm, Emily Todd, 314; see also Lincoln, Mary Todd
Henderson, Ky., 42
Hensley, Ed, 194
Henson, Josiah, 75
Herndon, William, 93
Heren, William, 245
"Hickory Hill," 18–19; see also Crenshaw, John Hart; "Reverse underground railroad"
Higgins, Allen, 205
Higginsville, Mo., 316–317
Hildebrand, Samuel, 245; postwar autobiography, 313; see also Guerrillas
Hill, Sarah Jane Full, 170, 204–205, 265
Hillenmeyer, Henry, 329
Hillsboro, Oh., 108
Hiram College, see Western Reserve, Eclectic Institute of
History of Morgan's Cavalry, 313; see also Duke, Basil W.; Morgan, John Hunt
Hobson, Edward, 259
Hodgenville, Ky., Abraham Lincoln birthplace monument, 323
Hoffman, Charles F., 21, 23
Holly Springs, Ms., 231
Holmes, Theophilus H., 248
Holt, Joseph, 124–125, 183, 225, 261
Home guards, 6, 129, 150, 151, 185, 243, 245; and Loyal leagues, 228, 280; as slave patrols, 131–132, 251–252, 255; class antagonisms, 188; infiltration by disloyalists, 245; politicization of, 228, 277–281; pro-Confederate, 188; see also Middle Border; Delaware; Kentucky; Maryland; Missouri
Home Missionary, 23
Hooper, Jim, 286
"Hoosiers," meaning, 42
Hopkins, John Henry, 177
Hopkinsville, Ky., 99, 134, 225; as African American enlistment site, 258, 262; executions of guerrillas near, 261; federal military enlistments in, 131; federal military occupation, 176; fugitive slaves, 258; Confederate military occupation, 116, 142, 205, 262
Hopper, Henry C., 129
Hospitals, in wartime, 119, 165, 178, 185, 272, 380n6

House, U.S., 48, 89, 104, 219; Committee of 33, 112; composition, 221; see also Congress, U.S.
Hoyt, Thomas A., 161, 230
Hulbert, Archer, 334
Hunter, David, 146
Hurlbut, Stephen, 150

Illinois, xvii, 6, 7; abolitionism/abolitionists in, 70–71, 91, 115, 178, 212, 227; African Americans in, 31–32, 223–224, 302; Alexander County in, 26; "American Bottom" in, see also Illinois, slavery/indentured servitude in, 32; and Middle Border, 144–147, anti-black immigration law in, 20, 41, 102, 223–224, 225; antislavery influences in, 34–35, 40, 93–94; as source for western migration, 78, 96; antiwar meeting in, 271; Baptist Church in, 178; "Blue Grass" subregion in, 26; "Black Code"/Black Laws of, 10, 20, 41, 72, 223, 303; Black Hawk War in, 54; border patrols, 243; canals in, 53, 60–61; central counties in, 93, 179, 224, 227, 271, 306; comity laws in, 71; Confederate enlistments from, 129; constitution of, 31–32, 33, 38, 40; constitutional convention of 1824, 34–35, 36, 43; constitutional convention of 1862, 222; contract apprenticeship in, 17–20, 31–32; cotton production in, 51; Democratic party in, 83–88, 93, 129, 179, 221–222, 223, 224, 271; dissent/dissenters in, 227, 268–269; Edwards County in, 32, 37; election of 1860 in, 106; election of 1862 in, 221–222, 223; election of 1864 in, 281–283, see also Elections; federal military enlistments in, 129; federal military veterans, 304–311; federal troops from, 152, 169, 173, 209, 217, 233, 254, 274; federal reserve in, 16–17; Fifteenth Amendment, 299, 308; foreign-born troops in federal armies from, 160; Fourteenth Amendment, 299, 306; French influence in, 18, 31, 32, 34; fugitive slaves in, 74, 89; Fulton County in, 277; Gallatin County in, 16–20, 26, 32, 40; geo-political division of, 93; "Great Debates" of 1858 in, 11, 100–103; Grundy County in, 55; Hancock County in, 179, 274; home guards, 243; involuntary servitude banned in, 20; Jackson County in, 129; Jasper County in, 26; Jo Daviess County in, 55; land speculation in, 39–40; legislature of, 18, 20, 84, 105, 129, 232, 243, 270, 304, 308; Lincoln-Douglas debates in, 11; Madison County in, 65; Massac County in, 77, 129; Methodist Church in, 179; Native Americans in, 54; northern

Illinois (continued)
counties in, 55, 85, 93–94, 142, 165, 218, 306; Ogle County in, 55; opposition to wartime emancipation in, 223–225, see also Emancipation Proclamation, Soldiers; Pope County in, 32, 77, 129; population migration to/growth of, 25–26, 34–35, 54, 55; postwar politics, 302–311, see also "Bloody shirt"; proslavery influences in, 34–35, 38–42, 43, 71, 84, 92, 208–209, 223–224, 228; racial violence in, 19–20, 77, 223–224, 280, 308; railroads in, 53; Randolph County in, 32; ratifies Corwin Amendment, 112; ratifies Thirteenth Amendment, 303; Republican party in, 91, 93, 109, 178, 179, 212, 221–222, 224, 227–228, 294, 302–311; Rock River subregion of, 54; salt-making in, 16–18, 40; Sangamon County in, 60; Sons of Confederate Veterans in, 316; secession support in, 128–129, 130, 223, 228; slavery/indentured servitude in, 31–32, 34, 40, 77; slavery politics in, 3, 29, 34–35, 65, 84, 89, 93–94, 108, 223, 223–224; southern counties in, 15–20, 24, 38, 39, 40, 54, 77, 89, 93, 108, 128–129, 130, 155, 156, 164, 173, 175–176, 195, 214, 223–224, 228, 231–233, 269, 274, 302, see also "Egypt"; southern cultural influences in, 25–26, 34–35, 39, 55, 93, 108, 128–129, 214, 224–225, 306; state capitol in, 34, 60; statehood of, 16, 17–18, 29, 31–32, 34, 43; supreme court of, 40, 77; territorial legislature of, 16, 31–32; Underground Railroad in, 71; Union County in, 224, 271; Union leagues in, 227–228; Union party in, 221–222; United Confederate Veterans in, 316; western counties of, 89; western migration to, 22–27; Whig party in, 84–88, 89, 93–94; Williamson County in, 26, 129, 306, 308

Illinois, Military District of (federal), 276

Illinois Republican, 19

Illinois State Journal (Springfield, Il.), 89

Illinois troops; 5th Cavalry Regiment, 221; 11th Infantry Regiment, 154; 24th Infantry Regiment, 160; 31st Infantry Regiment, 217; 109th Infantry Regiment, mutiny, 231–232; 128th Infantry Regiment, mutiny, 231–232

Illustrated Confederate War Journal (Louisville, Ky.), 319

Immigration, foreign, 44, 57–58, 310; as enlistees in federal armies, 160; see also German Americans; Irish-Americans; "Know-Nothings;" Nativism; West, American

Independence, Mo., 238; as Quantrill reunion site, 321; "Confederate tradition" in, 330; Woodlawn Cemetery, as site of first Confederate memorial, 315

Indian Territory, 221, 282; see also Native Americans; West, American

Indiana, xvii, 2, 7, 84; African Americans in, 29–31, 302; anti-black immigration law in, 41, 302; as source for western migration, 78, 96; "Black Code" of, 10, 29, 30, 41, 72; Benton County in, 55; border patrols, 243; Brown County in, 26; canals in, 53; Clark County in, 30; Confederate enlistments from, 129; constitution of, 33; constitutional convention of 1816 of, 30–31; Democratic party in, 2, 83–88, 89, 221–222, 223, 232, 271, 279, 302; dissent/dissenters, 268, 274, 279, 280; election of 1860, 106; election of 1862, 221–222, 223; election of 1864 in, 281–283, see also Elections; federal military enlistments in, 129, 164; federal military veterans, 304–311; federal troops from, 169, 209, 231–232, 254, 272, 273, 274, 281; Fifteenth Amendment, 299, 308–309; foreign-born troops in federal armies from, 160; Fourteenth Amendment, 299, 302, 306; French influence in, 29; fugitive slaves in, 74; Jasper County in, 55; Johnson County in, 276; Knox County in, 30; legislature of, 38, 105, 129, 271; Marion County in, 129; martial law in, 271; northern counties in, 55; population migration to/growth of, 25–26, 54; postwar politics, 302–311, see also "Bloody shirt"; proslavery influences in, 29–29, 30–31, 38, 43, 92, 208–209; Quakers in, 63, 92; railroads in, 53; ratifies Thirteenth Amendment, 302; Republican party in, 91, 109, 195, 221, 223, 232, 302–311; Rush County in, 280; Scott County in, 26; Sons of Confederate Veterans in, 316; secession support in, 129, 130; slavery/indentured servitude in, 29–31, 34, 36–37; slavery politics in, 3, 28–29, 30–31, 84, 85, 108; southern counties of, 23, 38, 76, 92, 108, 121, 130, 164, 165, 179, 214, 232, 274, 333; southern cultural influences in, 25–26, 108, 214; state militia, 129–130, 243; statehood of, 29, 30–31; supreme court of, 31; territorial government of, 29, 30–31; "Union festivals" in 1860 in, 1–3; Union meetings in, 108; Union party in, 221–222, 223; United Confederate Veterans in, 316; western migration to, 22–27; Washington County in, 280, 333–334; Wayne County in, 276–277; Whig party in, 84–88, 92

"Indiana Legion," see Indiana, state militia

Indianapolis, In., 144, 304, 333; and Lincoln's funeral train, 284; German Americans in, 106; Masonic Temple, 303; Republican party in, 106; response to war in, 126–127, 272; wartime race riots in, 223

Indian Nations, see Indian Territory

Individualism, see Southern

Index

Ingersoll, Robert G., 304
Internal improvements, 60–61; see also Canals; Railroads; Turnpikes; Middle Border; West, American
Iowa, xvii; border patrols, 243; federal troops from, 148–149, 159, 254; home guards, 243; Republican party in, 226; violence with northern Mo., 148, 243, 247
Iowa troops: 2nd Infantry Regiment, 149
Irish Americans, 26, 58, 129, 223; and dissent, 268; see also Immigration, foreign; "Know-Nothings;" Nativism
Ironclad Oath, see Congress, U.S.
"Irreconcilables," 293
Irreconcilation, 7, 291, 310
Island Mound (Mo.), battle at, 221; see also African Americans, federal military enlistment of, as federal soldiers; Middle Border, African American troops in
Island No. 10 (Mo.), battle at, 199; contraband camp at, 217, 224, 258

Jackson, Andrew, 61, 282
Jackson, Claiborne F., 80, 302; as proslavery "Ultra," 87, 96, 111; at Planters' House conference, 25; driven from office, 141; elected/inaugurated as governor, 111–112; efforts to effect Missouri's secession, 136–137, 139–141; efforts to gain Confederate support for Missouri, 110, 141; issues call for militia volunteers, 141; loyalty of questioned, 186; resolutions to support slavery, 87, 236
Jackson, Jim, 296
Jackson, Mo., 180, 186
Jacksonport, Ar., 173
James, Frank, 248, 321
James, Jesse, 248, 313
Jayhawkers, 100, 148, 153, 154–155, 216, 237, 239, 245, 247, 252, 329; see also Kansas, border war with Mo.; Missouri, border war with Ks., federal troops in
Jefferson, Thomas, 17, 28
Jefferson City, Mo., 111, 140, 141, 260; Lincoln Institute, 294
Jefferson Inquirer (Jefferson City, Mo.), 98
Jeffrey, Alexander, 199
Jennison, Charles, 148, 153, 220, 237; see also Jayhawkers
Jewry/Jews/Judaism, 44; see also Immigration, foreign; German-Americans
"John Brown's Body," 289, 292
Johnson, Allen P., 135–136, 140
Johnson, Andrew, 282–283, 311; "Swing around the circle," 306
Johnson, George W., elected Confederate governor of Ky., 144; death of, 199

Johnson, Waldo P., 148, 301; expelled from U.S. Senate, 182, 214; in Confederate Congress, 182; expatriation, 293
Johnson's Island (Oh.), prison camp at, 172
Johnston, Albert Sidney, 117, 175; death of, 199
Johnston, Annie Fellows, 322; see also *Little Colonel, The*
Johnston, William Preston, 137–138
Joint Committee on the Conduct of the War, see Congress, U.S.
Jones, John S., 82
Jones, Martha M., 160
Jonesboro, Il., 273; Lincoln-Douglas debate at, 100, 103
Journal (Cincinnati, Oh.), 45
Journal (Louisville, Ky.), 247, 317; see Prentice, George D.; Watterson, Henry
Julian, George W., 92, 214, 219, 230, 303, 309

Kansas, xvii, 7, 337; as destination for contrabands/fugitive slaves, 216; border war with Mo., 78–82, 328; emigrant aid societies to, 79, 95; federal troops from/in, 136, 148, 155, 159, 169, 216, 220–221, 282; fugitive slaves to, 237; home guard, 237; Lecompton Constitution, 11, 93, 98–99; national cemeteries, 310; proslavery influences in, 95; "Red-Legs," 238, 330; slavery politics, 78–82, 94–99, 329; statehood of, 11, 98–99, 110; Territory of, 78–82, 94–99; violence in, 99
Kansas troops: 1st Colored Infantry Regiment, 220–221; see also Lane, James Henry
Kansas City, Mo., 156, 238; and Order No. 11, 238, 240; "Confederate tradition" in, 329, 337
Kansas City (Mo.) *Star*, 320
Kansas City (Mo.) *Times*, 313; see also Edwards, John Newman
Kansas-Nebraska Act (1854), see Congress, U.S.; Kansas
Kaskaskia, Il., 28
Kautz, Emma, 287
Kees, John W., 273
Kellogg, William, 213
Kentucky, xvii, 7, 16, 33, 47; abolitionism/antislavery in, 64–65, 66, 103–104, 115, 234; admission to Confederacy, 7, 144; African American military enlistment/troops in, 7, 258–262; African American population in, 293–294, 296, 298, 308–309, 330; anti-free black immigration law, 41, 72–73; anti-abolitionist violence in, 103–104; Appalachian mountain counties in, 85, 121, 244; as source for western migration, 25–27, 30, 38, 50, 66, 80, 84, 93,

Kentucky (*continued*)
98, 108, 144, 301; avoidance of military service in, 205; Baptist Church in, 175, 176, 179–180, 183; Bluegrass subregion in, 23, 75, 88, 121, 164, 166, 200, 205, 244, 258, 296, 322; "Bluegrass System" in, 49–50, 52, 59; colonization societies/colonizationism in, 63, 64–65, 114; commissioners to Ohio from, 3; Confederate Association of, 331; Confederate commissioners to, 121; Confederate military incursion into, 116–119, 165–168, 181, 200–205, 208, 245; Confederate military recruitment in, 165, 202–204; Confederate military enlistments from, 7, 8, 111, 135, 205; Confederate military occupation of, 11, 116–119, 142, 164–168, 181, 200–205; Confederate military veterans in, 294–298, 300, 316–317, 322, 326–327; "Confederate tradition" in, 6, 7, 310–325, 329–330, 330–332, see also Middle Border; Conservative party/conservatives in, 226, 294, 300; constitutional convention of 1849, 87–88; Constitutional Union party, 234; cotton production in, 51; Democratic party in, 83–88, 222, 226, 293, 300; disfranchisement of Confederates/sympathizers, 182, see also Expatriation Law; eastern counties, see mountain counties; economic base of, 50–51, 52; election of 1859 in, 105; election of 1860 in, 105–106; election of 1864 in, 282–283; election of 1870 in, 308–309; elite in, 50–51; emancipation of slaves, 293, 294–296; Emancipationists in, 64, 87–88, 92, 109, 226, 294, 295, 300; Expatriation Law, 182, 296; federal military enlistments in, 131, 205, 207; federal military occupation of, 11, 117–118, 142–143, 144, 165–166, 181–199; federal military veterans in, 294–298, 300, 318–319; federal troops in, 169, 209, 232–234, 277, 295; Fifteenth Amendment, 299, 308–309; first state constitution, 30; Fourteenth Amendment, 299, 306; free blacks in, 41, 64–65, 72–73, 87, 295–298; Freedmen's Bureau in, 296; fugitive slaves in, 74–75, 161, 218–219, 220–221, 225, 254, 258, 295, see also African Americans, as wartime fugitives; Gallatin County in, 187; Garrard County in, 139; German Americans in, 117, 137; Grant County in, 187; Grayson County in, 295–296; Green River subregion in, 168; Green County in, 259; guerrilla violence/guerrillas in, 152–153, 243–253, 290, 295–298; Hard-line warfare in, 11, 117–118, 144, 147–157, 182–199, 211, 237; hemp production in, 51, 60, 81, 88; Henry County in, 261; Home for Confederate Veterans, 316–317; home guard/county militias in, 139, 193, 225, 245; legislature of, 3, 64, 71, 104, 111, 142, 182, 293, 295, 296, 300, 317, 323, 330–331; Logan County in, 163; McCracken County in, 175; Madison County in, 75, 99; martial law declared, 261; Mason County in, 23; Meade County in, 122; Mercer County in, 163; military arrests in, 182–183, 187, 209; military confiscation in, 218–221; national cemeteries, 310; National Legion, 309; northern counties of, 273; neutralism in, 120, 122–123, 130–131; neutrality of, 128, 142, 143, 145; neutrality violated, 142–143; Owen County in, 187; Pendleton County in, 263; Pewee Valley in, 265, 326, 327, see also Home for Confederate Veterans; political contests in, 57–59; population migration to/growth of, 22–27, 93; postwar politics in, 299–300, 311–327; postwar violence in, 294–298, 302; Presbyterian Church in, 66, 207, 230; proslavery influences in, 85–88, 92, 99–100, 109–110, 111, 114, 115, 209–210, 217, 218, 225, 253–262, 294–298, 299, see also Unionism/Unionists; provisional (Confederate) government of, 143–144, 169, 199; racial violence in, 99, 225, 258, 259–262, 294–298, 299, 302, 308–309; railroads in, 53; river frontage mileage in, 130; Republican party in, 178, 179, 221–222; response to John Brown's Raid in, 103–104; postwar return of former Confederate troops, 293–297; revivalism in, 16; Scott County in, 298; secession convention in, 144, 181; secessionism/secessionists in, 114, 115–116, 120, 121, 130–131, 138–139, 142, 164, 179–180, 225; settlement of, 22, 28–29; slave hiring in, 51–52; slave revolts rumored in, 99, 103, 132; slave trade in, 64, 259, 267; slaveholding in, 86–87; slavery in, 10, 37, 41, 42–43, 51–52, 85–87, 294–296, 322; slavery politics in, 3, 64–65, 66, 87–88, 99–100, 105–106, 114–119, 208–210, 294–298; Sons of Confederate Veterans in, 316, 330–331; southern counties of, 163, 169, 205, 243, 258, 295; States' (or "Southern") Rights Party in, 125, 144, 226, 256, see also Conservative/Democratic Party; southern sympathizers in, 123, 181, 203; State Guard militia in, 111, 266; state militia in, 245; "sunk country" in, 16; test oath in, 182; Thirteenth Amendment rejected, 293, 295; tobacco production/culture in, 51; towns/cities in, 55; turnpikes in, 52; *Uncle Tom's*

Cabin Law, 330–331; United Confederate Veterans in, 316–317, 323, 331; United Daughters of the Confederacy in, 315–316, 325, 330–331; Union (or Loyal) Leagues in, 245; Union Democratic Party in, 115, 125, 222, 226, 234; and "Union festivals" in 1860, 1–3, 5; Unionism/unionists in, 6, 115–119, 120, 121–125, 130, 131, 132, 139, 142, 143, 152, 163–164, 179–180, 181, 182–183, 187–188, 197, 198, 204–205, 208–210, 225, 227, 256, 293, 295, 300, 318–319; Warren County in, 158; wartime emancipation of slaves in, 87–88, 254–262; wartime trade interruptions, 196–199, see also Trade permit system (federal); western/Purchase Region in, 81, 85–86, 132, 139, 156, 181, 190, 196, 245, 251, 259, 260–261, 325; Whig party in, 84–88, 91, 114; white residents' views of Confederacy, 120–122; Women's Confederate Monument Association, 320

Kentucky and Virginia Resolutions, 61

Kentucky, Department of (federal), 139

Kentucky, District of (federal), 139

Kentucky "Legion," see Louisville, Ky., home guard militia in; Rousseau, Lovell L.

Kentucky Loyalist, The, 195

Kentucky Military Institute, 131

Kentucky River (Ky.), 22, 163, 168, 202

Kentucky State Flag (Frankfort, Ky.), suppressed, 195

Kentucky Statesman (Lexington, Ky.), 103

Kentucky troops, Federal: 2nd Infantry Regiment, 131; 3rd Cavalry Regiment, 207; 17th Infantry Regiment, 232; 20th Infantry Regiment, 209; 22nd Infantry Regiment, 232; 24th Infantry Regiment, 232

Kentucky Yeoman (Frankfort, Ky.), 139

Key, Thomas M., 127

Key, V. O., 6

Kiefer, Joseph W., 318

Knights of the Golden Circle, 269, 275–276, 283

Knott, J. Proctor, 142; as Mo. attorney general, 138, 142, 182; arrest for refusing Mo. Convention oath, 142

"Know-Nothings," 44, 91, 92, 93; see also American party

Knoxville, Tn., 267

Ku Klux Klan, 296, 297–298, 300, 308, 309, 310, 325, 333; see also Kentucky, racial violence; Missouri, racial violence; Regulators; "White caps"/white-capping

L and N Railroad, see Louisville and Nashville Railroad

Lake Erie, 53, 54

Lancaster, Ky., 309

Lancaster, Oh., 76

Land Ordinance of 1785, 16

Lane, James Henry, 146, 148, 153, 216, 220–221, 238, 239, 247; Kansas Brigade of, 216

Lane Theological Seminary, 68–69, 70; "debates" over slavery, 68–69; see also Abolitionism/ Abolitionists; Cincinnati, Oh.

Lawrence, Amos A., 79; see also Emigrant Aid Societies

Lawrence, Ks., survivors reunions, 321–322; wartime raid on, 13–14, 237–240, 321–322; see also Order No. 11; Quantrill, William C.

Lawrence Massacre, see Lawrence, Ks., wartime raid on

Lawrenceburg, In., 145

Lazear, Bazel F., 239

Lebanon, Ky., African American enlistment violence, 260; Confederate raid on, 210

Lecompton Constitution, see Kansas

Lee, Robert E., 283, 311, 318

Leftwich, William M., 314–315; see also *Martyrdom in Missouri*

Leonard, Abiel, 51–52, 122

Leonard, Nathaniel, 51–52

"Les Pays des Illinois," see Louisiana, Colonial District of

Levies, see Assessments

Lewisport, Ky., 247

Lexington, Ky., 22, 33, 40, 50, 52, 61, 64, 99, 110, 191, 224, 258, 284, 316; African Americans in, 293, 295, 309; and Bragg's Confederate invasion of Ky., 166, 200–201; as African American enlistment site, 258; as "Athens of the West," 50; Baptist Church in, 180; "Confederate tradition" in, 329; economic competition with Louisville, 161; federal military enlistments in, 131; Presbyterian Church in, 178; racial violence in, 309; refugees in, 173; United Daughters of the Confederacy in, 329

Lexington, Mo., 79–82, 180, 225, 316; battle at, 237; "Pro-Slavery Convention of Missouri" in, 79–82

Liberia, 63; see also American Colonization Society; Colonization/colonizationists

Liberal Republicans, 299, 309, 332; see also Republican party

Liberty, Il., 175, 272, 279

Liberty, Mo., 191, 240; arsenal raided, 187

Liberty party, 66, 72, 85

Lieber, Francis, W., 249; "Code," 249, 263; see also Guerrillas

Limbaugh, Jefferson W., 96; see also *Southern Democrat* (Cape Girardeau, Mo.)

Limerick, Patricia Nelson, 9

Lincoln, Abraham, 5–6, 8, 13–14, 135; administration of, 122, 124, 126, 130, 139, 144, 147, 179, 184, 188–189, 196, 197, 198, 200, 221, 222, 226, 227, 234; and black enlistment, 13–14, 219–221; and Border States/politicians, 213–220; and civil liberties, 211, 214–221, 273; and confiscation of property, 219–221; and colonization of freed slaves, 63, 221; and compensated emancipation, 214–215, 216, 219–221; and conscientious objectors, 168; and Constitution, 220; and Corwin Amendment, 112; and Declaration of Independence, 102; and dissenting editors, 273; and election of 1864, 282–283; and free labor ideology, 102; and Henry Clay, 91, 100; and John Brown, 103–104; and Mo. Radicals, 255; and national reconciliation, 283–284; and Republican party, 91–93, 100–102, 103–104; and U.S. Constitution, 102; and war powers, 144–145; and wartime emancipation of slaves, 13–14, 214–221, 224, 255, see also Emancipation Proclamation; and federal commanders, 145–146; and Whig party, 91, 100, 102–103; antislavery moderation of, 90, 91, 93, 100–104; approves General Orders No. 100, 249, see also Lieber Code; as commander in chief, 7, 129, 137; as Illinois state legislator, 18, 60–61; as legal counsel for railroads, 144; as regional antislavery symbol, 36; as U.S. congressman, 84; assassination of, 15, 283–284; authorizes bombardment of Maryland cities, 145; authorizes distribution of arms to Kentucky unionist militia, 139; birthplace monument, 323, see also Hodgenville, Ky.; calls for military volunteers, 116; debates with Stephen A. Douglas, 11, 100–103, see also "Great Debates"; election as U.S. president, 105–106, 144; funeral train, 284; "House Divided" speech of, 103; inauguration as U.S. president, 108, 124, 126, 145, 317; offers compensation for voluntary emancipation, 214–216; opposition to Mexican War, 84; orders wartime hanging of Dakota Sioux, 335; orders martial law, 145; participation in Black Hawk War, 54; presidential cabinet of, 109; racial beliefs of, 100–102; Reconstruction plan of, 283–284; reelection as president, 13; response to Baltimore Riot, 145; response to Lawrence, Ks. raid, 238, 239; river trade policy of, 196; second inaugural address, 283; suspends habeas corpus, 145, 221; view of neutrality as disloyalty, 144–145, 146; views of by proslavery residents, 105–108, 115, 138, 224
Lincoln Farm Association, 323
Lincoln, Ill., 178

Lincoln Institute (Mo.), 294; see also African Americans, as federal military veterans
Lincoln, Mary Todd, 314
Lincoln, Thomas, 37
Lincoln, William W., 284
Lindley, James J., 98
Lists, 185, 192, 194; see also Dominion system; Loyalty/disloyalty; Military occupation
Little Colonel, The, 322; see also Johnston, Annie Fellows
"Little Dixie," see Missouri
"Little Giant," see Douglas, Stephen A.
Living Age, The (New York), 328
Loan, Benjamin F., 237, 250
Locke, David Ross, 299, 309–310; and Abraham Lincoln, 299
Lockland, Oh., 46
Logan, John A., 89, 217, 304, 318
Logan, Mary, 89
Loguen, Jermain, 76–77
Lord, Nathan, 177; see also Churches
Lost Cause, 312–314, 315, 322, 326, 329, 331, 332; and guerrillas/partisans, 313, 320–322; see also "Confederate tradition"; Kentucky; Middle Border; Missouri; Southern; Southerners
Lost Cause (Louisville, Ky.), 319
Louisiana, 19, 28; Colonial District of (French), 15, 16, 27–28, emancipation of slaves in, 292; federal occupation of, 199; see also Illinois, Indiana; secession of, 108; Territory, 28, 63, 90
Louisiana Purchase, 28, 63
Louisville and Nashville Railroad, 1, 114, 115, 116, 196, 200, 210
Louisville and Portland Canal (Ky.), 53
Louisville Pike (Ky.), 117, 201
Louisville, Ky., 171, 306; African Americans in, 77, 258, 293; and Bragg's Confederate invasion of Ky., 200; as African American enlistment site, 258; American Legion, 326–327; Catholic influence in, 58; Confederate enlistments in, 244–45; Confederate parolees in, 244–245; "Confederate tradition" in, 316, 320; Confederate military veterans, 326–327; Democratic party, 303; draft evasion in, 275; economic competition with Lexington, 161; election riots in, 92; Emancipation Day celebrations, 304; Emancipationists in, 92, 304; federal military prison for women, 263 102; federal military veterans in, 326–327, see also Grand Army of the Republic/encampment in; federal troops from/in, 117, 139, 154, 213, 254, 262, 289; foreign-born population of, 58, 117; freedmen's

convention in, 293; fugitive slaves in, 74; Galt House in, 234; German Americans in, 58, 92, 117, 137; Grand Army of the Republic/encampment in, 319–320, 326–327; home guard militia in, 139; military arrests in, 189; military prison, 171; neutralism/neutralists in, 127; New Englanders in, 92; peace convention at, 271; population of, 57; proslavery influence in, 159, 294; racial violence in, 261–262; refugee camp, 267; river trade in, 196; secessionism in, 181; slave population of, 86; slave trade in, 258; Sons of Confederate Veterans in, 320; Southern Expositions in, 318, 331; "Union festival" in 1860 in, 1–3; Unionism/unionists in, 126, 127; United Confederate Veterans in, 331; United Daughters of the Confederacy in, 320, 327; wartime refugees in, 173;
Louisville (Ky.) Journal, 62, 89
Lowell, James Russell, 145–146, 151
Lovejoy, Elijah P., 70–71, 115, 178
Lovejoy, Owen, 71, 91, 212, 219
Lovie, Henry, 204
"Loyal leagues," see Union leagues
"Loyal West," 231, 307, 309, 332; see also Middle Border, war memory in; Military veterans
Loyalty/disloyalty, measures of, 11, 120, 132–133, 147–157, 165, 169, 177, 173–199, 209–210, 225–235, 268–284; and slavery/wartime emancipation, 132, 133, 171, 184, 208–210, 226–235, 249–252, 255, 257, 259–260, 262–268 see also Middle Border; Dominion system; Hardline war; Military occupation; Union leagues
Lundy, Benjamin, 65; see also *Genius of Universal Emancipation*
Lyell, Charles, 44, 57, 75
Lyle, Joel K., 105, 134, 178; driven from Ky. church for Republican politics, 178
Lynchings, postwar, as politicized violence, 287–290, 297–298, 302, 308; see also Guerrillas; Ku Klux Klan; "White caps"/white-capping
Lyon, Nathaniel, 138, 140–141; at Planters' House conference, 140; death, 141; expedition into Mo. interior by, 141, 147; Monument Association, 310–311, see also Springfield, Mo.

McAfee, John, 150
McCabe, John Dabney, 114
McCarroll, Annie Leslie, 181

McClellan, George B., 147, 218; as commander of federal Division of the Potomac, 150; as commander of federal Department of the Ohio, 139, 142, 143; as Democratic presidential candidate in 1864, 234, 281–283; neutrality agreement with Simon B. Buckner, 141–142
McClernand, John A., 129, 217
McCormick, Cyrus, 55
McCulloch, Ben, 199
McCready, James, 322
McDaniel, Reuben, 39
McDonald, Donald, 149
McDowell, Nelson, 250
McElroy, C. H., 190
McEuen, Oliver H., 179
McGuffie, William H., 71; *Eclectic Readers*, 71
McHenry, John, 232
McKown, Bethiah, 194
McLeansboro, Ill., 273
McMullen, J. W. T., 177
McNeil, John, 147, 193, 315
McPheeters, Samuel B., 178
McPherson, James M., 125, 146
Madison, In., 24, 57; contraband camp, 302
Madison, James, 16
Magoffin, Beriah, 105, 123; and secession, 110, 123, 136–137; loyalty questioned, 142, 146; proclamation of neutrality, 137; resigns as governor, 182
Maine, 70; Kennebec subregion, 24
Malvin, John, 73
Marion College (Mo.), 64; see also Palmyra, Mo.
"Man Without a Country," 8; see also Hale, Edward Everett
Manchester, Mo., 173
Mangrum, Dick, 289–290
Mangrum, George, 285–290
Mann, Alfred M., 176
Mann, Horace, 48
Mann, John Preston, 175, 221
Mann, Nancy, 176, 273
Manumissions, see Emancipation; Slavery; Delaware, emancipation of slaves in; Maryland, emancipation of slaves in; Virginia, emancipation of slaves in
Maple, Joseph C., 190
Marietta College (Oh.), 334
Marietta, Oh., 65, 278, 311
Marion, Ill., 129
Marion Record (Marion, Il.), 195
Markham, Norman G., 152
Marmaduke, John Sappington, elected Mo. governor, 301–302
Marshall, Anne E., 310
Marshall, George C., 186
Marshall, Humphrey, 200, 201

Marshall, Mo., 180
Marshall, Thomas, 179
Martial Law, 185, 194–195, 314; see also Dominion system; Loyalty/disloyalty; Military occupation
Martial Law, or Order No. 11, 314; see also Bingham, George Caleb
Martin, Helen, 209–210
"Martyr Monuments," 315; see also Middle Border, "Confederate tradition";in; Public Monuments
Martyrdom in Missouri, 314–315; see also Leftwich, William M.
Maryland, 22, 34, 75; African American enlistment in, 256; as source for western migration, 26, 30, 41; election of 1864 in, 283, see also Elections; emancipation of slaves in, 37, 41, 292; free blacks in, 87; habeas corpus suspended in, 145; legislature of, 145; military arrests in, 145; neutrality stance of, 145; ratifies Corwin Amendment, 112; slave population of, 37, 41, 86; slavery in, 37, 42
Mason-Dixon Line, 5, 132, 334
Massie, Nathaniel, 32, 33
Massachusetts, 47, 48; emancipation of slaves in, 36; supreme court in, 36
Mattoon, Il., 269, 281
Maximilian I, 293
Mayslick, Ky., 27, 51
Maysville, Ky., 75
Measles, as wartime epidemic, 168
Memorialization, see Public Monuments; see also Middle Border
Memphis, Tn., 3, 115, 133, 155, 221, 267; smuggling to, 196; surrender to federal armies, 221
Menard, Pierre, 32
Mennonites, 120; neutrality of, 164; see also Conscientious objectors
Mersman, Joseph J., 58
Metcalfe, Leonidas, 254–255
Metes and bounds, 25
Methodist Church/Methodists, 16, 177; African Episcopal, 189, 280; slavery politics in, 66, 179
Mexican War, see Mexico, U.S. war with
Mexico, as locus for postwar Confederate expatriation, 293, 313; U.S. war with, 84, 142, 184, 243, 248
Miami Canal (Oh.), 44
Miami, Mo., 180, 254; African American enlistment at, 257; contraband camp at, 254, 257, 258
Michigan, xvii; federal troops from, 169, 232, 254
Middle Atlantic region, as source for western migration, 22, 44, 55; defined, 22

Middle Border, 1–4, 110; African Americans in, 72–77; antislavery influences in, 35–36, 90; as "Dixie Frontier," 22; Black Laws in, 69, 72, 87; Confederate commissioners to, 121, 134; Confederate military occupation of, 11, 12, 164–168, 199–205; "Confederate tradition" in, 6, 7, 305, 311–325, 329–330, 330–332; cultural pluralism in, 22–27, 58–59; defined, xvii, 7; drought in 1862, 166, 200, 221; economy of, 50–51, 52; election of 1860 in, 105–112; emancipation politics in, 211–241, 268–284; federal military enlistments in, 127, 129, 140; federal military occupation of, 11, 12; foreign-born population of, 58–59, 106; Hard-line warfare in, 11, 12, 211; idea of middle confederacy in, 94, 110; internal improvements in, 52–53; land sales/valuation in, 53, 81–82; Liberal Republicans and, 309; loyalty/disloyalty in, 11, 12, 115–116, 231, 307, see also Military occupation; memorialization in, 305, 311–325; national cemeteries in, 310; neutrality/neutralism in, 120, 122, 123; "New Departure," 309; opposition to Republican party in, 121–123, 125–126, 135–136, 309; neutrality/neutralism in, 125–126, 130–131; opposition to emancipation, 211–216, 221–226; population growth/migration to, 22–26, 54–55, 57–59; postwar politics in, 291–325; proslavery influences in, 37–42, 44–48, 90, 93, 94–105; racial views of whites in, 47–48, 50, 52; racial violence in, 19–20, 223–224; response to war in, 126–140; slavery/servitude in, 42–43; slavery politics in, 78–113, 211; secession crisis in, 105–113, 120–126; views of South, 52; Unionist war memory in, 231, 307, 311–318; Union Tradition in, 333–338; see also Illinois; Indiana; Kentucky; Missouri; Ohio; West, American
Middle States, 22, 50, 146; see also Illinois; Indiana; Middle Atlantic region; New Jersey; Ohio; Pennsylvania
"Middle West," 9, 337; defined, xvii, 332
Middletown, Oh., 308
Midway, Ky., 261
Midway College (Ky.), 190
Midwest, 9, 337, 338; defined, 334; and slavery narratives, 35–36
Military Academy, U.S., 94, 134, 139, 142, 147, 187, 212, 234, 276
Military arrests (federal), 181–182, 188–189
Military commissions (federal), 185, 195
Military confiscation, 12, 211; of slaves by federal armies, 217–221; see also Congress, U.S

Military conscription, 12, 165, 211, 221–222, 244–245, 280; commutation fees, 275, 276; enrollment, 245, 274–275 95, 100; evasion, 8, 179, 243–246, 274–276; opposition to, 224, 280; seen as inferior to volunteer service, 208; substitutions for, 245, 275, 276; violence as resistance to, 275; see also Dissent/dissenters
Military desertions/deserters, Confederate, 243–244; federal, 8, 247, 274–277; see also Military conscription
Military districts (federal), 185
Military enlistments, across state lines, 131, 140; see also Illinois; Indiana; Kansas; Kentucky; Missouri; Ohio
Military garrisons (federal), 185–186, 254, 276–277, 296; African Americans as, 259, 295–298
Military impressment, see Slaves
Military occupation, 12, 184–199, 206; of civilians' homes, 185; physical effects of, 172; see also Middle Border, Confederate occupation of, federal military occupation of; Civil liberties; Kentucky; loyalty/disloyalty, measures of; Missouri
Military paroles/parolees; Confederate, 243–244; see also Prisoners of war
Military patrols (federal), 186
Military Tract, see Ohio, Military (or Virginia) Tract in
Military tribunals, see Military commissions (federal)
Military veterans, Blue-Gray reunions, 320; "Loyal West" trope, 231, 307; postwar politics, 302–328; organizations, federal, 304, 305, 307; organizations, Confederate/ guerrilla, 316–317, 320–322; see also Commemorations; "Confederate tradition"; Middle border, war memory; Union Triumphant
Militia, state, 188, 245; as slave patrols, 255; class antagonisms in, 188; desertions, 247; racial politics in, 251–252; see also Indiana; Illinois; Kansas; Kentucky; Missouri; Ohio
"Militia draft," see Congress, U.S., Militia Act; Military conscription
Mill Springs (Ky.), battle at, 170, 175, 199
Millikan, Elizabeth, 224
Milton, In., 67
Milwaukee, Wi., 333
Mine Creek (Ks.), battle at, 282
Ministers, see Abolitionism/abolitionists; Churches/faiths; Dissent/dissenters; Proslavery; Slavery; Unionism/unionists
Minnesota, federal troops from, 159
Mississippi, 1, 12; cotton production in, 81; Delta counties in, 81; secession of, 108

Mississippi, Army of (Confederate), 201; see also Bragg, Braxton; Kentucky, Confederate incursion into
Mississippi River, 13, 15, 16, 21, 23, 27, 28, 50, 51, 52, 70, 86, 89, 116, 130, 175, 191, 221, 337; "American Bottom" of, 32; Confederate chain blocks, 142; Kentucky Bend of, 258; Lower Valley of, 163, 200, 232, 243; Upper Valley of, 15, 17, 27–28, 32; wartime trade interruptions, 196, 197
Missouri, xvii, 7, 16; abolitionism/abolitionists in, 64, 78–82, 180, 232, 234; admission to Confederacy, 7, 144; African American population in, 298; African American enlistment in, 256–262; African American troops in, 7, 294, see also African Americans, veterans; and Border State Convention, 138; Andrew County in, 245, 256; anti-free black immigration law in, 41; avoidance of military service in, 205; and Crittenden Compromise, 11; as northwestern state, 94; Boone County in, 94; Boon's Lick subregion of, 24, 38, 39, 50, 53, 78, 79, 86, 154, 246–247, 292; border war with Ks., 78–82, 94–99, 100, 148; Buchanan County in, 157; Burnt District in, 240, 330, see also Order No. 11; Callaway County in, 255; canals in, 53; Cass County in, 239; "Charcoals," see "Radical"/ Republican party; Chariton County in, 251; Clay County in, 240; "Claybanks," see Conservative party; colonization of freed slaves to, 63; contested secession of, 143, 150; controversy over Kansas in, 94–99, 236; Confederate commissioners to, 121; Confederate military incursions into, 51, 61, 104–105, see Price's Raid; Confederate military enlistments in, 7, 8, 181, 205; Confederate military occupation of, 11; Confederate military veterans in, 300–302, 316, 322; Confederate Soldiers Home, 316–317; "Confederate tradition" in, 7, 293, 301–302, 311–322, 328–329, see also Middle Border; Conservative party in, 226, 301; constitutional convention of 1849 in, 72; constitutional convention of 1865 in, 292–293; constitutional convention of 1875 in, 301; Convention government in 141, 143, 182; Convention ("test") oath in, 182, 189, 237, 256, see also Oaths of allegiance; Democratic party in, 84–88, 98, 105, 221–222, 236, 300–302; disfranchisement of Confederates/sympathizers in, 283, 309; Daughters of the Confederacy in, 315, 316; "Drake Constitution" of 1865, 292–293, 300–302;

Missouri (*continued*)
see also Drake, Charles D.; election of 1860 in, 110; economic base of, 50–51; election of 1860 in, 106; election of 1864 in, 283 105, see also Elections; emancipation of slaves in, 213–214, 292, see also Frémont, John C., emancipation proclamation in Mo.; Emancipationists in, 98, 226, 234, 236; Equal Rights League, 294, see also African Americans, citizenship rights pursued, postwar "colored conventions"; federal military enlistments in, 131, 205; federal military occupation of, 11, 143, 181–199; federal troops in, 11, 150, 169, 173, 180, 232; Fifteenth Amendment, 299, 308–309; foreign-born troops in federal armies from, 160, 180; Fourteenth Amendment, 299, 306; free blacks in, 72–73, 87; Freedmen's Bureau in, 296; French colonial governance of, 15; fugitive slaves from/in, 216–221, 256–258, see also African Americans, as wartime fugitives; German Americans in, 15, 78–79, 137, 140, 160, 162, 180, 225, 230, 245, 253–254, 301; guerrilla violence/guerrillas in, 13–14, 152–153, 217, 242–253, 298; Hard-line warfare in, 11, 144, 147–157, 211, 237, 254; hemp production in, 51, 60, 78, 81; home guards in, 137, 138, 150, 245–246, 247; House of Representatives of, 150; Howard County in, 53, 122; Johnson County in, 239; ironclad oath in, 292, see also oaths of allegiance; Jackson County in, 82, 155, 239, 254; Lafayette County in, 82, 186; land values in western counties, 81–82; legislature of, 64, 70, 87, 111, 236, 292, 295; Liberal Republicans in, 309; Linn County in, 260; "Little Dixie" in, 337; martial law declared, 194–195, 213, 261; military arrests in, 188–189; Militia Act of 1858 in, 137; Mormon War/Mormons in, 79; neutrality stance of, 130–131, 145; neutralism in, 120, 130–131; northern counties of, 78, 149, 150, 192, 193; northwestern counties of, 251–252; Order No. 11 in, 239–241, 250, 251 85–87, 101; Ozark subregion of, 78–79, 132, 243, 244, 332; "Paw Paw" militia in, 251–252; Pettis County in, 82; Pike County in, 179; Platte County in, 95; Polk County in, 132; population migration to/growth of, 50, 54, 55, 57, 78–79; postwar expatriation of former Confederates, 293; postwar politics in, 299–302, 305, 311–325; postwar return of former Confederate troops to, 293–297; postwar violence in, 294–298; Presbyterian Church in, 178–179; "Pro-Slavery Convention" in, 79–82, see also Lexington, Mo.; proslavery influences in, 34–35, 70–71, 78–82, 83–99, 110–113, 123–124, 140, 225, 251–252; provisional government of, 141, 182; racial violence in, 132, 294–298; "Radical"/Republican Party in, 94, 180, 221–222, 226, 234, 240, 245, 255–256, 260, 292–293, 295, 298, 300–302, 309; railroads in, 53, 78; Ralls County in, 260; removal of federal troops, 296; river frontage mileage in, 130; "rump" legislature of, 150, 169; St. Louis County in, 192; Saline County in, 186–187, 236, 328, 329; Sons of Confederate Veterans in, 316; secessionism/secessionists in, 120, 123, 131, 132, 136–137, 140, 186–187; southeastern/Bootheel subregion of, 141, 142, 156, 171, 241; slave hiring in, 51–52; slaveholding in, 86–87, 246–247; slave population of, 85–86; slave trade in, 81–82; slavery in, 10, 42–43, 51–52, 78–82, 85–86, 94; slavery politics in, 34, 60, 64, 78–82, 87, 92, 94–99, 123, 225, 292; socio-economy of, 50–51, 60, 80–82; southern counties in, 169; Spanish colonial governance of, 15; state convention of, 123, 125, 137, 138, see also Convention government in; State Guard militia in, 137, 138, 139–140, 141; state militia in, 137, 138, 147, 239, 247–248, 251, 328, see also Enrolled Missouri Militia; statehood of, 35, 41, 62, see also Missouri Compromise; "sunk country" in, 16; supreme court, 328; territorial period of, 32; Thirteenth Amendment, 295; towns/cities in, 55; tobacco production/culture in, 51; United Confederate Veterans in, 316; United Daughters of the Confederacy in, 315–316, 321, 322; "Ultras," 87, 105, 236, see also Democratic party, Proslavery influences in; Union Leagues in, 111; Union Party in, 221–222; Unionism/Unionists in, 120, 121–125, 131, 140, 143, 174, 194, 213, 237, 239, 252, 300–302; Vernon County in, 239; vigilance committees in, 95–96; wartime emancipation of slaves in, 87–88, 254–262; wartime trade interruptions, see Trade permit system (federal); western counties of, 78–82, 95–97, 154, 156, 194, 216, 221, 237, 245, 257–258, 296, 313, 329, see also Order No. 11; western migration to, 26–27, 35, 78, 80–81; Whig party in, 84–88, 91, 133, 180, 236

Missouri, Army of (Confederate), see Price, Sterling, raid in Mo. in 1864
Missouri Compromise, 35, 90, 109; see also Missouri, statehood of
Missouri Democrat (St. Louis, Mo.), 94
Missouri Herald (St. Louis, Mo.), suppressed, 195
Missouri Intelligencer (Fayette, Mo.), 23
Missouri Republican (St. Louis, Mo.), 93–94, 313
Missouri River, xvii, 21, 38, 53, 78, 79, 130, 141, 186, 236, 282, 329; valley of, 236

Missouri State Journal (St. Louis, Mo.), suppressed, 195
Missouri Statesman (Columbia, Mo.), 144
Missouri troops, Confederate: 1st Infantry Regiment, 116–18; Federal: 2nd "Horse" Infantry, 186–187; 9th Infantry Regiment, 131; 13th Infantry Regiment, 131
Missouri Vindicator (St. Joseph, Mo.), *The*, 300; see also Donan, Peter
Mitchel, Ormsby M., 155, 234
Moberly, William, 251
Montague, Lydia, 260
Montgomery, James, 100, 148; as federal commander, 216; see also Jayhawkers
Monuments, 113; see also Middle Border, "Confederate tradition" in
Mooneyham, Daniel, 275
Morehead, Charles S., 188
Morehead, James T., 3
Morgan, John Hunt, 106 18; and Bragg's invasion of Ky., 166, 167, 168, 200, 203–205; as idealized Confederate, 202–204, 262, 313; characterized as guerrilla, 247, 264; racial violence by troops, 251; raids into Ky., 194, 202–204, 205, 210; veterans, 320, 329
Morgan, Thomas Hunt, 106; death of, 210
Mormons, 79, 282; see also Missouri, Mormon War in
Morris, Robert, 122
Morrison, John I., 273
Morrison, William, 32
Morton, Lizzie, 273
Morton, Oliver P., 223, 270, 280, 303; elected to U.S. Senate, 303
Moulder, Jacob, 158
Mound City, Il., 260
Mount Air, see Underwood, Warner L.
Mount Pleasant, Oh., 65, 67; see also Quakers
Mount Sterling, Ky., 160
Mount Zion, Ky., 187
Munfordville, Ky., battle at, 166, 201
Murray, Amelia, 73
My Life at Oxmoor, 331; see also Bullitt, Thomas W.
"My Maryland," 283; see also Randall, James Ryder
"My Old Kentucky Home, Good Night," 327; see also Foster, Stephen; Kentucky, "Confederate tradition" in

Napton, William Barclay, 78–80, 95, 97, 110–111, 112–113, 132, 236, 328–329; Elkhill as home, 328
Napton, William Barclay, Jr., 328–329
Nasby, Petroleum V., 298–300; books, 317; "Letters," 299; see also Locke, David Ross

Nashville, Tn., 3, 200, 317, 319;basin of, 50; smuggling to, 196; Southern Convention in, 94, 123
Nast, Thomas, 317
National Republican party, see Whig party
National Road, 22, 52, 53, 60, 85, 129
National Union party, see Republican party
Native Americans, 16, 25, 54, 63; enslavement of, 28; in Confederate armies, 170; see also Trail of Tears; West, American
Nativism, 44; see also "Know-Nothings;" German-Americans; Immigration, foreign; Irish Americans
Nebraska, xvii; bushwhackers in, 243, 245; refugees in, 245
Neely, Mark E., Jr., 189
Neil, John B., 131
Neil, Robert, 277
Nelson, William "Bull," 139; and Bragg's Confederate invasion of Ky., 200–201; death of, 234
Neosho, Mo., 143, 150; see also Missouri, rump legislature of
Neutrality/neutralism, 6, 11, 120, 121, 124, 181–182, 237; see also Border States; Delaware; Kentucky; Lincoln, Abraham; Loyalty/disloyalty, measures of; Maryland; Military occupation Missouri;
Neville, Oh., 290
New Albany, In., 22, 100, 171, 176, 234; wartime race riots in, 223
New Bedford, Ma., 24
"New Departure," 309, 318; see also Democratic party; Liberal Republicans
New England/New Englanders, 13, 24, 47–48; antislavery activism in, 71, 89; as source for western migration, 23, 24, 25–26, 44, 45, 55, 57, 68, 78–80, 92, 187; emigrant aid societies, 79, 94–96; views of American West, 22, 23, 71, 79, 83, 229; views of slave state residents, 151; see also Northern; Northerners; Southern; Southerners; West, American; Westerners; Yankee/yankees
New Hampshire, 45
New Jersey, 13, 22, 27; as source for western migration, 22, 23, 25–27, 51, 65, 328; emancipation of slaves in, 36; legislature of, 36; slavery/indentured servitude in, 36–37; supreme court of, 36; Thirteenth Amendment, 295
New Liberty, Ky., 187
New Lebanon, NY, 168; see also North Union; Quakers
New Lisbon, Oh., 279
New Madrid, Mo., 15–16, 258; earthquakes at, 15–16

New Orleans, La., 46, 48, 53; battle at, 199; Customs House in, 82; federal occupation of, 199; slave market in, 81; smuggling to, 196
New Richmond, Oh., 70, 285–290
"New South Creed," see South, American; Southern
New York, 13, 284, 323; as source for western migration, 23, 24, 57, 180, 228, 299, 322; "Burned Over District" in, 68, 72, see also Abolitionism/abolitionists; federal military enlistments in, 129; railroads in, 53; western counties in, 228
New York, NY, 55, 70; as source for western migration, 55, 98; emancipation of slaves in, 36; wartime riots in 1863 in, 13; western counties of, 55
New York (NY) Herald, 225
New York (NY) Times, 48
Newport, In., 67
Newport, Ky., foreign-born population of, 58; federal barracks at, 183; federal military prison, 183; federal military prison for women at, 263
Newspapers, 163, 170, 179, 183; suppressions of, 195, 273
Niagara Falls (NY), 263
Niagara River (NY), Roebling suspension bridge at, 162
Nicolay, John, 139
Niles, Hezekiah, 55
"No Party Now But All for Our Country," 249; see also Lieber, Francis W.
North, American, xviii, 2, 5, 44, 47–48; "Lower" states of, 7; "One North" model of, 7
"North and the South, The," 47–48; see also Fisher, Elwood
North Carolina, as source for western migration, 25–27, 37, 78
North Union, NY, 168; see also Shakers
Northern, meanings of, 8, 9–10, 229–231; and exclusivism, 9–10, 13, 307, 309–310; and modernity, 310; and slavery/emancipation, 159, 230–231; as political descriptor in West, 104, 159, 230–231; collectivism as a cultural facet of, 8, 102, 231; Republican party as representative, 310; "regiments," 159; respect for law as facet of, 310, 332; restraint from violence as facet of, 310, 332; southerners as negative reference, 309–310, 332; see also northerners
Northerners, xviii, see also North, American; Northern
"Northwest Confederacy," see Dissent/dissenters, and secret societies
Northwest Ordinance (1787), 10, 17–18, 37, 43; Article VI of, 28–29, 31, 32, 34–36, 39, 43; see also Old Northwest; Slavery

Northwest Territory, 25, 28, 29; see also Old Northwest
Noted Guerrillas, 313; see also Edwards, John Newman
Noyes, Edward F., 156

Oaths of allegiance, 156, 185, 189–192, 244, 253; see also Dominion system; Loyalty/disloyalty; Military occupation
Oberlin College, 69, 74, 294; see also Lane Theological Seminary; Weld, Theodore Dwight
Observer (St. Louis, Mo.), 70
Occupation, see Military occupation; see also Martial Law
Official Records (OR), 249
Ogden, George W., 24
Oglesby, Richard J., 231
Ohio, xvii, 7, 150, 284; abolitionism/abolitionists in, 3, 64, 65, 69–70, 71–72, 100, 222; and comity laws, 71; anti-black immigration law in, 41, 89; as source for western migration, 55, 78, 96, 100, 117, 157, 190, 238; Anti-Slavery Society of, 69, 70; Ashtabula County in, 70; "Black Laws" of, 3–4, 10, 73, 74, 89, 103, 109, 303, 307; "Black Swamp" subregion of, 54, 55; Brown County in, 65; Butler County in, 279; canals in, 53; Clermont County in, 285–290; colonization societies in, 63; Columbiana County in, 45; comity laws in, 34, 109; Confederate military enlistments from, 136; congressional delegation from, 62, 109; constitution of, 31, 32–34; Delaware County in, 74; Democratic party in, 4, 46, 84–88, 103, 107, 109, 127, 221–222, 260, 276, 305–311, 333; economy of, 47–48; election of 1860 in, 106; election of 1864 in, 282–283, see also Elections; federal troops from, 154, 169, 223, 320; federal military enlistments in, 127, 129–130; federal military veterans, 304–311, 320; Fifteenth Amendment, 299, 307–308; foreign-born troops in federal armies, 160; Fourteenth Amendment, 299, 303, 306–307; free blacks in, 34, 41, 73; fugitive slave law of, 3–4, 109; fugitive slaves in, 74–75, 88–89, 161; guerrillas in, 290; Hamilton County in, 46, see also Cincinnati, Oh.; home guards in, 290; House of Representatives of, 1; legislature of, 1, 3, 4, 61, 89, 129, 161; Lincoln's speeches in, 103; Military (or Virginia) Tract in, 22, 25, 26, 32–33, 108, 128, 222; municipal elections of 1861 in, 108; neutrality/neutralism in, 136; opposition to wartime emancipation, 222; population

migration to/growth of, 25–26, 54, 55; postwar politics, 302–311, see also "Bloody shirt"; proslavery influences in, 32–34, 43, 74–75, 109, 128, 223, 299; railroads in, 53; ratifies Corwin Amendment, 112; ratifies Thirteenth Amendment, 303; Republican party in, 103, 127, 221–222, 230, 318, 333; Ross County in, 25, 311; Sons of Confederate Veterans in, 316; secession support in, 128, 129, 130; slavery/indentured servitude in, 32–34; slavery politics in, 3, 4, 29, 32–34, 44–48, 62, 65, 67, 68, 84, 85, 103, 104–105; southern cultural influences in, 25–26, 214, 299; southern counties of, 55, 90, 109, 128, 129–130, 136, 214, 230, 305; state capitol in, 1; statehood of, 29, 32–33; supreme court of, 71; territorial period of, 32–33; Trumbull County in, 67; Underground Railroad in, 67, 333, 336; "Union festivals" in, 1–3, 5; Union party in, 127, 221–222, 307; United Confederate Veterans in, 316; violence over slavery in, 100; western migration to, 22–27; Western Reserve in, 2, 25, 65, 67, 69, 70, 73, 85, 89, 108, 127, 147, 163, 311; Whig party in, 84–88, 108

Ohio, Army of the (federal), 208; and Bragg's Confederate invasion of Ky., 200; Society of, 304; see also Buell, Don Carlos; Perryville (Ky.), battle at

Ohio, Department of the (federal), 139, 254, 280

Ohio River, xvii, 1, 2, 3, 5, 6, 10, 15, 16, 21, 22, 23, 24, 25, 26, 27, 32, 34, 37, 38, 52, 57, 86, 127, 130, 161, 215, 288, 307, 320; and fugitive slaves, 41, 73–77; Valley, 1, 17, 22, 37, 54, 88; wartime trade interruptions, 197

Ohio State Journal (Columbus, Oh.), 54

Ohio troops: 2nd Infantry Regiment, 131; 20th Infantry Regiment, 215

Old Northwest, 25, 26, 35, 36, 37, 39, 41, 47, 52, 79; see also Northwest Ordinance; Northwest Territory

Old Republicanism, see Proslavery; Unionism/unionists, and slavery

Old Southwest, 54, 86

Olds, Edson B., 222

Oliver, William, 38

Olmsted, Frederick Law, 23

Olney, Il., 273

Order of American Knights, 268

Order No. 11, 239–241, 250, 251, 263, 321, 330; see also Ewing, Thomas, Jr; Missouri; Quantrill, William, raid on Lawrence, Ks.

Orphan Brigade (Ky.), Confederate, 323

Orth, Godlove S., 90

Orphan Brigade, 55; see also Kentucky, Confederate military enlistments from

Osage River (Mo.), 148

Osceola, Mo., sack of, 148, 237; see also Jayhawkers; Lane, James Henry

Owens, Cora, 135, 159, 265

Owensboro, Ky., 3

Oxford, Oh., 71

Oxmoor, see Bullitt, William C.

Pacifism, see Conscientious objectors

Paducah, Ky., 74, 77, 105, 228, 259; federal military occupation of, 142

Paine, Eleazer A., 260–261

Palmer, John M., 234, 294, 304, 309

Palmyra, Mo., 64, 151, 191, 248; Confederate Monument Association, 315; martyr monument at, 315; mass execution at, 248–249

Panics, of 1819, 61; of 1837, 53

Paris, Il., 273

Paris, Ky., 75, 203, 293, 309; African Americans in, 293–294, 309

Parke, Thomas Moore, 24–25

Parker, Daniel, 289

Parker, John P., 67, 73

Parsons, John, 22, 67

Parsons, Thomas W., 132, 160

Partisan Ranger Act, see Confederate States of America

Partisans, 152, 186; as guerrillas, 247; idealization by southerners/southern sympathizers, 203, 247; politicized violence, 204–205, 238; racial violence, 251; Union, 238; see also Confederate States of America, Partisan Ranger Act of; Guerrillas; Morgan, John Hunt; Quantrill, William C.; Red-Legs

"Pathfinder of the West," see Frémont, John C.

Patrols, see Military patrols

Patterson, Robert, 33

Patriot (Boonville, Mo.), suppressed, 195

Paul the Apostle (Saul of Tarsus), 15

"Paw Paw" militia, see Missouri

Payne, Robert G., 3

Pea Ridge (Ar.), battle of, 170, 199; see also Elkhorn Tavern, Ar.

Peace Convention, 123, 188; see also Unionists; Washington, D.C.

Peck, John Mason, 50

Pekin, Il., 228

Pennsylvania, 13, 22, 33, 92, 112, 114, 284; as source for western migration, 22, 23, 25–27, 55, 57, 68, 135; Bucks County in, 45; emancipation of slaves in, 36; federal military enlistments in, 129; federal troops in, 169; railroads in, 53

Personal liberty laws, 89; see also Congress, U.S., Fugitive Slave Act (1850)

Perryville (Ky.), battle at, 167–168, 201, 208
Peter, Frances Dallam, 176, 191
Pettus, Euphrasia, 265
Phelps, John S., 51, 132, 140
Philadelphia, Pa., 70, 92, 161; response to Fort Sumter in, 161
Philanthropist, The, 45, 48, 70, 74; see also Birney, James Grandison
Phillips, David Cleaver, 294, 295–296
Phillips, Wendell, 216, 309
Phinney, Jerry, 75
Picket Guard (Chester, Il.), suppressed, 275
Pillow, Gideon, 200
Pilot Knob (Mo.), battle at, 282
Pinckney, D. J., 64
Pirtle, Alfred, 232
Pittsburg Landing (Tn.), battle at, 169; see also Shiloh (Tn.)
Pittsburgh, Pa., 16, 24, 92
"Plan of salvation," see Guerrillas, counterinsurgency against; Kentucky, guerrilla warfare/guerrillas in; Paine, Eleazer A.
Planters' House conference, see St. Louis
Platte City, Mo., 315
Platte County Conservator (Weston, Mo.), suppressed, 195
Pleasant Hill, Ky., 163, 164, 166–168; see also Quakers
Poague, John, 129
Point Pleasant, Oh., 142
Poison Spring, Ar., racial atrocity at, 241, 260
"Political prisoners," 200; see also Habeas corpus suspensions; Military arrests (federal);
Polk, James K., 84
Polk, Leonidas, 116, 143
Polk, Trusten, expelled from U.S. Senate, 182, 214; in Confederate Congress, 182; expatriation, 293
Pollard, Edward A., 312; see also Lost Cause
Pope, John, 146, 150, 311; and assessments, 192
Popular sovereignty, 78–82, 90, 100; see also Democracy, and slavery; Douglas, Stephen A.; Kansas, slavery politics of
Porter, William S., 57; see also "Cincinnati Panorama of" 1848
Posey, Thomas, 30, 32
Potter, David M., 8, 229
Powell, Lazarus W., 193, 212–213; proposes amendment protecting slavery, 212–213; temporarily expelled from U.S. Senate, 182;
Prairie du Rocher, Il., 28
Pratt, William Moody, 139, 180
Prentice, George D., 247, 317
Presbyterian Church/Presbyterians, 22, 46, 207; slavery politics in, 64, 66, 161, 178–179
Presbyterian Herald (Louisville, Ky.), 195

Preston, Margaret, 263
Preston, William, 135, 138; expatriation, 293; joins Confederate army, 135
Prickett, Thomas, 177
Price, Sterling, 79, 136, 175, 178, 240; at Planters' House conference, 140 25; campaign in Missouri, 141; chairman of Mo. secession convention, 136, 147; commander of Mo. State Guard, 139–141, 188; neutrality agreement with William S. Harney, 140, 142; expatriation, 293; Raid into Mo. in 1864, 281–282
Princeton, In., 179
Princeton, Ky., 27
Princeton (NJ) Theological Seminary, 70
Prisoners of war, 171–172;
"political," 200; see also Military arrests
Prison camps/prisons, 171–172
"Pro-Slavery Convention of Missouri," see Missouri
Proslavery, defined;xvii and conservatism, 12, 226; and loyalty/disloyalty, 11, 183–184, 221–235; in Middle Border, 37–42, 44–48, 78–88, 94–99; in South, 48; ministers, see Churches/faiths; Old Republican beliefs, 226, see also Unionism/unionists, and slavery; opposition to wartime emancipation, 211–216, 222–235, 253–262; politicized use of terms abolition/abolitionist, 107, 115, 116, 124, 132, 135, 136, 144, 149, 159, 160, 161, 165, 178, 179–180, 222; see also Illinois; Indiana; Kansas; Kentucky; Missouri; Ohio; West, American
Protection organizations, see Dissent/dissenters; Home guards; Union leagues; Vigilance committees
Provisional Enrolled Missouri Militia, 251; see also Enrolled Missouri Militia; Missouri, state militias in
Provost marshals, 32; and military enlistment of African Americans, 259; federal, 151, 185, 190, 191, 225, 244, 251, 281; killed in Ky., 260; see also Dominion system; Loyalty/disloyalty; Military occupation
Provost marshal generals, 199
Public monuments, 310–311
Pugh, George E., 107, 311
Pulpit Politics, see Christy, David; Churches/faiths
Purcell, Edward, 302

Quakers, 24, 37, 42, 65–66, 67, 84, 89, 92, 120, 168, 257; and slavery, 45, 63, 66, 67, 89, 92, 99, 163; Cincinnati (Oh.) Meeting, 45; federal military enlistment of, 164; South River (Va.) Meeting, 45

Quantrill, William C., 240, 245, 315, 321; postwar idealization of, 313, 330; raid on Lawrence, Ks., 237–238, 321–322; veterans reunions, 320–322; see also Edwards, John Newman; Guerrillas; Order No. 11
"Queen City of the West," see Cincinnati, Oh.; Ohio River
Quincy (City), Il., 23, 275–276, 280, 281; Lincoln-Douglas debate at, 100
Quincy (Il.) *Herald*, 275

Rabbis, see Jewry/Jews/Judaism
Race and Reunion, 6; see also Blight, David W.; Reconciliation
Radicalism/radicals, as pejorative term, 226; see also Republican party, Radical faction in
Railroads, 53; see also Illinois; Indiana; Kentucky; Middle Border; Missouri; Ohio
Randall, James Ryder, 283–284; see also "My Maryland"
Rankin, Adam, 22
Rankin, John, 63
Rawlins, John, 304
"Rebel Democracy," see Kentucky, Democratic party, postwar politics in; Missouri, Democratic party, postwar politics in
Reconciliation, 6, 7; see also Irreconciliation
Reconstruction, 299, 300, 303, 306–307, 310, 317–318, 330, 331, 332, see also Fifteenth Amendment; Fourteenth Amendment; South, American
"Red-Legs," 238; see also Kansas; Partisans
Reed, Henry, 127–128
Reed, John Shelton, 6–7
Reed, Mary Louisa, 175
Reeves, Tim, 246
Refugees, 172–175, 239–240; African Americans, 296
Region and regionalism, defined, xvii, 9–10
"Regulators," 19–20, 77, 280, 296, 308; "Negro," 251, 296; "Union," 298; see also Illinois, racial violence in; Home guards; Kentucky, racial violence in; Vigilance committees; "White caps"
Reid, John W., expelled from U.S. House, 214
Religious revivals, 16; see also Kentucky, revivalism in
Renan, Ernest, 6
Republican Party, 8, 12, 83, 91–113, 220–222; abolitionist wing of, 106, 177, 212; and election of 1862, 221–222; and federal military veterans, 304–311, see also "Bloody shirt": and National Union party, 13, 282–283; and wartime emancipation, 12, 226–232; Conservative faction in, 12, 92, 226; control of U.S. Congress by, 107, 211; in Congress, 214; Liberal faction of, 299, 309, see also Liberal Republicans; ministers as, 177–181, see also Churches/ faiths; moderates in, 211; postwar politics, 299–301, 303–308, 309, 311, 318, see also "Bloody shirt"; Radical faction of, 13, 92, 109, 155, 220, 222, 299, 303, 306–307, 313, 318, see also Missouri; Union Leagues as arm of, 227–228, 281–283; western influences/origins of, 91–92, 100–103, 211, 226, 299; see also Abolitionism/Abolitionists; Delaware; Kentucky, Emancipation Party in; Maryland; Missouri; Union Party
"Retaliatory Tax," see Assessments
"Reverse underground railroad," 18–20, 74, 77; see African Americans, free; Crenshaw, John Hart; Slavery; West, American, slavery in
Reynolds, Henry R., 42–43
Reynolds, Thomas, 64
Reynolds, Thomas Caute, 301
Rhode Island, emancipation of slaves in, 36
Rhyne, J. Michael, 291
Rice, David, 64
Rice, James, 154
Rice, John, 154
Rich, Lucius L., 117
Richardson, William A., 223
Richmond, In., 99, 277
Richmond (Ky.), battle at, 166, 200–201, 203
Richmond, Va., 48, 141, 319; slave population of, 86
Ridgway, Lizzie, 175
Rio Grande River (Tx.), 335
Ripley, Oh., 63, 67, 75; see also Abolitionism/ abolitionists; Antislavery; Underground Railroad
Ripley (Oh.) *Bee*, 109
Roberts, St. Clair, 121
Robinson, James F., 256
Robinson, Marius R., 67, 69
Robinson, Stuart, 178
Rock Island, Il., prison camp at, 171, 172
Rockport, In., 127, 176, 273
Roebling, John A., 161–162; Ohio River bridge at Cincinnati, 162, 332
Rolla, Mo., 140
Rollins, James S., 91, 94
Roosevelt, Theodore, 323, 327
Rosecrans, William S., 168, 232; as commander of federal Army of the Cumberland, 267; as commander of federal Department of the Missouri, 260, 261, 282
"Rose-water policy," 153; see also Conciliation; Confiscation; Middle Border, federal military occupation of;

500   *Index*

Rousseau, Lovell H., 137, 139, 300; see also Kentucky "Legion"
Rowan, John, 336; Federal Hill as home, 336; see also Bardstown, Ky.; Foster, Stephen
Ruffin, Edmund, 48, 130
Russellville, Ky., 143, 181, 297; see also Kentucky, secession convention in

St. Clair, Arthur, 29
Ste. Genevieve, Mo., 28
St. Joseph (Mo.) *Herald*, 301
St. Joseph, Mo., 149, 300
St. Louis, Mo., 23, 28, 35, 52, 54, 63, 92, 156, 171, 184, 301; African American population in, 293, 298 3, 110; and Price's Raid in 1864, 282; Anti-Abolitionist Society in, 71; Black Code in, 71; Camp Jackson riot in, 138, 181; dissent/dissenters in, 178, 314–315; election riots in, 92; Emancipationists in, 309; freedmen's convention in, 293; GAR national encampment, 319; manufacturing in, 57–58; federal arsenal in, 136; foreign-born population of, 58; fugitive slaves in, 74; Gateway Arch in, 336–337; German Americans in, 58, 78, 92, 137–138, 226, 301, 309; Gratiot Street prison, 171, 189; Irish Americans in, 58; Liberal Republicans born in, 309; Lindell's Grove near, 137; martial law in, 194; ministers, 178, 314–315; municipal election of 1861, 138; New England influences in, 57, 78, 79, 153, 213; Planters' House conference, 140; population of, 57, 78; prisons in, 171, 189, 277; proslavery influences in, 159, 224; refugees in, 173, 328; Republican/Radical party in, 94, 226, 309; river trade in, 196; secessionism/secessionists in, 137, 138, 194; slavery in, 70, 73, 86; slavery politics in, 70–71, 78, 80; southern sympathizers in, 178, 265–266, 328; Union League in, 298; Unionists/Unionism in, 153, 178, 194, 225, 298
St. Louis (Mo.) *Times*, 70
Salem, Il., 273
Salem, In., 273
Salem, Oh., 89; Western Anti-Slavery Society of, 89; see also Quakers
Saline City, Mo., 186
Saline River (Il.), 16, 18
Salt, in history, 15; distribution in West, 17; making of in Illinois, 15, 16–18; see also Illinois
Sand Creek (Co.), atrocity at, 335
Sandersville, Ky., 105
Savannah, Ga., 82; Johnson Square in, 82; slave population of, 86

Sawyer, Samuel L., 82
Sayre, Mildred, 130
Schofield, John M., and guerrilla warfare, 247–248, see also Enrolled Mo. Militia; as commander of Department of the Missouri, 193, 196, 234, 238–239, 243, 247–248, 260; as commander of Mo. State militia, 157; issues General Orders No. 135, 256, see also Missouri, African American enlistment in
Schools/colleges, 131, 159, 176, 190, 201, 259, 294; freedpeople's, 260, 294
Schurz, Carl, 301, 309
"Scioto gentry," 32; see also Ohio, slavery politics in
Scioto River (Oh.), 25
Scott, Elvira A. W., 180, 247, 253, 254, 257, 264
Scott, Ettie, 192
Scott, John P., 180, 188
Scott, Winfield, 88, 145, 248
"Scouts," see Military patrols (federal)
Scrogin, Susan Terrill, 181
"Secesh," 116, 129, 130, 155, 156, 160, 168, 173, 174, 175, 176, 177, 180, 181, 191, 222, 230, 245, 258, 264, 266, 268, 272, 275; defined, 151; see also Loyalty/disloyalty; Secession; Soldiers, federal, views of slaveholding/slavery; Unionism/unionists, views of
Secession, 107–112, 121, 125–126, 128–129, 131–132, 135–136
Secessionism/secessionists, 194; cultural arguments of, 133–134; racial foundation of, 121; see also Middle Border; Illinois; Indiana; Kentucky; Missouri; Ohio
Secret societies, see Dissent/dissenters; see also Knights of the Golden Circle; Order of American Knights; Sons of Liberty
Sectionalism, defined, 9; in middle border, 83
Second Confiscation Act, see Military confiscation, of slaves by federal armies
Sedalia, Mo., 156; Union league, 298
Senate, U.S., 112, 222; Committee of Thirteen of, 123; Committee on the Territories, 90; composition of, 221; "Crittenden Compromise" in, 109
Seven Years' War, 27
Seward, William H., 145, 147
Shakers, 120, 163–168, 251; and slavery, 163–164; federal military enlistment of, 164; unionism of, 164; White Water, Oh., 276; see also Pleasant Hill, Ky.; South Union, Ky.
"Shakertown," see Pleasant Hill, Ky.
Shane, John Dabney, 22
Shannon, Wilson, 3–4, 71, 80

Shawneetown, Il., 16, 17, 19, 280; Bank of Illinois in, 17
Shelby and His Men, or the War in the West, 313; see also Edwards, John Newman; Shelby, Joseph O. "Jo"
Shelby, Isaac, Jr., 132–133
Shelby, Joseph O. "Jo," 187, 240, 250, 301; postwar idealization of, 313; postwar exile, 293; see also Edwards, John Newman
Shelby, Thomas H., 121
Sheridan, Philip, 7, 335–336; and "Great Triumvirate," 304; and Union Triumphant trope, 304
Sherman, John, 181, 212
Sherman, William T., 7, 149–150, 154, 181, 189, 238, 319, 335; and "Great Triumvirate," 304; and hard-line war, 154, 181; and military confiscation of slaves, 218; and Union Triumphant trope, 304; March through Ga., 241
Shiloh (Tn.), battle of, 170, 171, 199, 208; see also Pittsburg Landing (Tn.)
Sigel, Franz, 146
Sides, Henry, 77
Siebert, Wilbur H., 332–333
Simpsonville, Ky., racial atrocity at, 260, 262
Sioux, Dakota, wartime hanging of, 335; see also Lincoln, Abraham
Skiff, John, 198–199
Slave catchers, 73, 74, 76, 100; see also Fugitive Slave Law
Slavery, 45; abolition of in British West Indies, 76; and Native Americans, 28; and Northwest Ordinance, 17–18, 35–36; and "reverse underground railroad," 18; as democratic principle in West, 78–82, 228; as facet of regionalism, 10; as positive good, 47–48; forms of maintenance of, 73; French practices of, 18; in American West, 35–42; in middle border cities, 73, 85–86; indentured/contract servitude as, 29–32; on middle border, 21, 27–36, 73–77; politics of, 2–4, 34–42, 72, 78–113; see also African Americans; Abolitionists, Abolitionism, Antislavery; Delaware; Emancipation, Emancipationists, Kentucky; Maryland; Middle Border; Missouri; Native Americans; Proslavery, South, American, slavery in; Thirteenth Amendment; West, American, slavery in
Slavery Inconsistent with Justice and Good Policy, 64; see also Rice, David
Slaves, as informants, 173; fugitive, 62, 65, 73–77, 88–89, 95, 100, 109, 119, 125, 172, 216–221, 222–226, 254, 289; hiring of, 73–74; impressment as military laborers, see Military impressment; in western river trade, 74, 89; post-Revolutionary emancipation of, 36–37; preachers, 75; wartime emancipation of, 253–262; see also Emancipation; Slavery, wartime erosion of
Smith, Edmund Kirby, 166, 200, 201, 202
Smith, Caleb B., 92, 220; resigns from cabinet post, 220
Smith, Thomas C. H., 311
Smithland, Ky., 42; federal military occupation of, 142
Smuggling, see Contraband goods; Trade permit system (federal)
Snedecor, Issac M., 255
Snowden, Jacob, 245
Society of Friends, see Quakers
Society of the Army of the Cumberland, see Cumberland, Army of the (federal)
Society of the Army of the Ohio, see Ohio, Army of the (federal)
Society of the Army of the Tennessee, see Tennessee, Army of the (federal)
Soldiers, federal, views of emancipation, 227, 231–234, 247, 275–276; views of slaveholding/slavery, 151–152, 155, 156, 173–174; voting in 1864 election, 282, 283; see also Armies
Sons of Confederate Veterans (SCV), 316; see also Kentucky; Middle Border, "Confederate tradition" in; Missouri
Sons of Liberty, 269, 280; see also Dissent/ dissenters
South, American, xviii, 5; as source for western migration, 79, 268; Border region of, 6–7; Deep region of, 105; middle border relations with, 46; "One South" model of, 7, 315; "New South Creed," 317–318, 320; plantation agriculture in, 47–48; slavery in, 2, 47–48; see also Confederate States of America; Secession; Reconstruction
South Carolina, 15, 19, 48; as source for western migration, 22, 26–27, 66, 98, 150; secession of, 262; slavery in, 85; towns/cities in, 55
South Union, Ky., 163, 164–166, 251; see also Shakers
Southern, meanings of, 2–3, 6, 7, 8, 9–10, 96–98, 132–136; and exclusivism, 9–10, 13, 131, 290, 309–310; antimodernism as facet of, 160, 309–310, 312–313; as negative reference point for northerners, 309–310; as political descriptor in West, 46, 96–98, 104, 152, 157; as region, 22; conceptions of Union within, 134–135; Confederate service/sympathy as facet of, 165, 296; ethnocentrism as facet of, 160; individualism as cultural facet of, 8, 96; localism as cultural facet of, 310, 329–330;

Southern, meanings of (*continued*)
  "New South Creed" and, 317–318;
  slaveholding/slavery as foundation of, 96, 115, 135–136, 152, 158–159, 312;
  victimization as cultural facet of, 96, 158, 312; violence as a cultural facet, 309–310, 332; war sacrifice as facet of, 314–316, 320, 322; see also Southerners
"Southern Convention," see Nashville, Tn.
Southern Advocate (Weston, Mo.), 97
Southern Bivouac (Louisville, Ky.), 319
Southern Democrat (Cape Girardeau, Mo.), 96
Southern Press (Washington, D.C.), *The*, 48; see also Fisher, Elwood
Southerners, xviii, 6–7; as western migrants, 22; idealization of Confederates, 203–204; of culture, 12, 115, 116–117, 132–35, 157; political, 12, 134, 157–61, 203, 205, 206; politicized use of abolition/abolitionist, 107, 115, 116, 124, 132, 135, 136, 144, 149, 159, 160, 161, 165, 178, 179–180, 206, 210, 228, 264, 296; as unionists, 115, 116–117, 134–135, 204–205; views of Lincoln, see Lincoln, Abraham; see also South, American
Southernization, see Southern, and exclusivism
Spain, U.S. war with, see Spanish-American War
Spanish-American War, 326
Speed, James, 87, 220, 226
Speed, Joshua F., 124, 139, 212, 214, 220
Speed, Thomas, 318; see also *Union Cause in Kentucky, The*; *Union Regiments of Kentucky, The*
Springfield, Il., 13, 89, 91, 103, 108
Springfield, Mo., 140, 141, 156; see also Wilson's Creek (Mo.), battle of; national cemetery, 311, 316
Squatter Sovereign (Atchison, Ks.), 95; see also Stringfellow, John H.; Kansas, proslavery influences in
Stanbury, Henry, 75
Stanton, Edwin M., 168; as U.S. secretary of war, 183, 192–193, 200, 220, 224–225
Steamboats, 74, 76; see also Slaves, in western river trade
Steel, Frank F., 136
Steele, R. B., 191
Stephens, Alexander H., 201 Stevens, Thaddeus, 303 Stewart, Robert M., 98, 111 Stewartsville, Mo., 149 Stinson, Caleb, 295–296 Stowe, Harriet Beecher, 70, 89, 327; see also *Uncle Tom's Cabin* Stratton, Paulina, 155, 256 Streiff, Leonard, 137 Stringfellow, John H., 95, 96, 98; see also *Squatter Sovereign*; Kansas, proslavery influences in Stuckey, William R., 273
Sudduth, Ellen, 175

Sumner, Charles, 303
Supreme Court, U.S., 4; *Dred Scott v. Sanford* (1857), 11, 100
Sutherland, Daniel E., 242
Switzler, William F., 133, 143–144

Tappan, Arthur, 68, 69
Tardiveau, Bartolomei, 29
Tarpley, Charles C., 274–275
Taylor, Zachary, 84, 88
Tecumseh, uprising of, 16; see also Native Americans
Tennessee, 266; and desertions/draft evasion, 244; as source for western migration, 25–27, 37, 50, 78, 80; Confederate troops in, 141; eastern counties of, 200, 219, 267; federal occupation of, 199; fugitive slaves from/in, 258; middle region of, 267; provisional army of, 137; slavery politics in, 2–4; state militia of, 116; towns/cities in, 55; "Union festivals" in 1860, 1–3; western region of, 141
Tennessee, Army of the (federal), 30; Society of (SAT), 304
Tennessee River, 52, 74, 86, 130, 142; valley of, 17
Terre Haute, In., 28, 222, 272, 273
Terrell, Bettie, 190
Test Oath, see Congress, U.S., Ironclad Oath; see also Missouri
Texas, annexation of, 84, 97; secession of, 108
Thayer, Eli, 79; see also Emigrant Aid Societies
Thirteenth Amendment, 6, 293; see also Corwin, Thomas, U.S. Constitutional amendment protecting slavery by
Thomas, Daniel L., 280
Thomas, Lorenzo, 147
Thompson, Richard W., 84
Thwaites, Reuben Gold, 334
Timberclads, see Western Flotilla
Times (Chicago, Il.), *The*, 273
Titus, Charles H., 24
Tocqueville, Alexis de, 35
Tod, David, 109, 127
Todd, George, 315
Toledo, Oh., 299; wartime race riots in, 223
Toombs, Robert, 48
Tourgée, Albion W., 318
Trade permit system (federal), 185, 196–199; loyalty politics in, 197–199; see also Dominion system; Loyalty/disloyalty; Military occupation
Trail of Tears, 63; see also Native Americans
Trans-Mississippi Department (Confederate), 248
Transylvania Colony, 28; see also Kentucky, settlement of

Travellers' Rest (Ky.), 266, 267; see also Warren, Susan Shelby
Trenton, Mo., 305
Tribune (St. Joseph, Mo.), suppressed, 195
Trimble, John Allen, 108–109, 130
True American, The (Lexington, Ky.), 64–65, 104; see also Clay, Cassius M.
True Presbyterian (Louisville, Ky.), 178
Trumbull, Lyman, 234, 309
Turner, Frederick Jackson, 337–338
Tuttle, James M., 149, 319
Twain, Mark, see Clemens, Samuel L.

Über der Rhein, see Cincinnati, Oh., foreign-born population in
Uncle Tom's Cabin, 89, 327, 335; as play, see Kentucky; see also Stowe, Harriet Beecher
Underground Railroad, 62, 67, 71, 333, 336
Underground Railroad from Slavery to Freedom, The, 333; see also Siebert, Wilbur H.
Underwood, Johanna L. "Josie," 114–119, 133, 176
Underwood, Joseph, 114
Underwood, Lucy, 115, 117
Underwood, Warner L., 88, 114, 116, 117, 119, 262; Mount Air as home of, 114–119
Underwood, Warner L., Jr., 116, 117
Union Cause in Kentucky, The, 318–319; see also Speed, Thomas
Union Humane Society, see Mount Pleasant, Oh.; Lundy, Benjamin
Union, national, concept of, 2, 3
"Union festivals" in 1860, 1–3, 5, 6; see also Indiana, Kentucky, Ohio, Tennessee
Union leagues, 227–229, 249, 278, 293, 298, 304; African Americans in, 298; as home guards, 228, 272, 277, 279, 280; membership of, 228; see also Republican party; see also Unionism/Unionists, unconditional
Union meetings, 108; see also Secession
Union Party, 127; in Congress, 214; see also Delaware; Kentucky; Maryland; Middle Border; Missouri
Union Provost Marshal Papers, 250; see also Provost marshals
Union Regiments of Kentucky, The, 318; see also Speed, Thomas
Union Tradition, 333–338; see also Middle Border; Union Triumphant
Union Triumphant, as postwar Republican trope, 303–304, 310, 311, 318, 320; see also "Bloody shirt"; Exclusivism; Northern

Unionism/unionists, 121–125, 131; conditional, 121–125, 133, 209–210, 220; Conservative, 226–227; and guerrillas, 262; and slavery, 121–125, 133, 209–210, 226–227, 228–229, see also Proslavery; and wartime emancipation, 209–210, 219–222; as military informants, 185; home guards of, 129, 228; ministers, 177–180, 181, 183, 190, 216; suppression of secessionists in Border States by, 129; unconditional, 114, 120–121, 124–125, 127–128, 131, 137–138, 139, 197, 221–222, 227–229, 230–232, 237, 249; vigilance committees of, 129; see also Conservatism/Conservatives; Delaware; Kentucky; Maryland; Middle Border; Missouri
Unitarian Church/Unitarians, 62–63, 66, 153; Western Conference of, 63, 66
United Believers in the Second Appearing of Christ, see Shakers
United Confederate Veterans (UCV), 316; see also Missouri; Kentucky
United Daughters of the Confederacy (UDC), 315–316, 323–325; see also Daughters of the Confederacy; Kentucky; Middle Border, "Confederate tradition"; in; Missouri; Women, commemorative organizations
Unterrified Democrat (Linn, Mo.), 300; see also Zevely, Lebbeus

Vallandigham, Clement L., 8, 104–105, 222, 230, 311, 337; and "Copperhead Convention," 281; death, 311; exile to Confederate states, 8; see also "Man Without a Country"
Van Buren, Martin, 85
Van Wert, Oh., 308
Vandalia, Il., 34–35; and National Road, 52; see also Illinois, state capitol in
VanDyke, Henry J., 177; see also Churches/faiths
Vanice, James M., 215
VanLandingham, Oliver C., 32
Van Meter, Mary E., 172–173, 206, 265
Van Meter, William, 172
Vermont, 55; as source for western migration, 122
Versailles, Ky., 267, 309
Vest, George G., 301
Vicksburg, Ms., 13, 45, 183; battle at, 211
Vigilance committees, 95–96, 129, 143, 246, 272, 277, 279; as slave patrols, 131–132; see also Home guards; Union leagues
Vincennes, In., 28, 30; French in, 29; proslavery "faction" in, 30–31, see also Indiana, slavery politics in

Virginia, 2, 22, 28, 47; as source for western migration, 22, 26–27, 38, 39, 41, 44, 50, 55, 78, 80, 84, 108, 114, 121, 135, 160, 276;Bedford County in, 45;economic base of, 50–51; free blacks in, 87; fugitive slaves from/in, 65; military campaigns in, 208; Prince George's County in, 39;proslavery sentiment in, 48, 103; Shenandoah valley in, 26, 192; slave population of, 37, 86; slavery in, 37; Southside subregion in, 45; slavery politics in, 103; towns/cities in, 55; western counties of, 200, 219, see also West Virginia

Virginia, Army of (federal), 50

"Virginia Tract," see Ohio, Military (or Virginia) Tract in

"Voluntary servitude," see Illinois, contract apprenticeship in

Voorhees, Daniel, 222

Vox Populi (McLeansboro, Il.), 273; see also Morton, Lizzie

Wabash River, 22, 28, 29, 31, 50
Wade, Benjamin, 222, 335
Walker, William, 95
Wallace, Albert, 205, 225
Wallace, Ellen, 225, 258, 262
Wallace, John, 247
War Department, U.S., 138, 139, 140, 196, 197, 208, 218, 220, 249, 259, 276, 282, 302, 317; removal of federal troops from Ky. and Mo., 296
War memorials, see Public monuments
War of 1812, 184
Ward, William T., 194
Ward, Williamson D., 152
Warren, Robert Penn, 5, 6, 323, 325
Warsaw, Ky., 215, 296
Washburne, Asa, 108
Washburne, Elihu, 93
Washington, D.C., 48, 108, 115, 314, 317; Ford's Theater in, 283, see also Booth, John Wilkes; Lincoln, Abraham, assassination of; Lincoln Memorial, 323; Peace Conference in, 123
Washington, George, 22; as Confederate ideal, 329
Watchman (Circleville, Oh.), *The*, 273; see also Kees, John W.
Watson, Peter H., 153
Watterson, Henry, 317–318, 319, 320; "New South Creed," 317–318; see also *Journal* (Louisville, Ky.)
Waverly, Mo., 186
Weekly Caucasian (Lexington, Mo.), *The*, 300
Weld, Theodore Dwight, 68–69, 70; see also Lane Theological Seminary

West, Department of the (federal), 137, 213; see also Western States
West, American, African Americans in, 11, 29–32, 50; antislavery influences in, 34–35, 37–39, 40–41, 46, 49, 62–72, 88–89, 90; as destination for Confederate sympathizers, 245; as locus for postwar Confederate expatriation, 328; as "white man's country," 41, 42; "Black Laws" in, 40; canals in, 52–53; Civil War in, 5, 8–9, 14; cultural folkways in, 22–24, 130; cultural pluralism in, 22–27, 58–59, 163; defined, xvii, 335; foreign-born immigration to, 44, 57–59; French influences in, 27–28; German Americans in, 58–59; internal improvements in, 52–53; modernization in, 49–62; Native Americans in, 16, 25, 28, 54, 63, 221, see also Trail of Tears; politics/political parties in, 59–62, 78–82, 83–105, 126, 221–228, see also Democratic party, Republican party, Whig party; proslavery influences in, 37–42, 45–48, 62–72, 78–82, 89–115, 122, 209–210, 227–228, 230–232; racial traditionalism in, 47–48, 50, 58, 59, 60, 62–77, 84, 90, 109, 115, 208–210, 222–226; rivers as highways in, 52; sectionalization of, 104–105; settlement of, 21–27; slavery in, 17–19, 27–35; slavery politics in, 11–12, 34–42, 44–48, 49, 62–72, 77, 78–113, 121–122, 150–151, 208–209, 221–228; Spanish influences in, 28; views of New England/ New Englanders, 23–25, 35, 55, 78–80, 93, 130, 159, 203, 228, 230, 302, see also Westerners
West Liberty, Oh., 178
West Point, see Military Academy, U.S.
West Virginia, emancipation of slaves in, 292
Western Citizen (Paris, Ky.), 105
Western consensus, 41, 42, 47–48, 62–77, 84, 90, 106, 108, 109, 211, 212; see also West, American, as "white man's country,"; racial traditionalism in, slavery in
Western Flotilla, 142, 143, 196; see also Cairo, Il.; St. Louis, Mo.
Western Freedmen's Aid Commission, 257, 268
Western Journal and Civilian (St. Louis, Mo.), 62
Western Monthly Magazine (Louisville, Ky.), 52
Western Sanitary Commission, 174
Westerners, 24; racial views of, 47–48, 58, 59, 302; Unionism of, 55; views of New England/ New Englanders, 23–25, 35, 55, 78–80, 93, 130, 159, 203, 228, 229, 230–232, 302
Weston, Mo., 94, 315
Westport, Mo., 186; battle at, 282
Western Reserve, see Ohio; Eclectic Institute of, 2
Western States, defined, xvii

Wheeling, Va., 52, 197; Ohio River (Roebling) suspension bridge at, 162
Whig Party, 11, 48, 50, 57–61, 62, 93, 98, 114, 227; and free-soil politics, 80, 90, 92; decline of, 91–93; economic platform of, 46; see also "American System;" Clay, Henry; Kentucky, Opposition Party
"White caps"/white-capping, 308; see also Ku Klux Klan; Regulators
White, M. Todd, 253
White Water, Oh., 276; see also Shakers
White, William Allen, 334
Whittier, John Greenleaf, 84
Whittlesey, Charles, 147–148, 187, 215
Wickliffe, Robert, 64
Wilderness Road, 22, 28; see also Appalachian Mountains; Cumberland Gap; Kentucky, settlement of
Willard, Ashbel P., 2
Williams, Charles C., 152
Williams, George, 285; see also Mangrum, George
Willcox, Orlando B., 280
Wilmot Proviso, 84
Wilson, Augustus, 322
Wilson, Ephraim J., 151
Wilson, Joshua L., 46
Wilson, William, 32
Wilson's (or Wilson) Creek (Mo.), battle of, 141, 156, 243, 311
Winchester, Ky., 209
Wingert's Corners, Oh., see Nasby, Petroleum V.
Winn, Amelia, 207
Winn, Martha, 207
Winn, Robert, 207–209, 297
Winslow, Ill., 106–107
Wisconsin, xvii, 66; federal troops from, 151, 159, 232, 254; State Historical Society of, 334; 1st Cavalry Regiment, 151
Wise, Isaac M., 108
Women, African American, 267–269, 327; and African American military enlistment, 262; and antislavery, 69–70; and children, 265–267; and "Confederate tradition," 314–319, 320–322, 323–325; and contraband goods, 263–264; and fugitive slaves, 70; and guerrilla conflict, 238, 239; and loyal leagues, 272–273, 278; and loyalty/disloyalty, 263–268, 279; and postwar politics, 306; and war casualties, 171; as abolitionists, 69–70; as Confederate sympathizers, 195–196, 266; as home guards, 272–273, 279; as hospital nurses, 119, 165; as war refugees, 239–240; as wartime dissenters, 13, 175–176, 183, 262–268, 272–273; as widows, 266, 314, 322; commemorative organizations, 304, 314–317, 321, 323–325; exiled, 263; suffrage, 69; union aid societies, 174, 272; wartime experiences of, see Middle Border; see also Dissent/dissenters
Worthington, Thomas, 33
Woodson, Samuel H., 82
Woodward, C. Vann, 331
Wright, Elizabeth "Lizzie," 176
Wright, Horatio G., 254
Wright, John Stillman, 24
Wright, Joseph A., 63
Wright, Uriel, 138
Wyandotte, Ks., 95

Yale College/University, 64, 94, 135, 334
Yancey, William L., 106
Yankee/yankees, 23–25, 55, 78–80, 130; as southerners' term of opprobrium, 159, 203, 229, 230, 318, 329; as western descriptor, 24
Yates, Richard, 93, 106, 109, 223, 258, 270; opposition to, 275
Young, Bennet H., 316; and Confederate St. Albans Raid, 323
Younger, Cole, 245

Zanesville, Oh., 67
Zevely, Lebbeus, 300; see also *Unterrified Democrat* (Linn, Mo.)
Zollicoffer, Felix, 199, 297